KRLA ARCHIVES

KRLA
Chronological Archives
Volume 2
July 31, 1965 to November 6, 1965

KRLA ARCHIVES

PROTESTOR Barry McGUIRE: NEW TARGET

Elvis-Ten More Years as King of Pop?

Back in the early days of Rock & Roll, radio stations played a huge role in preomoting artists. Now that may sound obvious, but radio is an audio media, so it makes sense that they played music over the airwaves. What may be less obvious is the riole some some radio stations played in other media.

KRLA was one of the leaders on the West Coast in bringing not just music, but the artist persona to their audiences. Radio stations had long since learned that printed "playlists" were one way to expand their reach and influence. But after a while, they realized that playlists weren't the only thing worth printing.

The KRLA newsletter started out as a self-promotional piece, but evolved into what its audienced really cared more about: news on their favorite artists.

Okay, maybe it wasn't hard news and maybe it was barely a step above (if at all above) what the fan magazines like FLIP and 16 were going to start offering. Still, it offered a way for the station to connect to the audience outside the radio waves. It offered a way to engage teen boys better, as well. And that was a powerful thing.

Back in April of 1965, the KRLA Beat had changed formats and ran more pages, and by July it had upped its page count once again. There were more bands to cover and so they did. The Djs at the station continued to get their coverage, as that was part of the reason for the newsletter when it had started.

In presenting these original issues, we've moved a few of the pages around to ensure that the spreads still lined up. Not a big deal to most people unless you are severly OCD and have access to the original issues.

KRLA ARCHIVES

KRLA BEAT

Volume 1, Number 20 • Los Angeles, California • 15 Cents • July 31, 1965

FROM SHOWER TO STARDOM

LOOK WHAT ELVIS STARTED — Page 3 • **BRIAN JONES' PAST** — Page 7
WHY JACK GOOD LEFT SHINDIG • WHY BOYFRIENDS HATE STARS — Page 7
also — BEATLES • HERMAN • ELVIS • MARIANNE FAITHFULL

KRLA BEAT

LOS ANGELES, CALIFORNIA — July 31, 1965

AMERICAN FANS may be grateful for a chance to see the Dave Clark Five again, but British fans, who wonder why the group has so little time for their own country, shout "Stay home traitors!"

Dave Clark's Tours Irk Fans In Britain

By Alix Palmer

(A BEAT exclusive from Manchester, England)

"Traitors . . . Why don't you stay home!"

This is the response the Dave Clark Five got here before their hasty return to the United States only six days after their last tour.

Despite their prolonged absence, "Catch Us, If You Can" the title tune from their new film, earned itself a Tip for The Top in Britian's most popular pop show.

When I caught up with Dave at the television studios in Manchester, a week before he returned to the States, he summarized their reasons for the second tour.

"So many important dates had been arranged for us in America that we felt we would be letting people down if we skipped them," he said.

During our conversation, Dave also confessed nervousness about the show we was to do in California.

"We've got a marvelous performance in California coming up. But we can't get used to the outsize audiences. One hall will take 50,000 people. When we first started in Britain, we found 2,000 terrifying.

Overpowering Bigness

"This bigness of everything American strikes all the English groups who go over. It's almost overpowering," said Dave.

"I'd never settle there. Not that I've got anything against the American people — except that they can't make a decent cup of tea," he continued.

The film, with Dave as the hero aided and abetted by Dennis, Mick, Rick and Lenny, was released on July 8.

"It's alright, I suppose. "I only hope the critics like it," Dave said, commenting about the film.

What will the boys do when they finish their three weeks in America?

"Come home for a holiday," said Dave.

All the Five have bought large houses not far from London.

"I'm sure the Americans would like mine," said Dave. "It's very Oldie Worldie, with oak beams and things. Pity I can't take it back with me."

Red-Hot Cher Top Girl Star

A bewitching brunette with Indian eyes, a French name and a far-out appearance has suddenly become the hottest female vocalist in the U.S. Cher is suddenly Queen of the record world.

Few people know her last name (formerly Cher La Pierre, now Cher Bonno) but almost anyone who listens to a radio or a record player recognizes her voice and styling immediately.

Currently she has three records on the charts, two of them as Sonny & Cher (duets with her singer-producer husband, Sonny Bonno and the third one featuring only her, which is expected to become number one nationally at any day.

It's called "All I Really Want to Do," and it's one of the most unusual discs ever recorded. Bob Dylan wrote it, but he certainly wouldn't recognize it unless he listened closely to the lyrics.

Both Parts

Cher sings two parts — high and low — and combined with Sonny's arrangement and production it's like nothing else ever recorded. The Byrds had originally recorded "All I Really Want to Do" as a follow-up to "Tambourine Man" and at first it appeared they had another number one record.

But Cher's "cover" recording of it caused such a sensation that Columbia didn't even try to make a fight of it. They switched the flip side of the Byrds' disc and began pushing "Feel a Whole Lot Better," as the "A" side.

Dylan's "All I Really Want to Do" is such a strong song that both versions are doing well, but it's Cher's record that is causing the sensation.

As Sonny & Cher, the husband-wife team has two other numbers climbing the charts—"I've Got You" and "Just You." Many believe either one of these two numbers could become most as big as "All I Really Want to Do."

Like Beatles

It marks the first time since the Beatle explosion in 1964 that any artist has caused such a sensation in the record world.

But while the Beatles developed **TURN TO NEXT PAGE**

EVERYTHING'S SUNNY for Cher since her sudden boost in record sales, but how about Sonny? Once the star of the duo, he is now beginning to take a back seat to his chart-climbing wife.

Groups to Flood U.S. With Waves of Music

American television producers have found a way to beat the ban placed on some English artists. Instead of having the British artists come Stateside, the American television units will go to England!

"Shindig" has used this method before and will use it again. In fact, a "Shindig" unit is expected in London during the latter half of July. Among those filmed will be Sandie Shaw, Adam Faith, and Manfred Mann.

Gary Smith, producer of "Hullabaloo", has already been to England to audition lesser-known groups for his show.

Smith has also come up with a rather interesting idea which he has been discussing with Rediffusion TV executive, Elkan Allen. It concerns the possibility of exchanging film clips between "Hullabaloo" and the top British TV pop show, "Ready, Steady, Go."

Ian, Casey Track Down Squealers

British Recording Star Ian Whitcomb went to the KRLA station in Pasadena recently, to visit with the KRLA deejays.

Ian and Casey Kasem, were discussing his latest hit, "You Turn Me On," when they were interrupted by loud shrieks and screams of ecstacy.

"Could some of my fans know I'm here?" Ian wondered.

"Could be some of my fans too," Casey pointed out modestly.

Then they heard a distinctive voice screaming, "Look! Look what's here!"

"Why that sounds like Charlie O'Donnell," Ian said

"I haven't heard the Emperor scream like that for years," said Dave Hull. "Let's go see what's happening."

The two followed the happy laughter out into the KRLA waiting room.

"Well, well," chuckled Casey, "So this is what all the noise is about."

"Let me at one!!" cried Ian.

"Hey save one for me. I work here you know!" The two then rushed into the crowd of screaming girls and boys to join in the fun.

To see what was causing all this excitement, turn to page 9.

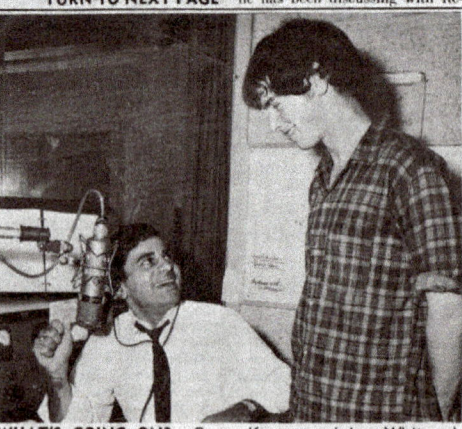

WHAT'S GOING ON? Casey Kasem and Ian Whitcomb wonder when their shop talk is interrupted by loud screams and laughter coming from the waiting room outside the KRLA control room in Pasadena.

KRLA ARCHIVES

THE GROWTH OF ROCK 'N ROLL

by Jerry Naylor

(Editor's Note: Jerry Naylor, was born in Texas and began his fantastic musical career in the South-Central U.S. area. When Buddy Holly of the Crickets died in 1959 Jerry, then working in Los Angeles radio as a KRLA deejay, was offered his position and since then has done most of the lead singing on the Cricket's singles and albums. Their latest recording, "Raining In My Heart", a Paul Anka composition and former hit recording for Buddy Holly, promises to take Jerry and the Crickets to the top of the charts.)

The seeds from which the great crop of English record successes have sprung, were sowed not in Liverpool, but in the Tex-Mex area, the testing grounds from which the hard "rock" beat and the swiveling hips of rock and roll singers were launched.

A great many tunes from the South Central United States, New Mexico and Texas give testimony to the great influence the Tex-Mex area has had on the British recorders.

The Beatles' "Words of Love", is a revision of a Buddy Holly-Cricket recording and The Rolling Stone's record "Not Fade Away", is again a revision of a Buddy Holly-Cricket composition and a hit of the past.

The most recent example of the British revision of the Tex-Mex sound is heard in "True Love Ways", a new Peter and Gordon chart offering, originally written and recorded by Buddy Holly.

Proving Grounds

The Tex-Mex area had long been a proving ground of one kind or another, from the testing of atomic energy to the recent NASA program. In the late 1950's it was a proving ground of another sort, and leading the parade of side-burned scream-getting performers who came there to prove their worth was the King of Rock n' Roll Elvis Presley.

After a fairly successful recording on Sun Records, he drove all the way from Memphis, Tenn., with accompanists Scotty Moore and Bill Black, for a tour of the one-nighters.

His price in those days was 80 cents a performance, just enough to pay for the gas and oil eaten by his hungry 1952 Lincoln, which faithfully, though sometimes frantically, brought them to each stage door.

Added Attraction

I first met Elvis at the stage entrance of the Memorial Auditorium in my home town, San Angelo, Tex. My job was to collect tickets for what was advertised as a great "Country and Western show," headlining Hank Snow and Johnny Horton, with added attraction (in very small, last-minute letters), Elvis Presley.

Some added attraction! Elvis Presley, followed by Scotty and Bill, wandered on stage before a puzzled and somewhat disinterested audience and gave a preview of a sound soon to be

JERRY NAYLOR

blared across the world—rock and roll.

Inspired by Elvis' new sound, a crop of entertainers began to pop up all over the area. From Wink, Texas, a small oil and wool center, came a young man to join the Presley package with his latest songs "Ooby Dooby" and "Rock House". Roy Orbison was his name, and along with his group, "The Teen Kings"; he not only sang and played the pulsating beat, but proved that a dance could go with it. The "Ooby Dooby Bug Dance", caught on, and made Roy Orbison's name and performances remembered by millions.

Next to pass through the Tex-Mex testing grounds was a college student from Texas whose "Party Doll" was being aired by every radio station in the Texas, New Mexico area. The student, Buddy Knox, along with Jimmy Bowen and their group "The Rythmn Orchids", traveled to Clovis, New Mexico, the only recording studio for hundreds of miles, to record two self-written songs, "Party Doll" and "I'm Sticking With You". Both sold over one million copies and established an even newer trend in rock and roll—the "Tex-Mex" sound.

Rock Empire

Norman Petty, father of the Tex-Mex sound and owner of the recording studio in Clovis, looked into the future and saw a rock and roll empire looming ahead. The Tex-Mex sound now proved, he had only to find new talent to spread the new beat.

Then Don and Phil Everly, who have recently seen their record "Price of Love", hit the top of British charts, recorded "Bye Bye Love". The record proved to be the foundation for their million dollar career and almost immediately the two Kentucky boys were one of the hottest rock and roll groups around.

Among the many song writers from all over the country who began submitting material for the Everly's to record were Buddy Holly and Jerry Allison from Lubbock, Texas.

Songs For Everlys

The two wrote a couple of songs they thought would fit the Everly Brothers perfectly and along with Joe B. Mauldin made the trek to Clovis to record some demonstration records for Norman Petty.

After a few "takes" with Buddy singing out, "Well That'll Be The Day", and Jerry and Joe B. joining in to fill the background, the "demo" was completed and each had visions of hearing "That'll Be The Day" introduced on their favorite radio program as a new Everly Brothers hit.

But keen-eared Norman Petty had other ideas. "Why not send your record to New York to be considered for a single record release with Decca Records," he suggested to Buddy and Jerry. After quickly summarizing the advantages of having their own hit, he was able to swing them over to his way of thinking.

Buddy, Jerry and Joe went back to Lubbock, Texas, and "That'll Be The Day" went off to New York. And after many pleading phone calls from Norman Petty, the record was given the go-ahead for release.

The Crickets

A group with a Decca Records has to have a name, so Jerry and Buddy began hunting through the encyclopedia to find one. Their search ended in the C's, where they found their new name—the Crickets.

"That'll Be The Day" sold well over two million records in the United States and England and engraved another name in the gold record business of rock and roll. The Crickets followed their first hit with many other million sellers and made the Tex-Mex sound known and copied the world over.

The Beatles freely admit that Buddy Holly, a great admirer of Presley who tried to pattern his own style after him, greatly inspired their style of singing and credit the inspiration for their name to the Crickets.

Meanwhile, Norman Petty's Studios were stampeded by recording artists around the world who wanted to capitalize on the Tex-Mex sound. And thus, this small New Mexico proving ground became another recording center, ranking with Hollywood, Nashville, Memphis and New York.

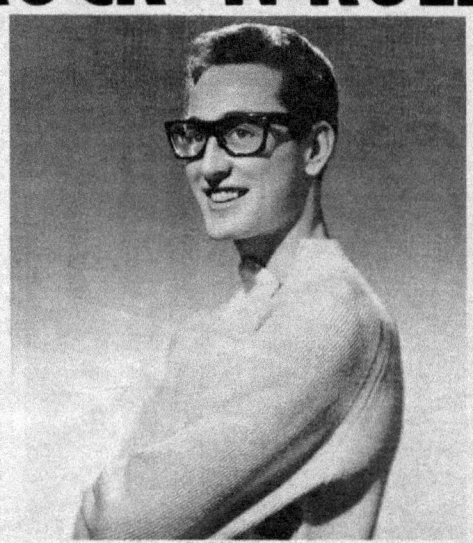

...BUDDY HOLLY

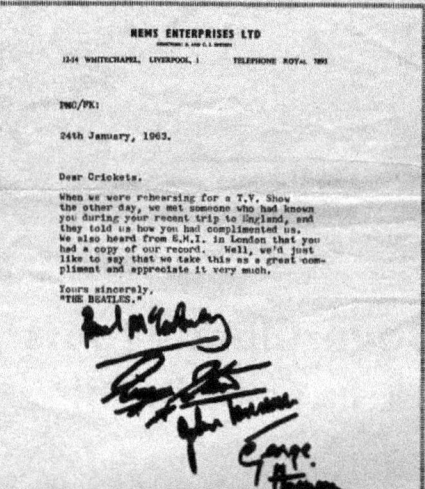

Cher Sizzles -

(Cont. from preceding page)

ed their styling in The Cavern in Liverpool and The Top-Ten in Hamburg, Chere received her training in quite another manner.

Sonny and Cher first met each other two years ago at a recording session for the famed Phil Spector. Sonny was doing one of the background voices and a female voice was needed. Someone asked Cher whether she had ever sung before.

"Well," she replied, "I sing a lot in the shower."

Cher's shower training has now paid off. She has put aside her acting ambitions and dramatic training to reign as Queen of the Record World.

This may result in an increase in water consumption and some of the cleanest young girls in the country.

Now they will all be practicing singing in the shower.

...ORIGINAL CRICKETS

KRLA ARCHIVES

– FROM ELVIS TO THE BEATLES

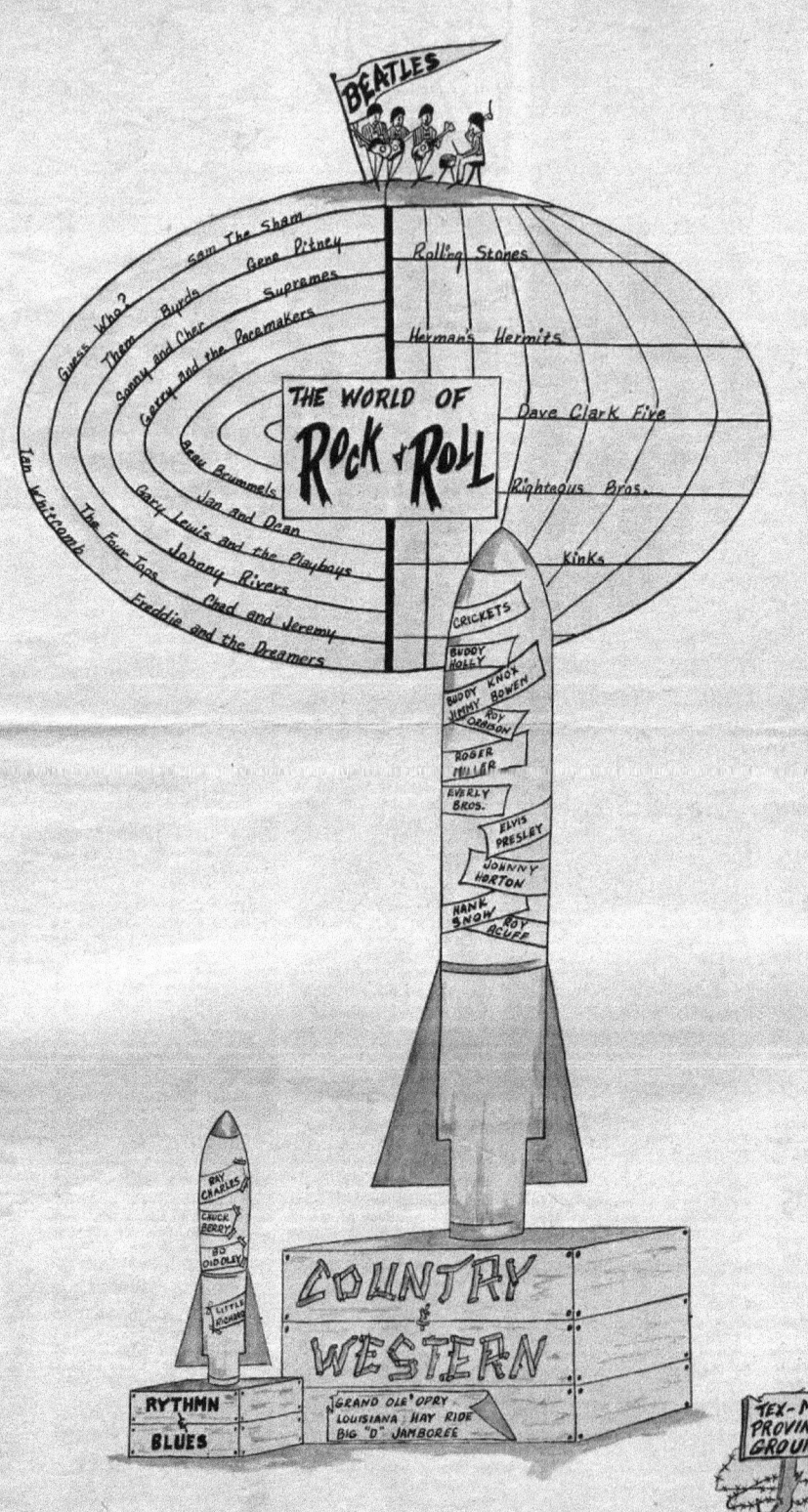

KRLA ARCHIVES

DONOVAN

Donovan Confesses Fears About Visiting United States

By Alix Palmer

(A BEAT exclusive from Manchester, Eng.)

Donovan, another British artist hitting the American pop scene, is scared stiff.

While he uses his first name only because he doesn't like his last name, he is referred to by most people over here as "the British Bob Dylan."

And that is exactly the reason why he has hesitated so long before going to America.

"The Americans are bound to think I'm trying to copy their Dylan," he told me.

"But I was writing and singing folk songs in Britain long before Dylan was heard of over here," he explained.

Donovan was born in Glasgow, Scotland, just 18 years ago. He first made the charts with a soulful record called "Catch The Wind", his own song and his first record.

Then came "Colours", which has been in the British charts for weeks and is still No. 5.

Dressed always in denim, with longish black hair, Donovan is very much a lone walker.

"I don't object to people," he said. "I just prefer to be by myself. I like sitting in some corner, watching and playing my guitar."

Three months ago, Donovan was literally singing for his supper. Now he is earning almost a thousand pounds a week (about 3 thousand dollars).

"I don't care about money," he said. "It probably hasn't hit me yet. I haven't bought anything, not even a car. I'm just thankful to be able to afford something to eat."

What does the British Bob Dylan think of his American counterpart?

"His songs are marvelous, much better than mine," he said. "But I don't think much of him as a performer."

ROYALTY ATTENDS PREMIERE OF HELP

Royalty announced it would attend the premiere of the Beatles' second film, "Help," at the London Pavilion on July 29.

Members of the royal family were expected but had not officially confirmed their invitations until just recently when Princess Margaret and Lord Snowdon announced that they would be at the premiere.

Both Princess Margaret and Lord Snowdon attended the premiere of "A Hard Day's Night" last year in the same theater.

Also attending the premiere of "Help" were all four of the Beatles.

EPIC RECORDS

Q: How often should you give yourself a manicure? How about pedicures? (Carla A)
A: Your nails are due for a manicure about every two weeks, and you should have a pedicure at least once a month if you really want to keep on your toes beauty-wise.

Q: I have to wear glasses about half of the time, and the rest of the time I have two red marks on the bridge of my nose. Makeup doesn't seem to cover them, and they look horrible. What can I do to keep this from happening? (Anne C)
A: Most stores sell tiny pads to keep glasses from leaving marks. If you can't find some by shopping around, stop by an optometrists' office and ask for help!

Q: I've always had a fairly nice complexion, but I've started breaking out all of a sudden. I haven't changed any of my habits that I can think of, except I've been drinking a lot of coffee lately. Could there be any connection between the coffee and the break-out? (Joann S)
A: There sure could! Coffee contains a great deal of oil and can cause skin eruptions. Try cutting down on the number of cups you drink (cups of coffee, of course) and see if your complexion doesn't go back to normal.

Q: My boyfriend gave me a bracelet for my birthday, and for some reason it makes my wrist itch when I wear it. This doesn't make sense because I know he paid quite a bit of money for my present. He keeps asking why I don't wear it, and I'm embarrassed to tell him. What can I do? (Deedee M.)
A: You're probably allergic to one of the metals contained in the bracelet. Coat the inside with clear nail polish and see if the irritation doesn't stop.

Q: I've tried all the popular dandruff shampoos on the market and nothing seems to work. I'm so self-conscious about this problem, I even hesitated to write you about it, so I hope you can help. (Sylvia D.)
A: The Fuller Brush Company has a new dandruff shampoo that works wonders, and isn't drying. The next time a Fuller salesman calls at your home, ask him about this product. If you'd rather not wait, call the nearest office of the company and see if they can arrange a short cut.

Q: I have a very weird problem. One of my eyes is blue and the other is brown. This always causes a lot of commotion, and I'd like to know how much it would cost to buy a colored contact lens to sort of even the score. (Joyce B.)
A: Prescription lenses cost around $200, so the cost of one would probably be a little less than half. But, why bother? Your "condition" isn't really a problem, it's an attraction. Why not enjoy the commotion? It sounds like fun!

HINT OF THE WEEK

I sat down the other day and figured just how much time I spend on my hair. It takes about forty-five minutes to set it every night, and I spend nearly that long combing it out in the morning, to say nothing of about a million re-combs during the day. That is an awful lot of time to spend, and I've thought of a way to cut down on it. When my hair doesn't turn out, instead of wasting hours in front of the mirror fussing with it, I now comb it into a very unflattering style and then back to normal. This makes me realize I don't really look that bad at all, after seeing myself *really* looking terrible, and I spend about half as much time primping! Try it!

(Doris D.)

GREAT BRITAIN OFFERS INEXPENSIVE HOTELS

If you're planning a trip to England, or just dreaming about planning one, you've come to the right place.

This week's problem is how to remain there as long as possible without going into debt for the next thousand years.

It's best to start well ahead of time and make your reservations (or "bookings" as they're called in Jolly Olde) some time in advance.

There are a number of bookings to choose from. If you're planning a short stay and have part of Aunt Hazel's inheritance to tide you over, hotel accommodations can be found through the London Hotels Information Service, 88 Brook Street, London, W. 1, England. The service provided by this agency costs nothing, but is a lot of help because it lets you know what accommodations are available when and where.

Hotel Prices

In the city of London, a hotel room will cost approximately ten dollars per night (per person). The price is sometimes a bit less, sometimes a bit more, but always in the neighborhood of this amount. Incidentally, England's hotels differ from most of our's as the price of a night's lodgings includes a full breakfast.

If Aunt Hazel has been kind to you, or if you plan on saving up several hard-earned dollars before beginning your trip, it would be wise for you to send for a copy of the British Travel Association's Guide To Hotels And Restaurants In Britain. A stamped, self-addressed envelope sent to the Association (nearest office is 612 South Flower Street, Los Angeles) should insure receipt of a copy, and if you'd like the deluxe edition which describes the English countryside and helps you plan a traveling itinerary, enclose $1 with your request.

Outside of the Metropolitan areas, you'll find hundreds of beautiful old inns with very sensible rates. During the tourist season, the average price per night is $5, and when business is a little less brisk (during the fall and winter months) the prices dip even lower.

Farmhouses

One of the nicest places to stay while you're larking about the countryside is one of the many farmhouses in Britain that have room for private guests. Here the price dips to between two and three dollars per night, or 20 dollars per week with two meals a day included in the bargain.

(If you're still on a booklet kick, there's another you can order free of charge from your British Travel Association. It's called Caravan And Camping Sites and Farmhouse Accommodations In Britain.)

The least expensive accommodations available in England are the best of all. All over this magic country you can find private homes happy to take in a paying guest for between 10 and 15 dollars a week, and sometimes even less.

Other Ideas

If one of your English pen pals doesn't know of a family you could board with, try writing to the Non-Commercial Accommodation Service, British Travel And Holidays Association, 64-65 St. James Street, London, S.W.1, England. Tell them what area you're interested in visiting and they'll send you several addresses of private homes in the vicinity. It's then up to you to write to the families and make arrangements.

Since it's impossible to send a stamped, self-addressed envelope to another country, send an International Reply Coupon (available at any post office) with your above request. It isn't completely necessary, but it's a small favor in return for the service and might help your answer arrive faster.

Now that we have you in England and safely encamped for the duration of your stay, stay tuned for the next BEAT where we'll be going into more detail about the second greatest country in the world.

See you then, old bean.

KRLA ARCHIVES

Fairy Tales Can Come True -- Look at Marianne Faithful

By Louise Criscione

Well here we go again. This time we're off to an exclusive interview with a girl who looks like a refugee from a fairy tale and has a story to match.

A rather petite and delicate blonde with a soft feminine voice, Marianne is currently riding a crest of popularity which few girls in the recording industry have been able to achieve.

But it wasn't always that way. In fact her whole career began almost completely by chance and sounds like a typical Hollywood fairy tale.

It all began at a St. Valentine's Day dance in 1964, where she met John Dunbar, a university student who happened to be a school friend of Gordon Waller's. Sometime later, Marianne was invited to a party with John and Peter and Gordon. Also attending this party was one Andrew Oldham, recording manager for the Rolling Stones.

Oldham took one good look at Marianne and came to an immediate decision — she would make a perfect recording artist.

"Andrew Oldham came up and asked me if I would like to make a record," she explained.

"And you said yes?" I asked.

"Yes, well why not?"

And so like all good fairy stories, the record, "As Tears Go By", was a big hit in both England and America and Marianne Faithfull's career had now officially begun.

First Visit

This was Marianne's first visit to California and also her first visit to the U.S. What did she think of our slice of America? "Oh, it's lovely. Really beautiful."

Although Marianne is sometimes labeled a folk singer, she says she does not consider herself one. But since she lists her biggest personal influence as Joan Baez, it is not too surprising that all of Marianne's records have had a kind of folksy sound to them—that is, all except her next release.

"It's more of a rock sound." Marianne laughs, in England, they call it 'convent rock.'" It seems that Marianne was educated at St. Joseph's Convent School, and thus the name "convent rock".

Andrew Oldham was the man responsible for launching Marianne's career, but for lots of reasons the two parted company before Marianne recorded "This Little Bird". And then an odd thing happened. Well, maybe not odd, but certainly uncomfortable. Oldham produced the Nashville Teens version of "This Little Bird", released the record, and placed it in direct chart competition with Marianne's record.

Marianne's position was uncomfortable enough without being further complicated by the fact that the Teens had once been employed by her father on his farm!

Two Birds

The incident received plenty of press in the English music papers, and anxious eyes watched the charts to see who would top who.

"The Nashville Teens' record was very good," Marianne said graciously. Apparently it was not good enough because Marianne's "Little Bird" flew a lot higher in both England and America.

Is it true that Marianne did not want to make "This Little Bird" in the first place because she doesn't like birds?

"It wasn't that I didn't want to make the record. It was just that after it was made everyone started talking about birds, and well I thought perhaps I should have made "This Little Snake" instead," she explained.

As always when two girls get together, the talk inevitably turned to fashion.

"What's 'in' in London right now?" I asked her.

"Well, it's sort of a whole look, with people like Mary Quant and Caroline Charles. And the big thing is little white boots. They're boots which have cut-out toes. They're very comfortable, and they're quite the big thing now," she answered.

Favorite Shops

Marianne says she doesn't really pay all that much attention to what is "in" fashion-wise because she just wears what she likes and what suits her best.

The recording star likes to do her clothes buying in those small London shops. "I'm lucky because where I live in Knightsbridge-Chelsea there are all kinds of small boutiques. There is one I especially like which is very close to where I live."

Marianne, who came to L.A. specifically to do a "Shindig", found two aspects of American pop shows which differ from the British variety.

"They take longer to make! Another thing is the color, everything is so colorful. In England, everything's beige!"

Does Marianne have other favorite singers besides Joan Baez? "Oh, yes, I like Jackie DeShannon and Nina Simone. And the Hollies. They're fabulous! I don't think you've heard much of them here, but they have the number one record in England, 'I'm Alive'. It's very good; I heard it here on the radio yesterday. You should tell them to play it more often!"

While reading a copy of the BEAT, the huge front page picture of Sonny and Cher caught her eye. "We met them, and they're very nice. They're coming to England, and I think they'll do very well there. I'm interested in recording one of Sonny's songs myself," she said.

Most Exciting

Lots of exciting things happen to people who make records, and especially to those who make hit records. What is the

TURN TO PAGE 15

WITH THE BEAT, Marianne Faithfull chats with BEAT reporter Louise Criscione about some of the stories inside. The two met on the patio of Marianne's hotel room for an exclusive BEAT interview.

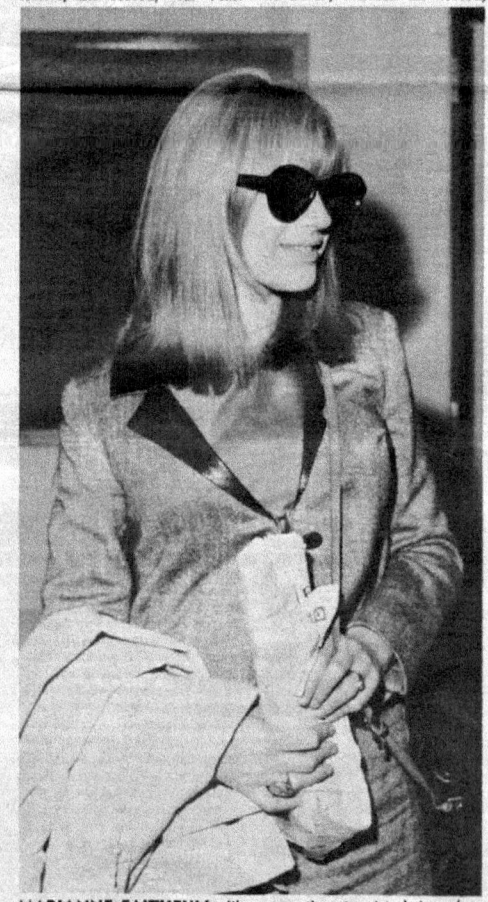

MARIANNE FAITHFULL, like any other tourist, brings her camera and sunglasses upon arriving in California. Direct from London, Miss Faithfull came to the U.S. via Pan American to do a Shindig Show.

ARRIVING AT SUNNY CALIFORNIA, English recording star Marianne Faithfull removes her coat and pops on a pair of sunglasses. After all — when in California, do as the Californians do.

KRLA ARCHIVES

MICK AND BRIAN

The Rolling Stones Story: First Part

By Louise Criscione

(Editors Note: This is the first of a three part series on the lives of the four Rolling Stones, which will be continued in the next two issues of the BEAT.)

They make girls sob, parents seethe and cash registers ring in record shops all over the world.

And like many internationally famous stars the Rolling Stones frequently find themselves on the front pages of newspapers. In stories which tell how they were ejected from "high class" restaurants for their refusal to come properly attired or how they have had their hotel reservations cancelled "in consideration of the hotel's other guests".

Parts of it are true, but plenty of it is false. It's really about time that someone set the record straight and followed the Stones through their growing pains, through their school years, and through their painful struggle to reach that top berth which they now occupy. The BEAT has decided to do just that, so here is the first installment of the amazing, often funny and sometimes sad Rolling Stones' story.

Mick Jagger

The Stone who stands in the center of the stage, who sings lead, who shakes the maracas, and who does "the dance" is Mick Jagger. He was born in Dartford on July 20, 1944 to Joe and Eva Jagger and christened Michael Philip.

Mick first saw the light of day just as World War II was slowly grinding to a halt. He doesn't remember much about the war. "I suppose the only thing I can remember was my mum taking down the blankets from the windows when all the fighting was over. They'd been draped round the windows because of the blackout regulations."

War all over, an all-grown-up Mick started his schooling at Maypole County Primary School. "I wasn't mad about school in those days. . . . I suppose it was because I was a bit scared. But soon I settled in. It wasn't, I decided, so bad after all. But I'm not going to say I was a marvelous scholar," he said, speaking of his school days.

From Maypole, Mick proceeded on to Wentworth County Primary School. Here Mick found the school uniform distasteful: "It was a drag—all that peaked cap stuff."

Bad Sport

Wentworth completed, Mick went on to Dartford Grammar School where he ran into a bit of trouble in the form of school sports.

"Though my dad was a physical training teacher, his job didn't really rub off on me. I didn't believe in running if there was a chance of walking. So, naturally, organized games were not my cup of tea," he explained.

Enjoying subjects such as history, which gave him a chance to day-dream, and hating others, Mick found himself facing his GCE examinations. The headmaster frankly informed him that he possessed only a fifty-fifty chance of passing his exams. But Mick was not particularly worried—he'd just do his best and see what happened.

To the surprise of many, Mick did so well that he found himself going to the London School of Economics with a grant to cover his fees and expenses!

And so Rolling Stone number one arrived in London and was more or less on his own.

While the first Stone was rolling passively through school, Stone number 2, Brian Jones was busily rubbing a lot of his headmasters the wrong way.

The Stone with the long blonde hair, who alternates between playing rhythm and lead guitar, Jones, was born on February 28, 1944, in the town of Cheltenham, some ninety-eight miles from London.

Brian's mother was a piano teacher who specialized in teaching children how to play. His father was, and still is, an aeronautical engineer.

Brian began his school career at an esablishment know as Dean Close Public School. Brian got away with a lot as far as his teachers were concerned because of that innocent look and kind of

...BRIAN JONES

A Few Notes On The Stones

Charlie Watts and Bill Wyman are both house-hunting. Charlie is looking for a kind of old-world house in London's West End. Bill who is just looking for anything big, is not particular where he finds it!

Stones' recording manager, Andrew Oldham, is the proud papa of a baby boy. Oldham's wife, Sheila, gave birth to the boy on May 25. The baby is being christened Sean, and Oldham says Sean already has long hair!

"Satisfaction" will not be released in England until August.

Suppose the BEAT can consider itself pretty lucky for those line-up shots of all the Stones which they allowed us to take, because their road manager, Ian Stewart, says: "They have a sort of plan which makes it completely impossible for them all to be together at the same time. Right — some pictures can be taken of them in small groups. But getting 'em all there in a line is just impossible." Yet the Stones were most obliging for the BEAT photographer they just lined up and smiled as pretty as you please. Makes us kind of proud.

Bill got himself a new guitar. It's a smaller model of the same make he had before, a Framus.

During their last American tour, the Stones received all sorts of souvenirs, trophies, and awards, but apparently Charlie came home with the biggest haul. No wonder he is looking for a new house — with all his own Civil War items, he probably can't even find a place to sit down in his own home.

Stones' first movie will be in black and white and will feature the boys in realistic roles. It will not be one of the usual run-of-of-the-mill pop films with all songs and no story. The movie will be shot mostly in England, but part of it just may be filmed here in America.

In answer to a request Reprise Records, Mick and Keith are writing an answer lyric to their current smash, "Satisfaction," which will be recorded by one of the Reprise artists.

— *Louise Criscione*

...MICK JAGGER

Best Beau Vs Favorite Star

Has your boyfriend spoken to you for the past several weeks? Is he planning to "divorce" you at the earliest possible moment?

If so, could this possibly be happening because he is faced with the humiliating prospect of sharing your love with a Beatle, King and/or Hermit?

He doesn't like this at all, does he? In fact, he's been known to moan openly at the mere mention of your true luv's name, while preparing to stalk off into the sunset.

Well, surely you aren't going to let a thing like that occur. You're going to placate that poor wretch, and quickly, before he finds someone else to take to dances and buy hamburgers for while you're waiting for that Beatle, Kink and/or Hermit to come along on a white charger and spirit you away.

What To Do

True, it isn't going to be easy to assuage his ego, but there are ways. Here, for your convenience (and downfall) are five of them.

1. It makes your boyfriend feel unimportant when you burst into wild applause at the mention of your favorite star's name. From now on, burst into equally wild applause at the mention of your boyfriend's name, too. This will make him feel *important*, just as soon as he finishes fainting from embarrassment.

2. Think back on all the times you've raved on to your boyfriend about how you'd give several right arms for your favorite's autograph. Aren't you ashamed of yourself? Don't you think it's about time you asked your boyfriend for *his* autograph, just to make him happy? Since happiness should not be one-sided, have him write it on a check.

Build Him Up

3. The main reason your boyfriend feels inferior is because he *is* inferior. Not really, but when compared to your favorite, let's face it, he isn't *quite* as clever, handsome and talented. It is up to you to make him think otherwise. Keep telling him that he *is* clever, handsome and talented, and have all your girlfriends tell him the same things. He'll probably get so conceited he'll have to start wearing a wash tub for a hat, but you'll be able to make an appointment to see him if you really try.

4. It hurts your boyfriend deeply to know that when he takes you home from a date, you sit down and write your daily letter to your favorite. Soothe his ruffled feathers by dashing a loving note off to him now and again, on highly perfumed stationery. He'll certainly appreciate it. Almost as much as his big brothers will.

5. You know how it is when your boyfriend takes you to a movie starring your favorite. You sit there and shriek and he sits there and glares. This is because he thinks that he is sane and you are nuttier than a fruitcake. Well, next time you go to a movie starring *his* favorite, secretly nudge him with a large knitting needle until he roars loudly. Then glare at *him* in disgust. Perhaps he will get the point.

TURN TO PAGE 16

angelic smile which he would spread across his face if punishment seemed about to catch up with him!

He was good at music and English, but like Mick he didn't care all that much for sports. "I couldn't stand all that organi-

KRLA ARCHIVES

THE BEAT GOES TO THE MOVIES

Shenandoah

By Jim Hamblin

There have not been very many times that actual warfare has ever been experienced inside the United States. The most notable exception was the Civil War of the 1860's.

This new Universal Pictures film eloquently describes some of the gritty horror of war, especially when it erupts in your own backyard. It tells of the rape and plunder of both people and the land that seems to always occur in wars — by men who have no stake in the fighting in the first place.

Film star James Stewart, in one of the best roles of his career portrays Virginia rancher Charlie Anderson, who is determined that the war with the "Yankees" just go on by his farm.

As portrayed in the movie, Charlie makes a good case, and the audience is almost ready to sympathize with him.

Son Captured

But then Yankee soldiers capture one of his boys and make him a prisoner of war — and suddenly our peaceful rancher has a real stake in the war.

What happens in the aftermath and the terrible violence of war is carried off very well on the screen by Director Andrew McLaglen (son of the famous Victor McLaglen).

In every respect, this is a good family film, produced in the finest tradition of good entertainment. Its story is about real people and the things that happen to them. Sometimes sad, sometimes happy, SHENANDOAH is a master stroke, and makes another impressive addition to the line-up of great films that we'll be able to see this summer.

New Actress

WHAT TO WATCH FOR: Performance by "newcomer" Rosemary Forsyth in her very first film. The studio has had her under contract for a year, waiting for just the right part for her. They picked it. She is busy now, has just finished WARLORD, with Charlton Heston.

Incidentally, we are in one of the best times in many long years for good movies. It's our suggestion to try to catch as many of these films as possible. The studios are quite capable of drying up soon!

It's been a long time since we have had so many excellent motion pictures playing. By the time we get around to a review on all of them, they will be reruns on television, so here's a check list of the best bets:

DRAMA:
In Harm's Way — excellent war film about naval action.
The Pawnbroker — very serious film about a man's memories of the past and how they affect his life now.
Von Ryan's Express — one of Sinatra's best.

COMEDY:
This category is really having a heyday.
The Great Race — action and color and wonderful story.
Magnificent Men In Their Flying Machines — just about the same thing and almost as well done.
What's New Pussycat? — definitely for 18-year-olds and above, but a wild and funny movie.
Cat Ballou — (already reviewed) — just might be funniest movie of the year.

That's a quick check list of the recommended features from the BEAT.

DOUG McCLURE, who has been seen in "Virginian" TV series, stars in this epic film along with James Stewart, Glenn Corbett, Patrick Wayne and Rosemary Forsyth. The Civil War drama was produced by Robert Arthur and directed by Andrew V. McLaglen.

A POINTED MOMENT in the film occurs when the Yankee Army overruns the Southern Position and the young man stares death in the face. In spite of appearances, Shenandoah is a good family picture and all the girls should take along a dry hankerchief. (Did all Union soldiers wear Beatle boots?)

KRLA ARCHIVES

This Is What They Saw

IT WAS THE BEATS that were causing all the commotion at the KRLA radio station that day. The papers had just arrived and when the kids and Emperor Hudson spotted them, the fun began. They were soon joined by Ian and Charlie O'Donnell.

PERSONALS

To Sandra Browitt of Wigan, England:
I thought you'd like to see your name in the BEAT, so here it is.
Your California pen pal,
Kathy Torres

Keith Richard:
Guess What??
Love Flo

To Brian Jones:
I love you. I love you. I love you.
A TRUE Stone Fan,
Cindy Farrow

To Dick Biondi:
What ever happended to Rita March?
Curious

To Mr. Robertson of the Marina Palace:
Thanks so very much for getting Robin and me backstage to meet Ian Whitcomb. We luv Ian, he's the greatest (and so are you.)
Shorty and Robin

To The Rolling Stones:
Please Hurry Back To California. I Love You.
Becky Armond

To Vicki Pinner:
I don't care if you don't like the FAB Stones.
STONES FOREVER
BEATLES NEVER
A True Stone Lover

Ti Harrison:
Hope you didn't hurt yourself when you bumped into Jeremy. Good luck in the future.
Your neighbors,
H. and P. Mc.

To Robin Kingsley:
We heard you at the Hollywood Bowl. We like you.
Marianna and Stephanie

To Jerry Shapiro:
Welcome back from Mexico. You sure took a long time to get back.
Freddie N.

To Herman:
Please forgive me for bothering you all the time, but "I Can't Help Myself." If you'd stop long enough, maybe you wouldn't want to keep running.
Sylvia P.

MAIL BOX

Stone Story

Dear Beat:
This May, I among many other Rolling Stones fans, was lucky enough to go to the Rolling Stones Concert in Long Beach. The program was great and included the Byrds and Paul Revere and the Raiders. But the highest point of the show was when the Rolling Stones made their appearance.

Today, when I started reading "On the Beat," Bill Wyman's comments about their close call at the Long Beach auditorium caught my attention. Especially the line that was printed where Bill comments, "There must have been a hundred teenagers on the roof and more piling on top of them."

I was back there and I got pushed against the car. There were no teenagers on the roof. Instead there were a couple of Long Beach policemen up there. They were pounding on the car with their bully sticks and just about knocking everyone around the car almost unconscious.

After being pushed around like crazy, the policeman who wasn't on the car started pushing everyone out of his way. I had bruises on my shoulder for a week afterwards. That policeman almost broke my back when he pushed me.

I hope the Rolling Stones will understand. We admire them, respect them, and above all, love them. If we had wanted to kill them we might have tried climbing up on the station wagon. It is something very special to all of us to be near them. With everything the way it is now, who knows when we might see them again.

We love them, so Rolling Stones, come back to California and soon.
Sincerely as a Stone fan can be,
Jo Anne Orijel

BEAT Fans

Dear BEAT:
"GREAT" is the work for the BEAT. We all want to tell you of the neat job you're all doing by bringing rising pop groups to the teen scene. It's great to hear about all of them. Stay tops-cuz we know you will!
Yours,
The Neatbeats, Anaheim

Dear Editor:
I would like to say that you have been doing a fine job with your newspaper. I eagerly look forward to reading it every week and find everything in it to be writings of sheer genius.

Your fine writing and clever jokes are exceeded only by your sincerity and desire to serve the public.

The BEAT will go down in history as one of the finest newspapers to ever serve the teenage buyers.

Keep up the good work.
Love,
Mother

AUTOGRAPH PLEASE, two U.S. fans asked Herman. The English recording star quickly obliged them by signing one of his newest albums, "Herman's Hermits On Tour," which is just where they are.

KRLA BEAT SUBSCRIPTION

you will SAVE 60% of the regular price!
AN INTRODUCTORY SPECIAL . . . if you subscribe now . . .

☐ 1 YEAR — 52 Issues — $3.00   ☐ 2 YEARS — $5.00

Enclosed is $............

Send to:.. Age:..............

Address:..

City:.............................. State:.................. Zip:..............

MAIL YOUR ORDER TO: KRLA BEAT
1401 South Oak Knoll Avenue
Pasadena, California 91106

Outside U.S.: $9.00 — 52 Issues

CASEY'S QUIZ

By CASEY KASEM

The last thing this internationally famous singing star ever wanted to be is an internationally famous singing star. His father, an oil well driller, taught him to play the guitar as a child and by the time he'd reached his teens he was conducting a talent show over local radio. He was most interested in writing songs, not recording them, but fate had other things in mind. He recorded one of his own compositions and suddenly found himself at the top of the charts. Now he's so busy, he's been forced to rent his Tennessee home (which has, of all things, a swimming pool in the living room.)

KRLA ARCHIVES

Sisters Win Carton Match

Congratulations to sisters Marilyn and Susan Kane of Long Beach, the first two winners of the KRLA BEAT Cartoon Contest.

Marilyn, 15, attends Long Beach Poly High, while her sister Susan, 13, attends Hughes Junior High. Since both sisters are talented art majors, and since it was a draw between the two, we feel sure they will be happy to share the two albums.

While there were many other clever and well-drawn cartoons submitted to the BEAT, the Kane sisters won easily because their cartoons were among the few reproducible for newspapers.

"You idiot! Why didn't you tell our readers that the cartoons have to be drawn in pen or ink of some sort," my editor boomed.

"I'm sorry sir . . ."

Not Reproducable

"Sorry! Look at all these wonderful cartoons that these poor, hard working, earnest Beat Readers have slaved over," he said, waving some of the many cartoons which were drawn in crayon, colored pencil or pencil.

"And we can't even use them."

"Yes sir."

"See that you do it right this time."

"Yes sir."

So you see readers, the cartoons must be drawn in pen or ink of some sort in order to be reproducible. Sorry about that.

Raise Money For Your Club

Want to raise extra money for your club treasury? You could easily make several hundred dollars.

Write to: Fan Club Funds, KRLA, Sunset-Vine Tower, Suite 504, Hollywood, California — 90028.

KRLA BEAT

The KRLA BEAT is published weekly by Prestige Publishing Company; editorial and advertising offices at 6290 Sunset Boulevard, Suite 504, Hollywood, California 90028.

Single copy price, 15 cents.

Subscription price: U.S. and possessions, $3 per year or $5 for two years. Outside U.S., $9 per year.

HELP!

HELP! We are in need of a drummer (boy or girl) and a girl bass guitarist.

They must be 14-16 years-old and live in the Torrance-Gardena area. Anyone meeting these requirements, write to Sylvia Araujo, 3826 W. 184 St., Torrance, Calif. 90504.

HELP! My name is Josephine Porraz. I am sixteen years-old and I need "Help". I would like a summer job or any kind of job you have to offer. Josephine Porraz, 54 North Grand Oaks, Pasadena, Calif. 91107.

CASEY'S QUIZ ANSWER

(Don't peek unless you've read the question elsewhere in the BEAT)

Roy Orbison

Back issues of the KRLA BEAT are still available, for a limited time. If you've missed an issue of particular interest to you, send 15 cents for each copy wanted, along with a self-addressed stamped envelope to:

KRLA BEAT
Suite 504
6290 Sunset Blvd.
Hollywood, California 90028

ISSUES AVAILABLE
- 4/14 — INTERVIEW WITH JOHN LENNON
- 4/21 — INTERVIEW WITH PAUL McCARTNEY
- 4/28 — CHIMP EXCITES TEEN FAIR
- 5/5 — HERMANIA SPREADS
- 5/12 — HERE COMES THE BEATLES
- 5/19 — VISIT WITH BEATLES
- 5/26 — FAB NEW BEATLE QUIZ
- 6/2 — L.A. ROCKS AS STONES ROLL
- 6/16 — BATTLE OF THE BEAT
- 6/23 — P. J. — HERO OR HEEL
- 6/30 — PROBY FIRED
- 7/7 — SONNY & CHER vs. THE BYRDS

?Beatle Quiz?

Okay Class, come to order. It's KRLA Beatle Quiz Time and we have five more questions for the most educational and rewarding contest in Beatleland.

You Beatle Students who missed the first eight weeks of the Beatle Quiz can still catch up by ordering the July 24, July 7, June 30, June 23, June 16, June 9, June 2 and May 26 issues of the BEAT.

The winner of the quiz will be rewarded with a personal interview with the Beatles for the BEAT when the group arrives in August and along with a friend will be invited to attend the Beatle Concert as guests of the KRLA Deejays.

Additional prizes will be provided for runner-ups and in case of a tie there will be additional questions or a drawing to decide the final winner. The contest will cover a ten-week period, with at least five new questions asked each week.

Beatle Quiz
KRLA BEAT
Suite 504
6290 Sunset Blvd.
Hollywood, Calif. 90028

CONTEST EDITOR:

Below are my answers to the fourth set of questions in the BEATLE QUIZ CONTEST.

My Name .... Address ....

City .... State .... Zip Code ....

I (☐ am) (☐ am not) presently a subscriber to the KRLA BEAT.

NEW QUESTIONS

1. The Beatles starred in a TV spectacular, seen on the American airwaves last fall, and did a series of hilarious parodies. What was the title of the show?
2. What famous American Bandleader did the Beatles invite backstage during their 1964 tour of the States?
3. Which Beatle has a passion for modern art and used long rolls of paper instead of canvas?
4. Which of the Beatle's special favorite, whom they have never met, has sent them several congratulatory telegrams?
5. One of the Beatles is rumored to have two identical wardrobes, for both on and off-stage wear, because of his tendency to gain weight. Which Beatle has this problem?

KRLA ARCHIVES

Guess Who?

YES, ITS HERMAN doing a show with the Dick Clark Caravan of Stars. Herman and his Hermits made such a hit in the United States, they have come back for another tour.

Herman Slates Heavy Schedule

Herman and his Hermits, are following up a successful tour with the Dick Clark Caravan of Stars, with another tour from July 22 through August 15.

The popularity of the group in America, in addition to influencing a second tour, landed them spots on three television shows. They will be on the Al Hirt Show on July 24, the Danny Kaye Show on October 13, and a TV special, "Herman's Wonderful World."

Herman's place in the hearts of U.S. fans seems to be second only to the Beatles and the Rolling Stones. His "Wonderful World" is still climbing the national charts, and his latest, "I'm Henry VIII, I Am", could land him on the top of the charts.

Album Numbers

"Henry VIII" is Herman's second hit to be forced off an album, the first being the fantastically popular, "Mrs. Brown". When disc jockeys began playing the "Mrs. Brown" track off the "Introducing Herman's Hermits" album, MGM Records had absolutely no intention of releasing it as a single. However, when the requests (and in some cases demands) reached such gigantic proportions that they had no choice, "Mrs. Brown" was released and soon after became number one in the nation.

"Henry VIII"

Now it's happening all over again. "Henry VIII" is off the "Herman's Hermits On Tour" LP. Again, disc jockeys picked it up, requests flooded MGM, the record was released as a single, and in just two weeks it had made it within the top fifteen on all three of the national charts, and all the way up to number three on the Cash Box Top 100. This makes "Henry VIII" one of the fastest rising records of all time.

No wonder Herman is touring the U.S. again—this guy is popular and you spell that with a capital "P"!

—*Louise Criscione.*

Beatles Talent Boost Exports

The British Broadcasting Corporation recently announced that recorded Beatle programs will be used in an attempt to boost exports.

The programs will be aired all over the world, in forty-one different languages, and here's hoping some of them will be heard in the California area.

The Beatles are being used because of their universal appeal, which the BBC feels will help present the correct picture of modern England. The director of the airway feels the Beatles have helped make much of the world far more aware of Britain, and what it is really like.

The plan has the backing of many government agencies in England, and is expected to result in a tremendous upsurge in export sales.

It's nice to know that Britain's faith in the Beatles equals our own after all, and that everyone in merry England isn't busy griping because the foursome won an award they're about to earn all over again!

British Seaside Hotel Hosts Several Recording Groups

(Manchester, Eng.) Gerry and the Pacemakers, Freddie and the Dreamers, Billy J. Kramer and the Dakotas are all doing summer shows in the same seaside resort — Blackpool, Britain's major holiday center.

Everyone is wondering when Gerry will marry pretty Pauline Behan, his fan club secretary. They announced their engagement at the beginning of the year.

"We're in no hurry," said Gerry.

"The boys and I have got to sort out our careers first. The big problem at the moment is whether to make another film. The public didn't seem to like the last one much, and films take up so much time."

On the same bill as Gerry is America's Gene Vincent, who, judging by the standard of his performance, might well make a comeback over here.

But Gene, who announced his engagement to singer Jackie Frisco here just recently, also has a problem. In 1960, he was injured in the car crash which killed singer Eddie Cochran. Now Gene has been told his left foot will have to come off.

"I've been walking with the leg in irons," said Gene. "Now the pain has got too much for me, and the doctors have advised I have it off."

RUMORS BLOOM IN STRANGE SOIL

By Louise Criscione

Ever wonder about those rumors which continually travel the circuit and become so lodged in people's minds that even the truth will not dispel them? Where do these rumors come from? Who starts them and why?

Rumors are vague things — they hardly ever reveal the culprit who starts them. But in general—rather than in specific—there are some very interesting possibilities to explore.

Rival entertainers have been known to start rumors about their competitors. What easier way to kill competition—that is, if you want competition killed—than by simply dropping a casual "Did you know that . . . ." to the right person?

And many times that "right" person is the newspaperman. A reporter is always looking for a story—it's his business. And just like any other business, there are the good and the bad. There are reporters who check their facts as best they can, but there are other reporters who are so anxious to grab the "scoop" that they fail to properly check their sources. This oversight, of course, is the lifeline of the rumor.

Wedding Rumors

Way back in February 1964, a noted newspaperman obviously failed to check his sources well enough and consequently initiated the first of the "Paul McCartney weds Jane Asher" rumors. Just how many people believed that story—how many Paul McCartney pictures were torn to shreds before the truth was learned? Plenty.

That case was probably nothing more than misinformation. But many times rumors are deliberately written to plant a doubt in people's minds, and usually they do just that. "Are Chad and Jeremy really splitting up?" A simple question — that's all it takes. Quickly the question transforms itself into an alleged statement of fact: "Chad and Jeremy *are* splitting up." Rumor started—it's as easy as that.

In fact, just such a thing did happen and Chad and Jeremy were forced to chase the rumor all over England and America denying everywhere that they were splitting up. But despite all their denials, no doubt some people still believe that they are breaking up, or at least that there is trouble brewing in their camp. Because for some reason, the denial just never seems to travel as far or as fast as the rumor.

Wrong Quotes

Another huge factor in the rumor department is the misquoting, quoting out of context, or the failure of the reporter to explain the circumstances under which the quote was made.

Just a raised eyebrow or a facial expression can change completely the meaning of a statement. Take for example this quote by Dave Davies of the Kinks when asked if the Kinks were happy: "No, Pete attacked me with a knife yesterday!" Now that was said jokingly—it was a put-on. It was meant to be funny and it was. But do you see what could happen if that was taken out of context and used in some reporter's "scoop" of the Kinks breaking up? It could plant a lot of doubts, make a lot of trouble, and require a lot of explanations.

So why don't entertainers do something about these rumors? Well, what can they do? Sue? Sure, they could because in some cases careers have been ruined by a particularly vicious and false statement. But a law suit is a costly and drawn-out affair. And a career is sometimes short-lived anyway, so a law suit really doesn't pay. Also, a suit means more publicity, and if by some chance the rumor has missed some corners or if it has died down, it is certain to rise again with the suit.

Can't Be Erased

Okay, so why don't artists at least answer the lies written about them? Ray Davies of the Kinks puts it very simply: "What can you do about stuff like that? I suppose if I answer back people will think it's true. No smoke without fire, and so on and so on."

Unfortunately, whoever thought up that old saying, "The truth never catches up with the rumor," knew exactly what he was talking about. Because somehow people are just more eager to believe the rumor than the truth.

Since it is impractical to sue and impractical to answer back, most entertainers have learned to accept the rumor as an occupational hazard.

Still, it's a shame that people in the spotlight cannot be protected from those with the false and vicious tongues. Kinda makes you wonder just who you can believe.

Yeah, the rumor is a lousy deal all the way around.

BEATLES AGAIN PROVE THEY'RE STRONG AS EVER

For approximately 18 months now, the Beatles have been going around setting precedents and breaking records like nobody's business. One of the toughest precedents they have set for themselves is selling enough copies to insure a gold record for each of their albums. In order to receive this coveted gold record, one million copies must be sold. To date, every single Beatle album released by Capital Records has sold the necessary million.

The newest Beatle album, "Beatle VI", is not deviating one inch from the established Beatle tradition. After only five days of taking orders, the half-million mark was reached. And by the time the album was finally released on June 14, it had qualified for a gold record!

Who says the Beatles are losing popularity?

KRLA ARCHIVES

EXCLUSIVE INTERVIEW
Jack Good With The BEAT

By MICHELLE STRAUBING and SUSAN WYLIE

(EDITOR'S NOTE: The following is a series of excerpts from a conversation between Jack Good, former producer of Shindig, and BEAT Reporters Michelle Straubing and Susan Wylie.

Q: *Why are you leaving Shindig?*
A: I am dying faster than I should have died. An hour show is too much to do and I cannot take it.
Q: *What kind of training did did you have?*
A: I was at the BBC School For Producers for six months. Although I learned very little from this, this was my official training. I don't think anybody needs training as a producer. They just have to have a certain sense of what is show business and what is show people. They also have to have a common humanity with other people in order to give them what they want.
Q: *Do you feel that your leaving will affect the show?*
A: I would be a super human if I thought it wouldn't affect the show. I can't help feeling it might hurt the show, which is no reflection on Dean Whitmore and one always hopes that one is indispensible; one rarely proves to be so. I hope in an off beat sense that Shindig will carry on endlessly. When in one of my more selfish moments I wouldn't mind it dropping dead next Thursday.
Q: *Is the new producer going to be able to be as much of a public figure as you were?*
A: No, but he's going to have the intellect to persuade someone else to do it for him.
Q: *What were some of the first shows you ever produced?*
A: The first show I ever produced on television was called "East Side Special" in 1957. I was the first one to ever have Elvis Presley and Little Richard perform on TV in England.
Q: *Did you produce live shows before you did TV?*
A: Oh yes, a lot of live plays before that, particularly when I was at Oxford University.
Q: *Why was P. J. Proby forced off the stage at the Freedom From Hunger Concert?*
A: He wasn't forced off the stage. He could have stayed there endlessly.
Q: *Then why were the girls allowed to run on stage?*
A: They weren't allowed to come on stage. They just came on stage as far as I could see.
Q: *Where did the proceeds from that show go?*
A: The proceeds went to the United Nations Freedom From Hunger Foundation. There could not be a better cause. The actual proceeds from this show will not be enough to keep any significant number of starving people from dying of hunger, but we are hoping the number of people who came to see this program will promote this cause and make people realize while we're leading the good life, millions of people abroad are not just hungry, but actually dying of hunger. Mothers with children in their arms are dying of hunger and their children are dying of hunger. We can do something about this by promoting the equipment. We're not giving it, we're lending it on a long term basis along with seed and know how to show the people abroad in order to keep themselves alive this is a very important cause.
Q: *I've noticed that many of the Shindig people seem to stick together. Can you explain this?*
A: That's because we're a big, happy family. We really are a party. We have a lot of parties together and we really live out of each other's pockets. We have a great time together. There's nobody in the cast who doesn't love each and every one of us.
Q: *What do you do to further the careers of the regulars on Shindig?*
A: We don't feel it's necessary. We believe that everyone on Shindig has enough talent to make it on their own. We're not here to promote each other. We are here to promote Shindig and the fact that we're living together in harmony.
Q: *Are you married?*
A: Yes.
Q: *Do you have any children?*
A: Yes, I have three children and I hope they never have to die of hunger.
Q: *Are you going to produce*
TURN TO PAGE 16

ON THE BEAT

By Louise Criscione

Well, I finally got Kinked! After listening to Kinks albums for hours, and after witnessing their performance "live", I have come to the somewhat belated conclusion that the Kinks are fabulous! Only thing I can't figure out is why they aren't more popular in America. Granted, they have had some huge hits and both of their albums have done very well on the national charts, but I still think that the Kinks are an extremely underrated group! Maybe it's because they haven't had enough television exposure, nor have they made nearly enough personal appearances in the States. But whatever the reason, it is certainly not because of a lack of talent—'cause talent is one thing which the Kinks possess in abundance!

...DAVE DAVIES

Isn't the Beau Brummels new record a direct attempt to sound just a whole lot like the Byrds?

There is a very logical reason behind Sonny & Cher's failure to make their scheduled appearance on the Kinks' Reno, Nevada show. Seems that just before they were to board the plane, they heard of the tragic El Toro plane crash and Cher absolutely refused to fly! Since they had to go to Reno by plane and since Cher simply would not set foot on one, the Kinks' show was forced to proceed without the services of Sonny & Cher!

Spanish Location Nixed

The Beatles were previously set to begin shooting their third film, "A Talent For Loving", this autumn after returning from their U.S. tour. The western was to be filmed on location in Spain—that is, until it was discovered that the Spanish weather is not too reliable in autumn. So that's out. Alternate plans are now being made and will be announced shortly.

QUICK ONES: Well, the Stones should have gotten some satisfaction out of the fact that "Satisfaction" made it all the way to number one on the national charts . . . Roger Miller has been appointed Ambassador-at-large by his home state of Oklahoma . . . Terry Black is now living in Southern California, Huntington Harbour to be exact . . . Sign in a British paper read: "Welcome back Stones, your country needs you" . . . George Harrison spends his leisure hours shooting potatoes off the trees in his garden in Surrey . . . Of all the songs which he has written, Gerry Marsden likes "Ferry Cross The Mersey" best because "the lyrics represented my true feelings about the people who live on the banks of the Mersey" . . . The Supremes have been booked into the Copa from July 29 to August 4 . . . Verdict on Tom Jones' tonsils—out they go!

John Lennon

The rest of ON THE BEAT is devoted to John Lennon because John has been kind of busy lately. First off, he sold his old Rolls Royce to Ringo and purchased a brand new one. John's new Rolls is completely black — black upholstery, black windows, and black hub caps! Not to memtion a TV and a built-in bar.

John has been invited to Lund, Sweden by the students of the Royal University. Reason for the invitation: to speak on the subject of being an author! You realize, of course, that John's second book, *A Spaniard In The Works*, has been published and is now on newsstands everywhere. John's comment on his new book! "It's the usual rubbish, but it has more pages!"

And finally—people are still talking about why the Beatles won the MBE awards. Mr. Lennon himself has a few words to say on that subject: "I don't think we got ours for rock 'n' roll. On that basis, we'd have got OBE's (a higher award), and the Rolling Stones MBE's! I reckon we got them for exports, and the citation ought to have said that."

Yeah, well you tell 'em, John.

A BEAT EDITORIAL

Fads and Fleecing

Fads can be fun, but some of them are also becoming outrageously expensive. Greedy manufacturers are turning out cheap novelty items and then selling them at prices which are ridiculously high.

For instance, a new line of kooky sunglasses priced at $10 to $15. They cost less than one dollar to manufacture.

Some of our very high-minded and moral elders are setting quite an example in ethics as they use every device to fleece us out of our hard-earned money and allowances. Worst of all, too many of us seem to be falling for it. We rush out and buy the latest do-dad, regardless of cost.

It's time we wised up. In far too many cases, the price is *not* right. But as long as we keep playing their game, these unscrupulous manufacturers will continue playing use for suckers.

Ridiculous Ads

Speaking of people who seem to regard teenagers as brainless nitwits, how about some of the advertisements you see and hear these days. A particular cosmetic, toothpaste, mouthwash, deodorant or hair rinse is supposed to change your entire life.

If teens who encounter such offensive advertisements would simply refuse to buy the product — regardless of its quality — the advertising agencies would soon get the message and start approaching us as adults.

Then we could be treated to such mature approaches as the nut in a tin suit who rides a horse across people's lawns to sell soap.

Turn-About

The old-fogey dictators who screen foreign artists to decide whether to allow them into this country to perform use one basic yardstick for their decisions: Is the performer talented enough and is he or she sufficiently well-known.

In most cases their decision is no. Some British groups have been denied work permits in the U.S. even when they had the number one record in this country.

The men who make these recommendations are members of the American Musicians Union. And if the public were to judge them by the same yardstick, not a single one of them would be sufficiently well-known to pass the same test.

British Refuse Work Permit To Singer Bobby Vinton

Bobby Vinton, going to London to promote his new British made single, "Don't go away mad," was told by the British Government to go away.

Denied a work permit, the recording star was forced to cancel his scheduled appearances on radio and television.

But all was not lost. While in London, Vinton taped interviews for the British pirate radio stations, which don't particularly care if you have a work permit or not since the stations are illegal anyway.

Meanwhile, Bobby's manager contacted the Variety Artists Federation to discover why Bobby's work permit had failed to come through.

The American Federation of Radio and Television Artists had not replied to recent Variety Artists Federation letters concerning British artists being prevented from receiving American work permits, he was told.

KRLA ARCHIVES

...THE RAIDERS

Methods to Take Off Those Extra Pounds In Order to Fit Into Summer Fashions

Weight is becoming more and more of a problem in the teenage world, and summer is the world's worst time for gaining just that. If your clothes are starting to get a big tight around the middle, here are ten good ways to help you fight the battle of the bulge.

See your doctor before going on any kind of a diet, then try these helpful hints. They help you *stay* on it!

1. Dieting can be interesting. it can even be exciting if you're willing to work at it. Start by buying an article of clothing, something you've been wanting for ages, only buy it the size you'd *like* to be. Try it on every day so you'll be able to tell how much progress you're making, and get ready to flip the day it fits!

2. Weigh yourself every other day and keep a chart of your weight losses. This is especially interesting if you're quite a bit overweight. When the pounds start rolling off, keeping your chart up to date becomes a pleasure to look forward to.

3. Don't tell everyone you're dieting. Wait until they start noticing the difference for themselves. This helps make a diet interesting because it's such a good feeling to know you're looking better, and it's an even better feeling when the compliments start coming.

Count Calories

4. Get a pocket calorie counter and keep it with you at all times. Some foods can really surprise you when it comes to the amount of calories they contain, so do not take the chance of ever being uncertain. The chart will probably separate the carbohydrate foods from the protein foods, so stay with mostly proteins and the weight will disappear faster.

Keep Busy

5. Don't get down in the dumps about your weight. When you're dieting, you're going to be twice as conscious of your figure, and you'll be upset every once in awhile because you didn't start your diet sooner. You're doing something about it, and that's what matters most. If some upleasant soul calls you "Chubby", don't give in to the natural urge to rush home and eat three layer cakes. Just consider the source and keep dieting.

6. Since so many over-weight people are compulsive eaters, keep yourself busy so you won't be so aware of being hungry. You might even try putting a bell on the door of the refrigerator, to remind you to reach for a salad instead of a leg of lamb.

7. If you do go off your diet for a day, don't stay off it. Go back on the next. After all, "starving" isn't easy, and you're only human. Just give yourself a good talking to and get with it!

8. Talk your diet over with your folks and arrange not to be home for certain meals that would be just too much temptation to resist. And ask the shopper in your family to pick up some of the dietetic foods available in most super markets. They don't taste bad at all!

Salad Dressing

9. If you can't stand the somewhat gluey low-calorie salad dressings, try lemon juice and salt. It sounds ghastly, but isn't. It may take a little getting used to, but the chances are good that you'll end up liking the combination. Lemon juice is good on nearly every vegetable, raw or cooked.

10. Get lots and lots of exercise. Most everyone says that walking won't burn off calories, but it will strengthen muscles and keep you in better physical shape. It takes between a half hour and forty-five minutes to walk about two miles, depending upon your speed. Driving may be easier, but standing on your own two feet and hiking it off gets results!

If, of all things, you aren't trying to lose weight, but gain it, prepared diet foods like Metrecal and Sego are helpful. One 300 calorie meal a day can help take off the pounds, and an additional meal (besides the other three) of Metrecal can help put them on. (You lucky, lucky character!!)

'Othello' to Rock London Or Roll on Broadway?

Will "Othello" rock in London with Proby or roll on Broadway with Jerry Lee Lewis?

Jack Good's hankering to produce a rock n' roll version of this Shakerspeare play has given birth to countless rumors.

According to some, the ex-producer of Shindig was going to make his play a London-based production and many believed that Brian Epstein purchased the London West End Theater for Good's production and was going to personally back the show.

And the star Good reportedly wanted for his show — P. J. Proby.

These rumors were quieted recently when Ray Brown, booking agent for Jerry Lee Lewis released the news that Good wants to produce "Othello" on Broadway, with Lewis as the star.

"It's in the talking stage. I recall Jerry Lee told me sometime ago that he'd try anything once." said Brown.

Since everything is still "just talk," only time will tell.

Tall Tale of Paul Revere Not to Mention His Raiders

Sixteen year-old Paul Revere tossed a typewriter out of the window, thusly realizing his youthful ambition to get expelled from school.

This was not his first attempt. He had been trying for some time. But insolence, insubordination, rebellion and even revolution had failed to impress his elders that he was not a worthy schoolboy.

At last he had hit upon a successful plan. Out the window went a school typewriter, breaking the window, the typewriter, and ending his career as a student.

"A great day in my life", recalls Revere, now the revered leader of a swinging booming group, named the Raiders. "I was free of school but I had no job and little education. What was I to do?

What indeed, you may ask indignantly. And so Revere continues to elaborate the curious tale of his career.

Golden Comb

"I went where all dumb kids go if they have no talent or ambition, to hairdressing college. But the amazing thing was that I turned out to be a brilliant barber. I was a new Perry Como.

After graduating with the Order of the Golden Comb, he took $500 left to him by his grandmother and went into the barber business.

"This succeeded well," Revere reported. "I was, by then seventeen, and I was able to buy a second shop, then a third. By the time I was eighteen I was making a lot of money."

But besides money he also liked playing piano and since the age of seven had been playing boogie, blues and, when playcraze started, rock n' roll.

So at the age of eighteen, a businessman and a piano player, he sold the barber shops and bought a a drive-in restaurant in Boise, Idaho.

Bread Boy

And guess who was delivering bread to his drive-in?

A swaggering eighteen-year-old with dark eyes, a way with girls, and the name of Mark Lindsay.

"He begged to be allowed to sing and because he was bigger than we were, we let him. He was good. Very good, said Revere.

"But I was a greedy man so I said to myself in a low avaricious muttering voice: Why let this bum sing with us for money when he could play an instrument as well. That way we get double value.

"Thus did Mark Lindsay become a saxophonist of great style and a guitarist too. Also, he stopped delivering bread and became a handsome pop singer whose depths are still unknown."

Temporary Retirement

Then for twelve months, and without apparent reason, Paul Revere said goodbye to success and retreated to a log cabin in Oregon where he sulked quietly and counted his takings from the drive-in restaurant.

Mark Lindsay, who had become impossibly handsome, decided that it was easier to live on no money at all in Hollywood than to deliver bread in Idaho. So he hied himself to the movie capital of the world and began to search under the front seats of cars in quest of pennies and nickels dropped by spendthrifts from Bel Air and places of that sort.

He disguised himself as a bum, which with his wild hair, wicked eyes and general air of debauchery, was not difficult. Then one day a terrible yearning overcame both himself and Paul Revere. So they joined up and **TURN TO PAGE 14**

...PAUL REVERE

KRLA ARCHIVES

THE BEST QUOTE OF THE WEEK comes from Ringo Starr, who says wisely, "Once you are deaf to your public, you might as well retire because you'll give them nothing. Judging from that quote, Ringo and the other Beatles plan to be in business for quite a while.

The Curious Ride to Top Of Paul Revere, Raiders

(Continued from Page 13) re-started their music.

There was a teenage club in Portland, Oregon where the worst group in the world used to play the most hideous music Paul had ever heard.

Third Raider

One of the guitarists was a small tough man called Mike Smith who asked to be called "Smitty".

"Smitty—you are a lousy group but you have it made here. I would like to be in on what is happening," Revere said to him in his gentle way.

Revere takes up the story: "What was happening was that Smitty was packing the club. The kids were going wild. Yet the group was so bad. No one played in tune, in time or anything.

"So I took over the club and Smitty joined us. I said: 'Just because you are a terrible guitarist doesn't mean you need be a bad drummer. Be a drummer.' And it came to pass that Smitty became a clever drumming man and Paul Revere and his group were now three."

Smitty had two friends who were even worse than he was. Naturally Paul took them on. In this way, he reckoned, he would be able to shine.

This he did and, to his amazement and the delight of the youth of the North West frontier, Paul Revere became a very big local star.

Mushrooming record labels promised him great fame and immense riches, but because he had an eye for business, he rejected most of the offers and has now ended up with Columbia Records, who had been established for many hundreds of years, long before the dog sat with his ear cocked in front of the phonograph.

Choose Name

Paul Revere, having for a long time wondered what on earth to do with his name, decided to call his group the "Raiders". Though he had little education and no sense of history, there was, at the back of his mind, a faint recollection that a man named Revere had figured somewhere in the history of America.

The group's name caught on, and so did their music. And from a sound-proof booth in Portland's KISN radio station, stepped a nervous, reed-thin opportunist - disc - jockey called Roger Hart, who became the group's Epstein but who, surprisingly, did not believe himself to be more important than God.

Hart diligently and honestly began to mold the group into a salable product and planned to retire by the age of 30 with a million dollars in the narrow leather pockets of his narrow leather coat. To date, he has not succeeded, but give him time.

After the Raiders had totally conquered the North West corner of the Union, Hart met another man who also would not be visible were he to stand behind a telegraph pole.

Derek Taylor

By name: Derek Taylor—erratic publicity officer for the infamous Beatles whose dramatic rise had been so parallel to Revere's ride to fame.

Hart, in a torrent of disc jockey glibbery, convinced Taylor, that the group was worth hearing.

"I believe every word of what you say," cried Taylor with abandon, and immediately deserted his ill-paid job with the Beatles. He emigrated to Hollywood with his wife and four children, leaving a trail of debts and regrets behind him, in London.

The group was strengthened when Smitty's two friends were replaced by two eighteen-year -olds called Drake Lewin and Philip Volk (good Anglo-Saxon names) and they are, to use the one of the world's great cliches, "on the threshold of big things."

Believe what you wish of this awful narrative; the only thing that really matters is that here America has a wonderful group of artists who can take on the best people State-side and any one of the European invaders.

Take it or leave it.

Major Lance, The Vibrations, The Dave Clark Five Bobby Vinton, Adam Wade, Billy Butler, and The Yardbirds

From Furniture to Beatles Mr. Epstein Manages Well

A British businessman who gave up peddling records in favor of pushing recording artists, has made pop history.

The ex-furniture pusher is Brian Epstein and since 1963 his artists have emerged, one by one and group by group, as hit parade champions.

Among the artists he has handled are the Beatles, Gerry and the Pacemakers, The Fourmost, Billy J. Kramer and the Dakotas, The Big Three, Cilla Black, Tommy Quickly, The Sounds.

Within twelve months has been associated with 12 number one recordings. This is a feat unmatched by any other manager in the pop music world.

How did this man from Liverpool become one of the most important figures on the British entertainment scene in such a remarkably short space of time?

Record Shop

The first few years of his career he tried selling furniture, acting and interior decorating. Then, with one assistant, he took charge of his family's first record shop. Soon trading under the name of NEMS, it became the dominant record retailing organization on Merseyside.

One of the keys to the success of the business was Epsteins efforts to satisfy individual customer requests. As it happened, it was also his desire to keep his customers happy which led him to the Beatles.

German Beatles

A smattering of Liverpool fans began asking for the Beatles who had recorded on a Polydar disc in Germany. With no idea that the four were living a few hundred yards from his store he went to their performance at the Cavern Club under the impression that they were German artists.

At this point he casually drifted out of the record selling business and into the artist's management field with an informal personal agreement with the Beatles.

Soon he realized the group's potential, but this was no over night success story. Epstein spent a year preparing the Beatles for the future and not until 1962 did he travel to London for talks with record company producers.

One Failure

One major label refused to go beyond the audition stage with the boys, but at the office of E.M.I. he met with a more enthusiastic response.

The Beatles taped their first single, "Love Me Do", and Epstein's venture, which began as the management of one single group, became a large and successful organization of rare force and unique acheivement in the entertainment world.

...BRIAN EPSTEIN

KRLA ARCHIVES

MARIANNE DISCUSSES HER WORLD
(Continued from Page 8)

most exciting thing that has happened to Marianne as a recording artist? The question took a lot of thinking and remembering back over the past year since "that party". Finally she had the answer: "I think it is being able to accomplish all this myself. I mean, at eighteen being able to come over to Los Angeles because of my recordings."

According to Marianne, being a pop star isn't all a dream come true. "I hate touring," she said. "It's terrible, especially for a girl. It's not so bad for a boy, but for a girl it's just horrible."

Marianne would like to branch out in show business and try her luck at movies. But she is in no great hurry. "Maybe next year."

Mrs. John Dunbar

The future looks pretty bright for Marianne Faithfull. At eighteen, she is already a recognized star, the maker of hit records, and most important of all—Mrs. John Dunbar. Marianne and John were secretly wed on May 6, a little over a year since she had first met him at that St. Valentine's Day dance.

John accompanied Marianne to L.A. He is an extremely nice guy who prefers to let the limelight fall exclusively on Marianne. When our photographer asked John if he would pose for a picture with Marianne, John replied simply: "I'd really rather not."

The newlyweds have been so busy that they have not as yet had time for a honeymoon. "I don't mind. You know, it really doesn't matter," said Marianne.

Nevertheless, the Dunbars will be taking a belated Mexican honeymoon in August.

A lucky girl—that Marianne Faithfull.

For Girls Only
By SHEILA DAVIS

Calling all boys. I'll make you a bargain! If you'll stop reading this column, I'll send you a brand new dollar bill. You might have a little trouble spending them (I printed them up myself) but it's the thought that counts.

The mail was really great this week, and I'd like to start off this chat with an excerpt from one of your letters. The girl asked me to withhold her name, but here's what she had to say about a problem many of us have.

"I have never been able to get along with my sister, who is two years older than I am. Our battles were keeping the whole household in an uproar, So I decided to try and solve our personality problem.

"I made a list of all the things I don't like about her and studied them carefully. This made me realize that most of my complaints weren't really faults on her part. They were just things we didn't see eye to eye about, and things we don't have in common.

"It also made me realize that if she and I weren't related, we probably would never be good friends; we're too different. After thinking it all over, I made up my mind not to expect so much from her and respect our differences. Now we get along fine. We'll never really be close, but we do love each other and are finally able to let it show even if we are about as similar as night and day."

Separate People

That letter is so true, I can't believe it. Most brothers and sisters don't get along because they expect too much from each other and forget they are separate people.

This isn't the case with me however. All I expect my brothers to be is human, and I guess that's asking too much (har). Incidentally, I've been having a nice rest the last few days. My sixteen-year-old brother isn't speaking to me.

He asked how to spell the word *flavor* and I told him f-l-a-v-o-u-r (you know me and my English phase). He wrote it that way on his summer school homework and his teacher marked the word wrong.

Gee, I wonder if he'll ever speak to me again? Let's hope not.

Do you love to buy presents? I do! I think it's more fun than getting them. Well, almost. Next to buying gifts, I love to hide them. When I bought a locket for my mother, I sewed it into the hem of one of my skirts so she wouldn't find it and spoil the surprise. I'm beginning to wonder if I'm clever or just plain sneaky.

Pen Pals

I think pen pals, friends you have never met in person, are the hardest to buy for. If you're planning a surprise, you can't come right out and ask obvious questions or they'll know something's going on. Last time I had this problem I settled for a big box of stationery and then put stamps on all the envelopes. I was tempted to address all the envelopes to me, but I thought that would have been a bit much. Anyway, my pen pal loved the present! Another good idea might have been personalized stationery, but that'll have to wait until her next birthday.

Back to the mail bag. I received a ten-page letter from a thirteen-year-old girl from San Pedro, and it was actually stained with tears!

Wearing Braces

The girl had just come from a dentist appointment and was thunderstruck by the fact that she was going to have to wear braces for the next two years. And she felt that wearing them was literally going to ruin her life.

I sympathize with her point of view because this same thing once happened to me. It does give you a pretty awful feeling to know you're soon going to be walking around looking like you have swallowed a wrought iron fence.

But I don't sympathize with the "ruining her life" feeling. At least I don't agree with it. I'd be a sorry sight today if I hadn't worn braces, and although it certainly was no fun at all, it was certainly worth it.

I know more young adults who'd give their eye teeth to go back a few years and start over with braces. A smile is something that has to last a lifetime, and I figure any amount of discomfort is not too high a price to pay for making sure that your smile will always be pretty. Wearing braces is like bracing yourself for the future, so my advice to the girl who wrote the letter and to anyone else about to be wired for sound is to grin and bear it. Someday you'll be glad you did! Which is so much better than having to be sorry you didn't.

Fan Clubs
(For information from any of the listed fan clubs enclose a self-addressed, stamped envelope.)

...CILLA BLACK

CILLA BLACK
c/o Francie Kruge
8692 Falmouth Ave., #4
Playa Del Rey, Calif.

THE BEATLES
c/o Sharon Owens
4821 Audubon
Warren, Michigan 48092

THE PREACHERS
c/o Kathy West
1528 Pas and Covina
Valinda, Calif.

DONOVAN
c/o Jeanne Shields
8927½ Krueger
Culver City, California.

ROLLING STONES
c/o Susan Hayward
1507 E. Romneya Dr.
Anaheim, Calif.

CHAD & JEREMY
c/o Madeline Jen Kin
1800 Orange Grove
Orange, Calif.

The above information is provided as a service to our readers. Accuracy of the information you receive is the responsibility of the officials of each club.

Sonny & Cher Visit London

Sonny and Cher, having just finished cutting their newest record album, "Look at Us," are on their way to London where they will do several television shows.

Plans in England for the married duo include "Ready Steady Go," the British version of Shindig and "Disc a Go Go" and Tops in Pops.

Going along for the ride are York-Palta executives Charles Greene and Brian Stone. Meanwhile, stay-at-homes from Atco and Imperial Records are going crazy trying to rush releases of Cher's new album and "Look At Us."

Taping British shows should be easy for the pros. They have been appearing on the tube regularly and recently have had two Shindig pics of the week in a row.

KRLA ARCHIVES

KRLA Tunedex

EMPEROR HUDSON — CHARLIE O'DONNELL — CASEY KASEM — JOHNNY HAYES

BOB EUBANKS — DAVE HULL

DICK BIONDI — BILL SLATER

KRLA BEAT
6290 Sunset, No. 504
Hollywood, Cal. 90028

If you were a KRLA BEAT subscriber your name and address would be printed here and you would receive your copy at home, saving 40%.

BULK RATE
U.S. Postage
PAID
Los Angeles, Calif.
Permit No. 25497

1	2	ALL I REALLY WANT TO DO	Cher
2	5	HOLD ME THRILL ME, KISS ME	Mel Carter
3	1	SATISFACTION	Rolling Stones
4	7	I'VE GOT YOU	Sonny & Cher
5	6	YES, I'M READY	Barbara Mason
6	3	I CAN'T HELP MYSELF	The Four Tops
7	4	ONCE UPON A TIME/WHAT'S NEW PUSSYCAT	Tom Jones
8	12	I'M HENRY THE VIII, I AM	Herman's Hermits
9	9	I'M A FOOL	Dino, Desi & Billy
10	11	WHITTIER BOULEVARD	The Midnighters
11	10	LAURIE	Dickie Lee
12	16	CARA MIA	Jay & The Americans
13	15	WOLLY BULLY	Sam the Sham & The Pharoahs
14	14	CRYING IN THE CHAPEL	Elvis Presley
15	8	WHAT THE WORLD NEEDS NOW IS LOVE	Jackie DeShannon
16	13	THIS LITTLE BIRD	Marianne Faithfull
17	27	SAVE YOUR HEART FOR ME	Gary Lewis & Playboys
18	20	SEVENTH SON	Johnny Rivers
19	18	WONDERFUL WORLD	Herman's Hermits
20	26	HUNG ON YOU	Righteous Brothers
21	25	YOU BETTER COME HOME	Petula Clark
22	19	JUST YOU	Sonny & Cher
23	17	HELP ME, RHONDA	Beach Boys
24	29	ALL I REALLY WANT TO DO	The Byrds
25	21	HUSH, HUSH SWEET CHARLOTTE	Patti Page
26	22	MR. TAMBOURINE MAN	The Byrds
27	30	LET HER DANCE	Bobby Fuller
28	35	TO KNOW YOU IS TO LOVE YOU	Peter & Gordon
29	—	YOU WERE ON MY MIND	We Five
30	36	PAPA'S GOT A BRAND NEW BAG	James Brown
31	32	TAKE ME BACK	Little Anthony
32	34	PRETTY LITTLE BABY	Little Anthony
33	39	EASY QUESTION	Elvis Presley
34	—	I WANT CANDY	The Strangeloves
35	—	I HAPPENED JUST THAT WAY	Roger Miller
36	40	DOWN IN THE BOONDOCKS	Billy Joe Royal
37	—	LET THE WATER RUN DOWN	P. J. Proby
38	—	DON'T JUST STAND THERE	Patty Duke
39	—	IT'S GONNA BE FINE	Glenn Yarbrough
40	—	I DON'T BELIEVE	The Guilloteens

KRLA ARCHIVES

KRLA BEAT

Volume 1, Number 21 — LOS ANGELES, CALIFORNIA — 15 Cents — August 7, 1965

DYLAN - "THAT'S WHERE IT'S AT BABE"

BRITISH POP STARS RAP U.S. -- 2 • ARE BEATLES WASHED UP -- 13
THE FAMOUS DAVE CLARK TELEPHONE HOAX -- 3

KRLA BEAT

Los Angeles, California — August 7, 1965

DYLAN POP IDOL

Folk King Now Hottest Thing In Rock Field

A strange and sensitive young man who uses bad grammar to read beautiful poetry and a rough-edged voice to sing spellbinding songs has done an impossible thing.

He has bridged the gap between the folk world and the rock world and has bound together the tastes of adolescence and maturity.

Suddenly it's all one world listening to the musical stories, preachings and scoldings of 24 year-old Bob Dylan, a runaway from Minnesota who has become the dominant voice in music, from the Beatles to Baez.

Already dominating the commercial record charts in England, he has suddenly ignited a similar enthusiasm in this country. Dylan (pronounced "Dillon") no longer belongs to the folk musicians. He is now being claimed by everyone. As a writer and entertainer, one after another of his songs is becoming number one on both sides of the Atlantic.

His latest Roman candle is one which he sings himself, a driving, rocking ballad called "Like a Rolling Stone." It took only one week to reach the top ten in many record surveys throughout the U.S.

It threatens even to out-sell the other Dylan songs which have been propelling other performers up the charts — the Byrds' recording of "Mr. Tambourine Man," the Byrds' and Sonny and Cher's recordings of "All I really Want to Do," and the Turtles' "It Ain't Me, Babe," to name only a few.

Many Records

Commercial success as a song writer is nothing new to Dylan, of course. Top artists have been recording them for the past several years and many of them, such as "Don't Think Twice, It's All Right," and "Blowin' in the Wind" have become classics.

But it is the personality and raw, rough-edged vocal stylings of Dylan himself that the public now seems to be clamoring for.

With a messed-up shock of hair topping gaunt, sensitive features, dressed in beat-up blue jeans, boots and wrinkled shirts, Dylan appears an outlandish figure.

Classed strictly as a folk entertainer until recently, he has just returned from an enormously successful tour of England, where he managed to surpass the Beatles, the Rolling Stones, the Animals and all the rest of them on the record charts. Suddenly people have stopped dancing and started listening.

How did he do it? Teenage fans don't throw penny candy at him or scream while he performs, yet the talk in both England and America is all about Dylan. He has received the plaudits of almost everyone in the business, including the Beatles. They acknowledge him as a great influence on their

TURN TO PAGE 9

TASTING SCUZZIES at Baskin-Robbins, while Scuzzy fans join in awe, Dave Hull enjoys the sweetest recognition ever won by a personality of his fame and status.

... BOB DYLAN

HAS OWN ICE CREAM

'Sweet' Honor For Hull

Dave Hull has finally been recognized as Southern California's outstanding personality.

True, the Hullabalooer hasn't made "Who's Who" or the Hall of Fame, but he has drawn a far sweeter recognition.

Dave is the first man ever to have an ice cream flavor named after him.

Baskin-Robbins (31 Flavors) ice cream stores have invented an entirely new flavor in honor of him. It's called — naturally — "Scuzzy" ice cream. "Scuzzy" is Dave's favorite word, and Scuzzy ice cream is already a favorite at all the 31 Flavors Stores.

KRLA Recipe

One reason the flavor is so wild, *anything* named "Scuzzy" would have to be wild), is because all the KRLA deejays got together and made up the recipe. Each supplied his favorite ingredient, and then the Baskin-Robbins people mixed them all together to come up with an ice cream that's something else!

And no wonder — just listen to the ingredients: roasted almonds, cream caramel, maraschino cherries, crushed coconut, fresh lime juice, macadamia nuts, tropical fruit punch and English toffee.

And to really make it exciting, Baskin-Robbins is offering fabulous prizes for the first people to guess which ingredient was suggested by each of the deejays — Dave, Dick Biondi, Bob Eubanks, Emperor Hudson, Casey Kasem, Charlie O'Donnell and Bill Slater.

Grand Prize

The grand prize winner will receive $500 plus two tickets to see a KRLA Beatle concert at the Hollywood Bowl! There will be 50 runners-up, and each will receive two Beatle concert tickets for the Hollywood Bowl! And for those who fail to win any of those fantastic prizes, there will be hundreds of additional winners who will receive 45 RPM records and Beatle pictures.

You can rush right out to your nearest Baskin-Robbins store and pick up a free entry blank. And while you're at it, try some of Dave's Scuzzy ice cream — if you have the nerve, that is.

After all, not even the Beatles have an ice cream named after them. Nor Elvis Presley. And did you ever hear of Sandy Koufax ice cream? Of course not!

Only Scuzzy.

Beat Plans New Column For Surfers and Beach Bunnies

The BEAT is picking up on the action by joining the surfing set. And you're invited to join with us.

Whether you are a real hot-dogger or strictly a sun-bather, whether you like riding the waves or simply walking the sand, we think you'll enjoy the surfing reports beginning in next week's BEAT.

Surfing Illustrated Magazine, one of the most popular surfing publications in the world, will provide a special column each week devoted to every form of activity at the beaches. It will include reports on surfing conditions, competition, special events, contests and lots of exciting pictures.

Even surfing fashions, surfing songs and surfing social life — things you can enjoy without ever getting your feet wet. All the things that combine to make California the surfing capital of the world.

So join us next week as the BEAT goes to the beaches. Until then, watch out for wipeouts.

KRLA ARCHIVES

THE DAVE CLARK FIVE sing "Catch Us If You Can," the title song from their new movie, during a taping for "The Dean Martin Show." The boys spent their free time in California playing golf and singing "Happy Birthday" to wrong numbers.

SINGING 'HAPPY BIRTHDAY'
Dave Clark 5 Dial Wrong Numbers

Has anyone sung "Happy Birthday To You" over the phone recently? If so, there are three possible explanations.

1. It was your birthday and someone decided to honor you with a singing telegram.

2. It was your birthday and a friend decided to sing happy birthday to you over the phone, thus saving the price of a singing telegram.

3. It wasn't your birthday, but The Dave Clark Five was playing a joke on you.

It seems that after The Dave Clark Five had finished shooting for The Dean Martin Show, there was an hour lull in which they had to wait around to see if the tapes came out okay.

With an hour to kill and nothing to do, the mischievous five decided they might as well practice their singing.

They picked up the studio telephone and dialed at random. When someone answered the phone, they burst into song. "Happy Brithday To You", they would sing boisterously.

Wrong Number

"You have the wrong number," people would protest throughout the song. Finally after their singing was done, they would let the person speak.

"It's not my birthday, you have the wrong person," the victim would say.

"Well, why didn't you say so? You mean we did all that for nothing?" They would answer indignantly.

Their mischief wasn't a hundred per cent successful however. The Dave Clark Five were disappointed to find that in the United States most people aren't home on Saturday night and all they got on most of their calls were dial tones.

During the Dean Martin Show, in which they appeared with Phyllis Diller, Eddie Fisher and Abby Lane, The Five sang "Wild Weekend" and "Catch Us If You Can," the title song from their new movie.

Past Careers

The Dave Clark Five weren't always five. Before they formed a group three years ago, Dave Clark was a film extra, Mike Smith was a correspondent for a finance company, Lennie was a cost clerk, Rick was an abstract lighting designer and Dennis was an electronic engineer.

"How did the five come together?" the BEAT Reporter asking naively.

"Ah, that's an interesting story," Dave baited her.

"I saw Rick scrubbing floors outside the studio where he was working. Instantly I could tell he had great potential," he explained.

"I said 'come with me and I will make you a great star'. Then Lennie was teaching at an all-girl school in England. . . ."

Mike Smith grabbed the pencil from the reporter, who was feverishly taking notes.

"He's just kidding you know. You must understand us." Mike Smith then began talking about the picture they just made.

Catch Us

"I can't tell you about the plot, except that it's a cross-country chase that is set all along England. There were lots of stunts in the film," he explained. (Here's where the Dave Clark Five could show off their skill in judo and karati.)

"I had to wake up an hour before the others because my make-up took so long to put on. It got awfully embarrassing," Smith continued.

"I had to wear a padded bra in the movie. I'd have to ask the wardrobe man, 'Would you do me up please.' It was very embarrassing for a big guy like me," he explained.

Being the biggest guy in the group has had other disadvantages for Mike Smith.

"I almost got killed trying to get off the stage a couple of weeks ago," he said. "There were scratches all along the back of my neck."

Biggest Bloke

"I always seem to get the worst of it. The biggest bloke is the easiest one to grab," he continued.

Eager fans were not the only hazards the group faced while touring the U.S. They have had equally harrowing experiences while traveling from place to place on airplanes.

"We were flying somewhere at night, I don't remember exactly when, and one of our engines dropped out. As we landed, the other one stopped as well," Mike Smith shuddered.

"During another one, the cylinders blew up and we smashed one of our wings," he reminisced.

Speaking of exciting experiences, what kind of girls does the unmarried Mike Smith like?

Natural Girls

"A natural girl. Someone who is herself and doesn't put on any kind of front," Smith explained. "Not one like that," he said pointing out a heavily made-up girl who walked by the CBS studio where they were shooting a tape for "T.J.'s", a new series that might be shown this fall.

Apparently the tastes of the rest of the five run in the same direction. They like their girls to be "wholesome." They also love their fans, but dislike immensely girls "throwing themselves at them."

During a two and a half-hour break in the shooting of the Dean Martin Show, the five experienced another first. They walked over to a neighboring golf center and played a round of pitch and putt.

The game consisted of balls being shot from one end of the course to another. The victor of the game? Mike Smith, with the fabulous score of 43.

Pity Poor Parents In Idol Crisis

Last week we gave you five very helpful hints (oh, *sure* we did) on how to keep your boyfriend from divorcing you because he has to play second fiddle to your favorite star. We're sure that our hints completely eliminated that problem (and your boyfriend.)

Is it possible that you are experiencing equal problems with your parents because of your devotion to that certain someone?

If so, you had better (1) run and look to make sure they did not move out in the dead of night last evening, (2) follow simple (decidedly) instructions we're about to give you or they might move out *this* evening.

Exterior Decoration

1. It upsets your parents *terribly* when you paste pictures of your favorite star all over the freshly-painted walls of your room. How are they ever going to rent it out to a boarder when they finally get you married off? Resolve this situation by pasting your star photos on the *outside* of the house.

2. Appeal to your parents' sympathy and sense of fair play. Some evening after they've been doing a lot of complaining about your "star-gazing" habits, take all of your records and pictures and magazines outside and tearfully build a large bonfire. Sob extra loud as you're about to light it, and your parents will come running. Just don't get all burned up if they bring matches.

3. It is ridiculous the way you practically blast your poor parents out of the house, playing your favorite's records at ear-shattering volumes. Have the good grace to fix up a comfortable place in the garage. Then ask your folks if they'd mind moving into it.

Another Track

4. Do not let your parents worry that you have a one track mind, and that you think of nothing besides your favorite's movies and records. Buy a recording of the "1812 Overture" and play it at least once a day, and stay up until all hours watching Spencer Tracy (your new fave) on the late show. This will completely convince your parents. (That your one track mind has been de-railed, that is.)

5. Your parents wouldn't be so dead set against your favorite if they got to know him better. *Insist* that they accompany you to one of his movies. How you are going to accomplish this feat we really can't say, but a loaded revolver might prove helpful.

MICK HAS BEST QUOTE

The Best Quote of the Week comes from Mick Jagger: "A friendly face in the audience to smile at. You've got to have someone to sing to—not just a sea of swaying faces. Laughter's important. A wrong note, a false start, pulling faces—anything will start us off. If you can't find a joke in most things, you are dead, man."

August 7, 1965 — THE BEAT — Page 4

KEITH, CHARLIE, BILL

BEAT Continues 2nd Part Of The Rolling Stones Saga

By Louise Criscione

(EDITOR'S NOTE: This is the second article from a three part series on the Rolling Stones.)

Last week we began the Rolling Stones' Story. We watched as Mick Jagger worked his way through School, Wentworth Primary School, Wentworth County Primary School, Dartford Grammar School, and finally into the London School of Economics.

Then we followed Brian Jones through Dean Close Public School and Cheltenham Grammar School. We watched him develop an interest in music, and we accompanied him on his travels around the Continent, then back to Cheltenham, and finally on to London. And now we are ready for Rolling Stone number three.

The Stone with the dark hair who plays a mean lead guitar, who sometimes stares impassively out into the audience, and who at other times spreads a grin across his face which literally extends from one ear to another, is Keith Richard. Keith is the youngest Stone, born December 18, 1944 in Dartford, England to Doris and Bert Richard. Actually, their last name originally had an "s" tagged onto the end of it, but somewhere along the way that "s" was lost and so the name stands as simply "Richard."

No Electrical Engineer

Keith's grandfather ran a dance band in the 1930's, and perhaps this is where Keith picked up his love for music. One thing for certain, he did not pick it up from his father. For Mr. Richard was an electrical engineer and as most fathers do, he hoped his only son (and his only child as well) would follow in his footsteps. But Keith had a mind of his own, and that mind did not turn naturally toward electrical engineering.

Keith first went to Westhill Infants' School and then on to Dartford Primary School. His best subjects at school were art, history, and geography. One of Keith's schoolmasters remembers him as being a straight-forward person, one who "laughs when he is happy, cries when he is sad. He's open and frank."

As far as school sports went, Keith had this to say: "It was okay when I played ordinary football. That went on till I was about thirteen and, though I wasn't really much good at it, I quite enjoyed the idea of getting out of the classroom into the open air. But when we switched over to Rugby football —well, that was too much."

Richard Special

"But cross-country running! That was different."

At least, for Keith it was different. He ran his own kind of race—one which can only be described as a "Richard Special". He would start off with the others, then lag behind until he found some tree or bush big enough to hide behind. And once hidden, Keith would produce a pack of cigarettes and have himself a solitary smoke! "It was a matter of hanging on till the others came back, all blown out and exhausted—then tack myself on to the last few and accompany them back to school."

Keith's first guitar was a $30 Spanish Rosetti purchased by his parents. He had, by this time, become a staunch Chuck Berry fan. So between his Berry records and his grandfather's patient instruction on primary chord production (not to mention Keith's own enthusiasm and determination), he finally learned to play.

After Dartford Primary came Dartford Technical College. However, Keith's stay at the college was cut a little short, for it seemed that Keith was fond of skipping school for more pleasurable pastimes. And so Keith moved on to Sidcup Art School. It was here that Keith met up with Dick Taylor, a fellow student. Dick remembers, "Keith had this natural talent which way above what you'd expect from a lad who'd never even played with a band."

Common Interest

It was also about this time that Keith met up with one Mick Jagger, and indirectly Chuck Berry was the cause. Keith had a Chuck Berry album tucked securely under his arm and Mick, being another avid Berry fan, spotted the album immediately.

"What you got there—Chuck Berry?" Mick asked.

"Yep", replied Keith. "Like him?"

"You bet," grinned Mick.

Just two school boys who had found that which makes for friendship—a common interest. An everyday occurance? Perhaps, but this everyday occurance marked the beginning of a group which was to much later rock the pop world.

Keith's mother remembers that first meeting between Keith and Mick. "I can't remember him being more excited than he was the day he met up with Mick and they started talking about music. I was very keen on Keith keeping on with his music because he really did show a lot of promise."

So Mick, Keith, and Dick Taylor began practicing. In fact, before Keith ever met up with Mick, Dick had been trying unsuccessfully to persuade Keith to join a group, but Keith was too shy.

Mad Rehearsal

"But Mick snapped him out of it. And soon the three of them were rehearsing like mad—Mick on his harmonica and the other two on their guitars," Mrs. Richard said.

At first the only thing the three budding musicians made was noise, causing their sessions to be ejected from the Jagger household, then from the Richard household, and finally forcing the boys to go to the Taylor house for their rehearsals. It was not that the Jaggers and Richards did not want the boys practicing in their homes—it was just that the neighbors' complaints had reached the point where it was really better that the three removed themselves and their "music" from the near vicinity!

By the time the boys had reached the Taylor house, they were mad for some real equipment. But they faced one slight problem—money. The three talked over ways of earning the necessary capital, but they decided that everything would take too long and they wanted that equipment NOW.

Getting Equipment

Mick then came up with an idea—maybe, just maybe, his parents would kick in the money. And so Mick talked on and on about how much they really *needed* the equipment, and how much better *everything* would be if only they had that equipment. On and on until finally, for one reason or another, his parents agreed. It was an elated Mick Jagger who met Keith and Dick and yelled: "It's okay. My folks are going to stake the money so we can get some good equipment. 'Course it's only a loan, so we've got to pay it back as soon as we can."

So two Rolling Stones (though, of course, they were not known as that yet) marched onto the London Beat scene of 1962. Although they rehearsed and talked R&B continually, they were still just school boys and not real musicians. Mick was at the London School of Economics

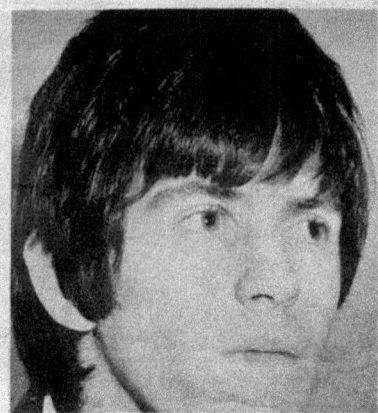

... KEITH RICHARD

and Keith was studying for a career in advertising.

But the day of the Rolling Stones (as we know them now) was drawing nearer. There were already three of them (Brian, Mick, and Keith) in London and crazy for R&B. And two of them already together. That leaves just two Stones unaccounted for.

Charlie Watts

The Stone who sometimes sports the shortest hair, who most often wears a suit complete with white shirt and tie, who digs Civil War antiques, and who pounds the drums as well, if not better, than anyone else around, is Charlie Watts. He was born Charles Robert Watts on June 2, 1941 in the section of London which is called Islington.

Charlie's family was not musical at all. His father was a truck driver for the British Railways, and his mother admits that the only musical instrument she could play was the phonograph.

Charlie claims two distinctions which separate him from the other Stones. First, he is the oldest. And second, he was the first to go out with a girl, (or so he says anyway)!

First Date

"She was the daughter of a next door neighbor. I was three and a half years old. Goodness knows how old she was. But all I can say is that I have always been very mature for my age. Trouble is that I can't remember now even what she looked like."

Charlie's first taste of school life came at the Tylers Croft Secondary Modern. He didn't like mathematics or science, but he did do well in history, art, and handwriting.

Charlie has always been one for clothes, and although he did not have much money he did dress smartly. He says: "Don't put me down as Little Lord Fauntleroy. It is just that I always preferred being smartly dressed to being comfortably dressed."

He was serious-minded and rather reserved. He didn't rebel openly, instead he kept his complaints inside himself. It was quite obvious by the time that he had finished Tylers that Charlie was going to be artistic and so he moved on to Harrow Art School.

By this time, Charlie had his own drum kit. He says: "It was a gift from my dad. It wasn't a complete kit—not the shiny sort of gear you see in the shops today. But it was really all there. Cymbals, bass drum, snare, bass pedal—I could get all the sounds I wanted. And I could sit in with the greatest musicians in the world simply by sticking on records."

Charlie wasn't a R&B fan right off, he liked jazz and held the great Negro jazz musicians as his idols. By the time he was nineteen, Charlie had left school and was working for an advertising agency, Charles Hobson and Gray, and earning the incredible sum of about $42 a week.

But Charlie's mind was also on the drums and jazz, so when his advertising day was finished, he would hurry off to some club where he would play with different jazz groups all around Chelsea.

That makes four potential

TURN TO PAGE 8

... BILL WYMAN

... CHARLIE WATTS

KRLA ARCHIVES

...JACKIE DE SHANNON

Jackie DeShannon Previews Yesterday, Today, Tomorrow

By Michelle Straubing and Susan Wylie

(EDITOR'S NOTE: Jackie De Shannon took time out from a rehearsal for the Dick Clark Caravan to talk to BEAT Reporters Michelle Straubing and Susan Wylie on her past life and future plans. Here are a few excerpts from that conversation.)

Q: Do you think the Beatle tour you were on last summer helped your career?

A: Yes, I think it helped it an awful lot. I really do. I got to appear in front of 25,000 to 40,000 people. Maybe some people who didn't get to see me before got a chance to see me. And of course, being on the first Beatle tour meant a lot to many of the kids.

Q: How do you go about writing a song?

A: It's very hard. I don't know. I've been writing for about nine years and I just started writing. I don't know what to tell you. It's just things you feel inside and what happens to your life. That's the way I write.

Q: Do you write both the music and the lyrics?

A: Yes, I do.

Q: What do you think you would do if your career was suddenly all over?

A: Well, I'm very interested in art, and I'm going to art school. I don't think there is such a thing as a career being over. I mean once you're established as a personality or once you've been in the public eye there is no such thing as a career being over. You may not be as popular because anything that comes up has to go down or cool off. Once you have been established, there's no such thing as being over. You may quit, or you may not want to work as much, which a lot of the acts do. After they make it, they get very tired and they don't want to work anymore.

Q: What do you think has been the biggest influence on your career?

A: There's no one thing. I've just always been interested in learning and developing myself better as a person and as a talent. I think constant digging for new things to learn and being around people who are very bright has helped a lot.

Q: How did you get started in your career?

A: I just started singing everywhere and anywhere I could. I just kept going and then one job would lead to another, and one person would hear of me and go on and on. Then I got a record contract and I made records until they hit.

Q: Then you were singing before you were writing?

A: Yes, I was. I couldn't get any material because I wasn't a name. So I started writing for myself.

Q: What is your favorite song that you've recorded and written?

A: My favorite song that I've recorded is, "What The World Needs Now Is Love", and my favorite song that I've written was recorded by Marianne Faithfull called, "Come Stay With Me".

Q: What is your preference in music?

A: I love all kinds of music actually. It's whatever I'm in the mood for. I think this year I'm leaning toward Elizabethan folk music.

Q: Do you think folk music is becoming more popular? for about four years. I think people are becoming more fond of folk rock which is folk music, or folk changes with a beat. I'm glad to see it because I've learned to love that kind of music. I'm glad to see it's really coming in although I was doing it a long time ago, so it isn't new to me. But I'm glad a lot of people are broadening themselves and picking up on it.

Q: Are you planning on doing any more writing?

A: Yes, I'm writing a book now.

Q: What kind of a book?

A: Well, I've just started. It's a philosophy book, and poems, and drawings. It's going to be a mixture of everything.

Q: Have you titled it yet?

A: Yes, it's called, "No Curls For Jacqueline".

Q: Do you know when it will be out?

A: Oh no, I have to finish it. I have several people interested in it, but I haven't sold it yet.

Q: Do you think you had to make any sacrifices for your career?

A: Yes, my childhood. I did not play. It's a big thing with me, and now I play. I have lots of dolls, I make lots of time to go to the park in, and just do things I would've done when I was little. I didn't actually sacrifice it then, I just miss it now. At the time I wasn't interested in doing it and I was really pure. I devoted my whole self to whatever I was really interested in. But now I miss the things that I would've done when I was

TURN TO PAGE 6

ON THE BEAT

Congrats to the Byrds — they made it to number one in England with their "Mr. Tambourine Man!"

Bob Dylan, currently the rage of England, has a new record, "Like A Rolling Stone," which looks like it will be his first really huge smash single here in the U. S. It is certainly one of the most commercial records to date. Also, if you enjoy getting the most for your dollar, you really should pick up "Like A Rolling Stone" — it's six minutes long! And it contains some pretty great lyrics as well. Watch for it to go.

Beatle fans should be glad they're not in Mexico. "A Hard Day's Night" has been branded there as "not suitable for children". Reason for this label: Alleged sexy dialogue. I'll tell you one thing, I'm gonna go straight back and see that movie again because I must've missed something those first ten times around!

BOB DYLAN
...Set for Hit

Studio Address

Did you know that 2120 South Michigan Avenue — besides being a cut off the "Rolling Stones 12 x 5" album — is also the address of the Chess Recording Studios in Chicago where that particular cut plus lots of their other hits have been recorded?

Speaking of the Stones, they have done it yet again, haven't they? Their new album, "Out Of Our Heads", is fabulous! 'Course, that's really nothing new for the Stones — all of their records are fabulous.

Britain's Animals would like to be cowboys! It's true — on their last visit to the U.S., the boys headed for parts West, stopping off at such "wild places as Denver, Cheyenne, and Laramie. In Laramie they purchased the whole traditional cowboy outfit including levis, stetsons, and six guns! But Hilton Valentine soon became disillusioned with his outfit — wasn't authentic enough he decided. So, he trade his store-bought clothes for a really authentic suit of clothes which he bought from a really authentic cowboy who had just come off an authentic cattle drive. And you just can't get much more authentic than that!

ERIC BURDON
...Cowboy Animal

Cowboy Animals

After their shopping spree and a several day stay in the Wild West, all five of the Animals looked and felt very much like true American cowboys. Only had one minor problem — everytime they opened their mouths out came a flood of the Queen's English! Oh well, they still *felt* like Westerners anyway.

Ever wonder why Jay and the Americans chose "Cara Mia"? Jay himself gives us the answer: "Well, 'Cara Mia' has been a favorite of mine since I was a kid. I finally talked the other guys into doing it in the act, until enough people had heard it and demanded that we record it." Very clever, Jay — and also very smart. The record is currently in the national top ten and is also climbing up the charts in England. This, of course, makes Jay most happy cause now that "Cara Mia" is such a huge success he can put on a very smug grin and say "I told you so" to the other four Americans!

Narrow-Minded Adults

It is absolutely amazing how obnoxious some adults can be! No offense intended, but really if they don't like our music, why listen? They know how to switch the dial, don't they?

And another thing—people who are too narrow-minded to accept any other kind of entertainment except that which they personally enjoy should learn to keep quiet and let each person like what he wants to.

QUICK ONES: The editor of a very well-known American teenage magazine wrote a letter to a British music paper declaring that Herman and his Hermits are the most popular British group in America. Really? Well, that's news to a lot of people—Beatles, Stones, and three-fourths of the teen populace included . . . Gene Pitney thinks the group scene is dying . . . Watch for Sonny & Cher to go over really big in England during their August visit . . . The Bobby Fuller Four have been set as headliners on a live package show which will hit the Fox West Coast Theaters in August . . . John Lennon thinks that touring Europe was just like starting all over again . . . George Harrison said he didn't really expect anything big in Spain, France, or Italy—"They're so far behind there with the music, anyway." George says the reason for the Beatles going in the first place was to promote their new movie . . . Come on, Dave Clark, tell the people the *real* reason why your Pasadena Civic show was cancelled.

KRLA ARCHIVES

... WE FIVE

Leave Rover, Bring Money When Visiting Gt. Britain

Before we go any further into the subject, we think the time has come to go into detail about a few of the adjustments you'll have to make while traveling through the second greatest country in the world.

Each country is different in many ways, and one of the major adjustments for American visitors in Britain is getting used to their money system.

When you enter Britain, you can bring as much money as you like (we'll go into detail about how much money you can take *out* of Britain in future issues). The rate of exchange (American currency for British) varies a few cents from time to time, but the approximate figure at this writing is: $2.83 equals one pound.

The pound sterling is divided into twenty shillings (20s) and pound notes are issued in the denominations of one pound, five pounds and ten pounds. Shillings are divided into twelve pennies. Silver coins issued in England are "Half-A-Crown" (two and a half shillings), the "Florin" (two shillings), a one shilling coin and a sixpence (six pennies) coin.

English Coins

Two copper coins are issued: the penny (1d) and the halfpenny, which is often pronounced "Hay-Penny." There is also a nickle coin worth three pennies.

One of the most confusing things about English money is the constant reference to the term "guinea". Many prices in stores are marked in guineas, but there is no actual note or coin for this amount. A guinea is one pound, one shilling.

To avoid confusion when you start spending your British currency, here are a few helpful hints as to how much some of your everyday expenses will amount to.

You'll be wanting to write home and brag about your experiences, and each letter will cost you six pennies in British coin for the first ounce, and 1½ pennies for each additional ounce. (This is the air mail rate.) Postcards can be mailed for four pennies.

When making telephone calls, local calls from a telephone booth cost four pennies. The price of long distance calls varies according to distance, and an extra three cents is charged if a long distance call is made from a telephone booth.

Busy Signal

British telephones are somewhat the opposite of our's. When you hear what sounds like a busy signal, this means the line is clear and your call can be put through. (This reminds us of the first time the Rolling Stones were in California. One of the boys made a call — his first — from his hotel room and the number was busy. He stood, waiting patiently for his party, thinking this signal meant the call was going through.)

Transportation is another area in which confusion reigns for the weary traveler. The cost of traveling by bus within a city is very small, but you don't pay your fare when you get on the car, as you do in America. In some areas of Britain, a conductor will come by and pick up your money. In others, you pay as you leave the bus.

Long distance travel by bus costs between two and three cents a mile, and a reservation is encouraged. If you plan to do a lot of cross-country motor coaching, there is a Coach And Bus Guide available for $1.50 from The American News Company, 131 Varick Street, New York, N.Y., 10013.

If you want to rent a car and do it yourself, the price per week will be somewhere in the neighborhood of $60. This includes insurance, but you buy your own gasoline. Gas for an eight hundred mile trip would cost you about $14. Car rental prices might be slightly more in the summer months, but are less the rest of the year.

Train Traveling

Traveling by train, second-class, costs approximately four cents (American money) per mile. Anyone planning to do a lot of train traveling in England should buy Thrift Coupons here in America before setting off for Britain. The coupons are exchangable for train tickets throughout England, and will save money in fares, but they must be purchased in the visitor's own country. Thrift Coupons are available at many travel agencies in this area.

Taxi fares in London are two shillings (30 cents) for the first three-fifths of a mile, and 6d (seven American cents) for each additional three-tenths of a mile. If the journey goes over six miles, there is no set rate for fares, and the prices depend upon whatever agreement is made between the passenger and the driver. An extra sixpence is charged for each additional passenger.

If you plan to take a taxi from the London airport into town, seven American dollars is a reasonable price to suggest to the driver.

Tipping The Same

Tipping in Britain is much the same as in America. Ten or twelve per cent of the entire amount is acceptable.

Two unexpected rules to remember when entering Britain are:

(1) All cats and dogs must be kept in a British kennel for six months before being allowed into the country, so leave Rover at home unless you intend to stay a long time. This rule is in effect to keep rabies out of Great Britain. (2) If you take more than a half a pint of perfume or toilet water into England, you'll be charged an import duty fee on the items!

Stay tuned to the BEAT for more about England next week!

New California Group Soars Across Charts

California has spawned still another hit group.

They're called "We Five," and although they have only one hit to their credit so far, many predict they will become one of the hottest groups to hit the world pop scene.

They made their first big splash a few weeks ago when the four guys and a girl took a Sylvia Fricker folk ballad, gave it a hip beat arrangement and turned it into one of the fastest chart climbers around.

"You Were On My Mind" was an instant hit up and down the West Coast. It's popularity rapidly spread eastward.

Where did the We Five come from and who are they? Mike Stewart, Beverly Bivens, Bob Jones, Pete Fullerton and Jerry Burgan were the first of a series of artists to be signed up by Frank Weber, the manager of the Kingston Trio.

The lead singer and arranger, Mike Stewart comes from Riverside, California. He went to Pomona Catholic High School where he served as president of his senior class and was a letter athlete in track.

From there he went to the University of San Francisco and Mt. San Antonio College. His brother, John Stewart is a member of the Kingston Trio and Mike wrote several songs for the trio.

The only girl in the group, Beverly Bivens was born in Orange, California, and attended Santa Ana High School.

Bob Jones comes from Honolulu and went to high school there. When he left the islands to attend The University of San Francisco, he met Mike Stewart.

Football Star

Pete Fullerton, who plays bass for the group, attended Claremont High School where he was the star of the football team. From there he went to Mt. San Antonio College, where he earned a degree in art and was a classmate of Jerry Burgan.

Guitarist Jerry Burgan was born in Kansas City but was raised in San Diego and attended Pomona Catholic High. Also a college boy, he went to the University of San Francico and Mt. San Antonio College.

What Jackie Gave Up To Start Her Career

(Continued from Page 5)

around 12, 13, 14, and 15. Now I just do all those kind of things like . . . like crazy things . . . you know, to do, I have collections of all sorts of things and I cut out things in fan magazines. I like to just do things that are casual, go to a lot of foreign films . . . But I guess you have to be sort of successful before you have the time to do it. It worked out very well, but at the time it was kind of a sacrifice. When everyone else was going to dances and things, I couldn't go because I was singing somewhere. I kind of missed proms and things like that which I have kind of a thing about. I didn't get to go, but it was well worth it.

Q: *How old were you when you first started?*

A: Two and a half years!

Q: *You weren't singing then, were you?*

A: Yes! I was a very unusual child! I was on a radio station and I had my own radio show when I was six. I used to sing gospel music and things like that. I'd just sing everywhere—church socials, and all sorts of things. I was kind of a weirdo because no one was singing the kind of music and the type of music I was doing. Now it really is nothing. People think it's great, but at the time when I was going to school, like junior high school, they thought I was really a nut. I lived in a small town and I was always singing. One year I was a cheerleader and a captain and all that, just going through that phase. Then I just stopped altogether, and they all thought something was wrong with me. I was always going on tours with rock 'n' roll groups and singing everywhere and they thought I was a nut. Now they don't think it's so funny.

Q: *Where were you living at this time?*

A: In Illinois, about 50 miles west of Chicago.

Q: *Do you ever have time to go on vacation?*

A: Oh yeah. I don't vacation like take two weeks per vacation. I vacation during the week. I take time off to do whatever I want to do. I do mostly what I want to do anyway.

Q: *Have you ever been mobbed by any of your fans?*

A: Yes. Once when I was on the Beatles' tour it was really frightening. I came out the wrong door and about 3,000 people chased me. It was amazing. I was crying and everything. They were just trying to be friendly, but 3,000 of them at once is pretty hard to take. It's very dangerous.

Q: *Was there anything particularly interesting or funny that happened on the tour?*

A: I think probably one of the funniest things was this. You know they have the stages up high so the kids couldn't get to the Beatles. One time they built the stage up so high we had to go up about 30 steps. It was like singing 2 stories up. The audience was down below in little chairs, and the wind was blowing very hard. I almost blew off the stage, and Ringo's drums blew off. It was very funny.

EPIC RECORDS

KRLA ARCHIVES

CALIFORNIA CACTUS amused the Sir Douglas Quintet. Although they hail from Texas, this was the first time they had ever seen the prickly plant, so they had to have pictures of it.

Sir Douglas Quintet Real Texas 'Movers'

By Jean Watson

The Sir Douglas Quintet, of "She's About A Mover," fame hail not from Great Britain, but from San Antonio, Texas.

Since when, you may wonder, do boys from Texas have titles added to their name?

The answer is simple. It seems that when Douglas Wayne Sahm, John George Barker, August E. Meyer, Frank Morin and John Perez were recording their first record they had no name to tack onto it.

"How about the Sir Douglas Quintet," Huey Meaux, their Cajun manager and ex-deejay jokingly suggested. Due to the boom of British artists in the United States, they figured a "Sir" would add distinction to their title.

Happily, the record they were cutting, "She's About A Mover," became an overnight hit, and the boys weren't about to change their name. And thus they became "The Sir Douglas Quintet," with Sir Doug playing the guitar and singing, Sir August at the organ, Sir John playing bass guitar, Sir Frank at the sax and another Sir John playing the drums.

Girl Movers

"She's About A Mover," which was written by Sir Doug himself, was inspired by no one girl in particular and by all girls in general.

However the boys might have been thinking of girls with long straight hair and Mod clothes, because they think the English influence looks great on American girls.

"They look with it, you know ... in the groove," said Sir John.

During their tours around the U.S. the boys feel they have gotten their most enthusiastic audience response from the Southern states.

"The kids are much more excited in the South. They really yell and scream, especially in Georgia and Florida," said Sir Frank.

"In the North the kids like to dance to our music rather than sit and listen."

High School Friends

The boys all went to the same high school in San Antonio, however they did not form the quintet until about ten months ago.

Since they have become five, everything has been more or less rosy for the Sir Douglas Quintet, and they hope to follow their first hit with a new one, "The Tracker."

Meanwhile they are touring around the United States and making plans to make California their permanent home.

"The weather is great here, especially at night," Sir Doug said, adding that nights are hot and muggy in Texas.

"Everything is in the groove here, things really swing," interrupted another member of the quintet.

Loves Dances

Speaking of swing reminded the Quintet of rock n' roll music, which they especially love to play at dances.

"You can really tell when your music has hit a nerve. There's a certain reaction that you get from your audience."

If they continue to cut records such as "She's About A Mover," a lot of nerves across the United States will continue being hit.

VIEWED AT CLOSE RANGE
Stars Lose Glitter For Fan

(EDITOR'S NOTE: This letter, received by the BEAT from a very intelligent and mature young lady, is one we think should be shared with all of our readers.)

Dear KRLA BEAT:

Please publish this letter in the BEAT. I had a very jolting experience, and I know other girls can learn by what happened to me.

After months of plotting and planning and scheming, I finally got to meet my favorite group. I'm not going to tell you which group it was because if I did, this letter might make them feel embarrassed, but I am going to tell you I wish I had never met them in person, and why.

I met the group by sneaking into their dressing room after a concert, and I wasn't disappointed in them because they weren't nice to me. They were nice, and under the circumstances I would not have blamed them if they'd been anything *but* cordial.

My disappointment happened after I got home and put one of their records on my phonograph. It was my favorite song at the time, and when I heard it I started crying. I don't know if I can explain how I felt, but it was like all the magic was gone and they were just real people to me.

Nightly Dreams

I've never felt the same about them. I used to get a funny feeling in my stomach everytime I heard one of their songs, or even heard their names. And I used to lie awake every night dreaming of getting to know them. I'd even plan what we were going to say to each other. (Do you do that too, or I am nuts or something?)

Things are different now. Because I did get to know them, and that gulpy feeling is gone forever.

I guess this happened because of the scene in the dressing room. They came tearing in after the show, and there I was. They said hello, and I said hello, and there really wasn't much else to say. All I did then was watch them racing around, trying to get everything ready to leave before the crowds started trying to break in. They were nice enough to let me stay and watch, but I wish they hadn't.

My special favorite of the group was in a terrible mood because he had this awful cold and was about ready to collapse from holding his breath on stage. (It was the only way he could keep from coughing and sneezing.) He was nice, as I said, but all pale and drawn and tired-looking; nothing like I'd dreamed he'd be.

Looked Beat

The other members were tired too. And they looked like they hadn't had a square meal for months. There were cokes waiting for them in the dressing room and they fell all over each other trying to get to them.

Right in the middle of all the excitement, one of the guys said "I can't stand another night of this" in a real funny voice. Then he looked at me and smiled kind of sheepishly and said "Oh, I guess it's worth it."

That was really about all that happened. About then one of their managers came in, saw me and politely ushered me out of the dressing room. The whole group said goodbye, and that was really all there was to it.

I suppose you're wondering why I'm making such a big deal out of all this. I didn't see anything out of the ordinary; just several very tired people who were going to get a lot more tired before their tour was over.

But that's what makes it a *very* big deal. I expected to see something extraordinary, and didn't. And I'd give anything to be able to go back and do it all over and just be content to watch them on stage where they *are* extraordinary.

Magic Lost

Really, I'd give *anything* to have that gulpy feeling back. I called it "magic" a few paragraphs ago, and I guess that's about the best word I've ever heard for this feeling.

On stage, in movies, on records they're so exciting, I'd built up an image of them in my mind, or maybe my heart, and I loved the way I felt about them. Now I know they're just people, and I feel empty every time I think about all this.

Before this happened, I had all sorts of sneaky plans made to get to meet the Beatles in person. Now I wouldn't do that for the world. I love them too much to see them any other way than the way I see them now.

If I'm still not reaching you, and you still can't see what was so jolting about this experience, look at it this way. When it gets dark tonight, go outside and take a look at the stars. They're so shiny and beautiful when they're far away, out of reach. Then go inside and take a close-up look at a picture of a star in the encyclopedia. It isn't beautiful now, is it? No, it's just a bunch of burning metals and gas and there's nothing magic about it. (Just like the moon isn't as romantic now that you've seen every pore of its surface on television or in newspapers.)

Far Away Stars

It's the same thing with stars of the human variety. They give so much more happiness when they're far enough away to let you use your imagination about what they're really like.

When you get too close to a star, either variety, a part of the enchantment dies. You never really know how much you have to lose until its lost, so if you want your starlight to stay bright, just go on *wishing* you could meet him. In this case, the wishing is so much more pleasant than having that wish come true.

Cheryl Johnson.

A RARE COMBINATION of talent, Chad and Jeremy have soared to the top of the charts in both England and the U.S. with such hits as "Willow Weep For Me" and "If I Loved You." They are also good sports, in typically Yugoslavian style, good-naturedly overlooking a rather spectacular boo-boo in the BEAT which somehow credited them with recording the Peter and Gordon hit, "True Love Ways." Peter and Gordon are the only ones who got sore about it.

KRLA ARCHIVES

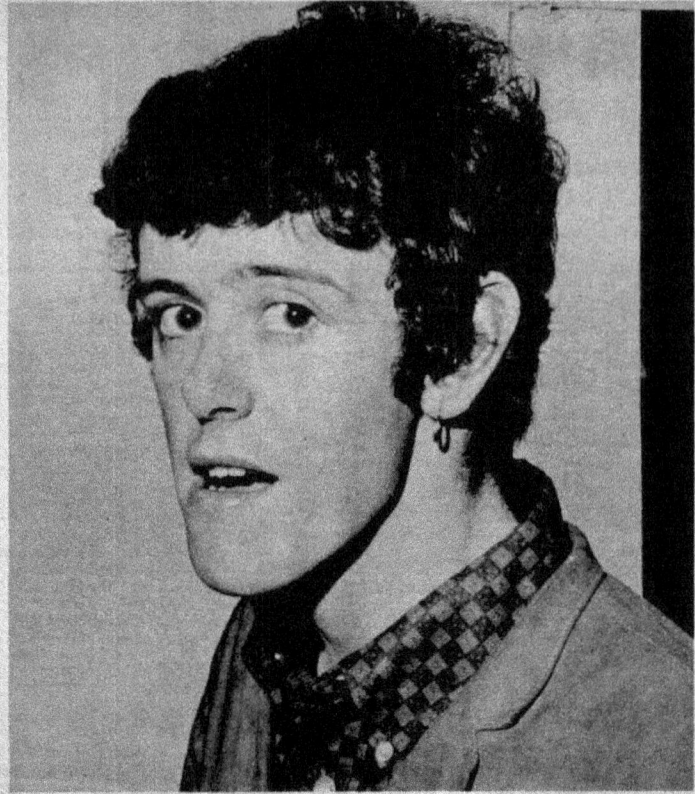

... DONOVAN

Donovan Serious About Music But Says He Has An Easy Life

By Michelle Straubing/Susan Wylie

(EDITOR'S NOTE: During Donovan's first trip to the United States, he took time out from a Shindig rehearsal to talk to BEAT Reporters Michelle Straubing and Susan Wylie. Their trusty tape recorder yields the following conversation.)

Q. — What are your first impressions of America?
A. — It's too fast. It's not slow enough. Too much high pressure advertising. Apart from that, it's a gas.

Q. — Where are you going to be going in this country?
A. — I'm coming back for the Newport Folk Festival. Then I'm coming over here to California after a TV show in New York, and I'll be doing some Hollywood TV shows.

Q. — Can you compare your American fans to your English fans?
A. — Yeah, they're both wild. They're wilder here because the guards who hold the kids back are crueler.

Q. — Have you gotten mobbed, out here yet?
A. — Not yet, but I'm expecting it any time now. I was literally unknown here until I came out.

Q. — Do you feel you had to make any sacrifices for your success?
A. — No, actually. I don't work as much as the public seems to think.

Q. — Do you consider yourself to be a folk singer more than anything else?
A. — A contemporary folk singer.

Q. — How would you define a contemporary folk singer?
A. — I can't define folk music, therefore I call myself a contemporary folk singer. They are songs that are not made to be commercial, they just happen to be.

Q. — Have you written any songs?
A. — Yeah, I wrote both my records that are out now.

Q. — Do you have an album coming out?
A. — It's out now.

Q. — What's the name of it?
A. — "Catch The Wind"

Q. — What were you doing before you were singing?
A. — I was singing.

Q. — What would you do if something happened to your career and you couldn't sing any more?
A. — I don't know. I'd just continue what I'm doing, but I wouldn't be paid as much money.

Q. — What part of England are you from?
A. I'm from Scotland. I moved down to England and lived in Manchester and places like that until I lived in London, where I made it big.

Q. — When did you first get interested in music?
A. — When I left home at fifteen and travelled about singing blues and folk music and things.

Q. — Are you interested in other fields of entertainment?
A. — Yeah, acting. But not like Elvis movies. We're going to be making films, but they're going to be sort of art films — a bit of culture.

Q. — How do you feel about being called Dylan's protege?
A. — We get along splendidly. We're the best of friends.

Q. — Do you feel you learned a lot from him?
A. — I learned a lot from him, but you don't learn from just one person, you learn from everyone.

Q. — Do you think teenagers over here are wilder or more mature than in England?
A. — In England they dig much more blues records. They like the colored sounds. They like songs with big feeling. I don't hear much of that over here. I'm sure they can get turned on to it. Like the Stones are playing blues, and you like that, so maybe you'll like other blues, which is good.

Q. — Is there anything you particularly like or dislike about your work?
A. — I don't like the fast pace that much. You've got me pegged wrong actually, because I don't really work in the business all that time. I'm only in the business when I'm doing things like records. The other times I write and paint and things like that.

Q. — Are you writing a book?
A. — Well not a book, it's poems. They're going to publish. It's Jonathan Cage, John Lennon's publishers. I'm going to be with John, see.

Q. — What's the name of it?
A. — I don't know. It's just a book of poems with illustrations by a girl I know.

4 Stones In London— Wyman Will Follow

(Continued from Page 4)

Stones now on the London scene, and that leaves us with only one more to go.

Bill Wyman

The Stone who stands on the extreme left corner of the stage, who plays bass guitar, and who is noted for his deadpan expression and his considerable gum-chewing ability is Bill Wyman. He was born in Lewisham, South London on October 24, 1941. His father was a bricklayer.

Bill comes closet to equaling Charlie's two distinctions. For Bill is the second oldest Stone, and he took out his first girl at the tender age of four. She too was his next door neighbor, and Bill says: "She had strikingly colored hair. A definite ginger nut. We used to cuddle behind the bushes near our homes—and I've got a strange feeling that I offered to marry her."

Bill first went to Oakfield Junior School and then on to Beckenham Grammar School. Of his school days, he says: "I didn't kick up too much. There wasn't any point. If there was an argument going, I'd just try and look the other way. I used to get a bit short-tempered when I was pushed into something I didn't like, but fortunately I had plenty of time to give to the subjects I was best at. Like math, art and music. Fooling about on the piano gave me a kick, I suppose, but again I was not really dedicated enough to worry about whether I was doing the right thing."

Wasting Time

"Around the time I was thirteen, I had this feeling that I wanted to play in a group, maybe lead my own outfit. My family seemed to think I was stark raving mad. I suppose they did not want me to chuck away all that education by making music a full-time job, and they could not see much point in me wasting time on it if I wasn't going to stick at it."

So Bill temporarily shelved his ideas, but not for long. His first guitar was a Broadway, and along with the guitar he got himself a $66 amplifier. Besides learning to play the guitar, Bill also became interested in electronics and thereupon made it a point to study his amplifier both inside and out.

Still, Bill was not absolutely set on a career in music. "Trouble was that I didn't have the faintest idea what would happen to me when I left school. I did not reckon I was good enough to force my way into the music business, and I wasn't interested in putting in a life's work using my knowledge of maths. I mean, there are figures and figures and the mathematical ones didn't seem right for me."

Office Job

While making the rounds of the various jazz clubs, Bill also had managed to find himself a job in an office. But it was definitely not for him. "I hated it," Bill recalls. "Absolutely detested every minute of it! It all seemed such a waste of time. I didn't seem to be learning anything, there was no future in it—and when I got my pay packet . . . well, it was just ridiculous! And the only thing which lightened my little old load was playing my guitar, mostly for my own enjoyment at home, and listening to records, or the radio."

And so now all five of the Rolling Stones were in London and crazy about music. Two of them were already together, a third was about to make their acquaintance, and the other two were busy developing their own musical abilities. A lot was to happen to all five of them before they actually got together and tasted their first success as recording artists.

Next week we will delve into their struggle to claw their way to the top—past the barriers placed, sometimes deliberately and sometimes unintentionally, in their path. We'll follow along as they make their first attempts at success. We'll watch as they fail—we'll smile as they succeed. But that's all next week in Rolling Stones' Story—Part III.

British Stars Rap, Praise United States

British entertainers have brought home impressions about the U.S. which range from unbridled admiration to shocked disgust.

According to Gerry Marsden, of Gerry and the Pacemakers, America is a great place to visit, but no place to live in.

"I'd hate to live there—could not stand the pace, but it's a great place for a visit," he told Britishers following his third tour of the U.S.

American fans also amazed Marsden, who found them to be much more demonstrative than their counterparts in Great Britain.

"It's a great experience, even if we feel a bit scared from time to time," said Gerry, commenting on his reactions when a whole auditorium of U.S. fans came charging onto the stage.

Mixed Reactions

The Hollies, one of England's top rock n' roll groups returned home from their first U.S. tour with mixed emotions. Tony Hicks, who hated the U.S., was annoyed at the price of food and the people in the street who, "call you Beatles if your hair is a bit long."

Graham Nash who thought the U.S. was "Great, Better than England," was taken back by some of the teenage fans. "Little girls write their names and number down and ask you to call them that night. They're only nippers," he said.

"It's a great feeling to be in America and see the place," said Bobby Elliot. "Everything British is the thing."

Herman thinks the U.S. is fabulous, and said that Herman's Hermits have to change their act for the American audiences.

"You put more into it," he explained. "After travelling six hundred miles a day in a coach or on a plane, you're shattered, but they expect a lot more because they only get one chance to see you, then you're gone."

KRLA ARCHIVES

MAIL BOX

Adult Readers
Dear Editor:

Just to let you know that there are many of us in our early 20's who like current pop music too. Not all the popularity of the top sellers is confined to teenagers alone. The music of the English groups has caught the fancy of many adults.

My own personal taste in music runs the gamut from classical to the top 40. My favorites are the English groups. They have a special meaning for me since my pen pal in England is an English girl. We have become very good friends over the mail.

I enjoy reading the BEAT and getting the facts about what's what in pop music. Your articles are written intelligently without sensationalism. It's nice to know where we can read the real facts instead of listening to a lot of hearsay.

Keep up the good work and I hope you always keep the facts straight. Do you have any idea how many of your readers are not teenagers?

Sincerely, an oldtimer at 24,
Thomas Vincent Quiroz.

☆ ☆ ☆

More Spats Please
Dear Editor:

I love the BEAT, it's really fab. In the July 7 issue of the BEAT you printed a picture of the "Spats". They're groovy. I hope you will print more about the "Spats" in the BEAT soon. I will continue to love the BEAT and will look for more on the "Spats".

Sincerely,
A BEAT Lover,
Cathy Sweeney, Anaheim.

☆ ☆ ☆

No More Tickets
Dear Gentlemen:

We believe in our own mind that we are truly Beatle fans. Naturally like any other noble fans we wrote away for tickets. The anxious weeks of waiting were almost unbearable. Then finally we received a reply. Our eyes and hopes dropped a little when we found we could get no tickets.

As we listen to our favorite radio station, KRLA, we hear everything about the Beatles. How does this station get the right to give away all these tickets free when the thousands of kids who paid a lot of money did not get any, because you claimed there were no more. Is this fair? We think not.

Thank you,
Two True Beatle Fans,
Barbara and Roberta Tilles.

Dear Barbara and Roberta:

I am truly sorry that you were unable to go to the Beatle Concert and know how disappointed you must be. I only wish there was something I could do.

However, I am surprised that you protest us giving free tickets to the Beatle Concert in our contests. As you know, the tickets were sold out almost immediately after the Beatle Concert was announced. We knew that a lot more kids would want to go to the Concert than there would be room for. Therefore we held back a few tickets to offer as prizes. We are not making any money by giving these tickets away free. We just thought that the kids who didn't get to buy these tickets would appreciate the chance to win them in a contest. If we had sold these few extra tickets, there would still not be enough to go around. We hope you realize that we are not giving these tickets away to be mean, but as a favor to KRLA listeners.

Sincerely,
The BEAT.

☆ ☆ ☆

Nice People
Dear BEAT Editor:

Did you ever wonder how many nice people there are in the world?

Maybe it's just an accident, but I don't think so: there are a lot more than you think.

As a KRLA Suzuki representative, I have had the opportunity to go into many homes and sit five, six, sometimes seven hours with one family.

It hasn't failed yet that every one of them has been as nice as if they were my own family, as a matter of fact, after a day of playing cards, swimming, or monopoly, I felt bad when someone else won it.

But that was not a factor in the warm personalities of these people. Win or lose, they were the greatest to be with. When I left, I felt as if I had known them for years.

There was no guarantee, and as I said, maybe it was just an accident, but I don't think so. To all the people who hid Suzukis in their homes and let us stay with them, a salute for being among the nicest people in the world!

Fred Broson,
Culver City

Fan Clubs
(For information from any of the listed fan clubs enclose a self-addressed, stamped envelope.)

DONOVAN
c/o Francie Kruge
8692 Falmouth, Apt. 4
Playa Del Rey, Calif.

IAN WHITCOMB
c/o Alice Mang
1409 San Carlos
Arcadia, Calif.

DENIS PAYTON OF DAVE CLARK FIVE
c/o Joanne Binder
5937 S. Honore
Chicago, Illinois 60636

THE BANSHEES
c/o Lynne Wells
319 Noren Street
La Canada, Calif.

ROLLING STONES
c/o Bill Wilkinson
425 Fairway Drive
Brookfield, Wisc. 53005

HERMAN'S HERMITS
c/o Marry Garra,
9123 Morehart Ave.
Pacoima, Calif. 91332

ELENA NOEL
c/o Pilar Lopez
540 N. West Knoll Dr.
Los Angeles 48, Calif.

CHAD & JEREMY
c/o Madeline Jen Kin
1800 Orange Grove
Orange, Calif.

THE BEATLES
c/o Sharon Owens
4821 Audubon
Warren, Michigan 48092

The above information is provided as a service to our readers. Accuracy of the information you receive is the responsibility of the officials of each club.

"SUZUKI SYNDROME? Nah! — It's just that the Hullabalooer and I can't leave our Suzukis behind without a leash," Charlie O'Donnell tells curious onlookers, who wonder why the deejays are sitting on their Suzukis instead of working behind the microphones. KRLA gave away 30 motorcycles just like these handsome models during their July Suzuki contest.

Bob Dylan Rockets To Top In Pop Field

(Continued from Page 2)

own music and on the whole Mersey sound.

Driving Beat

He has changed his vocal style recently, dropping most of the wandering troubadour overtones and picking up a sharp, driving rhythm and blues beat accentuated by electric guitars.

But the messages in the lyrics are still there. Dylan is one of the outstanding modern poets — much more a poet than a singer or songwriter — and this appears to be responsible for changing the trend of pop music.

More and more of the successful songs being written by others are also folk message ballads. But they have changed the beat, hardened it. The lyrics are folk, but the music is rock and R&B. Dylan, incidentally, doesn't call them songs. To him they are stories.

Born in Minnesota, Dylan lived off and on for his first 17 years in Hibbing, a mining town "way up on the Canadian border." In an often hilarious summary of his early experiences called "My Life in a Stolen Minute," he wrote, "Hibbing's a good ol' town. I ran away from it when I was 10, 12, 13, 15, 15½, 17 and 18. I been caught an' brought back all but once."

His first jaunt was to Chicago and before the police found him, the 10 year-old runaway had gotten his first guitar. By the time he was 15 he had taught himself piano, autoharp and harmonica and had written his first song, dedicated to Bridgette Bardot.

Thereafter, his restlessness took him to a series of towns and states, winding up in Burbank, California. Later he moved to New York's Greenwich Village, where his coffee house performances gained him a devoted following which has grown steadily in numbers ever since.

The KRLA BEAT is published weekly by BEAT Publications; editorial and advertising offices at 6290 Sunset Boulevard, Suite 504, Hollywood, California 90028.

Single copy price, 15 cents. Subscription price, U.S. and possessions, $3 per year or $5 for two years. Canada and foreign rates, $9 per year or $14 for two years.

Exclusive distribution handled by Miller-Freeman Publications, 6328 Lewis Avenue, Long Beach, Calif. Inquiries should be directed to the attention of David Thomas.

KRLA BEAT SUBSCRIPTION

you will SAVE 60% of the regular price!
AN INTRODUCTORY SPECIAL . . . if you subscribe now . . .

☐ 1 YEAR — 52 Issues — $3.00   ☐ 2 YEARS — $5.00

Enclosed is $..........

Send to:..Age:..........

Address:..

City:...................... State:.................. Zip:..........

MAIL YOUR ORDER TO: **KRLA BEAT**
1401 South Oak Knoll Avenue
Pasadena, California 91106

Outside U.S.: $9.00 — 52 Issues

CASEY'S QUIZ

CASEY KASEM

When the Rolling Stones left England's Crawdaddy Club and went on to bigger and better things, the owner of the rock nightspot had to go looking for a group that could replace the famous five. It wasn't easy. In fact, it was next to impossible. But he finally found another fivesome who were able to pick up where the Stones left off. This same group is now riding high on both the English and American charts. One of the members closely resembles Brian Jones, but the group's sound is all its own. Oddly enough, the group's trademark is short hair and American Ivy League suits!

Answer on Page 10

KRLA ARCHIVES

BEATLE QUIZ!

Final Questions

Woody Alexander

Beatle Quiz
KRLA BEAT
Suite 504
6290 Sunset Blvd.
Hollywood, Calif. 90028

CONTEST EDITOR:

Below are my answers to the set of questions in the BEATLE QUIZ CONTEST.

My Name .... Address ....
City .... State .... Zip Code ....

I (☐am) (☐am not) presently a subscriber to the KRLA BEAT.

NEW QUESTIONS

46. The Beatles almost didn't get through one of their American concerts last summer. The high altitude got to them and they had the feeling of "floating off" all during their performance. In what state did this happen? ....

47. Which of the Beatles recorded a conversation that was released as one whole side of an intreview album. Also, what was the album called? ....

48. A famous American entertainer once said he dug the Beatles because his kids would take away his television set if he didn't. Who was he? ....

49. When the Beatles were quizzed about possible female co-stars for their second movie, John Lennon remarked, "We're trying to get _____."
Name the famous personality mentioned in his quip. ....

50. What is the brand name of the drums Ringo plays and how many are there in the set he most often uses? ....

CURVACIOUS TANYIA CALLAHAN of Santa Maria is the winner of KRLA's "GIRL ON THE BEACH" contest. For sending in her winning picture to Deejay Bill Slater, Jerry Clark of Santa Maria wins a custom-built surfboard from Jacobs Surf Boards in Hermosa Beach. Tanyia wins a $200 wardrobe from Bullock's Downtown.

HELP!

Dear BEAT:
HELP! I've got a band with two guitars and a drummer and we desperately need a bass guitar player.

If anyone is interested he should have his own guitar and amplifier. He doesn't have to be great because we're not the best band in the world. We want a boy between 14 and 16 who lives in the South Inglewood area.

Anyone who is interested in joining the "Arragons," please write: Rick Heltebrake, 1222 S. Inglewood Ave., Inglewood, Calif. 90301.

★ ★ ★

Anyone who is interested in making amateur motion pictures for kicks should contact Imperial Pictures, 5240 Wood Avenue, South Gate, California. We welcome everyone. There is but one requirement: they must live in the South Gate area.

★ ★ ★

HELP! Beatle Fan wants to buy a ticket to the Hollywood Bowl Beatle Concert for either the 29th or 30th. Write to: Beatle Fan, 717 Carhart, Fullerton, California.

Music Pro Joins BEAT Staff

The BEAT has expanded again, adding experience, depth and knowledge of the recording industry to its staff in *Julian Portman*, former west coast manager of Record World Magazine. Portman will assist in production of the BEAT, as well as writing a weekly gossip column entitled "Platter Pot" that'll talk about new platter releases and the artists who create them.

Portman was also former west coast editor for Music Business Magazine and worked as a reporter for several newspapers in the East.

His appointment is effective immediately.

CASEY'S QUIZ ANSWER
(Don't peek unless you've read the question elsewhere in the BEAT)

The Yardbirds

Back issues of the KRLA BEAT are still available, for a limited time. If you've missed an issue of particular interest to you, send 15 cents for each copy wanted, along with a self-addressed stamped envelope to:

KRLA BEAT
Suite 504
6290 Sunset Blvd.
Hollywood, California 90028

ISSUES AVAILABLE

4/14 — INTERVIEW WITH JOHN LENNON
4/21 — INTERVIEW WITH PAUL McCARTNEY
4/28 — CHIMP EXCITES TEEN FAIR
5/5 — HERMANIA SPREADS
5/12 — HERE COME THE BEATLES
5/19 — VISIT WITH BEATLES
5/26 — FAB NEW BEATLE QUIZ
6/2 — L.A. ROCKS AS STONES ROLL
6/16 — BATTLE OF THE BEAT
6/23 — P. J. — HERO OR HEEL
6/30 — PROBY FIRED
7/7 — SONNY & CHER vs. THE BYRDS
7/24 — BEATLES TOP STONES
7/31 — CHER

KRLA ARCHIVES

For Girls Only

Calling all boys! How did you find my column this week? Yes, yes, I know. You just open the KRLA BEAT and there it is. And I wish you'd STOP finding it!

Speaking of boys, and I've been known to a time or two, how do you feel about the subject of accepting last minute dates? Some girls are violently against this practice, and others sort of take the late-comers with a grain of salt.

Personally, I don't think there is anything wrong with accepting this kind of date if you really *want* to go out with the boy in question. If he's some creature from the lagoon that you would not *dream* of dating, you can always draw yourself up virtuously and say "I don't accept last minute dates" (or figs) (do not say that!) and get off the hook.

What I'm trying to say is this. I think this is just one of the many subjects that's been blown all out of proportion. It really isn't that big a deal. It's sort of like the big tizzy some girls go through when they're trying to decide whether to accept a car date. You know, rather uncalled for. It isn't the car that's really the crux of the matter, it's the boy. There are some boys you could drive from here to Timbucktoo with and never have a fear, and there are others you couldn't trust on a Schwinn. What really matters is the boy, and how well you know him.

Why Refuse

To close this confusing monologue, I think a girl who refuses a last minute invitation from a boy she's been dying to date is out of her tree! Which just has to be the most confusing thing I've said so far, but in my opinion, the most true.

As you may have noticed, this isn't my day. I mean, I'm saying everything backwards again, so bear with me. Oh well, some have it and some don't, and guess who doesn't!

Oh, before I forget, I'd like to ask you a favor. I collect match book covers with restaurants on the front. Wow. See what I mean? Can't you just imagine a match book cover with a restaurant on the front? Like, that would have to be the world's largest matchbook. Anyway, let's make that *names* of restaurants on the front.

Send Matches

I'd really flip if you'd drop such a match book in the mail to me (take out the matches or burn them first or the Post Office may come for you with a long rope) for my collection. I'll try to help with your hobby in return.

Hey, remember last week when I told you my little brother isn't speaking to me because I told him flavor was spelled f-l-a-v-o-u-r and got him into trouble with his summer school teacher? Well, at the time I was overjoyed because he'd stopped speaking to me, but now I'm beginning to get worried. He *still* isn't speaking to me, and this morning he gave me a note that said "You have been sent to Coventry. Har."

Anyone going through an English phase similar to mine knows that being sent to Coventry means no one will speak to you because of some gross boo-boo you've made.

I made the boo-boo of being born in the same family as that nutty brother of mine, so I guess I'm getting my just desserts. And the thing I'm beginning to get worried about is that I might someday have to *return* from Coventry, and why should a thing like that have to happen to a nice kid like me?

Cool Parents?

Never, never answer that question, but do answer this one. I'm going to take a poll about parents, and I'm really curious how it will turn out. As you know, no one is perfect (except George Harrison, maybe) no matter what age they happen to be, and there are very few teenagers who get along with their folks every single minute of every day.

Now, think about this. If you *had* to choose between parents who take a dim view of your teenage activities and parents who go overboard in the other direction (you know, like if your folks can do the Freddie better than you can, and your friends think *they're* a lot more fun than *you* are), which two-some would you choose? I've had letters complaining about both types of parents, and like I said, I'm really curious as to which side will win this poll.

Please let me know how you feel about this subject soon, so we can talk more about it.

I wonder how long it will be before permanents are a thing of the past? I know it will be at least another hundred years before I have another one. I splurged at the "beauty salon" about two years ago and I've been moaning ever since.

Permanent Mistake

At the time, I asked for a "body perm", but I don't think the beauty operator paid much attention. After I finished fainting about the results, I figured well, it'll go away in a few months. I later found out that a permanent *never* goes away. The curl does, in time, but the chemical process of the hair is changed and the only way to get rid of the damaged hair is to have it chopped off.

Never again!

Oh, before I bring this to a shuddering halt, I've seen another of those falling-off-the-couch-laughing commercials. A nice litle old lady walks up to her teenage grandson and says "Johnny, could I have bad breath?"

I hope that someday he smiles and says "Sure, if that's what you want!"

Oh, boy. I've blabbed on much longer than I'm supposed to! I'm going (fast), but keep your letters coming! See you next BEAT!

PEN PALS FROM ENGLAND, INDIA

(Here are several English girls who would like American pen pals.)

Ruth Spencer, 16
Brooklyn
Nursery Lane
Near, Maresfield
Sussex, England

Diana Blunder, 17
Pinhay
43 Chesterfield Road
West Ewell
Surrey, England

Annette Stargroom, 14
225 Llole Drive
Speke
Liverpool 24, England

Jennifer Payne, 14
2 Hockley Lane
Netherton, Dudley
Worcs, England

Pam Vesty, 15
60, Narford Road
Clapton, London E.5.
England

Betty Whitehouse, 17
36 Old Hall Road
Featherstone NR.
Wolverhampton
Staffs, England

Wilma Bell, 16
10, Urswick Green
Barrow-in-furness
Lancashire, England

Shirley Ford, 16
1, Somerfield Close
Burgh Heatt
Tadworth
Surrey, England

Margaret Heaney, 15
44 Oldbridge
Speke
Liverpool 24
Lancashire, England

(These boys from India would like to write to American girls.)

Brijesh Mongal
112/290 Swaroop Nagar
Kanpur, India

Kuldip V. Accanoor
c/o Mr. A. S. Vithala Rao
6, Greeta Niketan
266, Linking Rd.
Bandra, Bombay-50, India

R. K. Arora
Chawla Street
Jagraon,
Ludhiana, India

Inder Jit Dutt
59/28 Rohtak Rd.
New Delhi-5, India

T. K. Bhattacharya
4/90 Chandi Tala Lane
Regent Park,
Calcutta-40, India

Neel Kamal Verna
11 Hanuman Rd.
New Delhi-1, India

Subhaash A. Palekar
Radha Bhuvan
Siddhanath Rd.
Baroda, India

Most Claims Long Contract

Mickie Most, independent record producer and the man responsible for producing all of Herman's hit records, has won an injunction in London restraining Herman's Hermits from recording with anyone else.

Most claims that he has an exclusive contract with the group calling for him to produce all of their records for the next four years.

However, Harvey Lisberg, one of Herman's managers, declares that this just isn't so. Lisberg says that the group will file to get the injunction removed.

Animals Eagerly Await First Harlem Concert

The Animals, one of England's most popular groups, will record a "live" concert at the Apollo Theater in New York which will be waxed when the group returns to America on September 12.

To record "live" at the Apollo (located in New York's Harlem) is a group ambition which was frustrated earlier this year when U.S. Immigration authorities turned thumbs down on the idea. However, they have now gained Immigration approval, and the session is to be supervised by Mickie Most.

The Animals have just returned to England from a very successful tour of Japan. In fact, Eric Burdon declares that "it was the best tour we ever had!" The boys were especially knocked out by a Japanese girl who kept telling them that "you English are so quiet". Somehow, the Animals were not aware that they were all that quiet!

While in Japan, Eric became fascinated with those steel helmets which the Japanese construction workers wear. "I got one to wear when we go to America next, in front of all the governors. It will have NAACP and Freedom Now written in Japanese on it."

They told me they needed a mathematician to work on it as there are three Japanese characters to every Western letter.

Wow! That really ought to be some hat!

The Animals' biggest American hit to date has been "House Of The Rising Sun", but for some reason the boys are definitely off that record now. Eric says: "We've been trying to forget the number. I'm all against it."

Rather ironic, isn't it?

—Louise Criscione.

THE ANIMALS (from left) John Steel, Dave Rowberry, Eric Burdon, Chas Chandler and Hilton Valentine, will appear this fall on alive concert taped in New York.

KRLA ARCHIVES

   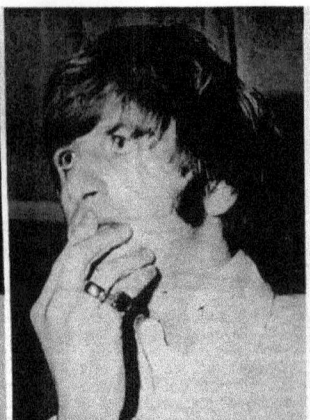

...JOHN   ...PAUL   ...GEORGE   ...RINGO

IS BEATLEMANIA DYING?

Beatle rumors are flying again, and it's the same old story. According to the latest rumblings from the grapevine, "the Beatles are slipping in popularity."

These rumors are no doubt being manufactured by the same people who said "Elvis will never last", and the Beatle gossip is no more fact than the Presley predictions were.

Rumors aren't completely fabricated out of thin air. They usually spring from acorns of doubt and grow into towering oaks of confusion.

One of the reasons behind the most recent crop of rumors is the fact that concert tickets have not yet been sold out in all the cities on the Beatle itinerary. Tickets are still available for concerts in Portland, Oregon and Kansas City, Missouri and one or two other cities.

This is causing a bit of speculative whispering, but no matter what is being said, the availability of tickets in some areas does not mean the 1965 American tour will be the Beatles' swan song.

Tickets for some Beatle concerts have always sold out in a matter of hours, but this has not always been the case throughout all of the country. During the last Beatle tour, tickets were available in some cities as late as the day of the concert, but were always sold out by the time the great moment arrived.

Beatled Areas

Some areas are simply more Beatled than others, causing tickets to be sold at a faster and more furious pace. Last year many California Beatlemaniacs got to see John, Paul, George and Ringo only because it was still possible, at the last minute, to purchase tickets for the Las Vegas concert at Convention Hall.

The availability of tickets in some places is only an acorn, but because the situation is being looked at through misinformed eyes, the rumor-bearing oak is already beginning to take root.

It needn't bother. The tickets will be sold. They always *have*, and the chances are good that they *always will!*

As always, the proof is in the pudding. If the Beatles were in any sort of slump, their latest album wouldn't be the number one LP in the nation, and "Beatles VI" wouldn't have climbed to this spot in three short weeks when it often takes as long as three months for an album to rise to the top.

Beatle Albums

Where other Beatle records are concerned, "Beatles 65" is still the number twenty-five bestseller in the country, after seven months on the charts. Another Beatle album, "The Early Beatles" is also selling well (number fifty-three after three months on the charts), in spite of the fact that it includes no new Beatle songs and is a reissue of early album tunes like "Anna."

The most recent Beatle single, "Ticket To Ride" has finally dropped off the national American charts, after reaching the number one slot, but is still riding high on many foreign charts. To mention a few, "Ticket" is number one in Holland, number four in Hong Kong and number seven in Malaysia.

The new Beatle single was released on July 19, and a world of loyal Beatlemaniacs eagerly awaited its arrival. (Don't have to tell you where you heard it first, do we?) (Hardly!!)

Illegal in Indonesia

There is only one place we can think of where the Beatles may be having a problem, and that's in Indonesia. The Indonesian government has outlawed the sale of rock and roll music and recently staged a raid on a black market storehouse of rock tapes. Many Beatle tunes were confiscated in the raid, which proves that the foursome is popular even in places where it's against the law to be a Beatlemaniac!

Now that you know the whole truth and nothing else but, you will have something to fight those rumors with, and don't hesitate to quote the BEAT when you're standing up for John, Paul, George and Ringo. The information printed in this article isn't just our opinion. It's fact!

And so is the fact that the Beatles are here to stay!

KRLA ARCHIVES

TIPS TO TEENS

Q: My mother is always lecturing me about going to bed earlier than I do, but I can't sleep more than six hours at a time. If I go to bed at eleven, I wake up at five a.m., which is LOTS of fun. How can I convince her that she has nothing to worry about?
(Dana H.)

A: Some people need less sleep than others, although it is a little unusual for a teenager to need only six hours of snoozing. Tell your mom to check with the family doctor about this. He'll probably confirm what I've just told you, which should keep her from worrying about your health.

Q: I bought a jersey dress, and it's really cute, but I about go nuts when I wear it. The seams are bound in a weird kind of thread that hurts when it touches your skin. It's worst of all in the sleeves. What can I do?
(Virginia B.)

A: Rebind the seams with seam binding (which figures) or wide, soft ribbon. If you're not good at sewing, apply iron-on tape with a warm iron (which also figures). Jerseys are often bound with this "weird thread" because the material is too slippery for ordinary thread.

Q: I'm letting my hair grow, and it's about half way down my back (don't worry, I'm a girl). It doesn't bother me except at night; then I can't sleep because that mop of hair is really hot. I can't put it in a pony tail because the rubber band leaves a mark on my hair the next day. Any suggestions?
(Diane M.)

A: Try stuffing your locks into a pretty nightcap, and if that doesn't work, tie your hair up with a ribbon—in a pony tail, or two pigtails. The ribbon will probably fall out during the night, but you'll be sound asleep by then and won't know the difference.

Q: No matter how often I wash my hands, my fingernails always look grubby. This is because I have funny streaks in them. What causes this and what can I do about it?
(Vera L.)

A: Streaked nails are caused by a number of things, such as a temporary upset in your body chemicals, or a fever. Try using the new "nail-white" product that comes in cream form instead of the not-very-effective pencil. You can buy it at most drug stores, and if all else fails, a beauty supply house will have it.

Q: I have two questions about getting a tan. First, do you recommend those fake tanning products that are supposed to tan you overnight? Second, last summer I did something really moronic. As a joke, I taped Paul McCartney's initials on my back and then sat out in the sun. I still have P. M. across my shoulders; it's not too noticeable, but people still wonder. How can I get rid of the initials?
(Ursula B.)

A: In answer to your first question, I don't recommend the tanning products you mentioned. They work for some people, but in others they turn purple and orange wherever the skin is slightly roughened (knees, elbows, etc.). If you're going to try this kind of product, make a test by putting some of the lotion on your arm and seeing what develops. About your initial problem, the letters should fade if you get enough sun this year. If they don't, cut a hole in the back of an old blouse and give that part of your back an extra dose of sunshine.

Q: I'm going to have a party soon, and I'm tired of serving the same old cokes. Can you think of something different I could serve without going broke?
(Karen K.)

A: Try making a giant float. Put about three quarts of ice cream in a punch bowl and pour any carbonated beverage over it. Then supply lots of glasses and straws and watch your masterpiece disappear in seconds! Speaking of seconds, better plan to make another batch because your guests will be coming back for more!

HINT OF THE WEEK

Maybe this is just wishful thinking, but I think I've discovered a new fashion idea! I was sewing two shifts at the same time, one polka-dotted and the other striped, and I sewed the wrong pieces together. I ended up with a shift with a polka dot front and a striped back. At first I was about ready to tear my hair out, but when I tried my mistake on, it looked kind of sharp. I sewed the other one the same way, only with the stripes in front, etc. I ended up with two of the wildest outfits and I'm always getting compliments on them!
(Sharon B.)

A PRETTY CONTRACT may be in the making for Roy Orbison, one of the hottest American artists on the international scene. The singer may break with Monument Records and sign a million dollar contract with MGM Records.

A BEAT EDITORIAL
The Spoilers Return

It seems there are "spoilers" who delight in giving a black eye to everything decent. Take the case of motorcycles.

In the eyes of some people anything with two wheels and a motor is a monster. With a worse monster on its back. This attitude has been brought about by the recent rash of stupidity displayed by some cycle clubs — one in particular. They are the spoilers, and they couldn't possibly have acted at a more inopportune time!

It came just as the cycle industry was finally getting to its feet again as a respectable institution. The 'wild one' image had become something you thought about only while watching the late show. People no longer went into a panic when they heard the familiar roar. They no longer automatically figured the driver was a "bad guy" to be watched at all times.

They simply thought "Hmmm, that looks like fun." It was . . . and still is. We're printing this editorial in hopes of helping it stay that way.

Not All Hoodlums

A motorcycle is not a monster. It becomes one only when the person at its controls has no control over himself. Every person who rides a motorcycles isn't a hoodlum. And anyone who thinks so is making the error of judging everyone by the actions of a few.

Unfortunately, motorcycle gangs do exist. Fortunately, however, it isn't considered hip to belong to one. It's considered just exactly what it is — utterly ridiculous.

Most motorcycle owners are respectable, law-abiding citizens. Students, teachers, businessmen — people from all walks of life. People who use their cycles for transportation and recreation, not as instruments of terror.

We hope the two-wheel trend will continue to grow. And it will — provided the public is willing to take a closer look at the situation to discover that most cyclists are people who use their head and wheels simultaneously.

FAMED SONS, Dino Martin (left) and Desi Arnez (right) along with Billy, the son of a California contractor, combined talents and came out with a hit, "I'm a Fool." The three should have no trouble making their own names in the pop music world.

KRLA ARCHIVES

Personals

Dear BEAT Readers:
A Manchester boy has written to me requesting a pen pal. As he says he is interested in film stars, I thought California to be the best place. He is 17 (will be 18 on John Lennon's birthday) and likes Beatles, Stones and all other Pop stars. He is very eager to learn about the States. Please write soon. Victor Bevan, 92 Frank Cowin Court, Sussex Street, Salford 7, Manchester, Lancs., England.
    Sincerely,
    Joyce Keen.

To Robin Kingsley:
  We like you!!
    Marianna and Stephannie.

Nancy:
  Larry loves you.
    Guess Who?

To Tim McGuinn and Mike Clarke:
  Well, we're sorry to bug you again, but we're glad we finally "met" (?) you after that disappointment of several months ago! Did you really remember us? Must've choked when you saw us. Sorry, but thanks for signing the autographs!
    Martha Aarons and
    Judi Weinburger.

To Bonnie and Marcy:
  Everytime anyone mentions Gerry and the Pacemakers I freeze and then check to see if I can breathe. YOU TWO know what I mean!!
    Ann Jordan.

Dave Davies Love:
  Wherever you are in this cruel hypocritical, heartless, cold intolerant world, I love you.
    Love from a Realy Kinky honest-to-goodness Kinker.

Mike Love:
  Here's hoping your 21st is a rave. Have a fab time though you're not here.
    J.

To Dennis of The Beachboys:
  I've got your fourth drumstick. You did just as well with the other three at the concert.
    The Girl Backstage With
    the Pink Scarf

To Mollie:
  Tuffy! I'd thought we'd won that "Bonanza" contest! Would have made me sing guitars to ya!
    Mike

To BEAT Readers:
  This girl would like to write to a tall and handsome boy about 15 or 16 years-old. She has blonde hair and is 14 years-old. She will give more information about herself when the boys writes. She will *only* write to a boy. Here is her address: Elizabeth Foulkes, 26 B Elloway Road, Speke, Liverpool 24, Lancs, England.
    Sher Owings

Tina Luv:
  Now how could Pauly have been at your house when you know he lives here? Say hello to John for me!
    Lorelle McCartney

To Jackie W.:
  I'm only dropping these few lines to thank you for being the dearest, sweetest person I know and for allowing me the pleasure of being your best friend.
    Hya

To Cal of "The Virtues":
  You're darling, but what happened to Mr. Tambourine Man"? Say "hi" to Chuck.
    The Three Girls
    In The Corner

THE BYRDS FLY TO THE NUMBER ONE SPOT on the English charts with "Mr. Tambourine Man," a Bob Dylan composition. They are (from left) David Crosby, Chris Hillman, Gene Clark, Jim McGuinn and Mike Clarke.

Tambourine Men Also Top British Charts

California's Byrds have made it a clean sweep with "Mr. Tambourine Man," hitting the top of the record charts in both the U.S. and Britain.

In the latest British surveys they jumped from number 3 to number one. Two weeks previously they had been listed at number 17.

Three American artists are among the top ten on the British charts — Elvis Presley's "Crying In The Chapel" is number five and Gene Pitney's "Looking Through The Eyes Of Love" is number eight.

Seven other Americans are included in the British top — 30: Sam the Sham "Wooly Bully" No. 11 ... The Everly Brothers "The Price of Love" No. 12 ... Joan Baez "There But For Fortune" No. 15 ... The Four Tops "I Can't Help Myself" No. 20 ... P. J. Proby "Let The Water Run Down" No. 23 ... Sir Douglas Quintet "She's About A Mover" No. 25 ... and The Beach Boys "Help Me Rhonda" No. 27.

British Top 10

1.	MR. TAMBOURINE MAN	The Byrds
2.	HEART FULL OF SOUL	The Yardbirds
3.	I'M ALIVE	The Hollies
4.	TOSSING AND TURNING	The Ivy League
5.	CRYING IN THE CHAPEL	Elvis Presley
6.	TO KNOW YOU IS TO LOVE YOU	Peter & Gordon
7.	IN THE MIDDLE OF NOWHERE	Dusty Springfield
8.	LOOKING THROUGH THE EYES OF LOVE	Gene Pitney
9.	LEAVE A LITTLE LOVE	Lulu
10.	ONE IN THE MIDDLE E.P.	Manifred Mann

☆ ☆ ☆

KRLA ARCHIVES

BEAU BRUMMELS DAZZLE FASHION WORLD

FAMED STYLIST CY DEVORE makes a final inspection of the new outfits he created for the Beau Brummels — (from left) John Petersen, Sal Valentino, Ron Elliott and Ron Meagher.

San Francisco's Beau Brummels are now setting fashion trends as well as music trends.

When they talk about aiming for the top-ten, they could be talking about the top ten best-selling records on the national charts or the list of ten best-dressed men.

As you may have noticed on their recent television appearances, they have new outfits — created by Hollywood's famed Cy Devore — which would dazzle the original Beau Brummel.

The B-B's who now have a third consecutive national hit with "You Tell Me Why," found it was easier to record a hit record than it was to persuade the Beau Brummel of the fashion world to design costumes for the Beau Brummels of the music world. Devore has previously rejected a similar request by the Beatles.

Carl Scott of Cougar Productions, who manages the Beau Brummels, says three factors persuaded Devore to accept the commission.

"He seemed to like the idea of designing outfits for a group of modern-day Beau Brummels," says Scott, "but for the most part we have two people to thank."

"One is his 14 year-old daughter, Lisa, who is a big fan of the group. The other is choreographer Charlie O'Curran — Patti Page's husband — who is a close friend of Devore and has been boosting the boys ever since seeing one of their early performances."

At the urging of his daughter and O'Curran, Devore agreed to add the Beau Brummels to his star-studded list of clientelle, which includes such names as Dean Martin, Frank Sinatra, Peter Lawford, Jerry Lewis, Elvis Presley and dozens more.

So, Ron Elliott, Sal Valentino, Ron Meagher and John Petersen now have a stunning visual image to go with their now-famous musical image.

And — speaking of the top-ten — they'll probably make it in both categories.

YEAH, YEAH, YEAH
ABOUT THE ROLLING STONES

by Louise Criscione

Yeah, well this week's column is dedicated to the Rolling Stones.

Charlie has a special room in his London flat where he does all his painting and drawing. Of course, he doesn't have too much leisure time nowadays, but he did find time to design some notepaper and cards for Bill. Yeah, well listen Charlie — I could use some notepaper myself.

The Stones find the Chess Studios in Chicago are best for recording their real R&B sounds, while the RCA Studios in Hollywood are definitely best for capturing sounds for release as singles. Yeah, well some people cut records in garages, and I have this real nice dirty garage which I would be very willing to let you use.

Brian says it does not really matter to the Stones where they are performing — they're a lot more interested in the audience. Yeah, well then how about performing at my house.

Dark Pictures

One of the Stones' fans wants to know why someone doesn't turn the lights on before the pictures for their LP covers are taken. She goes on to say, "We could see you much better then." Yeah, well that is a good idea. Somebody turn on those lights!

Keith's current pet peeve is the way some of his neighbors act. Says: "They've got some VERY funny habits but it's them who stare at us. We have to creep in and out of our place." Yeah, well I know a whole bunch of people who wouldn't at all mind being neighbors to the likes of Messrs. Richard and Jagger.

When asked what he thought of marriage, Mick said: It's all right for those who wash!" Yeah, well I wash, Mick!

Some other reporter asked Mick what he thought of his fans. And he said: "Silly question, isn't it? I mean, without fans . . . well, we're dead. 'Course I like them — only wish I could spend more time meeting them — the real real ones, that is!" Yeah, well I'm real real (whatever that means!).

Line Them Up

Charlie also had some choice comments on fans. "I'd like to get 'em all queued up and then thank them all for everything they've done to help the Stones. You get a marvelous feeling when you know that things are appreciated." Yeah, well the queue forms behind me.

About money, Charlie says: "Very useful stuff to have. 'Course, we married men have extra responsibilities! Actually, the more you earn, the less you seem to handle." Yeah, well listen Charlie — it is absolutely impossible to handle less money than I do!

A lot of people think that Bill is the quiet Stone who never says anything. Well, let me tell you — he's not! Fact is, he comes out with some pretty funny comments on some things which are not pretty funny to begin with. For instance on girls: "We married men don't answer questions like that. Just say I don't disapprove of them." And on dressing rooms: "If they get any smaller, we'll have to leave our guitars and cigarettes outside."

Mick is genuinely knocked-out by the success of "Satisfaction" here in the U.S. Says: "Our records usually go up quite slowly there. But this is going up really fast. Oh, fab gear!" Yeah, well fab gear!

Seems certain journalists are always trying to start trouble. Reports had the Stones allegedly snubbing Herman when both appeared on the same show in Philadelphia. Mick says: "Nonsense! I was the only one to speak to him simply because we never saw him. Our dressing rooms were miles apart at the show in Philadelphia. I saw him waiting to go on to face a 15,000 crowd. He looked shaky and said he was terrified. I said something about not to worry and he'd be great. This snub never happened."

Yeah, well some people just like to make trouble, that's all. Soreheads, idiots, poopoonasties, and all like that.

What kind of cars does Brian like? "I've gone overboard for American models. Out of this world. They look so great."

Yeah, well listen Brian — I've got this old American model car which is really out of this world, and I'd be more than happy to let you have it cheap.

THE ROLLING STONES — (from left) Charlie Watts, Mick Jagger, Bill Wyman, Keith Richard and Brian Jones.

KRLA ARCHIVES

BEAT GOES TO MOVIES
In Harm's Way
By Jim Hamblin

Created by Otto Preminger and produced for Paramount Pictures, this is probably the best war film Hollywood has come up with since the real thing. The story begins on the night of December 6, 1941, on the island of Hawaii, and takes us through the process of the naval war in the early months of the battle in the Pacific.

The heavyweight cast breezes through magnificent performances to come up with what feels like the shortest 3-hour movie on record. John Wayne heads the cast list, as first the disgraced Captain, later as the Admiral who bails out the Navy in the rising tide of ill-fortune at the darkest hour.

There virtually was no U.S. Navy after Pearl Harbor, and HARM'S WAY recreates the image, the confusion, the agony, some of the petty attitudes, and the *esprit de corps* of those days, with what at times seems like almost painful realism.

Peyton Place?

We are told that some of the local Navy brass are calling the film "The Peyton Place of Pearl Harbor," but nothing less than the reality of life is portrayed briefly with lovely Barbara Bouchet, in opening shots of the story. Some of the scenes we saw in the early preview of the movie have now been cut out of the film for its general release.

There are constant surprises throughout this film, as we discover such stars as Burgess Meredith, Kirk Douglas, Patricia Neal, and Dana Andrews. And oh yeah, don't forget that wonderful old Navy term "CINCPAC"!" That's Henry Fonda's role.

IN HARM'S WAY is first of all the kind of film that *entertains*. Beyond that it is also informative, and gives this generation of teeners a practical and authoritative look into life at the time of World War II.

Producer-Director Otto Preminger is a tough taskmaster who allows no temperamental outbreaks from any of his cast, except just possibly himself. But however he handles it, he's certainly coming up with a beautiful finished product.

Watch For Title

Unusual titles for movies are intriguing, aren't they? The one for this photoplay comes from a line by John Wayne near the beginning. You might watch for it, just for kicks.

You might also watch for some fine acting. Brandon de Wilde portrays a difficult role — a spoiled kid who learns that his father is more of a man than he thought — more so than any of his so-called heroes.

Brandon was that toe-headed fella so much talked about after the western flick SHANE. He's grown up now and for sure holds his own. Two years ago he was part of that actors company seen in another Paramount picture, HUD, starring Melvyn Douglas and Paul Newman.

As HARM'S WAY steams its way toward a dynamic closing it's hard to accept the fact that we will have to leave the realistic characters who have grown up in front of us.

There was one gent who got so interested he nearly forgot to buy any popcorn. . . . and man, that's attention!

As an historic record, and insight into the times, IN HARM'S WAY is a valuable contribution. The timeless John Wayne is a joy to behold.

CHRIS NOEL, a green-eyed blonde, has established he_____ and even do comedy in more than half a dozen feature pictures (including "Girl Happy" with Elvis Presley) and an impressive list of television shows. But despite her beautiful form (36-23-34), Chris says she wants to be thought of as an actress and not a pin-up girl. This is why she is careful to wear Mother Hubbard costumes such as the one above when she poses for publicity pictures.

FOUR AGAIN, the Hondells appear with singer Frankie Avalon in a scene from the movie "Beach Blanket Bingo."

HONDELLS AGAIN BACK TO FOUR

The Hondells, popular West Coast group, are back to being four again. They originally started with this number, but last Christmas Jerry Le Mire, was injured in an automobile accident.

News of the accident was withheld until doctors could make a definite diagnosis. Le Mire continued to make personal appearances with the group, but back pains finally necessitated his leaving the group in order to make a full recovery.

Le Mire's absence from the group was a very well-guarded secret and since he does not play lead guitar, it didn't alter the Hondells'.

The only trouble the boys had was with promoters and bookers. Naturally, the promoters were not too happy to find that the four man group which they had booked contained only three members! However, when the circumstances were explained to them, they were usually very understanding.

Everything is all right now. Jerry is fully recovered and has once again joined the group for all their personal appearances. And the Hondells have a very full summer schedule, which includes the television show, "Where The Action Is," a new record, "Sea Of Love", the chance to sing the title song for a movie entitled "Winter A Go Go," and a thirteen week advertising campaign for Pepsi Cola.

It looks like a really busy summer for the four Hondells.

PORTMAN PLATTER POT
By Julian Portman

Faro Records' *Eddie Davis*, bossman of *Cannibal and The Headhunters*, has added the wild-sounding *Zulu and The Warriors* to his label. . . . It's *Johnny Rivers* singing the title tune on that new fast action TV series "Danger Man" . . . *Melinda Marx*, (Groucho's offspring) and *Vee Jay* records may split. The label hasn't been active in promoting her new single "What" that was picked as a "hit" by almost everyone.

Capitol's Jody Miller filmed two Scopitones . . . *Gil Friessen* called to inform us that our review of *Yellow Rolls Royce*, the title tune "Mae," written by *Riz (More) Ortlani*, was played by *Herb Alpert's Tijuana Brass*, and could be another hitsville for A & M records . . . belated wedding congratulations to *Jerry Moss* on his recent marriage.

Colpix has released *Paul Peterson's* new single "You Don't Need Money" b/w "See the Ring" . . . *The Rising Sons*, a folk-rock quintet, joined the Columbia label . . . *Bobby Darin* returned to *Atlantic Records*, the home of all his hits. . . .

Herman and The Hermits are working on a flicker at MGM, with time-off to do one niters . . . *The Leaves* signed with *Pat Boone's Penthouse Recordings* . . . *Boone* has a hot single titled "Rainy Days" produced by that multi-talented *Norm Ratner* for *Dot Records* . . . "How to Stuff A Wild Bikini," the new American International Pictures release, not only has the grooviest looking chicks in captivity (bikinis), but the hottest sounds in music to go along with the sights. The toe-tapping, hand-clapping film is guaranteed to ring the cash register.

Leon Mirrell, executive producer of *Shindig*, off to London to tape top British and continental musical groups for the show . . . *Dick Howard*, talent coordinator for the same TV show, claims he has a look-a-like in TV. Could it be Flipper . . . ?

Barry Young, an underrated vocalist, brought by his new platter on *Dot Records* titled "One Has My Name." Barry is a Dean Martin sound alike . . . and where is the true *Sig Sakowicz* that comic *Jackie Vernon* talks about on all those network TV shows? Write and tell Portman. The funniest story will win a funny prize!

KRLA ARCHIVES

KRLA Tunedex

EMPEROR HUDSON

CHARLIE O'DONNELL

CASEY KASEM

JOHNNY HAYES

BOB EUBANKS

DAVE HULL

DICK BIONDI

BILL SLATER

KRLA BEAT
6290 Sunset, No. 504
Hollywood, Cal. 90028

BULK RATE
U.S. Postage
PAID
Los Angeles, Calif.
Permit No. 25497

This Week	Last Week	Title	Artist
1	1	ALL I REALLY WANT TO DO	Cher
2	4	I GOT YOU BABE	Sonny & Cher
3	3	SATISFACTION	Rolling Stones
4	2	HOLD ME, THRILL ME, KISS ME	Mel Carter
5	—	LIKE A ROLLING STONE	Bob Dylan
6	5	YES, I'M READY	Barbara Mason
7	7	WHAT'S NEW PUSSYCAT?	Tom Jones
8	6	I CAN'T HELP MYSELF	The Four Tops
9	9	I'M A FOOL/SO MANY WAYS	Dino, Desi & Billy
10	12	CARA MIA	Jay & The Americans
11	—	IT AIN'T ME BABE	The Turtles
12	8	I'M HENRY THE VIII, I AM	Herman's Hermits
13	20	UNCHAINED MELODY/HUNG ON YOU	Righteous Bro.
14	17	SAVE YOUR HEART FOR ME	Gary Lewis & Playboys
15	21	YOU'D BETTER COME HOME	Petula Clark
16	29	YOU WERE ON MY MIND	We Five
17	24	I'LL FEEL A WHOLE LOT BETTER	The Byrds
18	10	WHITTIER BLVD.	The Midnighters
19	30	PAPA'S GOT A BRAND NEW BAG Pt. 1	James Brown
20	16	THIS LITTLE BIRD	Marianne Faithfull
21	11	LAURIE	Dickey Lee
22	28	TO KNOW YOU IS TO LOVE YOU	Peter & Gordon
23	27	LET HER DANCE	Bobby Fuller Four
24	18	SEVENTH SON	Johnny Rivers
25	32	PRETTY LITTLE BABY	Marvin Gaye
26	31	TAKE ME BACK	Little Anthony & The Imperials
27	34	I WANT CANDY	The Strangelaves
28	36	DOWN IN THE BOONDOCKS	Billy Joe Royal
29	—	THEME FROM 'A SUMMER PLACE'	The Lettermen
30	—	WHO'LL BE THE NEXT IN LINE	The Kinks
31	—	YOU TELL ME WHY	The Beau Brummels
32	40	I DON'T BELIEVE	The Guilloteens
33	35	IT HAPPENED JUST THAT WAY/ ONE DYIN' AND A BURYIN'	Roger Miller
34	33	EASY QUESTION	Elvis Presley
35	38	DON'T JUST STAND THERE	Patti Duke
36	—	IT'S THE SAME OLD SONG	The Four Tops
37	37	LET THE WATER RUN DOWN	P. J. Proby
38	—	I PUT A SPELL ON YOU	Nina Simone
39	43	ONE STEP AT A TIME	Maxine Brown
40	—	CALIFORNIA GIRLS	The Beach Boys

KRLA ARCHIVES

KRLA BEAT

Volume 1, Number 22   LOS ANGELES, CALIFORNIA   15 Cents   August 14, 1965

**No More 'Little Boy' Image For Herman – He's Matured!
Oh Yeah! What's in His Right Hand? See Next Page**

KRLA BEAT

Los Angeles, California — August 14, 1965

BEATLES RECORD ANOTHER SMASH – NO 'HELP' NEEDED

Despite the panic-stricken titles of their two new songs — "Help" and "I'm Down" — the Beatles have no cause for distress.

Their latest single appears to be just as hot as all the other Beatle million-sellers, with heavy sales reported from the moment it was released. As usual, there was also a tremendous backlog of advance orders.

And with the boys scheduled to arrive shortly for their third American tour and the premiere of their movie, it looks like the U.S. is in for another epidemic of acute Beatlemania.

Aside from the commercial success of their latest single, both sides are also drawing raves from the music world.

"Help" — the title tune from the movie — is a prime example of their unique ability to cut a record which is unmistakably Beatles and yet "different" from their previous sounds.

New Bag

In "Help" (a Lennon-McCartney tune, naturally) the Beatles opened a brand-new bag. They used much stronger vocal backing behind John's solo voice. And it is this two-part vocal which gives "Help" that slightly "different" sound.

The flip, "I'm Down," is also a striking example of their versatility. It's a hard-rocker, as wild if not wilder than anything else they ever recorded. Paul takes the lead on this side, but he manages to disguise his voice so well that even the hard-core Beatle-buffs had a hard time deciding just which Beatle it was.

The McCartney voice which shouts out "I'm Down" sounds not even remotely like the McCartney voice which croons "All My Loving."

SUAVE HERMAN NURSES A LOLLYPOP

'CATTY' GIFT FROM FANS

Herman Meets Real Cat

On the first day Herman and his Hermits spent on the MGM lot in Los Angeles, 2000 screaming fans came to greet them, Herman got a new cowboy hat, and a kitten found a new home.

Upon arriving at the studios, where they did a three-day shooting for "When the Boys Meet the Girls," the group was rushed out of their black limousine and into the studio press office where they could speak to the fans collected outside over a loud speaker.

Hearing the fans singing, "I'm Henry The VIII," Herman stepped up to the microphone and sang a few verses right back. He was rewarded for these efforts when fans sent up presents which included cakes, a cowboy hat, a water gun and a live kitten.

While Herman appreciated all the gifts, he was especially floored by the kitten. "It's frightened," he murmered sympathetically, while the frantic cat clawed itself firmly onto his jacket.

"But you can't take the cat back with you to England. You won't be able to get him in," someone pointed out to Herman.

"Can anyone give this kitten a good home?" the fans were asked.

A teenage girl appeared out of the mass and Herman gratefully turned the kitten over to her.

It just goes to show, "Every cat has its day."

Boston Has New Version Of Tea Party

The Boston Tea Party has been repeated, giving the old hostility between Great Britain and the colonies a new angle.

In the Tea Party—1965 style —it was indignant Boston teenagers, not patriots, who marched on down to the harbor. And at this rebellion it was not tea, but Beatle records, which went floating down the river.

What is more, this tea party got the official stamp of approval from Boston's mayor and junior chamber of commerce because the teens were protesting Great Britain's refusal to grant Jana Louise a work permit.

Boston teenagers apparently think it is terribly unfair of the British authorities not to allow Jana Louise into their country to perform.

Likewise, many people, both here and abroad, think it's unfair for American authorities to bar well known English entertainers from the U.S. pop scene.

Fair or unfair, tossing Beatle records overboard seems to be a pretty drastic measure.

Bowl Show For Dylan

The Beatles' exciting performance at the Hollywood Bowl will be followed within a few days by another blockbuster—a Bob Dylan Concert.

"Bob Dylan will be at the Bowl on September 3," Bob Eubanks, producer of both concerts, announced.

While the Beatles are scheduled to leave following their Hollywood Bowl performance on August 29 and 30, Eubanks says he will invite them to stay and see the Dylan concert.

Tickets for the Dylan performance can be obtained at Mutual Ticket Agencies, The Automobile Club of America, Wallich's Music City and the Hollywood Bowl Box Office.

Tickets to the Beatle Concert were completely sold-out when the first day's mail arrived, so you'd better hurry if you don't want to miss this opportunity.

. . . ANOTHER MILLION - SELLER?

Star Booted From Club – Records Song In Protest

Eyes blazing with hurt and indignation, a familiar Hollywood figure dashed home late one night recently and began furiously writing verses filled with heart-rending anguish.

The events which had transpired that evening were almost too horrible to comprehend for Sonny Bono. One minute the shy and sensitive young composer, producer and vocalist was a top star — famed for his husband - and - wife Sonny and Cher recordings.

A moment later, zero. Ejected from the hallowed spaghetti-colored halls of the record industry's Valhalla. Kicked out of Martoni's.

To be so humiliated in front of a packed roomful of his disc jockey friends, fellow artists, fellow record producers, fellow record promoters and fellow pizza lovers was life's cruelest blow.

And the absurd excuse they gave for it all, the unmitigated gall of their reason for giving him the gate. Not for drinking too much . . . not for punching a Columbia man . . . not for spilling his lasagna on Natalie Wood's new bell-bottom outfit.

Not for any such commonplace, honorable reasons, but simply because they didn't like the clothes he wore (like a three-quarter length leopard skin

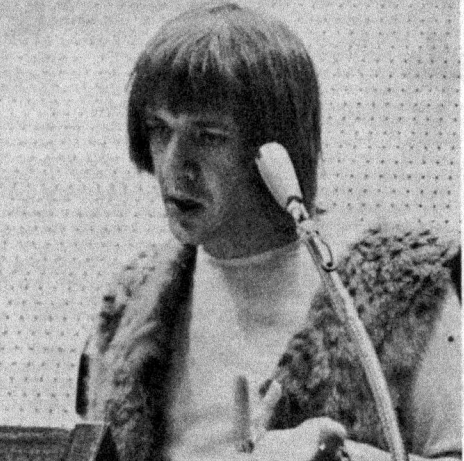

SONNY SAYS: "DON'T LAUGH AT ME"

TURN TO PAGE 12

KRLA ARCHIVES

EARLY STONES (from left) Charlie Watts, Bill Wyman, Mick Jagger, Brian Jones and Keith Richard, look quite different from the Stones of 1965. Today's Stones would never appear in look-alike outfits and short hair and are seldom found wearing white shirts and ties. Which Stones do you like best — the casual long-haired ones or the more formal looking Stones?

STONES' SAGA: Part III

Often Without Food Or Money

By Louise Criscione

For the past two weeks we have been following the Rolling Stones along that path which eventually led them to the success which they now enjoy. We trailed all five of them as they went through school, as Brian wandered around the Continent, as Charlie labored for an advertising agency while keeping one eye glued to those Dior models who kept parading by his office, and as Bill struggled through an office job which he "absolutely detested".

We watched as all five music-crazy young men stalked the streets of London anxious to play their instruments just anywhere that people would listen—really anywhere that they would be tolerated. Still, they were not a group. Only two of the present Stones—Mick and Keith—were together, but the third was about to meet up with them.

The year is 1962. Mick and Keith have finally made a decision—they want to make music a career and they want to form a group.

Brian Enters

Things were still in the talking stage when Mick and Keith met one Brian Jones in a pub in London's Chelsea, a place called The Bricklayer's Arms. He too was wild for rhythm and blues, he too wanted to form a group, and so now there were three Rolling Stones, though they still didn't have a name.

The three of them faced a bigger crisis than merely finding a name for their budding group —they first had to find a place to live. Flats in London are hard to come by anyway, but for the three boys with virtually no money and without noticeable hair cuts—it was a practically impossible task. But then they were used to impossible things, and so eventually a flat was secured. It wasn't much of a flat, to be sure, but it was a place where the three could plug in their record player and listen to that R&B sound for hours.

Keith's mother visited the boys every so often and stared in disbelief at the mess which she beheld. She recalls: "They'd say: 'Do have a cup of tea.' They'd look for the tea, then spend a lot more time hunting 'round until they could find a cup. Always a cracked old cup. If you got one with a handle on it you were lucky.

Marvelled

"I just marvelled at it all. How these boys could leave home and live in an indescribable place like this was beyond me. I offered to wash their shirts. I soon wished I hadn't. They'd send about a dozen to me and it looked as if they'd been strewn all over the garden during a rainstorm. If someone had thrown a bomb in the place, it couldn't possibly have looked any worse."

The fact that the flat looked so horrible did not bother the boys nearly so much as the fact that the cupboard was literally devoid of food. Mick was the only one with money because he was still going to the London School of Economics, so he still had that grant for his fees and expenses. With what was left, the boys bought the bare necessities. And as for food, they lived on potatoes.

Keith's mother would send over food, but still the boys were often hungry. Keith recalls: "Sometimes we'd be invited out to a party. That was a highspot because it meant that we could get a drink or two, or at least a snack. They reckon that a lot

TURN TO PAGE 6

BRIAN JONES exits from the Armored Truck that was used to transport the group to an engagement they had in Fresno during their tour of the United States. This may be the answer to avoiding problems with the Stones' avid fans.

KRLA ARCHIVES

Fan Sends Open Letter To Beatles
By Nancy Griffin

(Editor's Note: Thousands of letters questioning and criticising the Beatles' romantic lives, continue to pour into the BEAT office as the date for their fabulous arrival in California draws closer and closer. In answer to these protests, we are printing some remarks written to us by a very loyal 17-year-old Beatle fan.)

People who say that Paul and George must stay single make me furious, for unlike many other devout Beatlemaniacs, I do not feel that the Beatles belong to me and me alone.

Sure I love the Beatles, just as do millions of other girls around the world. But no matter how John, Paul, George and Ringo appreciate their fans, they still need another kind of love—the kind they can receive from their girls, wives, family and friends.

The Beatles deserve their own private lives and loves because they, like all human beings, have feelings—feelings which can be hurt ever so easily by so-called "fans".

Some, who claim to be fans of the Beatles, hurt them both physically, by mobbing them, and otherwise, by writing horrible letters criticising them for being in love with the girl of their own choosing. How would we feel if the "tables were turned?"

I may be strange or crazy, but I "luv" and respect these men because they are talented and because they are so happy in their "private lives." I admire them for shrugging off rumors and bad comments, while continuing to do so well in everything.

They are fabulous and deserve

... THE TURTLES — INDIVIDUALS WITH SIMILARITIES

RACING TO THE TOP
Nothing Slow About The Turtles
By Fred Bonson

While most turtles are noted for their tardiness, the singing Turtles are becoming noted for the speed in which they are rapidly ascending the record charts with their first record, "It Ain't Me Babe".

The Turtles have been together for two years, but the Dylan-penned "It Ain't Me Babe" is their first attempt at cutting a record.

The six-man group claims that they know exactly what they like and exactly what they dislike. They like Bob Dylan, Byrd-watching (that's the feminine type birds, of course), and switching signs on rest room doors. The boys dislike the military draft, cold chili, imported cigarettes, and rock 'n' roll groups with long hair and animalistic names!

Another group claim is that each member is highly individualistic. However, this claim is open to some argument. Read on, and you'll see why.

Lead Singer

Turtles' lead singer is 18-year-old Howard Kaylan, who stands 5'10" and sports long brown hair. Howard not only lends his voice to the group, but his pen as well. He writes all of the group's original material (including "Almost There"—the flip of "It Ain't Me Babe"). His trademark is his fuzzy fur vest; he likes Hoyt Axton, Astrud Gilberto, and Sonny Tufts, and he exclaims proudly that — "I'm a UCLA dropout!"

Mark Volman, also 18-years-old, is the Turtles' back-up singer and harmonicist. With eyes and hair of brown, Mark stands 5-feet-11 and likes Jazz Crusaders, Ola Tungee, and Bullwinkle. He also has the distinction of being known as the "bumbling idiot" of the group!

Dapper Dresser

The Turtles claim a Paul McCartney look-alike among their number. He is 19-year-old Don Murray, also known as the group's "dapper dresser". Don plays the drums and harmonica, stands 5-feet-9, and has long brown hair and brown eyes. He attended college for awhile, but he too is now a "dropout". Don's favorite artists include John Hammond Jr., Booker T & The MG's, and Dwight Fry.

The tallest Turtle is six-foot Jim Tucker, who reports that he chews gum 24-hours a day! Being a nonconformist, Jim is 18-years-old, has long brown hair, brown eyes, and is a college dropout. He plays rhythm as well as bass guitar, and Jim likes Andy Williams, Charlie Byrd, Melvin Mickadoo and the Mountain Men.

If any of the other Turtles start to "crack up", then Al Nichol can take care of them because Al is a psychology major at Valley State College. He is 5-feet10, has brown eyes and long brown hair (what else?), and he is 19-years-old. The lead guitarist, Al, also sings and plays the piano.

College Student

Rounding out the group is 20-year-old Chuck Portz. Chuck is still a college student, who is majoring in humanities. He plays bass and rhythm guitar for the Turtles. At 5-feet-9, Chuck has long brown hair and (just to be really different) green eyes. His favorite artists are Joan Baez, Buffy St.-Marie, and Batman.

So there they are — the six highly individualistic Turtles.

Albuquerque Teens Resist Chaperones

The teens in Albuquerque have quite a problem on their hands. It seems that in the city of Albuquerque, teens under 18 are not allowed to attend public dances unless accompanied by their parents.

This "under 18" law was enacted because of teenage drinking and other illegalities which had previously gone on before this law was passed.

However, the Albuquerque teens feel that they deserve another chance, and so 300 of them plus a few local disc jockeys recently staged an orderly protest before the city commission. Their aim, of course, was the repeal of the "under 18" law or at least its revision.

The city commission took no immediate action on the "forbidden" teens' request, but it did promise to "take the matter under study".

So, while the Albuquerque teens have not won a victory—they have managed to bring their problem to the attention of not only Albuquerque but also to the whole United States, which is not bad for just 300 kids and a couple of disc jockeys!

ALREADY A SMASH
in Los Angeles - San Francisco - Seattle - Chicago - Philadelphia

THEE MIDNITERS

Riding To Top of Popularity on

"WHITTIER BLVD."

CHATTAHOOCHEE 684

CHATTAHOOCHEE RECORDS

9165 SUNSET BLVD.   213-CR 5-5021   LOS ANGELES, CALIF.

KRLA ARCHIVES

PERSONALS

To BEAT Readers:
I would like to have pen friends in California as I will be there on September 6.

My particulars, if wanted, are as follows: Age, 25; sex, male; hair, black; eyes, brown; height 5 feet 9; occupation, technician.

I would like to correspond with females from 18 years and over. My hobbies are as follows: correspondence, cinema, dancing, football, baseball, jazz, beat groups, traveling and postcards.

Hope to hear from you. Please write to S. Vadivelu, 21 Battis Hill Islington, N.I. London, England.

★

Dear BEAT Readers:
I have a huge problem. A soon-to-be 16-year-old girl would like an American boy to write to. However, I am not an American, nor am I a boy.

Please write to Susan Fuller, 155 A. M.Q. Stratford Road, R.A.F. Gaydon, NR. Leamington Spa, Warwiskshire, England. She is mad about motorbikes, horses, guitars, pop music and American boys. If Susan does get a boy to write to, she would be quite pleased and thankful.
A Faithful Reader,
Suzy.

★

To Sky:
There's no escape from the fact that you're out of the question. Too bad, but I can't seem to make you mine. How can I be satisfied? I'm dreaming of your love, but I know you can't be trusted. But I'll continue to play with fire until I'm yours.
Daisy Mae.

★

Frank W. and Cole of the Tekneeks:
Stones and Donovan rule! Thanks for making that night perfect. I didn't get home until one a.m.
Your Donovan Fan,
Katy C.

Dear BEAT Readers:
I would like to have a boy pen pal from England, who might come to America this summer or anytime. He must be at least 17. I am an 18-year-old, 5-feet-2, green-eyed brunette.
Mary Managano,
348 Swanston Lane,
Gilroy, California.

★

To John and Robin in England:
Surprise? Isn't that tuff about me getting P. J.'s hair pin? See ya in a couple of years. Be good!
Luv,
Candy.
P.S. Have Mike tell the Stones hi for me.

★

To Randy Camp:
I'm going to stick a clothes pin on your heart of stone. You have a marvelous voice.
From an 11-year-old.

★

To The Missing Links:
"I Cried Goodbye" and "Heartbreak Hill" are groovy songs. Good luck with them on your new record.
Kathy and Nancy.

★

Dear Geoff:
How does it feel to see your name printed (and spelled right too!) in America's *only* top pop newspaper clear over there in London? Hope you enjoy the ever-fabby BEAT.
Your Beatle-Luvin Buddy,
Poo.

★

Dear BEAT:
I have been reading the BEAT and it is the greatest thing since Columbus discovered America. Loads of people probably tell you that, but I just thought I'd tell you again.

To get to the point, I would like to write a 12-year-old boy from England.
Mary Baldwin,
3344 Laurice Ave.,
Altadena, Calif.

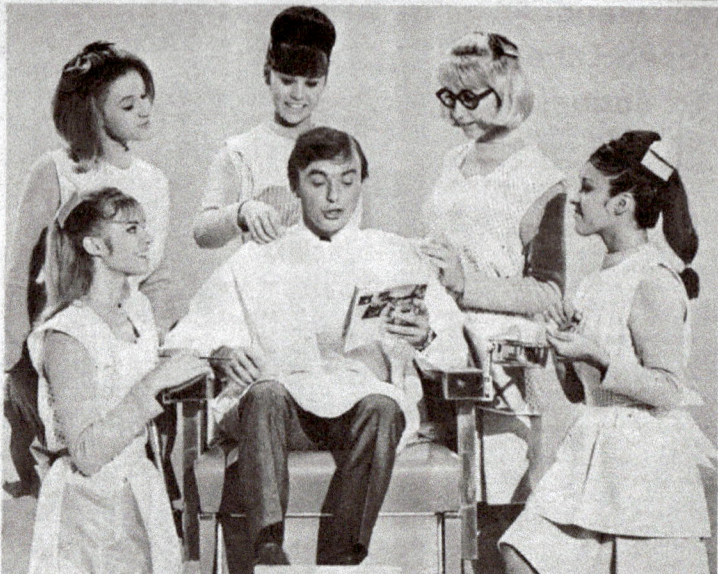

LIFE IN LIVERPOOL was never so good for Gerry Marsden. The BEAT photographer took this shot on the set of Shindig, where Gerry is being pampered and catered-to by a group of adoring females whom you'll recognize as the Shindig dancers.

Some Gifts Good, Others Bad For Sending To Stars

When your favorite star or group comes into town, the first wish that pops into your mind is to meet them.

This wish doesn't come true very easily or very often. You usually have to try the next best thing and make countless attempts to reach them on the telephone.

This carefully plotted plan doesn't usually end in success either, and you go on to the next-best-thing. You send your favorites a present. And after it's been delivered to their hotel, or back-stage, you feel a little less out of it, knowing they at least know you're alive.

Many of you are probably right in the middle of dreaming up a groovy gift for some lucky star. A remembrance from you and a friend, or a more expensive present from an entire fan club.

Need some help? We thought you might, so here's our two cents worth on the subject.

Many stars receive giant cakes, decorated with their names and faces, but these gifts are a lot less blessed to receive than they are to give. The stars appreciate all the work that goes into such a masterpiece, but they don't dare take one bite of it!

Cakes Taboo

This is nothing against the fans who cared enough to be thoughtful. It's a safety precaution necessary because there's always a chance that the food could have been prepared by someone who isn't a fan at all (there's always that ten per cent).

The "look but don't touch" law is an old rule in the show business world, and it has to be followed to the letter, whether the stars like it or not.

They usually don't like it at all, by the way. While a star is on tour, he rarely gets the chance to have a square meal, and there's nothing he'd like better than a large chomp of the goodies.

Having to stand around with his mouth watering isn't very fair to the star, and it certainly isn't fair to the fans who put a lot of time, effort and money into the project. So stay away from foodstuff gifts of any type (even sealed boxes of candy—they're also taboo) and you can avoid the unfairness on both sides!

Another popular gift that isn't as welcome as you think is a stuffed animal. They're adorable and appreciated, but the star can not take this kind of gift with him. He'd have to buy another suitcase in every town just to carry his zoo around in, and a group only has so much room for baggage. Because of this, a star usually has to give his furry friends away, and doesn't always have time to make sure they find "good homes".

When you're planning a gift for a favorite, make it something he *can* take with him. A small scrapbook of clippings is a most appreciated present. Stars can't possibly read every magazine or newspaper in the world, and only get to see a small portion of what's being written about them.

Make sure they're "nice" clippings, though. Stars may give the impression that they couldn't care less about what the press thinks, but they have feelings just like everyone else.

A great present for a fan club to give a favorite would be a box of pencils engraved with his name or the name of the group. Fans are always rushing up and pleading for something to remember a star by, and what would be nicer than to have a personalized pencil to hand over?

You can bet your star would never forget the thoughtfulness behind this gift.

Other Ideas

Other possibilities would be an address book with names and numbers of fans in the area (or maybe even all over the country) just in case the star gets lonesome. Or a small box of stationery with stamps already pasted on the envelopes (so many stars would answer the personal notes they receive while

TURN TO PAGE 13

THEE MIDNITERS, a California group, recorded one of the wildest instrumentals of the year with "Whittier Boulevard". It's beginning to move up the national charts following its initial success out here.

KRLA ARCHIVES

With Cold Potatoes, Stones Think Twice

(Continued From Page 3)
of musicians have to starve for their art, but honest—our situation was ridiculous!"

Occasional Egg

Brian remembers that occasionally the potatoes were decorated with a fried egg. "It sort of gave the spuds a colorful look. And also boosted the old calories. Of course, all this seems very funny to us now, but it was a terrible old drag at the time."

It was up in that bare-cupboarded, antique, and utterly messy flat that the name "Rolling Stones" was decided upon. They had been listening to a Muddy Waters' album, and when they came to the "Rolling Stones" track on the album they felt it would make a good name. Except that they didn't want to pinch the name just as it was, so they enlarged it to the "Silver Rolling Stones".

But the "Silver" didn't last long, and it reverted back to simply the "Rolling Stones".

Long discussions were held between Mick, Brian, and Keith. They were about a lot of things, but mostly about the future—that is, their future with rhythm and blues. Brian says: "I remember one chat between the three of us, with a Muddy Waters' long-player providing the background music. We thought about our parents, about the efforts they'd made in giving us a good home-life as kids and a good education. We wondered if we were doing the right thing by not getting into worthwhile jobs and forgetting all about this mad music bit."

"What If . . ."

"So we had to think hard. Suppose we failed. Suppose we went on not doing much, just soaking up music, for a whole year. That would be about the limit, we reckoned. We flopped—would it matter? At least we'd have tried. We'd have tried to the best of our ability and we would have had nothing to regret in later life—when possibly we'd all be working in offices and married and settled in some suburban house.

"But if we didn't give it a proper fling, we would probably end up kicking ourselves—like never knowing how good we could have been. And we figured that a lifetime of regret, of thinking back, just wouldn't work out."

And so the rehearsals continued. The group now contained (besides Mick, Brian, and Keith) Dick Taylor (Keith's old school friend) on bass guitar, Ian Stewart on Piano and organ, plus a continuous stream of drummers.

Wrong Move

They joined the National Jazz Federation, figuring that this was the best way of getting work. Unfortunately, their logic was proved wrong.

Mick says: "The problem was, as far as we could see, simple. The traditional boom was on the way out. . . . We knew, quite defintely, by going around the different clubs that audiences were looking for something as an alternative though most of them didn't really know what it should be.

"So here were we, youngsters, bold as brass when it came to shouting around about the sort of music we wanted to play. You can't really wonder at the fact that we were disliked—hated almost—by some of the guv'nor figures in the business.

"They, we were sure, simply wanted to keep the old scene going as long as they could. Wringing out the last of the big money. Sort of all mates in together—and we looked very much like proving a nuisance."

And so, by orders from the top, most doors remained closed for the Rolling Stones. But they did manage to get a foot in the door one night at a place called the Marquee Club in London.

First Break

It was their first real break, and they made about $60. Split between the six of them, it didn't amount to much—but it was a lot more than they were used to making.

Dick Taylor was at this time still attending the Royal College of Art, and being a student and being a Rolling Stone at the same time was just too much for him. And so he left.

Dick's departure left the Stones minus a bass guitar player—also they did not yet have a steady drummer. Messrs. Jagger, Jones, and Richard gathered together their scanty supply of money and placed an ad in a music paper calling for the services of a bassist and a drummer.

Bill Applies

Bill Wyman was playing with various rock 'n' roll groups, and he was also holding down a job in a department store which promised him security plus an increasing pay check. But R&B was ringing in his ears when he saw that advertisement in the paper.

He had heard of the Stones and thought of them as a "pretty rum lot". He felt it was a good idea for him and his own drummer, Tony Chapman, to make a grab for the two open positions with the Stones.

They met at a place called Wetherby Arms. Bill remembers: "There weren't many people about this time of the night. But over at the bar were two geysers with long hair and scuffy clothes. I mean, I was reasonably well-dressed, I suppose, because at least I was earning some money—but these two were ridiculous."

The "ridiculous" two were Brian Jones and Keith Richard. Soon a third made his appearance. Bill recalls that this third was "another long-haired scuff called Mick."

They talked awhile—then got down to playing a few numbers together. And before the fivesome left the Wetherby Arms, Bill and Tony had agreed to become Rolling Stones.

However, Tony's stay with the group did not last too long. He felt that he wasn't made to play with a far-out group like the Stones, and so he exited.

Needed Drummer

What the Stones really needed was a good steady drummer, and they had the one they wanted all

HOW TO MEET THE BEATLES

Faking An Accident Old Trick, But It's One Way To Be Noticed

By Sondra Lowell

You *can* meet the Beatles when they come here, get their autographs, even sit and talk with them. Getting into a Beatle press conference or even a Beatle party isn't nearly as difficult as getting into, for instance, Fort Knox. Of course, you have to be awfully lucky, but sometimes you can help luck along with careful planning. If you really want to meet them, there are all sorts of things you should be doing right now.

One thing you can do is study. Of course, the only way to get an "A" is to end up face to face with a Beatle, and knowing a lot about algebra and history won't do you a bit of good. But reading and rereading all your old movie magazines can be very helpful. It might help to read a few spying manuals, too, and maybe even a couple of books on voodoo or teleportation—that means traveling by mind waves or something.

Anyway, if another girl got to them in a certain way, that might just end up being the way you can meet them. Or somebody else's schemes might give you ideas for your own.

I read one story where a girl was invited to a big party at the Bel-Air hide-out in Southern California last year (and alone!) with the Beatles because Paul shook hands with her at a charity function and liked her. That story probably won't help you at all. Too far-fetched.

The ones about Pat Boone's kids meeting them in Las Vegas or Burt Lancaster's having them over for an evening aren't of much use, either—unless your father is a movie star. Well, maybe your parents are active in some big charity and you can suggest they invite the Beatles to a fund-raising affair.

Or, if your house is large and secluded, you can ask the group to stay with you. But that's pretty impossible too.

Success Story

Not that you shouldn't think up impossible brainstorms. Even if they're absolutely wacky and could never happen, it doesn't hurt to try. Last year five girls from Phoenix dreamed up something that couldn't work in a million years. They started getting ready for the Beatles in February, contacting the mayor of their town and doing a hundred billion other things so that when the Beatles came the girls could present them with the key to the city.

Well, the Beatles never even got to Phoenix so the girls went to Las Vegas, hoping against hope to give them the key there. The Beatles' press agent had been notified, but hadn't told them yes or no.

Then, during the performance, a few minutes before the boys went on, Derek Taylor came out to the girls in the audience and brought them backstage. He'd taken a vote of the Beatles, who agreed to see the girls. You can imagine how they felt! Ringo was lying down at first, but he got up and talked to them, and, along with the other Beatles, answered all their questions.

Each girl shook hands with each Beatle about five times and every girl got autographs of every Beatle on both her white gloves. The girls were especially delighted because they hadn't realized such big stars would be so nice and polite.

See what you can do if you really try? Not a single reporter was allowed inside the dressing room, and yet these teenagers made it. Afterward they got another treat. The Beatles asked where they were sitting and then waved to them from the stage.

Accidental Meeting

Oh, there are hundreds, even thousands of ways to meet the lads. Some girls bumped into them accidentally last year. Some caught up with their limousine in a race down the freeway. As the Beatles scrambled into an elevator in one city, a girl was almost pushed in with them by the crowd.

Paul picked her up and set her down outside the elevator. Granted, it would have been more exciting if he'd put her down *inside* the elevator, but when has he picked you up lately?

In most Beatle-meeting schemes, you're going to have to depend on luck, no matter how good your idea is. So figure out what things might happen that could help you. But don't waste your time waiting for the impossible.

Here are a couple of hints that were learned last year.

1. There's a rule against sticking heads out Beatle windows, and it's hardly ever broken.
2. It's awfully doubtful that you'll find a Beatle in a hotel swimming pool even in the middle of the night or traipsing around outside their hide-out even in disguise. I heard about Ringo combing his hair back and walking through an Atlantic City hotel unrecognized, but it's too hard to believe. Who could mistake a face like that? No, when they go anywhere, it's in freight elevators and limousines and anything else that's sneaky.

Next week I'll tell you how to meet them the way I did, at one of their parties.

figured out. His name, of course, was Charlie Watts, and he was at the time playing with the Alexis Korner band.

Charlie remembers when the Stones first approached him about joining up with them. He says: "So they asked me about kicking in with them. Honestly, I thought they were mad. I mean they were working a lot of dates without getting paid or even worrying about it. And there was me, earning a pretty comfortable living, which obviously was going to nosedive if I got involved with the Stones. It made me laugh to think of them trying to get me in with them too.

"But I got to thinking about it. I liked their spirit and I was getting very involved with rhythm 'n' blues. I figured it would be a bit of an experiment for me and a bit of a challenge, too. So I said okay, yes I'd join. Lots of my friends thought I'd gone stark raving mad."

Six Stones

Finally, the five Stones were together in a group. Actually, there were six Stones because Ian Stewart was still playing with them. They were a long way from that first hit, but their dates were becoming more regular. They played the Flamingo Club

TURN TO PAGE 14

KRLA ARCHIVES

Tips to Teens

Nail Buffing
Q: *I don't like to wear nail polish (even natural) because it always chips off, but I would like to have shiny nails. Would buffing them help?* (C.K.)

A: Definitely, especially if you use a buffing cream that puts a hard gloss on your nails. But don't buff them too much or you'll end up with a crop of hang-nails. A few moments a day is enough to keep them shining.

Hair Straightener
Q: *I want to let my hair grow long but I'm afraid to because it's naturally curly. Is there some kind of home permanent that straightens the hair or would I have to go to a beauty salon?* (S.A.)

A: As far as I know, there is no "home permanent" type hair straightener, but why don't you call any beauty supply house (see the yellow pages) and find out for sure? Even if there is such a product, I'm hesitant to recommend it. Hair damages very easily, and it's better to spend the money on a professional job than it is to spend it later to repair the results of doing it yourself.

Barefoot
Q: *I love to go barefoot in the summer, but after a few months of this my feet look like I've never worn shoes in my life. Is there any way I can keep from getting "callouses" or whatever they are, and also, is it true that going barefoot makes your feet bigger?* (F.H.)

A: Going barefoot over a long period of time, like years, would probably cause your feet to widen, but I doubt if you'll have this problem. About the problem you do have, there are two good ways to solve it. One is a little "sander" that polishes off the rough spots (I bought one at a drug store two years ago, and wouldn't part with it for anything—and it only cost $4), and the other is a cream lotion called "Pretty Feet". Either way, you can be barefoot *and* beautiful!

Unphotogenic
Q: *I am reasonably pretty, but whenever I have my picture taken, I look horrible. I always get this one silly look on my face and nothing seems to help. I'm going to have a portrait taken in about two weeks, so please give me some helpful suggestions.* (C.M.)

A: You probably get that "silly look" because you're trying too hard to come up with a natural expression. When the time comes for you to smile-at-the-birdie, try to forget you're in front of a camera and think of something or someone you especially enjoy. Think of a giant pizza, or your favorite Beatle, or some such, and you'll find yourself smiling quite naturally. This is an old trick, used successfully by many models and actresses, so give it a try!

False Eyelashes
Q: *I'm allergic to just about everything used in make-up, and I have to wear a special medicated kind. I don't mind this, but I do mind not being able to wear eye makeup. Do you think they'll ever make special mascara and liner for people with my kind of problem? And do you think it would look ridiculous for me to wear false eyelashes?* (E.N.)

A: False eyelashes are quite the vogue these days, but you don't really need them. There's a whole line of non-allergenic eye cosmetics! I forget the name of the company that manufactures them, but you should be able to find them at most good drug stores, particularly those which specialize in pharmaceuticals.

Hot Head
Q: *I'm saving my money to buy a wig, but now I'm getting leary about my goal. I've heard that a wig is very hot if you have long hair underneath it (mine is below my shoulders) and that wearing a wig can ruin your own hair. Is this true?* (K.H.)

A: Hair is an extension of your skin, and must be allowed to breathe in order to remain healthy. Wearing a wig won't harm your hair unless you wear it all day, every day. Wigs do get a bit warm at times, but no more so than a hat would. Not as much, in fact. If the hair under your wig is freshly shampooed, you'll stand a better chance of not becoming overheated and wanting to flip your wig. Clean hair retains less heat than an oily mop.

Dylan Doesn't Give A Hoot About Fame

Will success in the world of pop spoil Bob Dylan?

Not if Bob Dylan, of the wild hair, faded blue jeans and unpolished boots can help it. He states with obvious conviction that success will not change his life because "I stay out of it."

Yet now that the pop spotlight is on Dylan, it is highly possible that his hard-core folk fans will disown him. There *are* those kind of "fans", and they will immediately reject a folk singer if he so much as uses an electric guitar. Dylan however states that he really couldn't care less about that type of "fan".

"If they attack me just because I have some success with records, then they're entitled to. But I am equally entitled to disagree with them.

"Popular music — a lot of it is fantastically great music. Are these people trying to hate pop music, or what? I don't hate pop music," he argues.

Himself Only
Not only does Dylan not care if the die-hard folk fans reject him—the entire record-buying public can reject him!

"I have no responsibility to anybody except myself. If people like me—fine. If they don't, then maybe I'll do something else," he claims.

Besides dealing with those folk fans, Dylan must now deal with the numerous stories which are always written about those in the limelight. Haunting him wherever he goes are stories of the "Dylan image", the "Dylan message", and the "Dylan kind of freedom," and the performer is quick to repudiate such tales.

"Everybody is motivated to act a certain way. I don't try to prove anything about myself. I just don't ask people to study me. I don't know what my image is now. I could change clothes and look different, couldn't I?" he says of his so-called image.

No Message
Apparently, Dylan doesn't feel that he has any great "message" to offer the world because he says: "Don't put me down as a man with a message. All I can hope to do is sing what I'm thinking and maybe remind you of something."

Dylan's "kind of freedom" is simply the freedom of expression. "It's nothing to do with a political party or religion. It's in yourself," he explains.

Many have been unable to understand exactly what it is that Dylan is trying to get across in his songs. He explains his compositions this way: "Songs are just pictures of what I'm seeing—glimpses of things—life, maybe, as it's going on around me. They're not confined to words you hear. They are scattered between different things, and the lead for the listener will lie in the title of the song."

A little far-out, rather unconventional, most definitely controversial and hardly the world's best singer, Dylan secret to success may lie in his ability to write lyrics which most people, especially young people, can identify with.

Dylan, himself is realistic and critical when discussing his writings. "You know, every one of my songs could be written better. This used to bother me, but it doesn't anymore. There's nothing perfect anywhere, so I shouldn't expect myself to be perfect," he says.

Lives In Present
Only too happy to let others worry about what will happen to him in the future, Dylan lives only in the present, although he says that he does have some things ready—"plays and things".

There are some who regard Bob Dylan as a rebel, a fanatic, a kook. They see him as someone to avoid—someone to warn the sweet young things about. But in typical Dylan fashion, Bob answers these charges by simply saying: "I don't want to be regarded as a threat. I just hope that if people do listen, they'll think harder. I just want to see people happy."

To which we say—Amen.

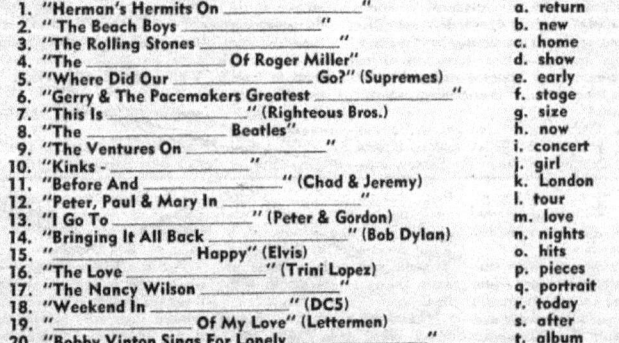

RECORD QUIZ

The single record business is booming, but so are album sales! Do you "know where it's at" where LPs are concerned? Find out by taking this simple (we said it, you didn't) quiz. The missing words left out of the album titles in the left hand column can be found (scrambled, of course) in the right hand column.

See how many of them you can match up. It shouldn't be too hard because all the albums mentioned are top sellers across the nation.

You won't win any prizes in this "contest", but if you score 15 or more points (count one point for each correct answer), just think how much fun you'll have, going around bragging about how brilliant you are!

1. "Herman's Hermits On _____"
2. "The Beach Boys _____"
3. "The Rolling Stones _____"
4. "The _____ Of Roger Miller"
5. "Where Did Our _____ Go?" (Supremes)
6. "Gerry & The Pacemakers Greatest _____"
7. "This Is _____" (Righteous Bros.)
8. "The _____ Beatles"
9. "The Ventures On _____"
10. "Kinks - _____"
11. "Before And _____" (Chad & Jeremy)
12. "Peter, Paul & Mary In _____"
13. "I Go To _____" (Peter & Gordon)
14. "Bringing It All Back _____" (Bob Dylan)
15. "_____ Happy" (Elvis)
16. "The Love _____" (Trini Lopez)
17. "The Nancy Wilson _____"
18. "Weekend In _____" (DC5)
19. "_____ Of My Love" (Lettermen)
20. "Bobby Vinton Sings For Lonely _____"

a. return
b. new
c. home
d. show
e. early
f. stage
g. size
h. now
i. concert
j. girl
k. London
l. tour
m. love
n. nights
o. hits
p. pieces
q. portrait
r. today
s. after
t. album

STOP READING UPSIDE DOWN AND TAKE THE QUIZ

(1) l-Tour, (2) r-Today, (3) h-Now, (4) a-Return, (5) m-Love, (6) o-Hits, (7) b-New, (8) e-Early, (9) f-Stage, (10) g-Size, (11) s-After, (12) i-Concert, (13) p-Pieces, (14) c-Home, (15) j-Girl, (16) t-Album, (17) d-Show, (18) k-London, (19) q-Portrait, (20) n-Nights.

KRLA ARCHIVES

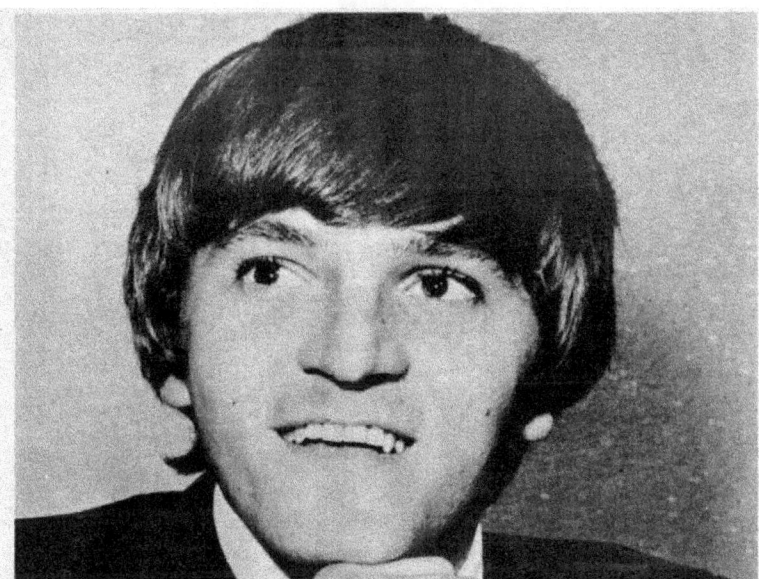

Joey Paige Finds Second Home With Rolling Stones In England

By Michelle Straubing and Susan Wylie

(Editor's Note: Joey Paige who's popularity began growing after his appearances at the World Teen Fair with the Everly Brothers, went to England four months ago to do promotion work with Eric Easton, manager for the Rolling Stones. During his visit Joey gleaned several impressions of British teenagers and artists which he shared with BEAT reporters Michelle Straubing and Susan Wylie and their handy tape recorder.)

Q: What were you doing over here before you went over to England? Were you singing?

A: No, I was primarily a musician. I played bass for the Everly Brothers. I wasn't thinking seriously of becoming a solo artist.

Q: What made you decide to switch?

A: I finally recorded and got a contract with Warner Bros. It was my first record, and it didn't do anything. My first job was at the Arch County Fair Grounds with the World Teen Fair. I did so well there, that I decided to go into it full time.

Q: Did your going over to England affect your career in any way?

A: That's actually where I first got started. I went to England with the Everly Brothers for the first time at the end of 1961. I started to get a following over there and when I went back the second time, it was amazing how the kids remembered me. I was really surprised. The agency that booked the Everly Brothers asked if I would stay over and do a tour. This was my first encounter of being a solo artist, which had a great deal of influence because I did very well and I can go back almost anytime I want.

Q: Why do you think you did better in England than over here?

A: I think it was the exposure with the Everly Brothers. We were touring around the country, and at that time American artists were very big over there. I think that's why.

Q: What is your connection with the Rolling Stones?

A: Just good friends, that's all.

Q: Can you compare American teenagers to English teenagers?

A: A couple of years ago, the teenagers here were more reserved. They didn't carry on as much and enjoy themselves as much. In England, they always tore the rafters, ripped up the seats, and all that. I think it's like they say—teenagers are basically the same all over the world.

Q: What about teenagers drinking?

A: I think teenagers drink for a kick at first. I'd hate to think we have a bunch of alcoholics for teenagers.

Q: Do you find the teenagers in England marry at an early age like they do here?

A: No. I think they get married at a much later age. I think the reasons are financial. Over there it takes them longer to get into position where they can afford to get married. That's what holds them back.

Q: Do you feel that the teenagers' dances are expressions of emotions or just a way to dance?

A: I think it's a mixture of both. When I get up and dance, I do what I feel. If the music makes you want to gyrate a certain way, you do it. I don't feel that there's any real significance to the way you move, it's just how you feel.

Q: Do you feel that if you were to get married it would hurt your career?

A: I think right now, yes. I don't think once you're established it matters so much. Once the kids get to know you, they sort of realize it's going to happen sooner or later. While you're becoming popular, it's sort of nice if the kids know you're not married.

Q: Have you ever been mobbed by any of your fans?

A: Oh yes, quite a bit. One night in Washington, D.C. with the Shindig tour, we were all waiting to get the bus near the stage door. It was really a wild show that night. I came out and they said take that bus over there. They had a couple of cops with me and it just wasn't enough. I got around to the bus, and everyone followed me around. I was standing there and the bus door was locked. There I am in the middle of a mob and one girl had a pair of scissors and she was cutting my hair.

Q: Do you feel you owe your fans the right to mob you and tear your clothes?

A: No, I don't look at it like that. I think you find a very enthused crowd lots of times, but you only find three or four that push the panic button and start the whole thing. It's unfortunate that you have to watch yourself. I don't mind them pulling at me. The only thing I don't like is like if they're trying to cut my hair and that scissors could jab someone in the eye or something.

Q: What do you think of the problem English groups have getting into the United States?

A: I don't think it's right. For so many years we went over there and we've done exactly what they've done here to the pop music industry as far as dominating it. It's a cycle that's changing now and I believe that it's coming back to America. On the English Top Ten, there are plenty of American artists. The Everly Brothers who started the whole thing were number one in England recently. So it's definitely a cycle. The cycle may come around and change a little bit, but music is definitely a cycle.

Q: How would you compare the British sound to the American sound?

A: The British songs are a lot deeper. They are more involved. You have to listen to the lyrics they have a lot more content. There is a definite English sound involved also.

Q: Do you feel that a song has

TURN TO PAGE 13

Boy-Catching Hints— Need Bait For Hook

By Janica Dark

Remember when there used to be a boy for every girl? Weren't those the good old daze?

Unfortunately, those daze seem to be gone forever!

The present surplus of girls in this world is just *fine* with boys, but things aren't quite so *fab* and *gear* on the opposite side of the situation.

But, all is not lost. It is still possible to trap the man of your choice by fighting off the competition. You must be more than just beautiful to do this. Your mind must be well-rounded, too.

In other words, you have to be *smart*.

Smart enough not to follow the the following helpful hints, that is!

Sporty

1. It is no longer enough for a girl to just *be* a good sport. A girl must also *know* about sports and not ask real cute questions at athletic events (such as "when does the quarterback come up to bat"?). Start with football and learn all the rules of the game. When you are an expert on the subject, don't *tell* your victim the news. Wait until he takes you out to dinner and asks you to *pass* him the salt! Then *show* him!

2. Display your knowledge of music and the object of your affections may change his tune about your I.Q. Listen to rock 'n roll a lot, but tell him you *prefer* the Three B's. He'll be shocked, thinking you mean Brahms, Beethoven and Bach. Providing, of course, that you don't slip and tell him you actually mean the Beatles, Bob Dylan and Barbara Mason.

3. Convince your prospective prey that you are extremely well-educated. Toss off a few author's names on each date, and use a lot of real big words. If he suspects you've been reading the dictionary, assure him you're waiting until they make it into a movie.

Current Events

4. Always be in the know about the current events of the day. Boys can't *stand* girls who don't know where it's at! Discuss the latest political and social happenings at great length, whenever possible. Your future one-and-only will be very impressed, and besides, he can use the sleep.

5. We live in a very scientific age, and boys admire girls who are interested in the space race. When your victim suggests that the two of you take a look at the moon, accept the offer graciously. When you arrive at your leafy destination, talk for hours about the most recent rocket launching. He'll be to shotdown to try any monkey business with *you!*

MARIANNE FAITHFULL, who recently released "Summer Nights", a follow-up to her hit record "Little Bird", is planning to fill her own summer nights with a long belated holiday in Mexico.

KRLA ARCHIVES

Staff Busy On Beat Rep Count

Attention all BEAT Representatives!

Since July 30, the deadline for the BEAT Representative contest, BEAT staffers have been frantically working on their adding machines to find the 31 representatives who sold the most BEAT subscriptions.

If you are anticipating winning first place, have no fear. We will notify you in enough time for you to swoon, revive, scream, and pick a friend to attend the Beatle Concert with you.

The ten second place representatives may choose between a wrist watch and an autographed Beatle album. The ten third place winners will receive autographed Beatle albums.

The KRLA BEAT is published weekly by BEAT Publications; editorial and advertising offices at 6290 Sunset Boulevard, Suite 504, Hollywood, California 90028.

Single copy price, 15 cents. Subscription price, U.S. and possessions, $3 per year or $5 for two years. Canada and foreign rates, $9 per year or $14 for two years.

Exclusive distribution handled by Miller-Freeman Publications, 6328 Lewis Avenue, Long Beach, California. Inquiries should be directed to the attention of David Thomas.

HELP!

SOMEONE HELP!
I received somebody else's camera at the Dave Clark Five Show at Melodyland. If you are missing a camera or have a strange one, please send a self-addressed stamped envelope and information to Sheri Robinson, 710 Driftwood Ave., Seal Beach, Calif.

Ticket To Ride
HELP!
I have one six dollar ticket for the Beatle concert on August 30, 1965. If anyone has one or more tickets to sell for the same price, please write to Joanne Morello, 11539 Elkhurst St., Santa Fe Springs, Calif. 90670.

Guitarist Needed
HELP!
Two 17-year-old girls in the Orange County area are in need of a male acoustic guitarist to back their singing duo. Professional experience is not necessary, but a reasonable knowledge of the guitar might come in handy.
Write to Patti Dwyer, 5430 W. Lehnhardt, Santa Ana, Calif.

Tickets To Trade
HELP!
I would like to trade two tickets to the Hollywood Bowl Beatle Concert August 30 for two tickets for the August 29 Beatle Concert. These tickets are *not* for sale. They are only for trade.
For further information call 883-0653, or write to Kris Schieb, 20444 Bassett St., Canoga Park, Calif. 91306.

Name Wanted
HELP!
We are two girls who would like to be singers. We tried, but couldn't think of a name. Therefore we would appreciate any suggestions we could get from BEAT Readers. If you can think up any names, send them to Barbara Sirchia and Sally Pensa, 10404 5th Ave., Inglewood, Calif. 90303.

CASEY'S QUIZ

By CASEY KASEM

Many of today's top singing stars are musicians by ear only, and are unable to read music. Not so with this miss. She holds a music degree from Hart College in Hartford, Conn. and is as expert at playing the piano as she is at vocalizing. Born in Orange, New Jersey, she's a hit on both sides of the Atlantic. Her tours of England and other points in Europe have been the most thrilling experiences of a lifetime, and considering her successes on the charts, that's saying a lot. Her first big hit was titled "Walk On By".

(Answer on Page 10)

KRLA BEAT SUBSCRIPTION

you will SAVE 60% of the regular price!
AN INTRODUCTORY SPECIAL . . . if you subscribe now . . .

☐ 1 YEAR — 52 Issues — $3.00   ☐ 2 YEARS — $5.00

Enclosed is $..........

Send to:.. Age:........

Address:..

City:.......................... State:.......... Zip:........

Outside U.S.: $9.00 — 52 Issues

MAIL YOUR ORDER TO: KRLA BEAT
1401 South Oak Knoll Avenue
Pasadena, California 91106

KRLA ARCHIVES

CASEY KASEM INTERVIEWS THE GUILLOTEENS on Shebang. The Nashville trio wasted no time in developing a following in Southern California. They've drawn good crowds in record with "I Don't Believe." The Guilloteens night club appearances and now have a hit r were first introduced to this area by a friend and fellow townsman — Elvis Presley.

KRLA / SCUZZY ICE CREAM CONTEST OFFICIAL ENTRY FORM

GRAND PRIZE WINNER — $500 and 2 Tickets to KRLA BEATLE Concert at Hollywood Bowl
50 RUNNER-UPS — 2 Tickets EACH to the KRLA BEATLE Concert at Hollywood Bowl
HUNDREDS OF ADDITIONAL WINNERS —
45 RPM Records and BEATLE Pictures

RULES:
1. Scuzzy Ice Cream is made with 8 different ingredients — each selected by a KRLA personality. The object of this Scuzzy contest, is to match up the ingredients, with the KRLA DJ who made the selection. For example, if you think that Dave Hull selected "Fresh Lime Juice", then you'll want to write the letter "E" next to the number "5".
2. Return your entry to any BASKIN-ROBBINS store, or mail to: "SCUZZY, KRLA, Pasadena", not later than midnight, August 15, 1965.
3. From all those who successfully match the ingredients with the KRLA personality who selected them, a drawing will be held, for the $500.00 Grand Prize, and 50 Runner-Ups who will receive 2 Tickets each to the Hollywood Bowl BEATLE Concert. All others who were successful will receive 45 RPM records and BEATLE pictures.
4. No purchase necessary.
5. All winners will be notified by mail by August 25, 1965.
6. Baskin-Robbins Inc., KRLA, and Baskin-Robbins franchised stores' employees and their families are not eligible.

Match The KRLA Personalities With Their Favorite Ingredient

KRLA PERSONALITIES	"SCUZZY" ICE CREAM INGREDIENTS
1. DICK BIONDI	A. ROASTED ALMONDS
2. BOB EUBANKS	B. CREAM CARAMEL
3. JOHNNY HAYES	C. MARASCHINO CHERRIES
4. "EMPEROR" HUDSON	D. CRUSHED COCONUT
5. DAVE HULL	E. FRESH LIME JUICE
6. CASEY KASEM	F. MACADAMIA NUTS
7. CHARLIE O'DONNELL	G. TROPICAL FRUIT PUNCH
8. BILL SLATER	H. ENGLISH TOFFEE

IMPORTANT: LISTEN TO KRLA FOR HELPFUL HINTS

MY SOLUTION: 1 2 3 4 5 6 7 8

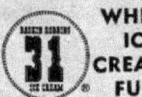

IT'S BASKIN-ROBBINS WHERE ICE CREAM'S FUN!

NAME
ADDRESS
CITY
PHONE

MAIL BOX

Dear Sirs:
Those people in England who are fighting the Beatles for getting that M.B.E. bestowed upon them have got to be kidding.

How can they possibly call them "vulgar nincompoops" or "stupid and hysterical?" That's not fair!

The Beatles, if anyone, deserve some sort of award. They have made people happy and kept kids off the street! The only stupid people are those who are fighting this.

Thanks for listening to what I have to say.
Sharon Watkins,
Manhattan Beach.

★
Fan Mail
Dear BEAT:
I want to say thanks for having the best teen publication on the market today. You have everything the younger generation is looking for in reading material. The writings are always interesting and every part of the BEAT deserves to be read. My congratulations to the staff for doing a fine job.

I might add that my mother likes the BEAT too. She doesn't consider it "rubbish" like a lot of other reading material available to the "youngsters" nowadays.

Personally, I think the BEAT is the greatest thing to come along since KRLA! I wouldn't miss a single copy. Keep up the good work!
Armi Santa Cruz,
Buena Park.

Dear Armi:
Thank you. And thanks to your mother too.
The BEAT.

★
Adult Failings Describing "Them"
Dear Editor:
I was reading over some of my BEATs and I came across a letter from a girl who wanted to know which was correct, "Them are great" or "Them is great".

I think it would be Them are great. You see, there is more than one member in Them. If there was only one person being referred to, you would use "is." Understand?
Evelyn Navarro,
Port Hueneme.

Dear Evelyn:
When you refer to a group as a whole the verb becomes singular. For instance The Dave Clark Five IS a great GROUP. But MEMBERS of the Dave Clark Five ARE great guys.
The BEAT.

THE GANG FROM SHEBANG!

By Famous Hooks and Sherry Goldsher

Hi There—
A lot of people have been writing in about the stars and the show, Shebang. In answer to your cards and letters we have started this column. We will try in each issue to answer as many questions as possible.

Lately, we have received quite a few letters about Steve Bates, Janice Garrett, Famous Hooks, Melody McMurray, Buddy Schwimmer, Mike Loyet and Richard Weizer.

The ratings are in and thanks to Casey Kasem, the Guest Stars and the Gang From Shebang, the show is a big success.

That's about it for this issue, and if there are any questions send your letters to....
Famous Hooks,
1154½ South Bronson,
Los Angeles 19, California.
Sherry Goldsher,
408 North Stanley,
Los Angeles 36, California.

CASEY'S QUIZ ANSWER
(Don't peek unless you've read the question elsewhere in the BEAT) **DIONNE WARWICK**

Back issues of the KRLA BEAT are still available, for a limited time. If you've missed an issue of particular interest to you, send 15 cents for each copy wanted, along with a self-addressed stamped envelope to:

KRLA BEAT
Suite 504
6290 Sunset Blvd.
Hollywood, California 90028

ISSUES AVAILABLE
- 4/14 — INTERVIEW WITH JOHN LENNON
- 4/21 — INTERVIEW WITH PAUL McCARTNEY
- 4/28 — CHIMP EXCITES TEEN FAIR
- 5/5 — HERMANIA SPREADS
- 5/12 — HERE COME THE BEATLES
- 5/19 — VISIT WITH BEATLES
- 5/26 — FAB NEW BEATLE QUIZ
- 6/2 — L.A. ROCKS AS STONES ROLL
- 6/16 — BATTLE OF THE BEAT
- 6/30 — PROBY FIRED
- 7/7 — SONNY & CHER vs. THE BYRDS
- 7/24 — BEATLES TOP STONES
- 7/31 — CHER
- 8/7 — DYLAN

KRLA ARCHIVES

... LESLIE GORE

Leslie Gore Launches Career With 'Sweet 16

Two and a half years ago a New Jersey teenager was asked to sing at her best friend's "sweet sixteen" birthday party.

Since that party, everything has been "Sunshine, Lollipops and Rainbows" for Lesley Gore, who's swift ride to fame sounds like a plot from an old Shirley Temple movie.

When Lesley, who was sixteen too, sang at the party, the guests leaped to their feet with applause and someone suggested that she cut a dub of one of the tunes and send it to a recording company.

A few days later the record was cut. A few weeks later the teenager had an exclusive recording contract with Mercury Records.

On May of 1963 Lesley sang at another party—this time her own 17th birthday—and the tune was her own hit platter, "It's My Party."

A five-foot-two strawberry blonde, Lesley's idea of a good time is stopping at a drive-in for a medium-rare hamburger with a wonderful date.

And what is a "wonderful date?" Lesley admits that she is usually attracted to good-looking boys but finds that they soon become superficial.

"A good personality and a good sense of humor is much more important for the attraction of good-looks wears off," she said.

Broadway Dreams

Like many teenagers, Lesley's life is also filled with dreams of the future and one of them is the hope of starring in a Broadway musical.

"When I was a child I dreamed of becoming a recording artist and it is coming true. Maybe my other ambition to become a star of Broadway musicals will come true too," she points out hopefully.

Why not? Anything can happen in a world of "Sunshine, Lollipops and Rainbows."

'Who' Go Wild Over Pop Art

The Who have gone completely pop-art.

For those of you who are wondering, Pete Townshend, guitarist for the group describes pop art in this way:

"It is representing something the public is familar with, in a different form."

The boys have a jacket made out of the Union Jack and another jacket which is covered with medals. They sometimes even smash their equipment for a visual pop-art effect.

"One gets a tremendous sound, and the effect is great," Peter explained.

The Who also claim that they live pop-art off stage as well as on — whatever that means!

HERMAN'S HERMITS TO BEGIN FILM SOON

If all goes according to plan, Herman's Hermits will begin filming their first starring movie in September. The plot will be built around the group, and will be filmed here in the U.S.

Although the title is not yet definite, tentatively it is to be called "There's No Place Like Space."

BEAT GOES TO MOVIES

VON RYAN'S EXPRESS

I should, of course, disqualify myself from all critical comment about Frank Sinatra, who stars in this wartime drama produced by 20th Century-Fox. I've got his portrait tattooed on both wrists and my record collection looks as if no one else ever made a recording! Be that as it may:

VON RYAN'S EXPRESS is a tightly drawn and exciting story about a group of prisoners of war who are led to freedom by an American flyer, Colonel Joseph Ryan, who crashed in Italy near the end of the war.

There are a couple of parts in the early stages of the film that get a little choppy and unconvincing, and they almost would really be best left out of the picture, but serve to enhance even further the wonderful pace and suspense of the finale.

The story of how the film was made is nearly as exciting as the photoplay itself. The train you will see in the film, used to haul the escaping prisoners out of Italy, is actually a portable movie studio. In shots where the boxcars are supposedly filled with the prisoners, there are really wardrobe departments, make-up men, technicians, and the other parts of the crew necessary for the production.

Vintage Train

The train moved at night on a regular schedule through Italy, stopping on a precise time-table for water and fuel. The train itself virtually an antique, was in both World War I and II. At any particular location, it might have to pack up and move out of the way for an oncoming passenger train. And, because of its age, it would occasionally slip off the track. (!)

Some of the special effects used in the film, notably the Nazi airplanes, and the crash scene where Sinatra first appears, are remarkably bad. They look like something straight out of a child's coloring book. But, by contrast, some of the other effects are up to the usual high standard of a 20th Century-Fox film.

Shot in wide screen CinemaScope and very good color, the film also is edited quite well. Watch for some very original camera work as the story moves along. The photographer likes to ride cranes apparently, because we are always being lifted up or around something, and it's kinda fun!

It is quite possible to get so involved with the story that when it's over you actually feel bad about the ending. After all that work and then look what happens to Colonel Ryan. But just what does happen you'll have to see for yourself.

MILLION-SELLER POP ARTIST Johnny Leyton, British singer who has turned to acting, meets with another fella who has sold a few records, too. Leyton appears as Lieutenant in "Von Ryan's Express".

KRLA ARCHIVES

Sizes, Money Change When Visiting Britain

Pour yourself a spot of tea and let's get on with our series of articles about traveling to England. Before we go on to how and where to look for a job in Britain (if you plan an extended visit . . . lucky one!) and the possibilities of attending school in Jolly Olde, here are a few more helpful facts you'll need to know before setting sail.

Many articles are subject to import duty when you're going through British Customs, particularly furs, jewelry, camera equipment, etc. But if the articles have been used previous to your trip, and you plan to return to America within six months, there will probably be no charge. Brand new items sometimes cause suspicion, and naturally so, because the Customs Officials don't know you from Adam, and might feel you plan to sell the items while in Britain.

Deposit

If you're staying for a longer time than six months, you may have to pay a deposit on a few items, refundable when you leave the country (if you still have the items with you, of course). But if you're just "traveling about", you'll probably have no trouble at all if you aren't toting a mink coat and several diamond tiaras.

As previously discussed, you can take as much money into England as you like, but when leaving, make sure you don't have more than fifty pound notes in your possession, because you can't take it with you.

You can bring out any uncashed traveler's checks you brought with you when you entered Britain, and up to the equivalent of 250 pounds (about $700 American dollars) in foreign currency (which includes American money).

Play It Safe

These regulations are a bit confusing, and the best thing to do is buy international traveler's checks with your funds. If you change too much of your American money into British money, and decide to leave the country before spending it all, an English bank will convert up to 100 pound notes into traveler's checks. The remainder of your British currency (above the just mentioned 50 pound note limit) may have to remain in Britain, and might not be returned to you.

Just remember not to cash more traveler's checks or convert more of your funds than you feel you'll need to spend during your stay.

When you're deciding what clothing to take on your trip, keep in mind that the weather in England is unusually mild. Average temperature for the winter months in the London area is forty degrees (above, of course) and it rarely gets higher than the mid-seventies in the summer. If you plan to be there during the winter months, take a warm coat, but don't worry about digging out your red flannels.

Forecast

When you're planning a weekend trip in the London area, and would like to know what to pack for your outing, a call to WEA-2211 will give you a complete weather forecast.

If you bring electrical equipment with you, such as irons, radios, shavers, be sure the appliances can be used on British voltages. Electrical equipment always has a tag when purchased, giving specifications as to where it can be used safely. The most common voltage in Britain is 200-250 V.A.C., 50 cycles. That probably means next to nothing to you, unless you're studying electrical engineering, but just take a look at the tag that came with the item when it was purchased. Or, if you lost the tag several thousand years ago, call an appliance dealer and ask questions. There is no point in your taking up space with items you won't be able to use.

Sizes Vary

If you plan to do a lot of shopping in England, remember to watch for the difference in our sizes and theirs. American sizes are now being used by the majority of foreign manufacturers, but not all.

Watch especially for the difference in shoe sizes. If you wear a size seven in California, you will wear a size five in London. And we wouldn't blame you if you did a lot of bragging about how your feet shrunk on the trip!

Shops in England usually close by 5:30 in the evening, and every town has an "early closing day" where the shops close at 1 p.m. In the London area, the early closing day is Saturday, but the days vary throughout the country.

That's all the news from Jolly Olde this week, but stay tuned for more about England next BEAT.

CAPITOL'S BIGGEST VOCAL GROUP—"The Fearsome Foursome" may play football during the fall season with the Los Angeles Rams, but are Capitol Records largest vocal group. The famed defensive line (in white uniforms) averages 6-feet-five-½" in height and 270 lbs. in weight . . . they gotta be the biggest vocal group in the recording field.

House of Commons, Oldham Join Attack On Enemy of Stones

A magistrate in Glasgow, Scotland, aroused the wrath of Andrew Oldham and the British House of Commons recently, when he referred to the Stones as "morons".

It seems that when a 15-year-old boy was hauled into court for allegedly breaking a shop window, Magistrate James Langmuir warned the youth not to let himself be carried away by "complete morons with hair down to their shoulders and filthy clothes".

Rolling Stone Manager Andrew Oldham, who also sports long hair, was quick to attack the magistrate.

"What gives him (the magistrate) the right to assume that long hair goes with dirt.? Does not his wife have long hair?" he asked indignantly.

"As far as I and the Stones are concerned, the man is dead, part of a dead generation. Any one who uses his position to attack people he does not even know and who have never done him any harm does not even deserve a reply," Oldham continued.

The British House of Commons got into the act when Laborite M.P. Tom Driberg accused the Glasgow magistrate of using his privileged position to attack the appearance and performance of the Rolling Stones.

According to the Laborite, the magistrate's comments were "irrelevant, snobbish and insulting personal comments".

Seems that the Stones have fans all over, even in the British government.

'They Laugh At Me,' Cries Unhappy Sonny

(Continued From Front Page)

pancho) and the way he wore his hair (like down to his shoulders).

Hair Flying

With hair flying behind him in his haste, he rushed home to describe the torment and agony of his plight to the world. Sonny wrote a protest song.

By dawn it was finished, a powerful epic of the soul which would make Dylan's best sound like a Sunday recital by Little Orphan Annie. It was a song which would arouse the conscience of all mankind. Even Mario and Tony from Martoni's.

Even then, after completing the lyrics and music to his epic, Sonny's mission was only half completed.

That same morning he made an immediate appointment at a recording studio. Within a matter of hours, his inspired song of protest would be on its way to the radio stations of America, for all the world to hear.

Facing the recording studio microphone — this time without the comforting presence of Cher beside him — Sonny Bono felt the goosepimples begin crawling up his left leg as his rich baritone voice reverberated through the studio with these immortal lyrics:

LAUGH AT ME

I never thought I'd cut a record by myself
But I got something I want to say
I want to say it for Cher
And I hope I say it for a lot of people.
Why can't I be like any guy?
Do they try to make me run? Sun of a Gun
Now what do they care about the clothes I wear,
Why get their kicks from making fun? Yeah?
This world's got a lot of space and
If they don't like my face
It ain't me that's going anywhere.
No — so I don't care.
Then leave that me.
If that's no fair I have to beg to be free
Then baby leave that me
I'll cry for you and
I'll pray for you and
I'll do all the things that the man upstairs says to do.
I'll do 'em for you, I'll do 'em all for you.
It's gotta stop some place,
It's gotta stop some time.
I'll make that other cheek mine and
Maybe the next guy that don't wear a sil tie
He can walk by and say hi
Say hi instead of why
Instead of why
Instead of why, baby
Instead of why
What do I do to you
Why, I don't know why
Tell me why.

Elvis Makes Another Film

It appears that Elvis Presley makes more movies than anyone else in Hollywood! He is continually finishing up one movie only to begin another.

In a relatively short time span, he has completed "Girl Happy", "Tickle Me", "Harum Scarum", and "Frankie and Johnny".

And now Elvis is all set to begin filming another picture. The new one is to be entitled "Hawaiian Paradise". It will be in color, and parts of the movie will be shot on location on the island of Oahu.

It is interesting to note that although Elvis grinds out those movies in rapid-fire succession, every single one of them has been a huge box office success.

Not one of them has ever flopped — and from the looks of things not one of them ever will!

KRLA ARCHIVES

For Girls Only

By Sheila Davis

Hi, boys! Even though you are invading our special corner of the BEAT, please don't stop reading! Instead, stick around! You might learn something! Like how to knit, and other fascinating things guaranteed to keep you in stitches!

Pardon the pun, but I had to get rid of them. Now onward to fascinating things, like knitting for instance.

I know knitting isn't really anyone's idea of a wild time, but if you learn to do it well, you can make a lot of sharp clothes that would cost mucho dollars if you bought them.

I only have one problem in this area, and it's really needling me (there I go again). I can knit just fine until it's time to stop. Then I don't know how to "bind off" or whatever you call it. I hope someone reading this will come to my rescue before the sweater I'm working on ends up being a tunnel instead!

Failing Friendship

Prepare yourself. I'm about to get serious for a moment. You know how it is with friends. Some people you get along with, and some you constantly clash with. This is just natural, and everyone accepts it. But it's really awful when you find yourself clashing with someone who is a friend, or who at least used to be one.

This is happening to me right now. A girl I practically went through school with is starting to get on my nerves, and whenever we go anywhere together, I have to grind my teeth to keep from telling her off. She's nice and all that, but we no longer have anything in common.

When all this started, I started making up excuses why I couldn't go places with her, and some of those excuses sounded pretty flimsy. Needless to say, this made our relationship more strained.

I've finally decided what I'm going to do about the situation. I'm just going to tell her we don't get along (although I'm sure she knows that) and ask her if she can think of a way we can get back on better terms, and have fun together again.

Fair To Both

This isn't going to be easy to do, but it's only fair to her (and to me) that I don't keep making up incredibly silly reasons why I'm "busy". I know this is hurting her, and it makes me feel awful.

Maybe we'll be able to work something out. After all, we've been friends for years. If not, at least we'll have been honest and won't end up hating each other with a passion.

If you're having this type of problem, please consider just coming out with it and being frank. I've been on the other end of a situation like this, and there's no more horrible feeling in the world than to call someone, ask them to go somewhere, and have them say "well . . . er . . . I can't go out because . . . ah . . . ummm . . . my little brother was run over by an elephant." (Don't I wish!)

Another thing that's very unfair to a friend is not to tell her (or him) if she has a personal problem that's all too noticeable. There's nothing any harder than to tell someone to "try Lavoris", etc. But you're no real friend if you don't. *Someone* is going to say something, and you can save your friend so much embarrassment if you let her hear it from you.

How About Me?

(I wonder if any of my friends who are reading this will have something "difficult" to "tell me" tonight. Hope not. But if there's any reason they should, I sure hope they will! If your best friends *don't* tell you, they are not all that "best.")

Remember when I raved on and on about the time I broke up a beautiful romance by writing to a boy too often and on perfumed stationery? Well, I received a letter asking for more on this subject. In answer to the question the letter posed, yes, I do think it's okay to write one letter if you and the boy have agreed to correspond. But if he doesn't answer, forget it! Because that's just what he's done.

If you can't resist the urge to write again, when a month or so has gone by, try harder. If the urge becomes uncontrollable, just say something light like "are you dead?", or something equally clever (ha!).

Study Steady

While I'm on the subject of boyfriends, if you're going steady with someone you can't seem to talk to, take stock of things quick! Too many steadies just sit when they're together at a restaurant or driving or something like that.

There's an old joke about always being able to tell married couples from twosomes on dates. If the couple isn't talking to each other, they're married! Well, chances are, they shouldn't be, and are probably both secretly miserable.

If you and your steady have nothing to say too often, it's because you don't have enough in common. The time to remedy this situation is *now*, so you won't miss out on any more fun and you won't take the chance of someday settling down for a quiet, boring life together.

Enough of this serious stuff! When I get up on my soap box, I don't know when to quit. But you can relax, because I just did.

Another "First"

Another remember. Remember when I told you I'd heard about spray-on nylons and planned to believe it when I saw it? Well, I still haven't, but I have heard about an actual product that's just about as kooky. It's an adhesive you use to keep your nylons up, and may already be on the market.

What are they going to think of next? Hmmm. I'm almost afraid to ask that question. Someone might answer!

Oh, my brother is speaking to me again, or was for a few short moments. He received a plaid Madras shirt as a present, complete with a tag that says "Guaranteed To Bleed".

For awhile he laughed about it, thinking someone was putting him on, but his curiousity finally got the best of him and he asked me about the tag.

I patiently explained that Madras weaves come from India and when washed they blend and bleed together, giving the material an even more unique pattern and color. I then asked him where he'd been all his life.

Guess who is never going to speak to me again? Again!

You guessed it, but don't you do the same! Keep your letters coming and I'll see you next BEAT!

Love Trip To England

(Continued From Page 8)

to be dirty to be popular?

A: I don't think so, you might get a giggle out of it. I'm sure that the kids are aware of what goes on. They shouldn't think the wrong way all the time unless it's out and out suggestive.

Q: Do you feel that this is a bigger problem in America?

A: The English kids will say, "Oh listen to the lyrics, they're suggestive." It doesn't mean that much to them. An American kid would say "Oh listen" and laugh about it. I know you're really talking about "Satisfaction". You must remember that I don't honestly think it's a suggestive song. Mick could be saying he can't get any satisfaction because he can't find a girl to fall in love with. The reason the record was number one is because they came here and did a fantastic show. They tore them up. It stands to reason that their next record would be number one.

Q: Do you feel if it was any other record, it would also have been number one?

A: Oh yes, definitely.

Q: Are you planning to do a movie?

A: I was just reading the BEAT and I noticed everyone is Maybe I better! Maybe a fun picture, a beach picture. It might be fun.

Gifts . . .

(Continued form Page 5)

they're in town if it were this convenient to do so). A selection of postcards for them to send back home would be nice, too. Stars have folks, just like everyone else, who worry when they don't hear regularly.

One of the most fabulous gifts we've ever heard of is the Star Emergency Kit, which could include things like a pen (to sign last-minute autographs), a pair of shoestrings, an extra set of guitar strings, dimes for emergency phone calls, an explanation of American money (if the star is from out of the country), a list of phone numbers for reaching long distance, information and such (these often vary even from city to city), a plan showing sneaky routes to his hotel, a map of the area (and of the U.S.), safety pins, a nail file, an extra tooth-brush, kleenex, bandages, a needle and thread, and any of the other jillion things a traveler rarely has right at his fingertips.

Just remember to make your gift something your favorite will really be able to use. That way he'll always remember who gave it to him!

ON THE BEAT

The Beatles have produced a lot of great records in the past, but "Help," which demonstrates the considerable song writing versatility of John and Paul, has got to be one of their best ever.

Anyone who can write "And I Love Her" and then turn around and compose "Help" (not to mention that wild flip, "I'm Down"), has *got* to be versatile!

Howard, the lead singer on the Turtle's hit "It Ain't Me Babe," explains how he happened to land the job of singing lead on that particular record: " 'Cause I'm the heaviest!"

Roger Miller, the man who likes to give the impression of a poor country boy, is apparently not so poor after all. A radio station in Norfolk, Virginia, seems to feel that "The King of the Road" can come up with one million dollars and is suing him for exactly that amount. They claim that Roger failed to make his scheduled appearance in a show which was sponsored by the radio station, thus causing them and their promotion agency to suffer losses amounting to one million dollars. Kind of wrecks Roger's image because many people like to think of him as a gypsy type character with no worldly possessions. Oh well, just goes to show that you shouldn't believe all that "image" stuff in the first place.

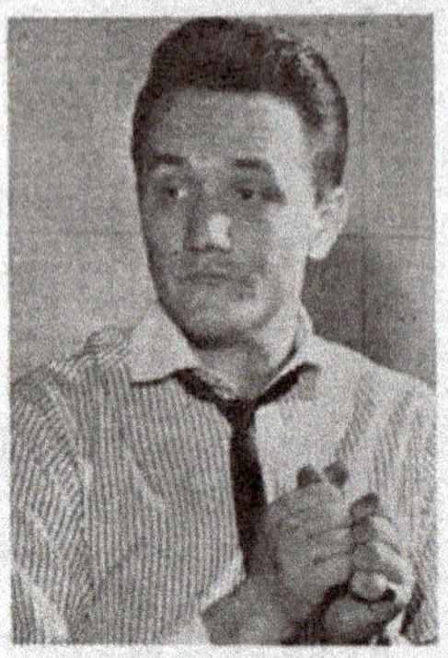

ROGER MILLER
. . . Some Hobo!

The West Germans have found an answer to the British James Bond. His name is Jerry Cotton, and he is an American who performs spine-tingling feats just like Bond. Only difference is that Cotton works for Mr. J. Edgar Hoover and the FBI instead of the British Secret Service. I've never seen a picture of Jerry Cotton, but if he looks even remotely like James Bond, I'm all for him!

QUICK ONES: Dick Clark will go dramatic again. This time it will be on a "Ben Casey" segment entitled "Then I, And You And All Of Us Fall Down" . . . I hope I'm wrong, but after their present tour of the U.S. we will probably not see the Beatles "live" again. Instead, they will concentrate on movies and give up touring, especially these strenuous American tours. . . . The Rolling Stones have won a gold record for selling more than a million copies of "Satisfaction". . . . The Kinks will return Stateside in October. . . . Glad to see that the Bobby Fuller Four have cut their hair. . . . Peter Sellers is cutting an album which makes fun of about twelve Lennon-McCartney penned songs. Supervising the entire production will be the Beatles' own recording manager, George Martin. It really ought to be some album!

DICK CLARK
. . . Action Man

There is a sharp promoter wandering around the Liverpool area who has come up with a wild idea. He is recording the different groups who appear on the Mersey ferry and selling the "live" records to the kids on the boat as a souvenir of their trip! Pretty clever idea—someone ought to put it into operation here in California.

WATCH OUT FOR: An album which you shouldn't miss. It's the "Rolling Stones' Songbook" by Andrew Oldham Orchestra and Chorus. The album is for real and features eight Stones' originals, two Oldham compositions and two other tracks. Oldham says he recorded the album "to prove that the Stones' music is not just noise, but that their melodies and idiom can stand up in any form."

Record Companies Fight Old Battle

Record companies in England blame their sharp drop in sales on the pirate radio stations anchored off-shore which broadcast a continuous stream of pop music just like our American stations. The BBC doesn't do this, of course. It has a lot of "interesting" talk programs to break up the music shows.

Record companies advanced the same argument in this country 40 years ago. They claimed that if the public could listen to records free, then no one would buy records. They even went to court in an effort to prevent radio stations from playing their records.

The American record companies soon discovered they were absolutely wrong. Offhand, it sounds like the British are about 40 years behind.

KRLA ARCHIVES

GEORGE HARRISON doesn't think that America is all that wonderful. "In the U.S.A. people are very hard to get through to, and when you do you find you've got hardly anything in common with them. The living is so fast over there I just can't keep up with it, and Americans who are geared up to it can't understand this," he said after his last visit.

A BEAT EDITORIAL
WE'RE READY

The first time we heard "Like A Rolling Stone" by Bob Dylan, we knew two things were likely to happen. One good and one bad.

The record would become an overnight hit — a good thing. But Bob Dylan would lose something because of this — a bad thing.

Bob Dylan has been one of the few remaining strongholds in the "folk world" for several years. Until now, he's been the idol of thousands rather than millions because he wouldn't "go commercial." Not good old Bob. Everyone else might subtract from their style and sound and\message, but not Bob. He'd sooner starve.

His cluster of fans used to say "he's too **talented** to be popular." Now that he has become one of the most in-demand artists in the world, they're saying he sacrificed his talent to **become** popular. Went commercial all the way.

They don't know what they're talking about. Nothing about Bob Dylan has changed. His style is still uniquely his own. His lyrics still have the impact of a lightning bolt. His "message" (although he denies having any) remains too powerful to ignore.

His fans also used to take great pride in saying the world wasn't ready for Bob Dylan. Well, the world is now. And perhaps that's something we can all be proud of.

Bob Dylan is saying the same things he's always said. He's become a major star because the rest of the world has finally started to listen and understand.

He hasn't changed. We have. And it's about time.

Early Rolling Stones Find First Success

(Continued From Page 6)

on Mondays, sometimes the Marquee on Thursday, occasionally the Red Lion on Friday nights, and the Ealing Club on Saturday nights.

While still at the Ealing Club, the boys were asked for their autographs for the very first time. Of course, they have signed thousands since, but they still remember that first one. Charlie says: "A girl who used to come and see us said she was knocked out by the stuff we played. Apparently she was feeling sad because she was due to move to Newcastle—and she wanted our autographs to remember us by. Well, honestly, I felt quite embarrassed about it all but I did sign.

Serious Musicians

"It's difficult to explain exactly how I felt. I supposed the main thing was that we were sort of characters who took the music seriously but certainly did not take ourselves, as individuals, very seriously. And to have this girl wanting us to write our names—it sort of shook me."

Meanwhile, the Stones wrote to various clubs trying to drum up a little more business for themselves. They felt that they needed a manager, but since none came forward, they plodded on alone. They were insulted from all sides, they were jeered at as they walked along the street, and the hard core jazz people still disliked them intensely.

In those days, they did not draw wild, screaming, capacity crowds. In fact, more than once a promoter lost money by booking the Stones. It is interesting to hear from one enterprising promotor who had booked the early Stones.

No Crowd

"The hall looked pretty well empty, and I thought to myself that this one was going to be a floperoo of an evening. I even had thought of quickly getting on to one of the better-known groups and trying to salvage at least my self-respect by laying on something good for the kids.

"Those Stones were so perishing casual about everything. Sure, they were careful about setting up their amplifier and so on, but they couldn't even tell me in advance what numbers they were going to include.

"But when the Stones got into their second number, things started to happen. The kids who seemed pretty blase at first seemed galvanized into action. They gathered 'round the stand, gazing in awe at Mick Jagger as he shook that hair around the place—for a moment he reminded me of a housewife shaking out a blanket.

Saw Appeal

"Obviously, it was too late for me to get anything much back at the box office, but I knew for sure that these boys would be a huge attraction once they'd got themselves a bit of publicity. What's more, I decided that I'd book them back as soon as possible."

So, the Rolling Stones played on. There was great potential there, and more people were becoming aware of that potential. They were making more and more fans locally, but the Stones had still not ventured far from their home-base of London.

We had previously planned to make the Rolling Stones' story a three-parter, but due to new and pertinent information from our sources in England, the BEAT has now decided to devote another week to the Stones.

So, next week we will conclude the Stones' story by watching the group become residents of the Crawdaddy Club, by looking on as Eric Easton and Andrew Oldham walk into their lives, and by sitting in with them as they cut their first record.

PORTMAN'S PLATTERPOOP

By Julian Portman

The Smoke Rises: Billy Harrison, guitarist for the Them, split . . . Freddie & the Dreamers are zero in England, and The Honeycombs, who couldn't buy a winner in the U.S., are now the top British group in Japan and Sweden.

Crescendo's Joe & Eddie, the top folk-blues duo, flying with so many TV-guest appearances for this coming season, soon to release their next album, "Walkin' Down the Line" . . . The Minutemen's new single on Keltone is "Thinkin' of You" b/w "Remember" . . . The Enemys film debut in Paul Newman's "Moving Target" . . . Gene McDaniels has a stroller in his latest Liberty disk "Walk With A Winner" . . . The Boss Tweeds', new pactees for Chattahoochee, "Little Bad News" is slated for September.

We Five, A & M records fast-selling group, are the "hottest" in California . . . "Fingerpopper" is the title of Columbia's picture that'll star The Righteous Brothers . . . Pushing aside their long black hair with white streaks, The Skunks inked with Era records . . . Lovable H. B. Barnum goes country/western for his next Capitol platter with "Dance With Me" b/w "I Can't Help It" . . . a world-wide news service in Europe created a laugh recently when in an exclusive bulletin they listed The Byrds as being five crew-cut boys from California. I guess according to the British The Byrds hair length is strictly crewish . . . Cannibal and The Headhunters follow their smash with "Nau Ninny Nau", or translated BEAT-style, "What's for Dinner"

Boomerang records inked Meep Meep and The Roadrunner and realeased "Justine" to compete with The Righteous Bros. . . . Paul Horn's music is not considered rock, but his new RCA Victor album "The Mass in Jazz" is the wildest . . . Kathy Kersh, Vince Edwards' recent bride, is appearing at the Red Velvet without going on a honeymoon, business comes first! The way she's constructed, one doesn't have to sing too well, but she does! . . . Herman's Hermits appear on the Al Hirt summer tv-show doing "Hello Muddah" (Allan Sherman's hit) Manchester-style.

Dean Martin continues with the new sounds on "Bumming Around" b/w "Houston" for Reprise . . . The Leaves master was sold to the new Mira label. It's a gasser of a single, with "Too Many People" b/w "zero Minus One" (a Dylan tune) promising to be a double hit . . . Johnny Tillotson warbles title to new tv-series "Gidget" . . . Jan & Dean now enter the publishing field via the comic book route . . . Don Grady, singer, songwriter, publisher, actor and one of the stars of "My Three Sons" tv series, goes the dancing route in one of the segments for next year . . . Chad of (Chad & Jeremy) goes the solo route for Columbia besides continuing with Jer . . . Paul Anka ankled MGM's "When The Boys Meet The Girls." Herman's Hermits may have offered too much competition!

The Supremes go big time when they open in New York's famed Copacabana nitery. It's a first, but the club must need the business . . . Johnny Rivers signed for an Ed Sullivan December 19 slot may experiment with Christmas Carols rock style . . . MGM, of the film industry, realized the strength of the teen market by adding another film for Herman's Hermits "There's No Place Like Space" and signing the fruggin' New Colony Six for "Penelope".

Colpix's Duane Eddy and The Rebels latest is "Trash" b/w "South Phoenix" . . . Hanna Barbera better hurry and release that sound track album "A Swingin' Summer", for the warm season is flitting by, but not fast enough for summer schoolers . . . Mercury's Hondells warble title song in "Winter A Go Go".

Didja Know Dept: When Capitol relased the "Beatles VI" album it sold a million copies the first day . . . and that The Beatles have never grooved a Capitol album that has failed to sell a million copies . . . who said all the gold is in Fort Knox?

Storm Warnings: California is battin down the hatches with Herman's Hermits leaving town, Donovan arriving, The Beatles on the way, and Mannfred Mann scheduled for September . . . the long predicted earth tremors (according to various cult prognosticators) may soon be felt . . . and what is a Sig Sakowicz? Don't forget to write the Platter Pot!

KRLA ARCHIVES

SURF BEAT

By Don Murray

(Editor's note: Surfing remains California's most popular pastime and fastest-growing sport. The information and photos on this page are furnished exclusively to the BEAT by Surfing Illustrated Magazine,

Busy Season For Surfers on USSA Schedule

Surfing is a year-round sport in California, but the United States Surfing Association (USSA) competition schedule is now in its busiest period.

The Carlsbad Contest was just recently completed, followed by the Third International Surf Festival Contest Aug. 7-8 at the new Hermosa Pier.

Also in August, on Wednesday the 11th and Friday the 13th, the First Annual U.S. Midget Surfing Championships Contest was scheduled at Zuma Beach for the preliminaries and Malibu Surfrider Beach for the finals. The age limit in it is 12 and under (competition gets younger and better every year).

Anyone may enter these contests, the only requirement being a membership in the USSA and a 1965 competition card. Both of these may be obtained with application for entry. The forms are available at most surf shops as well as the USSA at P.O. Box 59, Redondo Beach.

This column will keep you up to date on coming contests.

one of the world's most respected and popular surfing publications.)

WHEN YOU'RE SPEAKING of surfing, it's good to know what you're talking about. Like how many. Lots of people seem to think surfers are a small group, like the lady from the advertising agency in New York who called the USSA office recently to ask where the surfers were that day.

So — in case anyone asks you — there are 500,000 surfers in California, and at many beaches the surfers outnumber the swimmers. As you can see, they're a pretty big group.

Swimming Test

THERE'S TALK GOING AROUND of a voluntary swimming qualification test for surfers, and several clubs are interested in the idea. The test would be administered by the lifeguards, who feel that although the majority of surfers are capable of handling themselves in the water, they could prove it to themselves by taking the test.

This would consist of swimming out through the surf, around a buoy, and back again for a total of 300 yards. Any stroke, any style, but no stopping allowed.

An endorsement of water safety by surfers themselves would go a long way in showing the public that surfers are concerned with their sport.

School Sport

SCHOOL DAYS MAY BE happier days before too long. More and more school officials are considering adding surfing to the list of official sports.

This is a long way from the days when surfing was, generally, a dirty word among the faculty. This attitude seems to be changing to one of "if you can't lick 'em — join 'em."

With upwards of 70 per cent of the student body going surfing, school authorities can hardly go on opposing the sport. This might be a good time for some of the high schools to band together into surfing clubs!

Surfer Ads

NOTICE THE NUMBER OF companies now using the surfing theme in their advertising. Seems that something we've known right along, that surfing is great, has finally got through to Madison Avenue.

Of course their idea of what surfing is like sometimes is a little weird, but at least they are recognizing the sport. Surfing music has long been used in radio and TV advertising, which proves that it swings with the best, but direct reference to surfing has been rare until recently.

Nowadays, people like Kelloggs (electric guitars on surfboards, yet) and Buick (their "big-gun" Riviera billboards went right over the heads of most people) are spending fortunes on surfing commericals.

NO WONDER SURFING IS SO POPULAR

TORN WITH INDECISION

Why Surf Photographers Go Mad!

A strange breed of cat is the surfing photographer! We heard lately that couches belonging to coast-town psychiatrists are often feeling the weight of gibbering photogs with salt-spray in their hair.

Seems they are all torn up by an occupational hazard. Most surf photographers have to be pretty good surfers in order to know when to click the shutter for the best surfing shots.

Correct timing separates the surfing photographers from the beach snap-shooter. And that's the problem! They are torn between surfing and shooting pictures.

They still talk about the photographer who came down to a certain beach to shoot the swell that hit most local spots two or three weeks ago. The way it is told, he brought along his surfboard as well as his tripod and camera equipment.

He started shooting like mad as surfer after surfer took off for some great rides. Finally, he became so stoked about the surf that he grabbed his board and rushed out to do some surfing of his own.

Just as he reached the water's edge somebody took off on an all-time wave. Dropping his board he rushed back to his camera — to late to shoot the ride.

This kind of indecision went on all day and in the end he didn't get to ride much and he missed most of the good shots. He was probably one of those who finished up at the psychiatrist.

That same weekend revealed another mental weakness that seems to afflict surf photographers. They have a morbid fear that the surf is breaking much better elsewhere than it is on the beach that they're on.

The weekend we are talking about, the surf was up at nearly every beach along the coast. Rumors flew that it was overhead at such and such a beach, it was glassy at some other beach and it was uncrowded at another beach. Every photographer out figured he was missing the shots of a lifetime by staying where he was — no matter how good the surf was breaking.

The CHP had a ball handing out tickets to wild-eyed photographers rushing back and forth between various beaches.

Nuts or not, we love that tangled-haired photographer who risks his expensive equipment in the ocean's salt-spray. He chases a will o' the wisp — the perfectly-focused, perfectly-exposed, perfectly-lit, perfection wave being ridden by the best surfer around, taking the one ride that captures all the beauty, mystery and skill of surfing in one shot.

No wonder he flips now and then!

DR. DON JAMES of Santa Monica is generally recognized as one of the world's great surf photographers. He doesn't fit the description above (and, of course, half of that is spoof). He is a successful dentist whose long experience as a surfer has led him into many techniques to get the fabulous shots often seen on the covers and color center spreads of Surfing Illustrated.

... SURFER'S JOY

KRLA ARCHIVES

DEAR SUSAN:
Answers To Fans' Questions

By Susan Frisch

Could you please tell me Herman's real name?
Diane Hart.

Dear Diane: Herman's real name is — now get this — Peter Blair Denis Bernard Noone!!!!

What are Paul McCartney's favorite television shows in America? Brenda Carson.

Dear Brenda: Paul's favorite shows out here are Shindig and Bewitched, which are also aired in England on Monday nights.

Could you please tell me which one of the Kinks writes most of their songs and what was their first hit?
Lois Freedman.

Dear Lois: Kink Ray Davies writes most of the songs and their first hit was "Long Tall Sally".

Does P. J. Proby have a girl friend? If so, what is her name and could you tell me about her?
Randi Reeves.

Dear Randi: I hate to say it, but P. J. does have a girlfriend. Although it's nothing serious he is dating a seventeen year-old model and actress, Sarah Leyton, sister of actor John Leyton.

Could you please tell me about Jeremy, of Chad and Jeremy?
Mary Beemus.

Dear Mary: To begin with, Jeremy whose real name is Jeremy Thomas Clyde, was born in Dorney, 20 miles from London. He's mad about Lasagne, the color blue and listening to the Beatles (natch), Peter, Paul and Mary, and Dionne Warwick.

Does Bill Wyman have any children? If so, what are their names, and what is his wife's name?
Patricia Patterson.

Dear Patricia: Bill has a darling little boy named Stephen. His wife's name is Diane.

What is Herman really like off stage? Gail Edwards.

Dear Gail: That is really a difficult question to answer seeing that he is human and, as you know, people do get in many different moods. I would say he is a very sincere and gracious person. He is neither shy nor basically bold, but does enjoy meeting new people, especially GIRLS!

Does Paul McCartney have any brothers or sisters?
Francis Hannon.

Dear Francis: Paul has a brother named Mike McGear. Mike, like his brother Paul, is keenly interested in music. In fact he has his own group called "The Scaffold". Paul also has a new baby sister from his new stepmother. (lucky girl, huh?)

What are Herman's favorite foods and colors? Laura Fine.

Dear Laura: Herman's favorite foods are steak and curried rice. His favorite color is blue in all shades.

What kind of cigarettes does Paul smoke? Kathy House.

Dear Kathy: Last time the Beatles were here (last summer) I noticed that Paul smoked Marlboro. If he still smokes them is something I don't know, but do not worry — I'll find out this August!

THE BEATLES TAKE A BREATHER on Huntington Hartford's Paradise Island during the filming of "Help". Standing behind them is Jerry Pam, a fellow-Britisher who now lives in California and handles publicity for the Beatle films and other enterprises. John seems to fancy the odd hats the boys wear in the movie — he's wearing one of them now.

Byrds Remain At Top On British Charts

The Byrds have done it again, two weeks in a row. It's been a long while since the United States captured top honors on the British record charts for this length of time.

Coming up fast, and will probably cause the American Byrds some trouble in next weeks ratings, are *The Fortunes*, whose "You've Got Your Troubles" jumped to 4th from 28th and *The Animals*, who seem to have another hit record in "We Gotta Get Out of This Place". *The Animals* leaped to 7th from 26th.

The Dave Clark Five have a "biggie" on the way upward with an initial chart appearance of "Catch Us If You Can" in the 18th position.

Folk swinging groups have started to attact attention amid our normally "quiet" cousins with *Joan Baezs*', "There But For Fortune Go I" jumping to 8th position from 15th, and Australia's *The Searchers*, "He's Got No Love," kangarooing to 12th from 23rd.

It's not very sporting of the English to mistreat their American cousins with only five records among their Top 20. P. J. Proby, in 17th place, is the last of the five American artists.

This was not "The Week That Was" for American record artists in England.

British Top 10

1. MR. TAMBOURINE MAN — The Bryds
2. HEART FULL OF SOUL — The Yardbirds
3. TOSSING & TURNING — The Ivy League
4. YOU'VE GOT YOUR TROUBLES — The Fortunes
5. I'M ALIVE — The Hollies
6. IN THE MIDDLE OF NOWHERE — Dusty Springfield
7. WE GOTTA GET OUT OF THIS PLACE — The Animals
8. THERE BUT FOR FORTUNE GO I — Joan Baez
9. CRYING IN THE CHAPEL — Elvis Presley
10. TO KNOW YOU IS TO LOVE YOU — Peter & Gordon

KRLA ARCHIVES

KRLA Tunedex

EMPEROR HUDSON

CHARLIE O'DONNELL

CASEY KASEM

JOHNNY HAYES

BOB EUBANKS

DAVE HULL

DICK BIONDI

BILL SLATER

KRLA BEAT
6290 Sunset, No. 504
Hollywood, Cal. 90028

1	5	LIKE A ROLLING STONE	Bob Dylan
2	1	ALL I REALLY WANT TO DO	Cher
3	2	I GOT YOU BABE	Sonny & Cher
4	3	SATISFACTION	Rolling Stones
5	4	HOLD ME, THRILL ME, KISS ME	Mel Carter
6	11	IT AIN'T ME BABE	The Turtles
7	13	UNCHAINED MELODY/HUNG ON YOU	Righteous Bros.
8	16	YOU WERE ON MY MIND	We Five
9	6	YES, I'M READY	Barbara Mason
10	10	CARA MIA	Jay & The Americans
11	9	I'M A FOOL/SO MANY WAYS	Dino, Desi & Billy
12	12	I'M HENRY THE VIII, I AM	Herman's Hermits
13	14	SAVE YOUR HEART FOR ME	Gary Lewis & Playboys
14	7	WHAT'S NEW PUSSYCAT?	Tom Jones
15	15	YOU'D BETTER COME HOME	Petula Clark
16	40	CALIFORNIA GIRLS	The Beach Boys
17	8	I CAN'T HELP MYSELF	The Four Tops
18	17	I'LL FEEL A WHOLE LOT BETTER	The Byrds
19	19	PAPA'S GOT A BRAND NEW BAG, Pt. 1	James Brown
20	23	LET HER DANCE	Bobby Fuller Four
21	18	WHITTIER BLVD	Thee Midniters
22	36	IT'S THE SAME OLD SONG	The Four Tops
23	29	THEME FROM 'A SUMMER PLACE'	The Lettermen
24	30	WHO'LL BE THE NEXT IN LINE	The Kinks
25	26	TAKE ME BACK	Little Anthony & The Imperials
26	22	TO KNOW YOU IS TO LOVE YOU	Peter & Gordon
27	—	BABY I'M YOURS	Barbara Lewis
28	—	NOTHING BUT HEARTACHES	The Supremes
29	27	I WANT CANDY	The Strangeloves
30	25	PRETTY LITTLE BABY	Marvin Gaye
31	31	YOU TELL ME WHY	The Beau Brummels
32	32	I DON'T BELIEVE	The Guilloteens
33	28	DOWN IN THE BOONDOCKS	Billy Joe Royal
34	—	HELP/I'M DOWN	The Beatles
35	—	SUNSHINE, LOLLIPOPS & RAINBOWS	Leslie Gore
36	—	OO WEE BABY I LOVE YOU	Fred Hughes
37	33	IT HAPPENED JUST THAT WAY/ONE DYIN' AND A BURYIN'	Roger Miller
38	—	JU JU HAND	Sam the Sham and The Pharaohs
39	35	DON'T JUST STAND THERE	Patty Duke
40	—	THE LOSER	The Skyliners

BULK RATE
U.S. Postage
PAID
Los Angeles, Calif.
Permit No. 25497

KRLA ARCHIVES

KRLA BEAT

Volume 1, Number 23 — LOS ANGELES, CALIFORNIA — 15 Cents — August 21, 1965

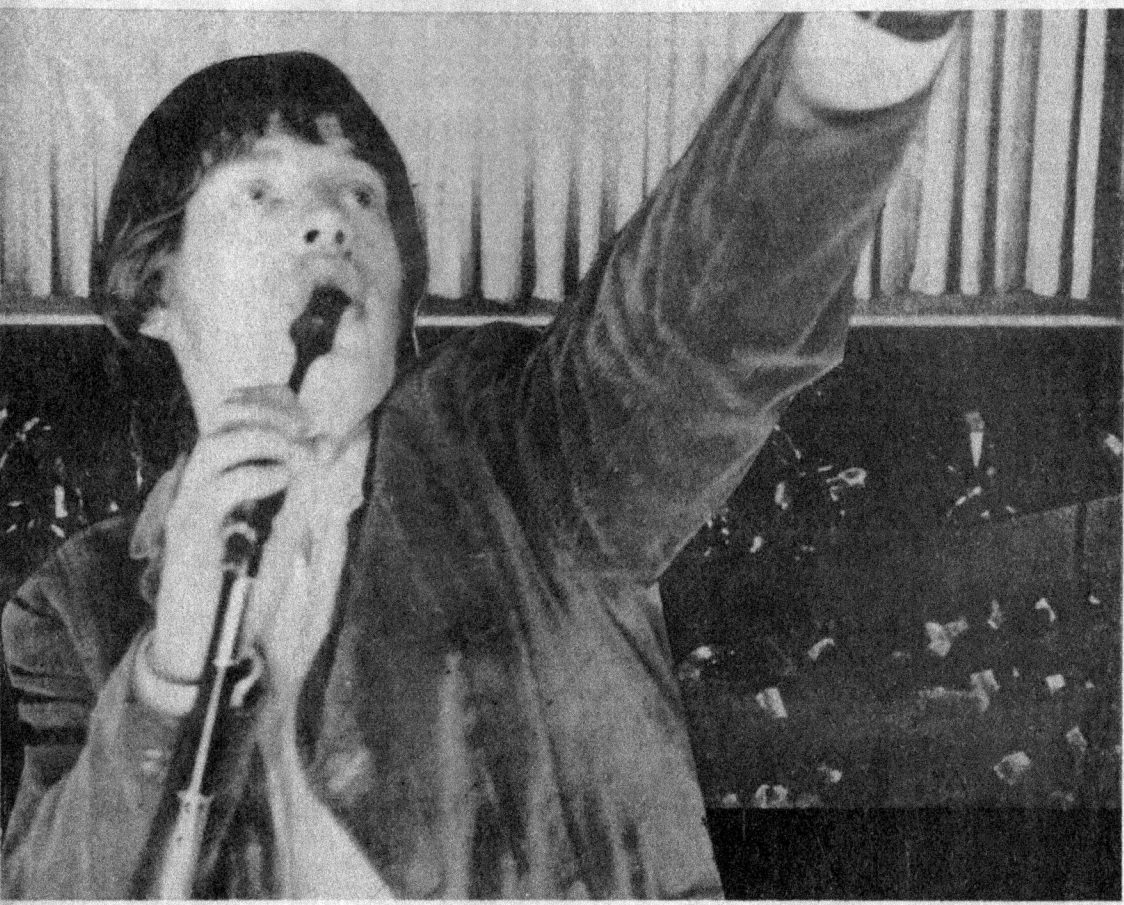

'NOW I GOT A WITNESS,' SAYS MICK; STONES TESTIFY ON THEIR PAST-5

KRLA ARCHIVES

KRLA BEAT

Los Angeles, California — August 21, 1965

BEATLES RUN FOR 'HELP'

HERE COME THE BEATLES, racing through deep snow in Austria in a scene from their new movie, "HELP," which is already drawing an enthusiastic response in England and will open in the U.S. shortly. The running practice will come in handy during their forthcoming American tour, when they will again have to evade hordes of fans. For more exciting photos from the Beatles' new movie, just turn the page.

A BEAT EDITORIAL
TODAY'S MUSIC

This editorial is for you, the readers of the BEAT, but it's mostly for your parents.

As we've said before, adults are finally beginning to accept teenage music and teenage favorites. This is the way it should be. We hope this editorial will remove the last mountain of misunderstanding and help speed up the process.

If we've heard the following statement once, we've heard it a thousand times. "I don't really mind the music any more, in fact I rather like it — of course it isn't really music." You've undoubtedly heard the remark too, voiced by adults who consider this opinion to be all too true.

It isn't. Today's music is a new breed that doesn't sound much like yesteryear's. But that doesn't mean it isn't really music. That would be like saying this year's fashions aren't really fashions at all, because they're different from last years'.

But there's a reason why many adults feel this way. Much of "our" music is presented with the accent on sound and beat rather than melody and lyrics.

We suggest that anyone harboring doubts give a listen to some of the instrumental versions of the current hits. Many orchestras, bands and solo instrumentalists are recording pop albums and the result is really something. The songs aren't just fun. They're also music, some of which is amazingly beautiful.

Today's music might not be the lost chord, but it's definitely something worth finding. And keeping.

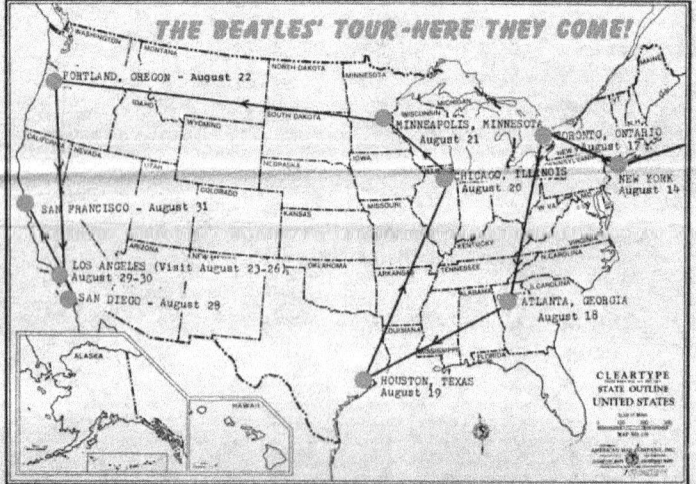

HOW TO MEET THE BEATLES - II
Party-Crashing Works

By Sondra Lowell

I know it sounds almost unbelievable, but one of the most common ways to meet the Beatles is to go to one of their parties. Well, I did. (Think I'm a snob, announcing it so casually? You should have heard me for about five months afterward. "Would you mind shaking my left hand? Ringo touched that one." Forgive me. I'm gradually rejoining the mortals.)

They were having a big party in one of their Las Vegas hotel rooms and I didn't even know till it was nearly over. But I heard a girl talking about being invited to it. Then a friend told her to go up to the Beatle floor and see Derek Taylor, who was in the hall and would let her in.

So I went up with two friends and asked for Derek. He wasn't there, but one of the guards told us a room number to call to get him. How easy! I thought. Little did I know that nearly every girl in the hotel was trying to call that number (most never reached it) and that you had to know a password to get it. I really made it into the party purely by luck, plus persistence. Somehow I got into the room without the password—which turned out to be "Liverpool"—and, after a billion other complications, got to the now-small party. By then Paul and George were gone, but John and Ringo were worth all the trouble. They were charming, wacky, and shook my hand. What more could a girl want out of life?

Employees Name

All day and night girls were paging Beatle employees to take them up. Sometimes it worked and sometimes it didn't. Making contact with them will be even harder if they don't stay in a hotel. Still, it's best to know their names, and to find out who they
(TURN TO PAGE 11)

GUESS WHO? Surely this couldn't be . . . But it is — the Beatles, thoroughly disguised in another scene from "Help"! You've undoubtedly recognized each one by now, despite the beards, but just to settle any arguments here's the correct indentification, from left to right: Ringo, Paul, John and George.

KRLA ARCHIVES

THE BEATLES

"HELP!" *Guess where the Beatles are now? Bermuda!! Austria!! And what are they doing there?*

Why are the high priests of the terrible Goddess of Kaili interested in the Beatles?
Why is Ringo being pursued to the ends of the earth by a gang of Eastern thugs?
What do they want of him—they aren't fans.
Two leading scientists hope to rule the world.
Paul is threatened by a beetle.
An Eastern beauty saves the boys' lives time and time again.
A channel swimmer ends up in an Alpine lake and Buckingham Palace has a busy day.

When Scotland Yard arrives in the sunny Bahamas after unsuccessful maneuvers on Salisbury Plain they find four Ringos but only one George, one Paul and one John.
When the power crazy scientists arrive in the Alps the boys miraculously escape their deadly weapons.
Will John live to sleep in his pit again?
Will Paul ever get back to his electric organ?
Will George be re-united with his ticker-tape machine?
And Ringo—will he ever play the drums again?

KRLA ARCHIVES

These are a few of the scenes from the year's most anxiously-awaited movie. In coming weeks the BEAT will present further previews of the fabulous Beatles' movie, which has been a world-wide sensation and is due to open in the U.S. shortly.

Many of these scenes also appear on the Beatles' new album, "HELP", which is taken from the sound track of the movie. The album is already a top-seller in both the U.S. and England, and the title song (issued as a single) is one of the most popular the Beatles have ever recorded. It reached the top spot in England 48 hours after its release.

As America prepares for the premiere of "HELP" and the arrival of John, Paul, George and Ringo themselves this month, it's evident we are in for another powerful siege of Beatlemania

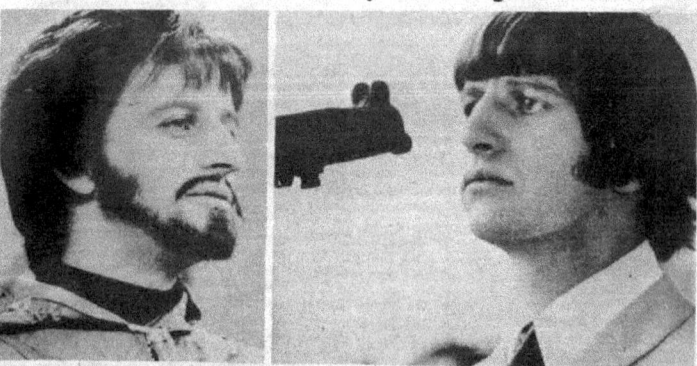

DESPITE DISGUISES, RINGO IS RECAPTURED

"SHOCKING" SCENE WITH POOR RINGO   **UNITED AGAIN, BOYS JOIN A PARADE**

KRLA ARCHIVES

PART IV:
THE ROLLING STONES SAGA

BREAKS ROLL IN STONES' WAY

By Louise Criscione

This is the fourth and last segment of the Rolling Stones' Story. In the third segment we reached the point where all five of the present day Stones were together and performing as a group.

Their dates were becoming more and more regular—they played the Flamingo, the Marquee, the Red Lion, and the Ealing Club. Still, that one big break which the Stones needed so badly was missing. It was to come in the form of one Gorgio Gomelsky. Gorgio ran a club—the Crawdaddy to be exact—which was located inside the Station Hotel in Richmond, some ten miles from the center of London.

Gorgio says: "These boys were really good. In fact, I had a verbal contract with them to be their manager—and that agreement suited me fine. I worked as hard as I could for the boys for a number of reasons. First, they were doing a great job for my club—really lifting it from the doldrums. Second, they were playing a brand of music that appealed to me personally and had fired me with an ambition to see it better appreciated here in Britain. And third, I was fed up with a lot of the insipid rubbish that was making the Top Twenty."

Wooing Reporters

In fact, Gorgio was so taken with the boys and their music that he decided to do his best to get some reporters down to The Crawdaddy to see the Stones perform. He managed to interest Peter Jones, a free-lance writer for many music papers, who spoke to the Stones.

"Brian sounded most despondent. He talked very quietly, very sincerely, about the Stones' beliefs. He spoke frankly about the blocks that had been put on their progress, but he spoke almost without anger. He talked about the following they'd built up at Richmond and tugged a newspaper cutting from his wallet to prove the point," Jones recalled.

More than talk was involved. Jones watched the Stones perform and saw their potential immediately. Soon he was at the Record Mirror office talking one of the Mirror reporters into making the trek to Richmond to see the Stones.

This reporter also liked what he heard, liked it so much that he went back and wrote a rather lengthy article predicting that the Stones would one day be the *Biggest* group on the R&B scene! It was a milestone for the boys—it meant that someone *inside* the record business had confidence in them, so much confidence that he was willing to stick his neck way out and shout to his thousands of readers that the Rolling Stones were going to be big—real big.

Another Favor

Peter Jones was not ready to walk out of the Stones' lives just yet—he was to aid their career along once again. The newspaper man knew Andrew Oldham and mentioned the Rolling Stones to him. Oldham, at this time an employee of Brian Epstein, was doing part-time publicity for the Beatles. Since the Beatles were becoming too big for just part-time publicity, Andrew was looking for another group and when Jones mentioned the Stones Andrew promised to talk to someone else about the group. That someone else was Eric Easton, an experienced agent with a notable list of clients to his credit.

Oldham talked fast and furious to Easton. He mentioned the fact that George Harrison had actually seen the Stones perform and was quite impressed with the group. Easton was not at all sure about it, but after thinking it over for a couple of days, he agreed to travel to the Crawdaddy Club with Oldham and at least have a look at the Stones.

What kind of a first impression did the Stones make on Easton and Oldham?

First Impression

Easton says: "It was absolutely jammed with people. But it was also the most exciting atmosphere I've ever experienced in a club or a ballroom. And I saw right away that the Rolling Stones were enjoying every minute of it. They were producing this fantastic sound and it was obvious that it was exactly right for the kids in the audience."

And as for Oldham, he recalls: "You hear these great adjectives kicked around in this business all the time. So when you really want to use them, they seem to have lost a lot of their meaning. But these Stones were just incredible, fantastic, fabulous. Communication—that's the one-word secret of what happens for them in a club setting."

Easton and Oldham had managed to speak to the boys briefly that night, and they had asked them to come up to the office as soon as possible. Next day found Mick and Brian in Easton's office. There was no run-around, no big promises. Easton simply stated the facts—he and Andrew were interested in the group, and they would do the best they could for the boys. Easton also made it clear that if the public did not like the Stones, that would be that—there would be nothing further they could do for them.

Pact Made

It was a good deal—the best the Stones had ever been offered. It didn't take long for Mick and Brian to make the all-important decision—yes, they would go along with Easton and Oldham.

The next step, of course, was to make a record. Easton and Oldham did not waste time pounding on recording company doors. Instead, they formed a new company, Impact Sound.

"This formation of a separate recording company wasn't a vote of no confidence in the existing companies. But we felt, Andrew and I, that the Stones were ahead of their time and therefore it was expecting a lot for ordinary A and R men to see eye to eye with the sounds they produced. By doing the whole thing ourselves, we had complete control," Easton explained.

So just thirteen days after Andrew and Eric had made that trip to Richmond, all six of the Rolling Stones (remember Ian Stewart was still playing piano with the group) made their way into the recording studio. One of the results of that session was an old Chuck Berry sound, "Come On." The record was released by Decca in the summer of 1963 but the boys were not happy with it and felt that they could have done much better. Still, the record strayed onto the charts and while it did not go much higher than number twenty it did manage to stay on the charts for three months!

Beatle Help

The Stones now faced the serious problem of finding a follow-up for "Come On." It was solved one day quite by accident when Andrew Oldham happened to run into two of the Beatles (John and Paul). He mentioned that he was looking for some new songs, the Beatles, who liked the Stones, and made no secret of the fact, saw the chance to help them materially. They told Andrew that they had some songs which they had just written and to which the Stones were certainly welcome.

Andrew said that he was very interested and, in fact, was about to meet the Stones in a place called the Ken Colyer Club. John and Paul agreed to go along. Inside the club they did a quick job of demonstrating one song in particular, "I Wanna Be Your Man." The Stones liked it, but there was just one problem. John and Paul, being their usual efficient selves, had not actually finished writing the song yet. However, the Beatles said that if the Stones really like the song, they would finish it up right away. And they meant that literally—they were back five minutes later with the entire song completed.

First Hit

"I Wanna Be Your Man" was duly recorded and became the Stones' first really big hit. About this time, the boys made their initial television appearance, and they also embarked on a tour with the Everly Brothers. This tour afforded them the chance to display their wares all over England. Up until this time, the Stones had not ventured too far outside of London. Now they had the opportunity to travel, and they naturally grabbed it.

It was a smart move, and the tour paid off handsomely for the Stones because they succeeded in making fans wherever they played. But don't get the idea that everything was rosy for the Stones. It was not. They were still ridiculed and jeered at (mainly by the older generation), and they were still not being accepted seriously by many people, including members of the press.

It was frustrating, maddening and it caused Brian to burst out with: "These ruddy reporters do **(TURN TO PAGE 15)**

. . MICK JAGGER

KRLA ARCHIVES

WE FIVE, A NEW AND EXCITING MODERN POP GROUP FROM NORTHERN CALIFORNIA, recorded one of the year's top songs with "You Were On My Mind," an affectionate rhythmic blueser which powerfully builds up to an exciting crescendo. On the flip side the crew dishes-up a moody version of "Small World." It's a talented group, and you'll be hearing much more of them.

EXCLUSIVE BEAT INTERVIEW

Chad Eyes Future Career During Split With Jeremy

By Louise Criscione

Because the recording duo of Chad & Jeremy are currently performing separate functions, many unfounded rumors have been traveling the record circuit.

The BEAT felt the best way to uncover the truth was to go straight to the boys themselves and simply ask. So bright and early one morning I traveled out to Chad's apartment and over coffee and donuts, managed to get the facts straight and clear up a little bit of the mystery which has been surrounding Chad & Jeremy.

First off, Chad & Jeremy are NOT splitting up. Although Jeremy is doing a London play, "Passion Flower Hotel", and Chad is in California, the two still record together.

"You know, when Jeremy decided to do this play, people started saying 'Oh, how can you do that? You'll break up the act.' But we don't think that way. We don't think a person should just stand still," Chad said.

Jeremy will be tied up with the play for nine months if it's successful. "That's the shortest he could get—that's the shortest time anyone is allowed. If it's not too successful, then he can leave in September. He does have ten days off in November, so we can make some personal appearances and one-nighters."

Broadway Doubtful

According to Chad, if the play goes on Broadway Jeremy will go with it. "But even if it is successful enough to go on Broadway, it takes a long time. You have to negotiate and it usually takes over a year or more. Anyway, I doubt if 'Passion Flower Hotel' will make it to Broadway," he added.

Chad himself admits he does not share Jeremy's enthusiasm for serious drama.

"I went to drama school, but when I discovered that I had no talent for acting I reverted back to singing," he explained.

Despite this there is a possible television series in the offing for the duo, which Chad says will be about two university students.

"They live in a college town with a professor and his wife. Some of the neighbors don't like us because we have long hair, and we'll just take it from there. But it won't be all comedy," he said.

Meanwhile, Chad is making plans to produce records for Columbia. "I'm too lazy to produce independently," he explained. "Of course, Phil Spector became a millionaire by being an independent producer," he reflected.

New Partner

The first person Chad will record will be his wife, Jill. She recorded for the first time in England with a vocal group. "It was a horrible record. Terrible. Of course, it wasn't Jill's fault," Chad commented, grinning sheepishly in the direction of his wife.

While Jeremy is tied up in London Chad will busy himself with solo records.

"You see, Jeremy is the star —he's the one that does all the funny bits on stage. Now I'm having to learn. I appeared in Chicago without Jeremy, and it turned out very well. There were capacity houses, which surprised me. I got Jill to come on stage with me and sing," he said.

Other activities keeping the California half of the duo busy will include looking for an apartment for him and his wife, "700 acres will do!" and counting calories.

Counting Calories

"I don't eat sweets. I eat fruit and salads and I'm always grabbing a piece of carrot or something. If I ate the things Jeremy does, I'd be rotund," he explained.

A man of many interests, Chad is also carrying on a private campaign against commer-

(TURN TO PAGE 8)

... CHAD and JEREMY

KRLA ARCHIVES

DICK AND DEEDEE are back at work again. Dick has recovered from his throat operation and DeeDee has returned from her honeymoon. The pair have just finished taping a Shindig show, making a disc and will leave for Europe this fall.
BEAT photo by C. Gunther

Pop Duo's Romance Takes Strange Twist

How's this for a romance story with an odd twist?

Thirteen-year-old boy meets thirteen-year-old girl and gives her his class ring. But puppy love is foiled, the two break-up, and for six years they go their separate ways.

But Kismet has written that they meet again, and so they do. Both land jobs in the same candy store, the hero doing odd jobs and the heroine working behind the counter.

By some strange coincidence, both are aspiring young singers. So naturally they get together and make a record. "The Mountain's High." Is it a hit? You bet it is.

And now they are an established couple, working hand in hand and producing hit after hit. Fate strikes again, this time giving the hero of our saga, a serious throat infection which means he must undergo a complicated operation.

Happy Ending

Don't worry, this story has a happy ending. He recovers, and the couple, along with two close friends, travel to the First Methodist Church in Las Vegas for a wedding.

The bride is DeeDee, the heroine of the tale, and the other half of the well-known Dick and DeeDee singing duo. And Dick's role in the wedding—Best Man of course.

Bill Lee, former manager of the two and present production manager for the Dick Clark office is the groom while Shelly Berger, present manager for Dick and DeeDee, rounds out the wedding party.

Long Courtship

Unlike many Hollywood marriages, this was no whirlwind courtship. The couple had been dating for some time and first met over three years ago when Lee started managing Dick and DeeDee. Therefore, with Dick in the hospital and their European tour cancelled, DeeDee had time on her hands and decided to fill it with wedding plans.

Dick and DeeDee, who are presently touring the United States, followed DeeDee's wedding with a Shindig show and some commercials for Triumph Motorcycles. And the European tour is still in the offing. The two will go to England in October after a tour of the Continent.

Clothes Don't Make The Hermit

Herman, after losing all of his clothes, was named one of the ten best-dressed men in England!

The award was made by the Clothing Manufacturing Federation which annually compiles the list and while Herman is usually very well dressed, when he was notified of his newly-won honor, he was in a very embarrassing position indeed.

"Gads, and all me clothes are missing," he exclaimed frantically from the dentist's chair he was sitting in when the good news was announced.

The trunk containing all of Herman's clothes was either mis-routed or lost somewhere between London and Los Angeles. So there sat poor Herman, one of England's best dressed men, with a toothache, no decent clothes, and throngs of newspapermen and photographers waiting outside for him.

What to do—what to do?

It posed quite a problem, but eventually it was solved and a properly-suited Herman emerged from the dentist's office. But unfortunately, Herman still had one slight problem—the toothache!

Successful But Lonely Future Seen By Vaulting Young Star

By Jean Watson

"And now little Mike Clifford will sing the Lord's Prayer," announced the principal of Hillcrest Grammar School.

The children waited. The teachers waited. Members of the PTA waited. But little Mike Clifford was nowhere to be found.

Thirteen years older and a seasoned performer, Mike Clifford still remembers that moment with fear.

"I was so scared when I heard my name that I ran back into the classroom and locked myself in the closet."

Mike's career didn't end in a closet. "Next week the principal kept me in the office before I was supposed to go on and shoved me onto the auditorium stage."

The first experience before an audience is the most memorable one and Mike recalls his with awe.

Nobody Laughed

"It was really weird, nobody laughed," he wondered.

There were a lot of Rubicons yet to cross, but from that day forward Mike Clifford realized that there was something which separated him slightly from the rest of his classmates—something which would bring him both excitement and loneliness—a talent for singing.

Since his third-grade experience Clifford says he has never been afraid of an audience. "I'm more relaxed in front of an audience than when I'm not," he admitted.

"In school I was a loner socially as far as the kids were concerned. But I was not afraid to go into public.

"At first it kind of threw me. I wondered why I was different. The guys seemed to resent the attention I got from the girls. Also I found myself before the others did. What they didn't understand they didn't like, so they rejected it."

Gradually Mike, engrossed in developing his career, drifted further and further away from the normal growing-up activities which monopolized the attention of his teenage peers.

First Break

Then in January of 1961 the 17-year-old had his first big break. He made a 16 city tour to promote his first record and made his first network appearance on Dick Clark's "American Bandstand."

The record, "Poor Little Girl," never got anywhere, but Mike did. He became friends with Dick Clark and began touring with his "Caravan of Stars," and one year and six records later, he had a million seller—"Close to Kathy."

Since then he has had two more hits, "What to Do With Laurie," and "All the Colors of the Rainbow," and one album which was aptly titled, "For the Love of Mike."

Now a handsome, slender young man, with brilliant hopes for the future, Mike admits that there were lots of sacrifices to be made and which he will continue to make.

No Girlfriends

"It's hard to have a steady girlfriend because the time you have to yourself in a week you could put in one hour.

Also you can't join any groups or clubs because you never know when you are going to have to run off. It's hard to maintain friendships and you lose the security of a certain schedule. In this business you can't count on anything being there," he said wistfully, summarizing the disadvantages in the life of a performer.

"But it's all worth it," he said quickly. "There's the excitement, the challenge, the hope of grabbing that brass ring. If I had it to do all over again, I'd do it exactly the same way."

"The worse time in my life was two years ago. I had fulfilled my ambititons to a point and there didn't seem anything left to do. Then I realized I haven't even started to do what I feel capable of doing," he said.

Brass Rings

Some of the brass rings presently intriguing the performer include dramatic acting, night club performances and of course, a few more million sellers.

Although he is now a veteran performer, able to face crowds with great poise and calm, there have been times when the young singer wished he were in third grade again and there was a closet handy.

During one of his shows, the boys in the audience were so annoyed because their girls were swooning over Mike, that they began throwing money at him.

Furious, Mike walked off the stage and the manager had to calm the boys down before he would return.

"I never have any trouble with the girls. Just the guys. I guess I don't blame them," he said frankly.

"What they forget is that they go home with the girl, and talk to her and laugh and whatever, while I go to catch a plane for the next performance."

... MIKE CLIFFORD

Personals

TO BYRDS Gene and Dave:
Thanks from the bottom of our hearts for the autographs and friendly smiles you gave us at Le Sourdesville! We love you.
The girls in Ohio
who had the BEATS

To BEAT Readers:
If you want a pen pal please write me. I'll try and answer all letters. I would like to write to all kids from the U.S. and England. I'm 15 years old and have brown hair and blue eyes. I love to dance, swim, play guitar, and write to pen pals. When you write, please send a picture if possible. Send letters to Christy Iversen, Mondamin, Iowa, 51557.
I'll be waiting to hear from you all.
Yours truly,
Chris.

☆

To Leslie:
You can have the Beach Boys. We love the Beatles!
True Mods.

Attention:
Would the blonde "surfer-girl" named Barbara, who lives by the water, please forgive the boy from England who is very much in love with her. He came back here to live because of you, you know.
A friend.

☆

To Maurice Banas in New York:
I bet you thought your name would never be in here. I'm glad you're going to subscribe to the BEAT. I know you'll love it and I'm glad you liked the issues I sent you.
Your pen pal in Santa Paula.

☆

To Ron Elliot:
Thanks so much for the interview.
Love,
Char and Freddie.

KRLA ARCHIVES

On The BEAT

By Louise Criscione

RINGO STARR

John and George are about to have a new neighbor—one Mr. Ringo Starr M.B.E. will shortly be moving into a $60,000 house which he has just purchased in Weybridge, Surrey.

The house currently has seven bedrooms, but Ringo is having two of them enlarged because he feels that five bedrooms, a nursery suite, two staff bedrooms, and a staff living room will be a sufficient number of rooms to comfortably house his entourage!

If you are the adventurous type who is thinking of making a thorough search of Surrey in the hopes of locating Ringo's new home, I'll give you a king-size tip. The house is surrounded by trees and stands on its own spacious grounds. There, that ought to help you searchers a little bit.

Of course, you know by now that Herman and his Hermits have completed a small role in the movie "When The Boys Meet The Girls," and that this September they are set to begin filming their first starring role in "There's No Place Like Space." But just exactly what kind of films are these, and is Herman possibly planning on reverting back to acting rather than singing?

Movies Suit Herman

Herman himself explains the situation for us: "These films are not the usual 'pop' films which to me anyway are the scourge of the earth. I hate them. Appearing in these films is no achievement. I would like to go on doing films although I have no definite ambition to be a movie singer, actor, or comedian. I would just like to do parts which suit me, and do them well."

Well that clears that up—I think.

The "Shindig" people said that they would beat the immigration ban placed on English artists and they meant that literally. A "Shindig" unit recently flew over to the Twickenham Studios in England and captured on tape such people as the Rolling Stones, the Kinks, the Hollies, the Who, the Moody Blues, George Fame, Manfred Mann, Sandie Shaw, Adam Faith, Dave Berry and Lulu.

Foggy Crystal Ball

Whatever crystal-ball gazer made the prediction that the Beatles were slipping and, in fact, were already dead should give her crystal ball a good washing because it is all fogged up! With virtually no television promotion for "Help," the record still managed to reach number one on the British charts just 48 hours after it had been released. That's slipping?

GENE PITNEY

Gene Pitney would like to be in the movies, but with his busy schedule he hardly has time to eat! He has just cut an album, is making a return trip to Europe, will tour the Far East making a stop in Australia, and will then return to England by way of India for a fall tour and some British television shows. And with that schedule, he thinks he has time for movies?

Quick Ones

Alan Price, who recently left the Animals for health reasons, has formed another group—the Alan Price Combo . . . His recent visit to the U.S. apparently did not impress Donovan much for he revealed that "I was not exactly knocked out with it, man" . . . Rolling Stones' film, originally set to be shot in August, has now been postponed because of time problems . . . John Lennon is buying a cottage in Corsica . . . On her recent tour of Japan, Brenda Lee broke all the previous attendance records.

WATCH OUT FOR: "Leaning On A Lamp Post" to be Herman's next U.S. release. It's a revival of an old George Formby song so it should be a lot like "Mrs. Brown," which was also borrowed from Formby.

SHINDIG SINGER DONNA LOREN dries her hair while with arranger Jack Nitzsche, who is responsible for such numbers as "Lonely Surfer," "Village of Giants" and "Needles and Pins." The arranger recently produced a recording session for the Shindig regular.

Chad Refuses to Stay Still While Jeremy Gets Dramatic

(Continued form Page 6)
cialism at Christmas time.

"I don't know why I especially chose that to single out. I guess it was because I was asked that question around Christmas time, and it was my first Christmas in the U.S. It's barbaric over here! It's commercialized in England too, but it's not taken into the homes so much."

While Christmas has gotten worse, Chad feels that pop music has improved greatly.

"That stuff before was absolute junk—apologizing to all those cats who went before! I really got to despise those dreary songs. There was nothing there,

Mob of Girls Scare Zombie

There is nothing the Zombies like better than meeting girls, but they had one experience which will reoccur in their nightmares for years.

As the five young men from Hatfield, England were leaving through the backstage door after a performance in Las Vegas, they had a harrowing experience in which they barely escaped being mauled by a group of admiring girls.

Not that the boys mind being mobbed or admired. But they did mind when one girl grabbed Hugh's hair and pulled him over backwards.

Hugh, the 20-year-old drum player, said it was a good thing he didn't get a hold of the girl because he "might of spanked her."

"Some girls go to too many extremes to see a group," he commented.

Luckily this experience hasn't marred their impression of American girls. The boys think they are "Corrrrrrr-WHaaaaaa," whatever that might mean.

it just didn't mean a thing."

Big Moments

Three experiences stand out in Chad's mind as his most exciting experiences as a performer.

"The first was landing in America for the first time. It's a childhood aim for everybody," Chad said. "The second was playing to one's first very large house. The third was playing our first campus date (Drake University in Iowa) and our first real concert."

The singer was inspired to go into show business, ironically enough, by his art teacher who suggested he would make a good teacher.

"I figured that was just like being dead," Chad shuddered, "so I went to drama school."

It was at drama school that he met both Jill and Jeremy. "Jeremy looked just like Bob Dylan, with the hair and all. We had a group and we played harmonicas," he recalled.

Reality soon reared its ugly head and coming to the conclusion that a folk singer can't make a decent living in England, Chad got a job with a music publisher.

"I arranged a Gilbert and Sullivan medley album. Then I really got the bug. During my lunch hours I would rush out and sing with Jeremy. The people I worked with thought I was crazy!" he chuckled.

Big Break

The duo's biggest break came the minute "Yesterday's Gone" was released in America.

There is one other thing which Chad considers quite a "break." "We had to pay $85,000 to get out of our three year contract with our lousy English management and our lousy English recording company. It was a small company—one which didn't believe in giving royalty checks! It's a relief being with Columbia and getting our royalty checks when they're due."

Chad finds that there are more opportunities for struggling young singers in the American pop scene then there are in England.

"It's very weird over there. England is very close-knit and very prone to crazes. In America, you can make all kinds of records and they sell. In England, you wouldn't dream of doing that because it just would not make it. In order to get a ballad on the charts, you almost have to be an estalished singer.

Beatles Tolerated

"The English kids are very kinky with Them and The Who. The Who wear pop art costumes and are very adventurous onstage. The big thing now is R&B. The Beatles are only just tolerated by the kids now because the Beatles have become accepted by the adults.

"I definitely think that America is the best place to get started because here you always have a fighting chance to get away. In England, there are too many monopolies. Only in America do you have all these small record companies. In England—never," he said, explaining the differences.

Chad, a particularly creative person, doesn't like just sitting still and not progressing. In addition to singing and producing records, he and Jeremy have already produced one film, and he has several plot ideas for other films. Then there is the possible television series. One thing for certain—Chad will not just sit and stagnate. He will move on.

"You have to go on. You can not just mark time, or else where would you be—aged and toothless!"

Somehow an aged and toothless Chad Stuart is difficult to imagine.

KRLA ARCHIVES

Dave Hull Calls Fans

As we all know, Dave Hull does not like to blow his own horn. In fact, he is so shy, modest, and retiring that his fans were literally forced to start a Dave Hull Fan Club in order to acquaint the world with this shy, modest, and retiring young man who absolutely refuses to blow his horn.

This they did, and the result is the Dave Hull International Fan Club which lists among its honorary members Gerry and the Pacemakers, Chad & Jeremy, Freddie & the Dreamers, Mrs. Louise Harrison (George's mother), Jack Good, and the Manfred Mann.

If you would like to blow Dave's horn, all you have to do is send one dollar and a self-addressed envelope to Colleen Ludwick, 6231 N. Ivar, Temple City, California.

For this extremely small fee, you will receive a membership card, pictures of Dave and a bi-monthly newsletter which is really more like a news*paper*. It contains the English Top Ten, news and gossip about all the groups, exclusive interviews, and contests. And, of course, for that one dollar bill you also get the enjoyable opportunity to blow Dave Hull's horn!

CASEY'S QUIZ

By CASEY KASEM

This star been one of the biggest names on the charts for the past few years, and recently made his nightclub debut at New York's famous Copacabana. But he still isn't too busy to come to the aid of a friend. When Pittsburgh disc jockey Bob Tracy was fighting a virus, this favorite sat in for his ailing pal and received over five thousand thank-you calls during his on-the-air good deed. The title of his first big hit record was taken from an old poem, and he got his career underway by organizing a group that hoped to bring back the big band sound. (See answer on Page 10)

FAN CLUBS

(For information from any of the listed fan clubs enclose a self-addressed, stamped envelope.)

GERRY AND THE PACE-MAKERS
c/o Ann Wilson
Post Office Box 92
Maplewood, New Jersey

BRUCE SCOTT
c/o Sonia Ruiz
1846 Lupine Avenue
Monterey Park 54, Calif.

BOBBY FULLER FOUR
c/o Pat and Pat
217 McCoy Road
Orange, Calif.

SONNY AND CHER
c/o Darlene LeBlanc
7116 So. Boar Ave.
Whittier, Calif.

HERMAN'S HERMITS
c/o Gree Eagleson
9191 Randall Avenue
Whittier, Calif.

GEORGIE FAME
c/o Cheris Zarr
28764 Fairfax
Southfield, Michigan

TURTLES
c/o Lee Bustos, National
Fan Club President
8647 Lincoln Blvd.
Los Angeles 45, Calif.

SONNY & CHER
c/o Barbara Messer
2829 East Walnut
Orange, California

PETER & GORDON
c/o Patti & Cathi
22126 Linda Drive
Torrance, Calif. 90503

BEAU BRUMMELS
San Bernardino Chapter
c/o Nan Wright, President
2052 Mallory Street
San Bernardino, Calif. 92405

IAN WHITCOMB
c/o Kathie Raisler
14720 Gandesa Road
La Mirada, Calif.

The above information is provided as a service to our readers. Accuracy of information you receive is the responsibility of the officials of each club.

KRLA BEAT SUBSCRIPTION

you will SAVE 60% of the regular price!
AN INTRODUCTORY SPECIAL . . . if you subscribe now . . .

☐ 1 YEAR — 52 Issues — $3.00   ☐ 2 YEARS — $5.00

Enclosed is $..........

Send to:.. Age:..........

Address:..

City:.................. State:.......... Zip:..........

MAIL YOUR ORDER TO: **KRLA BEAT**
1401 South Oak Knoll Avenue
Outside U.S.: $9.00 — 52 Issues   Pasadena, California 91106

KRLA ARCHIVES

"GREAT SCOTS," exclaimed KRLA Deejay Dave Hull when the group visited him at the studios recently. Dave bares his knee to Bill Schnear while the rest of the group, (from left) Dave Isner, Wayne Forrest, Rick Neli and Jerry Archer, look on in amazement.
BEAT Photo by C. Boyd

JUDY MANCZ, who calls herself "A Struggling Young Artist," sent this week's winning cartoon all the way from Dayton, Ohio. She will win two record albums from the BEAT.

Back issues of the KRLA BEAT are still available, for a limited time. If you've missed an issue of particular interest to you, send 15 cents for each copy wanted, along with a self-addressed stamped envelope to:

KRLA BEAT
Suite 504
6290 Sunset Blvd.
Hollywood, California 90028

ISSUES AVAILABLE
4/14 — INTERVIEW WITH JOHN LENNON
4/21 — INTERVIEW WITH PAUL McCARTNEY
4/28 — CHIMP EXCITES TEEN FAIR
5/5 — HERMANIA SPREADS
5/12 — HERE COME THE BEATLES
5/19 — VISIT WITH BEATLES
5/26 — FAB NEW BEATLE QUIZ
6/2 — L.A. ROCKS AS STONES ROLL
6/16 — BATTLE OF THE BEAT
6/30 — PROBY FIRED
7/7 — SONNY & CHER vs. THE BYRDS
7/24 — BEATLES TOP STONES
7/31 — CHER
8/7 — DYLAN
8/14 — HERMAN

HELP!

HELP!
I would like to run a poll on our fave singers. Would everyone please send their choice of favorite singing group, male singer, female singer and singing duo to Gigi Bell, 3534 Pershing, San Bernardino, Calif.

HELP!
Girls who can play the guitar or drums and live in the Redondo Beach area, we need you. If you are sixteen or over and would like to play in a group please write to Cheryl Burchiere, 508 Paseo de la Playa, Redondo Beach, Calif.

HELP!
I want to trade a $6 ticket to the Beatles Bowl concert on August 29 for a ticket on August 30. Will pay difference on a $7 ticket. I am NOT selling the ticket, so please don't write unless you have a ticket (even if it's a $3 ticket).
Write to Mary Ann Geffrey, 1122 W. Desford Street, Torrance, Calif. 90502.

HELP!
I am going to hold a popularity poll for Dino, Desi and Billy and would like fans to send in a postcard with their name and vote for one of the three. Please send the votes to Dino, Desi and Billy, c/o Carol Baggio, 12703 Lazard Street, Sylmar, Calif. 91342.

have you heard
'YOUR FRIENDS'
are coming?

The KRLA BEAT is published weekly by BEAT Publications; editorial and advertising offices at 6290 Sunset Boulevard, Suite 504, Hollywood, California 90028.
Single copy price, 15 cents. Subscription price, U.S. and possessions, $3 per year or $5 for two years. Canada and foreign rates, $9 per year or $14 for two years.
Exclusive distribution handled by Miller-Freeman Publications, 6328 Lewis Avenue, Long Beach, California. Inquiries should be directed to the attention of David Thomas.

MAIL BOX

Mutual Understanding
Dear Editor:
You said in your editorial "Teens Being Knocked" in the July 24 issue, that "The name of the game is Grab a Pen (Because it's Mightier Than The Sword) and Go-Go." That's exactly what I'm going to do and I'll start by saying thank you for standing up for teenagers.
The future leaders of America are teenagers. Teenagers are youth. Youth is fresh ideas. Could it be that adults are jealous of this. Or could it be that they just don't understand. If the former is true, adults are merely small and petty. If, however, the latter is true, a little effort on both sides is going to be needed.
Don't these magazine writers who write inadequate descriptions of teenagers realize that they are not only hurting us, but also adults? There is already an unnecessarily cool relationship between the young and the old. Some amount of friction is to be expected because of the vast difference of age. However there is no need to over do it!
Adults must understand that teenagers are going through an uninhibited and free time of their life. This shall soon be shattered by the heavy responsibility of adulthood. Teenagers must understand that adults have a great many responsibilities and because of this they often have an inadequate capacity for patience. This is usually accompanied by a lapse of memory. They forget that they too were once young.
There must be a conscious effort made by adult and teenager alike. Effort is the key to success. And success is what we need to turn this cold relationship into a warm one. So to my fellow teenagers and to adults I offer this plea . . . Help us get our feet back on the ground. Won't you please, please help each other.
Sincerely,
Cheryl E. Watson, Fullerton

Meeting Byrds
Dear Editor:
Just wanted to let you know what fab thing happened to my friends and I with the help of your BEAT.
We are subscribers and took some BEATS with us to Le Sourdesville, an amusement park in Ohio, to see if we could pass the good word about the BEAT.
We wanted to see those fab Byrds and hung around after the show till almost everyone was gone and finally saw Gene come out of hiding. He was signing autographs for a few fans still sneaking about so we meandered up to him too.
We had some BEATS which featured the Byrds and I handed them to him so he could sign the pix. He recognized the BEAT right away and exclaimed, "Way out here?" Then he proceeded to sign everything we handed him. He was very nice. We got Dave's autograph later.
We are planning on seeing them again and are sure Gene and Dave will remember us if we show them the BEATS again.
Thanks again,
Phyllis Manz,

Sheila Goofed
Dear BEAT Editor:
Each week I read the fabulous BEAT and enjoy it thoroughly. Your articles on England and English groups are fab. I especially enjoy reading Sheila Davis' "For Girl's Only" column. (I am a girl.) But while reading the August 7 issue I came across something terrible in her article. She said on page 11, column 2, paragraph 6, that George Harison was perfect!
Oh how ghastly! ANYONE in their right mind knows that David McCallum is the ideal of perfection!!!! I will admit that George is pretty neat but "Illya" is the living end!
Tell Sheila I will continue reading her great column but when she speaks of human perfection tell her ONLY to mention David McCallum.
Carole Statly

CASEY'S QUIZ ANSWER
(Don't peek unless you've read the question on Page 9.
Bobby Vinton

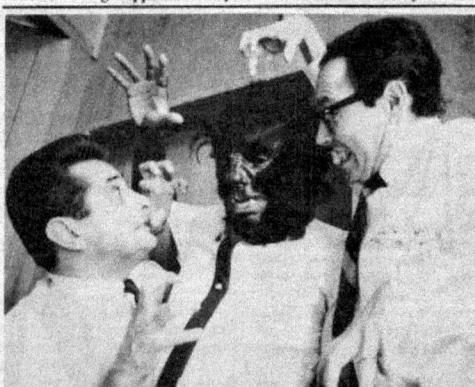

DAVE HULL AND DICK MORELAND are paralyzed with fear as the wolf man attacks. Fortunately, it turned out to be a joke, with Round Robin coming out from behind the monster mask. He was calling attention to his latest hit record, "I'm the Wolf Man," which looks like the biggest ghoul gimmick since Bobby Pickett's "Monster Mash." Naturally Clarence, Dave Hull's gruesome mascot, has made "I'm the Wolf Man" his KRLA "pick to hit."

Q: *My girlfriend left her sewing machine with me when she went away for the summer. Where can I take sewing lessons for the least money?*
(Edena F.)

A: The Singer Sewing Machine Company has offices all over the state and offers a special sewing course for teenagers. The course consists of eight lessons and costs a total of $10. You attend twice a week for a month, two and one-half hours at each visit, and learn all the basics you'll need to know to sew up a storm!

Q: *I have two questions about what to wear when. When a boy invites you out and doesn't say where the two of you will be going, how do you decide what to wear? Also, I have a "golf date" in about two weeks. I've never gone golfing before, nor have any of my friends. What would be the right outfit for this occasion?*
(Jackie C.)

A: When you're going on a Destination Unknown Date (which isn't very thoughtful of the boy in question, but very typical of too many) the best thing to do is wear something that isn't too dressed up or too casual. Stick with an outfit that has sort of an all-occasion look. About golf, a blouse (stay away from sweaters or you'll roast) and straight skirt or slacks will be fine. If you have long hair, wear it up and out of the way. Tennis shoes or any flats will do for footwear on the course.

Q: *I don't have a lot of money to spend on perfumes, but I would like to start buying some. Please recommend a few scents that don't cost too many cents!*
(Dorothy D.)

A: Avon manufactures one of the best lines of inexpensive colognes. If you aren't already on an Avon Lady route, call any office of the company and leave your name and address. Other nice scents you can buy for cents (well, almost) in most drug and department stores are Aquamarine—by Revlon, Blue Grass—by Elizabeth Arden, Heaven Scent — by Helena Rubenstein, or any of the Faberge products.

Q: *I'm fourteen, a boy, and just starting to date. Is it true that corsages are old hat with girls? If so, why?*
(Robert E.)

A: Corsages do seem to be a thing of the past, fashion-wise. Probably because the keynote of today's styles is simplicity, and a frilly corsage is anything but. Also, it draws attention to the girl which is nice but kind of embarrassing.
(Carolyn R.)

Hint of the Week

I've always had a terrible problem with my hair. If I put it on rollers at night, it's too curly the next day, and if I don't, it's too straight. I finally discovered the answer to this problem! I've been setting my bangs with Scotch tape for quite a while. Now I make big loops instead of curls and "paste" them with tape. The next morning, my hair looks the way it did the day before, just the way I want it to. Setting it with tape, without water, really works, so give it a try!
(Carol S.)

Look Sleek, Superior For Beatles' Parties

(Continued form Page 2)
are before everyone else does.

Here are a couple of names to remember besides Brian Epstin, who will be along, but will probably be unapproachable: Neil Aspinol and Malcolm Evans. Malcolm is the least well-known, so it might be best to concentrate on contacting him. You know, of course, that when you get to him you should act as calm as you can. Nothing will keep you away from the Beatles more successfully than screaming or giggling.

Even if you manage to get on the same floor as the Beatles, you're unlikely to catch a glimpse of them unless you're staying in the room next door and bore a hole in the wall. You might get up on the unguarded freight elevator, or if you're really lucky, you can do what a group of girls did in Las Vegas. They grabbed the key to a room on the Beatle floor off the front desk and went up to it. They had to leave when one girl's mother found out, but that really wasn't so horrible, because the guard in the hall saw to it that the girls (and every other unauthorized person) didn't go near the Beatle rooms, anyway.

Patti's Cousin

A lot of girls sent the boys notes, via the guards, but I don't think it accomplished anything at all. And one girl tried to get by as Patti Boyd. Naturally that didn't work. So she dropped the improvised accent and became Patti's American cousin. Somehow that did work and she was already at the party when I got there.

Since every situation has its own unforeseeable obstacles and possible loopholes, I can only give general information for your Beatle chase. One important hint is to eavesdrop. Hang around reporters and English-looking people and even mobs. I'm sure you know that hundreds of girls found out where the secret Bel Air house was last year. The only way they could possibly learn was through the grapevine.

And that's the main thing you will have to rely on for information. It should tell you, besides a lot of rumors, where the Beatles really are or if they're having a party or if they've just gotten in or just left.

Older girls usually know more than younger ones and might be telling the truth if they say they just got out from a Beatle party. When they do, don't ask questions. It will only make them feel superior and prompt them to carefully guard all their information on how to get in. Simply listen without much interest if you can, and think hard about how what you've heard can help you.

Here's another pointer—dress nicely. You don't have to wear a cocktail dress, but nobody's going to mistake a teen in bell bottoms for a Beatle guest. Don't look too young, either. If you're ten, better forget it. But if you're twelve or so you might be able to fake it, so that somehow, if the chance comes your way, you can say "oh, I'm eighteen," and slip inconspicuously into the crowd of party-goers.

Next week I'll tell you a foolproof method for Beatle-meeting. Honest, it can't miss.

YEAH, YEAH, YEAH
Beatles Are Okay

Yeah, well this week's column is dedicated to the Beatles.

When asked if Paul felt the Beatles had a responsibility to their fans, he replied: "No. It would probably be a nicer answer if I said yes we have a responsibility to fans. But I can't be noble for the sake of it." Yeah, well don't feel too bad, Paul, I'm more peasant than noble too.

John was asked recently what he was going to do with his M.B.E. award, and he said: "I think I'll have mine made into a bell push so that people have to press it when they come to the house." Yeah, well I happen to know a whole lot of people who would be more than willing to press your bell, John, no matter what it was made out of!

Financial Problems

George, the financial wizard, was giving everyone the lowdown on the Beatles' money scene. He said: "We all have some private investments. Believe it or not, we still haven't got a terrific amount of money in real capital." Yeah, well listen, George, I haven't got a terrific amount of money in anything!

Ringo was quoted recently as saying: "You can't go on getting number one records forever." Yeah, well then how come you guys keep on doing it?

Paul says: "Another thing I hate is where somebody tells you his opinion after the event. You know the sort—'Well, if you want my honest opinion. I didn't like it in the first place.' We've had a lot of that and we hate it. It's cowardly." Yeah, well listen Paul, if you want my honest opinion, I didn't like it in the first place either.

Home Movies

Ringo has purchased a movie projector and he rents first-run movies to show on it at home. Yeah, well listen Ringo—how about sending me over the first-run cartoons when you're done with them?

A sort of rumor has been floating around lately to the effect that the Beatles hate any kind of touring. Paul answers: "You see, this is a case of somebody twisting something we've said to make a story turn out THEIR way." Yeah, well I don't think that's quite true Paul. I mean, I twist and twist and nothing EVER comes out MY way!

Yeah, well that's all.

Beatles Back on Top

The Beatles have performed a feat which is next to impossible in England or anywhere else — they have jumped from nowhere to number one in 48 hours! And yet they cry "Help"?

It seems that American artists are coming back in vogue again. Sam The Sham is threatening to break into the top ten next week with his "Wooly Bully." He has already progressed to number 11 this week. That petite, big-voiced girl, Brenda Lee, is trying to make "Too Many Rivers" a trans-Atlantic hit. It jumps aboard the British survey this week at a mighty number 23.

Roy Orbison, who enjoys tremendous popularity in England, has released a new one, "Say You're My Girl," which is ascending the charts rapidly. This week finds it only one digit behind the lovely Miss Lee.

P. J. Proby is trying to force "Let The Water Run Down" to the top of the charts, but it refuses to go any higher than number 28. Someone really should tell P. J. that water just won't run uphill!

It looks like Marianne Faithfull has made a successful switch from folk to rock. Her "Summer Nights" is making twenty-place jumps each week, and if she keeps this pace up for just one more week, she will find herself right smack in the middle of the top ten!

British Top 10

1.	HELP	The Beatles
2.	MR. TAMBOURINE MAN	The Byrds
3.	YOU'VE GOT YOUR TROUBLES	The Fortunes
4.	WE GOTTA GET OUT OF THIS PLACE	The Animals
5.	TOSSING AND TURNING	The Ivy League
6.	HEART FULL OF SOUL	The Animals
7.	THERE BUT FOR FORTUNE	Joan Baez
8.	IN THE MIDDLE OF NOWHERE	Dusty Springfield
9.	CATCH US IF YOU CAN	Dave Clark 5
10.	HE'S GOT NO LOVE	The Searchers

KRLA ARCHIVES

For Girls Only

Greetings, boys! Now don't get me wrong. That opening line doesn't mean I'm welcoming you to our private corner of the BEAT with open arms. It means you've all been DRAFTED!

There. That took care of *them*. And it's a good thing because I don't feel like yakking *to* boys. I feel like yakking about them!

Isn't it weird the way girls don't like boys who are too nice? I started thinking about that last night and I still haven't stopped. I can't quite figure out why it happens this way, but it definitely does. If a boy is too polite or will do anything and everything you ask him to, he somehow loses a lot of his appeal.

I know I once had what would logically be considered the "ideal steady". He was always on time, always called me every day, took me wherever I wanted to go and never let me doubt for a minute that I was his one and only. And he was always bringing me some thoughtful little present, and driving me around to do errands and all that.

Not Ideal

Well, after a couple of months, he seemed anything BUT ideal. I got so tired of him being so sweet and understanding and predictable, I actually used to dream up ways to make him mad enough to tell me where to get off. Even that didn't work.

Just think. If only he'd displayed a little of his true nature (you can't tell me ANYONE is THAT agreeable) he might still be going steady with me. And what more could he possibly ask for?

I'm kidding, I'm kidding, but as I said, it's weird the way a girl doesn't like living on a pedestal. I wonder why. And something tells me I'll go right on wondering for a long time. The rest of my life, for instance.

That experience really taught me something though. It's more fun to stay home than it is to spend a lot of time with someone you don't like. I know a lot of girls who date guys they can't STAND just to have something to do.

When you're faced with the choice of being rather miserable and *really* miserable, the sensible thing is to choose the former. Besides, if you stay home, maybe someone you CAN stand will call!

Now that I've rattled on about boys, I think I'll continue to do a bit of rattling about girls.

Career Girls

I think every girl should make plans for some kind of a career after high school or college. There's nothing wrong with being a housewife and a mother, but there's a lot wrong with being nothing else.

There must be an awful lot of girls who get married long before they should because they've never learned how to make a living for themselves. It should not be this way, and doesn't have to be. There are too many fascinating careers open to the weaker (hah!) sex these days.

I spent several years yearning to be an airline hostess, but as my interest grew, so did I. Now that I'm an inch too tall, guess I'm going to have to make some substitute plans. Like maybe getting married to the Jolly Green Giant if I don't stop growing pretty soon!

That just reminded me of something. I have a close girlfriend who dates a boy about two inches shorter than she is, and he's really the greatest. In most cases like this, the boy practically has a nervous collapse if the girl happens to wear a pair of high heels. But not this boy. He takes the situation right in his stride and never even mentions their "differences".

Craddle Robbing

That reminds me of something else. Do you think there's anything wrong with dating a boy younger than yourself? I don't! Not unless you're seventeen and he's seven or something just about as ridiculous. The object of a date is to have fun together, in my opinion anyway. And I'm discovering that age has very little to do with just about everything. One of our neighbors is in her fifties, and there are times when I think she is a lot more hip than I'll ever be!

Wow, I'm really raving today. When I get started running off at the typewriter, I don't know when to quit!

Fortunately, I just did. On to something a little less opinionated!

Have you seen any evidence of the Pop Art fad in your crowd? Girls all over the country are starting to wear really kooky things as "decoration". The other night I saw a gal with a really cute pin on her dress. It was in the shape of a peanut (the pin, not the dress) and when I had the chance to see it better, I realized it was a REAL peanut! Sounds nutty (Oh brother), I know, but it isn't as wild as some of the things I've heard. Like wearing a stalk of celery, or a door hook, or a colored egg nesting in your hair. (SO HELP ME, I read where that egg bit actually happened!)

Identification Rings

Another rather kooky thing I just heard about are I.D. rings. They're shaped just like tiny identification bracelets and they look adorable if you ask me. I know, no one *did* ask me, but I still think they're clever. Maybe be a little *too* clever, come to think about it.

Speaking of things I've read, I'm surprised someone hasn't written an article about how much more time girls have to themselves these days. We used to have to spend hours setting our hair and then backcombing it and putting on makeup. Now that it's fashionable to just run a comb through your locks and dash on a few touches of this and that, we have more time to spend on the really *important* things in life. You know, chasing boys and that sort of thing.

Before I go, I have to tell you about a letter I received from this girl who has what she called "motion sickness." Her friends were always badgering her to go on the rides at amusement parks, and she knew what would happen if she did. But, they would not let the subject drop and kept calling her "Old Yaller". She finally solved the problem by going on just one ride. Chances are her friends will never bring up the subject again. NEVER.

Speaking of letters, keep your's coming! I don't know what's happening to me, but my new fave is Sean Connery; Who is yours? Let me know the latest and I'll see you next BEAT!

RECORD QUIZ

Heres' a just-for-fun quiz to test your knowledge of the record world. Put on your thinking cap and see if you can match the ten groups or artists with the discs that gave them their first big break in show business.

The answers are printed upside down below the quiz, but no peeking allowed!

1. Bobby Vinton
2. Little Anthony & The Imperials
3. Peter, Paul & Mary
4. Jay & The Americans
5. Elvis Presley
6. Righteous Brothers
7. Trini Lopez
8. The Miralces
9. Roger Miller
10. Dave Clark Five

a. Little Latin Lupe Lu
b. Heartbreak Hotel
c. Do You Love Me?
d. Dang Me
e. Shop Around
f. Lemon Tree
g. Roses Are Red
h. If I Had A Hammer
i. Tears On My Pillow
j. She Cried

ANSWERS (AND STOP THAT PEEKING!): 1-g, 2-i, 3-f, 4-j, 5-b, 6-a, 7-h, 8-e, 9-d, 10-c.

BRENDA LEE, a little girl with a big voice, returned from the Orient recently. "I'm seriously thinking of moving to Japan. They're all so small over there that for the first time in my life I could look someone in the eye when I'm talking to them," she joked.

PEN PALS...

AUSTRALIAN TEENAGERS WANTING FEMALE PEN PALS IN AMERICA.

Joyce Mills, 38 Grace Street, Toobul, Queensland, Australia. 16 years old; interested in the Beatles and pop music; would like girl pen pal of same age.

Patricia Smith, "Fernleigh", Tingha, Queensland, Australia. 17 years old; would like a girl pen pal of same age.

I. J. Godhold, 1 Jean Street, Kingaroy, Queensland, Australia. Interested in dancing, squash, basketball, records, and pop music; would like girl pen pal of 20.

☆

Robyn Muller, Maxmore Stud, Kelsey Creek, Proserpine, Nth Queensland, Aust. 14 years old; would like a girl pen pal of same age.

Maureen Corbett, "Elrington", Trundle, New South Wales, Australia. 14 years old; interested in dancing, the Beatles, pop and folk music, fashions and psychology; would like girl pen pal of 15.

Mary Warman, 37 Kedron Brook Road, Wilston, Queensland, Australia. 16 years old; interested in tennis, art, dancing and records; would like girl pen pal of 16.

Marilyn Reynolds, 12 Norfolk Avenue, Surfers Paradise, Queensland, Australia. 14 years old; interested in the Beatles; would like to write to a girl pen pal of 14.

AUSTRALIAN TEENAGERS WANTING MALE PEN PALS IN AMERICA.

Anne Barton, 46 Cadell Street, Toowong, Queensland, Australia. 15 years old; interested in reading, swimming, pop music and the Beatles; would like a male pen pal of same age.

Madonna Robinson, 23 Napier Street, Ascot, Queensland, Australia. 11 years old; interested in gymnastics, squash, records, pop music, bowling; would like a male pen pal of 11 or 12.

Donna McKay, 82 Allen Street, Hamilton, Queensland, Australia. 11 years old; interested in swimming, squash, pop music, and bowling; would like male pen pal of 11 or 12.

Loretta Comerford, Norman Street, Hamilton, Queensland, Australia. 11 year old; would like male pen pal of 11 or 12.

Michele Pascoe, 9 Shaw Road, Kalinga, Queensland, Australia. 16 years old; interested in surfing and the Beatles; would like male pen pal of 17 or 18.

Judy de Bakker, 36 Portwood Street, Redcliffe, Queensland, Australia. 14 years old; interested in pop music and the Beatles; would like male pen pal of 15-17.

KRLA ARCHIVES

BEAT Photo by C. Boyd

Will Success Spoil Three Little Rich Boys?

By Beverly Akins

Born with the traditional silver spoons in their mouths, Dino, Desi and Billy have no rags to riches story.

Dino is the son of Dean Martin and Desi is the son of Lucille Ball and Desi Arnez. Because the parents of the third member of the trio are not famous Hollywood stars, the question of the hour seems to be: "Who is Billy's father and what does he do?" The answer is simple—Billy's father is a man named Mr. Hinsche and he is an extremely successful Southern California businessman.

And now that we have the parentage thing all cleared up, we can go on to the boys themselves.

Two Secretaries

The three have captured the young record-buying audience in such a tremendous way that each one of the boys has *two* girls answering the huge amount of fan mail which is being written to them daily. Quite an achievement when you consider they've only released one record, "I'm a Fool."

The BEAT caught up with them at a recording session where they were putting the finishing touches on their first album. During the interview, the sheet music arrived causing quite a bit of excitement among the three. They huddled over one song in particular, "Like A Rolling Stone." The song will be featured in their album, and this was the first time that they had actually been able to make out all the lyrics!

School First

The boys, of course, are still attending school and this makes things a little rough. But whether it's rough or not, all of the boys' parents have decided that school definitely comes first. Like it or not, all three went to summer school and in September all three will march on back to school, full time.

Billy, who is 14, will attend Loyola in the fall. Dino, who is 13, will go to Rexford (a private school) and then join Billy at Loyola. Poor Desi is, to his frustration, still only twelve and, therefore, still attending Beverly Hills Catholic School. The other two boys consider this situation hilarious, but Desi himself is not so happy about being the "baby" of the group.

Future Plans

The future seems a long way off for the boys, but they *are* giving it a little bit of thought. In fact, Dino has his mind all made up: "I want to produce records," he states positively. Desi is not quite so sure, but he does know one thing: "I'll go on playing the drums. Oh, and I'd like to live in Hawaii."

Had he ever been to Hawaii before? "Yes, lots of times." To which Billy and Dino teased: "Oh, yeah, Desi's a world traveler"!

As for Billy's future, he says: "It's kind of early. I haven't really decided yet."

In the immediate future, Desi is eagerly awaiting their forthcoming trip to Hawaii, while Billy is looking forward to an up-coming stint in the Jan & Dean movie, "Easy Come, Easy Go."

Would this be the first time the boys had ever faced the Hollywood cameras?

Billy said: "I've done a couple of things. I was in a movie with Barbara Rush when I was five years old." Reminded that he had said a "couple of things" but had only volunteered information about one, Billy admitted that acting had made such an impression on him that he had forgotten what else he had "starred" in!

Acting Experience

Desi said that this would not be his first acting experience either: "I was on the 'Lucy Show' about five times. Then I was on 'Truth or Consequences'. I was behind this curtain playing the drums, and the contestants were supposed to guess how old I was. They were all guessing ages like 54"!

Well, that leaves Dino—had he ever acted before? "I never did anything exciting," he moaned.

Billy had obviously been giving those "couple of things" some more thought for all of a sudden he blurted out: "I just remembered that I was a swimming baby with Esther Williams one time!"

All three of the boys have current pet peeves. Dino dislikes "corny jokes about our hair and our clothes"; Desi dislikes "dumb people"; and Billy dislikes "waiting to go on stage—that gets you."

No Allowances

As all of the boys come from well-to-do families, money is no problem. But do the boys receive an allowance or what? Desi says: "No, I've never had an allowance." Billy added that none of them get an allowance, but "when we need some money, we just ask for it." To which Dino replied: "Yeah, we ask for it, but we don't always get it"!

Dino, Desi and Billy each have their favorites in the entertainment field. Desi names the Byrds, Chad & Jeremy, and "for the movies I like Jack Lemmon and, of course, my mother"!

All the while Desi was answering the question, Dino was standing beside me repeating "Byrds" over and over in my ear until I somehow got the idea that he liked the Byrds a whole lot!

Billy lists his favorite entertainer as Bob Dylan, pronouncing him "really cool."

Group favorites are the Beatles and the Beach Boys. "And don't forget the Byrds", Dino quickly added. And Billy piped up with "and Bob Dylan." And Desi? He just laughed.

Free Time

The boys do not have much free time, but when that rarity does occur, they all enjoy doing something different. Desi can probably be found either surfing or go-carting. You might find Billy with his ever-present guitar strapped securely around his neck and coming up with new sounds on it.

And Dino will be found riding motorcycles. The BEAT reporter brought up the fact that he couldn't ride motorcycles because he was not yet sixteen. "Well, up in Palm Springs you can ride around the hills, and we own a lot of property up there," Dino explained. That last statement drew scornful looks and ridiculing sighs from the other two.

If you get the impression that a lot of teasing goes on among Dino, Desi and Billy—you're right. The boys have come a long way in a short time. They're young and they're impressionable—it would not be hard for them to become swell-headed and completely taken with themselves.

Kept In Line

But because there are three of them, and because they do not hestitate to put each other down for making what they consider to be a conceited or phony remark—I don't think that they will ever fall into that balloon-headed and egotistical trap. They bring each other down too much for that.

If they continue to progress as they have been doing, Dino, Desi and Billy are just liable to out-shoot everyone else in the record business. They have certainly made a good start as it is. They have appeared with the Beach Boys, they have completed a "Dean Martin Show" which will be aired on October 14, and they are set for a "Sammy Davis Jr. Special" which will be shown on Thanksgiving Day.

Already, people are starting to point a finger at Dean Martin and say: "I know you—you're Dino's father." Sounds a lot like an indication of big things to come for Dino, Desi and Billy—doesn't it?

KRLA ARCHIVES

Guilloteens Stick Necks Out For Interview With BEAT

By Susan Frisch

When the Guilloteens recently came west from Memphis their first claim to fame was the friendship and endorsement of a fellow-townsman, Elvis Presley. At first glance it appeared their only claim to fame.

But then someone heard them sing, and since then they have been rapidly establishing themselves as talented performers in their own right, both on the night club circuit and in the recording field.

Hanna-Barbera Records, expanding their Huckleberry Hound-Yogi Bear cartoon empire into the recording field, signed the three Tennessee lads as their first act. Shortly afterward they released "I Don't Believe," which is already making inroads on the national charts.

For the Guilloteens — Joe Davis, 20; Laddy Hutcherson, 20, and Lewis Paul, Jr., 18 — California has proven to be everything they hoped it would be. I visited them recently — tape recorder in hand — for the following BEAT interview:

Q — How do each of you feel before going on stage?
Laddy — In nightclubs or on stage I feel really nothing, but if it is in a concert or something I feel real nervous.
Joe — I guess I feel about the same as Laddy does.
Lewis — I feel nothing at all.
Q — Where have you toured up until now?
Laddy — Mostly in the South.
Q — Which place do you like best out of all the places you've been to?
Laddy — Miami Beach, Florida. But I like California too!
Q — What are your plans for the future?
Laddy — I want to get into radio or maybe be a disc-jockey.
Joe — I want to help make the Guilloteens an organization and a big success, then retire at the age of 30.
Lewis — I'm gonna try to make this group as big as we can get it and if it can't get any bigger I'll just go home and sweep streets.

Q — What was the most embarassing thing that has happened to you on stage while performing?
Laddy — Speaking for all of us I guess the time when the chord quit working, then the amp quit working, then the bass quit. Also one night the guitar was stolen.
Joe — I guess the most embarassing thing is watching Laddy and Lewis on stage.
Q — Who are your favorite singers or entertainers?
Lewis — Bobby Blue-Bland, he's just out of sight, he's the greatest.
Laddy — I like them all but my standouts are the Beatles and Dusty Springfield.
Joe — Elvis — and I also like the Beatles.
Laddy — Yes and we mustn't forget Yogi Bear! We love Yogi Bear!!!
Q — Do you date fans?
All together: NO!
Q — Why?
Laddy — I don't know, it's just that it's a bad scene, I guess. It really isn't fair to the girls when we have to leave. I don't know, but we just don't do it and we probably won't.
Q — What is the most attractive quality you find in girls?
Laddy — Big brown eyes.
Joe — Neatness and cleanliness.
Lewis — I better not answer that one. (Laughter)
Q — Do any of you have girl friends or going steady, etc.?
All together: NO!
Q — Now tell me honestly, what do you think of the girls that scream and practically go into convulsions?
Laddy — I love it!
Joe — I dig it except when they start pulling at that hair.
Lewis — I guess I like it too.
Q — Are plans being made for a second record?
Laddy — Yes, but we can't say the name yet. Also, we have plans for an album which will probably be called "I Don't Believe."
Q — What are your future plans in way of more tours?
Laddy — We don't know, where ever the money is and whoever makes the best offer. But the next one is being arranged in the Southeast.
Q — What kind of performing do you like to do best?
Laddy — We like concerts best 'cause they're easier and more fun. Also, I guess nightclubs 'cause it's fun when people come in and dance and have a good time.
Q — Why do you have long hair? Is it just because everyone else does?
Laddy — We have it because the public demands it and wants it. In fact we are all gonna let our hair grow longer.
Q — Where do you usually take a girl out for a date?
Laddy — Usually out to eat and to a show.
Joe — It depends on the girl and how much money you have.
Lewis — I refuse to answer on the grounds that it may incriminate me!

A REAL CLIMBER, Guilloteen Laddie Hutcherson uses singing partner Lewis Paul Jr. as a stepping stone to the top, while the third Guilloteen, Joe Davis watches with amusement. *BEAT Photo by Ted Schultz*

PORTMAN'S PLATTERPOOP

"Smilin'" *Ed Sullivan* who always has *The Beatles* first, taped them on August 14 for viewing on his fall TV show September 12 . . . Universal Pictures, not to be outdone by MGM's *Herman's Hermits,* brought *The Missing Links* in to create chaos at their studio. Tours were cut short as soon as the long-haired Links were spotted . . . Valiant's *Gil Shelton* signed to appear in "Young Hollywood."

The *Everly Brothers* latest "Beat and Soul" is already the talk of the East Coast . . . Reprise records have released a 3rd Kink album called "Kinda Kinks." Certainly it's selling! . . . *Barry McGuire,* former lead singer for the *New Cristy Minstrels,* has a controversial record "Eve of Destruction" . . . *Herb Alpert's Tijuana Brass* has been making the State Fair routes this summer!

The *Midniters* album based upon their hit single *Whittier Blvd.* will be released after Labor Day by Chattahoochee . . . The *Hondell's* Mercury single is "Sea of Love" . . . Hotels in most major cities do not wish to house the popular rock 'n roll groups, and you know why . . . *Dave Barnheizer,* producer of the *Lloyd Thaxton Show* eminating from Hollywood, reports that it goes color this fall.

Shindig's talent buyer *Dick Howard* rumored that each *Beatle* is worth over one million, and most of the loot has come from the Americanside. Lend-Lease, anyone? . . . Motown is not going square even though they signed *Connie Heines, Billy Eckstine* and *Tony Martin* . . . *Bud & Travis* furnish the singin gvoices for the new TV series "The Legend of Jesse James" . . . *Sonny & Cher,* the popular husband-wife singing duo, do not record individually on the same label. Sonny is an exclusive artist with Atco while Cher records singly with Imperial and with Sonny at Atco . . . U.N.C.L.E. co-star *David McCallum,* unleashes his pipes for MGM this fall . . . The *Righteous Brothers* were inked by Danny Kaye for several appearances.

It's become a fact that top star-hosted variety shows, in order to maintain high TV-ratings, have gone to the top teen vocalists for help. This insures them of large viewing audiences. How about a television program, with top teen-stars as hosts instead of the old hats who have to struggle through a show. As long as they recognize the strength of the teen market, why not develop a show around someone like *Vic Dana* or *Bobby Vinton,* for example, who can then introduce other teen recording artists. This could be a groovy show and a monster of a rating catcher.

On the subject of monsters, *Vic Dana's* "Moonlight & Roses" promises to be monstrous. It's taking off with giant steps . . . *Bill Black's* combo has a goodie in "Spootin" . . . Remember The *Flamingo's,* they're now on Philips and have a good first release "Call Her On the Phone" . . . *Herb Alpert* may go solo for his proposed role in the TV series Mr. Roberts . . . United Artists are going into a big build-up on *George Hamilton* for the teen market before the release of his film "Viva Maria" with a Miss Bardot. I guess they figure, with her figure, she doesn't need help.

Jan & Dean and *Johnny Rivers* were honored by the Boys Clubs of America for their work in its behalf . . . *Jewel Akens* has found the right material for his next single release . . . *Johnny Rebel* wrote the tune "Buy Me the Moon" that Tower is releasing for "Reb" . . . The *Turtles* hit "It Ain't Me Babe," a Dylan penned tune, will be the name of their soon-to-be-released album . . . Decca's young vocalist and guitarist and ASCAP's youngest songwriter, *Keith Green,* was inked by *Sammy Davis* for his first Fall special. Keith is 11 years old and has penned over 150 tunes. I wonder what he's going to do when he gets older?

Vic Dana does a two week bit in September for his favorite Uncle. It will be at March AFB and the commanding officer says, "they won't be bothered by the teen fans!" Wanna bet? . . . The *Fortune Cookies,* a cute female vocal group, have a smash in the making for their first release on Smash records titled "It Sould Have Been Me" . . . *Elvis Presley* sings 10 tunes in his forthcoming flicker "Hawaiian Paradise."

Hits in the Making: The *Supremes'* "Nothing But Heartaches" on Motown . . . *Gerri Thomas'* "Look What I Got" on World Artists . . . *Chad & Jeremy's* "I Don't Want You Baby" on Columbia . . . *Jewel Akens'* "It's The Only Way to Fly" on Era . . . *Marianne Faithfull's* "Summer Nights" on London . . . *Chubby Checker's* "Everything's Wrong" on Parkway.

Not to Miss Dept.: *James Brown's* "Papa's Got A Brand New Bag." It's exciting and sensational and should continue to climb to the top . . . The *Fearsome Foursome's* "Fly In The Buttermilk" on Capitol Records. These huge footballers, the one-half ton defensive line of the Los Angeles Rams, have a catchy tune in their first outing, with a record sleeve that should frighten away any monsters, providing you live in a haunted house . and as a famed rock 'n roll tunesmith would say, in the treasured words of one Sig Sakowicz, later baby!

LITTLE ANTHONY & THE IMPERIALS had their first hit record with "Tears On My Pillow," in 1958. After a six-year absence, they came back with another smash, "Goin' Out Of My Head," "On The Outside Looking In," and their latest, "Take Me Back."

KRLA ARCHIVES

SURF BEAT

By GENE VANGELISTI

SURFING HAS COME a long way from the days of wooden boards and uncrowded beaches. As you may know, the classic sport multiplies every day. Why?

There are a good bunch of why's and I don't have the audacity to ask you to sit through such a long tale as that. However, the big reasons should be gone over lightly to fully understand our sport.

Surfing is different — very different from practically any sport you can name. It is without a doubt one of the most individual sports that anyone can try — it is just the ocean, your board and you — no teamwork, no special equipment and no prepared area to practice it. No one can help you ride a wave.

Once you commit yourself and stand up, that's it. You are locked in a seemingly holy bond between you and "Mother Ocean." You fully control her daughter, "The Wave." You can either win this elemental battle or you can try getting off and walking.

The wave can be terrifying but she can also be a surfer's delight. She can supply you with untold experiences. Every wave has a personality of it's own — big, small, fast or slow — they are always different.

A surfer never rides two waves alike. He could ride every day of his life and never perform the same maneuver on two waves. This is what makes surfing a challenge — the ever-changing wave. She's wonderful, she's good and clean, always honest, never holding anything back. She sets a good example for all of us.

"Kooks" Not Wanted

This is surfing. It is not long blond hair, smoking before you're 16 and using foul language. These kind of people are not real surfers, they are known as "kooks" and real surfers sneer at them. It takes guts to be good at any sport and that is especially true with our sport.

The guy or girl who hits the water with the right attitude and seriously tries to ride every wave to the very best of his ability always comes out better, physically and mentally, for it.

He learns faster and will probably get more respect and help from his long time surfing friends. Actually it is nearly impossible for someone to explain how you should ride a wave. Ride the way you feel is the best and safest way you know.

Get a board that fits you, it doesn't matter what kind as long as it has a reputable name. In some cases a used board is like old clothes, either too long or too short and cheap new boards are not always the answer.

Other board manufacturers have followed the lead of the golf industry in recent months by using the "Pro" model. Hobie was the first with the Phil Edwards model which is perfection in riding.

Dewey Weber has gone into production of the Harold Iggy model which tops his line. If any of you have seen Harold ride you will agree that he is the most under-rated surfer around.

Gordon & Smith have the new Mike Hynson model which rides like a dream. Mike is a very experienced shaper and a great rider. The new member of the ever growing line of models is the new Donald Takayama model which is made by Bing. Bing makes some of the greatest boards in the world. This new addition should be very welcome to the surfing world.

Good Investments

These boards are naturally more expensive than the standards, but if you become capable and find you are not progressing as fast as you should be, maybe a good custom board would be a good investment. It is as though they surf themselves.

All of them will handle any wave to hit this coast except those surfed by the lucky guys in the Santa Cruz area. They are sometimes blessed with winter waves up to twenty feet and special boards are required for this kind of surf.

August and September are great months for surfing. Hot weather adds to good south swells, lots of surfing movies and contests. If you haven't had a chance to catch a contest in person — do it. You'll have a great time.

It's not just surfing, it is competition and tough competition at that. Clubs will enter as a team and the spirit runs high. They surf their hearts out and will usually perform tricks that you won't see at the beach.

Clubs play a big part in surfing today and they are a big help to everyone concerned. Most clubs run under the United States Surfing Association rules which provide uniform operations.

If you surf you should join the U.S.S.A., the reasons are many and it will help you later. If you have any intentions of entering a contest you must be a member of the U.S.S.A.

Windansea Good Example

I'd like to mention some names at this point as long as I have mentioned surfing clubs. The famed Windansea Surf Club was a leader in making a respectable sport out of surfing.

They hold surf clinics to teach the not-so-experienced surfer

MAN AGAINST WAVE — NO HELP AROUND

Battle Waged Against Stones By Indignant Parents, Press

... BRIAN JONES

... BILL WYMAN

safety and water rules. They can match any club in the world.

The club goes to the Islands every year from the profits gained from their many money-making events over the year. They have dances, show surfing movies and really use their heads when it comes to representing the sport of surfing. If you are in a club now and have any say at all, you might bring up some of their ideas and gain by their experience.

If you surf and don't belong to a club maybe some day you will be asked to join one. If you are not a person to join clubs you can still aid in building a good image for surfing by acting like a well-adjusted athelete.

Well, here's to surfing, all of the clubs and to you. It will be my pleasure to fill you in on the surfing happenings up and down the coast this summer. If there are any points that are unanswered and you would like the scoop, just say the word and I'll try. Good waves and thanks.

(Continued from Page 5)

not seem to want to take us seriously. Well, that's okay. We'll make them eat their lousy words one day. We'll make them take our music seriously."

Won't Change

People suggested, in fact people demanded, that the Stones cut their hair and wear stage suits. "You won't catch us falling in line like that. We're not interested in all that stage make-up either. So we've got pale faces. So some of the knockers say we look as if we've never been out in the sunlight—that's okay with us. People can say what they like," Brian answered.

"People" did say what they liked, and practically none of what they said was good. But the fans, the kids, the real record-buyers—these people liked the Stones. They appreciated and understood what the five long-haired boys were laying down. And little by little, these people made the Rolling Stones one of the biggest groups in the world, second only to the Beatles—and in some places second to no one at all.

They have made it to the top now. It took a lot of work, a lot of sacrifice, and a lot of sweat. But they made it. They sometimes still find themselves being ridiculed because they still refuse to wear short, neatly-barbered hair, because they still refuse to don look-alike suits on stage, and because they still continue to speak their minds.

Let Live

If they offend you with the way they dress, the way they look, or the way they talk—then just ignore them. Switch the radio dial or turn off the television —but quit knocking them. After all, they are only being themselves, and why shouldn't they? It's a free world, isn't it? And not everyone must conform — not everyone must do just as everyone else is doing.

As Eric Easton was heard to mutter: "They are the gentlemen of the orchestra."

They are indeed.

KRLA ARCHIVES

KRLA Tunedex

 EMPEROR HUDSON
 CHARLIE O'DONNELL
 CASEY KASEM
 JOHNNY HAYES
 BOB EUBANKS
 DAVE HULL
 DICK BIONDI
 BILL SLATER

KRLA BEAT
6290 Sunset, No. 504
Hollywood, Cal. 90028

BULK RATE
U.S. Postage
PAID
Los Angeles, Calif.
Permit No. 25497

This Week	Last Week	Title	Artist
1	1	LIKE A ROLLING STONE	Bob Dylan
2	3	I GOT YOU BABE	Sonny & Cher
3	6	IT AIN'T ME BABE	The Turtles
4	2	ALL I REALLY WANT TO DO	Cher
5	8	YOU WERE ON MY MIND	We Five
6	5	HOLD ME, THRILL ME, KISS ME	Mel Carter
7	22	IT'S THE SAME OLD SONG	The Four Tops
8	7	UNCHAINED MELODY/HUNG ON YOU	The Righteous Brothers
9	19	PAPA'S GOT A BRAND NEW BAG	James Brown
10	16	CALIFORNIA GIRLS	The Beach Boys
11	4	SATISFACTION	The Rolling Stones
12	27	BABY, I'M YOURS	Barbara Lewis
13	9	YES, I'M READY	Barbara Mason
14	14	WHAT'S NEW PUSSYCAT?	Tom Jones
15	10	CARA-MIA	Jay & The Americans
16	28	NOTHING BUT HEARTACHES	Supremes
16 (TIE)	15	YOU'D BETTER COME HOME	Petula Clark
17	34	HELP!/I'M DOWN	The Beatles
18	12	I'M HENRY THE VIII, I AM	Herman's Hermits
19	25	TAKE ME BACK	Little Anthony & The Imperials
20	13	SAVE YOUR HEART FOR ME	Gary Lewis & The Playboys
21	11	I'M A FOOL/SO MANY WAYS	Dino, Desi & Billy
22	31	YOU TELL ME WHY	The Beau Brummels
23	18	I'LL FEEL A WHOLE LOT BETTER	The Byrds
24	17	I CAN'T HELP MYSELF	The Four Tops
25	24	WHO'LL BE THE NEXT IN LINE	The Kinks
26	20	LET HER DANCE	Bobby Fuller Four
27	30	PRETTY LITTLE BABY	Marvin Gaye
28	29	I WANT CANDY	The Strangeloves
29	23	THEME FROM 'A SUMMER PLACE'	The Lettermen
30	33	DOWN IN THE BOONDOCKS	Billy Joe Royal
31	38	JU JU HAND	Sam The Sham & The Pharaohs
32	—	COLOURS/JOSIE	Donovan
33	—	LAUGH AT ME	Sonny Bono
34	—	RIDE YOUR PONY	Lee Dorsey
35	—	ANNIE FANNIE	The Kingsmen
36	—	SUMMER NIGHTS	Marianne Faithfull
37	—	SO SMALL	New Faces
38	—	DO YOU BELIEVE IN MAGIC	Lovin' Spoonful
39	—	SUMMERTIME GIRL	The Tradewinds
40	—	THAT'S WHERE IT'S AT	T-Bones

KRLA ARCHIVES

KRLA BEAT

Volume 1, Number 24 — LOS ANGELES, CALIFORNIA — 15 Cents — August 28, 1965

Southland Premiere! KRLA Presents— THE BEATLES in 'HELP!'

KRLA BEAT

Los Angeles, California — August 28, 1965

A BEAT EDITORIAL
NO CENSORSHIP

In the music world, this is the age of the protest. As an old Latin proverb observes, "It's What's Happening, Baby."

Bob Dylan was the first to break the sound-off barrier when his "Like a Rolling Stone" jumped overnight from no place to **top** place on the sales charts. Dylan has been protesting against various things for years, of course, but the masses are just beginning to listen.

But the real ding-dong daddy of protest songs is Barry McGuire's "Eve of Destruction," a rousing ditty talking up The Bomb — which also became an overnight sales hit and is unquestionably the most talked-about and controversial record of recent times.

But McGuire's protests about modern suicidal warfare were nothing compared with the protests which quickly came pouring in from those who were offended by the song, particularly conservative and right-wing groups.

Ashcanned

As a result, many radio stations throughout the country — and even ABC Television — have banned the record. Despite "Eve of Destruction's" huge popularity and heavy public demand for it on the airwaves, these stations absolutely refuse to play it.

But in spite of the heated controversy surrounding it KRLA is still playing the record, refusing to join the ranks of those who yanked it from their turntables.

KRLA Station Manager John Barrett, a long-time advocate of giving the public what it wants to hear, sums it up this way:

"Regardless of our own personal feelings about the record — pro or con — we don't feel KRLA has the right to tell our listeners what they can and cannot hear. KRLA doesn't believe in censorship and we will bend over backwards to play any record or form of music which is in public demand."

And he added: "Our listeners set the music policy. KRLA plays whatever records they indicate a preference for — so long as they are not distasteful or morally offensive — and the public can accept or reject each one on the basis of personal taste.

"If they decide they want to hear Chinese music, then that's what KRLA will play."

The BEAT echoes a hearty "Amen." But who knows — at this very moment someone may be penning a Chinese protest song.

WADING THROUGH THE SURF AT NASSAU, John, Paul, George and Ringo complete the Bahamas' segment of their new film ("HELP!") and prepare to fly to the frozen alps of Austria for more scenes from the fabulous movie. KRLA will present a special advance screening of the long-awaited Beatle movie on Aug. 23. Huge turnouts are expected when the film begins its city-wide showing on Sept. 1.

KRLA HAS PREVIEW OF NEW BEATLE FILM

KRLA will present the Beatles in another first next Monday (August 23).

The first Southern California showing of their exciting new movie ("HELP!").

And the timing couldn't be more perfect.

KRLA's special advance showing of the United Artists film is timed to celebrate the long-awaited arrival of the Beatles in Southern California on the same day.

It will be a special treat for 500 lucky Beatle fans who will not only be the first in this area to see "HELP!" but will be able to see it without charge. Every seat for the special advance screening is being given away free.

It will be shown at the Carthay Circle Theatre, 6316 W. San Vicente, starting at 10:30 a.m. All is not lost, however, for those who miss the KRLA preview of "HELP!" The movie opens its regular city-wide run on Sept. 1, and huge crowds are again expected — equal to the turnouts for the Beatles' first movie, "A Hard Day's Night."

The movie climaxes a frantic week of Beatle activity in Southern California.

Begins Monday

It begins Monday when the Fabulous Four arrive in the Los Angeles area for a six-day vacation.

Saturday night they are to travel by plane or helicopter to San Diego for a performance at Balboa Stadium, returning to their guest home in Los Angeles after the show.

Sunday and Monday they will perform for Bob Eubanks and KRLA at Hollywood Bowl, two performances which have been sold out since mail order ticket

TURN TO PAGE 10

BEATLE MOVIE REVIEW
'HELP' Fab Film, But Poor Ringo!

It is quite obvious to the BEAT that the Beatles' second movie will need no financial "help." It's sure to be a box-office smash. The photography, the color, the production and the direction are fabulous.

Walter Shenson and Richard Lester are again teamed as the producer and director of the film. These two talented Americans, of course, fulfilled the same two jobs in the Beatles' first, "Hard Day's Night." They did such a great job that a reporter from the London Evening Standard said: "If the Beatles were awarded the MBE for what they did for Britain, Walter Shenson and Richard Lester ought to get life peerages for what they have done for the Beatles."

And as for the Beatles, they are delightfully and tremendously the Beatles. They were even more relaxed and sure of themselves this time, and it shows.

Missing Ring

The movie opens in the Far Eastern temple of the Goddess Kaili. A human victim is about to be sacrificed to the Goddess when Ahme (Eleanor Bron) makes the startling discovery that the intended victim is not wearing the sacrificial ring.

The ring is, of course, in the possession of one Mr. Ringo Starr who is at that very moment banging away on his drums. Ringo, extremely attached to rings anyway, is especially attached to this special ring, a gift from a fan, because it has somehow become stuck on his finger!

The High Priest, one Clang, (Leo McKern) and his gang of

TURN TO PAGE 10

Beatles Lease House In Benedict Canyon

When the Beatles tour the U.S.—and particularly California—they don't stay at just any ordinary hotel. Why should they when they can live in plush private homes surrounded by movie stars?

During their eight days in California The Beatles will lease a mansion-type house in picturesque Benedict Canyon outside Hollywood.

Their sanctuary even comes equipped with a drawbridge and moat. However, the moat is not as hazardous as the real kind, for it contains no animals of the man-eating variety.

For the pleasure of living in this drawbridged mansion, the boys paid the mere sum of $3,500, plus an additional $2,000 for insurance to cover any damage which might be caused by their overly-enthusiastic fans.

But since they are receiving approximately $45,000 per concert this will not take quite their last cent.

The Beatles hope the insurance precaution will not prove to have been necessary. Last year thousands of fans found their hiding place in Bel-Air, but the boys didn't mind because nobody tried to mob the house, break windows or steal souvenirs.

They deserve the same courtesy this year.

KRLA ARCHIVES

BEATLES FIND MUSIC AND FUN

"ALL SOME TEACHERS EVER THINK OF IS HOME WORK"

"I'LL TAKE THE LEAD, GEORGE"

"YOU ALWAYS TAKE THE LEAD, DARN IT!"

KRLA ARCHIVES

WHEN NOT OFF HUNTING RINGO

... WHO NEEDS AN AUDIENCE?

... "PLEASE DON'T TAKE MY TAMBOURINE, SIR"

KRLA ARCHIVES

Turtles Race With Success, Uncle Sam Waits At Crossing

By Louise Criscione

There is an unfortunate situation which reoccurs much too often in the recording business. A group or an individual makes a record and it's a real smash. Everyone plays it, buys it, and sings along with it. Then suddenly it disappears from the airwaves and the artist who recorded it likewise vanishes into oblivion.

There is a record out now which is a hit. Sooner or later it will stop being played, but I doubt seriously if the group which has recorded it will be a one-hit wonder. The record is "It Ain't Me Babe" and the group is the Turtles.

The BEAT recently interviewed the boys at a local club, and amid the empty tables and loaded ash trays, we had quite a little talk. And from that talk emerged the safe assumption that the Turtles will be around long after "It Ain't Me Babe" has died its natural death.

Play What's In

There are six Turtles, they all wear relatively long hair, they do not wear stage suits, they have a folk-rock sound, and they are extremely honest and frank. They admit that the reason they are playing folk-rock is simply because that's what is "in" right now. Jim says: "What were we playing before? Rock. Because that was what was 'in.'" Chuck pointed out that the Turtles "change with the times."

"It Ain't Me Babe" is a Bob Dylan composition. Bob Dylan is currently the "in" thing. Would this have anything to do with the fact that the Turtles chose that particular song to record? Mark answered: "We did it just to get off the ground." Jim disagrees with Mark saying: "No. We did it because it was a good song." Al added: "But we're not going to ride on it."

"We liked Dylan a long time ago—way before the public had even heard of him. We didn't start liking him just now because he is so popular," Don said.

Commercial Dylan

Wrinkling his forehead in thought, Don continued: "I've been thinking about it a lot lately. I mean, why Dylan has gone commercial. It's got nothing to do with money. How many people know him now? He's trying to reach more people, and he can do it this way."

Despite the fact that Dylan is their idol, the Turtles had a difficult time deciding if "It Ain't Me Babe" should be released as a single. They had cut three sides that night and there was a small amount of disagreement over which songs should be included on the group's debut disk. They finally narrowed it down to "It Ain't Me Babe" and "Almost There." Then they went into another huddle and eventually emerged with the Dylan-penned song as the "A" side.

The Turtles seem to be very sincere in trying to give the public the most for its dollar. They despise these one-song groups who do nothing but change the lyrics and use the same sound over and over.

No Fast Buck

I got the impression that the pet peeve of the group is record companies and record producers who are too lazy to make both sides of a record good enough to be the "A" side or who are too unimaginative to produce an album which has twelve good, but different, tracks. They deplore the fact that many Americans forsake originality, talent, and hard work just "to make a fast buck."

They are genuinely surprised and naturally thrilled that their record is doing so well. Mark says: "Well, it was all so quick. We still can't believe it."

Mark feels that the hardest decision they had to make in their career was finding a name, but Don thinks that it is trying to avoid the draft. The mention of the draft brought a cry of "help" from Jim, who declared confidently that "they'll never get me. I'll leave town first!"

Fear Draft

In fact, the group's deepest fear is that Uncle Sam is ready to call their number anytime now. Another fear is that maybe this is all a big dream, and tomorrow when they wake up they won't have a hit record at all. Howard was particularly alarmed when he learned that President Johnson had increased the draft! But Don is patriotic enough to allow the President to tell the Viet Cong that "the Turtles are coming." He feels certain that at the mere mention of the Turtles, the Viet Cong will all run away.

Al admits that the boys fight "constantly." And Don says: "Well, we have to. Especially now, I mean, we're together twelve hours a day." But Howard reassures us that once the group gets on stage everything is okay.

Howard is the "King"—the leader of the group. He reveals that he got that job for simply one reason—he is the biggest! However, Jim begs to differ with him and says that he prefers to call Howard the "spokesman" of the group and that all decisions are group decisions.

Biggest Mistake

Jim feels that the Turtles biggest goof was making "King" the leader. But Chuck feels that the biggest mistake is in letting people take free rides.

Mark is affectionately known as the "bumbling idiot" of the group. I asked why, but I need not have for I soon witnessed the answer. It is because Mark knocks over everything in sight! Howard calls him "Peter Sellers in disguise." Jim reveals that Mark is the only person who can walk off stage and knock down a whole row of tables!" And sure enough before the interview was over Mark had knocked over the same ash tray twice and had also succeeded in tipping over the microphone!

Gum Habit

Jim seems to be the Bill Wyman of the Turtles. On stage, and off stage as well, he constantly chews gum. "It's something to do. It's better than chewing cud," Jim explains.

"Yeah, because I was talking to cud," grinned Don.

Chuck (nicknamed "Animal") shows his folk influence by digging such people as Joan Baez and Buffy St. Marie. For those of you not familiar with Buffy, Chuck informs us that she is an Indian folk singer. Chuck thinks he looks a lot like Benjamin Franklin which make him rather happy because since Ben is dead he cannot possibly be drafted!

On stage, the Turtles wear the same "come as you are" type clothes which the Stones are well-known for. But apparently the Turtles do pay some attention to the way they look on stage because Chuck reveals that: "I al-

TURN TO PAGE 13

... THE TURTLES

KRLA ARCHIVES

FROM OUT OF THE WILD WEST The Bobby Fuller Four (from left) Dwane Quirico, Bobby Fuller, James Reeves and Randy Fuller, rode to success in the pop record world.

Bobby Fuller Four Reckon That Westerns Will Replace English

By Michelle Straubing and Susan Wylie

...(Editor's Note: The Bobby Fuller Four rode off from West Texas to sunny California where they fulfilled their dreams of success in the record world. Demonstrating that famous Texas hospitality, the four took time out from their busy schedule to predict the death of the English craze in a conversation with BEAT Reporters Michelle Straubing and Susan Wylie. The following are some excerpts from that conversation.)

Q: Are you interested in any other fields of entertainment?
Bobby: I have an ambition to act, but it's in the bag.
Randy: Bobby likes to shoot pool.

Q: What kind of musical training have you had?
Randy: Don't everybody speak at once. Actually, we three have been to school. Bob and I took music in college, but he took more than I did.
Duane: As far as I'm concered, I just taught myself. Bob has really taught me a lot on the drums.
Bobby: Duane has a lot of natural ability on the drums. That's one of the reasons I hired him. In my group he learns fast.
Jim: Sometimes.
Randy: When you get a bull whip he learns pretty fast!

Q: How do you classify yourself as a singing group?
Randy: We play West Texas rock and roll and it's nothing new. We've been playing it for years.
Duane: The same thing the Beatles have been trying to play and can't.
Randy: They've come close, but they're not from West Texas.

Q: Do you think that it's important to have a number one song?
Bobby: We'd love to have a number one song, but just to have one on the Top 40 is fine.
Randy: Some groups have a number one record, but they don't go over with the kids.

Q: Do you think the English trend will last?
Bobby: No, it's on the way out now.
Randy: What bugs me is some girls who come over and say we dig you, but the Stones have long hair and are English. What I tell them is someday all the American males are going to start digging foreign girls and just leave the girls in the cold like they did us. They're going to be sorry because those English aren't that good.

Q: What do you think about the way girls dress? Some people say that girls don't look like girls anymore.
Randy: That's because guys don't look like guys.
Jim: I don't like some of the styles they come out with.
Duane: I do.
Jim: I like some of them, but some I just don't dig. For instance, this high boot stuff. I mean they're fine if you're going trout fishing. I like girls to look a little bit feminine, but when they start wearing boots they look like fishermen. Then again, everyone has the right to dress the way they want.

Q: How do you feel about bell bottoms?
Jim: I like them. I liked them five years ago when the cowgirls were wearing them.
Duane: One thing I don't like is bell bottoms on boys. On girls, they're fine, but not boys.

Q: Is there anything you dislike about your work?
Jim: Yeah, loading up.
Randy: Our drummer is constantly beating on his drums. It irritates me.
Jim: Some boy keeps beating up on the drummer.

Q: Do you have any habits you would like to change?
Jim: Everyone has those.
Randy: I'd like to learn how not to grit my teeth when I tune my guitar.
Duane: I'd like to learn to control my temper. I just blow up. I get mad at myself when I mess around, not anyone else.
Randy: You take it out on everyone else.
Bobby: I'd like to have some time to myself.

Q: What would you do if you had to give up this career?
Bobby: I'd go into electronics or something like that.
Duane: I'd go into A and R. (An A and R man is someone in charge of record sessions.)
Jim: I'd never leave. I enjoy rock and roll. I love it. I've dug it all my life.
(Ed. note: Apparently, Duane was still thinking about our neighbors across the sea—for instead of answering the question which was asked, he was heard to mutter,
"Another thing we'd like to get straight with the teenagers and England. They think the English wrote all these songs, but they didn't. They're all Chuck Berry songs!")

On The BEAT

By Louise Criscione

Poor Donovan is having his share of trouble with officials both here and in England. He paid a very short visit to California and made such an impression that he was asked back to do all the pop television shows. Well, that's good, but what is bad is that in order to accept all the TV offers Donovan was forced to cancel an appearance in England. That was definitely bad because Donovan's loyal fans, after hearing the sad news, staged a huge riot and demanded their money back. If this was not horrible enough, Donovan was bombarded with two other misfortunes which occurred in rapid-fire succession, First off, the BBC after hearing of his cancellation, promptly banned him from their television network. All of this Donovan could take, but the really crushing blow came when he made the long trek out to Disneyland only to be refused admission because of the length of his hair! I guess Donovan has now learned that some weeks are just lousy all the way around.

DONOVAN

Byrds Welcomed

The Byrds were actually afraid of the reception which they would receive in London when they arrived for a three-week visit. But they really shouldn't have worried. There to greet the California five were several hundred fans plus a whole horde of newspaper reporters and photographers!

From the airport, the Byrds traveled on to a press conference which was described by one British newspaperman as "brilliant." They next moved on to the one place which they had all been dying to visit—not Buckingham Palace, not the London Bridge. No, the Byrds were off to Carnaby Street to purchase tons of new clothes.

We will soon have the five newly-clothed Byrds back in the U.S., so we can judge for ourselves if Carnaby Street really has such great clothes or not!

American Differences

One can always rely on Herman to come up with some interesting quotes. When asked if he felt that there is any difference between American and British girls, he replied: "Yeah, they're American here." Then when asked if he was a Mod or a Rocker, Herman answered: "No, I'm nothing." He then went on to explain: "But Karl and I used to be Rockers. We wore real tight pants, and with my legs they sure looked good!" I'll just bet they did, Herman!

... HERMAN

Quick Ones

Jimmy O'Neill has been signed for his second season as host of "Shindig." . . . Desi Arnez Jr. told me that he hates the odor of trucks. . . . Don Murray of the Turtles likes Dwight Fry, that character straight out of Dracula. . . . Patty Duke moved into a place of her own. . . . The Yardbirds will guest on this season's first "Hullabaloo." . . . Also signed for "Hullabaloo" next season are those fabulous Righteous Brothers, which is rather interesting because last season found the Brothers as regulars on the rival "Shindig." . . . Barry McGuire is really cashing in on this "protest" boom with his "Eve Of Destruction." . . . Elvis won his 45th gold record for "Cryin' In The Chapel" and Sam the Sham won his First gold one for "Wooly Bully." . . . Did you know that after the treatment the Stones received on "Hollywood Palace" many British artists are extremely reluctant to appear on that show?

WATCH OUT FOR: Haley Mills to hit Hollywood without a chaperon and with a 14 pound weight loss. Haley is currently putting the finishing touches on "Bats With Baby Faces" a film written by her mother and directed by her father. I'd say that's a real family enterprise, wouldn't you?

KRLA ARCHIVES

Q: *I don't know what my problem is, but I can't STAND to wear necklaces. They make me nervous or something and I can only keep them on for a few moments. I've never told my boyfriend about this (there was no reason to mention it) and he just bought me a beautiful strand of pearls for my birthday (not real ones, of course). I have to wear them, so can you suggest how?*
(Mary Lou D.)

A: People on the "high-strung" side often have trouble wearing jewelry. Start by wearing a longer type necklace OVER a blouse, so no part of the jewelry touches your skin. Try this experiment while you're doing something that will keep your hands busy and your mind off your phobia—like you're washing dishes or typing a letter. Leave the necklace on as long as you can, and next time you try this, you'll be able to leave it on longer. Then progress to a necklace that does touch your skin. When this has ceased to bother you, you're ready to wear the pearls on a date without taking the chance of having to remove them before the evening is over. Practice makes perfect!

Q: *I have one soap I use for my face, another for my hands and still another for taking a bath. Isn't there just one product I could use instead of having to keep track of three bars of soap? I've tried all the ordinary soaps, and none of them work.*
(Cynthia B.)

A: There's a great new soap that's perfect for all-over. It's called Safeguard and it contains both medication and deodorant protection. If you can't find it on sale in the nearest department store, any drug store should carry it.

Q: *I am about fifteen pounds overweight and our doctor has put me on a diet. It isn't too bad and I'm supposed to lose about a pound a week. The only problem I'm having is how and when to exercise. He says I have to do this every evening if I want to look nice when I've lost the weight. I don't have my own room (I share one with my sister) and I get embarrassed when I have to exercise in front of anyone. Any brilliant ideas?*
(Barbara K.)

A: Several! Your doctor probably told you it's a good idea to exercise at the same time each day. If he did, the main reason was because setting a particular time for this chore makes it a lot harder for it to "slip your mind." The exercise is valuable whenever you do your deep knee bends. There must be plenty of times during an average day when you can have a few moments to yourself in some room of the house (retreat to the bath if all else fails). Do your exercises during those moments if an audience gives you the jitters. By the way, did you know that exercising can really be a lot of fun if it's done to music? We know of a girl who lost twenty pounds to the tune of a Beatle album ("Hard Day's Night" — it has great exercising music)!

Q: *I just hate to get new shoes because every time I do, I get blisters on my heels. With all the cute new styles that aren't very expensive, I'd love to overcome this problem and start looking a little more well-heeled. Please help!*
(Kerry T.)

A: Try a little preventive medicine! You probably plaster your heels with band-aids after you've come down with a crop of blisters. Well, just do an about face and put a band-aid on each heel BEFORE the problem starts. Shoes, particularly the inexpensive kind, take the shape of your foot in just a day or two, so you won't have to keep this up for long. The protection should keep blisters from forming, and after all, that's the rub!

Q: *I have terrible posture and I'm about as graceful as a plow horse when I walk. Besides this, I'm always dropping stuff and am so uncoordinated I can't believe it. I guess I'm just a general mess and I hope you can help me do something about this!*
(Susan E.)

A: The first step toward solving your problem is to stop thinking you're a mess. Coordination and self-confidence go hand in hand! About posture, practice sitting in a straight-backed chair with both your shoulder blades touching the back. Then remember to keep this position when you're sitting elsewhere (not to the extreme, of course, there's nothing graceful about looking as though you have swallowed a two-by-four). The book-on-the-head method may be straight out of the last century, but it's still a step in the right direction. Practice walking with a volume of Shakespeare on your bean and you'll soon be poetry in motion. And please pardon that pun! Where your lack of co-ordination is concerned, take us up on our first suggestion first. Then make a more conscious effort to be coordinated. Don't do things too fast and keep clam. If you wear glasses, have them checked to make sure your prescription is up to date. If you don't wear them, have your eyes checked. Incorrect lenses or a need for glasses can cause a lot of physical disorganization.

Hint of The Week

I was always breaking out every time I took a breath, and my folks finally sent me to a dermatologist. I was embarrassed to go and kind of mad about the whole thing until the day I saw this older woman in the office. She was very nice and started a conversation and when she told me she was eighty years old, I about fainted! My grandmother is sixty and this lady didn't even look that old (I hope my grandmother isn't *reading* this). She must have read my mind (or my face, probably) and she told me, without my asking, that she'd taken good care of her skin all her life. Boy, I will never gripe about going there again! This really happened to me and I'm writing it in case any other BEAT reader is still complaining.

... KEITH RICHARD

Keith Richard's Girl Must Have Patience

If you are patient, energetic and beautiful you might be just the girl that Keith Richard is looking for.

Of course there was a period when the Stone was too wrapped up in his guitar to pay attention to any girl, no matter how perfect.

"For a long time I had to put a guitar before girls. And to tell the truth, when all the fellas I knew started going out with girls I was still at the bashful stage," Keith admitted recently.

Even now that he is out of the bashful stage and doesn't have to devote all of his time to practicing the guitar, Keith still feels a girl would have to be pretty patient to put up with him.

"I'm very untidy. I just sort of drop things all over the flat and rely on Mick to pick them up. I'm terrible in the morning. I just can't get up. If I arranged to take a girl out for the day she'd just have to come round, make cups of coffee and hope for the best."

Adjust To Keith

Besides putting up with Keith's habits, his girl would have to like staying in hotels because he is "not at all domsticated." She would have to be a girl with plenty of go who would like the "mad things" Keith does and a girl with a talent for fitting into the way Keith feels.

"Someone who'll sit at home with me playing records instead of going to mad parties. A girl who likes me the way I am and doesn't try to change me. Who isn't concerned with who I am on the group scene so much as who I am at home, behind all the publicity," Keith said, describing his dream girl.

And that's not all! "I like beautiful girls," Keith said, stating his final qualification.

It's a tall order but Keith need not worry. There are probably plenty of girls who would love to try and fill it.

Beau May Show You Chivalry Never Died

What's all this we hear about chivalry being dead? Let's not start having any funerals until we give those red-blooded American lads another chance to prove themselves. Next time you go out on a date, follow these five simple (definitely!) rules and give the poor guy the opportunity to be a gentleman.

1. Begin your campaign at the very outset of your date. When you-know-who (or you-know-what) arrives and honks his horn for you to come out and get into the car, go to the front door and glare at him. Then sit down on the porch and wait for him to come and claim his lady fair. Take a pack of cards with you. A rousing game of Solitaire will help pass the time when he drives off in disgust.

Sit Quietly

2. When you have arrived at your destination, providing you ever do, do not leap out of the car in an unladylike fashion. Sit quietly and wait until he comes around to your side and opens the door for you. If you have to wait for more than an hour, don't give up hope. He's bound to miss you sooner or later.

3. When, and if, the two of you ever reach the point of having a post-date snack, it is customary for the waiter to seat the lady of the twosome. However, since there are no waiters at the places *that* wretch takes you, it is up to your date to pull out your chair for you. If he forgets, teach him a lesson by doing an about face. Pull *his* chair out for *him*! It would be most effective when he is least expecting it.

Proper Exit

4. When it is time to leave  the restaurant, hand your coat to your date so he may help you into it. What you are going to do when he absent-mindedly puts it on and walks out is not our problem.

5. Even if your whole campaign has been a miserable flop up to this point, all is not lost. There is still the doorstep and the last chance for him to be that knight on a white charger. He can prove he is really interested in *you* by at least *asking* if he can kiss you goodnight. If he does so without asking, slap him gently. If he doesn't do anything, with or without asking, rejoice! Chivalry is not dead! Then get a new boyfriend.

KRLA ARCHIVES

Thrush, Teenages Tremble At Sight of Dave McCallum

"UNCLE'S" DAVID McCALLUM

Most actors are taking a back seat to recording stars these days, but not David McCallum! He's never made a record, but he's busy breaking several! His co-starring role on NBC-TV's "Man From U.N.C.L.E." series has won him one of the largest fan followings in television history and he receives more mail than M-G-M Studio (that's where his show is filmed) knows what to do with.

The reasons for David's appeal are obvious. For one thing, he has the popular look of the day. He's handsome, but not *too* handsome, sports a European mop of blond hair and an undercurrent of Merry Olde England ripples to the surface every time he speaks.

Many of his fans luvingly refer to him as the "Blonde Beatle"!

David is even more where-it's-at because the character he portrays is universally interesting. Illya Kuryakin, super-secret agent, is a hip sort whose appeal isn't limited to girl viewers only. His cool way of getting into and out of the most hair-raising scrapes imaginable has made him equally popular with guys.

Besides all of this, he's also one of the most gifted and versatile actors to ever hit the airwaves.

Natural Fascination

David was born in Glasgow, Scotland on September 19 (he's about thirty now, give or take a year or two) and his passion for acting was born shortly thereafter. His parents, both members of the London Philharmonic Orchestra, met in an orchestra pit, so the fascinating world of the theater was naturally David's cup of tea.

By the time he was fourteen years old, he was working in a British theater as an electrician and from there he went to the Royal Academy of Dramatic Arts in London. He then joined the British Army and spent two years as a lieutenant with the Royal West Africa Frontier Force.

British Films

After his discharge he took an acting job with a stock company touring the English provinces. This lasted for three years, until he was discovered by famed producer J. Arthur Rank, who launched David's career by giving him featured roles in several British films.

David came to Hollywood to play the role of Judas in "The Greatest Story Ever Told" and while he was here the "Man From U.N.C.L.E." creators took one look at him and knew he'd be perfect for the part of Robert Vaughn's right hand spy.

They couldn't have been more correct. The show was a smashing success and so was Illya. It was such a sleeper that it has been given a prime time slot for this coming season. From now on you'll be seeing your "Man From U.N.C.L.E." riding the world of bad guys every Friday night at 10 in *color!*

When David isn't rushing from one nail-gnawing adventure to another in front of the cameras, he lives with his wife Jill Ireland (a British actress who appeared with him on the show several times last season) and three sons in a 10-room house in the Hollywood Hills.

His fans don't seem to mind his being married, probably because they don't hear much about it. David keeps his private life *very* private and won't allow his family to be photographed or interviewed.

Thrush Beware!

All things considered, he's one of the greatest things that's ever happened to teenagers and television, and if THRUSH ever so much as harms one hair of his thatch-topped head, they're going to have to answer to us!

Wouldn't it be great if David could be persuaded to add another facet to his career and make a record? He does come from a musical family and studied the oboe as a child (at gunpoint), and we'll just bet he can sing up a storm.

We hope he'll stop confining his musical talents to the shower and let us in on the McCallum sound. It couldn't be anything but the best! If you hope so too, drop him a note and a hint in care of M-G-M Studios, 10202 West Washington Blvd., Culver City, Calif.

Maybe he won't take you up on the offer, but it's worth a try. Whether he does or not, David McCallum still rules!

Marianne Taking Rest

Marianne Faithfull, who is expecting a baby in the early part of 1966, collapsed before her scheduled appearance at the Winter Gardens in Scarborough.

Marianne's fans needn't worry—she is not seriously ill, but she has cancelled all her up-coming appearance for some time. However, Marianne will make some single appearances after she takes a long and well-deserved rest.

... MARIANNE FAITHFULL

Faithfull Scorns Spot On Peak Of Charts

While most performers, including the Beatles, break their necks trying for the coveted number one spot on the charts, Marianne Faithfull couldn't care less.

"I'm glad I haven't got one. I'm certainly not crying for a number one record. They can be a bit of a bore—you have to live up to them," Marianne said.

"Like the Beatles. Everybody keeps saying, 'They are slipping,' and 'The Beatles are finished,' they're so keen to knock someone who has a good number one record. Obviously, I'd like one from the point of view of status but otherwise no!" she continued.

The Beatles, on the other hand, admit that everytime they release a single they *hope* that it will reach that sacred number one spot.

"When you've got a new record out you can't wait to hear how it does after the first week. It doesn't matter how many number ones you've had, the next one is always the most important," George said.

Paul reveals that the Beatles are surprised each time they successfully make that long climb to the top of the charts. They really shouldn't be surprised. They've never failed to get there yet.

NEW MEMBER FOR MITCHELL TRIO

The Mitchell Trio, formerly the Chad Mitchell Trio, has a new member. He is twenty-two year old John Denver who replaces Chad Mitchell, the man who founded the Trio several years ago when all three of the original members (Mitchell, Joe Fraizer, and Mike Kobluk) were still attending Gonzaga University in Spokane, Washington.

Sometime ago, Mitchell announced his intention to leave the group in order to try his luck as a solo performer. He is already set for a stint on Broadway in a new play, and he will also record as a single artist.

It's a very lucky break for the young Mr. Denver because the Mitchell Trio is one of the most popular folk groups around.

"IT'S THE SAME OLD SONG" is the misleading title of the Four Tops' latest hit. Actually it's a brand-new song but it's following in the footsteps of their other world-wide hit, "I Can't Help Myself." It looks like these four just can't help themselves. All their records are winners.

JOINING EMCEE CASEY KASEM at the surprise party celebrating the 100th anniversary of Shebang are Lulu Porter and Freddy Cannon. Shebang is shown daily at 5 p.m. TV 5.

BEAT Names 21 Winners Of Representative Contest

Carol Bruesch of Hemet is the envy of her neighborhood.

And with good reason, for Carol is the grand prize winner in the KRLA BEAT Representative Contest. Her array of fabulous prizes includes two tickets to the KRLA Beatles Concert at Hollywood Bowl, an opportunity to interview the Beatles in person, and a lovely wrist watch.

All this for being the champion BEAT Representative from her school and selling the most subscriptions.

The next ten BEAT Representatives are second place winners in the contest and will receive their choice of engraved wrist watches or two tickets to the Beatles Concert at Balboa Stadium in San Diego.

They are Shirley Hess, Van Nuys; Sharon Wiley, East Los Angeles; Betty Raymond, Pasadena; Eunice Slagle, Highland Park; Robert Dressen, Buena Park; Anne Roberts, Los Angeles; Margaret Mendoza, Long Beach; Dina Pomeroy, Los Angeles; Estelle Brown, Canoga Park; and Elizabeth Collier, South Gate.

Third place winners, who receive their choice of autographed Beatle albums or two tickets each to the San Diego Beatles Concert are:

Mandy Humphrey, Alhambra; Donna Allbright, Santa Ana; Jean Bridges, Pasadena; Billie Hart, Los Angeles; Mary Guiterrez, Los Angeles; Susan Jamison, Burbank; Eileen Jones, Glendale; Arlie Clannahan, Beverly Hills; Bobbie Arlington, Oxnard; and Jan Silverton, Hollywood.

As a special bonus, the BEAT is also awarding two tickets to the Beatles Concert in San Diego to the following runners-up:

Margie Mormino, Covina; Pat Holladay, Santa Paula; Barbara Bates, Los Angeles; Jan Macquary, Pasadena; Cindy Annis, Woodland Hills; Linda Dunlap, Sylmar; Karen Yurko, Granada Hills; Laurel Sercomme, Arcadia; Eileen Rockman, Santa Ana; and Carol Ogren, Torrance.

If you missed out on the prizes for the current Beat Representatives Contest, don't be disheartened. Another one is scheduled for this fall, with another round of prizes.

Freddie and the Dreamers have been signed by Dick Clark for a month-long series of concert and college dates to begin in November.

MAIL BOX

Why Go To England
Dear Editor:
Many thanks to KRLA for publishing such a nice little paper. I find it very interesting. However, I have noticed recently in the BEAT and among the teenagers here, especially the girls, a frantic desire to go to England.

Why do these girls want to go to Britain? As an English girl myself (my family has lived here for two years), I cannot understand it.

Believe me, one has just as much chance, if not more, to meet a personality here in Los Angeles.

After all, when a "star" is here he is at least in a certain area. You can see all the personalities when they are here just as much as in England, and the tickets are easier to get. Also the native Californians don't know what glorious weather and climate they have here. If they ever do go to England they will come back here and never want to leave. It's fabulous land here and the Americans are daft to want to give it up.

Take it from me, California is a marvelous place to live. It's even better than Britain.

Thank you.
Misses KRLA
Dear BEAT:
Two weeks ago I moved from L.A. to Salt Lake City and in my opinion KRLA rates higher than the stations here. I'm going to try to get something for my radio so I can get KRLA up here. Please wish me luck.
Rosemary Skjalm,
Salt Lake City, Utah.

Dave And Dinah
Dear Editor:
"I'm Glad All Over" because of Dave Clark. My name is Dinah Clark and my birthday is December 15, the same as his. Not only that, but Barbara Ferris, who stars in the D.C. 5's movie plays the part of a girl named Dinah! I hope someday to really meet Dave!
Yours truly,
Dinah Clark, El Monte.

Freeburg Guests at KRLA

KRLA listeners were surprised to hear a new deejay sitting in as a guest on the Dick Biondi show recently. And nobody was more surprised than Biondi when the guest turned out to be Stan Freeburg.

The recording and television star was having dinner with KRLA Manager John Barrett and Program Director Mel Hall when he mentioned that he had been refused a job at KRLA 15 years ago because he "didn't have enough experience."

Barrett and Hall loaded Freeburg into a car, drove him to KRLA and said, "You've got the job!"

Dick Biondi stepped aside and watched open-mouthed as Freeburg took over for 15 minutes.

The famed comic (Freeburg, not Biondi) declared afterward, "I've had so much fun that I'd like to do the Dave Hull show when Dave goes on vacation."

We'll take you up on that, Stan.

CASEY'S QUIZ

By CASEY KASEM

Several years ago, when this star had a full-time job acting on England's "Robin Hood" TV serial, he never even dreamed that he would later become one of the best known singers in the entire world. He is now part of a famous duo that got its start through a recommendation by another famous duo. Ironically, the two twosomes sound nothing alike but look almost like brothers! This favorite began his acting career at the age of eight and intended to keep at it until he met a friend at school and decided to take advantage of his childhood music lessons. (See Answer on Page 10)

KRLA BEAT SUBSCRIPTION

you will SAVE 60% of the regular price!
AN INTRODUCTORY SPECIAL . . . if you subscribe now . . .

☐ 1 YEAR — 52 Issues — $3.00   ☐ 2 YEARS — $5.00

Enclosed is $......................

Send to:...Age:...............

Address:...

City:...State:..................Zip:...............

MAIL YOUR ORDER TO: **KRLA BEAT**
1401 South Oak Knoll Avenue
Outside U.S: $9.00 — 52 Issues   Pasadena, California 91106

THREE MORE KRLA listeners try Dave Hull's new ice cream flavor, Scuzzie, as Dave rubs his hands in glee. Within two weeks after it went on sale at Baskin-Robbins' 31 Flavors ice cream stores, Scuzzie led all others in sales. The Baskin-Robbins' stores are offering a huge array of fabulous prizes to the first persons who can guess the various ingredients suggested by each KRLA deejay. Entry blanks are available at each store.

KRLA ARCHIVES

PERSONALS

To Ron and Rick of The Barons:
You guys really tore Disneyland up. You guys are really great.
 Sue, Carol and Pam,
 Long Beach.

★

To Mick Jagger:
Thank you for answering my letter. You're a *deer* too! See you in October.
 Teresa.

★

To Pam of Los Altos:
Did ya know our tickekts for for August 29 are in Section P, Row 7, Seats 12 and 14?
 Barbie.

★

To Dave Hull, my favorite deejay:
Thanks for inspiring "Scuzzy." It's really great! My mom and dad like it too. That kinda makes us a "scuzzy" family!
 Scuzzily Yours,
 Jayn Fiore.

★

To Dick Chamberlain:
Hope you liked the ballet as much as I did. Weren't they great?
 A Nureyev Fan.

★

To Bob Dobes of the Wildcats:
You are without a doubt the most fabulous drummer I have ever seen. I love you. And so do all 35 members of your fan club.
 Love,
 Denna Owens.

★

To Whom It May Concern:
Eric Burdon is mine. Any objections? Then write to me —
 Claudia Burdon, 2381 Manchester, Cardiff, Calif.

★

To Dick Biondi, the guy with a heart as big as my home state of Texas:
Give my love to Johnny Rivers when you see him!
 Your Lovin Miss Galveston.

★

To Ringo Starr:
I have written a poem for you. I hope you like it.
 Ringo Starr is a fabulous drummer
 Ringo Starr is also my lover
 There are others who love him too
 But I don't think of them because it's so true
 These few words were meant to be for Ringo
 My dear will always be.
 See you at the Bowl
 Lov ya,
 Gloria Castillo.

★

To Mr. and Mrs. Joe Jagger:
Thanks for doing such a WONDERFUL job in raising Mick. He turned out perfect!
 Linda Wilson.

★

To Lynn in her new house:
Thanks for the fab dedication! Dick Biondi is the greatest, right?
 Diana.

★

To Dean of Jan & Dean:
Thanks for signing autographs outside Gazarris on Tuesday.
 The Five Girls in the Blue Fairlane.

DID YOU EVER SEE SUCH A CAR? It's the new KRL-"A", a perfectly-restored and beautifully-customed Model-A which is being admired and inspected here by KLRA Deejays (from left) Dave Hull, Dick Biondi, Casey Kosem and Johnny Hayes. You'll be seeing a lot of the KRL-"A" arond town in weeks to come. Behind its 1929 license plate is a new Corvette engine, surrounded by gleaming chrome. Note the "racing slicks" on the rear wheels. What'll it do. Frankly, we don't know yet. So far none of the deejays has been brave enough to take it to the track. We hope to be able to announce in the BEAT soon that some lucky KRLA listener can win this handsome chariot, one of the most unusual in the world.

'Help' Fab Film, But Poor Ringo

(Continued from Page 2)

no-gooders, set out to find Ringo, and all sorts of strange things begin happening. When Ringo is asleep, a weird "thing" comes through the wall and attempts to recapture the ring, but Ringo wakes up only to find himself on the floor and the ring still on his finger.

Enter Foot

Being extremely clever, the Beatles pay a visit to Professor Foot (Victor Spinetti) and his able (?) assistant Algernon (Roy Kinnear) in an attempt to get that ring off of Ringo's finger. But alas, none of Foot's wonderous machines will do the job. Foot himself becomes somewhat power-hungry and decides that if he can capture the ring, he will have the power to rule the world.

So now poor Ringo has two groups of bad-guys after him. The four Beatles put their think-ink caps on and again they come up with a plan — they all head for the Alps where they are positive they can escape the evil forces. However, quickly following in the Beatles' bootsteps are both Clang and Foot.

Scotland Yard

When in trouble in London the first place one should go to is Scotland Yard — and this the Beatles do. They explain their problem to the patient Superintendent who, after a small amount of persuasion, agrees to give the boys the full protection of the British Army to insure that their recording session on Salisbury Plain will be safe. But Clang, attired in the Army uniform, places himself in a strategic position on the Plain and is just about to capture Ringo when who should drive up in a tank to rescue the boys but Ahme.

Next the Beatles are off to the Bahamas, but right on their trail are Clang and his buddies and the Professor and his assistant. Since all Beatle movies must end happily, Ringo learns the magic formula, the ring slips off his finger, he passes it on to Clang who passes it on to Foot who passes it on to Algernon who passes it on to . . .

---

have you heard
'YOUR FRIENDS'
are coming?

The KRLA BEAT is published weekly by BEAT Publications; editorial and advertising offices at 6290 Sunset Boulevard, Suite 504, Hollywood, California 90028.

Single copy price, 15 cents. Subscription price, U.S. and possessions, $3 per year or $5 for two years. Canada and foreign rates, $9 per year or $14 for two years.

Exclusive distribution handled by Miller-Freeman Publications, 6328 Lewis Avenue, Long Beach, California. Inquiries should be directed to the attention of David Thomas.

'HELP' PACKED WITH THRILLS

(Continued from Page 2)

applications were first accepted back in May.

Favored Hollywood

Last year the Beatles stated publically that their Hollywood Bowl Concert was the highlight of their tour. This was not only because they loved the Bowl, the weather, the well-behaved crowds and their first sight of the movie capital of the world, but because of the smoothness in which the concert was handled by KRLA and Bob Eubanks.

Fans who were lucky enough to obtain tickets for the Hollywood Bowl concerts are requested to follow three general rules:
(1) Scream as loud as you like, but remain seated.
(2) Do what the police and security men say so that no one will get hurt.
(3) Treat the Beatles as nicely as you would wish people to treat you. Remember, they are coming to Southern California to entertain us, and they are here as our guests.

CASEY'S QUIZ ANSWER

(Don't peek unless you've read the question on Page 9.)
PETER ASHER of PETER & GORDON! The other twosome? Chad & Jeremy, of course.

Bob Eubanks brings the Beatles to Los Angeles

THIS WEEK'S CARTOON CONTEST WINNER is Chery Parker of Granada Hills, California. Miss Parker will receive two record albums for her winning cartoon of Bob Eubanks and his presentation of the Beatles at the Hollywood Bowl.

KRLA'S DAVE HULL is on the receiving end of some dance music for a change, instead of spinning records for others to dance to. The occasion was a party for disc jockeys and entertainers in Hollywood, and Dave was the belle of the ball as he made a courageous attempt to do the jerk with pretty Shindig Dancer Virginia Justis. He won a standing ovation, but later learned it was in admiration for his taste in dancing partners instead of his own dancing.

Back issues of the KRLA BEAT are still available, for a limited time. If you've missed an issue of particular interest to you, send 15 cents for each copy wanted, along with a self-addressed stamped envelope to:

 KRLA BEAT
 Suite 504
 6290 Sunset Blvd.
 Hollywood, California 90028

ISSUES AVAILABLE

4/14 — INTERVIEW WITH JOHN LENNON
4/21 — INTERVIEW WITH PAUL McCARTNEY
4/28 — CHIMP EXCITES TEEN FAIR
5/5 — HERMANIA SPREADS
5/12 — HERE COME THE BEATLES
5/19 — VISIT WITH BEATLES
5/26 — FAB NEW BEATLE QUIZ
6/2 — L.A. ROCKS AS STONES ROLL
6/16 — BATTLE OF THE BEAT
6/30 — PROBY FIRED
7/24 — BEATLES TOP STONES
7/31 — CHER
8/7 — DYLAN
8/14 — HERMAN
8/21 — STONES TESTIFY

KRLA ARCHIVES

For Girls Only

By Susan Frisch

Could you please tell me the truth about what's going on between Twinkle and Herman?
Rona Resnick.

Dear Rona: I hate to let you down but I don't know how much of all the talk that is flying around about the two is fact and how much of it is fiction. I do know that Herman and Twinkle have exchanged I.D. bracelets and that they like each other and their relationship is more than platonic. But cheer up. At least she doesn't travel with him so we must still have a chance.

Is it true that Roy of Freddie and the Dreamers wears a toupe?
Marsha Abramson.

Dear Marsha: The first time I ever saw Roy he had a Beatle hair-cut. I saw him again a few hours later and he was practically bald. So figure that one out for yourself.

How long have Sonny and Cher been married and do they have any kids?
Ellen Altschuler.

Dear Ellen: Sonny and Cher have been married since September 9, 1963, however, they do not have any children yet.

Could you please tell me what the real Brian Jones is like?
Barclay Davis.

Dear Barclay: Seeing that I have only one column to write in, it is rather impossible to answer your question. To sum his personality up with as few words as possible, he is great, fantastic, good-mannered, considerate and GROOVEY!!!!

Could you please tell me what a groupie is?
Betsy Goldberg.

Dear Betsy: A groupie is a girl (and in rare cases a boy) who uses sneaky means to meet the groups. Somehow she always manages to find out where and when these groups are coming in town and then makes a mad dash to meet them. I hope you're not one, because personally I think it's a bad name to be branded with.

Guess What! I'm going to stop starting this column with a special message to the boys who are sneakily reading our private corner of the BEAT. Know why? My brother, that's why. He finally did me the good deed (his first in history) of telling me that boys couldn't care *less* about *For Girls Only* and only read it to see what smart remark I've thought up for them this week!

Remind me to do him a return favor sometime. Like never speaking to him again, for instance.

I received the strangest letter this week. It wasn't signed and it was composed of six words printed on a sheet of stationery. Those words were . . . *Why do boys like pretty girls?* Judging from the handwriting, I'd say the "author" has yet to reach her teens, and reading between the lines, I imagine she means why do most boys go for pretty girls only?

I hope she was young enough not to know better, because isn't it common knowledge that this situation exists because boys will be and always have been boys?

A teenage male is about three million times more self-conscious than a teenage girl. You know what I mean—if you embarrass a boy just the tiniest bit, he practically breaks out in hives right in front of your face. He can embarrass you, but not vice versa.

Self-Conscious

Well, I guess they really can't help it, but this is a pretty good reason why a lot of them won't even go out on a date with a rather ordinary girl, or someone who has a "great personality." They're afraid of being laughed at by their friends, or that someone will think that's the best they could come up with. Lots of times a boy will go out with a girl he secretly can't stand just because she's extremely attractive.

But never fear, they do grow out of this phase. You've probably seen this happen to someone you know. When a boy gets out of school and on his own, he often marries someone who isn't any raving beauty compared to the girls he used to date. He looks for different things in a wife than he does in a girlfriend and I'm sure glad to hear it. Maybe there's hope for me!

Speaking of being gorgeous, isn't it the worst crime of all time when a boy is unbearably handsome and otherwise a total waste? This doesn't happen often, but I'll bet each person reading this knows of some boy who is just *too much* to look at and a real creep underneath it all. There was a boy like that in my school when I was a freshman. If you didn't know him you would really wilt, but once he said about two words, you just joined the crowd and walked away talking to yourself.

Hey, let's stop talking about boys for just a moment (but no more than that)! Have you ever heard of a Footprint Party? Well I went to one the other night and really did some high-stepping (OH BROTHER). My girlfriend's dad is building a recreation room with a concrete floor and he allowed her one end of the room to have all her friends put their foot and paw prints down for posterity and then sign their names.

Understanding Parents

It's sort of like owning your own Grauman's Chinese Theater! See if you can't talk your dad into this the next time he gets the building bug. I think it was really understanding of this girl's father. Too many parents just don't seem to understand how a little thing like this could make someone happy. I used to have a mad crush on her dad when I was about eleven, and I'm happy to say it has now matured into undying luv.

Here's another one for the record. Do you have an old album you can't bear to part with but just don't play any more? If you do, you'll be interested to hear this groovy idea (wow, am I full of bad jokes today). Make a bowl out of the album by following these instructions (if I can write them down sensibly enough to follow—I never could explain things right). (1) Find a rather large empty can—like a large pork and bean container. (2) Put the can in the oven on a cookie sheet, then put the record on top of the can. (3) Turn on the oven, keeping the temperature low, and keep peeking until you see the sides of the record starting to droop. When they have drooped to just where you want them, make a wild grab for the potholders and remove your masterpiece.

It should harden almost instantly and you should end up with a really attractive decoration for your room. If you don't let me know and I'll try to explain it better.

Freckled Pajamas

I recently saw two things I've really flipped for. One is the new freckled pajamas that are made out of white material with trillions of tiny red dots. I think they're supposed to look like measles because the name of the line is Quarenteens, but I like freckles more. Whatever the case, they are adorable!

The other thing is a new product called Faberge Nail Makeup. It comes in every color in the rainbow and you can do the wildest things with it! You can paint your nails one color and make polka dots with another. I hope this fad catches on because it sure would be fun. I don't suppose it would last long, but it would be really wacky while it did!

I've also gone wild over those wild stockings in all those wild colors. I know one girl who mixes and matches them and has the most looked-at legs in town. There's something about the fabric in some of them that rather drievs me nuts, but I finally had sense enough to wear a pair of plain nylons under the ones that did bother me and presto! No more problems! Just stares.

Well, I'm doing it again. Running off at the typewriter, I mean. Please keep in touch and I'll see you next BEAT!

. . . THE SUPREMES

Supremes to Reign At Top English Club

America's most popular female singing group, The Supremes, are set to visit England in October for a month-long engagement at London's famous Talk Of The Town.

Appearing at the club is quite an achievement for the girls because the Talk is the English version of New York's famed Copacabana. The Supremes should feel right at home because they have just completed a three-week stint at the Copa where they drew standing-room-only crowds every single night! And not only was the Copa packed, but it was packed with many of today's top stars.

Before flying off to foggy London Town, the Supremes will tape a "Hullabaloo" and will also fulfill a club date at Grand Bahama Island.

Busy girls, these Supremes. Busy traveling and busy making number one records. Their latest effort, "Nothing But Heartaches," looks as if it will run true to form and produce another chart-topper for the three hit-makers from Motown.

P. J. Loses Following In England

P. J. Proby, once the biggest single act in England, is seeing his following shrink drastically in size.

While he gave two shows in one week recently, he didn't draw more than 400 people. In fact Proby himself admits that at the second show there were only twenty people in attendance.

P. J., understandably reluctant to admit that he has anything to do with the poor attendance, is placing the blame squarely on the shoulders of the promoters. He accuses them of charging such terribly high prices that it is impossible to fill the house.

This accusation brought the wrath of one promoter who kindly suggested that if P. J. wished the promoters to lower their prices then he should lower his!

Proby has made no response to this "kind suggestion."

BEATLES WIN FIVE AWARDS AT LUNCHEON

The Beatles, who seem to specialize in receiving awards, have received yet another one. Well, actually another five.

The song-writing team of Lennon-McCartney received five Ivor Novello awards at a recent Variety Club luncheon honoring Britain's top musical composers.

"Can't Buy Me Love" earned John and Paul two statuettes. One for the Most Performed Work of 1964 and another for the Biggest Selling Single.

They won certificates for "A Hard Day's Night" as the second Most Performed Work of 1964 and as the Outstanding Theme of 1964.

Their fifth award was a certititicate for "I Feel Fine" which was voted the second Biggest Selling Single of the year.

KRLA ARCHIVES

SURF BEAT

By Gene Vangelisti

SEPTEMBER IS A GREAT month for our sport with a lot of big surfing contests, leading off with the one at Malibu. However, before dealing with the contest situation we'd like to pass along a conversation we had with Harold Iggy, who is a shaper and professional surfer.

The conversation was about a question that bothers a lot of non-surfers—why relatively expensive hand-shaped boards are preferred even for the novice surfer and why there is a need for the even more expensive special "signature" models.

Q.—Iggy, How long did it take you to learn to surf as well as you do?

Iggy—I started surfing in the fifth or sixth grade. Right now I have been surfing for about eleven or twelve years.

Q.—You have developed a different style of surfing compared to other surfers of your caliber. You are manufacturing a board for Dewey Weber called the Iggy model. What, do you think, makes your board ride differently than any other board? You seem to turn with the rail instead of the tail block on a bottom turn and you get an awful lot of speed.

Iggy—My boards are shaped differently from a regular Dewey board. They are about an inch or two smaller than normal and I make the board a little thicker in the middle and at the nose. The belly I put in the board gives it the speed by making it softer on the wave than a flat bottomed board.

Q.—What makes a board faster than another board...

Iggy—A fast board will not turn as well and limits a surfer from a maneuvering point of view. A fast board is over-sized and thin.

Q.—Iggy, do you think that the waves are harder to ride on the coast than in Hawaii?

Iggy—The waves in Hawaii are a lot thicker and stronger. The waves along the California coast are thinner and harder to ride.

Q.—Would you say that you need a different board in Hawaii or do you just have to change your surfing style?

Iggy—A different board is necessary to change your style somewhat. I've been back and forth about three times now and I've changed my style of surfing each time. When you surf in Hawaii you need to get speed out of a bottom turn. That's one of the reasons why the board I build now is that shape.

MANY PEOPLE HAVE wondered at the rapid growth of surfing and want to know why it has expanded at the rate it has. There are a lot of good reasons and Harold Iggy represents some of them. He is a craftsman and his thoughts and logic are respected all over the surfing world. He is a perfectionist who is always looking for a better wave to ride. A surfboard is one of the last hand-crafted products made in the U.S., and the men such as Iggy who put all their knowledge, experience, and enthusiasm into producing a perfect board demand our respect.

The Summer Surf

We have had a "zero" summer so far. For several weeks there has been a small south swell bearing the "red tide." We might get some big waves in September if previous years are any guide.

Some of the events coming up are the Hermosa Beach Surf Contest, the Ocean Beach Contest, the Windansea Invitational Surfing Contest for members and other top surfers. Next month will start out with the Malibu Surfing Association's Invitational Contest. If you get a chance, see if you can make it. The definite date will be set when they can figure out when the waves are going to be consistent.

Next comes the Huntington Contest, the "Big Daddy" on the Coast. You can find any surfboard or any surfing celebrity in the world at this contest which will be televised. After that comes the Makaha International Surfing Championships in the Islands. As you can see, surfing ends the summer with a big bang. If you are able to take part in some of the contests, even if just as a spectator, you will probably enjoy them.

Next Week

Next week we will have an interview with a shaper of Iggy's caliber, a gentleman from Hermosa Beach named Donald Takayama who makes a surfboard called the Takayama model for Bing Copeland of Bing Surfboard. If you are interested in buying a board, the information we will be giving you in the next couple of weeks will be a help to you in selecting a board. Before you buy a board, talk to one of the custom board manufacturers, they have knowledge that will help you.

Until next week—good surf and good rides to you.

... LOVIN' SPOONFUL

Spoonfuls Get Taste of Life .. 'If You Believe In Magic'

By Louise Criscione

It is really rather hard to believe. Things like this just don't happen — do they? The four unusual boys who perform collectively as the Lovin' Spoonful couldn't have possibly led those kind of lives or done all those things — could thhey? Read on and see what *you* think.

John Sebastian, the twenty-one year-old guitar and harmonica player, was born in Greenwich Village and began blowing into a harmonica during his tender childhood years. He mastered the guitar by the time he was twelve and sailed off to Italy where he lived for five years.

While in Italy he became a guitar maker's apprentice, then he worked on his own as a studio harmonica player. But "driven to despair by the byzantine power play of commercial folk music," John headed off for Marblehead, Massachusetts to become a sailmaker. However, when John reached Marblehead a truly horrible thing occurred. The man who had advertised for a sailmaker really didn't want a sailmaker at all — he wanted to paint the bottoms of boats with rust paint. Unfortunately, poor John was allergic to rust paint so he headed back to New York where he met up with Zal Yanovsky.

Laundromat Life

Zay is the twenty year-old lead guitarist of the group. He started playing folk music when he was fifteen years-old, and one year later quit high school to become a folk singer. John then left for Israel where he spent ten months. He returned to the U.S., lived on the streets for a while and as John put it, "then I lived in a laundromat for seven months."

Tired of laundromat life, the guitarist secured a job as an accompanist for the Halifax Three for ten months. He crashed in flames in California and then returned to New York in a two passenger MG along with two other people and all of their luggage, no less.

The group, surviving a snow storm in Albuquerque, finally arrived in New York safe and sound. From the big city, Zal made it to Washington, D.C. where he started playing electric guitar.

There is something of a gap in his story at this point, which he explained thusly: "someone gave me thousands of dollars, a fat pad with four telephones, and a twelve string guitar and bins full of assorted electric musical equipment." Apparently unimpressed, but well equipped, he went back to New York and joined forces with John.

Family-Tree

Steve Boone is the twenty-one year-old bass guitarist, who swears that he is a relative of Daniel Boone's brother. He also claims that his family once owned the Times-Tower building in New York, as well as one-fifth of Delaware.

While in traction for two months, after an accident at the tender age of seventeen, Steve spent the time learning to play the rhythm guitar. The accident was also financially rewarding and Steve ended up with thousands of dollars and the chance to spend the next several years playing in a band and spending money.

Steve's next stop was Europe, but since nothing much was happening, he came right back to the U.S. where he met up with John and Zal.

Joe Butler was the last to join the group. He started playing drums when he was thirteen and sang and played in a twist band in a number of Long Island clubs during his college years. While working these clubs, Joe met Steve and thus we have a "Lovin' Spoonful."

However, the group was not an automatic success. Far from it, actually about as far from it as you can get. They did manage to get a job at the Night Owl Cafe, but they soon (very soon, in fact) left the Owl and hid themselves in the basement of the Albert Hotel to practice with the lower echelons of the hotel staff cheering them on. A soft rain of plaster, vibrated loose from the ceilings during their practice sessions, covered the Lovin' Spoonful like dandruff. To keep their hair clean they started wearing different funny hats.

After two months of this they emerged, pale and blinking, and marched straight to the Night Owl Cafe for a second try at it. So impressed by their new professionalism, the owner cheerfully and readily rehired them and even went so far as to have 1000 balloons printed with "I LOVE YOU - THE LOVIN' SPOONFUL."

Their professionalism sparked others in the entertainment field it seemed as, "Record companies began making offers."

I don't know whether I believe that or not. It's pretty far out, huh? I wonder if it has anything to do with the Lovin' Spoonful picking "Do You Believe In Magic" as their first record.

KRLA ARCHIVES

Liverpudlians Drive For View of U. S.

Steve Laine, Kenny Cox, Ron Henley, Dave Burgess and Jimmy May, met in Liverpool. They numbered five. The name, LIVERPOOL FIVE, was, therefore, a natural result.

Steve, lead singer and leader of the group, who boasts that he can run fastest from an avalanche of screaming fans organized the group and is its spokesman.

Ron Henley, of the broad smile and romanesque nose, is the tallest of the FIVE and doubles on electric piano and saxophone, as well as participating in the harmonies.

Kenny Cox, lead guitarist, explains why The LIVERPOOL FIVE toured the Pacific Northwest in preparation for their debut on the national scene. "It's given us a chance to really get to know your country and its people first hand. Particularly since we've chosen to travel by car rather than flying. Its' a big and exciting country and we don't intend to miss any of it, if we can help it," he insists.

Jimmy May, the drummer for the group, thrives on the day and night pace of their North American adventure, admitting that it allows little or no time to date or develop steady girl friends.

Dave Burgess, bass guitarist, adds that they all agree they have a commitment to their new fans to postpone any present thoughts of marriage.

Germany was the scene of the FIVE's first great success. Their records jumped to the Top Ten and before embarking on their globe-circling crusade, they found time to make a film there.

With the release of their first record, the group moved south for television and personal appearances and then took off for a tour of the East Coast. Traveling between four and five hundred miles a day they will see a great deal of America, for America will demand seeing a great deal of them in the future.

RIVERS JOINS GUARD

Popular recording artist, Johnny Rivers, has joined the California Army National Guard. This means that Johnny must serve from four to six months active duty beginning sometime in either September or October.

WATCH OUT FOR THE LIVERPOOL FIVE! The official rock and roll representatives at the Olympics in Japan, they incited riotous adulation during a six month tour of the Orient. Besides that, they now have a new Bob Dylan record, "You've Got To Stay All Night."

Turtles Off To A Fast Walkover

(Continued from Page 5)

ways make sure that the hole in my jacket is in the back!"

English Conformists

The Turtles admit that they are "slightly" influenced by the English. Chuck even goes so far as to say: "We are conforming to the English groups with our hair and our clothes." Jim disagrees "slightly" and says: "I wear my hair long because it keeps my ears warm!"

Howard summed up the Turtles' feeling about the tremendous success of their first record by saying: "Thanks to everyone who supported the record. We hope that we can continue putting out records which people will like."

With the determination, drive, and talent which the six Turtles possess—it is pretty obvious that they *will* continue making hit records. You can't keep a good Turtle down, you know. They *always* win the race in the end!

James Brown Makes Tours Worthwhile

Energetic James Brown probably makes more personal appearances than any other performer in the world today and specializes in breaking attendance records throughout the United States.

But this time the tall-haired master of rhythm and blues has really outdone himself. During personal appearances in Atlanta and Milwaukee Brown managed to gross $70,888. No wonder he likes to travel! For that kind of money who wouldn't.

HERMAN NOW FREE

The restraining order which Mickie Most has placed on Herman's Hermits has been removed.

It was lifted when Herman's managers and Most reached a new agreement which was more beneficial to both sides.

Beatles Still On Top

The four Beatles have managed to hold down that number one spot for yet another week. A two-week residency at the top of the American charts is not at all unusual, but a two-week chart topper in England is a rare occurance so the Beatles can pat themselves on the back for having done it. It will be interesting to see if they can do it again next week.

The top ten remained stable this week with only one change —the Searchers were knocked down to 12 and replaced at 10 by "Everyone's Gone To The Moon" by Jonathan King.

Coming up very fast are "Zorba's Dance" by Marcello Minerbi and "Too Many Rivers" by Brenda Lee.

An interesting point is number 20. It is occupied by the late Jim Reeves and his "This World Is Not My Home." Jim, of course, enjoyed tremendous popularity in his native America but it was as a country and western singer and not as a pop star. However in England he is constantly found on the pop charts, especially since his death. Strange, isn't it?

P. J. Proby is still attempting to make water run uphill and he has partially succeeded for "Let The Water Run Down" has swum up three points and now finds itself at a mighty number 25.

British Top 10

1. HELP — The Beatles
2. YOU'VE GOT YOUR TROUBLES — The Fortunes
3. WE GOTTA GET OUT OF THIS PLACE — The Animals
4. MR. TAMBOURINE MAN — The Byrds
5. TOSSING AND TURNING — The Ivy League
6. CATCH US IF YOU CAN — Dave Clark Five
7. THERE BUT FOR FORTUNE — Joan Baez
8. HEART FULL OF SOUL — The Yardbirds
9. IN THE MIDDLE OF NOWHERE — Dusty Springfield
10. EVERYONE'S GONE TO THE MOON — Jonathan King

KRLA ARCHIVES

HERB ALPERT and his Tijuana Brass debuted in San Francisco instead of Mexico but they still play that South of the Border music like real natives. They currently have a best-selling album on the charts, Whipped Cream And Other Delights."

IF YOU'RE HIP . . .
the LEAVES are Happening
with a SMASH SINGLE

"TOO MANY PEOPLE"
(Rinehart & Pons)

B/W

"LOVE MINUS ZERO"
A DYLAN TUNE

Mira Records

9145 SUNSET BLVD. ☆ ☆ (213) CR 8-1125 ☆ ☆ LOS ANGELES, CALIF.

HOW TO GET A HEAD
Travel Through Minds Of Top Personalities
By EDEN

Ever wish you could drill a hole in the head of your favorite star so that you could climb inside and see what was going on in there?

Well don't look now but the other day while casually browsing through the merchandise at my local Good Will relief store, I came across a handy-dandy Ben Casey medical kit. Need I say more? C'mon gang—let's go drilling!

For our first head—shall we examine Mick Jagger?

"It's the getting up there and the first reactions. Just waiting to go on, killing time that makes you nervous. Once you're on, it's different, another world."

"Laughter's important. A wrong note, a false start, pulling faces—anything will start us off. If you can't find a joke in most things, you're dead, man."

Okay kids, careful for the cerebellum as you leave. Oh yes—thinks, Mick.

Hey, do you see what I see? It's P. J. Proby. C'mon let's go. With all that hair, this should be a *real* challenge! It certainly is dark in here. Mmmm—there are some interesting thoughts over there.

. . . P. J. PROBY

"Every girl I meet is a potential bride. I wish I was married again but I'm not because I haven't found the right girl. I don't know if I ever will — but I'm looking. There wouldn't be another woman in the world once I was married."

Very interesting, P.J. Ta. Well, c'mon group, we have a date with a cool head for some hot quotes. Yes — it's Ringo, it's Ringo!!! (Please step *over* the nose on your way up, friends!)

"I'm more conceited than I was, but I'm not so much that I forget people I've known for years, or make scenes in public places thinking it won't matter because I am me."

"To expect success in pop is madness. We certainly don't because success for us is "more" than for other groups—like having to go straight in at number one. That's tough, even for us."

Hear, hear!! You lay it on 'em, Ringo baby!

Hey, speaking of babies, there's Herman. Oh Herman—wait up. Alright everyone, all aboard. (Careful for his fang—I hear it's dangerous! Oh, Look. He's had it removed!)

"I'm warm and sincere and tremendous fun."

"People ask me what it is like being a star twice over as an actor and now a singer. I don't know because I don't think about it."

"They all say me tooth was a gimmick. But when I asked my dentist what's a gimmick doing growing in me mouth he said he didn't know, so he yanked the bloomin' thing out by the roots."

"People tell funny stories about me, but deep, deep down I really am nice. Aren't I?"

Yes, Herman, you are. Wierd — but nice! But we must be going now. Indeed, I think I spy a loyal soul just ahead. Yes — and if it isn't Paul McCartney, M.B.E. Alright friends, last one in is an old stethoscope!

"If anything happened to one of us we wouldn't go on. It's true. When Ringo was ill we didn't want to do the tour of Holland and Australia. It'd be a drag without him, we thought. If it hadn't been just a temporary illness, then that would have been it. We'd all have packed in. If one of us dropped out the group would break up. We definitely wouldn't perform as three Beatles."

. . . PAUL McCARTNEY

Well spoken, Pauly, and thank you. Hey kids — we still have time for just one more and I know just the one. Heads up, eyes right, attack front and center — it's John Lennon. All aboard.

"Women should be obscene and not heard!"

Uh oh—I think it's *curfew* time for us, kids. Alright—everybody out! Now, if you will form a single file line on the right you can all scrub down and remove your surgical gowns.

Strictly from a medical standpoint, wasn't it a wild trip? Unusual specimens, everyone of them.

Clever way to get a head.

KRLA ARCHIVES

JAN AND DEAN in happier days. Jan (right) is now recovering from a compound leg fracture which has temporarily halted work on their new movie "Easy Come, Easy Go." Fifteen members of the Paramount movie crew were injured in a freak accident when a locomotive rammed their flat car during filming of a scene.

Get Paid to Meet Beatles By Playing Brenda Starr

By Sondra Lowell

What's the best way—and the only way—to be *sure* you'll meet the Beatles? Become a reporter. (but don't call the BEAT — we're on to that trick). It isn't as hard to do as it sounds. A lot of girls did it last summer, including Donald O'Conner's daughter Donna. A neighborhood paper might be interested in a story on their appearance. And they might be especially interested in a review of the concert by a teenager.

Go to all the papers in town, although the biggest ones will most likely have their own reporters. If that doesn't work, ask your school paper to give you a press card. Even though it's summer, the Journalism teacher can probably be persuaded into at least considering your story for the first fall issue.

Dress and act the way you would if you were applying for a regular job. Try to sell them on your qualifications, like for instance, you're an authority on this type of music. Well, aren't you? You know all about the different sounds and performers and what makes the Beatles great.

Beatle Expert

Even your age is in your favor for this job. Not only do you understand the music, but you also understand the people who understand it. You know *why* they scream and absolutely adore four "mop-haired" (a common adult phrase, as you must have noticed) British singers. Now, how many adult reporters can say that?

And you know just the right questions to ask them at the press conference, because you're really interested and not just doing a job. Plus, of course, teenagers will buy the paper just so they can read a story on their idols, particularly when it's written by a fellow fan. If you've ever written for a paper before, that's another point in your favor.

With all these qualifications, you really should be able to get an assignment from a newspaper somewhere. So don't get discouraged if the first one or two turn you down.

Once you get the press card or official letter, have the paper contact the people handling the press conference so you can get a press pass. This won't admit you to the Beatles' quarters or very many other places. In Las Vegas last year, reporters were invited to a party with Connie Stevens and other stars, but that isn't too common. The card *will* get you into the press conference, where you can ask all the questions you want. You'll have the thrill of knowing that John and Paul and Ringo and George are talking and looking right at you.

Front Row Seat

Just to be sure they will be, get close to the stage or wherever they'll be as soon as you get into the conference room. Don't worry about what door they'll be coming out of because they'll be well-guarded and you probably won't get a word out of them on their way to the stage. You wouldn't even *want* to reach out and touch them. It would ruin your professional image. Besides, as soon as they arrive, everybody will start pressing toward the platform, and getting lost in the crowd is too unspeakable a fate to hazard.

You'll have enough troubles being right up next to the Magnificent Ones, especially if there aren't any chairs. Reporters and photographers will shove you and shout questions as fast and loud as they can. You'll be competing with experienced star-meeters, so don't get shy at the last minute.

Bring along a notebook of prepared questions, but if writing down the answers prevents you from asking more, wait and do that later. Directing each question to a specific Beatle will give you a better chance of getting an answer. As for the questions you ask, they can be anything you want. These young men have already been asked everything imaginable anyway.

Interesting Characters

You'll learn a lot more once you get into the frantic swing of the hunt, and you'll meet a lot of interesting people. There will be boys with long hair and rings on both hands who'll try to fool you, and girls like yourself, and a Liverpudlian reporter named—of all things—George Harrison. He'll tell you everything there is to know about the four except how to get to them.

But the most interesting people you can hope to meet are, of course, the Beatles themselves. Once you meet them you'll know you'd love them even if they were not the Beatles. Talk to Ringo and he'll tell you how funny you sound as he mimics your accent and dances by himself. Talk to John and you'll get a dryly comical (to everybody else) insult or a negative opinion on press conferences.

Talk to George and Paul and tell me what they say. I'm dying to know. That's why I'm going Beatle-chasing again this summer. See you then!

Money, Clients Worry Top English Haunts

Two of England's famous clubs, the Cavern and the Crawdaddy, give testimony to the fact that patronage can make or break a club.

Byrds Fly, Right 'In' At Britain

The Byrds emerged from their initial stage fright during their first tour of England to discover that they were as far "in" as you can get.

The California group's biggest thrill came when they were performing in a London club. The boys strolled on stage, stared out into the audience and completely flipped, for seated there before them were the Beatles and Rolling Stones.

If that were not enough, after the show was over the Beatles sent a note backstage asking the Byrds if *they* could meet *them*. Of course, you know what the answer to that was!

After a small conference the entire group (Beatles, Stones and Byrds) traveled to Brain Jones' Chelsea pad where they threw a party.

And to think that the Byrds actually worried about how the English would treat them!

Liverpool's well known Cavern Club, the place which sired the Beatles, was in the red and practically closed down until 23 local Liverpool groups came to the rescue.

Trouble At The Clubs

The Cavern meant a lot to these groups so they decided to play a 12 hour session for free with all of the proceeds going to the club. It was highly successful and although the Cavern is still not completely out of the woods, they have emerged far enough to see a shaft of sunshine through the trees.

Richmond's famed Crawdaddy Club, the scene of the Rolling Stones' first triumphs, has officially closed its doors. Not because of financial problems but because of the thoughtless behavior of a few.

A spokesman for Richmond Athletic Association, which owns the property on which the Crawdaddy was situated, gave the reason behind the shut-down: "It was due to a small handful of idiots doing silly things like breaking windows and driving cars across the rugby and cricket pitches. They have no respect for other people's property. We also had a fight—the first incident in three years and the Richmond Athletic Association decided to close us down," he said.

"But we shall open a new, much more exclusive club in the same area just for the nice genuine people who are in the majority," he promised.

PORTMAN'S PLATTERPOOP

Hollywood—Hoorah, *The Beatles* are here! They're serenading Angelinos, with *Bob Eubank's* aid, August 29-30. Then off to *Pete Marino's* home town, San Francisco on the 31st . . . Tipsville, U.S.A. *The Beatles* will be snuggling-up in a pad in in Coldwater Canyon, and pleeze, don't wake the neighbors when prowling . . . *Buddy (Party Doll) Knox* penned a contract with the hot Warner Bros. label. *Jimmy (I make the hits) Bowen* immediately rushed him into a session and out comes his first goody "A Housefull of Love."

Everyone's talking about *The Supremes*, just wonderful gals. They're heading into the Bay area on Sept. 17 for a one weeker at the Safari Club in San Jose . . . One of the more talented record arrangers and producers is Colpix's *Hank Levine*. His talent glows brightly in *Paul Petersen's* "You Don't Need Money" . . . Versatile *Stan Worth's* "Fingers" on RCA Victor is worth the investment . . . *The Leaves* are happening is a most profound statement. Their record "Too Many People" is happening! . . . Columbia Records initialed *The Rising Sons* to a four page contract . . . *Sam The Sham and The Pharaohs* are competing with *Herman's Hermits* in MGM's "When the Boys Meet the Girls" . . . A note for Herman's fans, he speaks in the new "Girl Crazy" flicker. Yep, he's one and two lining it.

Herb Alpert and His Tiajuana Brass are guest-starring on five networks TV shows this Fall: Al Hirt, Danny Kaye, Hollywood Palace, Andy Williams and Red Skelton. All love that Mexican sound . . . Guess What?? Why keep you in stitches, two new teen dance shows, the local type, are set for the fall season: "Boss Set" and "Hollywood Discotheque" . . . Medical Info: *Vince Edwards* has a new Colpix elpee "For Lovers; Just What The Doctor Ordered" . . . so wife, *Kathy (Body Beautiful) Kersh*, signed with *Dick Howard* for a Shindig appearance.

A new dance step called "Mermail" is featured in MGM's "Glass Bottom Boat." An illustrated booklet with instructions is free for the asking. Don't call or write us, contact the publicity office of MGM in Culver City . . . *Roy Orbison* John Hancocked on MGM pact, for both recordings and films. Now everyone's getting into the film act . . . *Jill Stuart* has waved her first for Columbia. Doesn't mean anything to you well, she's Mrs. Chad Stuart of *Chad & Jeremy* . . . Coosome twosome. *Jackie De Shannon* and a chap named *Sam*, so the story goes . . . "How To Stuff A Wild Bikini" by *The Kingsmen* on Wand is selling like a low cut bikini should . . . "Flipper" TV series will have a title tune sung by RCA's Frankie Randall.

Jackie & Gayle are flying high, all big TV shows are seeking this talented and lovely duo . . . Courage pleeze, this is not platter news, but they'll be making a pilot about the "hero" of all red-blooded youth, *Feerless Fosdick*. I had to relate! . . . A new book is called "Hollywood Kook Book" and it's not about food, but the "A Go Go" set . . .

Artists attention: Free copy, to first 25 Scribblers, who can best depict the author of the "Platterpoop" of "Fly in The Buttermilk" by *The Fearsome Foursome* . . . funniest one will be shown in The BEAT . . . and in the immortal words of Sig Sakowicz as he summed up *The Beatles'* appearance, "It's like being in the State Home of the Screamers" . . . later baby!

KRLA ARCHIVES

BEAT GOES TO THE MOVIE

How To Stuff A Wild Bikini

By Jim Hamblin

If taken seriously, this could turn out to be a rather corny picture about life as it really isn't.

But it was made by American-International and all in fun. And that's just what the audience has—fun.

The story sort of involves Boy Friend Frankie Avalon on a South Sea island on Naval Reserve duty, with only girls to take up the slack time. Lovely hula-hipped sarong-wearing Polynesian lovelies, with no "slack" at all!

Back at the ranch (Malibu) girl friend Annette Funicello (former Mickey Mouse clubber) is holding off the advances of dashing Dwayne Hickman, who has about the same philosophy toward girls as those Polynesian girls have toward men.

Frankie baby, worrying whether or not his girl back home is being faithful (?) has a witch doctor who looks like Buster Keaton (by golly, it IS Buster Keaton!) whomp up a brew that will let him look in on things.

Malibu has rocks and the story line hits them once in a while, but who really cares. The world's oldest kid, Mickey Rooney, also makes an appearance as an advertising executive promoting a cross-country cycle race.

And therein lie the thrills and mucho spills. Annette thinks it's fun to ride on a Honda, so off she goes with Dwayne baby.

There are certain other plot complications, as explained by the witch doctor, but we don't need to go into that now.

The only problem with this picture is the fact that *Life* is never like that. Which makes it entertaining, and that's what movies are for.

But has anyone EVER seen girls like that on the beach, or anywhere else? They're just too much. But don't stop the projector!

The wiggy title (done in colored animated putty) gets WILD BIKINI off to a delightful start, and we are rarely left alone after that.

American International is the studio that makes the Vincent Price—Edgar Allan Poe horror pictures and they stuff the same know-how even into wild bikinis, including fine original music (Les Baxter) and plenty of it.

The pelican never gets any screen credit, and we think he ought to sue. He turned in one of the best acting jobs in the whole film. The bird, by the way, is a spy. Watch out for him.

HOW TO STUFF A WILD BIKINI is one of the most pleasant instructional films any student ever saw.

STRUMMING HIS GUITAR, John Ashley leads Jody McCrea, Ed Garner, Mike Nader and the Beach Boys, showing us what happen when you know how to stuff a wild bikini.

WHILE THE BOYS FROLIC ON THE BEACH, the lonely Dee Dee (Annette Funicello) serenades her friends. Annette stays covered up in capris and sweater all the way through the picture, but it would take more than that to hide her talent.

KRLA ARCHIVES

KRLA Tunedex

EMPEROR HUDSON

CHARLIE O'DONNELL

CASEY KASEM

JOHNNY HAYES

BOB EUBANKS

DAVE HULL

DICK BIONDI

BILL SLATER

KRLA BEAT
6290 Sunset, No. 504
Hollywood, Cal. 90028

This Week	Last Week	Title	Artist
1	1	LIKE A ROLLING STONE	Bob Dylan
2	2	I GOT YOU BABE	Sonny & Cher
3	3	IT AIN'T ME BABE	The Turtles
4	5	YOU WERE ON MY MIND	We Five
5	8	UNCHAINED MELODY/HUNG ON YOU	Righteous Brothers
6	4	ALL I REALLY WANT TO DO	Cher
7	10	CALIFORNIA GIRLS	Beach Boys
8	12	BABY I'M YOURS	Barbara Lewis
9	17	HELP/I'M DOWN	The Beatles
10	7	IT'S THE SAME OLD SONG	The Four Tops
11	16A	NOTHING BUT HEARTACHES	The Supremes
12	11	SATISFACTION	The Rolling Stones
13	6	HOLD ME, THRILL ME, KISS ME	Mel Carter
14	9	PAPA'S GOT A BRAND NEW BAG	James Brown
15	—	EVE OF DESTRUCTION	Barry McGuire
16	33	LAUGH AT ME	Sonny Bono
17	22	YOU TELL ME WHY	Beau Brummels
18	16B	YOU'D BETTER COME HOME	Petula Clark
19	36	SUMMER NIGHTS	Marianne Faithfull
20	14	WHAT'S NEW PUSSYCAT?	Tom Jones
21	15	CARA-MIA	Jay and The Americans
22	30	DOWN IN THE BOONDOCKS	Billy Joe Royal
23	19	TAKE ME BACK	Little Anthony & The Imperials
24	25	WHO'LL BE THE NEXT IN LINE	The Kinks
25	13	YES, I'M READY	Barbara Mason
26	20	SAVE YOUR HEART FOR ME	Gary Lewis & The Playboys
27	18	I'M HENRY THE VIII, I AM	Herman's Hermits
28	23	I'LL FEEL A WHOLE LOT BETTER	The Byrds
29	26	LET HER DANCE	Bobby Fuller Four
30	38	DO YOU BELIEVE IN MAGIC	Lovin' Spoonfull
31	31	JU JU HAND	Sam The Sham & The Pharoahs
32	32	COLOURS/JOSIE	Donovan
33	—	ROSES AND RAINBOWS	Danny Hutton
34	—	I'LL ALWAYS LOVE YOU	The Spinners
35	—	LOOKING THRU THE EYES OF LOVE	Gene Pitney
36	—	I'M A HAPPY MAN	Jive Five
37	40	THAT'S WHERE IT'S AT	T-Bones
38	—	HEART FULL OF SOUL	The Yardbirds
39	—	MY GIRL SLOOPY	Little Caesar
40	—	I'M THE WOLF MAN	Round Robin

BULK RATE
U.S. Postage
PAID
Los Angeles, Calif.
Permit No. 25497

KRLA ARCHIVES

KRLA BEAT

Volume 1, Number 25   LOS ANGELES, CALIFORNIA   15 Cents   September 4, 1965

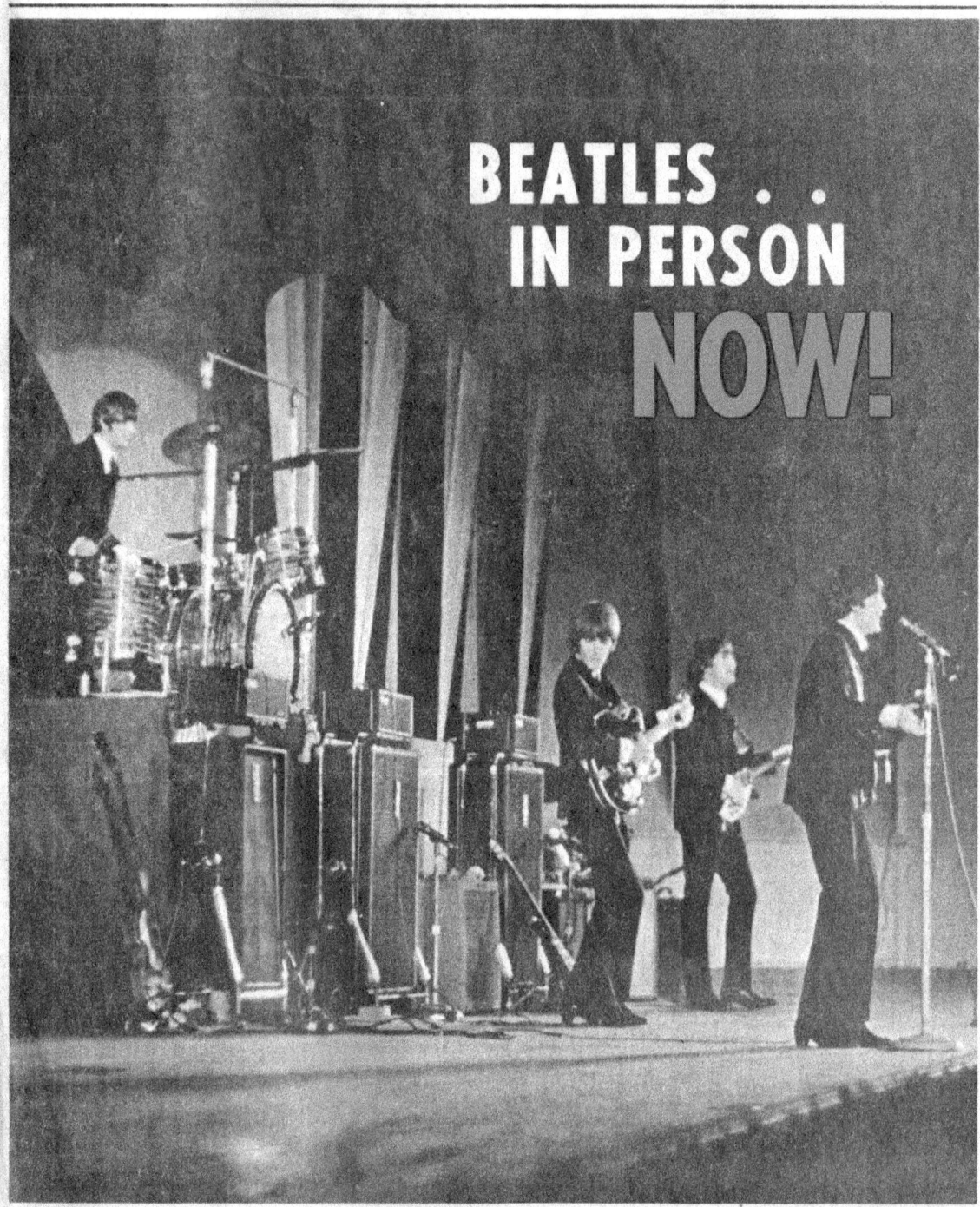

BEATLES.. IN PERSON NOW!

KRLA ARCHIVES

KRLA BEAT

Los Angeles, California September 4, 1965

'A-Beatleing We Go'

A-Beatleing we did go,
 A-Beatleing we did go;
All around the actors homes —
 A-Beatling we did go.

Thru' the bushes and 'round the stones,
 Over the fence we flew;
Thru' mud, and leaves, and poison plants —
 For a better Beatle view.

Sloshing thru' the slushy ravine,
 A-Beatleing we did go;
Over the fence with the barbed-wire top,
 A-PAINFULLY did we go!

A bottle, a battle, a Beatle at last,
 A policeman who doesn't care;
The city has laws and they have clubs,
 There'll be no Beatleing there!

A roar of motors, a cloud of dust,
 Ten cars all driving slow;
A flash of black, and then — they're gones
 A-Beatleing we did go!!

NEIGHBORS UPSET
George Has Problems With His Home Life

By LOUISE CRISCIONE

Those of you planning on traipsing to England to visit George Harrison had better beware — George's neighbors are furious!

Too many of George's devoted fans have been driving, walking, or hitch-hiking out to his house in hopes of at least capturing a fleeting glimpse of the distinguished Mr. Harrison M.B.E.

That was all fine and good (at least from the fans' standpoint) but in the process of tracking down George, his fans have also been trampling down all of his neighbors' petunias, chysanthemums and daisies.

All in all, since George's advent there has been nothing but trouble in that particular corner of the once quiet and reserved Surrey countryside.

His patient neighbors stood the noise, the trampled flowers and the wailing girls for quite awhile. They didn't dig it, but they they hoped that maybe if they just avoided it, it would go away.

Neighbors Explode

So they gritted their teeth and waited and waited AND waited. But each day only brought another horde of fans and another patch of trampled petunias.

It was inevitable — the spark finally reached the dynamite and the neighbors exploded. They held a kind of block meeting to chart their course of action.

Everyone spoke his piece and after hours of deliberation a decision was reached: War was officially declared on all George Harrison fans!

Neighbors' Union

Near-by neighbors banded together in a sort of Neighbors' Union which organized complete with by-laws and the whole thing. And the very first by-law instructed all to summon the police at the first sign of anything which looked suspiciously like it might be a Beatle fan.

Anyway, we just thought we'd warn you. The Neighbors Union is now in full operation — so don't visit George. And if you're abroad and determined to visit him anyway, then at least make sure that you don't look to much like a Beatle fan.

Oh, and one more thing — please be careful about trampling George's neighbors' petunias, chrysanthmums and daisies.

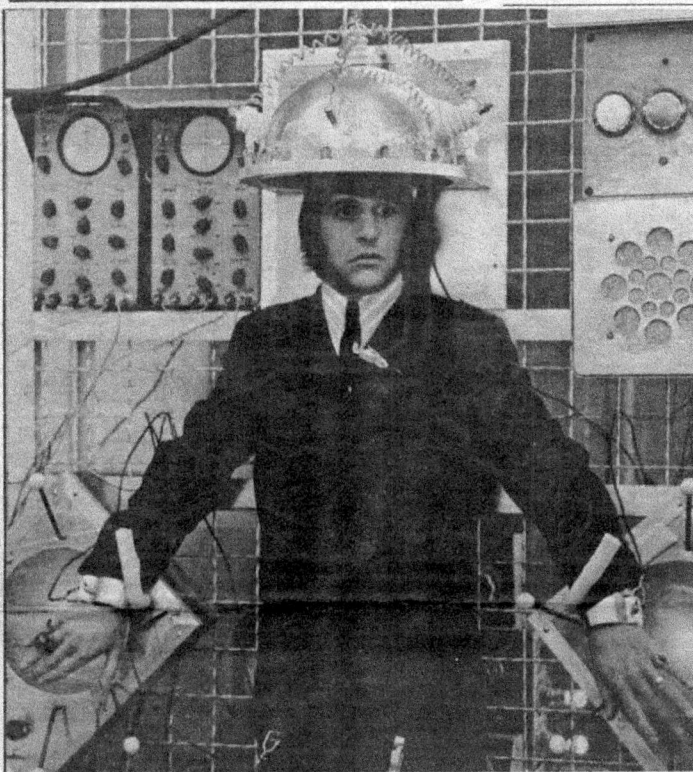

"HELLLLPP" . . . RINGO GETS A CHARGE OUT OF MOVIE ROLE

LOOKING AHEAD
Will Beatles Return? They Came This Year

Beatlemania is made up of many things. One of them is anticipation.

We wait breathlessly for them to come to America. When they arrive we're overjoyed to see them, but we start waiting for them to come back again long before they even leave our country.

The Beatles have just arrived in California, and we are already wondering when we'll get to see them again. And some of us aren't just wondering when. We're wondering IF.

The arguments against a third tour are reasonably sound. Beatlemania has become permanent. The Beatles need never worry about their popularity dying, and no longer have to work so inhumanly hard at being the world's star attraction.

It makes sense. The Beatles have every right to stop rushing all over the globe, and nothing to lose if they choose to take a well-deserved rest on their laurels.

But if this possibility is worrying you, stop and remember how long ago the concrete of Beatlemania hardened.

Was it before plans for this present tour were cemented? Or was it after?

It was before. When the Beatles returned from America in 1964, they had our country in the palms of their hands. And they still do.

The Beatles don't have to be here next year. But don't let it keep you up nights. They don't have to be here this year either.

If you want to start waiting for Beatles 1966, feel free to. We started weeks ago!

FLANKED BY PROFILES of John (left) and Paul (right), Beatles' manager Brian Epstein (facing camera) and KRLA's Bob Eubanks iron out final details in preparations for the Beatles' eagerly-awaited concerts at The Hollywood Bowl.

Huge Crowds Expected At Beatle Film

"Help," a most unsuitable term for the Beatles' second movie financially speaking, has opened in theatres across the United States to rave reviews and bulging box office registers.

From the initial box office returns in both the U.S. and England, "Help" is running way ahead of the Beatles' first movie, "A Hard Day's Night," so far as the gross intake is concerned.

KRLA Scoops

The technicolor Beatles opened their citywide engagement on September 1 — but, of course, KRLA helped 500 of you Beatle fans drool at the Fab Four at an exclusive premiere at the Carthay Circle Theatre on August 23 — thus scooping everyone else in Los Angeles by a full nine days!

By giving KRLA the Los Angeles premiere of "Help"; and by allowing us to present them at the Hollywood Bowl for two years in a row (despite many other offers), it looks as though the Beatles are trying to tell us something — like KRLA *is* the number one Beatle station in the whole world!

KRLA ARCHIVES

LOVE, NOT DESTRUCTION, IS BARRY McGUIRE'S MESSAGE

By Eden

(Editor's Note: A burly ex-construction worker has caused an overnight sensation with his recording of "Eve of Destruction." Barry McGuire has also caused a raging controversy.

Does he really believe we are on the the "eve of destruction?" What are his beliefs? What is he really like as an individual? Most of the answers are contained in this exclusive and highly interesting BEAT interview.)

Beauty is a fragile and sometime very abstract thing. It is found in all forms of nature—in flowers, in twilight skies, and occasionally in human beings. Today I met a beautiful human being.

Barry McGuire's appearance is deceptive, for he looks too manly and masculine to be called beautiful.

His own words provide a far better picture of his thoughts and personality—a much more accurate description than anyone else could ever provide. Thus, with few comments or translations on the part of this reporter, you may form your own impressions by listening in on one side of a conversation with this remarkable, interesting and compelling young man.

A Child Again

Speaking lightly of his childhood, Barry laughs.

"I'm still having it," he chuckles; "I haven't grown up yet! I almost grew up about five years ago, and I caught myself just in time. So now I'm happy to say that I'm a child again!

"I used to work in construction. I had to buy sandwiches off a lunch wagon and eat my lunch every day, and that didn't show me too much! Then every Friday when I got paid—by Monday I was broke again. So I had to borrow money from the guys at work so I could eat all week and this went on for four or five years.

"One day I was in a folk house —a coffee house—down at Laguna Beach and I heard some people singing that I really enjoyed. Everybody would just sit around and sing; it was like a non-competition hootenanny, where no matter who you were or what you sounded like—if you only knew two chords on the guitar—that was great. Somebody let me borrow their guitar so I played four of the strings and sang a song, and everybody liked it so much that my ego went crazy! I thought; 'Aw, that was really great!' so I bought a guitar that following week for ten dollars, from a guy at work—plus he bought my sandwiches that day!!

Joins The Christies

"One thing led to another and I went to a party about two months later and somebody at the party owned a club and asked me if I wanted to work one night a week in his club. I said 'sure' and for five hours I sang the same fifteen songs! But people kept teaching me new ones, and then—on to the New Christy Minstrels. I had been working with Barry Kane; he and I had a duo called 'Barry and Barry'—it sounds like some weird disease! — and Randy Sparks heard us and invited us to try with the Christies.

"I used to sing in the center of the group and all the promotions said 'under the direction of Randy Sparks;' so, I'd go to parties and everybody would call me Randy. Then I'd try to tell them who I was and nobody would believe me; they thought I was putting them on! I even got a review one time down in the South which said, 'Big, blonde-haired Randy Sparks looked the part with his baggy pants.' So I sent the review to Randy and I said, 'Would you please try dressing yourself a little bit better when you go onstage!!'

Conquers Temper

"I have gotten to the point now where I can catch my temper, stop it, and turn it around; turn it into love. I think when you're mad you're out of line with yourself. Y'know what causes temper? Fear. And fear always turns into rage. If you get mad, and then the other guy gets mad—well, what have you got? It's so much better to love. If you're insecure, you're afraid. I do what pleases me, and if someone else enjoys it—great!

"Everybody has their ups and downs; sometimes, when you're down, you don't realize how groovy everything is. So, you try—when you're feeling down, when you're feeling blue, when you feel that you don't have the capacity to compete—then you seem to go around (I've done

..... BARRY McGUIRE

it) and you try to bring everybody else down to your level. You don't want to be alone in your misery. So, hey—I'm just a person; that's all. I've had my ups and downs.

"You can't change the way people think; you can't tell them what to think or how to think. But you can show them a way, or offer them a door and then it's up to them. They can open the door and look through it and see what's on the other side, and then if anything there strikes home, or there's anything they can identify with—well then, it's up to them whether they retain it or not. But you yourself can't change anybody— except yourself.

"The most important person in the world is myself—and yourself. After me comes everybody else, and every*thing* else, everything that exists in the entire universe, galaxy, all the stars, and that goes into the microscopic in both directions; because, we're only living in just one little portion of infinity. We have the world that we live in, and when you really start thinking about it, it's infinite. So, there's really no good, and there is no bad; there are only *things, things*. And maybe some things you don't enjoy—so, don't do those things. And if you enjoy things, you *do* them. But you

TURN TO PAGE 6

'DESTRUCTION' COMPOSER

Eve Of Destruction
By P. F. Sloan

The Eastern world it is explodin'
Violence flarin', and bullets loadin'
You're old enough to kill — but not for votin'
You don't believe in war but what's that gun you're totin'
And even the Jordon River has bodies floatin'
But you tell me over and over and over again, my friend
Ah you don't believe we're on the Eve of Destruction.

Don't you understand what I'm trying to say
Can't you feel the fears that I'm feelin' today
If the button is pushed there's no running away
There'll be no one to save with the world in a grave
Take a look around you boy it's bound to scare you, boy
And you tell me over and over and over again, my friend
Ah you don't believe we're on the Eve of Destruction.

Yeah, my blood's so mad — feels like coagulatin'
I'm sittin' here just contemplatin'
I can't twist the truth — it knows no regulation
A handful of senators don't pass regulation
And marches alone can't bring integration
When human respect is disentegratin'
This whole crazy world is just too frustratin'
And you tell me over and over and over again, my friend
Ah you don't believe we're on the Eve of Destruction.

Think of all the hate there is in Red China
Then take a look around to Selma, Alabama
You may leave here for four days in space
But when you return it's the same old place
The pounding of the drums, the pride and disgrace
You can bury your dead but don't leave a trace
Hate your next door neighbor but don't forget to say Grace
And tell me over and over and over again, my friend
You don't believe we're on the Eve of Destruction.

KRLA ARCHIVES

WE GOT YOU BACK AGAIN!

KRLA ARCHIVES

...MICK JAGGER ...BILL WYMAN ...BRIAN JONES ...CHARLIE WATTS ...KEITH RICHARD

THE ROLLING STONES — R & B IMPORTERS

English Artists Find 'Soul' Music Is More Than Skin Deep

By Louise Criscione

The soul of today's music, the place "where it's at" is rhythm and blues. The type of music, this "soul," has been around the U.S. for decades now and it has always captured a small number of hard core fans, but it has only recently gained acceptance by the whole pop scene.

Ironically, R&B has been introduced to the American teenager by the British! Both the Rolling Stones and the Animals, in particular, are responsible for bringing American blues back into the spotlight, back before the eyes and listening ears of the Stateside teenager.

This situation brings up an interesting question—can a white group, and particularly an English group, successfully imitate the American Negro blues sound?

Eric Burdon, lead singer for the Animals and probably one of the most "soul" singers around, does not feel that just any Caucasian can sing the blues with the authentic feel of the American Negro.

Must Feel It

"Not unless he feels it deeply or is intimately acquainted with it. So that's why the trip to the deep South was especially important to us. It gave us the opportunity to do both," Eric explained.

Hilton Valentine, lead guitarist for the Animals, elaborated on Eric's statement: "There's no escaping the fact that the blues is the music of the colored man. It has a deeper meaning in the States, especially in the deep South, where they have the racial problem and widespread discrimination against minorities."

Eric believes that in England the racial problem is entirely different. He says: "So the difficulty has been in relating ourselves to a problem across the ocean."

Perhaps the biggest and most popular R&B group on the American and English pop scene is the Rolling Stones.

The sound of the Stones has undergone something of a change. But the Stones still play "soul"—"soul" which is strongly influenced by American Negroes such as Muddy Waters, Otis Redding, and Howlin' Wolf.

No Resentment

How do these colored blues artists feel about this adoption of their sound by people within the pop field? Mick reveals: "Muddy called us 'his boys' in a magazine article so we must have some acceptance with those people."

Brian Jones agrees with Mick that the Stones have gained a certain amount of acceptance in the dark world of R&B. "We went to the Apollo Theater for the NAACP benefit show and Wilson Pickett introduced us to the audience and then did an imitation of us.

"And if James Brown is around town he calls us and leaves messages. They accept what we're trying to do," Brian continued.

The Stones now record exclusively in the U.S. Why? Do they feel that they can get their "soul" sound here and not in England?

Brian answers that question by saying: "It's a great place to cut a record and America is a great place to be generally."

R & B Capital

Although R&B has finally got a foothold in Britain, America is still the soul of the "soul" sound, and don't ever let anyone ever tell you any different.

Brian admits that: "You can't get a lot of this blues stuff back home, any more than you can go to a club and find an artist that you can learn something from."

Do the English groups learn from other English groups who attempt to make the same sort of sound, or are they exclusively tutored by the American Negro singers?

Mick answers that question by saying: "We all love to dig the real sounds of R&B, to hear the groups and the bands that have something to say. But there isn't really anything in England today that any of us would go to see expecting to learn something."

Mick summed up the entire question of Englishmen attempting to sing American "soul." "It's all right here in America. You've got to come here to get the real thing."

Room For All

But R&B is a big world—in it there is room for everybody. At least, there is room for such people as the Animals and the Rolling Stones. These people have spread the gospel of R&B to places where it had never before been preached. In doing this, they have inadvertently helped American R&B and our American R&B artists.

So next time you start to accuse the English of doing nothing but imitating the Americans—stop and think about it. Remember that such names as Muddy Waters, Wilson Pickett and Howlin' Wolf were once totally alien to the average American teenager. And now these greats in the R&B field, although still underrated and under-appreciated, are becoming much better known.

You can consider the entire question now resolved—The roots of the "soul" sound are deeply embedded in American soil, but it's branches have now spread across the ocean to England.

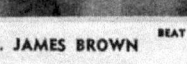

....JAMES BROWN   BEAT Photo by C. Boyd

KRLA ARCHIVES

Tips to Teens

Q: *Is it harmful to shave your legs every other day? Also, isn't there some product a girl can use to make this necessary chore a little less difficult (and painful)?*
(Olga M.)

A: Every other day is quite a rigid scedule for leg-shaving, but during the summer months, many girls don't have much choice. It won't really hurt anything, except make your legs a bit raw, and yes, there is a product you can use to make all this a lot more pleasant. It's by Clairol and it's called Ultra Smooth. It serves as both a shaving cream and an "after shave" lotion. (You just rub in what's left of the cream.)

Q: *This isn't a beauty question, but I hope you will answer it just the same. What is a girl supposed to do when she's out with a boy and he offers an opinion that you completely disagree with? I mean about something like "girls shouldn't do this" or about politics or prejudice. Are you supposed to not say anything, or should you go ahead and offer your own opinion, knowing it might start an argument?*
(Penny R.)

A: Wow, that's a question and a half. When any person ventures an opinion on a "controversial" issue, that person is asking for it, and you have a perfect right to counter the opinion with your own. However, if the boy is someone you'd like to get to know better, it might be a good idea for you to wait and express your own feelings after your relationship is a bit closer. If you just can't resist expressing them now do it in a nice way and maybe you can avoid the discussion turning into a battle.

Q: *I once bought a bar of transparent soap that was tan in color. It worked very well, but I don't remember the name of it and don't know what to ask for. Can you help me?*
(Elaine R.)

A: Many complexion soaps are of the amber transparent variety, so there's no way for us to tell which one you're on the look-out for. We can recommend a good one though. Neutrogena, which sells for one dollar a bar, and is more than worth it.

Q: *I like to wear my hair in a pony tail, but I'm afraid my hair will start breaking if I wear this style too often. I've heard that rubber bands are very bad on the hair. Is there some other way I could keep a pony tail neat?*
(Marsha K.)

A: Try putting several strips of scotch tape around your pony tail, and then tying it up with a strong ribbon. Unlese your hair is very heavy, this should work. If it doesn't, try putting the rubber band over the scotch tape.

HINT OF THE WEEK

I read in the BEAT about a girl who has a lipstick problem. I used to have the same difficulty. No matter what color lipstick I bought, it always turned red when I put it on. Then I discovered a specially-formulated lipstick base which prevents the top lipstick from darkening. It's called "Lights Up Yellow" by Dorothy Gray and you can buy it for $1.25 at any cosmetic counter. The reason why lipstick turns red on some people is because their lip coloring has a more bluish tint than others. This product really takes care of the problem and fast!
(Alice L.)

If you have a question you'd like answered or a hint you'd like printed, please drop a line to Tips To Teens c/o The BEAT.

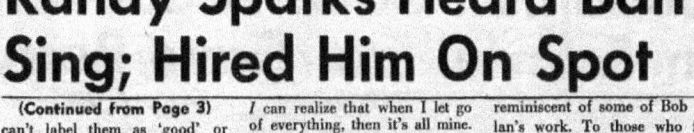

Randy Sparks Heard Barry Sing; Hired Him On Spot

(Continued from Page 3)

can't label them as 'good' or 'bad.'

Why Hate, Killing?

But why is it that other people hate and kill?

"Because they feel inferior," Barry explained. "Because they have been told so from the time they were a baby. They've been restricted; they've been told they can't do things; they've been told they don't do the things they do as well as other people do. So they feel inferior and they don't even want to do those things, because other people do them so much better.

"It's the pleasure, the enjoyment, that the individual soul gets out of the individual act. There's so much more beauty. It's just like the flower: One flower doesn't taste good, another flower does. So you eat the flower that does. And it is the same way with love and hate. Hate doesn't feel good. It does not sit right with me. And so I'd rather love than hate. If everybody loved, and if everybody thought that everybody else comes first, that would mean that everybody in the world would think that you come first, so you'd really never have to worry about yourself. You could just go around doing things for other people and everybody else would be doing things for others, and *I'm* others. So that means I would be taken care of. And the only way that I can *start* that, is to believe in it myself and to do it myself. Now if other people don't want to like me, if they don't dig the way I wear my hair, clothes I wear—well, that's okay! Because it doesn't change the way I feel about them.

"As soon as people realize— I'll bring this home—as soon as I can realize that when I let go of everything, then it's all mine. Everything then becomes mine— a *free* mine, an *honest* mine. It's mine to play with, it's mine to enjoy. Because I know that it doesn't belong to me. I'm just gonna use it for a little while, and as soon as I get through, somebody else will come along and use it. Whatever it is—a car, a house, the enjoyment of another person's company. I'm not going to be with you for but just a few minutes, and then you will be with somebody else; talking to them. So my pleasure right now—that I'm getting from you—is *my* pleasure. Everything I say to you is for *me*, and everything you say to me is for *you.*"

As a child, Barry did a great deal of travelling and moving about, and he attended five or six different grammar schools. Although he remembers having regretted the fact that he was unable to make and maintain many lasting friendships then, he finds himself grateful for the experience now.

"I want to take my little boy with me when I start travelling again. I found out that all the things people told me about other people being different than me is wrong. Everybody gets hungry, and wants a home and laughs; just like me. Everybody is just like me, therefore I *am* everybody and I have to love everybody."

Controversial Disc

Much controversy has been stirred up by the lyrics of Barry's first solo record—"Eve of Destruction," produced by Lou Adler on Dunhill Records. It was written by a brilliant nineteen-year-old by the name of P. F. Sloan, and is somewhat reminiscent of some of Bob Dylan's work. To those who find the song too depressing to be enjoyable, Barry says:

"Of course there is the possibility that we are on the eve of destruction; but it doesn't have to be. I don't think it does. I recorded it so people could see that while there *is* that possibility, there are also *better* alternatives. Now we don't have to wait till 'the sun comes up,' or a 'new day dawns' to do something about it.

"I think the Beatles have helped to start a whole new exciting thing for the teenagers which is gonna take over: it's happiness.

"Yes, I would like to be a big star. I would like to be big because I could do so much more; I could communicate with so many more people. Communication is very important.

"Yes, I like money very much. I like all the toys you can buy with it, and all money is for is to buy toys. The whole world is a toy.

"If we can wait around for all the kids to grow up—if we can hang around for just one more generation—it'll be a pretty good world!"

As with a thing of beauty you observe Barry McGuire as a human being. You listen to his records, you read his words and a few of his many concepts, Then you stop and think for a moment and realize that you have only just begun acquaintance with a compelling, talented, and dynamic young man.

Dear Susan:
By Susan Frisch

Dear Susan:
Could you please tell me how I can meet Herman's Hermits, and do they all have girlfriends, or is there still hope for me?
(Marsha Abrumson.)

Dear Marsha:
When you ask whether they have girlfriends I really can't say. Here in California they do each have a girl that they are particularly interested in. The girls that they date are also fans of theirs but not in the same way you are.

I'm sure Herman and the others have seen loads of girls that they would like to take out, but half the time these girls scare them to death.

I can't tell you how to meet them, because I myself am not sure but when and if you do, DON'T start screaming and running all over the place. This is why they come to see the same girls all the time when they are here, because these girls are quiet, subdued and act as though they couldn't care less about Herman and his silly old Hermits. So good luck and remember, act like a lady.

☆ ☆

Can you please tell what Donovan is really like off stage?
(Louise Davis.)

I am happy that someone finally asked me this question, for after interviewing Donovan last week I have nothing to say except the best about him. He is one of the nicest and friendliest persons I have ever met. He can't do enough for people and he really is what he appears to be.

There is no front about him, and the character he portrays on stage is really Donovan. I hope you can meet him some time and see these things for yourself.

☆ ☆

Could you please tell what the English Beau Brummell's real name is and little bit about him.
(Paula Derfich.)

Dear Paula:
Beau says his real name *is* Beau Brummell. He was born on September 26, 1942, and is 22 years old. He was born in England, but I don't know where.

☆ ☆

Will you please tell me where I can write to Marianne Faithfull and be sure of getting an answer.
(Barbara Fineman.)

Dear Barbara:
The best way to write to Marianne is to her London address: Marianne Faithfull. c/o Miss Brenda Howard, 18 Hearne Road, Chriswick, London, W. 4.

☆ ☆

Could you please tell me about the new movie that Herman and the Hermits just made?
(Jackie Jackson.)

Dear Jackie:
Boy, have I got news to tell you about their movie! As you may already know, it's called "Where the Boys Meet the Girls," and along with the Hermits it stars Connie Francis, Harve Presnell, Sam the Sham and the Pharaohs, Louis Armstrong, and Liberace.

The Hermits will play college students at a Western college, and they also will be doing two songs—one which is new, "Listen People"—"Bidin' My Time," from the play "Girl Crazy." It will be in Panavision and Metro-Color and should be released around Christmas time.

In September the Hermits will be back to begin filming another movie called "There's No Place Like Space," which will be shot on location. It will be released around the first of the year.

TALENTED BRENDA HOLLOWAY is on a dream tour which makes her the envy of every other female vocalist — and yet it's a tough assignment to appear on the same program with the Beatles. The Tamla-Motown recording star is touring the U.S. with them, appearing in each of their concerts. It's quite an honor. With their choice of just about any girl singer in the world to appear on their programs, the Beatles immediately chose Brenda.

KRLA ARCHIVES

Buddhism Gains A Convert In Colorful Star Dave Berry

One of the most popular solo artists in England and one of the most unusual young men on the pop scene is a lad by the name of Dave Berry.

If you are not immediately familiar with Dave, he is tall and unconventionally good-looking, and as he sings he moves about the stage in a way which can only be described as slow motion.

Nearly as off-beat as his maneuvers on stage are some of Dave's own ideas. Speaking of loneliness he philosophizes:

"Sometimes I think about the 'lonely' bit. I think you're born alone, die alone . . . . and you might as well live alone. But that is not ALWAYS my attitude. For instance I have terrible nerves before going on stage. That's one time when I really need somebody with me.

Tough Problem

"That's when I think about marriage. It's a tough problem for me. Sometimes I think how much I'd like to be married, to have a girl with me all the time. Then things change . . . and I think it might be a bit of a drag.

"I like sitting up, by myself, in the middle of the night. I'm definitely a night person. You can sort of think about life. In the daytime . . well, there's too much going on to think. To sort out your innermost thoughts."

Buddhist Convert

Aside from his contemplations on loneliness, Dave has also given much thought to religion. In this area as well as in others, Dave is somewhat off-beat and unconventional, and he is the first to admit it.

"I'm a Buddhist. I know that sounds a bit odd, coming from a Sheffield lad. But really what I mean is that I follow the Buddhist way of life. It all started with watching a religious program on television. Mr. Christmas Humphreys was talking about how he became a Buddhist — a Far Eastern religion. I thought it was right. And I bought some books about it. It's a very practical way of life. No demands are made upon you except that you simply lead a good life. You become nicer to other people; think about them more. You don't try to tread on other people.

"These are things about the inner me that I've not talked about really before. It makes a change from talking about my big feet — you probably know that my size twelves are about the biggest tootsies in the industry. I find it difficult to get shoes ready-made. Funny thing is that a family friend actually KNITTED me a pair recently — and very comfortable they are, too. I'm thinking of fitting them with leather soles and marketing them. 'Dave Berry's knitted boots'. How about that?"

Stage Routine

As an entertainer, Dave sums up his unusual stage routine for his fans.

"People keep asking me about how I got all those movements on stage. Like hiding behind my upturned coat collar and so on. Well, the honest truth is that when I first started working in clubs in the Sheffield area, the stages were much too small for me to move my gigantic feet around. So I had to make do with standing quite still — and letting my hands and eyes do the rest: It's stuck. But I'll just say that when I'm on stage, I regard every single moment as being part of the act, even the introductions. I love working . . but when I'm starry-eyed and stage-struck.

"Even though, as I was saying, it can be a very lonely life."

Perhaps it is a lonely life at times, but Dave Berry has brought a lot of warmth and happiness to his many fans in the past, and unless his size twelve knitted boots get in the way somehow — there is a good chance that he will go right on doing just that.

In America, Dave has been seen on Shindig and the special Beatle program. He is due to appear on Shindig again this fall.

A BEAT EDITORIAL

TOLERANCE

Hate is a powerful word and an even more powerful emotion; so powerful as to be awesome at times.

There are some people who are very sensitive to, and appalled by hate, and find it difficult to rationalize its existence.

P. F. Sloan is such a person. He is young — just nineteen years old — talented, and very sensitive, And he has written a song called "The Eve of Destruction," recorded by Barry McGuire.

The song has been called a "protest song" and has been denounced by certain extremist groups. It has been labeled a "message song" which mirrors all of the hatred in the world today.

For many people, however, it is simply an expression of truth which vocalizes their inner feelings and then defines the problems at hand and warns that destruction is one possibility if a better alternative solution is not sought.

Barry McGuire says of the song: "I think this is a song people have been singing for a long time, only they haven't known it. I was once looking for somebody's house with some other guys, and we couldn't find the place. I couldn't say exactly what we were looking for. All I could say was 'when I see it, I'll know.' I could never tell anybody what I wanted to say until I found this song. This says it all."

Yes, it does seem to say it all — for some people. For its singer, Barry McGuire, and certainly for its talented composer, P. F. Sloan, it concisely sums up many serious thoughts and opinions.

But what about you? Does it say anything to you, or for you? Or does it merely offend you?

In either case, if you listen to the words carefully and give them very serious consideration, the song is bound to give you some stimulating ideas for sober contemplation.

Whether you believe in it or not, it is still an important emotional spokesman of our time, speaking with the voice of many people. People who care if there is going to be a next time.

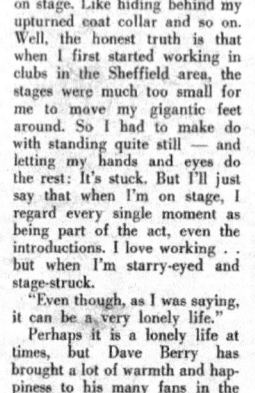

RECORD QUIZ

Boy oh boy. Just LOOK at you. Stretched out there in that hammock, under those tall shade trees, drinking a frosty glass of Goofy Grape. (Okay, okay, so it's a frosty glass of Rootin' Tootin' Raspberry — will you stop bothering us with details?)

Well, if YOU think WE'RE going to let you loll around while we're sweltering in this office, you have another think coming!

Tell you what we're going to do. We're all going to quit our jobs and join you, so you'd better put up another hammock if you don't like a lot of company!

Now, we won't be able to get there for a few hours, but until we do, we don't want any more of this lounging around bit. We've prepared the following record quiz just for you, to make sure you aren't going to just be sitting there enjoying yourself while we're getting all hot and gritty on the freeway.

Do the quiz this instant and we'll see you soon. And none of your "not if I see you first" stuff either!

Record Quiz

Just to make things difficult, we've taken all the members of five of today's top singing groups and mixed up all their names. Now it's up to you to unmix them (or else) and re-group them correctly.

The five groups are The Beatles, The Byrds, Sam The Sham and The Pharoahs, Herman's Hermits and Jay And The Americans. (If we have to work on a day like this, so do you!) And here are the 24 mix-up members!

A. Howie Kane
B. George Harrison
C. Jerry Patterson
D. Derek Leckenby
E. Jay Black
F. Mike Clarke
G. Ray Stinnett
H. John Lennon
I. Keith Hopwood
J. Marty Sanders
K. Karl Green
L. Domingo Samudio
M. Chris Hillman
N. David Martin
O. Gene Clark
P. Paul McCartney
Q. Peter Noone
R. Ringo Starr
S. David Crosby
T. Kenny Vance
U. Butch Gibson
V. Barry Whitwan
W. Jim McQuinn
X. Sandy Deane

ANSWERS (WHICH YOU HAD BETTER NOT BE PEERING AT UPSIDE DOWN OR WE'LL NEVER SPEAK TO YOU AGAIN) (WHICH HAS TO BE THE BEST OFFER YOU'VE HAD ALL DAY): The Beatles are B-H-P-R- (honest!). Sam The Sham and The Pharoahs are L-N-G-C-U (Domingo S. is Sam's real name). Herman's Hermits are Q-K-D-V-I. The Byrds are F-S-W-M-O. Jay And The Americans are E-T-X-J-A. If you made more than four mistakes, you'd better brush up on your group therapy while you're anxiously awaiting our arrival! And while you're at it, mix up another pitcher of Goofy Grape.

"CALIFORNIA GIRLS" DIG THE BEACH BOYS

KRLA ARCHIVES

NEVER QUIT HOPING

Yardbirds' Faith Gave Them 'Soul'

The pop scene of today is a rapidly-changing world in which there are few permanent residents. Singing today and silent tomorrow.

The Rolling Stones left the Crawdaddy Club and the Yardbirds were forced to fly in the airwaves vacated by the Stones, but they're flying high and alone now—and they're glad and we are glad.

Basically, the Yardbirds are an R&B group, but they cut their ties with other British groups by revealing that R&B is an instrumental form of music and vocals should not overpower the sound.

The five Yardbirds dig "raw" American blues and obscure Negro blues singers who formed the basis for the sound which is now being so widely accepted in the pop field.

Success did not come easily for the Yardbirds. They made three records which went absolutely nowhere due mainly to the fact that the group was way ahead of its time. They were attempting to play basic R&B at a time when the kids were just not ready to accept that kind of music or the people who play it.

First Hit

But perserverance does pay off — so the Yardbirds perservered and 16 months later they had a hit with "For Your Love."

Individually, the Yardbirds number five. Keith Relf resembles Brian Jones to some degree so Keith is automatically "in" with the girls. Being born on March 22, 1943 Keith is 22 years old.

We wears his blonde hair long and his blue eyes are clear. Keith sings lead for the group, but his real claim to fame is the fact that he is somewhat of an expert at faking worm-holes in antique furniture.

The remaining four Yardbirds are extremely adept at playing all sorts of weird instruments. Jeff Beck (who is the newest member of the group) plays lead guitar, violin and electric saw! Jeff caught his first glimpse of sunshine on June 24, 1944. His brown hair hangs long and his blue eyes sometimes become black.

Jeff's one ambition in life is to own "a big American car" so that he can practice that for which he is famed—looking innocent when stopped by an irate policeman!

Sound Effects

Friend Jeff has one other little novelty which makes his guitar playing rather unique — on his guitar he can make the sound of a chicken chasing a steam roller. Anyway, he says he can!

Chris Dreja plays rhythm guitar, maracas and foot. He does not mention how he plays foot, but I'm sure he does it very well!

Chris is a mere lad of 19, who celebrates his birthday on November 11. He wears his blonde hair relatively short (well, relatively short for a Yardbird anyway!) and he wears his blue eyes bloodshot. Chris maintains that he is the best-dressed man on the scene, but he fails to mention just which scene!

The Yardbirds' bass guitar and buffoon player is one Paul "Sam" Samwell-Smith. Paul says he was born somewhere in London but he's not exactly sure just where this blessed event occurred. However, he is quite positive that it happened on May 8, 1943.

Since all of the Yardbirds have distinctions, Paul felt that he should be no exception. So he reveals to the world that he comes equipped with built-in negative and positive fingers and voltmeter feet!

Drums?

Jim McCarty is supposed to be the drummer for the group but occasionally one finds him playing triangle beer cans and bath stoppers instead.

Jim states positively that he *does* have eyes and hair, and that he was born in Liverpool July 25, 1943.

After spending two years on the stock exchange (doing what he doesn't say), Jim pronounces show business "a piece of cake."

The Yardbirds are now flying so high up in the stratosphere that it doesn't look as though they will ever come in for a landing!

They are winging their way to America with a whole "Heart Full Of Soul," and assured guesting on this season's first "Hullabaloo," and the sincere hope that the American teenagers will appreciate the type of music which they are laying down.

We're pretty hip—I think we will understand the Yardbirds, don't you?

YARDBIRDS ... LOOKING AHEAD

THE TELEPHONE NEVER STOPS RINGING FOR THE BEATLES, even in remote areas such as this one where they filmed a portion of "HELP." Paul doesn't seem a bit surprised to find a ringing telephone hidden in the tall undergrowth — but he was a little peeved to discover the call was for someone else.

KRLA ARCHIVES

Beatlenotes

Remember when you ordered your Beatle tickets? You probably enclosed a note to the fab foursome, didn't you? Well, you weren't the only one! Nearly every single order contained a personal line or two just for the Beatles and we'd like to share some of those notes with you!

Here are some of the kookiest notes from several kooky folks we're sure you'll recognize.

Jello To Hohn, Paul, Heorge and Ringo:
Hust a note to tell you how jappy I will be to see you. Jurry and send the tickets and please stay in my jotel soon. I will be your bell boy for free if you won't tell the manager. He's a herk!
— Jose Jiminez.

* * *

Messrs. Lennon, McCartney, Harrison and Starr:
I hope you will not think it odd for an English teacher to be ordering tickets to your concert.
Being thought of as a square is the sort of thing with which I could not put up with.
— Mr. Novak.

* * *

Dear Beatles:
I plan to attend your concert, but should I find myself all tied up, I will pass the ticket on to Lt. Gerard. Please let me know if you happen to run across any one-armed men.
— Dr. Richard Kimble.
P.S. I didn't do it.

* * *

Gentlemen:
The party of the first part requests that the four parties of the second part keep him in mind should any trouble result from parties hosted by the parties of the second part.
Huh?
— Perry Mason.

* * *

Dear Boys:
My family and I can hardly wait for your concert. We don't get out much because my wife becomes nervous in strange surroundings, but we feel seeing you in person is well worth the risk.
I regret that Grandpa will be unable to attend, but he thinks rock and roll is terrifying. (He's sure an old bat about some things.)
Incidentally, I have a Beatle cut too. It helped me get ahead in life also.
— Herman Munster.

* * *

Greetings!
Just a line to let you know I'm looking forward to attending your opening.
— Dr. Ben Casey.

"Whatever's Right"

"WHATEVER'S RIGHT" — means that Marli Cooper of 20838 Exhibit Court, Woodland Hills, has won this weeks BEAT cartoon contest. Marli will be receiving two record albums compliments of the BEAT.

The KRLA BEAT is published weekly by BEAT Publications; editorial and advertising offices at 6290 Sunset Boulevard, Suite 504, Hollywood, California 90028.
Single copy price, 15 cents. Subscription price, U.S and possessions, $3 per year or $5 for two years. Canada and foreign rates, $9 per year or $14 for two years.
Exclusive distribution handled by Miller-Freeman Publications, 6328 Lewis Avenue, Long Beach, California. Inquiries should be directed to the attention of David Thomas.

DANCING 7 NIGHTS A WEEK — PANDORA'S BOX — 8118 SUNSET STRIP

Back issues of the KRLA BEAT are still available, for a limited time. If you've missed an issue of particular interest to you, send 15 cents for each copy wanted, along with a self-addressed stamped envelope to:

KRLA BEAT
Suite 504
6290 Sunset Blvd.
Hollywood, California 90028

ISSUES AVAILABLE
- 4/14 — INTERVIEW WITH JOHN LENNON
- 4/21 — INTERVIEW WITH PAUL McCARTNEY
- 4/28 — CHIMP EXCITES TEEN FAIR
- 5/5 — HERMANIA SPREADS
- 5/12 — HERE COME THE BEATLES
- 5/19 — VISIT WITH BEATLES
- 5/26 — FAB NEW BEATLE QUIZ
- 6/16 — BATTLE OF THE BEAT
- 6/30 — PROBY FIRED
- 7/24 — BEATLES TOP STONES
- 7/31 — CHER
- 8/7 — DYLAN
- 8/14 — HERMAN
- 8/21 — STONES TESTIFY
- 8/28 — KRLA PRESENTS THE BEATLES

KRLA ARCHIVES

KRLA'S CASEY KASEM interviews Jewel Akens (center), who gives inside story on his latest Era click, "It's the Only Way to Fly." Jewel also revealed that he'll be winging to Australia Sept. 4 for 10 days. The admiring audience is from Casey's "Shebang" television show.

PERSONALS

Dear KRLA D.J.'s:
I just want to thank you for bringing the Beatles back this year.
Yours truly,
Carol Marquette.

To The D.C. 5's:
To the greatest guys on this earth. I love you and especially Mike!!
A Smith-stricken D.C. 5 fan.

To Dave Hull:
Where's our stamp? Please urn it. Like on a letter maybe? e're waiting, The United ..uzz.
P.S. On second thought—how about you bringing it? Still waiting.
U. S.

To Robin Kingsley:
Thanks for the interview and for showing us how kind you are! Sorry about pushing you in the pool! Tell Ian to write me.
Ian's prez,
Kathy.

To Tommy of the Pool:
"If you need me," "tell me," 'cause my "empty heart" is going "around and around" thinking "it's all over now." I know "we've got a good thing going" so give it just "one more try." Don't let this be "the last time,"
please "have mercy baby." "You can make it if you try" 'cause "everybody needs somebody to love" and "I need you baby."
"That's how strong my love is,"
Lyne.

To All Mick Jagger fans:
We all can't have him, so I'll compromise and show him "How strong my love is." Cheer up, it could be worse. He could get married, you know.
The Mick lover,
Anaheim, Calif.

To Eileen Elson of Walsall, England:
How does it feel to have your name printed in the greatest newspaper ever? Remember, the Byrds and the Beatles rule!
Your Friend,
Susie.

Dear Miko:
We'd love to hear from you.
Luv,
Pam and Linda.

To Denise Kronig of H.B.:
I changed my mind, luv. I'll be taking Fitzie's class again next year with you and Joe (I mean Bruce). See you then.
A Lennon Lover,
(Guess who??)
P.S. Sure wish I had my green squirt gun back.

Beatle Quiz Winner!

We've got one a BEATLE QUIZ WINNER!
mail man is pooped from carting.
We all are sure tired. The ing bags and bags and bags full of Beatle Quiz entries up to us, and we at the BEAT are literally BEAT 'cause we've been correcting all of those Quizzes which he has been so laboriously carting up to us!
Okay, we've made you wait long enough. The winner of the Beatle Quiz Contest is the very lucky Miss Marilyn Wilcox of 1208 San Mateo Drive, San Luis Obispo, California.
Congratulations, Marilyn, from all of us here at the BEAT. We know you will have an absolutely fab time interviewing the four Beatles and watching John, Paul, George and Ringo perform at the Hollywood Bowl in living Beatlecolor!

We'd like to thank all of you (and there were thousands) who entered the Beatle Quiz. You really kept us busy doing our homework but then you know our motto: "Anything for our BEAT readers." Well, almost anything!
Besides Marilyn, we have also chosen two runners-up who will receive record albums and two tickets each to the Beatles San Diego Concert. These lucky girls are Miss Rita Van Voorhis of 2308 Laurel Avenue, Manhattan Beach, California and Miss Maria Inverso of 6724 Tobias Avenue, Van Nuys, California.
Our BEAT congratulations to Rita and Maria — happy listening girls!
And we'll see ya all at the Beatle Concerts, okay?

HELP!

HELP!
I'd like to start a fan club for Limey and the Yanks 'cos I love 'em. For information please write to:
Patty Luna,
909 South 4th Street,
Montebello, Calif. 90640

HELP!
All girl rock 'n' roll group is very interested in knowing what other people think about the idea of female groups. No matter who or where you are, drop us a line. All opinions are welcome. Write to:
Peggy Marcy,
16886 Sausalito Dr.,
Whittier, Calif. 90603

HELP!
Looking for a girl drummer who lives in the Westchester area. If you are between the ages of twelve and fourteen and want to help form a group, please write to:
Judy Leopard,
7939 Chase Ave.,
Los Angeles 45, Calif.

HELP!
Are you a member of a musical group that's looking for a manager? I have absolutely no managing exeperience but plenty of ideas. This inexperience can even be an asset—not knowing the things that "can't be done," we may wind up doing them! I have signed to handle one group but they are not active yet. If you're interested in discussing this, contract:
Diane Snelling,
12131 Roseglen,
El Monte, Calif.

MAIL BOX

Dear BEAT:
I'm writing this letter in hopes that all adults who condemn teenagers will think twice. Let's turn the tables on them.
The other night I attended a baseball game. The majority of spectators were adults and their behavior caused me to write this.
We found our seats all right, but many people were not as fortunate. All night long, people were roused from seats which were not theirs. Just because their seats weren't suitable to them, they would move into better seats which belonged to others.
You have to admit that at teenage concerts we have a sense of fair play. We accept our seats and our luck in getting them (good or bad) and try to make the best of it.
Throughout the game, airplanes, paper balls and empty peanut bags were thrown on the field. Now at our concerts are we cheap? Certainly not!
Why, when we throw stuff at our favorites it costs us something. Maybe it's candy, sandwiches, stuffed animals, or our shoes or boots—but it costs us a pretty penny.
Another point I must bring up is noise. At the game, everyone was yelling. Usually the men seemed to think they knew how to run the game. They were yelling orders to the ball players and telling them what to do at each point in the game.
Now, at our concerts we certainly make noise. But is it the shouts of disagreement? We do not tell the groups how to sing, what to sing, where to stand, etc. If they hit a wrong note, what difference does it make? They're before us in person and that's all that matters.
Now, I know a lot of adults have shunned the very thought of a teenage concert. Well, everybody think about it. You adults go to see your favorites, we go to see ours. It's the same idea, isn't it? We just happen to have different interests.
I guess that's about it. I just had to let the adults think about something. They're just as wild as teenagers when given the chance. So next time, think twice before condemning teenagers' behavior and think about how yours has been lately.
A. M. Richatts.

Hee-Howing Adults

Dear BEAT:
I do hope that you will print this letter in hope that it will make people (especially adults) think. I have just finished watching the Rolling Stones on a certain television show and I am shocked, angry and disgusted.
Honestly, you'd think "adults" would just grow up! They are always saying how rude we teenagers are and that we should follow their "good example." Well, if we are going to be like them we are going to be a bunch of pretty rude and immature people!
As the Stones were putting all they could into a fabulous performance, I was really enjoying myself and happy that the mostly adult audience were grinding their false teeth silently and politely.
Then as Mick was "dancing" the audience burst into laughter. I was really shocked. I could tell the Stones were angry (and I don't blame them one bit) even though they tried to hide their feelings.
And the audience laughed again. Is this what is called "polite manners?" Is that how we are going to act if we don't happen to like an act or because the performers don't look like everyone else?
I myself have sat through acts I didn't care for, but I knew other people enjoyed them and I was not about to hurt the hardworking entertainer's feelings by doing something ridiculous like hee-howing out loud in his face.
I only hope that when we are old and gray and go to see our favorites or watch dogs performing tricks we will have a little more consideration for the other acts on the show.
Teenagers—let's set a better example for adults to follow!
Laurie DeVault.

BEATLE TICKETS FOR SALE
2 for AUGUST 30 Performance (together)
1 for AUGUST 29 Performance
Call Virginia 472-8214
or Barbara 276-7821

KRLA BEAT SUBSCRIPTION

you will SAVE 60% of the regular price!
AN INTRODUCTORY SPECIAL . . . if you subscribe now . . .

☐ 1 YEAR — 52 Issues — $3.00   ☐ 2 YEARS — $5.00

Enclosed is $...........

Send to:..Age:...........

Address:..

City:..................................State:..............Zip:..........

Outside U.S.: $9.00 — 52 Issues

MAIL YOUR ORDER TO: KRLA BEAT
1401 South Oak Knoll Avenue
Pasadena, California 91106

KRLA ARCHIVES

POP QUEENS RAID

The boys sing and the girls scream. This has been the iron-clad law of the record kingdom ever since Frankie Sinatra first opened his baby-blue eyes and crooned to mobs of swooning females.

Have the men won the battle of the sexes in the record industry. We think not. For it is the women, being the main source of record sales, who dictate who will hit the charts.

Yet despite the male monopoly on the rock n' roll industry, groups like the Supremes, female halves of singing duos, like Cher of Sonny and Cher, and women who go it alone, like Lesley Gore, Petula Clark, Brenda Lee, Marianne Faithfull and Cilla Black, manage to break through.

This week the BEAT would like to take a look at some of the female voices who make the charts and add glamour to the world of pop music.

Song Sweethearts

Say top female group and you are speaking of the Supremes. The three, often referred to as "America's No. 1 Sweethearts of Song," have rung up an unparalleled string of winners and should continue to do so.

Female thrushes across the Atlantic have been making more and more of an impression on the American pop world. Among them is Petula Clark, who with "Downtown" was the first British girl to hit the No. 1 spot on the American charts for 12 years.

Another British import, this time from the folk scene, is convent-educated Marianne Faithfull, who once shocked British television viewers by describing a record as "lovely to hear when getting stoned at a party!"

A dangerous contender for Dusty Springfield's title of top British female singer is Sandie Show. Discovered by Adam Faith, Sandie has had several top-five discs on the English charts, despite the fact that she is a comparative newcomer to the pop world.

Miss Dynamite

Meanwhile female vocalists in the United States aren't sitting back while the British take over. A pro in the pop world, Brenda Lee, known as Miss Dynamite, has been scoring points in the record kingdom long before the Beatles were ever heard of.

Recently returned from England with her husband and singing partner Sonny, Cher stepped out of the shower and into the recording studio to become the hottest female voice in the U.S.

Recently she's had as many as three records on the charts at one time. Two of them were sung with spouse Sonny while her solo, "All I Really Want To Do," hit the coveted number one spot.

Party Girl

Lesley Gore, who sang her way into the charts with "It's My Party" in 1963, is still there offereing "Sunshine, Lollipops and Rainbows" to music lovers.

Other female voices, like Jackie De Shannon with "What The World Needs Now Is Love," Barbara Lewis with "Baby I'm Yours," Patty Duke with "Don't Just Stand There," and Barbara Mason with "Yes, I'm Ready," can also be heard crying, demanding and wooing amid the masculine booming, protesting and threatening.

So while the pop record kingdom may be a man's domain, there is still room for a few ambitious female trespasser.

... CONVENT GIRL

... DANGEROUS CONTENDER

... SWEETHEARTS OF SONG

KRLA ARCHIVES

MAN'S DOMAIN

... WANTING YOU

... PARTY GIRL

... ICE BREAKER

... MISS DYNAMITE

KRLA ARCHIVES

For Girls Only

By Sheila Davis

I can't believe it! I just got a letter from a real live boy! I mean, this *column* got a letter from a boy.

Remember when I told you about my hobby of collecting match books from different restaurants? Well, in this morning's mail, I found the following terse note.

"Greeting,

I'm a boy and I never miss ... reading your column, but I thought you might want a match book cover from an authentic Japanese restaurant."

The note wasn't signed, but there was a P.S. which stated: "Please withhold my name. I did." (Well, *I* thought it was funny!)

By the way, the match book really was from Yokohama, Japan. Funny thing though, the name of the restaurant was *Jack's*. Anyway my sincere thanks to the mystery man who never misses .. er .. reads my column. Also to BEAT readers Jayn Flore and Linda Prara for sending lots of match books for my collection! I'll return the favor by helping with your hobbies soon.

I know you aren't going to believe this, but incredible as it may sound, I have finally done something RIGHT! (You know me, I mean well but I'm not very.) The other night I had a date with this boy I've had my eye on for over a year. I was scared half to death that I'd do something ridiculous (the chances were good), but instead I did something almost human.

Snorting Car

About five minutes after the boy picked me up (wow, that sounds bad, but what I mean is *for a date*) his car started sort of snorting once or twice in every block. It ran okay most of the time except for these periodic spasms, but I could see he was really worried that it was going to collapse or something, right there on the spot!

So, I calmly turned to him and said "Oh, don't worry, it's only your fuel pump. You can have it fixed tomorrow."

Well, he gave *me* a look. Like, *get serious, old girl*. But about five minutes from then, when he stopped at a gas station and had the attendant look at the car, he suddenly found himself looking at me through new eyes.

The attendant calmly turned to him and said "It's only your fuel pump." And guess who I have another date with for next week? The attendant! (No, no, I'm kidding.)

I don't know why boys always think girls know absolutely nothing about cars. We don't, but that's beside the point. I just hope my new flame never finds out that I recognized his car problem because my dad just had our fuel pump replaced. If anyone reading this tells him, I'll never speak to you again. (This is bad?)

Before I forget, I need help (this is news?). A few months ago I saw a magazine advertisement for pendants you wear around your neck with perfume in them. (Bear with me, I'm saying things backwards again

today.) I thought they were just gorgeous, but I've never been able to find them on sale anywhere. Please let me know if you have information as to where I could buy one of these gear goodies.

Back to Boys

Now, back to boys. Did I tell you that I have a new idol? (Well, he's more of a second-fiddle favorite because no one will ever take George Harrison's place in me life.) Anyway, my additional fave is Donovan. I just loved his record of "Try And Catch The Wind" but I never really flipped for him until I saw him do the song on one of those teenage-type TV shows. I don't remember which one it was—there are so many of them these days, I don't know whether I'm coming or go-going. But whatever the show, Donovan was just darling. Especially when he played that mouth harp that hangs around his neck on that wire thing. And at the end of the show when all the performers stand up and flail their arms around, Donovan didn't quite know what was coming off, but he gave this sheepish kind of grin and flailed along. Gee, he's cute.

After the show I was trying to tell someone about him playing the harmonica and the guitar at the same time, and I couldn't explain it any better than I did just a moment ago. So I called a recording company and asked them to give me the correct name for a harmonica holder.

The guy on the other end of the wire paused for a moment and said in disgust, "A harmonica holder is called a harmonica holder." Well, it does sort of figure.

Oh, I just have to tell you about another of my kooky letters.

The Sister Problem

One of our readers has finally been able to come up with a way to solve the "sister" problem. She and her sister share a room, and since they haven't seen eye to eye about anything since the early spring of 1947, things are a bit strained a lot of the time.

The girl solved this problem by rigging up a heavy string from one end of the room to the other, right over her bed, and then hanging a sheet over it. I can't explain it very well, but the end result was a tent right over her bed.

The purpose of it was to keep her from having to see her sister, but when she was all ready to move into her teepee, both of them took one look at it and started howling. And they've been getting along ever since!

I'm running off at the typewriter again, but before I go, have you seen that commercial about a hair-set product called Dippity-Do? Well, I counted how many times they say Dippity-Do in that commercial and it's a grand total of thirty-two, which isn't easy because the commercial is only about thirty seconds long. It's probably a good product, but I swear I'll never use it until they lock that announcer in a closet with a tape recording of his commercial for at least a week!

Gotta go this instant. Please keep writing to me and I'll see you next BEAT!

GORGEOUS KATHY KERSH surprised everyone recently by revealing she had secretly married heart-throb Vincent Edwards — Dr. Ben Casey. Then she surprised **him** by suing for a divorce.

PORTMAN'S PLATTERPOOP

HOLLYWOOD ... School Days Are Near: *The Beatles* appearances in California hiked the "Help" album sale to one million the first week. Not bad for four young men from the old country. ... A bikini-clad *Patty Duke* has said goodbye to kiddie roles. ... *The Supremes* may have roles in the *Beatles* next picture. The threesome is the foursome's favorite singing group.

Songwriter, arranger and man of many talents, *Kim Fowley*, was one of the survivors of the mad rush made on *P. J. Proby* several months ago in England. Kim stated that Proby was attacked by only 1,500 fans—and that's not bad, for 8,500 was the total attendance. ... *Danny* "Roses and Rainbows" *Hutton*, Ireland's export to California shores, was a hero-type high jumper backer in the land of the shamrock. ... *Glen Yarbrough* has a smash RCA Victor album on the way. The title is appropriate, "It's Gonna Be Fine." ... That weird, but exciting drumming on U.S. Royal tire TV commercials is the work of famed H'wood drummer *Shelly Manne*. He did it on piccolo Boo-Bams to create those fascinating sounds.

Cannibal and The Headhunters are grateful to the *Beatles* for participating on their tour. ... *Lloyd Thaxton* will be the first TV personality to be enshrined at the Hollywood Wax Museum. ... *The Back Porch Majority* makes it to the front with several scopitone appearances. ... A lunch with *Harry Belafonte* is almost exciting as viewing this great performer work. He puts mucho feeling in a wee conversation. "Matilda" anyone? ... Eurasian actress-singer *Kieuh Chinh* has given up her budding career to carry a gun for her country in the Vietnam police action. ... MGM records swallowed *The Lovin Spoonfuls* to their label.

James Brown and The Flames almost burned Los Angeles down, like a cow did to Chicago so many years ago, when he drew more than capacity audiences to a club where the waitresses usually outnumber the paying guests. ... *Thee Midniters* album, based upon their hit single "Whittier Blvd." has just been released by Chattahoochee Records. ... *Milton Berle*, no fool he, signed *Sonny & Cher* to headline his stint as M.C. for an October "Hollywood Palace" date. ... the initial *Bob Eubanks* "Hit or Miss" panel will be *Roger Miller, Cathy Nolan, Chad Stewart, Molly Bee* and *Jerry Naylor*.

TV appearances: *Righteous Bros.*, October 25, "Andy Williams Show," ... *The Supremes*, November 18, "Dean Martin Show." ... *Sonny & Cher*, October 9, "Hollywood Palace."

All That Glitters Is Gold Dept.: In the Motion picture "*Beach Ball*," the following artists reputedly were paid the following amounts. *Righteous Bros.*, ($500), *The Supremes* ($2,500), *The Hondells* ($400), and *The Four Seasons* ($2,500). In a November release of "Wild, Wild Winter," the salaries for the talent are *Jay and The Americans* ($5,000), *Dick & Deedee* ($500), *Jackie & Gayle* ($400), *The Beau Brummels* ($1,500), and *The Astronauts* ($1,500).

Capitol Records had a phoney bomb scare in August. Must have been a mad record buyer. ... *Peter Fonda's* signature was barely dry on a Philips pact, when they released his "Blue Ribbon" and "We're Not Friends Anymore." ... *The Youngfolks* newest release is "That Lollypop Feeling" b/w "Mr. Tambourine." ... *Paul Petersen* passed his physical and will be donning khaki's shortly. ... *Petula Clark* warbles the title tune to *Alan King's* new TV series "The Impossible Years." ... it's supposed to be a secret, but the guy that did those wonderful arrangements for *David McCallum's* MGM record debut is *Hank Levine*, Colpix's music master.

Dean Martin, always in good taste, both in spirits and talent, asked *The Supremes* to join him in a milkshake? ... *The Good Time Singers*, regulars on the Andy Williams Show, owned by the Andy Williams Management firm, signed a recording pact with the Andy Williams dominated label, Columbia. ... *Jackie & Gayle* (Miller & Caldwell) firmed for a October slot with Red Skelton and at the same time signed their Mainstream record contract.

Joe & Eddie have a "big one" starting on Crescendo Records titled "Walkin' Down the Line." ... *Liz Minnelli* has a large size bomb on Capitol in "Did I Hurt Your Feeling." ... *The Astronauts* RCA Victor's newest, "La, La, La, La,", is starting to soar. ... *Ian Whitcomb's* "N-E-R-V-O-U-S" on Tower is one to keep an eye on. ... *Sonny & Cher*, togetherness personified on Atco with "Look At Us," will see the disc become a blockbuster. But why so glum on the album cover, Sonny? That might be a moneytree!

KRLA ARCHIVES

On The BEAT

By Louise Criscione

Heard quite an interesting story from Mr. Hinsche (Billy's father) on how Billy finally got his first electric guitar. It seems that Dino Jr. had acquired a brand new Fender guitar and so, naturally, his friend Billy felt that he too should have an electric guitar. Billy hinted to his father, who informed him that *he* was not about to spend $500 on a new guitar, especially since Billy could not even play one!

However, Mr. Hinsche did give his son's request a little more thought and finally came up with a solution to the problem. So, early one morning he and Billy made a trip down to one of the Main Street hock shops and purchased a $65 guitar!

After obtaining his precious guitar, Billy set out to teach himself to play (and play pretty well too). Now that Billy is such a star he has four secretaries answering his fan mail—and he finally did get that $500 guitar!

Puts Down Violence

In his hotel room, Donovan confided to the *BEAT* that: "I don't think violence is a pretty thing or bearable, and our children shouldn't see or learn it."

One English reporter wrote that the Byrds are "the greatest impact-making group to emerge from America for years."

"On The Beat" reported about a month ago that John Lennon had purchased a new Rolls Royce which he had completely blacked-out.

... BILLY HINSCHE

Apparently the London police do not read "On The Beat" for as John was speeding (Well, maybe not *speeding*) through London, he was stopped by the police because they thought that his blacked-out car was "suspicious."

Now how could anyone possibly think that a shaded Lennon in a Blacked-out Rolls was suspicious? I mean, how could *anyone*?

Quick Ones

Two of the Kinks are keeping themselves pretty busy — Pete Quaife is building an airplane in his backyard and Ray Davies is writing a musical . . . Tom Jones is set for a "serious" throat operation upon his return to England in the early part of September. Seems Tom's tonsils should have been removed months ago . . . Sonny & Cher went down *very* well in Britain, but were a bit overshadowed by the fantastic reception given to the Byrds. However, Sonny & Cher did create enough of a stir to be invited back to England in October for a full tour . . . By the way, did you see the film clips of Sonny & Cher's arrival in London? There to greet the duo were English fans reading the *BEAT!* Just goes to show you —they read us all around the world!

Dusty Springfield is another pop star who is paying a big price health-wise. She reveals: "I've been to see lots of specialists, had X-rays and so on. Nobody tells me anything. I'm just supposed to rest."

Paul Revere and the Raiders are being sought by Merv Griffin for three fall dates and by Dick Clark for three *years!* The group's manager says they are "seriously considering" Clark's offer.

Both of the Stones who were house-hunting have found what they were looking for. Charlie Watts has purchased a 15th Century house in Sussex and Bill Wyman has already moved into a $36,000 home in Beckenham.

All five of the Stones have re-signed with British Decca Records. The five year contract calls for a $1 million guarantee! Not bad for a group who once performed for free, is it?

... WATTS, WYMAN

The Beatles were mobbed by 10,000 fans when they showed up for the London premiere of "HELP." Ambulances were called to remove the casualties from the battlefield where 14 girls had fainted! Powerful stuff, those Beatles.

FLASH! EXCLUSIVE TO THE BEAT — Directly from where it's all happening, baby: New York, N.Y. Paul Revere and The Raiders here prance through their paces putting in some practice for their forthcoming performance (by invitation) to play a concert Sept. 4 between games at the Yankee Stadium for the healthy fee of $50,000. Think of it, Paul — with four more guys in your group, **you** could hire the Yankees to play halftime entertainment for **you**.

British Top 10

1. HELP — The Beatles
2. YOU'VE GOT YOUR TROUBLES — The Fortunes
3. WE GOTTA GET OUT OF THIS PLACE — The Animals
4. CATCH US IF YOU CAN — The Dave Clark Five
5. EVERYONE'S GONE TO THE MOON — Jonathan King
6. MR. TAMBOURINE MAN — The Byrds
7. THERE BUT FOR FORTUNE — Joan Baez
8. TOSSING & TURNING — Ivy League
9. IN THOUGHTS OF YOU — Billy Fury
10. WITH THESE HANDS — Tom Jones

Beatles Still Ride High

The Beatles are sure riding high on the British charts. Not only have they had the number one single for three weeks in a row, but they have also managed to do the impossible — their "Help" L.P. has debuted on the *singles* chart at an astounding number 22!

Occasionally the E.P. will hit the singles chart in England, but an L.P. — NEVER! That is, never before the Beatles. Of course, the Beatles specialize in doing "never" things, so the record industry really shouldn't be too surprised.

The Dave Clark Five moved up two points and landed in the number four spot this week with what is undoubtedly going to be the Five's biggest hit to date, "Catch Us If You Can."

Visiting England seems to be helping American artists tremendously on the British charts. The Byrds' chart-topper, "Mr. Tambourine Man," is slowly descending the charts, but is still securely lodged in the top ten at number six. Their "All I Really Want To Do," released to coincide with their visit to Britain, jumped aboard the survey this week.

Roy Orbison, who is usually assured of a British top ten record the minute he releases a single, seems to be having a bit of trouble trying to move his "Say You're My Girl" any higher than number 21, and this week the record dropped down to 24.

The swingin' Righteous Brothers jumped on this week at number 26 with their "Unchained Melody." Several months ago the Brothers set the British record world on its ear by knocking Cilla Black's version of "You've Lost That Lovin' Feeling" right off the charts! Perhaps they'll speed all the way up and knock off the Beatles next week?

KRLA ARCHIVES

Surf Beat

By GENE VANGELISTI

I wonder how many people realize that surfing is not only a sport, but something that goes a lot deeper. In many cases it is a way of life. There is more than one guy who lives just for waves. He is not a beach bum or a person who lives off others, he works hard all week just for those two days when he can ride to his heart's content. This is not an uncommon way of life on the West Coast. Surfing does become a part of your life and not just because it's a a fad. After you reach the point when you can ride a wave and understand what is happening, the feeling that you get is so fantastic you can't describe it. Surfing is without a doubt the cleanest sport known and you very seldom see a surfer who is out of shape.

The Surfing Look

Almost anywhere in the United States you can spot someone with all the trademarks of a surfer — the long blond hair, bermuda shorts, and no shoes. It has become a fad to act and dress like a surfer; surfing is the biggest fad to hit the U.S. since the Hoola-Hoop. What does the real surfer wear? That is up to the individual. Surfing is a sport for individuals; no one can tell you when to stand up, they can't tell you which wave to take — you have to think by yourself. Surfing, like many other sports, has its own special look. First you will note the ever-present tennies; blue, red, green, or white. Red is the latest on the West Coast because they stay cleanest looking. Next come the socks; a pair of cotton or white wool socks with stripes on the stretch band will do, although this isn't too important. What the surfer wears depends on his own individual personality. A typical high school boy may sport a pair of Madras bermudas and a white T-shirt. You will find that there isn't much you can wear Madras bermudas with except a white shirt. At this point he might decide to wear his "blues." Next comes the white shirt with the tails out or a shirt with competition stripes on it.

Board Test

Last week I had the pleasure of testing the Donald Takayama model surfboard manufactured by Bing Surfboards. This board is different than any other "signature" model in that it incorporates many new ideas. Donald is originally from the island of Oahu and has been shaping boards for six years. He left the Islands about seven years ago and went to work for Velzy in San Clemente. Since then he has worked for some of the biggest name surfboard manufacturers. He is a member of the Windansea Surf Club.

I think that this trend of "signature" models is one of the best things that has ever happened to surfing. Boards in this category, such as the Phil Edwards model, the Mike Hynson model and the Harold Iggy model, allow a surfer of professional ability the extra little touch it takes in a surfboard to maneuver, to turn and to ride. If you are thinking about getting a new surfboard and you are a good rider, one of these boards would more than likely solve any surfing problem that you have.

That First Board

When you get your first board you go down to the beach, put your board in the water, totter a little bit and finally get your balance, then start paddling out to get past the break. Then the questions start. What do I do next? Should I paddle for the waves? There are many questions and you may wonder how to get the answers. It is fairly simple. There are surfers on the beach who will help you, that is one of the nice things about the sport. If you are not too proud, walk up to someone and ask him to help you learn. He may say that he is too busy and doesn't have the time, then again he might say "Sure . . . let's go out." After you are out in the water he may teach you water Safety First or maybe how to paddle. But please, when you go out in the water make sure you know the basic fundamentals before you go out.

P.S.A. Needed

There is a definite need for a Professional Surfing Association on the coast, but it is a long time in coming. When you first consider the idea of professional surfing the average reaction is — why? The surfer who has been surfing for years can enter any contest — why should he go into a professional situation? Already most of the surfers in the United States are of professional ability and have accepted money from time to time. The problem with this is that the AAU standards and the Olympic possibility for surfing would make it impossible for them to compete in an Olympic category. Which is better: enter a contest and win a trophy, or win $500.00 or more while building up points toward a grand prize, maybe a car for the circuit champion? This is what surfing has in its future. A regular circuit with ten or more contests held all over the world patterned after the Professional Golf Association. Maybe surfing isn't going to make it into the Olympics in our life-time, but professional surfing is a likelihood.

If you have any questions on surfing, please write, we'd like to hear from you.   'Til next week — ride well.

Understanding For Stars Is Urged In Answers To Cheryl

(Editor's Note: In the August 7 issue of the BEAT, we printed a letter from Cheryl Johnson expressing the disappointment and dissillusionment which she felt after meeting her favorite group. The BEAT has since been flooded with letters from readers who have also met their favorite group and who disagree with Miss Johnson. We don't have space to print all the letters, so we have chosen two letters from girls who do not think that "Stars Lose Glitter For Fans.")

Dear BEAT:

I am writing this letter in answer to that letter you printed by Cheryl Johnson.

I can sympathize with her a little because I can imagine what it must feel like to suddenly discover that what she had mistaken for starlight was really just an electric lamp.

Still most of my sympathy goes to the artists—the one she met, and the many others. They keep telling people that they aren't gods and idols. They keep saying "We're human," but too many fans won't believe them.

If their fans are disappointed after meeting them, it's their own fault. And if they lose the magic feeling when they discover that the boys have been telling the truth (they *are* human) then I feel sorry for them.

I can't understand what Cheryl meant when she said they were "just real people to me." Just(?) real people? Is there anything more wonderful?

They Are Human

I know what Cheryl was trying to say, but to me part of the magic I feel comes from the very fact they are human. If they were tin gods, or if they were folded up and put away between performances I wouldn't like them.

I like to know that they can get angry and fed up, that they can laugh and cry, that they can even become ill (although I die when I hear that one of my favorites has a hang-nail!).

Since reading that the one member of the group had to hold his breath to keep from coughing and sneezing, I keep wondering, "Would I, *could* I, care that much?" He could probably have gotten someone to take his place, but perhaps he felt that he would be cheating his fans.

Before I close I would like to say just one more thing—and I certainly don't mean it as a slur on Cheryl Johnson.

I can't see how anyone with an imagination could ever be disappointed to find that stars aren't really "diamonds in the sky" and that the moon is just one big mass of craters and rock dust.

To me it seems like meeting your favorite star would be more like the feeling shared by a married couple who are truly in love. The first years are thrilling, complete with sky-rockets and moonbeams, but later the moonbeams are lost in the glow of love and understanding they share and the sky-rockets slow down (though they never really stop).

Yes, I really am glad that stars are human, aren't you?

Diane Snelling.

More For Cheryl

Dear BEAT:

(I'd like to write this letter to Cheryl Johnson but the BEAT is the only way I know of reaching her.)

Dear Cheryl:

I'm a normal, American teenager who has had more than my share of luck when it comes to meeting my favorites. I won't mention any names either, especially since I know the group you were talking about is one of the ones I have been lucky enough to meet.

Yes, I said "lucky enough." I consider meeting the various performers a highlight in my life and I have some wonderful memories of some truly wonderful people.

Like you, I didn't meet most of them under the most desirable circumstances, but I went looking for *people* and not "something extraordinary."

Just because a group of four or five men get together and make a record that sells a million copies doesn't make them any less human than you or I. Certainly—picturing a Rolling Stone, a Beau Brummel, or a Kink as being hungry, tired, lonely or just plain sick is not exactly glamorous or exciting but let's face it—even singers are human.

Rate Medals

Cheryl, you were disappointed because your favorite was "all pale and drawn and tried-looking" from trying to keep from coughing while on stage. Did you consider that he risked an even more serious sickness by even coming that night? Do you realize that most of these men rate medals for working for you above and beyond what is good for them?

You've certainly heard of riots at some concerts. Who is there to promise these fellows that they won't be killed or seriously injured?

You went looking for something out of the ordinary. I'm sorry. Sorry for you because you didn't see how out of the ordinary those men were. Sorry that you didn't realize that they must be out of the ordinary to do for you and I what they do. And I'm sorry for them. Sorry because I realize that most of their fans expect supermen—not people. For them to be people is almost a crime because they are the images that most teenagers look to for fun and a good time.

Cheryl, I know how you felt. Your stars came out of their sky and you weren't prepared for what you found. Certainly, you were let down. Maybe this letter has helped you bear your disillusionment. Perhaps it did not. But thank you, Cheryl, for reading this.

Katie Fontana.

. . . DAY'S END

KRLA ARCHIVES

THE BEAT GOES TO THE MOVIES
HARLOW

This film has been argued and fought over since the day rotund Joseph E. Levine announced he was making it.

Levine first said he was paying $100,000 to author Irving Shulman for the book written about Jean Harlow, a silver screen idol of bygone days of Hollywood. But, said Levine, "only to use the title." Fortunately, that's all they did use of a rather tawdry book that is at least 50 per cent fiction.

Then Levine, producer of a long string of successful pictures, announced that the film would be ready in August, only weeks away from the day it started production at the Paramount lot.

And he made it. The picture has arrived in much shorter time than it usually takes for an important movie, as a significant contribution to the art of storytelling.

Of the dozens of film critics in New York, only one, writing for the *New York Post*, has said he liked the picture. The lone approval came from a man who charges that the other critics were not reviewing HARLOW, but the reputation of Joseph Levine and whatever else they don't like about Hollywood.

Our man from the *Post* is very right.

HARLOW is an excellent film.

Every teenage girl, somewhere along the way, dreams of being the silver-haired movie star, with Cadillacs and furs, chauffeurs and servants, the 50-foot swimming pool and hilltop villa overlooking the twinkling lights of Southern California.

Every girl can vision herself the idol of millions of American men, stared and pointed at, admired and swooned over.

It has actually happened before, and perhaps some young girl reading this very paper will one day be another of the great stars of motion pictures.

Jean Harlow, who grew up in Kansas City, became such a star, and she was given the extravagant material rewards for hitting the top of her profession.

But she never found love and inner peace for herself, and the search, soon to become frantic, finally destroyed her.

That's the Jean Harlow that this new Paramount picture paints, and it's as good a Harlow as anyone else could come up with, for who knows what a person is really like?

The publicity campaign launched by the studio won't do much justice to the story. The billboards appeal to the same crowd that go for burlesque shows, but in spite of the shoddy image they give it, the picture is honest in its simplicity about telling a story about a tragic lady.

Young adults especially are attracted to the film, and the theaters are being filled by teens who have come perhaps because they are curious to know what the "real" Jean Harlow was like, or because they're curious about life in Hollywood of the early 1930s.

Whatever their reason, they'll come away learning a little something about life, and how important it is to be true to yourself, and what loneliness can do to the human spirit.

And no one is as lonely as the person in a crowd by himself.

That is the lesson we can learn from the unhappiness of the little girl from Kansas City who became the modern American Love Goddess, and who brought a new dimension to entertainment —desired by men around the world.

Joe Levine, with his reputation for sex movies and putting anything on the screen that will make money (including some of the best pictures) has given dignity and style to the twice-told tale of HARLOW.

And every man will always believe that if only she had known *him*, everything would have been so different!

THE GIRL WHO DIDN'T CARE — What was she really like?

THIS IS HOW THE STORY ENDS . . . a story about a search that led its way to tragedy and death. Carroll Baker plays the famous movie star of the 1930's, JEAN HARLOW.

AT HOLLYWOOD PREMIERE glamorous film star JEAN HARLOW steps from limousine. Film recounts the life of a controversial star.

EPIC'S BOBBY VINTON sings a haunting melody from the new Paramount Picture . . . "HARLOW." Bobby is heard singing the song "Lonely Girl," as the life story of one of Hollywood's most famous stars comes to its tragic ending.

Beat To Host Shindig Stars

Dig, Dig, *SHINDIG!!*

Yes, *everybody's* digging the hottest show in all of television, and now *you* can dig it right here in the BEAT.

Beginning next week and continuing every week thereafter, the fab regulars and guests on Shindig will all be popping in for a little chat right here in their own column. We'll be gabbing with Bobby Sherman, Donna Loren, the Zombies, and — many, *many* more.

So why don't you plan to join us every week from now on, 'cause this is where it's *happening*, Beaters!

We'll be digging you right here and every Wednesday night so, 'til next time, Beaters — ROCK ON!!

KRLA ARCHIVES

KRLA Tunedex

EMPEROR HUDSON

CHARLIE O'DONNELL

CASEY KASEM

JOHNNY HAYES

BOB EUBANKS

DAVE HULL

DICK BIONDI

BILL SLATER

KRLA BEAT
6290 Sunset, No. 504
Hollywood, Cal. 90028

BULK RATE
U.S. Postage
PAID
Los Angeles, Calif.
Permit No. 25497

This Week	Last Week	Title	Artist
1	1	LIKE A ROLLING STONE	Bob Dylan
2	2	I GOT YOU BABE	Sonny & Cher
3	3	IT AIN'T ME BABE	The Turtles
4	4	YOU WERE ON MY MIND	We Five
5	5	UNCHAINED MELODY/HUNG ON YOU	Righteous Brothers
6	8	BABY I'M YOURS	Barbara Lewis
7	10	IT'S THE SAME OLD SONG	The Four Tops
8	9	HELP, I'M DOWN	The Beatles
9	15	EVE OF DESTRUCTION	Barry McGuire
10	16	LAUGH AT ME	Sonny Bono
11	6	ALL I REALLY WANT TO DO	Cher
12	11	NOTHING BUT HEARTACHES	The Supremes
13	7	CALIFORNIA GIRLS	Beach Boys
14	13	HOLD ME, THRILL ME, KISS ME	Mel Carter
15	14	PAPA'S GOT A BRAND NEW BAG	James Brown
16		YOU TELL ME WHY	Beau Brummels
17	12	SATISFACTION	The Rolling Stones
18	19	SUMMER NIGHTS	Marianne Faithfull
19	22	DOWN IN THE BOONDOCKS	Billy Joe Royal
20	33	ROSES AND RAINBOWS	Danny Hutton
21	22	TAKE ME BACK	Little Anthony & The Imperials
22	30	DO YOU BELIEVE IN MAGIC	Lovin' Spoonfull
23	24	WHO'LL BE THE NEXT IN LINE	The Kinks
24	31	JU JU HAND	Sam The Sham & The Pharaohs
25	38	HEART FULL OF SOUL	The Yardbirds
26	32	COLOURS/JOSIE	Donovan
27	—	CATCH US IF YOU CAN	Dave Clark Five
28	35	LOOKING THRU THE EYES OF LOVE	Gene Pitney
29	—	WE GOTTA GET OUT OF THIS PLACE	The Animals
30	—	LIAR, LIAR	The Castaways
31	34	I'LL ALWAYS LOVE YOU	The Spinners
32	—	YOU'VE GOT YOUR TROUBLES	The Fortunes
33	39	MY GIRL SLOOPY	Little Caesar
34	—	I'M ALIVE	The Hollies
35	40	I'M THE WOLF MAN	Round Robin
36	37	THAT'S WHERE IT'S AT	T-Bones
37	36	I'M A HAPPY MAN	Jive Five
38	—	HOME OF THE BRAVE	Bonnie & The Treasures
39	—	THE GIRL FROM PEYTON PLACE	Dickey Lee
40	—	RIDE AWAY	Roy Orbison

KRLA BEAT

Volume 1, Number 26　　LOS ANGELES, CALIFORNIA　　15 Cents　　September 11, 1965

**THE THREE FACES OF BOB DYLAN
... POET, PERFORMER, PROTESTOR**

KRLA BEAT

Los Angeles, California — September 11, 1965

DYLAN HERE ON BEATLES' HEELS - WHAT A WEEK!

What a week! The Beatles setting new records in frenzy and excitement at Hollywood Bowl, only to be followed four days later by the incomparable Bob Dylan.

Preparations for the Beatles' second appearances at Hollywood Bowl had been carefully planned months in advance. Both their shows were sell-outs, of course. They had been since that very first day's mail came pouring in when tickets were placed on sale months ago.

The usually tranqil and serene Bowl was braced for this invasion by the Beatles and their frenzied throng of followers. The excitement of last year — the screams of ecstacy which had filled the Bowl with a deafening roar and could be heard throughout Hollywood — was well remembered.

Somehow, however, this year seemed even wilder. No one who attended either performance will ever forget it.

But even as the last Beatle scream was dying down preparations were underway for another momentous evening — the Dylan concert, also sponsored by Bob Eubanks and KRLA, at Hollywood Bowl on Friday, Sept. 5.

The huge, enthusiastic crowds mark the only thing the two sister concerts could share in common. The Beatles' shows are always wild — filled with screaming, waving, frantic girls. And noise — nothing but total noise.

But with Dylan it's different. When he saunters onto the stage, alone with only his guitar and harmonica, there is a hush of respect from the audience after the initial thunder of applause. While the Beatles' songs are usually drowned out by their frenzied fans, the audience listens to Dylan and to what he's trying to say.

Although he professes not to have a message, the listeners still search for one. And if anyone sheds a tear, it is a real one. For Dylan tells it like it is.

When his show is over, Dylan ambles off the stage in the manner that he came on. When the final encore is done his audience sits spell-bound, discussing his songs and the performance.

Yes the Bowl is accustomed to the world's great entertainers. But even so, this will go down as The Week That Was.

PAUL AND RINGO look like a couple of tourists as they catch their first sight of the California Pacific during their week-long visit here. While Southern Californians were seething with Beatlemania, the Beatles calmly basked in the sunshine at their Benedict Canyon retreat.

SHOW AT MELODYLAND

Animals Coming to Southland

Watch out — the Animals will soon be invading the Southland!

But don't worry — these are not the man-eating variety, they're the blues singing kind. Led by Eric Burdon, the five-man group will fly into Los Angeles for a September 20 appearance at Melodyland.

The Animals currently have one of the hottest records on the scene, "We Gotta Get Out Of This Place," but they are the best known for their fantastic version of "House Of The Rising Sun" which vaulted them to the top of the American charts.

A new image Lesley Gore, complete with a new hairdo and a much more assured stage presence, will compliment the English-born Animals.

By co-starring Lesley Gore who is typically pop and the Animals who are strictly rhythm 'n' blues, the Melodyland audience is guaranteed a varied show — one which will undoubtedly run the gamut from "Sunshine, Lollipops and Rainbows" to "Please Don't Let Me Be Misunderstood."

Along with the Animals and Lesley Gore will be appearing the Challengers and The Four Castaways.

The BEAT has learned exclusively from The Liverpool Five that they too will be billed on the same show, but Melodyland refuses to confirm the group's appearance, so you will just have to be patient until September 20 and find out for yourselves.

And until then your question of the week can be—Will The Liverpool Five or won't they?

Ilya Featured As Guest-Host On 'Hullabaloo'

David McCallum fans . . . Attention!

Gary Smith, producer of the top-rated TV series, "Hullabaloo," just signed the blond co-star of "The Man From U.N.C.L.E." to be the special guest-host of the program to be seen shortly. The segment of "Hulabaloo" starring Napoleon Solo's partner begins taping in Hollywood Sept. 1.

For "Ilya Kuriakin," incidentallly, "Hulabaloo" set a precedent: The series normally is taped in New York but this time the entire production company is being transported to California. Reason is that David is much too busy with his role in the cloak-and-dagger series to take time out and travel East.

Since Mahommet could not go to the mountain, the mountain went to Mah . . . er, McCallum.

BEATLEMANIA IN ADVANCED STAGE. Shrieking, screaming, crying, laughing — all symptoms of the violent disease which caused pandemonium at Hollywood Bowl during KRLA's two Beatle performances.

KRLA ARCHIVES

ESKIMO BOOTS

The Stars And Kooky Garb: Do Clothes Make The Man?

By Louise Criscione

Do clothes really make the man? Are they *that* important? Or are they merely for decoration?

Since the Rolling Stones first rolled upon the American scene with their "come as you are" attire, people have been noticing, commenting, approving and jeering at rock artists who prefer to wear casual clothes.

"Appalling" Sight

Because they don't wear just what everyone else is wearing, these artists have been asked to leave restaurants and hotels in case the other guests might object to viewing the appalling sight of a Sonny Bono or Brian Jones minus white shirt and tie.

But how did this all evolve? Why did certain artists choose now, today — 1965 — to break away from the traditional suit.

The Stones seem to have spearheaded this "clothes war," yet at one time in the group's career they *almost* purchased stage suits.

Brian says: "We just couldn't agree on a style, or even a color. You see, we've all got different tastes. And none of us wanted to become a carbon copy of the others.

"But looking at all the other groups going on stage in their mohair suits and their highly-polished boots—there are so many of them, it's impossible to tell them apart."

So the Stones chucked the stage-suit idea and instead showed up in just whatever each one personally felt like wearing.

Harsh Criticism

Of course, they have been vehemently criticized by many people who obviously feel that a performer *has* to wear a stage suit because it is the normal, "natural" thing to do—the thing which has been done for years. They feel that if this tradition has managed to survive all these years, a handful of "youngsters" has no right to change it now.

Mick Jagger questions their reasoning. "Does *everybody* in the business have to follow the same line? We play music—that is what people pay to hear. We are not dressing up like tailors' dummies just for the sake of it."

Many of you *BEAT* readers feel as Mick does. You've been writing to let us know.

An Individual

Just such a reader is Sandie Lockwood who wrote: 'To me, a boy who wears his hair long or dresses differently is showing that he is not a non-conformist but an individual. He is a person who can stand up and tell the world that he is not like anyone else.

"He is a person owned by no one but himself. I look up to such a boy. I really hope that someday people will be free enough to say and do and dress as they wish."

A popular California twosome, Sonny & Cher, wear stage-suits. But they are rather unique stage-suits and this puts the duo on the receiving end of many comments (both good and bad) concerning their particular mode of dress.

Of course, everyone knows the story of Martoni's and the subsequent Sonny-penned "Laugh At Me." And probably many of you have heard about the London Hilton canceling Sonny & Cher's hotel reservations because of the Hilton's disapproval of the American duo's "unusual" dress. The hotel management felt that it was "not tidy enough" to grace the stately Hilton.

Many Problems

This canceling of hotel reservations is just one of the many problems facing an individual who dares to be a little bit different.

Naturally since performers are human, they pretend that this kind of insult does not bother them in the least—but it *does*

TURN TO PAGE 8

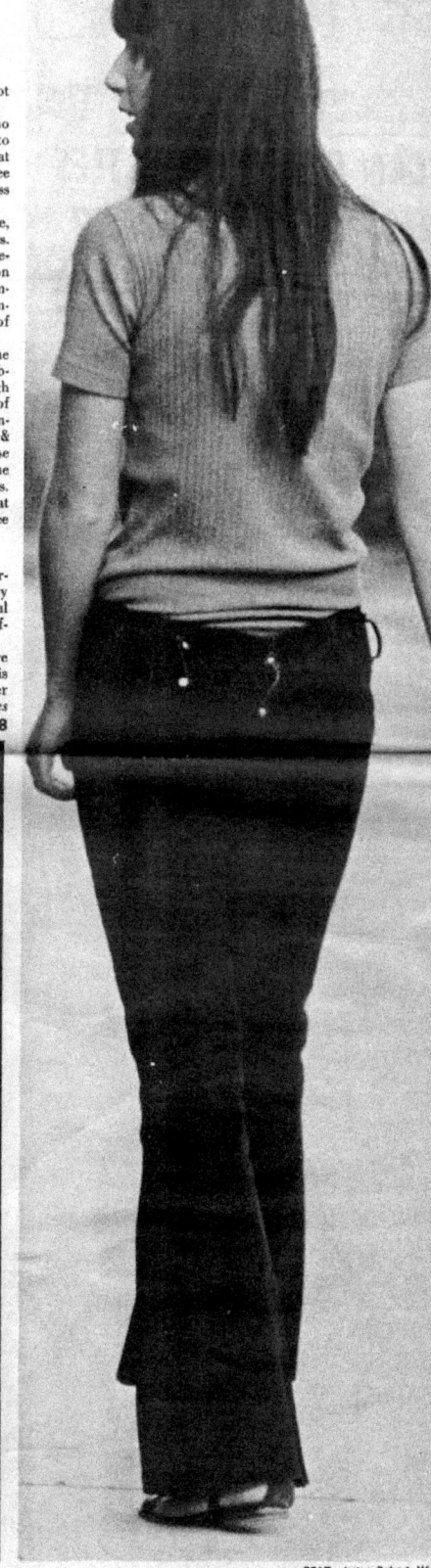

"BUT WHAT HAPPENED TO THE ESKIMO...?"   BEAT photo: Robert W. Young

CHER: NO HIP-HUGGERS FOR HILTON   BEAT photo: Robert W. Young

KRLA ARCHIVES

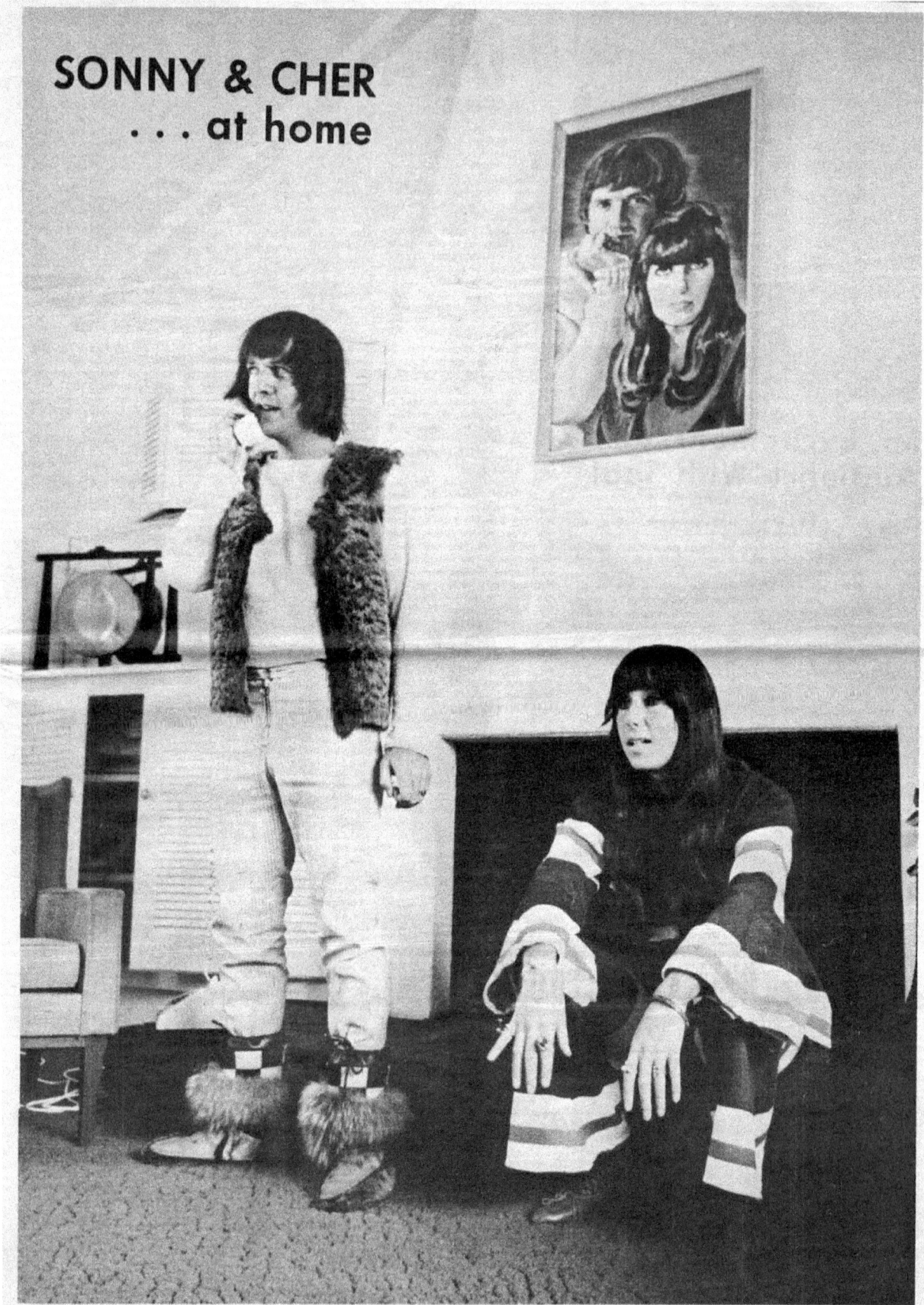

SONNY & CHER ...at home

KRLA ARCHIVES

JAMES BROWN

Mr. Excitement Stirs Audience With Soul

By NIKKI WINE

He's Mr. Excitement, an entertainer's entertainer, a singer with a lot of soul — he's James Brown.

For one and a half action-packed hours on a recent night in Hollywood, James Brown occupied the stage of the Tiger Crescendo and completely captivated the large group of fans who were jammed into the popular night spot on the famed Sunset Strip.

He began his one-night performance with a number on the piano-organ and a little drum-pounding and then he displayed his talent and versatility as an entertainer further with an electrifying medley of his world-famous hit records, both past and present, finishing with a rebel-rousing rendition of his latest smash — "Poppa's Got a Brand New Bag."

Audience Clamors

The one and only Mr. Brown sang up a storm — dancing all the while with his well-known version of the Mashed Potatoes. The stage rocked, the music rolled on, and before you could say "James, You're Out of Sight!" the audience was on its feet — not to mention chairs and tables — dancing, clapping and singing along with the dynamic young man on the stage.

In the audience that evening were several important people in the music industry as well as several well known entertainers. Among those who were paying tribute to the talents of James Brown were Joey Paige, Jimmy Boyd, and Phil Spector, and by the end of the show they were exclaiming "He's great, fantastic!" right along with the rest of the exuberant audience.

Devoted Fan

One devoted fan in the audience summed up Mr. Brown's performance for the Beat:

"He was completely involved in his performance and he completely involved his audience in it as well. He has incomparable rhythm and he just puts everything into his performance. It's just soul plus soul!"

"Soul plus soul," a lot of rhythm, and an enormous amount of talent — if you add them all up, the result is Mr. Entertainment: James Brown.

DEAR SUSAN:

By Susan Frisch

I would appreciate it very much if you could tell me how I can write to the Supremes. I tried Motown-Tamla Records, but that failed.
(Jan Genchon.)

Dear Jan:
I'm sorry that the result of your writing proved negative, but there must have been some mistake. The Supremes receive all the mail that comes there. Do you have the right address? It is Motown Tamla-Records, 2648 W. Grand, Detroit, Michigan. Try again, and if this fails too, write me again and I will see what I can do.

I read in the BEAT that the Beatles are not coming back next year for an American tour. Whose idea is it anyway, and is there anything we Beatle Fans can do to help bring them back next year live?
(A Beatle Fan.)

Dear Beatle Fan:
The person whose idea this is is Brian Epstein. He must have his reasons for doing so and although I really hate to admit this to myself and others, there is nothing we fans can do. I doubt that all the letters in the world would do that much good, but you can give it a try. You can write to Brian Epstein at: 5/6 Argyll, London, W.1., England.

Does Gary Lewis have a girlfriend? Do you know who she is? Can you also tell me if Gary and his Playboys will ever be up here, soon, for any shows? If so when and where?
("Gary.")

Dear Gary (???):
Well, Gary does have many girls that he dates, but no one girl in particular. He isn't going steady or anything like that. So I will say there is still hope!!! As far as I know Gary and the Playboys will not be up in Millbrae soon.

I was wondering if you knew anything about David McCallum, and if so I would like to know where I can write to him?
(Saundra Caron.)

Dear Saundra:
That sure is a loaded question. Seeing that David is one of the biggest stars in Hollywood it would be kind of hard to summarize him in this little space. I would like to say one thing to you and to the other readers. If you would like a personal reply from me about anyone or anything send me a self addressed envelope and I will write back. Now to get down to the question. He is married to an actress, Jill Ireland, who has also starred in "The Man From U.N.C.L.E.," and they have three little boys. This may interest you though: In Peter Ustinov's movie, "Billy Budd," David played a naval officer. And although the part was minor, he became noticed by thousands of fans. You can write to him in care of David McCullum, MGM Studios, 10202 Washington Blvd., Culver City, California. And if you are interested in joining a fan club for him the address is: David McCallum, 727 N. Fuller Ave., Los Angeles, California, 90046.

Could you please tell me everything about George Harrison? And could you please tell me where The Beatles are going to stay?
(Stephanie Berks.)

Dear Stephanie:
To be honest with you I don't know any more about George than you do, probably. Just look in any magazine and you will find out all you want. The Beatles will be staying in a private home in Benedict Canyon, but I'm sorry I can't tell you the exact address. Without doubt I am sure that you and a thousand others will find it by the second day they are in town.

I have the maddest crush on George. Could you please tell me his home address and if he and Patti Boyd are going steady? Could you also tell me where I can write to him so I can join the fan club?
(Christie Abames.)

Dear Christie:
George's new home address is not yet available. I'd give you the old ones, but I don't think they would do you much good. In regard to your question about George and Patti Boyd, I have this much to say: I don't think, in fact I will bet my bottom dollar, that he and Patti are still dating. I don't care what you or anyone reads, I still say they are not, at least I gather this from the people I have talked to. You can join any fan club for the Beatles to get in contact with George, and to list them would be absolutely ridiculous seeing that there must be at least a BILLION!!! Just look in any magazine and then choose from them all!

Please tell me who started the long haircuts. I say the Beatles did, but my girl-friend says no. Also did they go to college?
(Sandy Miller.)

Dear Sandy:
When you say who started the long haircuts I take it you are referring to the English singing groups. If this is so I would say the Beatles were actually the first group that ever brought attention to the public concerning the long hair. But by no means did they invent the long hair cuts. John is the only Beatle that went to college and it was an art college.

Is it true that John, Paul and George have turned in their MBE medals and Ringo kept his?
(Linda Gissible.)

Dear Linda:
This is a nasty rumor that has been going round. None of it is true! They all intend to keep their medals and are not thinking of giving them back, so don't worry about it, cause it was nothing but a rumor.

Could you please tell me if it is true that George and Patti Boyd are married, I read it in a newspaper the other day. And also what kind of cigarettes does Brian Jones smoke?
(Carry Rothmen.)

Dear Carrie:
Again I have to say that this is nothing but rumor. George and Patti are not married, and I personally think that they are not even dating anymore. Last time the Stones were in town I think I had noticed Brian smoking Pall Mall. Whether he still does, I don't know.

Could you please tell me one thing that I would like to clear up. Last week in your column you said that Paul McCartney's brother was a singer. I had heard he was an actor. Could you please clear this up for me and the rest of my friends?
(Sherry Buhens.)

Dear Sherry:
Well I must admit, I made my first mistake. To you and all of the readers I want to say I am sorry for giving you the wrong information. Mike McGear otherwise known as Paul McCartney's brother, is an actor and not a singer. He and the rest of his group, called the Scaffold, do mostly stage work and a lot of comedy. Please accept my apologies.

JERRY NAYLOR, former lead singer for the famous Crickets, has now gone solo and in the process has managed to snatch up a two-year contract with ABC-TV's "Shindig." What a break for Jerry! These long-term TV contracts are rare indeed, so the recipient of such a contract can consider himself extremely lucky!

SOON - BABY - SOON!!

BRAD BERWICK'S
"God, Country And My Baby"
B/W
"Are You Glad"
ON
DEEM RECORDS

PINE KEY PRODUCTIONS
8440 SUNSET BOULEVARD   LOS ANGELES, CALIFORNIA
(213) OL 6-1189

A NEW BEAT SPECIAL
Shindig Set Is 'Like A Family'

By The Shindigger

Hello and welcome, Shindiggers everywhere! Today is the big day for our very first Shindig column, and things are really jumping around here!

This week we're going to take you for a tour around the Shindig set and introduce you to some of the regulars who appear on the show.

Walking down towards the stage now, we can see the cameramen setting up their shots and—oh! there are two of the Shindig dancers, Pam Freeman and Maria Ghava. Hi, girls! Can you come over and say hello? Pam, what's it like to work on Shindig?

"It's fun—and tiring—and not at all like work. It's very exciting." And how do you feel about the show, Maria?

"It's great! We're all just like a family. We celebrate birthdays and we do have good times!"

Oh, I think that they're calling you to the stage now. Thanks girls.

Chat With Kathy

Wow!—if I'm not mistaken, we have a very special treat in store for everyone today. For the boys, we are going to drop in for a little visit with gorgeous Kathy Kersh in the make-up room, and for the girls—we're going to have an intimate little chat with John Paul Vignon. Need I say more? Well, what are we waiting for. Shindiggers? Let's go!!

That's the make-up room at the far end of this long, dark corridor. Shall we go in? Hi, Kathy, got a few minutes to chatter with the group I've brought along? Great.

Since not many of the kids are very familiar with you, why don't you tell us a little about yourself and your background?

"I was born on December 15, 1942 in Los Angeles, Calif. I have been acting for two years in such shows as "Man From U.N.C.L.E.," "Wendy and Me," "Ben Casey," and "Burke's Law," to name a few. Also in the movie, "The Americanization of Emily." I have been singing for about nine or ten week professionally in clubs such as The Pink Carousel and The Red Velvet."

Career to Continue

Well you have certainly had an interesting beginning. Do you have any hopes for the future?

"I hope to be recording this summer and continue with my singing career, and go back to acting a little later when my career in singing is established."

Guess you have a busy future in store for you! Good luck Kathy, and thanks for speaking with us.

We'd better hurry along now or else we are going to be late for our date with John Paul Vignon, and he is one Frenchman well worth being on time for! Oh, there he is now. Hi John!

"Hello, and how are you?"

Sigh!!! Just fine, thank you!! Are you ready to spend some time chatting with us? Good, why don't we begin now? What do you have hidden deep in your past?

"I was born January 30, 1939, in Dire-Daoua, Ethiopia, and I went to school at Avignon until I was seventeen. Then my parents sent me to Paris to study medicine. I was there for one year, and then I left to begin my career as an entertainer."

Just curious, John—how does the American field of entertainment compare with that of the French?

America Leads

"France follows America. Every American hit is translated into French and becomes a hit in France. Rock 'n' roll is the biggest thing over there now." Also, the American audience just wants to be entertained and it is much easier to sing for them."

Are there any shows such as Shindig on the French television now?

"Not yet, unfortunately."

Do you have any personal ambitions for your career in the future?

"Yes, to get a hit record in the American hit parade because no French singer has ever gotten one. Also to do a movie—a musical comedy."

We'll all be looking forward to that, Monsieur Vignon, but until then—Au revior et merci beaucoup! (For those of you who do not speak French, all I said was, 'Sigh, drool, growl!)

Well Shindiggers—it's been an exciting "first-nighter" here for us and now our time is running short. We'll be back again next week with more special guests and regulars and also we will have a very special surprise. Beginning next week, a young man named Bobby Sherman is going to co-host the Shindig column. So tune in next week for another fab visit to the halls of Shindig, and till then—ROCK ON!!!

CHER IN HER "WOTCHAMACALLIT" and Sonny in his animal skin tails and out-of-this world boots look on in mirth as the dressed-up Righteous Brothers do their stuff on 'Shindig.'

Seekers Rock From Down Under

By SUSAN FRISCH

The instant hit is by no means new in the unpredictable world of teen music. Why some records hit the best-selling charts immediately on release is a phenomenon probably never to be analyzed. The fact is that nobody—especially the lucky performers—questions an instant hit. When the performers are a brand new singing group, to boot, happy acceptance of their good fortune is a foregone conclusion.

In the case of The Seekers, an Australian group of three males and one female, their stroke of instant luck came in the sound of "I'll Find Another You," a first record that was a smash immediately on release in Great Britain and the United States.

Strong Opinions

The individual Seekers—Athol Guy, Judith Durham, Bruce Woodley and Keith Potger—voice strong opinions on the trend in music that has been so influential throughout the western world for the past two years.

"As long as people continue to write songs, and sing them with a special meaning to other people they will be accepted," Athol believes. "What it all comes down to," he explains, is the material. If you've got it, you're in. Unfortunately, America, like Britain, has been deluged by many 'one hit' groups who vanish after their first big records disappear from the hit charts." The bespectacled member of the group then spoke for the Seekers. "As for us," Athol said, "we feel reasonably confident that we can stay around .. we cant' sing anything that we don't like ourselves ... the type of songs we prefer are those in which the words mean something . . . like, 'I'll Never Find Another You.'"

Birthplaces

Athol, like the other members of the group, is very anxious to see New York. On this they are unanimous. New York is indeed half a world away from their birthplaces: Judith, Athol and Bruce were born in Austirilia where they met Ceylon-born Keith. At the time of the first meeting Athol and Bruce worked for an advertising agency in Melbourne; Judith was a secretary and Keith was a producer of radio shows. This was in the Year of the Beatles—early in 1964.

In Melbourne the group began to appear on several TV shows and worked in coffee houses. With some of this experience under the collective belt they decided for a try at the Big Town ... London. Three weeks following their arrival in Britain's capitol the quartet made its first important public appearance on the TV show, "Sunday Night at the London Palladium," the British equivalent of America's *Ed Sullivan Show*.

First Record

In December 1964 they recorded "I'll Never Find Another You" in England. Within three months following its release the record was well on its way to the top spot on the charts.

About the same time that the record had reached the hit spot in England, it was released in America, and as you all know the rest was history.

Soon they will be making another single, then a new Capitol album, which also is the label that they record under, and finally a world-wide tour that will include a return trip to Australia, and of course their first visit to the United States. Now to tell you a little about each one:

Breakdown

Athol was born on January 5, 1940, which also makes him the oldest, in Victoria, Australia. He is 6-ft. ½-in. tall with a shining cap of jet black hair and deep blue eyes. He loves golf, cars, and expensive nights out with girls! He also loves bird-watching, and hates his crooked nose!

Judith Durham saw light on July 3, 1943, making her the youngest, in Melbourne. She has dark brown hair, brown eyes, and is mad about ice in her drinks, classical and ragtime music, dressmaking, and her pet dog. She hates dirty rings around bathtubs.

Bruce, also born in Melbourne, met the world on July 25, 1942. Standing at 6-ft. 1-in., with brown hair and blue eyes, he loves to play squash and swim, loves cold beer, but will definitely let you know that he hates people who snore ... is that a hint, Bruce?

Keith Potger was born on March 2, 1941 in Colombo, Ceylon. He's the tallest of the group, standing at 6-ft. 1½-in., has brown hair, and green eyes. He loves vintage cars, Leonard Bernstein's work, surfing and driving. The one thing he hates most is getting up early, whether it's the morning, afternoon, or night!

One thing is for sure, though. Whether or not these four were seeking success or not, they sure FOUND IT!!!

THE SEEKERS

KRLA ARCHIVES

For Girls Only

I've promised myself I'm going to keep the pledge I made last week (or whenever it was that I experienced this particular weak moment) and not say one unkind word to the boys who are eavesdropping on this for-girls-only conversation.

I am, however, going to say two unkind words. GET LOST!

Now that we're rid of them, let's talk about them. No, on second thought, let's talk about us.

Flabbergasted

I read something the other day that really left me flabbergasted. Some famous male star (can't remember who, but he wasn't of the teenage variety) made the most brilliant comment I've ever heard about women. I can't quote him directly, but in essence he said that women stop being interesting when they fall in love. They lose their own identity and also their spark and independence and many of the things the lucky guy fell in love with in the first place.

Like I said, that is a brilliant comment. I'm sure he put it into words better than I did, but I've never heard anything so true in my life!

Naturally, I right away started thinking back to my own tragic loves, and if he didn't hit the nail on the head where you're concerned, he was dead right about your's truly.

One of my "memorable moments" was especially just like what he said. I always have been sort of a nut. You know, I like to horse around and joke and do semi-ridiculous things. Well, I finally succeeded in attracting the attention of a certain boy I'd been wilting about, and we went steady for about three months.

Play The Field

At the end of those three months, when he told me he thought we'd better "play the field," he did something that hurt my feelings for about three years! Right in the middle of this painful moment, he *yawned!*

I think, for the first time, I know why he did. When we first started going together, I was myself. You know, still kind of a nut. But one time he gave me a dirty look right in the middle of one of my capers, and I stopped kidding around. He also said something about liking a certain hairstyle, which I immediately copied, and a lot of other things now that I think about it.

By the time those three months were up, he wasn't going steady with *me*. He was dating the person I'd become in hopes of pleasing him. Boy, is that *dumb!* If the real me hadn't pleased him, he wouldn't have asked me to go steady in the first place. No wonder he yawned. He was probably bored to tears!

I know I've raved on and on about this subject for about a million paragraphs, and plan to shut up any second now, but it's really weird that I never really thought about this topic before. I would love to hear your comments, and if you feel like sharing a disastrous experience or two, feel free to bend my ear for pages and pages. After all, you'd just be returning the favor!

Solved Problem

Oh, I just have to tell you this before I forget it. I don't know if you have this next sort of problem (I used to, but now I have a car—such as it is), but if you do, I think my cousin from Dearborn, Michigan just solved it. (She's been writing me long letters ever since I started writing this column—I think she is hinting for a plug or something.)

Anyway, Mariette (that's her name—which rather goes without saying) lives about six blocks from her closest friend and often has to take long terrified walks home in the dead of night. She's sort of chicken anyway (to be truthful about it, this trait runs in our family) and kept harboring thoughts of buying fourteen-foot hatpins or some such item for protection.

Well, not thinking this was such a good idea, she sat down and analyzed the situation. And she came up with an answer that no one but a cousin of mine could think of (other things run in our family, too). Now, when she has to make the moonlit trek, she carries, clutched firmly in her small right hand, *a very large ball bat.*

All of her friends are in hysterics about this, but Mariette couldn't care less. She just grins fiendishly and stalks onward. No one has ever bothered her, before or after her turn at bat, but she keeps hoping.

Cherry Bombs

When I told one of my friends about this, she just scoffed and said she knows someone who has an even better bodyguard. A friend of her's carries a supply of cherry bombs, or whatever those firecrackers are that you throw to make them explode. (The kind that don't really hurt anyone but have been known to scare ten years off the life of everyone in a ten mile radius.)

Well, I've raved on again. I don't know what's wrong with me lately. When I sit down to write my column, I have about a million things in mind. Then I start rambling and pretty soon I've used up all my space with just two or three subjects.

Matter of fact, I think I also used up a lot of space talking about how much space I'm using up. (I think they're coming for me soon.)

One more thing. I'm all shook up about George Harrison being in town and have been watching a lot of television to quiet my nerves. It isn't working, but I have noticed something rather amusing. On TV, whenever teenage girls talk on the telephone, they always do so while lying on the floor with their feet in a chair. I don't do that, do you? If so, please write and tell me what I'm missing!

Gotta, go! Bye, ta, and see you next BEAT!

On The BEAT

By Louise Criscione

There are times when Mick Jagger is terribly quiet and mumbles only the bare necessities to injuring reporters. But there are other times when he openly speaks his mind becoming bluntly honest and unusually frank.

Mick was recently in just such a mood and so obligingly let off some Jaggersteam on a subject which has been disturbing him for some time now and is the apparent reason why the Stones make all their records here in America.

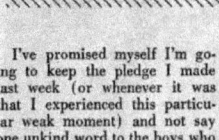

MICK JAGGER

"Recording in England—it's just one slow, painful drag. The whole scene is dead boring now, we're all waiting for something to happen but nothing does.

"For a start, the whole attitude of English recording engineers is simply slap dash. They just want to get the record knocked out as quickly as possible so they can all go home.

"They just don't care about what they are recording; they are not interested. In America, the engineers are just as excited over new sounds as we are. I'm not judging just by Rolling Stones sessions but other sessions I have been to, too."

Donovan's Doc

During the month of September, Donovan will make a 45 minute documentary for the BBC. Donovan will commentate the program which will depict he and some of his friends in typical situations. Donovan is reportedly very excited about the film and will title the show himself. It will be featured on on the BBC during prime time and will also be sold here in America thus allowing Statesiders the opportunity to view Donovan in his "typical situations."

The members of *Them* seem to be having some trouble with their personnel. Some time ago Billy Harrison left and was replaced by the Italian-born Joe Boni, and now the group's drummer, John McAuley, has left the group and is being replaced by London-born Terry Noon. This leaves only two members of the original *Them* still with the group, Van Morrison and Alan Henderson. No reason was given for this 50 per cent shake-up.

After the reviews his movie received, Dave Clark is temporarily off English movie critics. He says: "It's really ridiculous to send artsy-craftsy film critics to review our sort of film. It's meant simply as a vehicle for pop artists. You get some one along who normally does Shakesperian reviews and it's obvious he isn't going to like it."

Apparently the teenagers liked the movie all right because Dave reports that it has broken house records during its out-of-town English tour.

Burdon's Beliefs

Eric Burdon is putting the finishing touches on his book, to be titled "Going Out Of My Head." The book will be about a lot of things—discrimination, a plea for understanding and tolerance, Eric's experiences as

DAVE CLARK

a singer, Eric's travels with artists such as Carl Perkins, and the difference between American and English music.

Eric says: "As a rock 'n' roll singer I've met the highest and the lowest types of people. I wanted to tell people about my experiences through my book."

It really ought to be some book and I, for one, can hardly wait until it is released. Just goes to show that many pop artists are highly intelligent individuals and not just a bunch of dopes and high school drop-outs as many people would have you believe.

QUICK ONES: Watch for Jeremy's London musical, "Passion Flower Hotel," to be made into a movie. And they would like very much to get Dick Lester (director for both Beatle films) to direct the movie. . . . Ringo is so taken with go-karting that he is having a track built in his new Surrey home. . . . Remember Billy J. Kramer? Well, you probably wouldn't recognize him now—he's lost so much weight. . . . Brenda Lee is set for a November tour of England which will be filled with three weeks of ballroom and concert dates.

Love John Lennon's quotes—this guy has one of the quickest and cleverest minds around. When he was in New York for the Beatles' Shea Stadium concert, someone asked John what the thought about the promoter of the show, a man named Sid Bernstein, and John replied deadpan "I think 'West Side Story' is his best work."

Giggle of the Week . . .

The Ad Lib Club is one of the most popular young adult night clubs in London, and is noted for its famous patronage, having both the Beatles and the Stones as frequent customers.

On a pleasant evening not long ago, Mick Jagger and Keith Richard invited John Lennon and road-manager Neil Aspinall back to their flat for a final "coke for the road," after one of their gab-sessions at the Ad Lib.

After a long evening of talk and record-playing, the two Stone-men decided to do a fast disappearing-act as they headed for a long over-due rendezvous with the sandman. Although they were welcome to camp out on the couch, Neil and John decided to beat a path for home instead.

Due to the hour, they were unable to capture any runaway taxis, so the pair finally made for one of the "tubes," or underground trains, in the area. It was very early in the morning, and the "tubes" were just beginning to run. Neil reminisces, "It was amazing; there were loads of workmen and cleaners all over the place, but hardly anyone looked at John with the usual question mark in their eyes."

The funniest part of this After Hours Adventure came when the two weary travellers disembarked at a place called Tottenham Court Road. The escalator was not yet working so John and Neil trudged all the way to the top of the long, long, long flight of stairs, while a little man watched them from up on top. When finally, all out of breath and completely exhausted, they reached him, he placidly turned around and pressed a small button which started the escalator moving!!

Oh well, you were beginning to put on a few extra pounds anyway, John!

(Giggle, giggle.)

KRLA ARCHIVES

Rolling Stones, Sonny And Cher Lead In Far Out Trend

(Continued from Page 3)

hit home and it *does* hurt.

Sonny & Cher laughed, termed the entire incident "amusing" and went on to find much better accommodations anyway. Still, Sonny obviously gave the "amusing" incident some thought for he philosophized: "I think most people are afraid of doing anything which isn't conventional. It is they who have a complex, not people like us."

Clothes Don't Matter

Still another one of our readers, Jenny Anne Jones, feels that clothes don't have anything to do with what a person is. She writes: "The BEAT ran an old picture of the Stones showing them in a more formal attire and asked if we like them better then or now.

"Surely, the BEAT realizes it does not matter what the Stones look like but what they do and what they are that really counts. Since when have clothes taken on the job of giving instant biographies?

"To know someone requires much more time and effort than is put into a prejudiced glance at clothing and hair styles, which are matters of taste. If more people would stop being lazy and take the time to know people before judging them by such trivial things as their clothes, then all the Sonny Bonos in the world would not have to turn the other cheek. We would learn to appreciate a person for what he is inside, not just for what he happens to be wearing."

Dissenter

But apparently not all BEAT readers agree with Jenny' for a person who signed his/her letter "Jloonrod" wrote: "I have just read an issue of your paper and I must say that never in my life have I ever witnessed such a collection of Micro-cephalics. The collection of wooly idiots staring at me was frightening. I thought at first glance it was a publication of some sheep-growers association.

"With Donovan leading a cast of Bob Dylan, Mick Jagger, Cher—and his? or her?—husband even I could produce a movie which would scare the heck out of any teenagers!"

As far as the BEAT is concerned, Jloonrod stands alone. We have received no other letters endorsing his/her negative stand on the subject.

But we have been receiving stacks and stacks of mail voicing the opinion that a person should be able to dress exactly as he sees fit without being subject to ridicule by narrowminded individuals.

Clothes do NOT make the man—only the man can do that.

RIVERS JOINS GUARD

Popular recording artist, Johnny Rivers, has joined the California Army National Guard. This means that Johnny must serve from four to six months active duty beginning sometime in either September or October.

MICK: ". . . I'LL TAKE IT OFF AND SHOW YA!"

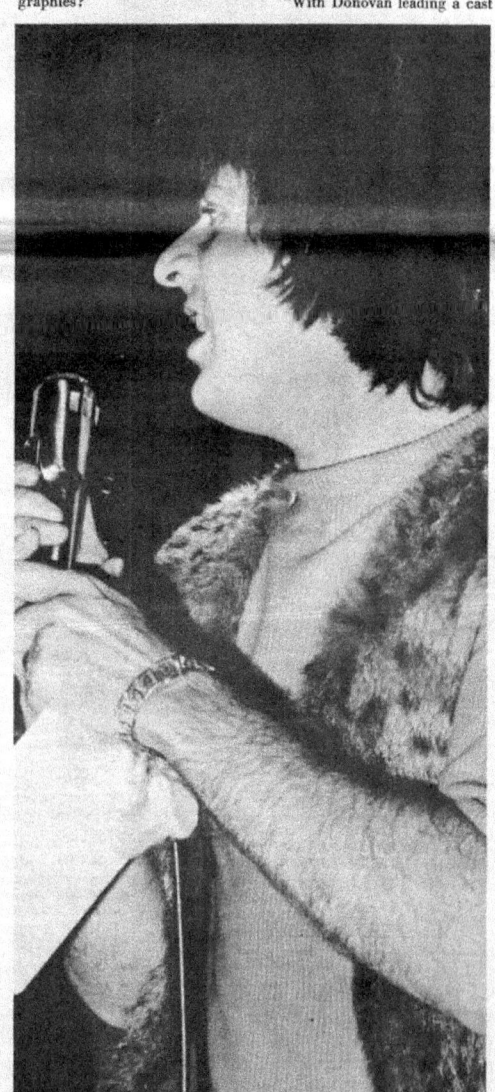

SONNY BONO — "NOT TIDY ENOUGH"

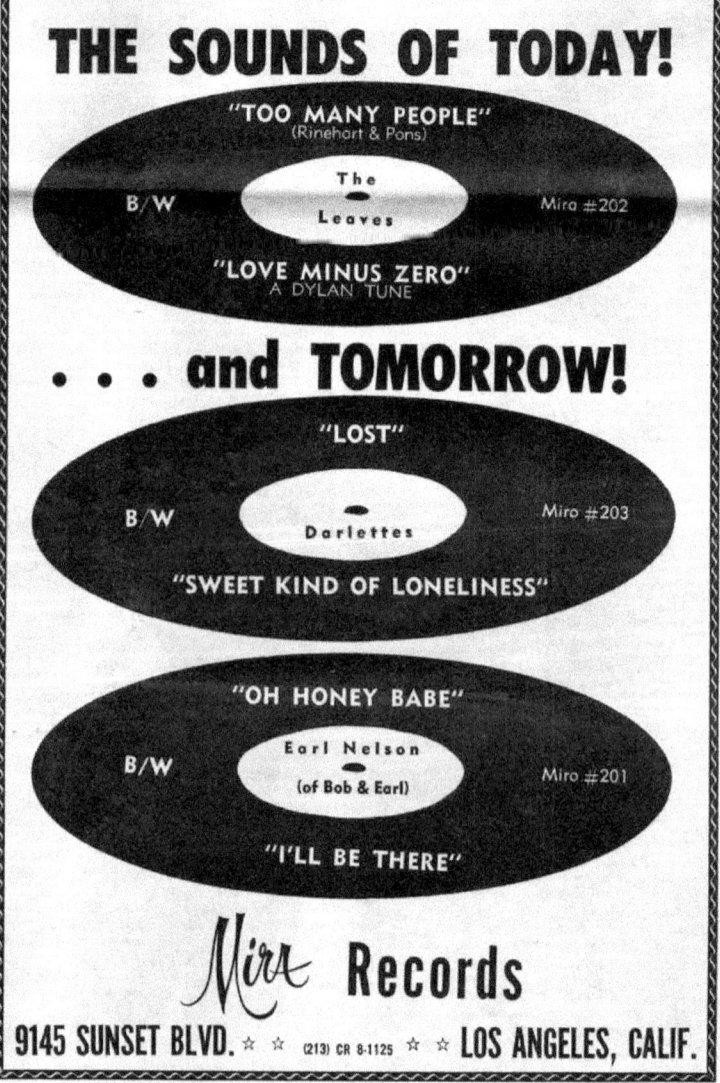

KRLA ARCHIVES

DAVE HULL, IAN WHITCOMB, CHARLIE O'DONNELL

MARIANNE FAITHFULL

DONOVAN TELLS CASEY KASEM and a "Shebang" audience how he writes and records such hits as "Catch the Wind" and "Colours." But the popular English star won't say where he got the shirt.

PEN PALS

Patti Carver, 1142 Fruitridge Road, Placerville, California, 95667, U.S.A.

Wants girl or boy pen pal from England, Canada, and U.S. between the ages of 15 and 17.

Dawn Voinovich, 10537 Danube Ave., Granada Hills, Calif.

Especially like George Harrison.

Anne Navarro, 317 So. Bush St., Anaheim, Calif., 92805.

Likes writing to people and will answer all letters. She is 16 and likes all pop groups.

Margaret Ruelas, 463 E. Kamala, Oxnard, Calif.

She is 14 years old and likes all English pop groups. She is looking for a girl or a boy pen pal.

Darlene Merrill, 3044 Cedar St., Bishop, Calif.

She is 16 years old, blonde hair and blue eyes. Darlene likes all English groups, and enjoys water-skiing and dancing.

Gloria Grimes, P.O. Box 2314 Oxnard, California.

Gloria would like a pen pal from England, preferably a boy.

Kathie Emery, 3903 Ashworth St., Lakewood, Calif., 90712.

Kathie would like a boy or a girl pen pal from England. She is 14 years old and loves the Beatles.

DANCING
7 NIGHTS A WEEK
PANDORA'S BOX
8118 SUNSET STRIP

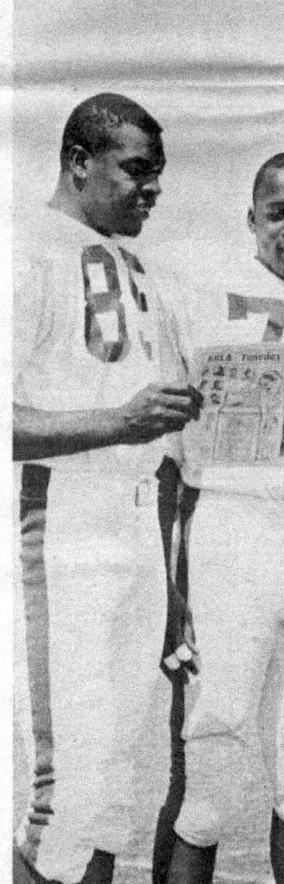

FOUR MORE BEAT READERS — the men, who also record for Capital, ca termilk." Opposing linemen will reco Jones, Merlin Olsen and Charlie "W

KRLA ARCHIVES

...EADS THE BEAT

BYRDS' JIM McGUINN

...AND EVEN HERMAN!

"Fearsome Foursome." The famed Los Angeles Rams defensive line- [take] time out to read about their first record release, "Fly In The But[ter ...recog]nize them instantaly as (from left) Lamar Lundy, David "Deacon" [Jones, ...De]ack" Cowan.

Personals

To Peter Noone:
Thanks for calling me up. I want to tell the world but no one would believe it. I luv you.
Luv, "Freddie."

* * *

To Annette McDonald in Southampton:
How does it feel to see your name in print? Se ya in '67, luv! Your pen pal in Covina, Merri.

* * *

To Robin Kingsley:
We're still rooting for ya!!
Your fans forever:
Menda, Linda, Rosie and Kathleen.

The KRLA BEAT is published weekly by BEAT Publications; editorial and advertising offices at 6290 Sunset Boulevard, Suite 504, Hollywood, California 90028.
Single copy price, 15 cents. Subscription price, U.S and possessions, $3 per year or $5 for two years. Canada and foreign rates, $9 per year or $14 for two years.
Exclusive distribution handled by Miller-Freeman Publications, 6328 Lewis Avenue, Long Beach, California. Inquiries should be directed to the attention of David Thomas.

Back issues of the KRLA BEAT are still available, for a limited time. If you've missed an issue of particular interest to you, send 15 cents for each copy wanted, along with a self-addressed stamped envelope to:

KRLA BEAT
Suite 504
6290 Sunset Blvd.
Hollywood, California 90028

ISSUES AVAILABLE

- 4/14 — INTERVIEW WITH JOHN LENNON
- 4/21 — INTERVIEW WITH PAUL McCARTNEY
- 4/28 — CHIMP EXCITES TEEN FAIR
- 5/5 — HERMANIA SPREADS
- 5/12 — HERE COME THE BEATLES
- 5/19 — VISIT WITH BEATLES
- 5/26 — FAB NEW BEATLE QUIZ
- 6/16 — BATTLE OF THE BEAT
- 6/30 — PROBY FIRED
- 7/24 — BEATLES TOP STONES
- 7/31 — CHER
- 8/7 — DYLAN
- 8/14 — HERMAN
- 8/21 — STONES TESTIFY
- 8/28 — KRLA PRESENTS THE BEATLES
- 9/4 — BEATLES .... IN PERSON NOW!

KRLA BEAT SUBSCRIPTION

you will SAVE 60% of the regular price!
AN INTRODUCTORY SPECIAL ... if you subscribe now ...

☐ 1 YEAR — 52 Issues — $3.00   ☐ 2 YEARS — $5.00

Enclosed is $..........................

Send to:...Age:............

Address:..

City:...................................State:...................Zip:.............

MAIL YOUR ORDER TO: KRLA BEAT
1401 South Oak Knoll Avenue
Outside U.S.: $9.00 — 52 Issues   Pasadena, California 91106

KRLA ARCHIVES

LESLIE GORE HAS A NEW IMAGE. The old one was fine, but the new one is like "Wow!" The "Sunshine, Lollipops and Rainbows" girl now includes a good selection of ballads along with her up-tempo teen material. Sporting a new hairdo and a polished stage presence, she will co-star with the Animals in a series of West Coast appearances this month.

RECORD QUIZ

Hi there! Yes, yes, we know! You've been expecting us and *where are we?* We *know* we promised to *resign from our* underpaid positions and join you on the green, but our plans have hit a *snag*.

When we went in to see the boss (that old snag!) to tender (not very) our resignations, he didn't even give us a chance. He fired us, with real matches yet.

In view of this, we are left with no choice. We can make you miserable by leaving, but we can make him *sooo* much *more* miserable by staying!

But don't think you're off the hook and can climb peacefully back into that hammock. We've thought up another record quiz to keep *that* from happening. After all, what do you think this is? A vacation or something?

ANOTHER RECORD QUIZ

Taking it from the top, see how many last names you can supply for the following singers. You'll find the answers printed upside down at the bottom.

1. Freddie .... (And The Dreamers)
2. Sonny and Cher ....
3. Peter .... and Gordon
4. Gerry .... (and The Pacemakers)
5. Chad .... and Jeremy ....
6. Dino ...., Desi .... and Billy ....

ANSWERS (AND DON'T THINK WE DON'T KNOW YOU'RE PEERING AGAIN): 1—Freddie Garraty, 2—Sonny & Cher Bono, 3—Peter Asher and Gordon Waller, 4—Gerry Marsden, 5—Chad Stuart and Jeremy Clyde, 6—Dino Martin, Desi Arnaz and Billy Hinske. Oh, by the way, all is not lost. We can always drop over *after* work. And none of your "not unless I live on a cliff" stuff either!

JUST PASSING BY . . .

By Eden

Paul McCartney has begun riding a collapsible bicycle which he bought recently. It seems that Paul Beatle, M.B.E. finds it much more convenient than a car when he is Beating it 'round Foggy London Town.

John Lennon has had a supply of brushes, paints, and canvasses delivered to his home in Surrey, England. Word has it that our Chief Beatle has decided to start dabbling in the ol' oils once again.

In the Beatles' new film, "Help," the boys are wearing some very special outfits. No ordinary business suits for our Beatle Bards! Instead, they are sporting matched outfits of their own design. For example, they have coupled corduroy suits with boots in the same fabric, matching suits 'n' boots of velveteen, and so on.

George H. claims to have had the idea over two years ago, but says that local bootmakers just gave him the cold shoe!

Quote from Richard Starkey, Esq.: "I think we opened up the way in America for English artists and it pleases me to see the lads riding high in the charts."

Eddie Hodges On New Tour

Eddie Hodges, the freckled faced, red-headed, 18-year-old, who became the heart throb of hundreds of girls through the movie, "Hole in the Head," is now on a two month tour of fourteen cities, beginning in Boston, and ending in Texas. Other groups and entertainers on tour with Eddie are The Kingsmen, The Guess Who, The Rocking Ramrods, Dion, and Barbara Mason.

Eddie, who records for Aurora Records, will be pushing his latest record, "New Orleans," once made big by Gary U.S. Bonds. Last summer, while Eddie was on another tour, it so happened he and the Kingsmen were on the same bill of stars. There formed a strong friendship between Eddie and the group and since that time they have been planning a tour for this year together again.

Some of you may know Eddie from television, as he has appeared on Hollywood A Go Go, Shiveree, Shebang, and most of the other teen programs.

THE KINKS — DAVE, PETER, MICK AND RAY.

FACTS ABOUT EACH MEMBER
Straight Scoop On The Kinks-Still Hot

Ray Davies, Dave Davies and Pete Quaife are the founder members of the kinks.

Ray Davies, the 21 year-old lead singer and Dave Davies, the 18-year-old lead guitarist, are brothers from the Muswell Hill area of London. Ray, who also writes the songs for the group, is the only married Kink. He married Rosa Dicpetri on December 12, 1964.

Devon Man

Pete Quaife, who plays the bass guitar for the group, was born in Tavistock, Devon and is the only Kink born out of the London area.

Mick Avory, drummer for the group, joined the Kinks in December of 1963. He is the only member of the group to have played with the Rolling Stones back in the days when only Mick Jagger and Brain Jones were in the group. "I played with them for two weeks while they were in London," he said. When the Stones went on tour he was unable to join them.

Before joining the Kinks, Mick used to work as an excavator on a building site. The ex-excavator is the only Kink without a sister. Pete has one sister—Anne. Ray and Dave have five: Rose, Doll, Cath, Vi and Gwen.

Ray and Dave were former art students and Dave is presently famous for being a camera bug.

The Kinks got started in London. Their Hits have been: "You Really Got Me Going," "All Day and All the Night," "Tired of Waiting," and "Set Me Free." "Set Me Free," their latest record, is currently number three in England.

Latest Single

In England they recorded for the Pye label and their latest single there was "Everybody's Gonna Be Happy," but the B side, "Who'll be the Next In Line," has had more air play here and seems to be the number preferred.

The Kinks press agent, Brian Sommerville, was formerly the press agent for the Beatles before Derek Taylor took on the job.

KRLA ARCHIVES

TEENS SIDE OF STORY

MAYBE IT'S TIME TO PROTEST

Please sit down and listen for a minute, Mom and Dad. And let's invite the teacher and perhaps the preacher, too, while we're at it.

We're going to sound off on something that's been bothering us a lot lately. We'll say this respectfully, but we mean every word of it.

You've been belittling teenagers for a long time now, saying contradictory things such as teenagers should be seen and not heard . . . that we need to shoulder more responsibility . . . that all we're interested in is having a good time, and the things that go on inside our own little world that we've created. You've said we're young and foolish, lazy and delinquent (recent FBI figures show that three per cent of the teenagers ARE, but that's far from the majority). And here lately we've even been accused of being radical because many of us like such songs as "Eve of Destruction."

True, we have our own "private world" where we have a great deal of fun. But that isn't all we have. We have also learned to cope with and solve a lot of ugly problems that you don't seem to be making much headway on.

Bigotry Acquired

We have learned to get along with each other. How did we manage that one? Quite easily. No person is born with feelings of prejudice, bigotry and intolerance. These things have to be acquired. Just as some of you acquired them. Only we haven't let that happen to us, because we learned from your mistakes.

We don't judge our fellow teenagers on the basis of race or religion or social standing. Look at the names and pictures on the best-selling record charts if you have any doubt.

A lot of you are stirred up because we are listening to protest songs such as "Eve of Destruction." You say this is a radical message, that it's a political philosophy or a conspiracy and that we're too young to meddle in politics because we don't understand what it's all about.

Listen, we're old enough to be called into the Army and to fight your battles. And if we're old enough for that, we're old enough to have a say in the way things are run. You fought a revolutionary war a couple of hundred years ago for those same principles — representation and self-determination.

As for being radical, what's so different about wanting a better world, or wanting to keep the old one in one piece? What's radical about being alarmed by the race to build even bigger bombs capable of wiping out civilization? What's radical about asking for a chance to vote, along with the chance to kill? What's wrong with being nauseated by the hatred and violence between fellow Americans in Mississippi or California?

Right To Listen

That's all that "Eve of Destruction" mentions. You may not like the song — and not all teenagers like it either — but at least you should be tolerant enough to allow others to listen to it. Or do you just want us to listen to "Lollipops and Rainbows"?

As a matter of fact, most teenagers don't think we're on the "Eve of Destruction." Most of us think we're on the eve of the greatest, happiest civilization mankind has ever known.

We think this because we're going to help make it that way. You admit you had great dreams when you were young of "changing the world." But you say you "outgrew" that phase. We're not going to outgrow ours. The world CAN be changed if we stop letting ourselves "outgrow" our youthful determination. "We" means all the people our age, in other countries as well as this one. The world of music and the world of I-C-B-Ms has brought us closer together.

We're going to work and struggle and protest and plan until we can somehow develop a workable way to begin substituting love for hate, happiness for misery and generosity for selfishness. This isn't a new plan. According to many books it was advanced two thousand years ago. You talk about it yourselves every Sunday, but you talk about it in the PAST tense instead of the present.

We're going to find some way to get together and work out a way to stop fighting among ourselves so that we can all work together in fighting hunger, poverty, disease and the using up of our natural resources, which threatens someday to make this world a barren plain.

Use It Right

Your generation has given us great scientific advances, but very few humanitarian ones. We're going to try to find a better way to use this knowledge.

Please let us make just three main points:

1. *Just because life has always been a certain way doesn't mean it always has to continue that way.*

2. *If you think wars are inevitable, then please try just one thing. Try fighting them with people YOUR age instead of OUR age for a change. If every country would do that we don't think there would be any more wars.*

3. *Since we have a pretty big stake in the future of this world too, and since you're calling on us to help you out of your scrapes, at least be tolerant enough and democratic enough to allow us to express our opinions too.*

Thanks for listening.

IN "HELP" JOHN CAME DOWN TO EARTH IN SNOW-CLAD ALPS

KRLA ARCHIVES

A DAY IN HIS LIFE
Joey Paige Finds Secret To Success: Plain Work

Even wonder how a pop personality spends his day? We did so we spoke to Joey Paige who obligingly let the BEAT follow him around on one of his "typical" days.

And, of course, where the BEAT goes—you go. So are you ready?

Up in Joey's apartment the alarm goes off and a sleepy and tousled-haired Joey squints an eye at the hands of the clock. They show a ridiculously early hour. He'd really like to go back to sleep, but a little bell goes off in his brain reminding him that today is the day he tapes "Shindig." So he drags his unwilling body out of the bed and into the shower.

After a quick cup of coffee, Joey heads out of the door and into his newly-purchased bronze and cream Cadillac Coupe de Ville. And Joey's off to be fitted for a tux. Tonight on "Shindig" they are going completely formal so Joey patiently waits while the ordeal of tux-fitting drags on.

Stage Clothes

Next stop—the cleaners. Joey's stage clothes were sent out two days earlier and he stops now to pick them up. With that out of the way, we board the Cadallic again and we're off to the studio.

It takes four days of rehearsals to get "Shindig" ready for the cameras. Today's Thursday—final taping day. This is the day that no one wants to make any mistakes because every mistake made today on tape costs the network money.

Joey arrives at the studio and the guard waves him in. The cast is gathered around Donovan who is giving an impromptu performance.

The last minute technical problems are hopefully ironed out by now and at 4 o'clock the cast assembles for a rehearsal.

Nervous

It's a nerve-racking business—taping a show. Joey waits around until it's his turn in front of the cameras. He's nervous. On the outside it doesn't show—being a performer he can't afford to let it show, but on the inside it's murder. This waiting around—he wonders if it will ever end.

Members of Joey's fan club are on the set. Many performers don't bother with their fans, especially on these nervous taping days. But Joey doesn't feel that way. He has a great bunch of fans behind him—and he knows it and not only does he know it, but he *appreciates* it.

He takes time out to talk to them. They want to know what's happening with his career, with him. "I'm going to Twenty Nine Palms for 30 days this month." So what's in Twenty Nine Palms, they ask. "The Marine Corps!" Joey explains.

More Questions

The girls want to know about Joey's famous bell bottom pants, is he going to wear them all the time now? "Sure, I'm the Bell Bottom Kid. I wear them all the time on stage."

Then come the inevitable questions about Joey's newest record—the best one he's ever done, "Goodnight My Love."

"I did it on my own. I paid for the session myself because I had so much confidence in it. I wanted it to come out just right, so I went ahead on my own and cut it.

"I do 'Goodnight My Love' in my act and the kids really dig it. When I went out on the 'Shindig' tour, it was the biggest number I did—it got the biggest reception."

Editor's Note: Joey's modest. It got the biggest reception on the entire show!)

Dress Rehearsal

He'd like to talk some more but it's now 6 o'clock and time for the dress rehearsal. It means more waiting, more mistakes, more problems.

And then it's time—time for the final taping. The show is taped in segments. It's Joey's turn now. Just as he steps in front of the camera he gets the news—in his segment they have *eight* minutes of tape left but *nine* minutes of show!

Joey was nervous before—now he's frantic! But again, no one knows for Joey's face relects nothing but calm. He takes his position, the camera's red light comes on and Joey launches into his song.

It goes down great. This is one of the most enthusiastic audiences that "Shindig" has ever had, even the television officials comment on it.

Joey's fans are packed into the audience, they wave banners at him, and he feels really good—it makes the whole thing worthwhile.

It's late now. The show's over and Joey and the Shindogs head for a nearby club, The Haunted House, where they try to rid themselves of the tension which has been building up all day long.

It's *really* late now as Joey leaves the club, it seems like years since his alarm clock went off this morning.

Wearily, Joey climbs into his car. He's looking forward to some sleep, but the minute he walks into his apartment the phone starts ringing.

It seems like it never stops. Joey wonders how so many people get his unlisted number and why they call at all hours of the day and night.

When the phone is finally silent, Joey crawls into bed and sets his alarm.

It'll go off early again tomorrow.

JOEY VIEWS LONDON FROM BRIAN JONES' APARTMENT

'Quips 'n Quotes'
by Eden

"Out of the mouths of celebrities," ad into your homes come the latest flashes from our Hotline to the world of entertainment.

Question for French sigh-guy John Paul Vignon: Do you speak any languages other than French and English? "Yes—the language of love! . . ."

Pity the poor beautiful blonde in Hollywood; it's a rough life all over! Says pretty Kathy Kersh: "Right now I'm concentrating on singing and I hope to combine singing and acting later. Part of the problem in acting is—if you are a pretty blonde in Hollywood—the producers refuse to take you seriously. But if you are talented, people in the music industry take you seriously immediately. Naturally I prefer to be regarded as a performer, not as some starlet." Oh, naturally!!

Speaking of his new son, who is just two and a half months old, Bill Medley of the Righteous Brothers says: "He plays the bass guitar and is forming a group with the kids around the block. I'd like to teach him to sing blues by the time he's six years old." OOHHHHHHH??? You aren't thinking of forming a new act, now are you?

George Harrison of the M.B.E. set proclaims: "We have a great hold in America and we like to see British artists coming up. We have never been jealous of anyone."

John Lennon: "I can do the Freddie dance now. Watch!" Freddie *WHO*, John-John??!!

ALREADY A HIT IN ENGLAND, JOEY REFLECTS UPON SUDDEN SUCCESS HERE

KRLA ARCHIVES

CAUGHT BETWEEN TAKES during a recent television taping, members of The Rolling Stones take time out to chat with some of the audience.

BEAT Photo by C. Boyd

British Top 10

1. HELP — The Beatles
2. I GOT YOU BABE — Sonny & Cher
3. EVERYONE'S GONE TO THE MOON — Jonathan King
4. WE GOTTA GET OUT OF THIS PLACE — The Animals
5. YOU'VE GOT YOUR TROUBLES — The Fortunes
6. CATCH US IF YOU CAN — Dave Clark Five
7. A WALK IN THE BLACK FOREST — Horst Jankowski
8. ZORBA'S DANCE — Marcello Minerbi
9. ALL I REALLY WANT TO DO — The Byrds
10. IN THOUGHTS OF YOU — Billy Fury

Four In A Row

Really didn't think that it would happen but it has—the Beatles are number one again this week, making it a total of four straight weeks at the top!

The way Sonny & Cher zoomed up from number 17 to number seven with "I Got You Babe" is a pretty strong indication that perhaps next week will find them in the number one spot.

Horst Jankowski and his "Walk In The Black Forest" moved all the way up to number seven this week, and Marcello Minerbi landed in the top ten right behind Jankowski with "Zorba's Dance."

The Byrds find themselves in a rather unusual but pleasant position. They have admitted defeat as far as the U.S. race of "All I Really Want To Do" is concerned, but in England it's a slightly different story which has the Byrd's version jumping from number 20 to number nine while Cher remains at number 22.

The Righteous Brothers moved from number 26 to number 17 with their "B" sided hit, "Unchained Melody."

Another American group, the Walker Brothers, are doing much better in England than they ever did here in America. They have already placed one hit on the British charts and now they seem to have another in "Make It Easy On Yourself" which debuted this week at number 23.

The Honeycombs, who have had only one big hit Stateside, "Have I The Right," have placed another on the English charts—"That's The Way," which jumped aboard this week at number 24.

Tied with Honeycombs at 24 are the Beatles and their "Help" album. The way it jumped on the charts last week, it looked as though it would make the long climb to the top in no time at all. But in this case first indications were all wrong, for this week the album has *dropped* two places from number 22 and number 24.

MAIL BOX

Dear BEAT:

For some time I have noticed the increasing hostility between Beatle fans and Stone fans. Frankly, I'm getting very tired of it!

For All Stone Fans

I'd like to say something to the Stone fans: I think you all should remember that we owe a great deal to the Beatles. Perhaps if it hadn't been for them we might not have the Stones.

The Beatles opened the door for all the many wonderful groups we now enjoy and the pop music world was changed by these four guys! There's also no doubt that they put out some great music. Far as I'm concerned, Lennon-McCartney, and Jagger-Richard are the two greatest song-writing teams around.

To those few Stone fans that raise such a ruckus—just stop and think. Do you think Mick, Keith, Charlie, Brian and Bill go around putting down the Beatles? They are intelligent and know this is senseless. I'm sure they expect the same of their fans.

Going around cutting the Beatle fans only casts a bad light on the Stones and their fans, and it gives the troublemakers some basis for their attacks.

For All Beatle Fans

What I want to say to the Beatle fans who cut the Stones is—why? Why must you attack the Stones, and write letters to DJs complaining about the 'rotten Stones' and their 'crummy music?' Are you so afraid that your faves are in such great danger of being made "unpopular?" Have you that little faith in the Beatles?

The music of the Beatles and the Stones is vastly different. As to which group is the best depends on the individual's taste in music.

I love the Rolling Stones and I don't want to see them ridiculed by a few thick-headed Beatle fans. And I don't want to see the Stones' fans make fools out of themselves with all this fighting.

So Stone and Beatle fans—let's quit arguing and just enjoy two of the greatest groups in the world!

Sincerely,
Linda Wilson.

Dear BEAT:

I am a Bob Dylan fan (I'm proud to say) and have been for months before "Like A Rolling Stone." In August 14 BEAT, page 7, it was stated that some "die-hard folk fans reject him" because he's 'in' now. Why? I know partly why but I'd like another opinion. For a few months I've been running around playing my Dylan albums for anyone who would listen and some of my friends are now pro-Dylan. We are glad "Like A Rolling Stone" is so popular for one major reason; vast numbers are beginning to listen to him. We think this is great.

There was something in the article I didn't agree with until I'd thought it out. BEAT's right. He hasn't any great message, just a vast number of ideas that start you thinking and you create your own "message." And when you listen to him, you do a powerful lot of thinking.

My parting thought is: If he uses electric guitars to reach more people or to enchance the song, I don't care because this is one fan who doesn't care if background is a dulcimer or 50 piece orchestra as long as the songs and voice are Dylan's.

Amen,
Leona.

MEL CARTER'S "Hold Me, Thrill Me, Kiss Me" has been one of the top songs of the summer. You'll be hearing it played for years to come as a "Golden Record" selection, bringing back memories of this summer which is drawing to a close. It has also firmly established Mel as one of the world's top vocalists.

KRLA ARCHIVES

Portman's Platterpoop

We've had the English sounds, now be prepared to dig the Irish sounds. Dee Gee Records just recorded *The Fenians* first stateside release "I've Got A Feeling" b/w "Love Our Love" ... *Roger Miller* inked for a fall Hollywood Palace appearance ... Hulaballoo is coming to the west coast for two fall appearances. The shows to be taped the latter part of September with audience participation. Write to N.B.C., not The *BEAT*, for tickets.

Colpix records completed the mopping of its worried brow when *Paul Petersen* received a last minute 1Y (student deferment) rating ... *Joy Paige* departed for the Marine Corps, and his fan clubs are clamoring for his locks that'll be shorn by a Marine Corps hair stylist ... Beauteous *Raquel Welch* goes the singing route on September 22d Shindig. This should be a must see! ... *Bobby Darin's* last platter release for Capitol Records is "That Funny Feeling". It's a Darin-penned tune and is also the title of a flicker with the same name that stars Mrs. Darin, Sandra Dee.

Cheryl Miller, MGM starlet, autographed a recording contract for the record arm of that film company ... *Ray Charles* was rushed in to record the title tune to "Cincinnati Kid" ... *Spanky Mc Farland's*, Deem Records, has *Brad Berwick's* newest release "God, Country and By Baby" b/w "Are You Glad" ... September 20 is the date that *The Animals* will appear at the Melodyland Theatre in Anaheim. They're bringing with them Mercury's *Lesley Gore* and Rampart Records *Cannibal and The Headhunters* for company.

They've finally set September 27 as the release date for *Randy Boone's* album "Ramblin Randy" on Decca ... *Frankie Lymon's* release for Columbia is "I'm Sorry" b/w "Let's Be More Than Friends" ... *Elke Sommer*, one of Hollywood's loveliest, has just finished recording her first MGM single. Names of tunes have been withheld to prepare for special promotion to introduce the singer to record world ... *Tony Harris*, DeeGee Records, young bundle of talent, wrote, arranged, produced and sang the label's hot-off-the-press release of "Honey".

It pays to know the boss, or How to Succeed In the World, American-way! *Nancy Sinatra, Jr.* and *Deana Martin* silently packed with the Warner Bros.-Reprise records family of artists. *Gary Lewis and The Playboys* newest for Liberty will be "Palisades Park". Could the fact Gary was raised in the Pacific Palisades (now lives in Bel Air) have anything to do with the selection? ... Hanna-Barbera records wisely signatured the talented *New Colony Six* ... *Frank Sinatra* huddling with *Jimmy Bowen* regarding his next sides for Reprise ... United Artists records okayed the release of *Patty Duke's* "Billie" motion picture soundtrack in which Patty chirps!

Capitol records *Liza Minnelli*, her mother Judy also records for that label, signed to appear on *Danny Kaye's* January 5th outing ... *Red Skelton's* producer airlined to England to film *The Animals, Freddie & The Dreamers, The Hollies* and *The Silkies* for future Skelton shows ... *Herb Alpert and his Tijuana Brass* have another monster for his A & M label in "The Third Man Theme" ... Hanna-Barbera's "Roses and Rainbows" was arranged by Colpix records many-talented *Hank Levine* ... Remember "Alley Oop"? The group that crated the sensational tune, the Hollywood Argyles, signed with Chattahoochee records. Their first release for *Ruth Conte* will be, are you ready for this, "Long Hair, Unsquare Dude, Called Jack" b/w "Ole". Later Baby!

RECUPERATING from a serious multiple leg fracture suffered in a Paramount Studio accident recently, Jan Berry (of the Jan & Dean partnership) stiffens an upper lip and wishfully makes like a mock dive into the pool at his San Fernando Valley home. Careful, Jan — one slip and that plaster cast will send you down to Davy Jones.

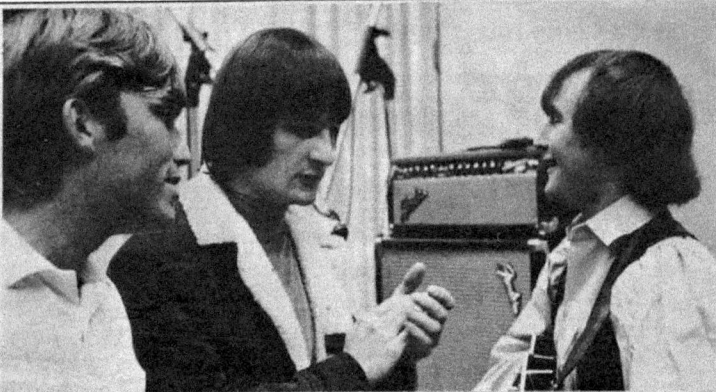

AS YOUNG A & R PRODUCER TERRY MELCHER (left) listens appreciatively, Byrds Gene Clark (center) and David Crosby monitor a "take" in the studio during the recording session recently of their trend-setting album for Columbia Records. The California group just returned from a smashingly successful British tour, their first trip overseas.

Q: I'm planning to have a party in about a month and I'm having invitation problems. First of all, there are two certain girls I want to ask, but they go around with three other girls all the time and I don't know if it would be polite to ask just two without asking the rest. Also, is it better to mail out invitations or just tell the guests when the party will be?
(Gail S.)

A: Where a crowd of five is concerned, it wouldn't be the slightest bit impolite to invite the two who are special friends of your's. When it's a twosome instead of a crowd, things can be a bit touchy if you invite one girl without also asking her constant companion, but in your case, don't worry about it. As for invitations, it would be better to mail them. Verbal invitations are fine except for one thing. The person you ask may be a million miles away when you mention the party, and could forget all about it and miss out on the fun.

Q: All the complexion soaps I've tried make my skin very dry. Can you recommend something that won't cause this problem, and also tell me how many times a day I should wash my face?
(Shirley P.)

A: There's a product called Velvet Foam (by Charles Of The Ritz) that would probably help your skin condition. It isn't a soap; it comes in tube form; and it's very non-drying. Since you don't have a surplus of oil, it might be best to limit your "facials" to one a day. If your complexion needs refreshing during the day, dash on lots of hot water and follow with cold.

Q: My mother and I have a big battle every morning and I am hoping you'll be able to settle our argument. I can't stand to eat breakfast and I feel just fine if I don't, but my mother about has a fit every time I skip this meal. As long as I feel okay without eating breakfast, I don't see why I should have to. I eat enough the rest of the day to get all my vitamins and all that. Please suggest something!
(Julie Fiore.)

A: Food is fuel and if you feel fine without re-fueling in the morning, you'd probably feel even better if you did eat breakfast regularly. Maybe the reason you avoid this meal is because you don't care for the sort of food that is synonomous with morning. Try something different, one of your favorite foods, and see if that doesn't help. You might also try Carnation Instant Breakfast, which is a whole meal in one glass, but do start the day with something. We're with your mom in that respect, because you need the energy even if you don't feel a lack of it.

Q: Do you know of a hair spray that doesn't make your hair stiff? No matter what kind I use, it always leaves a harsh kind of film, and this looks really terrible on long hair.
(Sandy R.)

A: Try Revlon's latest invention, a "touchable" sort of hair spray called Respond.

Q: I'm a sixteen year old boy and for about the last two weeks I've wanted to sleep all day and al night. And it doesn't matter if I do sleep for twenty-four hours; I'm still tired when I wake up. What is causing this and is there anything I can do about it?
(Jerry H.)

A: Unexplained exhaustion be caused by just about anything. The cause probably isn't too serious or you'd be having other effects also, but the problem is serious enough to get to the bottom of, and now.

Hint of the Week

I just recently started using a lipstick brush and I want to tell everyone what a God-send it is! It's almost impossible to just put on a "little lipstick" right from the tube, but with a brush you can make the color look so even, no one even knows you're wearing lipstick. I bought another lip brush to use for the kind of eye shadow that comes in tubes. I always got too much of it on, and in all the wrong places, before I tried this, and now I don't have that problem any more. It takes awhile to learn to use the brush just right, but it's sure worth the effort!
(Barbara G.)

... McGUIRE

McGuire Cuts New LP

From the "Eve of Destruction" to the brink of success is the road on which one Mr. Barry McGuire is traveling these days.

Barry has a brand new album titled "Eve of Destruction," and if his single by the same name is any indication, then Mr. McGuire has a best-selling LP on his hands.

Aside from the title song, the album includes selections such as: "Sloop John B.," "She Belongs to Me," "You Were on My Mind," and "What Exactly Is the Matter With Me?"

Six of the songs on the album were penned especially for Barry by P. F. Sloan, who is the author-composer of "Eve of Destruction."

KRLA ARCHIVES

THE BEAT GOES TO THE MOVIES

'SKI PARTY'

By JIM HAMBLIN

THIS IS ANOTHER ONE OF THOSE AMERICAN-INTERNATIONAL PICTURES, IN WHICH THE COLOR IS GREAT, THE STORY ENTERTAINS, AND THE GIRLS ARE TOO GOOD TO BE TRUE. LET'S GO ON A **SKI PARTY** OURSELVES . . . .

1. **IT ALL STARTED** when the two Football Stars in school could never make any time with the girls. These all-around athletes are perplexed . . . .

2. **AND THIS GUY** is the reason why (Aron Kincaid) and you can see he is very popular (Mary Hughes, Patti Chandler) with the young ladies . . . .

3. **SO WHY NOT** masquerade as girls (Dwayne Hickman, Frankie Avalon) when the gang goes on a SKI PARTY? That way, you will see what it is that Kincaid does.

4. **AFTER ALL,** no one (Deborah Walley) will really notice . . . .

5. **AND THERE'LL BE** music and (Leslie Gore) singing . . . .

6. **THE AMAZING JAMES BROWN** will entertain, and under the pie, we'll get to hear from ROBERT Q. LEWIS.

7. **AND THERE'LL BE GIRLS** . . . delightful charming . . . and in bikinis, too.

8. **AND A CHANCE** for some close investigation on how Kincaid really operates in the field . . . or by a pool, as in this unusual picture showing snowbound hills in the background.

9. **AND EVEN IF YOU DO** break your leg trying to get away when Kincaid decides to make a run on YOU, look what you'll have for consolation! Deborah Walley was the original "Gidget," remember, and won her life in Hollywood in a nationwide contest . . . .

10. **AND HERE TO WAVE GOODBYE** is JO COLLINS, who also just happens to be **Playmate of the Year** for that magazine . . . .

KRLA ARCHIVES

KRLA Tunedex

EMPEROR HUDSON

CHARLIE O'DONNELL

CASEY KASEM

JOHNNY HAYES

BOB EUBANKS

DAVE HULL

DICK BIONDI

BILL SLATER

KRLA BEAT
6290 Sunset, No. 504
Hollywood, Calif. 90028

BULK RATE
U.S. Postage
PAID
Los Angeles, Calif.
Permit No. 25497

This Week	Last Week	Title	Artist
1	1	LIKE A ROLLING STONE	Bob Dylan
2	4	YOU WERE ON MY MIND	We Five
3	2	I GOT YOU BABE	Sonny & Cher
4	6	BABY I'M YOURS	Barbara Lewis
5	9	EVE OF DESTRUCTION	Barry McGuire
6	5	UNCHAINED MELODY	Righteous Brothers
7	3	IT AIN'T ME BABE	The Turtles
8	8	HELP I'M DOWN	The Beatles
9	7	IT'S THE SAME OLD SONG	The Four Tops
10	12	NOTHING BUT HEARTACHES	The Supremes
11	10	LAUGH AT ME	Sonny Bono
12	13	CALIFORNIA GIRLS	Beach Boys
13	30	LIAR, LIAR	The Castaways
14	18	SUMMER NIGHTS	Marianne Faithfull
15	22	DO YOU BELIEVE IN MAGIC	Lovin' Spoonful
16	11	ALL I REALLY WANT TO DO	Cher
17	15	PAPA'S GOT A BRAND NEW BAG	James Brown
18	20	ROSES AND RAINBOWS	Danny Hutton
19	21	TAKE ME BACK	Little Anthony & The Imperials
20	25	HEART FULL OF SOUL	The Yardbirds
21	19	DOWN IN THE BOONDOCKS	Billy Joe Royal
22	14	HOLD ME, THRILL ME, KISS ME	Mel Carter
23	16	YOU TELL ME WHY	Beau Brummels
24	26	COLOURS/JOSIE	Donovan
25	27	CATCH US IF YOU CAN	Dave Clark Five
26	39	THE TRACKS OF MY TEARS	The Miracles
27	36	YOU'VE GOT YOUR TROUBLES	The Fortunes
28	29	WE GOTTA GET OUT OF THIS PLACE	The Animals
29	24	JU JU HAND	Sam The Sham & The Pharaohs
30	—	IN THE MIDNIGHT HOUR	Wilson Pickett
31	—	SINCE I LOST MY BABY	The Temptations
32	—	AGENT OO-SOUL	Edwin Starr
33	32	MY GIRL SLOOPY	Little Caesar
34	35	I'M ALIVE	The Hollies
35	—	HANG ON SLOOPY	The McCoys
36	37	MOHAIR SAM	Charlie Rich
37	38	DRUMS A-GO-GO	The Hollywood Persuaders
38	—	ACTION	Freddy Cannon
39	34	HOME OF THE BRAVE	Bonnie & The Treasures
40	40	I DON'T WANT TO LOSE YOU BABY	Chad & Jeremy

KRLA ARCHIVES

KRLA BEAT

Volume 1, Number 27 — LOS ANGELES, CALIFORNIA — 15 Cents — September 18, 1965

PROTESTOR BARRY McGUIRE: NEW TARGET

KRLA BEAT

Los Angeles, California   September 18, 1965

Gene Pitney: Mr. Success

No wonder Gene Pitney is grinning from ear to ear— Musicor Records has just released the sales figures of his single records.

In the U.S. and England alone Gene has a steady sales range of 300,000 to 800,000 on every single which he has ever released!

Gene's current hit, "Looking Through The Eyes Of Love," has already topped the British charts and the way it's now racing up the American charts it won't be long before it reaches that magic top-ten circle.

Who knows—Gene just might have himself a double country number one record. And it won't be the first time either!

...Gene Pitney

BEAT MUSIC BACKGROUND
Carnaby Street - New Way To Shop

While England has its huge department stores with multiple floors crammed with everything from needles and thread to tuxedos and minks, it also boasts a more modest but certainly colorful London attraction—unique Carnaby Street.

125 Yards Long

The busy little street — only 125 yards long — is the home of the hippies, the location where all the "in" people (The Beatles, Stones, Herman's Hermits, Animals and the rest) buy their "in" clothes.

To those of you familiar with London, Carnaby Street is situated in the West End, next door to Soho just off Regent Street.

The extremely narrow thoroughfare is solidly lined with small shops packed with the most modern of the ultra-modern clothing.

Beat Music

Beat music can be heard blaring from the shops at all hours of the day, and long-haired English citizens (both male and female) pause on the Street to talk, laugh and exchange the latest "in" gossip.

If there has to be a king of Carnaby Street, one person whose clothes stand stark against a backdrop of distinct clothes, it is 29 year old John Stephen.

Just 5 years ago, Stephen left his native Glasgow with only $36.40 in his otherwise empty pockets.

It was a wise step for Stephen — one which paid off handsomely—for today he owns several shops on Carnaby Street as well as 22 boutiques and two factories.

Spread To Us

Word of the fabulous clothes to be bought on Carnaby Street has spread to California by way of the visiting English groups.

Consequently, American visitors are making Carnaby Street their second home. The Byrds made a bee-line for Carnaby Street the minute their plane touched British ground. And Sonny & Cher wasted no time in buying enough clothes to keep them in new outfits for the rest of their lives!

Whoever said that designing and selling clothes especially for the younger generation, for the ones who really know where it's at, is bad business? Tell you one thing — it wasn't Carnaby Street. They're too hip for that!

Dylan Under Heavy Load - It's Money

When commercial success comes to a rock artist like Bob Dylan, it arrives wrapped in gold leaf and tied with a silk ribbon.

Dylan, who made his first appearance on our music scene as an impecunious protestor (he still protests, of course), now is as far from impecunity as the Beatles are from the Andrews Sisters.

Ascending Fortunes

A current breakdown of Bob Dylan's ascending fortunes show a picture like this:

Dylan is the principal reason for making Warner Bros. publishing company so very happy these days. The company owns no fewer than 78 Dylan songs. Currently the same company has eight tunes doing well on the best selling charts — of these, four are by Dylan. As of a couple of weeks ago, the author of "Like A Rolling Stone" had 16 singles on his songs and 28 of his songs in albums now on the market. Then Reprise Records (owned by Warner Bros.) rushed onto the market with the Dylan-penned "Chimes of Freedom" sung by Dino, Desi and Billy (Martin, Arnez and Hinsche, of course).

With all this activity, what else could be breaking for the lucky — and prolific — Mr. Dylan? Just this: Cher's next single (to be released in the very near future; the exact date has not yet been set) will be a release on Reprise of "Blowin' In The Wind." What's more . . . Cher will include three Dylan songs in her next album (release date to be announced).

Trend Continues

The trend to Dylan continues as famed conductor David Rose (who wrote "The Stripper" among many other numbers) rushes to record "Mr. Tambourine Man" and "All I Really Want To Do" in his forthcoming album for MGM Records. And The Liverpool Five, the latest in the British Brigade, chose the Dylan song, "You Gotta Stay All Night" for their first RCA

TURN TO PAGE 11

Bob Dylan — Protests Profitable

Fiendish Plan For Making Record a Hit

By Fred Bronson

Actually, this article will tell you how to make a record a *hit*, not how to make a *hit* record.

Haven't you ever been depressed because your all-time favorite only got to No. 39 on the radio station Tunedex? Wouldn't you like to see your next all-time favorite become No. 1? Okay, here are some helpful hints. Let's suppose you've heard that Clarence has just released a record, "Like A Mick Jagger." You want to make it a number one record, but nobody is even playing it yet.

Fiendish Plan

The first battle is won on the telephone. Begin calling all the record stores in the yellow pages and asking, "Do you have the new record by Clarence yet?" They'll say no, and you ask them when they'll get it.

Fine, that's part of step No. 1. The next day call them back again using your phoney English accent this time, and ask for the record, "Like A Mick Jagger." Tell them you're not sure who the artist is. Now you've got them worried — they don't want to lose out on any more sales!

The final part of step No. 1 is to have your brother or sister call back that night asking for the record again. Now they have had three telephone calls for a record which they don't have yet.

Extreme Caution

The next step must be performed with extreme caution, and the morning after your brother or sister has called. You must make an "in-person" appearance at all record stores within a 25-mile radius. This is a hard-operation. First, you will catch the boss opening in the morning. Rush up to him madly and scream, "Clarence! Clarence! Do you have his record yet?? I've *got* to have it!" The boss will apologize and say, "We'll have it tomorrow." Wait around 10 minutes until the boss takes a break and calmly walk up to the assistant. When he asks if he can help you, sedately say, "Oh, I was looking for, oh, now what was the name of it? Hagger? Magger?" The assistant will say, "Like a Mick Jagger!" By Clarence! Gee, we've had a lot of calls for that one. We'll have it tomorrow."

You now have all stores in town ordering at least five or ten copies of the record from the distributor. Sunddenly, the distributor figures he has a hot one on his hands, and he doubles his order for the company that makes Clarence's records, PUNK Records.

The promotion man suddenly has a live one too, so he doubles

TURN TO PAGE 10

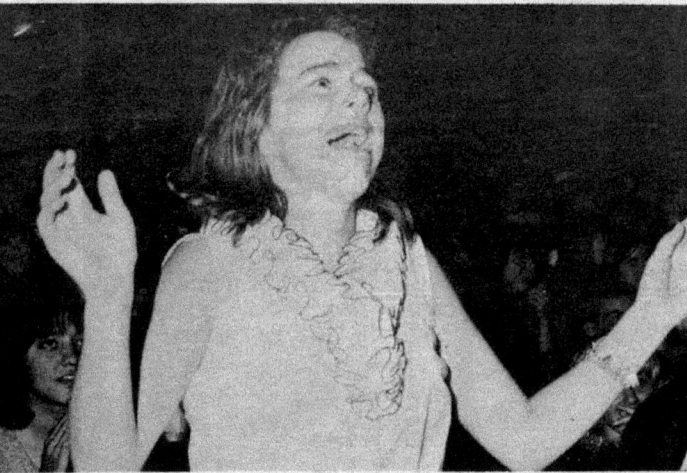
"LOOK OUT, RINGO!" An Alarmed Beatle fan screams a warning as pursuers close in on Ringo in "Help." Luckily, our heroes foil the plot.
BEAT Photo by C. Boyd

KRLA ARCHIVES

Ride In Space With Fab Four

By Nikki Wine
(Illustrations by Judy Manez)

This week, star-gazers, I though it might be fun to go on a space journey. Well, after all — if you can't beat 'em, JOIN 'em!! And what more interesting constellations could we visit than the meteoric Beatles? Right, so let's go! Everyone, all aboard our trusty spacecraft — Stranger 004 — and . . . BLAST OFF!!!

It certainly is a beautiful evening for a ride in space, isn't it though? Why, the heavens are so clear and the stars are so bright, they almost seem to be talking to one another. But wait! — I think they are!! Here — I'll turn up the volume on my super-keen snooper machine and coast right alongside that foursome over there so that we can all do some "high level" eavesdropping. Ah, they're coming in loud and clear now.

George: I just wanted to say something general about Number One records. The papers are making a lot more news out of the charts nowadays and this has two results. First of all, people who never buy any pop records know a bit more about the Top Twenty and this is a good thing. On the other hand when they read a story saying "Fred Nurke topples Elvis Bone" they think Fred Nurke is now the most highly-paid and highly-honored entertainer in the world and this guy Bone has had it forever.

John: We're quite safe at the moment. It's nothing to do with us. All we have cut is "HELP" — and it's certainly no threat.
(*Note: ?????*)

George: What I'm getting at is this. You can't blame anyone who isn't a fan for reading through the Top Twenty in the papers and saying to themselves "There you are, The Beatles aren't in the Top Twenty any more. They're right out of things. They've had it!" Or Elvis Bone has had it as the case may be!

Ringo: All right—so if "HELP" doesn't go to Number One straight away we're going to sit around and cry!"

(Ed. note: From out here in space—In England, "HELP" *did* go straight to Number One — within 48 hours of its release!)

Ringo: When we tell people we had a great big shindig to celebrate getting to Number One they can't understand it.

Paul: Yes — they say "Aren't you used to that yet?" I don't think we could ever get used to it. We hope for a Number One right away but it's still a surprise each time it really happens.

(Another unnecessary editor's note from out here in glorious space — Of course, Paul, if you say that it always comes as a huge Christmas-type surprise, well—whatever's right, baby!)

Paul: There must be a few less Beatle fans than there were, say, 18 months ago. Whenever there's something new happening you will find people sort of jumping on the bandwagon to have a go. I don't think you can get away from that.

Ringo: In other words, what we've got now are the REAL fans. The ones who don't just buy each Number One record BECAUSE it is a Number One record.

Paul: None of us minds criticism. We want that. We want to know what people think, whether they're fans or writers or whatever they are. It would be terrible if we just didn't want to know and tried to pretend we were little gods with a halo round each of our heads.

John: It's angels that have a halo.

Paul: It's just as bad to read stupidly good things about ourselves as it is to see stupidly wrong rumors.

(*Enter deep, spaceous voice from on high*—"This is your space-aged editor again. Since when does a Beatle ever do ANYTHING stupidly, stupid?!!!*)

George: It's bad when all the writers say wonderful things about something just because it's "in" and fashionable to do so. Constructive criticism is far more sensible than blind praise.

(Editor's note—All right my modest friends, we get the point. So I'm gonna fly home and spend a month thinking up something constructively bad to say about you. Now, on to something new — like rumors, f'instance. There's an ill smell currently floating about in the wind, hinting that you don't want to do any more tours. How 'bout it, huh?)

Ringo: No. Unture.

Paul: No, we're not against tours and we'll certainly be doing plenty more concerts here and abroad.

... Barry McGuire   Beat Photo: Chuck Boyd

Censorship 'Tool of Deception,' Says Outspoken Barry McGuire

By Eden

On a warm, sunny day recently the BEAT paid a return visit to the dynamic young man who has been the subject of much controversy of late.

Barry McGuire had spoken to readers of the BEAT (Sept. 4) in an exclusive and compelling interview which covered a myriad of subjects. Once again we spoke with Barry — this time among picturesque rocks and caves near a sandy California beach — to discuss further the controversy raging over his record, "Eve Of Destruction."

Animal Like

When he sings, Barry often sounds like a wild animal struggling to be free. He speaks with much the same passion and fervor. He is a man of firm convictions.

With the warm breeze from the Pacific humming soft accompaniment, Barry slowly vocalized his thoughts on the banning of his record for the BEAT.

"Well, that's what turns truth into controversy," he observed. "People who do not want to look at, or accept truth—then it's controversy." Bob Dylan was asked w h y he wrote controversial songs and he said: 'I don't write controversial songs, I write facts. If you can't look in the mirror that's your problem.'

"Censorship? I think it's a tool of deception. I can't imagine any person or group of persons, setting themselves up to tell any other person or group of persons what they can say or read.

Afraid Of The Truth

"When you start censoring it's because you're afraid of the truth or something. Censorship has a definite place in our society. You can see the results of censorship — and it's a great lesson. It will be its own doom.

"Every person should just keep asking himself until he comes up with the ultimate answer. I wish I had answers for them, but *nobody* really has the answers."

Another McGuire Protest Disc– Wait 'till You Hear This One

"Woodsman spare that tree,
Touch not a single bough;
In youth it sheltered me,
I shall protect it now."

Barry McGuire couldn't care less!

On the heels of the fantastic success of Barry's record, "Eve Of Destruction," Herb Newman of Era Records is re-releasing a single called "The Tree," which Barry recorded for Newman over four years ago.

Herb claims that the record is "weird, but a really *good* record." It tells, in folk style, the life story of a tree, which in the end finds itself sacrificed to the cruel axe of the woodsman.

According to Mr. McGuire, however, the record was a real bomb — then *and* now!

Well, don't let it worry you Barry — it just *might* sell a million, and there's no nicer plant than a money tree!

KRLA ARCHIVES

Good Taste Proves To Be Good Business For Busy Dick Clark

By Louise Criscione

He sits in a maze of plush offices with the French windows wide-open and the phone ringing incessantly.

Businessman

His name is Dick Clark and he's a shrewd and successful businessman, one who firmly believes in crediting his competitors with high intelligence and who also tries (and usually manages) to stay just one step ahead of them.

Clark knows teenagers — he's been working with them since he first began his famous *American Bandstand* show way back in 1956. During these nine years, Clark has made it his business to probe the teen-age mind, to search until he discovers what our segment of the American population will be digging six months or a year from now.

Dick Clark is a man of many faces. He *is* the smiling young host you see, and have seen, on television. But is *is* also a businessman who possesses the same kind of perception, initiative, know-how and money which has made Brian Epstein for example, the huge figure in the entertainment world he is today.

Epstein did it by making the Beatles professional giants Clark will do it by creating a new star. Oddly enough, he has chosen a Paul McCartney look-alike as his willing subject.

A New Star?

The young man's name is Keith Allison. He sings, plays the guitar and resembles Paul to such an uncanny degree that everyone turns to stare with the inevitable "is he or isn't he" look in their eyes.

Anyway, Dick spotted Keith when he was working with Jerry Naylor and the Crickets, the decision was made and "Operation Keith Allison" got underway.

You've seen Keith if you watch Clark's number one rated daytime television show, *Where The Action Is*. He's the one with whom the cameramen expertly tease you — the one they show just sitting in the audience.

It is all part of Clark's well-laid success plan, and before too long you'll see Keith bursting upon the pop scene with all the might of Dick Clark Productions behind him.

In addition to the perennial Bandstand, Clark also has his hands in pies you wouldn't believe! Of course, he's extremely happy with the tremendous success of *Where The Action Is*. In his back office there is a huge wall upon which Clark has posted small index cards explaining in detail *Action's* shooting schedule and guest list for weeks in advance.

Clark also owns the granddaddy of all the pop touring shows, *The Dick Clark Caravan Of Stars*. The *Caravan* has been on the road for a number of years now, always doing very well and always continuing to expand until today at least one of the shows has hit every single state in the Union.

Ever since the birth of the *Caravan*, Clark has made it a firm policy to present only the very best American pop talent available. With the upsurge of English popularity, Clark immediately jumped aboard that bandwagon, flew to England, and returned triumphant having booked such people as Herman's Hermits and Tom Jones for his *Caravan*.

Dick is right now in the midst of moulding a new tele-

TURN TO PAGE 11

...Behind Camera, Mussed Hair

...TAPING "WHERE THE ACTION IS" WITH CHAD (L.) AND JEREMY (R.)

KRLA ARCHIVES

THE BEATLES GO TO A PARTY

Police guard Alan Livingston home in Hollywood, where party was held.

DID THE EXCLUSIVE PARTY BACKFIRE?

When Alan Livingston, president of Capitol Records, tossed a Hollywood party in honor of The Beatles during their recent stay in California, all stops were pulled to make the event—hosted by Livingston at his Hollywood Hills home—as snooty and glamour-laden as they come in Tinseltown.

Creme de la creme was the guest list: Vince Edwards and wife Kathy Kersh (they're back together again and Mrs. Edwards is expecting), Dean Martin, Jack Benny, Bill Cosby, Polly Bergen, Hayley Mills, Suzanne Pleshette, Groucho Marx, Jimmy Stewart, Rock Hudson, and Gene Barry, to mention a mere few. Press was barred and Beatle fans were kept at a distance by courteous but firm police.

From all indications the planned event had earmarks of one whale of an evening in a town that's had more than its share of gay parties.

But something must have backfired.

Only three Beatles attended. George Harrison, in fact, was discovered by BEAT reporters at the Columbia Records Hollywood studios, an interested spectator at a recording session by the Byrds. John Lennon was observed leaving in evident boredom (see photo) before 9:30 p.m. Around 9:45, Ringo Starr and Paul McCartney followed John back to their secluded mansion on Benedict Canyon Road—or elsewhere, perhaps, to livelier happenings?

What happened? We probably shall never know. But we *can* conjecture that the boys weren't any too happy to see fans shivering outside the Livingston house in the night chill while they had to endure the boredom inside.

With the press barred, how then did The BEAT obtain these exclusive photos? Easy. BEAT photographer Chuck Boyd, intrepid and resourceful, merely disguised himself as a punch bowl. He returned empty, of course, but certainly not empty-handed.

Elated fans and amused policeman await arrival of the boys.

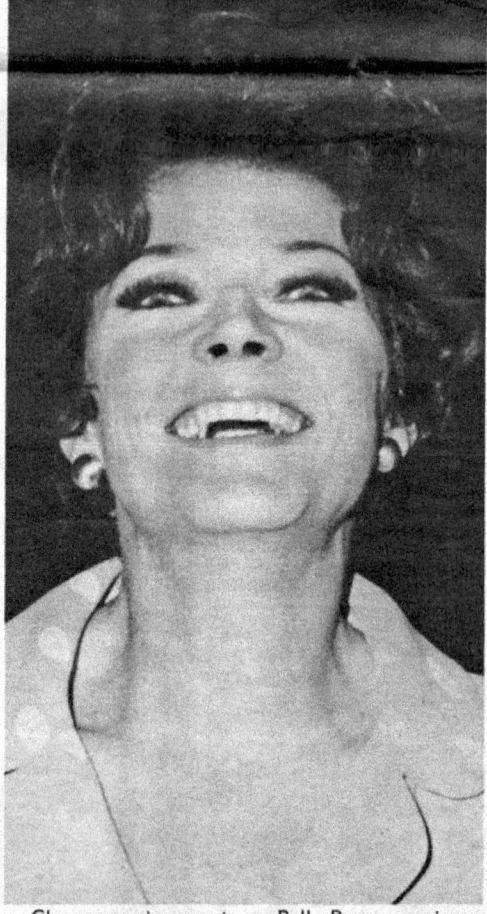

Glamorous singer-actress Polly Bergen arrives at the party

KRLA ARCHIVES

Bored, John Lennon leaves alone — and before 9:30 p.m., too.

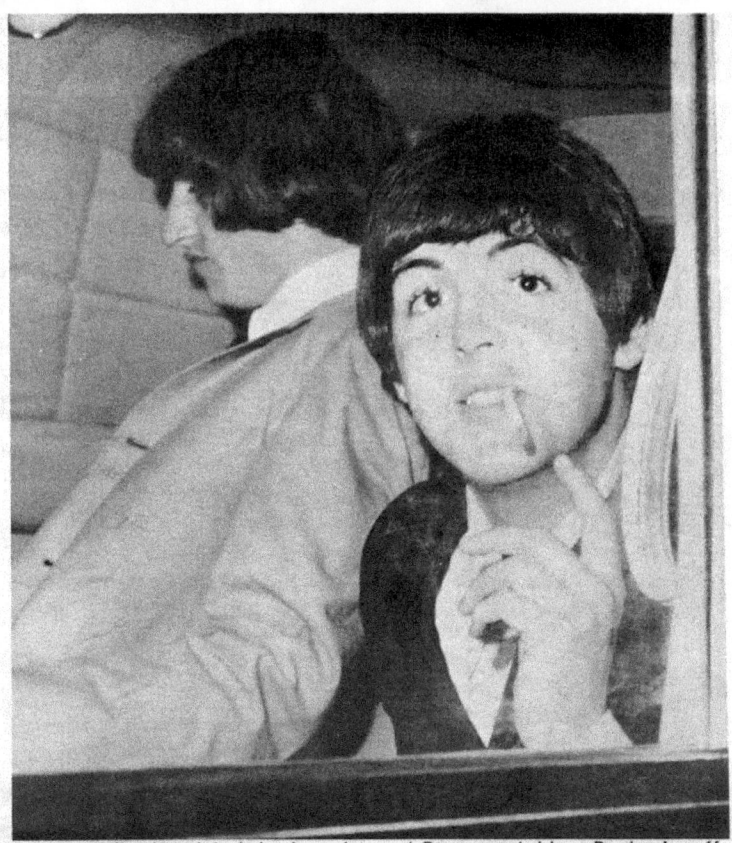
In car, hard on John's heels, a dejected Ringo and blasé Paul take off too.

..AND THE BEAT TAGS ALONG!

Departing stars (l. to r.) await their cars: Mr. and Mrs. Vince Edwards (she's Kathy Kersh), Dean Martin (chewing on toothpick), and comedian Bill Cosby.

KRLA ARCHIVES

LIVERPUDDLES
by Rob McGrae

The Clayton Squares

Undoubtedly, the number one group in Liverpool right now is a group called The Clayton Squares, or the "Squares," as they are known to their fans. Even now they are causing a good deal of commotion all around Liverpool, and people are tipping them to become very big stars indeed.

The "Squares" took their name from a well-known square in Liverpool—Clayton Square—and they are hoping that it won't be long before they are just as famous as their namesake.

Who's Who

There are six members of the group and the music they play is truly exciting. The line-up consists of the bass player, Geoff Jones, 18; Denny Alexander, lead singer and rhythm guitarist, 21; Pete Dunn, organist and lead guitarist, 21; Bobby Scott, a great Bob Dylan fan, who is the drummer and 20; Les Smith, alto saxophone, 21, and finally Mike Evans, the tenor saxophone player who is also the "Chief Square" for the group. Incidentally, Mike wrote the "B" side of their first record, about which more later.

The Squares have already appeared on American TV in the Discovery series, and in September they will be appearing in a documentary, "Liverpool Au GoGo," in which they will perform five numbers.

Book To Appear

The boys have also appeared on German, Australian, and French TV, and in September a book about them will be published to coincide with the release of their record, as yet untitled.

Just recently the Squares had one of their most embarrassing experiences. They were returning from an engagement in London when the van in which they were traveling broke down and they were forced to hitch hike back to London! Mike Evans says of this: "Due to being an ex-University student, I was used to hitching and soon managed to get a lift home."

I'll be back with more news from Liverpool's famous Cavern, and until then — Ta!

On The BEAT

By Louise Criscione

After the tremendous reception accorded the Beatles on their American tour, it appears that if all goes well John, Paul, George and Ringo *will* return to the States again next year!

During the filming of "Help," the Beatles as well as their Big Chief, Brian Epstein, let it slip that after this tour their personal appearances would be cut down to the absolute minimum by by-passing next year's U.S. Beatle invasion.

However, now all five of them have apparently changed their minds. Epstein predicts confidently: "They will be back here again next year."

Paul adds: "We love it here and I'm sure we'll be coming again as long as they want us." As long as we want them? He's *got* to be kidding!

Donovan Due

Attenttion Donovan fans—your boy's returning Stateside for a November 5 appearance at Carnegie Hall!

...Brian Epstein

Sharing the spotlight at Donovan's Carnegie show will be the fantastic American folk artist, Pete Seeger, but from then on out Donovan is going the solo route.

Immediately following Carnegie, Donovan will hit the American college circuit for a three week tour. All of Donovan's Ivy League dates will be a one-man Bob Dylan type concert with Donovan filling the entire bill himself.

Then in December Donovan will guest on the *Steve Lawrence Show* and sandwiched in his schedule somewhere is a week at the Sunset Strip's *It's Boss* club. Busy man, that Donovan!

QUICK ONES: Well, some unthinking "fans" have done it again—physically hurt a performer. The victim was Mike Smith of the DC5. Mike suffered two broken ribs when hysterical girls pulled him off the stage in Chicago. Won't these "fans" ever learn? . . . Sonny & Cher reportedly purchased a 1937 Rolls Royce when they were in England . . . Donovan thinks that Joan Baez helped Bob Dylan instead of the other way around . . . John Lennon, very pleased with his contact lenses, says: "They're marvelous! I can see things like bus stops and garden gates!" . . . Tony, co-owner of the famous Martoni's Restaurant—the place where Sonny met his Waterloo—is cutting an answer record to Sonny's "Laugh At Me." Should be very interesting!

Gerry and the Pacemakers are almost set for a Christmas season at one of London's West End theatres, the Saville. Brian Epstein, who manages the group, is part owner of the Saville and has already secured two writers to produce a script.

WATCH OUT FOR: Sonny & Cher to open a chain of boutiques around the London area. The American duo have thought of opening a small shop in Hollywood which would stock only the far-out type clothes which Sonny & Cher themselves wear.

But on their recent trip to Britain they discussed the idea with Larry Page (Kinks' manager) and he absolutely flipped! Matter of fact, he will be their London-based partner!

Kinks Berlin Alarm

The Kinks had a rather alarming experience when they performed in Berlin. Ray explains: "In Berlin we were met by the police and driven through a forest to a huge concrete bunker. Iron gates slammed behind us—that was the dressing room! We went out into the stadium through a network of tunnels. After the show about 50 fans pursued us back down the tunnel with the police looking on disinterestedly.

"All the restaurants refused to serve us a meal but they let us have drinks. Now I know why there are so many skinny people in Germany!"

Here's an interesting one for you. Jane Asher claims that she will marry Paul, but Paul says: "I've got no plans, but everybody keeps saying I have. Maybe they know better. They say I'm married and divorced and have 50 kids—so you might as well too!"

...Paul McCartney

Quips 'n' Quotes

"Out of the mouths of celebrities," and into your homes come the latest flashes from our Hotline to the world of entertainment.

Question for French sigh-guy John Paul Vignon: Do you speak any languages other than French and English? "Yes — the language of love. . . ."

Pity the poor beautiful blonde in Hollywood; it's a rough life all over! Says pretty Kathy Kersh: "Right now I'm concentrating on singing and I hope to combine singing and acting later. Part of the problem in acting is — if you are a pretty blonde in Hollywood — the producers refuse to take you seriously. But if you are talented, people in the music industry take you seriously immediately. Naturally I prefer to be regarded as a performer, not as some starlet." Oh, naturally!!

Speaking of his new son, who is just two-and-a-half months old, Bill Medley of the Righteous Brothers says: "He plays the bass guitar and is forming a group with kids around the block. I'd like to teach him to sing blues by the time he's six years old." OOHHHHH?? You are thinking of forming a new act, now are you?

George Harrison of the M.B.E. set proclaims: "We have a great hold in America and we like to see British artists coming up. We have never been jealous of anyone."

John Lennon: "I can do the Freddie dance now. Watch!" Freddie *WHO*, John-John??!!

FREDDIE CANNON found inspiration for his latest and fast-rising hit in a TV show title — Dick Clark's **Where the Action Is.** Now Freddie's got the action!

KRLA ARCHIVES

For Girls Only

By Shirley Poston

Oh, boy!

Now don't get me wrong. That opening sentence isn't an invitation to the opposite sex, welcoming them to our none-of-their-business corner of the BEAT.

It's an exclamation of sheer joy! Not only is George Harrison in town (or was) (more about that later) (faint, faint), but I also have something I'm just *dying* to tell you.

I got one of those one-in-a-jillion letters this morning. The girl who wrote it had just recovered from a whole year of hating the world because of a break-up with her steady.

They'd been going together two years, and the break-up happened because he suddenly started to change, almost overnight, into someone she didn't even know. Or like very much.

Gallon Of Tears

According to her letter, she cried a gallon of tears every night for about three-hundred-sixty-five in a row, and then woke up one morning her old self again. (Sound familiar? All-too, if you ask me.)

Now she's devised the greatest scheme to keep this from ever happening to her again.

As she put it, people don't change overnight. They just seem to. The qualities that make them turn out to be not-so-great were always in there somewhere, and from now on, she's going to serious *after* she gets acquainted with someone, not before.

I'm going to print her list of danger signals word for word. I just loved reading it, and I know you will too.

"Before-It's-Too-Late-List"

1. If you're starting to get serious about someone, first of all find out if he's serious about you. This isn't as hard as it sounds. Just take a realistic look at the way he treats you. If he's too thoughtless too often, I feel this means he just isn't that interested.

2. The degree to which he is jealous is also a lot of indication about a person. If he insists on having the name, rank and serial number of every boy you've ever smiled at in your entire life, he isn't just jealous, he's very insecure. Jealousy can be flattering in small doses, but if it's a constant source of argument between a couple, the boy has a lot of growing up to do and should be doing it at his own expense, not yours.

3. Also find out wheather his pet peeves are just ordinary gripes or if they're actually more petty than pet. You can tell a lot about someone by the things that annoy them, and by how annoyed they'll get before they lose control.

Look Out For Lies

4. Honesty is another quality to look for in a boy. If a boy tells you a little white lie now and then, it's no big crime, but if he makes a habit (whether he knows you're aware of it or not) of inventing stories, take warning!

5. This is really the second half of the last rule, but I'd be especially leery of a boy who did a lot of talking about his ex-girlfriends. This is an awful trait in anyone, especially when you might be next.

6. Talk to him about a lot of different subjects so you'll get acquainted with his views. If you're on the verge of falling in love, now is the time to find out if you have any violent differences of opinion, not when it's too late.

7. While you're at it, find out just how seriously he takes himself. I worry about any young person, boy or girl, who thinks they have *everything* all figured out. We all have opinions, but anyone who doesn't have enough flexibility to realize those opinions *could* be wrong, or could someday *change*, is too young to get serious or get serious about.

Don't Goad

8. Don't goad your boyfriend into getting furious, but keep your eyes open and take notice of how he acts when he gets mad. Some very calm people become raving maniacs when they lose their tempers. If this isn't a danger signal, I don't know what is.

9. Another good indication of a person's true self is how he treats other people. Most boys aren't glowing portraits of proper etiquette during their teenage years, and have a tendency to wise off. But you can tell whether he's kidding or whether he just couldn't care less about others if you really analyze a boy's actions.

10. Last but not least, listen carefully to his plans for the future. Maybe he doesn't really have any definite ones yet, but if he at least has an *attitude* that will be very revealing. If he has a "world owes me a living" outlook, or already feels he'll never really "be someone" without ever having tried, stick around at your own risk.

Well! If that wasn't a mouthful and a half! There are a couple of things I don't completely agree with, but most of it is so true it hurts! Now that I've shared her thoughts with you, I'm just *dying* again. To hear what you think of her method, that it, so let me know soonest!

George Who?

Now about George.

I still cannot believe it. I will not believe it until I am approximately four thousand years old, but *I touched George Harrison! With my own hand!*

I'm embarrassed to tell you how I managed that one, so I'll just admit that after a lot of begging and pleading and a few choice tantrums, I got to be introduced to him and I *still* have goose bumps (which look and feel a lot more like moose mumps to me).

He only had time to say hello, but I about *collapsed* anyway! I didn't do anything dumb, like faint or scream, but about five minutes after he left, I walked over and sat down in a chair that wasn't there. Boy, am I glad he didn't see that one!

Really, it was the thrill of a lifetime and I may never wash my hand (he HELD it for thirty seconds — I counted!) for the rest of my life.

Now that I've gone and told you how silly I really am (well, I can't help it — he's just *too much*. I'm going to tell you about this *really* moronic thing I always do George-wise.

When I'm trying to go to sleep at night, I lie there and make up big spectacular meetings between George and myself (in Cinemascope and Technicolor, yet) (never do anything small, I always say). First I decide what I'll be wearing, where it will happen, and when George finally appears on the scene, I plan out every single word we say to each other.

Terribly Clever

If that isn't crazy enough, I also do this, too. If, in my mind, I or George say something that just doesn't sound too brilliant, I don't just erase that moment of the day-dream and go on from there. *I start all over* and play the whole thing back, making terribly clever changes as I go along.

If, by any *remote* chance, you ever do this same thing about your favorite, *please* write and so I'll at least know I won't be alone in that padded cell when they come for me.

Naturally, this column is now about three miles long and I have a feeling the BEAT will soon be looking for a less long-winded "author." Just three more things before I go.

Beach Boy Bumps

"California Girls" by the Beach Boys gives me goose bumps, too. Not in Harrison proportions, but I do kind of get the shivers over this song. It really makes you feel great to be a girl from California even if you don't stand much of a chance to be one of the chicks they're singing about.

Second thing. I have always had a secret desire to be a singer. Is there anyone reading this who would be interested in getting a folk group together just for fun, the more-the-merrier type? If so, let me know. Just don't go around thinking I'm also having a secret desire to make a record and impress George. Nothing could be further from my mind. (Oh sure, sing it, Susan.)

Giggle of the Week
By Eden

Vincent Edwards has become famous for his surgical endeavors on the telly-bone, but some of his real-life operations are much more interesting!

For example, his separation from wife Kathy Kersh has been one of the more unusual in the wacky history of Hollywood. Even though the pair are estranged, they continue to share the same happy honeymoon cottage.

The punchline to this Surgeon's Saga? Well, back on August 24 while the Four Fab Fellas from Liverpool were in Los Angeles, Vincent took his "estranged" bride to a cocktail party for the Beatles. While there, Vincent went into operation and tried to obtain the theatrical services of one Mr. Richard Starkey, M.B.E. for the role of a singer with a brain tumor on an upcoming episode of Ben Casey.

Clincher for this Beatale: Vince would like wife Kathy to portray Ringo's girl friend!

Well, that's Hollywood, friends. (Giggle, Giggle!)

It's Happening . . .

It has been reported to the BEAT that the Ramsey Lewis Trio are beginning to Happen in a big way. According to our Agent 00-Snoop, the Trio's waxing of "In Crowd" has been outselling the Beatles in some areas of the mid-West.

★

The Supremes of Motown-Tamla records are happening big this year all over the world. The girls have just been signed to record the title tune to AIP's "Dr. Goldfoot and the Bikini Machine." Many c o n g r a t s, girls!

★

Speaking of the Supremes, the girls must really be Supremely happy about their new album. Entitled "Live at The Copa," it will have a certain Mr. Sammy Davis Jr. penning its liner notes. It seems that Mr. Davis is a great fan of the three talented girls from Detroit. Well, you're not alone, Sammy.

★

If you enjoyed Barbara Streisand's TV spectacular last season, you may just be treated to another Female Frolic on CBS in the near future. . . . The network with the Big Eye has offered Ann-Margaret one and a half million long greens to display her talents on a one girl show, a' la Streisand. Last report to the BEAT had Annie giving the matter one and a half million bucks worth of very serious thought!

★

April Stevens and brother Nino Tempo will make like rock 'n' rollers for Jack Rose in his upcoming "Around the World a' GoGo."

★

Anybody care to dance? Well, Herman (of the Hermits renown) does, and he has found himself a very pretty dancing partner. Blonde 'n' beautiful Shelley Fabares has just signed with Sam Katzman to join Herman in a new little toe-stepper called The Boston Dog. The two will put their dancing shoes into action in Katzman's new flick: "There's No Place Like Space."

★

Condolences from the BEAT to Soupy Sales. He will probably be cutting down on some of those creme pies for a while since the neighborhood medic discovered that Soupy is the proud (?) possessor of two gall bladders! Poor Soupy!!!

★

The Byrds are flying high these days after their overwhelming success in England. In one place, they broke all previous attendance records — including that of the Beatles!

★

No hard feelings between the two groups, though. While the Beatles were in Los Angeles last month, they sent a car to transport the Byrds to their not-so-secret hideaway. This was one up for our Feathered Friends as they were the very first guests of the Beatles in Los Angeles.

Jackie Boosts Career Anew

Jackie DeShannon, long time favorite in the pop music business, has decided to boost her shooting career-star even higher by conquering still another field of show business — the motion picture screen.

The blonde and extremely lovely Jackie has already completed a featured role in the soon-to-be-released movie, "Intimacy," which stars Barry Sullivan.

Song Writer

Besides cutting hit records, Jackie is also a prolific song writer with over 500 compositions to her credit. The majority of people who have written anywhere near that many songs rush right out and form a music publishing firm. But not Jackie. She explains: "I don't like to make too much money because that's unfeminine."

You you can take it from the BEAT — no matter how much money Jackie makes she will *never* be anything but feminine!

KRLA ARCHIVES

Kathleen Hietala — Opportunity Knocked

BEAT Prize-Winner Has Story to Tell

Dear J. Felice:

May I tell you a story?

It was ten minutes before the magic hour, midnight. All was still in the small white house on Cherokee Avenue. For once the record player wasn't going—not a Paul, or a John, or a Ringo, or a George could be heard. Kathleen was asleep. Father Fred? Ditto.

Bang! Bang! "Is the earth coming to an end?" gasped our heroine, little Kathleen. There was a mumble from the living room and "little K" knew that Father Fred, too, had been awakened from his beauty sleep.

After the mumbling had subsided, "little K" went into the darkened living room to find what had been the cause of the disturbance.

"Special delivery," he said. "You," he moaned, shoving it into "little K's" hand. "Zzzzz."

Well, when "little K" opened the letter what did she find? A beautiful green ticket and a letter from Judy Felice of the BEAT staff.

After waking Father Fred (and most likely the entire neighborhood) with a tremendous war-whoop (living on a street named Cherokee effects people that way) she sat down to write a letter of thanks. And she lived happily ever after. Ever after August 29, that is!

The End

So, thank you, thank you Judy Felice. You see, I didn't known I'd won! I hadn't looked at the contest winners' names because I knew I'd *never* win. Me and my ESP!

I love you, Lorne Green, the BEAT and the Beatles!

Ta and Ta Ta,
Kathleen Hietala.

HELP!

Attention Rolling Stones fans. I would like to have a poll on your favorite Stone. My "tabulated" results will be sent into the BEAT. Out-of-State replies truly welcome!

If you like, include some reasons for your choice. Write to Anne Weiss, 8843 Cashio Street, Los Angeles, Cal. 90035.

HELP!

I've been playing the drums for quite awhile and now I'm trying to organize a vocal-instrumental group. I need a guitar player, a bass player, an organist or pianist and a saxophone player. Anyone around 14 or 15 who is interested, phone me at AT 6-0890 and ask for Bruce.

HELP!

I was the girl who made it on stage at the Herman's Hermits Concert. While I was up there Herman talked to me and put his arm around me. Unfortunately, I have not been able to find anyone who has a picture of me.

If anyone does have a picture of me on stage please write to me at 6382 Reubens Drive, Huntington Beach, Calif. My name is Barbara Scott.

The KRLA BEAT is published weekly by BEAT Publications; editorial and advertising offices at 6290 Sunset Boulevard, Suite 504, Hollywood, California 90028.

Single copy price, 15 cents. Subscription price, U.S and possessions, $3 per year or $5 for two years. Canada and foreign rates, $9 per year or $14 for two years.

Exclusive distribution handled by Miller-Freeman Publications, 6328 Lewis Avenue, Long Beach, California. Inquiries should be directed to the attention of David Thomas.

The JOHN LENNON
SHIRTS
Small, Medium, Large
Available Now At
Beau Gentry
1523 North Vine

LAURA LEE WOJACK of Canoga Park says something in this drawing which could never be expressed in words. She's the winner in this week's KRLA cartoon contest. We hope you enjoy the album, Laura.

For the first time in L. A. . . . .

A NIGHT CLUB FOR YOUNG ADULTS 15 years of age & Over!

Continuous Dancing to LIVE Music
Seven Nights a Week, from 7 p.m.

★ *In Person:* ★

Aug. 27-Sept. 6	JERRY NAYLOR & THE CRICKETS
Sept. 7-12	BILLY JOE ROYAL
Sept. 14-21	THE WE FIVE
Sept. 22-24	TOM JONES
Sept. 25-Oct. 1	SONNY & CHER
Oct. 4-5	THE KINGSMEN
Oct. 7-10	PETULA CLARK
Oct. 25-31	IAN WHITCOMB

Plus THE REGENTS Nightly

IT'S BOSS!

84433 Sunset Strip
OL 49900

Back issues of the KRLA BEAT are still available, for a limited time. If you've missed an issue of particular interest to you, send 15 cents for each copy wanted, along with a self-addressed stamped envelope to:

KRLA BEAT
Suite 504
6290 Sunset Blvd.
Hollywood, California 90028

ISSUES AVAILABLE

- 4/14 — INTERVIEW WITH JOHN LENNON
- 4/21 — INTERVIEW WITH PAUL McCARTNEY
- 4/28 — CHIMP EXCITES TEEN FAIR
- 5/5 — HERMANIA SPREADS
- 5/12 — HERE COME THE BEATLES
- 5/19 — VISIT WITH BEATLES
- 5/26 — FAB NEW BEATLE QUIZ
- 6/16 — BATTLE OF THE BEAT
- 6/30 — PROBY FIRED
- 7/24 — BEATLES TOP STONES
- 7/31 — CHER
- 8/7 — DYLAN
- 8/14 — HERMAN
- 8/21 — STONES TESTIFY
- 8/28 — KRLA PRESENTS THE BEATLES
- 9/4 — BEATLES . . . . IN PERSON NOW!
- 9/11 — THE THREE FACES OF BOB DYLAN

KRLA ARCHIVES

THESE FOUR FAMILIAR-LOOKING BEATLEMANIACS were just as excited as everyone else attending KRLA's exclusive premiere of "Help". KRLA Teen Topper Vaughn Filkens (left) is flanked by Deejays Dick Moreland and Dave Hull and Newsman Jim Steck (looking the other way). Five hundred lucky KRLA listeners were treated to an advance screening of the new Beatle movie two weeks before its city-wide opening. Response to "Help" was even wilder than for "Hard Day's Night."

Hit Records Often Result Of Strategy

(Continued from Page 2)

the sales reports and mails it to the station. The librarian sees that the promotion man has a high sales report (which is probably doubled, anyway) and that all the stores are reporting that "Like A Mick Jagger" is a big request number.

Pick To Hit

BANG!! Clarence debuts first week at No. 32 and it is the pick to hit that week!

Now PUNK Records take out a full-page ad in all the national magazines, costing them a small fortune, saying "Break-Out in California! Guaranteed No. 1." Clarence is now No. 50 in the nation the first week on, debuting over The Beatles, The Supremes, and Bob Dylan.

Next week Clarence is on "Shindig," "Hullaballoo," and "Shebang!" Then it's Ed Sullivan, Dean Martin, and the "Tonight" show.

Yes, you've done it. Made a record a hit. Of course, now you are tired of the record, and it's time to start making a hit of your newest all-time favorite—"Sugar Pie Honeybun" by the Beeswax Three.

One final word of caution—don't waste all this effort on The Beatles, Herman's Hermits, or The Rolling Stones. They don't need *that* kind of Help!

Personals

To Donovan:
I'm glad you liked my chocolate cake, even though you did stuff yourself. Be sure to come for Jack Elliot's next birthday . . . it should be a blast.
Barb Scott from the Ash Grove

To L. C. and Danny:
It was great knowing you. Hope you read the BEAT and listen to Dylan. Hi to Wobert of San Diego, too.
Dano

★

To John H. English of the used-to-be Heathen's:
What happened to the group? Will we never hear your beautiful London accent again?
Chris Jones

★

To all Beatle Haters:
Get well soon!
A Faithful Beatle Fan

★

To the Fab Seeds:
We think you are all groovy and we luv all your songs, but we especially luv Rick and Sky.
Two Seed Luvers,
Barbara and Sue

CASEY'S QUIZ

By CASEY KASEM

Many record stars have been DISCOVERED by accident, but this personality became a musician by accident!! At the time he belonged to a youth club, and the athletic team he was a member of wanted to challenge a faraway team to a match. There were two problems, however. Distance and money. Our enterprising lad solved both by spending his last thirty dollars to start a band which played for dances until enough funds were raised to make the trip. Today, he's still the leader of this world famous group!

ANSWER: DAVE CLARK

A SECRET AGENT trailing a spy? No, just a not-so-secret deejay named Dave Hull broadcasting a report on one of his brushes with a gang of foreign agents known as the Beatles.

KRLA BEAT SUBSCRIPTION

you will SAVE 60% of the regular price!
AN INTRODUCTORY SPECIAL . . . if you subscribe now . . .

☐ 1 YEAR — 52 Issues — $3.00   ☐ 2 YEARS — $5.00

Enclosed is $............

Send to:..Age:............

Address:...

City:............................State:............Zip:............

MAIL YOUR ORDER TO: KRLA BEAT
1401 South Oak Knoll Avenue
Outside U.S.: $9.00 — 52 Issues   Pasadena, California 91106

SINGERS—SONGWRITERS—GROUPS
Give it the
"MILLION DOLLAR SOUND"!
PROFESSIONAL DEMONSTRATION RECORDING
AT REASONABLE RATES

ELDORADO RECORDING STUDIO
1717 N. Vine St., Hollywood   HO 7-6151

KRLA ARCHIVES

BIG PLANS AHEAD
Dick Clark's Story

(Continued from Page 4)
vision musical variety show, *Face The Music*, for CBS which will hopefully unite the "young" and the "old" by providing entertainment for both.

An Actor Also

All these projects are behind-the-scenes activities but don't get the mistaken idea that Clark always remains behind the camera. Not in the least! He has already enacted roles in two movies, "Because They're Young" and "The Young Doctors."

This season will find Clark in two more movies, "It's A Tough Life" and "Once Upon A Sandbox." And on the "little screen" watch for Dick to make guest appearances on *Ben Casey*, *Coronet Blue* and *Slattery's People*.

Only the powers above know what else Dick Clark has up his sleeve, but we *will* divulge one thimblefull of information: Be on the lookout for the *Dick Clark Teen World Fair*. As the date approaches and the schedule is finalized the BEAT will let you in on all the details first — 'cause Dick Clark promised us and we know he's a man of his word!

...DICK, DEEDEE AND DICK (CLARK) ON BEACH

Q: *I have problem skin and I would like to go to a dermatologist, but I'm afraid it would cost too much money. My folks want me to go, but we're not millionaires and I don't want to run up bills for them. Please tell me about what price I'd have to pay for treatments. (Penny R).*

A: Most dermatologists charge around $10 for the first visit (where they examine your problem and determine what's causing it) and between five and seven dollars for each following visit. It's thoughtful for you to think of your parents, but don't let that stop you from taking them up on their offer. The price of a few visits isn't that high, and the good that can be done is priceless.

☆ ☆

Q: *I read in this column where you suggested that a girl buff her nails (she didn't like polish). I took your advice too, but now I need more of the same. Do you buff your nails back and forth or what? (Dorothy C.)*

A: Buff them with a vertical rather than a horizontal motion. Buffing from side to side can tear the cuticle, and too much buffing in any direction. Next time you get ready for an at-home manicure, try using some Amaz-on Nail Cream. It leaves a hard finish that lasts for weeks.

☆ ☆

Q: *I'm fourteen and I'm often taken for seventeen or eighteen. Sometimes this is great, but most of the time, I don't like to look older than I really am. I have long hair, which I wear up, and I don't wear much makeup. How can I look younger? (Candy B.)*

A: Try cutting a heavy fringe of straight bangs to go with your upsweep (which is probably the cause of your "added years"). Bangs can soften a severe type hairdo and make you look girlish even if you aren't very.

☆ ☆

Q: *I'm just starting to wear mascara and my mother says not to wear it on my bottom lashes. Is this a rule in eye makeup and does it apply to everyone? (Teresa I.)*

A: Liner and mascara on the top lashes only was a rule of sorts for many years. The new trend in eye makeup is to wear what looks best on you. Considering the shape of your eyes and face, if you look better with mascara on the lower lashes, go ahead. Just keep it down to a dull roar or it will detract from your looks rather than add something.

☆ ☆

Q: *This is a crazy problem, but I have a dress with oversize pockets. Maybe I'm just clumsy, but I'm always ripping the pockets half off, catching them on something as I rush by. How can I keep this from happening? (Wendy M.)*

A: You just answered your own question when you said "as I rush by." Many people-in-a-hurry are pocket-rippers, and can find more hidden nails to snag their clothes on. Just slow down. Also, tack those pockets in the middle with a thread or two. This will help keep them from catching on everything.

☆ ☆

Q: *No one would believe my problem until my girlfriend and I tried an experiment. We both washed our hands, put on lotion and watched television for an hour practically without moving. At the end of the hour, her nails were perfectly clean and mine were already starting to look grubby! If you can explain that one (and it happens all the time), I'll believe it when I see it in print. (Mary Dell F.)*

A: Nails are an extension of the skin, and every person's skin has a different chemical balance. As a result, some people get "grubby" faster than others. To prevent this, wash your hands as often as possible and always use a nail file AFTER you've put on lotion. Even the slightest accumulation of oil under the nails can be a dirt-catcher.

HINT OF THE WEEK

I think I've discovered a brand new way to solve a very old problem. I used to panic every time a boy would ask me out to a restaurant, even if it was only a hamburger place, for fear I'd spend more money than he has (or wants to part with). I solved this by deciding to order something moderate in price at a snack-type place, and let him do the ordering in a more expensive restaurant.

When I say "you order for me," he orders his own dinner and then gets all befuddled and doesn't know what to order for me. So he naturally asks if I'm sure I wouldn't like to make my own choice.

By that time, I know what he is having and can make that choice in the same price range without anyone being the wiser or the poorer.

Clever, huh? I tried it three times already and it's never failed! (Barbara W.)

If you have a question you'd like answered, or a hint you'd like to share on any subject, drop a line to Tips To Teens, c/o The BEAT.

DYLAN

(Continued from Page 2)

Victor release. Don't look for that title, though, on the Victor single by the Five: For reasons best known to powers-that-be, the title has been changed to "If You Gotta Go, Go Now."

Does Bob Dylan care if one of his song titles gets changed? You'd have to ask him and these days you'd be lucky if he stopped in one spot long enough for an answer. Perhaps that spot might have been the Columbia Records studios where he just recorded yet another album for release soon.

Dear Susan

By Susan Frisch

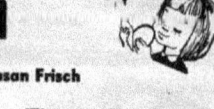

Can you please tell me how long Sonny and Cher have been married, and when will their next personal appearance be in Los Angeles?
Donna Kay.

Dear Donna:
Sonny and Cher have been married for 2 years, and their next personal appearance in L.A. will begin September 20, at the new teenage night club called "It's Boss." Hope to see you there 'cause Sonny and Cher are a great singing combination and it should be a wild time for everybody!!

Where can I write to Joe of the Gilloteens?
Rona Henley.

Dear Rona:
You can write to Joe in care of Hanna-Barbera Studios, 3400 Cahuenga, West Hollywood, California.

I would appreciate it very much if you could tell me if any of the Rolling Stones are married, and their ages.
Barbra Green.

Dear Barbra:
Charlie and Bill are married, and Bill is father to a little boy, Steven. The rest are single so we still have hope, huh? Mick, Brian and Keith were all born in 1944, which would make them 21 years old, but I don't know the birthdates. Charlie is 23, and Bill is 28.

What are Herman's favorite television shows and what are his favorite current records? Also, are he and Twinkle going together?
Caroline Newton.

Dear Caroline:
Concerning the question of Twinkle and Herman, I can only repeat myself for the millionth time. NO!!! He and Twinkle are not going steady, have not gone steady, and I am so positive without doubt, that they will *never* go steady. As for his favorites he feels that there are too many records that he likes and could not possibly narrow it down to one. As for the television programs I do think he likes *Shindig*, and — believe it or not — The Match Game.

Will it ever be possible to buy some of John Lennon's art work in stores? I love his work and I am sure that other people do too.
Steevie Witman.

Dear Steevie:
I seriously doubt that he will ever have any of his drawings in stores available to the public. However, I don't know for sure, but I will try to find out for you and the rest of the fans who want to know. I think they should be made public, but only time will tell, and one thing's for sure: he doesn't need the money!!!

MAIL BOX

Cavern Queries
Dear Editor:

Just recently I was fortunate to come across a copy of BEAT which I thought was really great.

My name is Robert McGrae and I am the manager of the famous Cavern Club in Liverpool where the Beatles, Gerry (and the Pacemakers), the Searchers, Billy J. Kramer, to name just a few, first started. I am sure that a great many of your readers must be interested in the Cavern and Liverpool, and I would like to say that I would be delighted to answer any queries which your readers may have. So if your readers would send their queries to me at: 17 Heydean Road, Allerton, Liverpool 18, England, I will certainly do my best to answer all the queries.

Any readers wishing to have pen pals from the Cavern could send details of themselves and I will have their names and addresses put on the Cavern notice board and I am sure that they will receive a lot of replies.

Robert McGrae

☆

Knocking Elvis
Dear Editor:

I don't see how anyone has the gall to say, "Elvis is *still* King". This statement is a farce — for Elvis reigns no more! He lost his crown last February when the Beatles conquered the hearts of America's teenagers. Let me point out a few questions to prove my point:

Did he have any hit records in the past year? No!

Can you actually say his records have truly *good* sound? No!

Do you ever see anybody wearing buttons bearing Elvis' name? Shoes, purses, notebooks, etc. with his face-printed on them? Gimmicks, such as Elvis wigs, Elvis dolls, or what have you? No!

Is he the topic of discussion in the music field?

Not only are his songs old fashioned, but his movies are unimaginative and basically the same. For instance, in each movie he stars in, he shows off his fighting talents, kissing talents, innocence and sex appeal to beautiful women.

Don't think I'm prejudiced when I say the Beatles are Kings. I can't really say I'm a true fan of the Liverpool four. In fact, my favorites are the Rolling Stones and I love them more than anyone!

In some cases the Stones are voted more popular than the Beatles. But I'm not able to argue the point that the Beatles are Kings.

Even if they do sometimes outsell Beatle records, (proof of outsell: a survey of record shops in New York; Stones outsell 3 to 1) they are not, (unfortunately) the Kings. The Beatles are and they shall be for sometime to come.

Margie Garcia

☆

Beatle Nuts
Dear Beat:

Last night I had the misfortune to see David Susskind's "Open End" opinion show. On it were eight New York and New Jersey teenagers who were to discuss the 'whys' of the Beatles success.

The discussion started out well, but was interrupted every few minutes by a rude young audience. It started out to be laughable because all eight kids were of the same opinion. All the 'whys' of the Beatles' success given by psychiatrists were *all wrong*, and they were *all right*.

They spoke of the Beatles being so kind, decent, and perfect. I started to feel sorry for they when they almost came right out and said they worshipped the Beatles, as if they were gods or something! A few of them had shrines in their rooms!

But the big burn was still to come! One of the girls started saying that the Beatles were the *only original* singing group and that everyone else IMITATED them! Then it exploded. Everyone started knocking the Rolling Stones, saying they were vulgar, dirty, slimy, ugly, real hairy and the scourge of the earth. All of a sudden, Mick Jagger was the biggest slob around.

Holy Cow! The Beatles are great but they aren't gods. Who wants to make Beatlemania a whole new religion?

There are other great groups like the Stones, the Hermits, Zombies, Unit 4 Plus 2 and the Yardbirds.

I don't feel that kids should be allowed to knock things they don't understand unless all America's youth is represented. No one there dug the Stones and I'm sure at least one in eight does throughout the pop world. Who agrees with me?

Cathy Gaugh

MEET THE STARS
Shindig's New Season Is Most Exciting Yet
By The Shindigger

Greetings, fellow Shindiggers. We've got lots of things to talk about today and lots of people for you to meet.

All the guests here at ABC-TV's Shindig studios in Hollywood are busy rehearsing their acts, so today will be the perfect time for you to meet more of our Shindig family.

Blossoms Bloom

The three girls who are on the stage now belting out a song are The Blossoms. From left to right they are Jean King, Darlene Love, and Fanita James, and they have been singing together for eight years. Did you know that the Blossoms are one of the most frequently heard female vocal trios in the country? They are also responsible for the vocalizing of the movie themes you heard while viewing such fab flicks "John Goldfarb Please Come Home," "Move Over Darling," and "Beach Blanket Bingo." The girls have also vocally backed many of the top vocalists in the country on their recordings.

Hmmmmm — even though there is no audience in the theater today I seem to hear screams. Oh — now I see why! Here come the Shindogs, Shindig's own singing sigh-guys.

All five of the Shindogs are from the Southern side of the ol' Mason-Dixon line; they are all fine musicians and performers as well.

Joey's Shades

The blonde Beatle-type who is playing rhythm guitar and singing the lead is Joey Cooper. You can always recognize Joey by the shades he wears 'round the clock.

Next to Joey is Delaney Bramlett, who plays bass guitar and occasionally raises his golden voice in song.

On the far left is Glen Hardin on the electric 88's and way in the back is Chuck Blackwell in charge of the skin-beating for the group.

Finally, on the extreme right is the very talented lead guitarist for the group, James Burton.

Put all five Shindogs together and that's a mighty powerful sound!

Soulful Donna

The pretty girl stepping into the spotlight front and center now is Donna Loren, a talented eighteen year old actress-singer. Donna is one of the most talented female vocalists around today, and when she sings, she really puts her heart and soul into the performance.

Aside from her singing, Donna is an accomplished dancer, and has also written about twenty songs, ten of which have been published. Donna is hoping someday to appear in a Broadway musical, but until then she'll stay right here with us at Shindig.

Wow! Before I forget, let me tell you about the swinging show next week. Shindig is going to really rock when such guests as the Everly Brothers, the Byrds, Jerry Naylor, Chad and Jill Stuart, Ketty Lester, and the McCoys drop in to say hello.

Well, until next week when we do it all over again, maintain your cool, Shindiggers, and—ROCK ON!!!

Beatles Now Talent Scouts

In addition to singing, writing, acting and playing musical instruments, the Beatles are also pretty fair talent scouts!

Thanks to the four, Brian Epstein's star stable now has another boarder — a three man group dubbed Paddy, Klaus and Gibson.

This is a case of knowing each other "way back when . . ." The two groups were friends during the days when the Beatles packed Liverpool's Cavern Club.

After the Beatles' meteoric rise, the two groups sort of lost contact with one another. Recently they met again when Paddy, Klaus and Gibson were appearing at the Pickwick Club in London.

The four Beatles decided right then and there that Epstein should welcome Paddy, Klaus and Gibson into his NEMS camp. And being a wise and shrewd businessman, Epstein seized upon their suggestion.

Of course, everyone is very pleased with the signing, especially Paddy, Klaus and Gibson!

Be on the lookout for these boys — with Epstein's protective wing about them they're bound to go.

THE BEATLES HIDEAWAY (shown here in this exclusive BEAT photo by Chuck Boyd) during their vacation-cum-work in Southern California is quiet once more now that the Fab Four have departed our scene. High above Hollywood the rented aerie was under police protection at all times during the Beatles' stay (note guard in photo).

Queen Sends For Fab Four

Millions of people (particularly girl-type people) would do anything to meet the Beatles. Teens, adults, tots, grandmothers and aunts would gladly travel half-way around the globe just to catch a glimpse of the fab four.

However, there IS one lady in this world who is making the Beatles come to her. She is the Queen of England and on either October 21 or October 26, John, Paul, George and Ringo will journey to Buckingham Palace to meet Her Majesty.

Investiture

The occasion is to be the investiture of the MBE awards which the Beatles won some time ago. The announcement of the Beatles' honor caused quite a bit of controversy when several of the previous MBE recipients threatened to return their medals because they felt that such a high honor to the four long-haired Beatles was unbearable and intolerable!

These people even went so far as to demand the Beatles refuse to accept the MBE's. But, of course, you *know* that the Beatles are not about to do anything as crazy as refusing their Queen!

KRLA ARCHIVES

THE BEAT VISITS SHiNdig

CAROLE SHELYNE typifies the famous **Shindig** dancers. A close-knit group — average age, 20 — they usually stay together socially and many share apartments or homes. Like Carole, most love dancing but also have hopes for acting or singing.

HANDSOME BOBBY SHERMAN, originally discovered at a party thrown by Sal Mineo, is one of the most popular **Shindig** regulars. In his spare time Bobby runs his own recording studio, produces film shorts and plays eight musical instruments.

PHOTOS BY ABC TELEVISION

These Men Help Make Show Tick

While the performers bask in the limelight and applause, a small army of men and women toil off-camera—unnoticed by the public—to keep *Shindig* at the top as television's most successful pop music show.

One of them is David Mallot, the young Englishman who is assistant producer. He is responsible for doing everything the producer doesn't have time to do. In addition to helping Producer Dean Whitmore plan the overall show, Mallot's duties include helping choose the people to appear each week, deciding how to "showcase" them and coordinating the various acts so that the show maintains the fast-paced, smooth-running format which it pioneered.

Another important key is Dick Howard, known as the "talent buyer." His job is to talk to dozens of agents and managers, to watch hundreds of acts in nightclubs and auditions, to listen to them on radio and to keep close watch on the record charts.

Only by being thoroughly familiar with what's happening in the pop world and by actually being able to predict who and what will be popular in the future can he do his job — to advise the producer and assistant producer on the type of entertainment and the specific acts to feature weeks in advance.

THE RIGHTEOUS BROTHERS always bring down the house on **Shindig**. They still appear frequently, even though filming their own movie (a James Bond type, of all things) and running their new record and publishing firm. **Shindig** gave Bill and Bob their first national TV exposure, bringing stardom.

BEAUTIFUL DONNA LOREN, another **Shindig** regular, leads finger-popping production number with the **Shindig** dancers and the Wellingtons. Donna is already a veteran performer at 18. She began her career at five, doing U.S.O. stage shows for servicemen.

KRLA ARCHIVES

A BEAT EDITORIAL
UNDERSTANDING

There's an old saying. It goes something like this ... You can't judge a book by its cover.

In fact, there are a lot of old sayings in that particular vein. Which figures. Since the beginning of time, people have been trying to get a point across. That the outside of people is usually very little indication of what's on the inside.

Well, the point still hasn't quite made it. Want proof? Just ask any teenage boy who doesn't have a crew cut. He'll be glad to tell you how it feels for a person to play second fiddle to a hairstyle.

Wonder why that is. Why longer hair is falsely considered a badge instead of what it really is — a fashion trend — Why most adults take one look at a stylishly shaggy mop and say in low whispers, "he's one of *those* nuts."

Most people, in spite of their don't-judge-a-book cliches, think longer hair automatically brands a guy as a kook. Nothing could be further from the truth. Some are kooks. Some are abysmal creeps. But many are intelligent, responsible young people who deserve a lot fairer shake than they're receiving.

You'd think people would have learned to practice what they preach. Unless you happen to know better. Then you just hope they'll start soon.

"We Found Elvis;" But He's Too Busy

By Sondra Lowell

I know Elvis' address, but I won't tell you what it is. Partly because it would be unfair to him if everybody knew, and partly because I'm just plain selfish.

Believe me, just knowing his address wouldn't help you much anyway. You might get a glimpse of him if you sat on his curb but, don't ring the doorbell and expect the King to answer. Or the butler to throw the door open and say, "Come on in. I'll tell El you're here."

Naturally, this sage advice comes from one experienced in such matters. And experienced I am. After all I've been turned away (thrown out) twice, haven't I?

The first time began as Sharon and I started meandering through Bel Air about 6:30 p.m. Sharon, a give-me-Elvis-or-give-me-death type, knew by heart every twist of the sidewalkless road. She'd walked and driven by I don't know how many times, but never before had she dared to approach the door. She was as terrified as I was, which didn't help my nerves any.

Campaign Pitch

All the way over I rehearsed my Elvis speech. It was awfully important that I say it just right. At school, you see, I was working with SCOPE, a national organization of college students who go South to register voters. We needed lots of money to get the volunteers down there and back, and to get them out of jail if we had to. Having Elvis' name connected with the project would sure reduce our fund-raising problem. Since Elvis is from the South, we were hoping he'd especially want to help freedom along, and maybe do a benefit to aid us in raising part of our $10,000 goal.

We'd be satisfied with a check from him, if he was too busy. We knew he makes three pictures a year, which is more than most stars do. But we also knew how wonderful he is about giving money to charity and helping so many people and organizations all the time.

The walk was so lovely, I was almost sorry to end it after half an hour. Sorry also because I was getting nervous about facing Elvis. He doesn't live in the mansion I expected. It's a modern, one story, black and white place, not at all pretentious. There's no private road or giant fence to keep people out. The driveway is large, shaped more like a parking lot. Several cars were parked in it, but not the diamond encrusted one I'd heard so much about. "Elvis" was scrawled on the mailbox post. It's a shame some fans can't respect peoples' property.

Door Opened

We walked to the door trying to look confident. I knocked and a young man with dark hair and beautiful blue eyes answered. No, not Elvis. We introduced ourselves, then said we were from UCLA and would like to see Mr. Presley about certain business matters. We were told to come back later, since Elvis had just gotten back from the studio and hour before and could not see us now.

"Later tonight or later in the week? I asked.

"Oh, later tonight or later in the week."

"Later tonight," Sharon and I decided. It was getting dark, so we didn't want to sit on the grass at the corner for two hours. The Bel Air Country Club was nearby, but we didn't happen to be members. We went over, though, to call a friend we suddenly remembered lived in Bel Air.

Mary Jo wanted to meet Elvis too, and she did have a car. So after we'd spent a while at her house, we all drove back to El's. We parked in the driveway next to some other girls who were sloppily dressed and came to ask the guy at the door to a party. He didn't go. He wasn't the same one as before.

Elvis still couldn't talk to us, but we could write a note. The notepaper handed us had "Elvis" printed at the top. When we finished the note which started with "I'm a neighbor of yours" for a friendly touch, and ended with Mary Jo's phone number, I handed him some pamphlets explaining the goals and organization of SCOPE.

Too Busy

"Well," the light-haired young man drawled, "it's not that El is prejudiced. He isn't. But he's too busy to do a benefit, and besides, he doesn't want to get publicly involved in something like this. All the stars who have lost a lot of popularity because of it. I'll give him your message. Maybe he'll want to help you if he can do it without getting any publicity. But he doesn't want to offend any of his fans."

Things are going well in Macon County, Georgia, where the UCLA kids are. Apathy is being overcome, voters are being registered, and there hasn't been any violence.

I know Elvis cares more about other people than he does about losing a few fans. He's too big a star for that to matter, anyway. He never called us, but that's probably because he has all his other good works to think of as well as his career and personal life. Besides, he can usually find time for only one benefit a year, in Memphis.

Maybe he sent a check to SCOPE headquarters in Atlanta and didn't tell us. Or maybe he didn't get our message. But Elvis has proven over and over that he isn't afraid to "get involved."

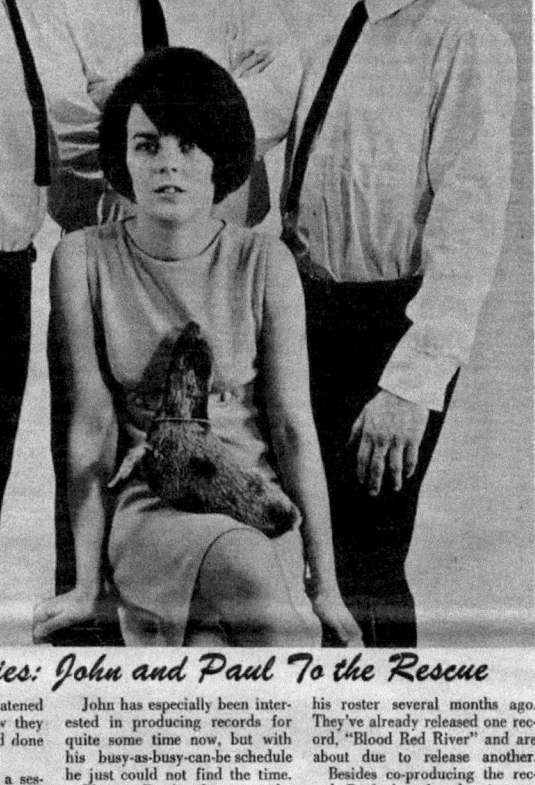

The Silkies: John and Paul To the Rescue

John and Paul have threatened to do this before but now they have actually gone out and done it — produced a record!

The two Beatles A&R'd a session in which another group member of the Brian Epstein family, The Silkie, cut the Lennon-McCartney penned "You've Got To Hide Your Love Away" from the Beatles' second movie, "Help."

John has especially been interested in producing records for quite some time now, but with his busy-as-busy-can-be schedule he just could not find the time.

The two Beatles chose to make their A&R debut with the Silkie for a number of reasons — first reason being the fact that friend Epstein manages both groups.

The Silkie is a three man, one woman British folk singing group whom Epstein added to his roster several months ago. They've already released one record, "Blood Red River" and are about due to release another.

Besides co-producing the record, Paul also played guitar on the session while George Harrison lent his hand to the tambourine.

Only Beatle not directly involved with the session was Ringo. Wonder where he was?
— Louise.

English Pen Pals

JANE RYDER
'Bryn Don'
Doncaster Rd.
Conisborough, Yorkshire
England

ANNE LIVERSIDGE
88 Howard Road
Mansfield, Notts
England

ANN MATTHEWS
29 Hanover Road
Tottenham
London, N. 15,
England

PATRICIA WRIGHT
78 Stainbeck Road
Meanwood, Leeds 7,
England

MAUREEN BALLARD
52 Vale Road
Haywards Heath
Sussex, England

SHELLY MAWBEY
84 Finchley Avenue
Mackworth Estate
Derby, England

have you heard
'YOUR FRIENDS'
ARE GREAT?

KRLA ARCHIVES

HELP – CLOSEUPS OF BEATLES

By The BEAT Staff

Everyone knows by now what this picture is all about, and millions of teenagers (and postteens) will go and see it just because it's there, and because the amazing Beatles are in it.

So we will not dwell on the story, except to say that some nasty fellows chase Ringo and his pals all over the world, trying to swipe a ring he's wearing.

At the time we saw "HELP!" the Beatles were actually living in Los Angeles, up in exclusive Benedict Canyon. There was some commotion at the rear of the theater, and rumor has it that one of the Liverpool lads snuck in to watch a part of it.

Hundreds Swarming

Police were up in the Canyon guarding the house, hundreds of boys and girls were swarming all over the hills around the house, sometimes getting in trouble, and all the time the Beatles quietly idylled away their few days off.

The long-haired imports from England continued to be the center of the world of show business, as they have been for the past two years.

Some of the girls kept up their vigil for 50 hours at a time.

The Beatles have become such super-stars that it is hard to imagine them as real people. We all get to feeling as though they are fluffs of talcum powder that we just read about all the time.

But they are real, and they seemed to have enjoyed their California vacation, and they

...Ringo

also seemed to enjoy making their second feature film.

Spark Is Gone

It will not live up to the promise of "*Hard Day's Night*," which surprised everyone by being so good. And even though the same production team also made HELP! the little spark is gone. But don't get us wrong: HELP! is an enjoyable picture, with lots of action and some amazing photography.

It's kind of like "*Mondo Cane*," only with Beatles. The camera stops here, then there, pops up, down, back, and around first focusing on Ringo's nose, then a musical instrument, then catching the vapor condensing from John's breath as he sings.

It's very much like writing poetry with a 35mm movie camera. Great artistry is shown in the filming of the various sequences, no matter how poorly their supporting cast may have acted the scenes. The Boys themselves hop-scotch through the whole movie with vitality — and with the detachment of the millionaires they are.

The story has at least three good belly laughs and a dozen or more chuckles, and any number of smiles. Interspersed by frowns when you cannot understand what they said or didn't catch the meaning of a fast-flying witticism.

In Full Color

But never mind. It's the BEATLES — right there in full color on the screen! When could you ever see them so clearly, or so intimately?

And who, in the name of the British Empire, can ever forget the famous Paul McCartney Nude Scene? It put Gina Lollobrigida to shame, at least as far as the girls are concerned.

This is the one great value of the picture — *we get to look at the Beatles*, while they cannot look back. We can examine this phenomenon of our age, this quartet that has stormed the gates of mankind and won completely, without ever firing a shot.

The Beatles have conquered the world.

What else is left for them, *except* making expensive home movies?

BEAT STAFFERS (l. to r.) Louise Criscione, Nikki Eden Wine and Susan Frisch clutch passes to "HELP!" as they patiently wait in line to see it again — and again and again!

WAITING FOR 'HELP' — "WE LOVE YOU, BEATLES"

KRLA ARCHIVES

KRLA Tunedex

EMPEROR HUDSON

CHARLIE O'DONNELL

CASEY KASEM

JOHNNY HAYES

BOB EUBANKS

DAVE HULL

DICK BIONDI

BILL SLATER

KRLA BEAT
6290 Sunset, No. 504
Hollywood, Cal. 90028

BULK RATE
U.S. Postage
PAID
Los Angeles, Calif.
Permit No. 25497

This Week	Last Week	Title	Artist
1	1	LIKE A ROLLING STONE	Bob Dylan
2	2	BABY I'M YOURS	Barbara Lewis
3	13	LIAR, LIAR	The Castaways
4	5	EVE OF DESTRUCTION	Barry McGuire
5	2	YOU WERE ON MY MIND	We Five
6	6	UNCHAINED MELODY	Righteous Brothers
7	3	I GOT YOU BABE	Sonny & Cher
8	8	HELP/I'M DOWN	The Beatles
9	15	DO YOU BELIEVE IN MAGIC	Lovin' Spoonful
10	14	SUMMER NIGHTS	Marianne Faithfull
11	9	IT'S THE SAME OLD SONG	The Four Tops
12	7	IT AIN'T ME BABE	The Turtles
13	10	NOTHING BUT HEARTACHES	The Supremes
14	18	ROSES AND RAINBOWS	Danny Hutton
15	20	HEART FULL OF SOUL	The Yardbirds
16	28	WE GOTTA GET OUT OF THIS PLACE	The Animals
17	—	THE "IN" CROWD	Ramsey Lewis Trio
18	12	CALIFORNIA GIRLS	Beach Boys
19	19	TAKE ME BACK	Little Anthony & The Imperials
20	11	LAUGH AT ME	Sonny Bono
21	21	DOWN IN THE BOONDOCKS	Billy Joe Royal
22	26	THE TRACKS OF MY TEARS	The Miracles
23	25	CATCH US IF YOU CAN	Dave Clark Five
24	27	YOU'VE GOT YOUR TROUBLES	The Fortunes
25	24	COLOURS/JOSIE	Donovan
26	30	IN THE MIDNIGHT HOUR	Wilson Pickett
27	—	TAKE ME FOR A LITTLE WHILE	Evie Sands
28	35	HANG ON SLOOPY	The McCoys
29	31	SINCE I LOST MY BABY	The Temptations
30	36	MOHAIR SAM	Charlie Rich
31	32	AGENT OO-SOUL	Edwin Starr
32	37	DRUMS A-GO-GO	The Hollywood Persuaders
33	—	TREAT HER RIGHT	Roy Head
34	—	HOME OF THE BRAVE	Jody Miller
35	38	ACTION	Freddy Cannon
36	39	HOME OF THE BRAVE	Bonnie & The Treasures
37	—	RIDE AWAY	Roy Orbison
38	—	TOO MANY PEOPLE	The Leaves
39	—	GIRL FROM PAYTON PLACE	Vickie Lee
40	—	TURN AROUND	Boo Boo & Bunkie

KRLA ARCHIVES

KRLA BEAT

Volume 1, Number 28 — LOS ANGELES, CALIFORNIA — 15 Cents — September 25, 1965

SONNY - HE AND CHER HAVE FIVE HITS!

KRLA BEAT

Los Angeles, California — September 25, 1965

THUMBS UP FOR FABULOUS CALIFORNIA COUPLE

BUT NOT SAN FRANCISCO
Beatles Say L.A. Was 'Just Great'

The Beatles are already talking of a return trip to America next year and another vacation in Southern California.

"It was tremendous," says Paul.

"Great, just great," says George.

Their only criticism of their ten-day American tour concerns the near-riot which broke out during one of their two performances at the Cow Palace in San Francisco.

At a London news conference Brian Epstein criticized the management of the Cow Palace for providing insufficient security." During the disturbance, which forced the Beatles to cut short the second show, the fans threw rings, pens, flashlights and teddy bears onto the stage, in addition to the usual fusilade of jelly beans.

Underestimated Appeal

"They may have underestimated the Beatles' appeal," he said of the management. "There is a problem here. Their adulation can be underestimated."

Epstein charged that barriers were only one foot in front of the stage at the Cow Palace and that security guards were unevenly distributed.

"Although I am told that the kids in San Francisco are wilder than elsewhere, the boys and I find it difficult to believe," he said. "The second show was so bad we cut three numbers. It was the very first time the boys have had to cut their own show. It could not have been very pleasant for the boys," he said.

But speaking of their two concerts at Hollywood Bowl (sponsored by Bob Eubanks and KRLA) Epstein said: "It was well-organized as well as enthusiastic . . . the highlight of our tour."

Epstein also announced plans for a seven-city tour by the Beatles throughout Britain this autumn. He said they expected to do one-night shows at Glasgow, Newcastle, Liverpool, Manchester, Sheffield, Birmingham and London.

Screaming Welcome

The Beatles were met by a screaming mob of several hundred fans on their return to London airport. Many of them had waited throughout a chilly night for the plane's arrival.

Ringo, George, Paul and John were whisked from the airport in a private car with a police motocycle escort.

They appeared tired, but in good spirits. Glad to be home again, but cheered by the memories of huge overflow crowds and an estimated $1 million from their U.S. tour.

The Beatles' elaborate departure plans in San Francisco almost misfired. The strategy called for them to take an elevator from their eighth floor hotel rooms, descend to the second floor, cross to a fire escape at the rear of the building and climb down to the ground to a waiting ton-and-a-half truck.

Everything went smoothly until the driver, apparently anxious to speed away before fans appeared on the scene, gunned his truck and started moving away from the hotel.

Ringo was only halfway aboard the vehicle and almost fell off before he was pulled inside.

. . . BRIAN EPSTEIN

Stones Prove They're Still Riding On Top

It took a long time for the Rolling Stones to reach the top, but it only took three weeks to prove that's exactly what they've done.

The week of August 7, their latest album, "Out Of Our Heads", hit the national charts at a modest number 93.

The following week told another story. The disc jumped all the way to the number three in the national slot, topped only by the number one "Beatles VI" and the number two "Herman's Hermits On Tour".

That's a lot of climbing for one little album to do in such a short period of time. But did that stop the Stones? Nope. They didn't even have to pause for breath before taking the final giant step toward having the Number One album in the country.

That happened the week of August 21, and it looks like the Stones can take a well-deserved rest. Because it looks like "Out Of Our Heads" is not only where it's at. It's also going to stay where it's at for a lot of weeks to come.

Sonny & Cher Have Five Hits At Once

When Sonny & Cher decide to make a hit record, they don't fool around. They take five and make four more.

BILL AND BOB STILL SETTING RECORD WITH LIVE SHOWS

Things couldn't be righter for the Righteous Brothers.

The California duo has not only become one of the world's most popular recording and television teams, but is setting new records in personal appearances as well.

They recently set new attendance records at the 500-seat Safari Room in San Jose, playing to standing-room-only audiences for ten consecutive days.

They have also been signed for the most coveted prize of all — to support Frank Sinatra for a month at the Sands in Las Vegas, starting Jan. 4. For an exclusive BEAT interview with Bill and Bob — including some fabulous pictures of them — turn to page five.

Unless memory fails us, this is the first time any group or singer besides the Beatles has had five hits on the national charts at one time. Herman was in there with four not long ago, which was a sensational accomplishment. But five? Wow.

Headed List

"I Got You Babe" headed the list by being the number one national hit, followed by Cher's "All I Really Want To do". Sonny's rendition of "Laugh At Me" came on next, like gangbusters, and within a few days, two of the twosome's previous recordings were slamming their way onto the charts.

Late Comers

The late-comers were "Just For You", and Sonny & Cher's very first release, "Baby Don't Go".

Baby, that's going and then some!

HERE THEY ARE — The Rolling Stones in action (minus Charlie Watts who is in the background beating his drums) performing their two-nation chart topper, "Satisfaction," without a doubt the biggest record the Stones have had so far.

Inside the BEAT

Vaughn vs. Women	3
John & Paul on TV	4
The Righteous Sound	5
Brenda's Beatle Tour	6
Beatles Sound Off	7
For Girls Only	8
News From The Cavern	11
Tips To Teens	12
Stones Rule England	14
Beatle Alphabet	15

ALSO — Supremes, Shindig, New Movies, Roy Head, 16 pages of news, pics of other top pop stars

The KRLA BEAT is published weekly by BEAT Publications; editorial and advertising offices at 6290 Sunset Boulevard, Suite 504, Hollywood, California 90028. Application to mail at second class postage rates is pending at Los Angeles, California, with additional entry privileges at San Francisco. Single copy price, 15 cents. Subscription price, U.S. and possessions, $3 per year or $5 for two years. Canada and foreign rates, $9 per year or $14 for two years. Exclusive distribution handled by Miller-Freeman Publications, 6328 Lewis Avenue, Long Beach, California.

WHAT HE BELIEVES
Robert Vaughn Digs Double Role In TV and Politics
BY NIKKI WINE

Any attempt to interview Robert Vaughn can be compared only to an attempt to interview the Encyclopedia Britannica if that were possible. Robert is a man to *listen to*, not to question.

Robert Vaughn is a man of deep thought and numerous words, which he employs articulately on every conceivable subject. He seems never to be caught off-guard by any question, and gives the impression of a man prepared for anything.

"A" Disgusting Bore

There is no beginning quite like that beginning which is tinged with controversy, and Robert's opening lines for The *BEAT* are certainly no let-down. On the subject of female actresses in Hollywood, Robert let loose with a verbal blast in explanation of remarks he had made previously to a national publication: "It is necessary for any woman to be overly-supplied with masculine hormones to be successful at any career position and probably much more so because they are competing directly against men in Hollywood, not only in *seeking* jobs, but when performing a job in a competitive sense as an actress. I also said that they were nervous, neurotic, self-pitying and I find the whole lot rather a disgusting bore!"

Robert Vaughn appears to be a man who has subjected himself to a good deal of thorough self-analysis and examination, and who now has a good sense of self-proportion.

In explaining his ideas on astrology to The *BEAT* readers, he also succeeds in giving his listener his own considered opinion of himself as an individual. It makes for a fascinating self-portrait. Is astrology merely a hobby with Robert Vaughn?

Stars No Hobby

"It is not a 'hobby' nor is it a way of life — it is simply one of my interests, and I find it to be programmed quite accurately as far as my astrological sign is concerned. Everything that I've read about my sign applies to me, and the other signs that surround my sign do *not* apply to me.

"I look at astrological charts in hindsight as to how they applied in a given situation in the past, because I think that that goes into the area of sorcery and witchcraft and fortune telling if you try to shape your future based upon the stars. They shape *you!*"

"I am the most representative of the fifteen-cent magazine version of a Scorpio. I'm right on the nose! I'm difficult to know well — even over an extended period of time. Fixed purposes; excessively organized; very dominant towards the opposite sex; the most obvious kind of Scorpio."

Fan magazines have had a hey-day lately with Robert's supposedly "delinquent childhood," claiming that he was both a thief and a juvenile drunk, and just about anything else they could think of.

A Different Picture

But turn around and ask Mr. Vaughn about his "bad childhood" and you will get quite a different picture of his "wayward youth!"

"This is a grave misnomer apparently started to excite the imagination of children who feel that they have a cameraderie — particularly if they're on the outside-looking-in, as far as society is concerned — with an actor who has started out poorly and been successful and gotten attention. This makes them feel that they too have that potential. I suppose that's the meaning behind the original stories concerning my wayward youth. My youth was *not* wayward in the least. I was shuttled back and forth between grandparents and parents; however I got a great deal of affection and kindness from both of them. I did moderate amount of petty theft, as virtually every young person I know has done — particularly males. I did a moderate amount of drinking — as the same applies.

"I was a good student from the time I was in school and was never at any time considered a juvenile delinquent or an insane youth, as has been ascribed to me by various fan magazines."

Political Interests

There has also been a great deal of discussion on the subject of Robert's interest in politics, and much comment has been rendered on Robert's identification with the Kennedy family. As to any political aspirations, he concedes: "If and when that time comes — and there are many things that would influence my decision to run for political office, not the least of which would be the fact that I knew the Democratic Party *wanted* me to! — I would probably like a situation on a state level first to acquaint myself with the various problems involved in handling legislation and people and I would like eventually to be involved in a federal situation of some kind where reasonable thinking and rational behavior was effective. But I have no fixed purpose as far as that's concerned. I think that will have a natural fruition in the next dozen years as a result of the work that I do now. Next year I'll be working with the Governor as his television advisor during the campaign."

As to rumors that Robert has an eye set on the Presidency, he smiles and says: "That's just another extension of a simple thing, because it's much more fun to say that a guy doing a television series that's essentially a cartoon show really wants to be President of the United States. Obviously it's good copy! I'd prefer to be Emperor anyway!!"

Working On Ph. D.

Robert is extremely well-read and well-informed and his views on the educational system are equally well-developed. He is now involved in obtaining his Ph.D. in the Philosophy of Communications at the University of Southern California, and already holds a Master's degree and a B.A. from Los Angeles State College.

Commenting on the present educational system, Robert says, "There should be some compromise between *no* grades and the present system of grading which causes so many drop-outs. I think that there should be some system that they have started in some of the UCLA branches — at Santa Barbara for one — they have an entire system there of no grading and it's working out very well. I think that it creates unnecessary early neuroses — and there are plenty to come! I don't think a fifteen-year-old should have to feel that his life is going to be a reflection of his grades."

Award Winner

Robert has appeared regularly in the TV series "The Lieutenant," and currently in the smash spy-series "Man From U.N.C.L.E." as well as several plays while in college. He won the acting award for "Hamlet" and the directing award for "A View From The Bridge" while completing his Master's degree.

He names such favorites as Dick Van Dyke and Johnny Carson in the field of comedy; Anne Bancroft, Kim Stanley, and Geraldine Page on the stage; and Katherine Hepburn, Ingrid Bergman, and Greta Garbo in motion pictures.

As for his own future in the field of entertainment, Robert tells *BEAT* readers: "I'd like to moderate a show — like the Joe Pyne show! *(Ed. note:* Robert was very dissatisfied with his own appearance on the show.

"I'd like to play Las Vegas as a stand-up comedian as Johnny Carson does and I'd like to do musicals. I'd like to direct.

Likes A Challenge

"I like to challenge myself in every way. I fail a lot! — but I challenge myself!"

Robert Vaughn appears to be a man of considered taste and opinion. But he was very adamant in demanding that his favorite performer be made quite clear to the public. In his emphatic manner he passionately declared: "Of all the people in all of the areas of show business, my favorite entertainer of all is Ming Toy Ginsberg."

Thanks to Robert Vaughn . . . and to Ming Toy Ginsberg —

Good-night Ming baby, *whatever you are!!*

. . . HANG ON, BOB.

. . . SHATTERING EXPERIENCE

September 25, 1965 — THE BEAT — Page 4

Hoops Are Happening!

As always, there are countless fads entered in the race for popularity. Some will lose out along the way, but you can bet the gold hoop earring craze is destined for the winner's circle.

Some say Bob Dylan started the whole thing by presenting gold hoops to two of his good friends. Like, when Phil Spector and Donovan started sporting Bob's rewards, ears started ringing all over the world.

Style Returns

The style is anything but new, except to us. It's come and gone several times, but it's come back again and how! And this time there's more to it than just a new look in lobes. The fad has turned into a game everybody can play (at their own risk).

There are two separate sets of rules which apply to the game. On one hand (er . . . ear), hoops help the girls get the message across to the boys. If a girl's wearing just one hoop, on her left ear, that means to keep your distance. If she's wearing just one, on her right ear, give her a ring! When she's wearing two hoops (on both ears) (where else, pray tell?) a bit of mystery enters the picture. She either *is* going steady or *isn't*, and it's up to the interested party to find out which.

Other Rules

The other set of rules gives the hoop craze a different meaning. A hoop on the left ear means the wearer is in a good mood. A hoop on the right means she's mad as a hornet. Two hoops signify a special occasion, but it's up to the rest of the world to determine whether it's a good one or a bad one.

Both sets of rules make the game portion of the fad fun but confusing. Put your imagination to work for a moment and you'll see why.

Say you're a boy and you see a cute girl wearing a hoop on her right ear. According to one school of thought, this means she's available, but on the other hand (sorry—ear) it could mean she's seething with rage.

How's He To Tell

How is a poor boy to tell which rules she's going by? And even worse, what if she isn't going by either and just happened to feel like wearing hoop earrings that day?

Running neck and neck with the hoop fad is a recent rash of black eyes adorning the countenances of boys who made the wrong guess.

Oh well, there's always one sure-fire life-saver if you happen to run into a member of the hoop-group who'd rather fight than switch.

Just offer to let her put one of those rings through your nose.

PITNEY GETS AWARD

Gene Pitney has received a "Shooting Star" award from the London Press Exchange, Ltd. The award was presented to Gene for his chart-topping English single, "Looking Through The Eyes Of Love".

THE BEAT'S RESTLESS REPORTER ASKS...

THE QUESTION OF THE WEEK

What Is Your Honest Opinion of the Beatles?

Answers:

"Who?"
—Cher Yuld (Computer Programmer)

☆ ☆ ☆

"Why should I think about it? Whenever I find one crawling in my kitchen, I spray it with insecticide."
—Farfel Smith (Housewife & Nuclear Physicist)

☆ ☆ ☆

"Beatles. Schmeatles. Why all the fuss about them when the world is just waiting for Pierre Salinger?"
—Jayne Klutz (Part-time Hollywood Sex Symbol)

☆ ☆ ☆

"Definitely not our type."
—The Roe Ling Stones (Las Vegas Sharecroppers)

☆ ☆ ☆

Readers of The BEAT are invited to send in answers to the Restless Reporter's next QUESTION OF THE WEEK, which is:

What would you do if your boyfriend showed up for a date dressed in animal skins like Sonny Bono?

Please keep your answers **short**. (All entries become the property of The **BEAT**. If your answer is printed in The **BEAT**, you will receive **free** in the mail one current LP record album. Mail your entry right now to THE QUESTION OF THE WEEK, The **BEAT**.

OK, KIDS, TAKE IT AWAY!

John And Paul To Be Hosts Of TV Special

Big things are happening in London Town these days for two of our favorite Mop Tops.

John Lennon and Paul McCartney will do their own hosting honors for a fifty-minute spectacular which will be produced by Granada television this fall.

To Pay Tribute

The special program will pay tribute to the talented team of composers and to their international success in the field of song-writing.

It is doubtful at this time that the two remaining Beatles will appear with messrs. Lennon and McCartney unless they have a new record released at that time.

The program will feature musical selections composed by John and Paul and the performing artists may include Peter and Gordon, Cilla Black, Billy J. Kramer and the Dakotas, the Fourmost, and the Silkie.

Clips Of Yanks

There is hope at the moment that the show will also include film clips of some American artists, possibly including Ella Fitzgerald.

It is not known at this writing whether or not the program will be aired in America, although several other Beatle specials probably will be seen here throughout the next few months.

TOUCH OF TRAGEDY

Accidental Meeting Kicked Off Career

He came into the *BEAT* office the other day. He had a story to tell and a record to push. We listened to his story, but only you can make the record a hit.

His name is Frankie Albano and he would rather not say where he's from. Guess it doesn't matter — it's kind of anti-climatic anyway.

Far-Out Story

The story itself sounds rather far-out, but it IS true. His father is a shoemaker and ever since Frankie could remember he always wanted a pair of Roman sandals. But his father, being extremely busy making customers' shoes, never had the time to make a pair for his son.

Frankie, like all of the other members of his family, had a great love of music. He picked up his basic sound by attending the Negro church as a little boy. There he would sit on somebody's lap banging his small hands against a tambourine.

He had the same kind of childhood as everyone else. Nothing unusual or different. When he grew older he found himself a girlfriend. Nothing strange about that, is there?

Then one day he and his girl had a big fight and Frankie decided that they should call it quits. He wanted to be a singer — wanted to be big-time.

Frankie Cuts Out

The day Frankie left, the girl handed him a box with a card which read, "For no other reason but love." Inside the box Frankie found a pair of Roman sandals, just like the ones he had wanted so badly.

With the sandals in his suitcase, he hitch-hiked to the tinsel city of Hollywood with his eyes full of stars and his pockets devoid of money.

He missed his girl, in fact he was downright miserable, but his pride wouldn't allow him to call her. He drifted into a Hollywood cafe and there found himself telling his story to a perfect stranger.

Meets Writer

Here Frankie himself takes up the story: "As fate would have it the stranger I was talking to was a songwriter and before I knew it he had written a song about my hurt and lost love.

"He called the song 'Forgetful One', and though I had never sung professionally before I soon found myself recording for the writer, Mike Curb.

...FRANKIE ALBANO

Calls Too Late

"The night after the session I couldn't stand it any more so I phoned her. She didn't answer — she couldn't, for I learned that the night before she had been killed in an automobile accident.

"Little did I know that the song which I had recorded for her that night would take on a completely different meaning.

"The only things I have left of her now are the Roman sandals, which I will always wear. And my song for her, 'She'll Never Know.'"

LIVERPOOL FIVE ON THEIR WAY

Watch out and listen for the newest release of one of the most exciting and interesting groups to come our way in a long time. The name of the group: The Liverpool Fvie. The title of their new RCA Victor release, "You Got To Stay All Night," written by the one and only Bob Dylan. It was released the 16th of August, and within the first week of its release it scaled the charts in Washington at number 39.

KRLA ARCHIVES

... RIGHTEOUS & RIGHT NOW!

BEAT photo: Robert W. Young

BROTHERS IN SPIRIT

'Whole Lotta Spirit' Heard In Righteous 'Soul Sound'

By Eden

Although talent is not necessarily hereditary, it is often said to "run in the family." In the family of the Righteous Brothers, talent runs rampant and it is evenly distributed between the two of them.

'No, Bill and Bobby are not really blood-relations, but they are brothers in spirit. Their spirit? Well, it's the "soul sound," brother, and that's a whole lotta spirit!

Brotherhood Formed

Bill Medley and Bobby Hatfield discovered one another in 1962 when each was playing with his own group in the Orange County area of California, and the brotherhood was formed.

Their first job as a team was at the Charter House in Anaheim playing at a big prom. Describing that evening, the Brothers Righteous say: "We had 10 fake songs and we were a group of strangers and we did some strange things, like singing the same songs several times around, dragging each one out for at least five minutes, and taking lots of breaks. When the kids asked for a cha-cha only one guy in the group knew one and we all came in on it. Then they asked for a march when the Queen of the Prom made her entrance. The only one we knew was 'When The Saints Go Marching In.' It was a gas!" gas!"

"Big" Take

Did you ever think that entertainers make a mint overnight? Well, for the group of five, the total take that evening was forty dollars!

Bill Medley was the first brother to branch out into songwriting, his first composition being "Little Latin Lupe Lu." This was the first single record for the boys, and at first it made very few ripples in the great pond of pop music.

But the Righteous Brothers were booked into the Rendezvous Ballroom in Balboa — this was the beginning of the big time.

"There were 300 kids the first night", they recall. "We kept coming back every weekend and after awhile, there were 2,000 kids. We did nothing but rhythm and blues and we pushed "Little Latin Lupe Lu." The kids began ordering it at the record shops and pretty soon we had a little Latin hit!

Found Their Name

About the name, boys. How did two "brothers" become so Righteous? It began at a six-month engagement which they played at the Black Derby in Santa Ana. Approximately twenty-five per cent of the crowd was Negro. "They were more soulful and their purpose in coming to hear us was to listen to and to enjoy the music. When we did something they particularly liked they'd say 'It's righteous, brother' and there was our name."

This has been just the beginning of the touching saga of the Righteous Brothers. Now, we will move ahead in time and space to the present day. Bill and Bobby are not just two rock 'n' roll singers; they are talented artists whose forte lies in a skillfully blended combination of jazz, gospel, rhythm and blues, and spiritual. Well, they do throw a *little* rock 'n' roll in here and there!

"We don't have any gimmicks. Our approach is with one specific quality in mind: the heart of the song. We stick to our bag — one type of song. We don't do surf or hot rod or skate board. People who hear us may like us or they may hate us and that's all right as long as they don't ignore us, as long as they remember us."

Their Sound

On the subject of their "sound" and their particular kind of music, the Righteous guys are far from silent. Bobby explains, "Yes, we have the soul sound. It's when you feel the music you sing. But we're singing more and more unsoulful songs now. You know, like 'hum along with the Righteous Brothers!' We're being produced like two good-looking guys who can't sing!"

Bobby was referring to their last three or four records, all of which were produced by the youthful rock 'n' roll magnate Phil Spector, on which the lyrics of the songs are nearly incomprehensible. The boys prefer to do good music with good lyrics which can be understood on the finished product. Bobby explains, "We don't record songs we don't undersand." Then he laughs and continues, "My Mother has finally become one of my fans. She heard "Unchained Melody" and discovered for the first time that I could sing!"

The humor of the Righteous Brothers falls on the weird side, and both claim such favorites as Phyllis Diller, Peter Sellars, Jonathan Winters, and Bill Cosby.

A Hip Baby

Mr. Medley, a recent entrant into the ranks of parenthood, says of his two-an-a-half month old son: "He's all hung up on Baby Ruth's right now. But he plays the bass guitar and he's forming a group with the kids

TURN TO PAGE 13

KRLA ARCHIVES

SINCERITY PAYS

Brenda Holloway Tells Inside Story of Career

She's really a nice person—one of the nicest in the business. She probably doesn't have any enemies — and that's rare.

Guess by now you've figured out that the girl we're talking about is Brenda Holloway. She's an extremely talented and a very lucky young lady of 19.

We recently caught Brenda at a recording session for the Supremes. As usual, Brenda was bubbling over with enthusiasm. Enthusiasm for the Beatles, for the tour, for her new record, for life.

Wanted To Sing

Brenda always wanted to be a singer, she says. In fact, she elaborates: "I used to watch all the shows on television and start crying because I wanted to be an entertainer. My mother used to get so mad at me!

"I used to get whippin's because I'd start crying and I wouldn't go to bed."

Brenda went to Jordan High School in Los Angeles and every time the school held a talent show, Brenda was the first to sign up.

Heard By Gordy

Then she happened to attend a disc jockey convention and Berry Gordy (head of Tamla-Motown) was also there. Gordy heard her sing. "He said I had a pretty good voice and so he signed me up," Brenda explained.

Her first record was "Every Little Bit Hurts" and her first professional appearance was at the Latin Quarter in New York where she joined the rest of the Tamla-Motown family onstage for the very first time.

A huge break came drifting Brenda's way when she went to Detroit and was told that the Beatles wanted her on their tour!

Brenda just couldn't believe that they really wanted *her* — but apparently they did, for plans were finalized and Brenda joined the boys in New York.

Beatles 'Real Nice'

Brenda thinks the Beatles are "real nice. They're down to earth. They're just people — that's why I like them. They're very friendly and I like them a whole lot!"

All the time the Beatles were staying in Los Angeles, Brenda did not go near their house. "I stayed away because of all their fans. I saw them everyday for about 10 days, so why go back? I don't like to bother them."

Brenda was really thrilled with the tour. "I loved it because we got to fly every place and eat on the plane. It's been a dream tour."

Criticism was voiced by some of the performers on last year's Beatle tour claiming that the fans didn't want to see anyone except the Beatles.

Tense Audiences

Brenda says: "Audiences were tense, but if you just did your best, you were all right.

"And now since they've seen the Beatles before, they can wait. They do just come to see the Beatles, but they're not so excited as last year."

Recalling more tour memories, Brenda chuckled: "Ringo borrowed my hairdryer to do his hair.

"We had pillow fights. George usually started them and then everyone joined in. And Ringo would walk down the aisle of the plane saying: 'Fasten your seat belts. Only doing my job!'

Prettiest Hair

"Ringo's hair is the prettiest. He doesn't have too much to say to anyone. Except one night he and the drummer from the King Curtis Band got into a long discussion on God and religion."

Brenda admits that the tour is "one of the most exciting things that has ever happened to me."

"I enjoy the Beatles. If they'd been crabs or mean I wouldn't have enjoyed it. I miss them now that the tour is over."

Brenda really won't have too much time to lament the end of the Beatle tour. She'll be much too busy.

She has a new record, "You Can Cry On My Shoulder," written by Barry Gordy.

Not "Done Right"

Of the record Brenda says: "I like it very much. It was on the market and then they took it off. I'm going to do it over again because it wasn't done right the first time.

"I sang it on the tour and I got pretty good response. The kids seemed to be listening to it."

And for the distant future? "I want to go into A&R work. Probably in the next year. I have a whole lot of ideas."

Brenda entered show business in the first place to try and make people happy —and she's done just that.

As I said — Brenda is a genuinely nice person. And those kind are hard to come by!

...BRENDA: GENUINE PERSON

★ NATIONAL RECORDING COMPANY IS LOOKING FOR ★
NEW TALENT - SINGERS - SONGWRITERS - GROUPS
CONTEMPORARY ROCK 'N' ROLL, FOLK OR R&B
EVERYONE WILL BE GIVEN AN OPPORTUNITY
CALL JOHNNY OTIS, ELDO RECORDS — (213) HO 7-6151

On The BEAT

By Louise Criscione

Herman is back Stateside to make a movie. "Naturally I've snatched the biggest part, but I used to be an actor so I'm not too nervous," Herman declares confidently.

Mike Jagger reveals that the Stones were not too jazzed over the idea of releasing "Satisfaction" as a single, "but now, of course, we are happy." They oughta be!

Ian Whitcomb, recently returned to England after a long and successful tour of the States, had quite a lot to say about Americans in general, but I thought you'd be more interested in what he had to say about us.

"But on the West Coast they're very hip. The kids are terrily pro-English; the Stones are bigger than the Beatles."

Observant boy, that Ian! Watch out for him — he'll be coming back in October.

Stones Re-Sign

The Stones have re-signed with London Records for a five year, three million dollar deal. London handles the Stones' record distribution for the U.S. and Canada.

In England and the rest of the world, the Stone records are released through Decca and this is where the good stuff comes in, for Decca has agreed to give the Stones five million dollars for independently produced films!

The first movie is scheduled to begin shooting in January and they are hoping for a mid-Spring release date.

The Stones were originally set for a movie to be filmed in August, but because of their tight schedule and also due to this better deal they dropped out of it.

Also tentatively set, but not yet confirmed, is a movie for Mick. Fashion photographer, David Bailey, is setting the film up and the working title for the movie is "The Assassination of Mick Jagger!"

Quick Ones

Donovan's book of poems may be delayed a bit. Seems he wrote the poems in manuscript and then promptly lost the manuscript "in London somewhere" . . . When the Animals are in Hollywood they will discuss plans for a possible MGM movie. Chas. Chandler says the boys have definite ideas on the kind of movie they want to make . . . When the Beatles' plane was forced to make an emergency landing in Portland, John quipped: "Beatles, women and children off first!" and George deadpanned: "This should stop them asking how much longer we're going to last!"

Never Still

They just keep moving, don't they? Those two beatles, Paul and John, are never still. They write songs, appear in movies, sing, play instruments, produce records and now they are set to host a television spectacular!

The 50-minute show will be a tribute to John's and Paul's fantastic song-writing successes. However, unless the Beatles have a new English single out during the filming of the show (in late October or early November) the Beatles will not perform.

Definitely appearing on the show will be practically all of Brian Epstein's proteges — Cilla Black, Billy J. Kramer and the Dakotas, the Fourmost and the Silkie.

Film clips of American artists will also be shown, but the only name released so far is Ella Fitzgerald. However, other top names are being sought.

The show will be produced for Granada TV, but it is quite possible that an American network will pick up the show for broadcast in the U.S. Sure hope so!

Sonny & Cher, just back from their triumph in England, had a lot of say about message songs — that is, Sonny had a lot to say:

"With us, I think, the universal message is really just love. I build everything around that. I don't think anybody really believes in war so I can understand why some of the war protest songs come about. But I don't really know whether it does any good to sing about it, you know."

...IAN WHITCOMB

...GUESS WHO!

KRLA ARCHIVES

A BEATLE'S PRESS CONFERENCE
WHAT'S IT LIKE?

BEAT photo: Robert W. Young

LET'S GO SEE . . . with Louise Criscione

Hollywood — Well, gang, we are off again and this time it's to a Beatles' press conference! Wanna come?

It's about 6:30 p.m. — a half hour before the press conference is due to get underway.

The location of this press conference is a well-guarded secret, but as always happens with anything concerning the Beatles the secret has somehow managed to get out, and throngs of teenage girls are lined up outside the door.

Not a Prayer

They really don't have a prayer of gaining admittance but they wait anyway — hoping that they will get at least a glimpse of the four Beatles as they make their mad dash from the armored truck to the door of the building.

Policemen group around the parking lot and solidly line the entrance to the building. At the door a girl stands with a list of invited guests and only those people whose name is on the list are allowed past the guards.

Each guest is provided with a gold press pass, and without this pass *and* your name at the door — you are completely out of luck. This year *no one* sneaks in. Even the Beatles themselves are on the list!

As the guests are checked in they are handed a press kit which contains the Beatles' well-known biography and also a copy of their latest album, "Help."

Room a Beehive

The conference room is a beehive of activity. Television cameramen are setting up their equipment, tape recorders are being readied, reporters are chatting and officials are checking and rechecking the microphones and amplifiers.

Nothing, absolutely nothing, must go wrong tonight. It's been planned too long to have anything go wrong now at the last minute.

More people are admitted, seats are rapidly filled, the clock is moving closer and closer to the time when the Beatles are due to arrive.

It's ten minutes to seven and Tony Barrow, publicist for the Beatles, steps up to the microphone and gives the press their last minute instructions.

A Roar Outside

Then suddenly a roar is heard from the crowd gathered outside and you know that the Beatles have finally arrived!

Two policemen run up the aisle clearing the way for the Beatles who are following close behind.

And then you see them! John, the undeclared leader, arrives first followed in short order by Ringo, Paul, and bringing up the rear is George.

Immediately the flash bulbs start flashing. The four make their way to the platform on which four microphones, four stools and four small desks have been placed.

Each Beatle waves hello, chooses a seat, and the photographers move up in front of the platform to take their alloted 10 minutes of shots.

The Beatles allow themselves to be photographed individually and in a group. And then it's our turn to ask questions.

Questioning Begins

Two microphones have been set up on the floor, and as Tony points to you the microphone is brought over and you ask your question. In this way every question as well as every answer is heard by everyone in the room.

It's going very well. The veteran newsmen comment on the smoothness and organization of the conference.

The questioning lasts for a little over an hour. Some of the questions have been asked a million times before, some are brand new. The Beatles answer all of them — sometimes with a laugh, sometimes very seriously.

They field all of the questions expertly. Some reporters attempt to put them down, but they are always on-guard. And they are never without an answer. John and Paul do most of the talking, with George coming in third and Ringo remaining the quietest.

Thank the Press

After a series of short television interviews, the Beatles thank the press for coming — the press thank the Beatles for inviting them — the conference room is cleared and the Beatles jump aboard their armored truck for a quick drive to the show.

We were sorry to see the conference end so soon. But they will be back again next year (they told us so!). And we can hardly wait, can you?

For Girls Only

By Shirley Poston

Special Message To All Boys Who Think I Don't Know They're Reading This Column Whether I Like It Or Not: After you finish this installment of "For Girls Only", I'd be only too happy to lend you my copy of "Little Women."

There, I guess that took care of *them* for another week.

Speaking of *them*, have you ever gone through a big trauma about buying a gift for a boy? Series of traumas, I should say, because that's usually the case.

Birthday Looms

It all starts when either Christmas or a birthday is looming on the horizon. About two months before the date, the girl stops *wondering* should she or shouldn't she and starts getting *panic-stricken*. It's all of a sudden so important that minor problems like earthquakes and tidal waves don't even faze her.

Then, one morning s h e wakes up, takes a steely-eyed glance in the mirror, notices that a tic has developed under her left eye, and comes to a decision.

"I will," she shouts. While the rest of the family wonders *what* she will, she proceeds to the next trauma. *What* to get him.

After about a month of this, during which large dark circles appear under both eyes, she decides what. It is then time to start worrying about when. Ultimately, she faces the final problem. How. Just hand it over or make a speech or what. Or put it on his doorstep like a May basket and hide in the ivy.

I don't know about you, but I've had several of these experiences, and so help me, I'm not having another one. Ever! It takes all the fun out of giving the present.

Solemn Vow

It is now several thousand shopping days until Christmas and I am making a solemn vow, on paper so I won't *dare* break it. If I am going steady with someone come St. Nick time, I am going to march to the department store and buy him a present. None of this lying awake nights wondering what, what, what to get him.

Then, just before Christmas, I am going to march up to him and present the gift. None of this dying a thousand deaths, wondering if he's bought something for me, and if he'll feel obligated if he hasn't.

THE MOTHERS

Then, when I have done all that, I am going to faint. From shock. Because I'll never believe it until I really see myself do something so simple without making a Broadway production out of it.

★ ★ ★

Oh, Brother!

My brother is going to kill me. I can feel it coming. And I can tell you exactly when it's going to happen. The very day he reads this particular column because I'm about to tell a good one on him.

This brother of mine thinks he's a real romeo, and last week he was walking around telling the whole family how this really great girl was just sitting by the phone waiting for him to call her again.

Well, about two days later this big envelope came in the mail for him. I'll never know where the girl got that big a sheet of paper because it was about the size of a wall.

Gets the Message

It was folded about fifteen times and he unfolded and unfolded and unfolded, expecting something really sensational. When he got to the message, he sure *got* the message.

There was one word typed dead center in the paper.

It said, and I quote, *BYE!*

I thought I was going to literally die laughing at the look on his face. And telling you about this is almost worth dying for.

There's only one thing that's bothering me. How did she get that great big paper in a typewriter?

Life is just one big mystery after another . . .

A Beautiful Farewell

Oh, just remembered another beautiful "farewell". A girl I knew had an after-school job in a drug store and she never told her boyfriend about it. A few days after he'd asked her to go steady, and she'd accepted, he came into the drug store with another girl. They sat down at the soda fountain and when his steady came over to take their order, he about collapsed.

He managed to keep control enough to order two malts, but when they arrived he really got shook up. When he got to the bottom of his, there was her ring in the bottom of the glass!

★ ★ ★

I'm talking about too few things for too long again and using up all my space. Between now and the end of this column, I am going to discuss five separate subjects.

One, do you know where you can buy the world's cheapest bell bottoms? At any Army-Navy surplus store, where else? They can be dyed any color and really look sharp. P.S. — I have a feeling that several sailors are never going to speak to me again.

Two, I heard of another great thing you can do with old records you don't have the heart to throw away. Make one of those hanging mobiles or whatever you call them. You know, those bunches of stuff that sort of hang from the ceiling and waft in the breeze?

Non-Sensible Manner

Three, why is it completely impossible for me to explain anything in a sensible manner? I'll bet you don't know many people who would refer to a mobile as those bunches of stuff that sort of hang from the ceiling and waft in the breeze. If this is the case, you don't know how very fortunate you are.

Four, see number five. I can't think of a number four.

Five, they are coming for me soon, I fear. Seriously (I was kidding??) I do want to tell you one sensible thing if I can manage it. I got a letter from a girl who was having this big problem redecorating her room on about a seventy-eight cent budget. There was a huge window in her room, with Venetian blinds that she just despised, but she didn't have enough money to buy drapes. I was about to write and suggest something ridiculous when I got another letter. She'd solved the problem by going on a paint hunt in the garage. She found leftover drips and drops of about seven colors and proceeded to paint the blinds, alternating the colors. She says it looks fantastic. Just thought I'd pass the thought on to you in case you're in a Venetian painting mood. If so, start by finding a Venetian who wouldn't mind being . . . Oh, good grief. End it all so someone else can get a word in edgewise this *BEAT*!

★ ★ ★

Six, (to make up for number four) please keep your letters coming and if I *don't* see you next *BEAT*, please plan to come round on visiting day.

In Love With A Star

DEAR BEAT:

Please print this letter. Something wonderful happened to me and I want all the other girls who read the *BEAT* to hear about it.

About two years ago, I fell in love with a star. I'm not going to say who, because that really doesn't have much to do with what happened.

I don't mean the crush kind of love. I mean the kind that lasts and lasts, and the longer it lasted, the more I cared.

Pain Of Loving

This was a lot of fun in a lot of ways, but it made me unhappy sometimes, to be honest about it. I'd about die every time I heard a rumor about him maybe getting married or going steady with someone, and I used to get a terrible feeling when I'd stop and realize that my chances of ever meeting him were about one in a billion.

Things finally got to a point where I was unhappy more than I was happy. I didn't know what to do about this, but I knew I had to do something besides sharing my problem with my friends (most of them had the same problem with other stars, so they were not much consolation).

I've never been the type to write fan letters. I know stars must receive more mail than they could ever possibly read, and I didn't see any sense in adding my letters to the pile.

But, finally I just couldn't stand the feeling of panic any longer. So I sat down and wrote a letter to my idol and told him just exactly how I felt about him. Not in a mushy way. Just that I loved him and would probably get over it someday and hoped to live through the time between now and then.

That Creepy Feeling

Right after I mailed it, I started feeling better, and whenever I'd come down with that creepy feeling again, I'd write him another letter.

I didn't even expect to get an answer (I didn't), but being pen pals with him, even if it was one-sided really changed things. I didn't feel so far away from him, or so helpless.

Now it's come to the point where I write him about other things. Not just problems or my caring about him. About myself and what I think, and about my friends and the fun we have. I just tell him anything and everything that's on my mind.

I discovered that this helps more than just my feeling toward him. By putting things on paper, I've been able to understand situations that were always sort of foggy to me. And I've learned not to take myself quite so seriously.

I don't know if he reads my letters (sometimes I write every day), or if anyone reads them, but even if they don't, this has given me a chance to get a lot of things off my chest.

My favorite was in town this summer, and I was dreading his visit before I started "corresponding" with him. I knew I'd get hysterical because he was so near and still so far away. But that didn't happen. I went to see one of his concerts and instead of getting all crazy and rushing up on the stage like I might have done a year ago, I just sat there and listened with this strange smile on my face. My friends stopped screaming every few minutes to ask what was wrong with me, but I just went on smiling.

Really Close

I don't know if I can explain how I felt, but I guess I just felt really *close* to him for the first time. I knew almost everything there was to know about him, and because of all my letters, there was a slim chance that he knew almost everything about me.

And even if he didn't, something very nice took the place of panic and now I like loving him because it no longer makes me miserable.

Maybe I've just grown up a little, I don't know. If so, then he's partly responsible for that, just by being there for me to confide in. And that makes me feel even *closer* to him.

If anyone is having this same problem, I wish you'd try and solve it with a pen and paper instead of tears. No one has to know your secret, and you'll be amazed at how much better you'll feel. I'd rather my name wouldn't be printed if you publish this in the *BEAT* (hope, hope). I'd like to keep my secret, too.

Name Withheld By Request,   Anaheim, California.

RECORD QUIZ

Do some of today's hit discs sound slightly familiar? Well, no wonder! Several of them are brand new versions of great old favorites.

Below you'll find a list of five favorite "re-makes", and the jumbled names of the artists who made them successful originally.

See if you can match them up! Answers appear below, too, but they're upside down because we know **your** type.

1. "Theme From A Summer Place" (Lettermen)
   A. Dobie Gray
2. "To Know You Is To Love You" (Peter & Gordon)
   B. Al Hibbler
3. "The In Crowd" (Ramsey Lewis Trio)
   C. Percy Faith
4. "Unchained Melody" (Righteous Brothers)
   D. Chris Kenner
5. "I Like It Like That" (Dave Clark Five)
   E. The Teddy Bears

ANSWERS: 1-C, 2-E, 3-A, 4-B, 5-D. Don't feel too bad if you didn't get more than three correct answers in this quiz. It's harder than it looks. We know, because we couldn't even remember the right answers ourselves! (We're dumber than we look.) (We sincerely hope so, anyway.))

KRLA ARCHIVES

FRUITS OF TALENT are enjoyed by artist Tommy Yamashita (center, holding LP's), winner of The Beatle Art Festival. Tommy was presented with a Vox guitar and amplifier, a box at the Hollywood Bowl Beatle concert and a complete collection of albums by his favorite foursome by KRLA's Dave Hull (l.) on the set of Casey Kasem's **SHEBANG** TV show. While Casey (r.) points to part of the loot, Dave puts some kind of good luck sign over Tommy whose winning painting is seen in all its gorgeous glory at right.

MAIL BOX

Dear *BEAT*,

I had to write this to someone because I'm too angry to keep it to myself. The other night, as I was watching the news on television, there were some girls who claimed to be Beatle fans.

In order to just catch a glimpse of the Beatles they had rented a helicopter and hovered over the Beatles' "hideaway." When a servant told them to leave because the Beatles were trying to sleep, these girls were offended because they had spent too much money to fly away without seeing the Beatles.

I know how much any Beatle fan wants to see the Beatles because I'm a Beatle fan and I'd do *almost* anything to see them.

But I certainly wouldn't consider a person a Beatle fan if she puts her own happiness so far above that of the Beatles' as to ignore their wishes completely.

With the Beatles here in L.A. as our guests, we should try to make them feel at home and at ease. How in heaven's name can anyone be at ease with a helicopter hovering about observing every little thing they do?

One of these girls also mentioned following the Beatles on the freeway last year at a ridiculously high speed. And I bet she wouldn't have cared in the least had she caused John, Paul, Ringo and George to land in a hospital — or a morgue. She wouldn't care, that is, as long as *she* got to see them. I only hope that the Beatles had a wonderful vacation here in spite of these girls and people like them and that they'll come back again soon.

Thank you for letting me vent my anger in this way.

Sue Bingham

Back issues of the KRLA BEAT are still available, for a limited time. If you've missed an issue of particular interest to you, send 15 cents for each copy wanted, along with a self-addressed stamped envelope to:

KRLA BEAT   Suite 504   6290 Sunset Blvd.
Hollywood, California 90028

ISSUES AVAILABLE
- 3/31 — BEATLE TITLE CHOSEN
- 4/14 — INTERVIEW WITH JOHN LENNON
- 4/21 — INTERVIEW WITH PAUL McCARTNEY
- 4/28 — CHIMP EXCITES TEEN FAIR
- 5/5 — HERMANIA SPREADS
- 5/12 — HERE COME THE BEATLES
- 5/19 — VISIT WITH BEATLES
- 5/26 — FAB NEW BEATLE QUIZ
- 6/9 — BEATLES
- 6/16 — BATTLE OF THE BEAT
- 6/30 — PROBY FIRED
- 7/24 — BEATLES TOP STONES
- 7/31 — CHER
- 8/7 — DYLAN
- 8/14 — HERMAN
- 8/21 — STONES TESTIFY
- 8/28 — KRLA PRESENTS THE BEATLES
- 9/4 — BEATLES . . . IN PERSON NOW!
- 9/11 — THE THREE FACES OF BOB DYLAN
- 9/18 — PROTESTOR BARRY McGUIRE

KRLA BEAT SUBSCRIPTION

you will SAVE 60% of the regular price!
AN INTRODUCTORY SPECIAL . . . if you subscribe now . . .

☐ 1 YEAR — 52 Issues — $3.00   ☐ 2 YEARS — $5.00

Enclosed is $..............

Send to:.. Age:..........

Address:..

City:........................... State:................... Zip:..........

MAIL YOUR ORDER TO: **KRLA BEAT**
1401 South Oak Knoll Avenue
Pasadena, California 91106

Outside U.S.: $9.00 — 52 Issues

KRLA ARCHIVES

TALENTED RON LIPKINS OF LOS ANGELES IS THIS WEEK'S ALBUM-WINNER FOR THE BEST BEAT CARTOON.

HELP!

I am starting to put together all my Beatle pics and articles in a giant scrapbook. If anyone has any Beatle pictures or articles pertaining to the fab four, please send them to me. Jori Page, 717 Carhart, Apt. E-4, Fullerton, Calif.

HELP!

I'm trying to find out who is more popular, the Rolling Stones or the Beatles. Cast your vote for either one. Write to: Lisa Smith, 11841 Runnymede Street, North Hollywood, California.

HELP!

I've just started putting together my scrapbook of Herman's Hermits and wondered if anybody would help me. I'm afraid that I couldn't possibly have all the articles or pictures of them and I'd really appreciate it if you could send anything you might have on them to me. I'll return anything which I already have. Jill Houghton, 3900 Lenawee Avenue, Culver City, California.

KRL"A" Contest A Challenge To All Model Car Builders

How often has Dad or Mom grumped, "Don't see for the life of me why you spend so much time fooling around with that old model. What that kind of time-wasting is ever going to get you, I swear I don't know"?

Sounds familiar, doesn't it? But if you're one of those guys always "fooling around" with customized models trying — and very often succeeding — to turn components into a replica of a top-dog of autodom, you've now got an answer for Mom and Dad.

Big Contest

Valuable cash and merchandise prizes may be waiting for you through station KRLA's new KRL "A" Contest, open to everyone who builds model cars in Southern California. For best entries there are five first prizes, five second prizes, five third prizes, and 75 honorable mentions.

The KRL "A" Contest is, of course, designed around the station's custom-built mobile unit, a street rod known around Los Angeles as the KRL "A". This is a stock Model "A" with a Chevy 283 engine, five-spoke mag wheels with cheater sticks on the rear. The drive train is Chevy automatic matched to a limited slip rear end.

Three Divisions

There are three separate divisions in the contest:

OOPS!

Gertrude, our devilish Gremlin who goofs type with wild delight, last issue dipped impish hands into the type box and scrambled the correct address of It's Boss — which should have read, of course, 8443 Sunset Strip. 'Cause that's where it's at, babe.

Replica — to be judged in comparison with the actual KRL "A";

Open — builders are permitted to design their own versions of the KRL "A", the only requirement being that all models must be built around a Model "A" radiator shell;

Operating — this division is for advanced builders who wish to include operating lights, doors, steering linkage and the rest of the jazz. This division is also known as Master Modelers Division Three.

General Rules

The general rules are simple. All models entered must have the letters KRLA or KRL "A" clearly visible on the car's exterior. No models will be accepted after the advertised closing date for entering the contest. Don't forget to put an I.D. tag on either the model or its display case. KRLA will not set up or decorate any special displays. Also, while you may use plastic display cases, these cases must be intact on delivery.

That's about it on the actual contest. Now . . . glance to the right. See the handsome Maltese Cross decal? It's yours for the asking — a sharp black-and-yellow on white decal designed to highlight any rod on the road — when you spot the KRL"A" in your neighborhood. Just tell Carson Schreiber at the KRL"A" wheel the BEAT sent you!

SEE YOUR OFFICIAL ENTRY BLANK BELOW.

YOUR MALTESE CROSS... Watch For It!

NEW NUMBER

KRLA has a new number for its contest telephones: 681-3601. And with the new number the telephone company is providing expanded service to accommodate the many thousands of callers who enter KRLA's huge array of daily contests.

This means that the KRLA switchboard will now be able to handle even more calls simultaneously, and each contestant has a better chance of getting through. A new contest will be coming up shortly, so how about giving the new number a try?

This may be your lucky day.

Official Entry Blank   KRL 'A' Contest

NAME_____ AGE_____

ADDRESS_____ PHONE____

CHECK APPROPRIATE SQUARE: DIVISION 1 ☐ JUNIOR ☐ SENIOR

DIVISION 2 ☐ JUNIOR ☐ SENIOR

DIVISION 3 ☐ JUNIOR ☐ SENIOR

HERE IS A BRIEF DESCRIPTION OF DETAILS JUDGES SHOULD LOOK FOR IN MY KRL "A":

_____

_____

THIS IS YOUR OFFICIAL KRLA BEAT ENTRY BLANK

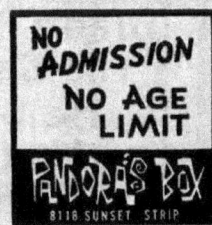

KRLA ARCHIVES

LIVERPUDDLES
by Rob McGrae

There is an exciting new group here in Liverpool called The Hideaways. Here in England, they have appeared on television more times than any other group in a commercial which was filmed at Liverpool's famous Cavern Club. There is just one little catch to that, though — through this commercial the group has come to be called The Tick-a-Tick-a-Timex boys. These boys really believe in the blues and their music shows this influence.

The line-up of the group consists of Judd Lander, 18, the harmonica player and also the comedian of the group; John Donaldson, 18, who acts as drum-beater for the boys; Frank O'Connor, the lead singer and rhythm guitarist; "Ossie" Yue, a Chinese boy who is 18 and is the group's lead guitarist, and John Shell, 18, who is the bass player.

Most people are amazed to see the enthusiasm and vitality the boys put into their act. This vitality of theirs is really a fantastic thing to see while they are performing and the wild reaction of their audiences is sound testimonial to this.

The boys have great ambitions and hope that their first record, which will be released in October or November, will be a large enough hit to insure them a trip to the States. Their wish will come true to some degree this September when Americans will be introduced to them for the first time on the Telly. The Hideaways will be appearing in a documentary film called "Liverpool Au GoGo," which is to be screened sometime in September. This show is certain to win them many new fans in America, and in the meantime, all of their fans here in Liverpool will be rooting for them.

Anyone wishing to contact The Hideaways may write to them at the following address: The Hideaways, Dept. H., 8/12 Matthew Street, Liverpool 2, England; or through their American fan club, which is: Miss Sue Franklin, 22858 Gault, Canoga Park, California, U.S.A.

Till next time then, this is Rob McGrae from the Cavern. Ta!

...THE HIDEAWAYS — OUT OF HIDING.

BRAD BERWICK
ANSWERS THE PROTESTORS

'GOD, COUNTRY and MY BABY'

Flip Side - "ARE YOU GLAD"

Brad's Proud of His Country He Sings About It!

DEEM RECORDS

Brad Berwick Fan Club
For Information Write
12345 W. Ventura Blvd.
Studio City, California

KRLA ARCHIVES

TIPS TO TEENS

Q: I am fifteen years old now and I respect my parents wishes, but they still treat me like a little kid. I want to let my hair grow to shoulder length and *they* won't let me. I've tried to explain to them that I am old enough to know what I want, but this doesn't seem to work. What can I do?
(Martha C.)

A: You'd better do some more explaining, and a lot of it! You are certainly old enough to choose your own hair style, among other things, and since your parents seem to think otherwise, it's up to you to convince them how wrong they are. Approach them on their own level. Don't cry or throw a snit. Talk. If that doesn't work, keep talking until it does. Also, while you're campaigning to prove you aren't a little kid any more, be sure you never act like one.

☆ ★ ☆

Q: In a recent BEAT, I read where this girl had trouble having a good picture taken of herself. You advised her to think of her favorite star. Now I want you to help me. I take lousy pictures myself and every time I think of the Beatles or darling George I get the dumbest looks on my face. Please tell me what I should do.
(Candy M.)

A: Well, this is probably going to sound semi-ridiculous, but have you tried saying "cheese" just as the camera clicks? It may be an old fashioned thing to do, but it's been working for several jillion years! If that doesn't work, try thinking of the funniest joke you've ever heard. Then drop by the office and tell it to us.

☆ ★ ☆

Q: To come right to the point, I have a large nose. I have earned such names as Hose Nose, Spout Snout, etc. I know there is plastic surgery, but could you recommend a less drastic method or a product I could buy to have a regular looking nose?
(Craig H.)

A: As far as we know, plastic surgery is the only method for solving the problem you speak of. If you feel this is too drastic, you can at least be comforted by the fact that the name-calling will cease. Your letter sounded as though you aren't too upset by it anyway, but in case you were just being brave, rest assured that if your nose doesn't change, other things will. The people who are still childish enough to be unkind to others, for instance.

☆ ★ ☆

Q: My English pen pal's birthday is coming up soon and I can't think of anything I could get her that she would like. Have you any suggestions?
(Donna M.)

A: We sure do, and here are as many of them as we have room for. How about a really nice pen (apropos and very easy to mail), or personalized stationery, or a subscription to an American magazine or newspaper (plug, plug), a piggy bank so she can start saving for a trip to the "colonies", a great big card signed by all your friends, or a scrapbook of the most popular fads and stars in America (so she'll really be in the know about what's happening on our side of the Atlantic). Oh, we just thought of a *really* great one! How about a hand-made thank you card with several pages. Like on the front it could say America Thanks England For ... then on the next page you could put a pic of the Beatles with a caption underneath, and you could have a pic of a girl dressed in English styles on the next, etc. It would really be a gas!

Q: I about go crazy every time I try to wear mascara. My lashes are quite long and they scrape against my glasses. I do not notice this until I put on the mascara, but then I can't stand it! I hope you'll be able to help because my eyes are very pale and need highlighting.
(Derry L.)

A: Why don't you substitute eye liner and a touch of shadow for mascara? When you wear glasses, you can get away with more eye makeup than most, because it isn't so visible. If you find you still prefer mascara, use the good oldfashioned cake and brush kind. After the mascara has dried, brush your lashes with a clean dry brush to remove the stiffness. Mascara has a tendency to dry in lumps, so carefully run a straight pin through any clogged lashes.

Q: I have naturally curly hair which I hate. When I go to the beach it gets wavy and fizzy. What can I do? It's medium length and I don't want to cut it or wear a bandana. HELP!
(Cathy S.)

A: See this week's hint, coming up next!

HINT OF THE WEEK

I read in the BEAT where you said you didn't know of any home permanent type hair straightener. Well, I had my hair straightened with Perma-Straiten or something like that and it worked! It only cost $2.25 and a professional job costs between $7.50 and $10.50 at a beauty college. I can imagine how much they'd charge you at a salon. I suggest people with this problem try this product before putting out all that money. Even if it doesn't help, I don't see what it could hurt!
(Paula S.)

If you have a question you'd like answered or a hint you'd like printed, drop a line to Tips To Teens, The BEAT, 6290 Sunset, Hollwood.

PORTMAN'S PLATTERPOOP
By JULIAN PORTMAN

"It's *The Beatles* 4 to 1", stated a Chicago Press agent. He did the promotion for both the *Dave Clark 5* and *The Beatles* during their engagements in the Windy City. "Both draw heavy attendances, but the *Beatles'* followers are too much, including the screaming department"... Joseph Levine's "Harlow", the highly publicized picture that has fared in the same manner as the star's life, still has the jinx following right along. *Bobby Vinton* smashed his Ferrari, a gift from "Harlow" producer *Levine* for making the theme song into a hit.

Lovely *Melody Patterson*, the young female lead of the new TV series "F Troop", pacted with Warner Bros.-Reprise Records. Her first single will be a rock 'n' roller... A great big hand to *Frank Sinatra Jr.* for heeding the talent call from the "Toastmaster General of the United States", *George Jessel*. He jetted out to perform for the soldiers in Viet Nam.

Two records to listen to: RCA Victor's *Frankie Randall*, a Lenny Poncher protege, "At It Again", and *Stan Kenton's* "Peyton Place Theme" on Capitol... The *Supremes* have another large album sale in "More Hits by The Supremes". They're in town to record the title tune to American International's "Dr. Goldfoot and The Bikini Machine". The gals have been spending so much time in H'wood that *Mary Wilson* told *Sig Sakowicz* that she may move here permanently.

Another tiger on the loose, or *Soupy Sales'* son has formed his own musical group, "Tony and The Tigers"... *The Young Americans* hit the H'wood Palace on Sept. 25... "The Young Man from Boston", the musical tribute to JFK, has been nabbed by 100 TV markets for October release. Musical director *Al Sendrey*, who wrote the background music is beaming with joy. He owns a few shares of sponsoring Plymouth autos high rising stock... *Hullabaloo's Joey Heatherton* waxed Paul Anka's "The Flippy" to be premiered on one of the October shows.

Sammy Davis' Thanksgiving Special "Sammy Davis and The Wonderful World of Children" is exclusively aimed at the youth market. Sammy will be the lone adult performing... *Hank Levine*, who ankled Colpix records after producing their only chart hit in 3½ years, is huddling with fast-growing, and fast-moving Dee Gee records... "Honey", Dee Gee's latest release by talented *Tony Harris* is quickly becoming a d.j. favorite around the country.

Nancy Wilson slipped into town to record the title tune to "Who Killed Teddy Bear", it'll be in her next Capitol album... The Slate Bros., a H'wood nitery that as a rule does not cater to the teen-set, did big box office business with a one week engagement for Lesley Gore.... It's bombs away for *The Cascades'* first release on Liberty, "I Bet You Won't Stay". They can do better, but this is not it... Two new vocal-musical groups to arrive on the scene are "The Gas Company" and "The Mothers". There'll now be clamorings for equal time... It's still in the rumor stage, i.e., the splitsville between *Chad & Jeremy. Chad* recently appeared as a duo on "Shindig" with his lovely wife *Jill*... *The Dave Clark Five* signed for many appearances on *Hullabaloo* starting in October.

Roger Miller, who does everything right, is rumored to be the replacement for the late *Nat (King) Cole* as the narrator in the "Cat Ballou" follow-up, "Kid Shelleen"... *Herbie Alpert and his Tijuana Brass* have all the luck. They're doing a *Danny Kaye Show* with beauteous *Elke Sommer*. Need anybody to lug the sombrero's? ... *The Spats*, the ABC-Paramount recording footwear, came into town to vocalize during a segment of the new TV series "My Mother, The Car"... *Jackie Vernon*, Ed Sullivan's favorite non-singer, signed to do a comedy album with Dee Gee records.

Judy Garland, a fine performer and outstanding showman, did herself proud by asking *The Young Americans* to appear during her Greek Theatre engagement. They were a perfect blend of harmony, youth and experience to make another evening with Garland memorable! Top young vocalist *Buddy Charles* (he has a Darin-like quality) bought back his contract from Liberty records. They wanted him to grow Beatle-like hair before they'd release a single. His manager nixed the idea!... later baby!

KRLA ARCHIVES

MAIL BOX

Dear Editor:

Stars Keep Glitter

I was a little disappointed when I read the letter from the girl, who had met one of favorite groups, and wasn't glad.

I haven't yet met my favorite group. But I have met other groups, and they were everything I expected, even when I only had the time to say "Hi" or get an autograph.

Most of them were just average nice people who were lucky enough to become big stars. I liked most of them better because of this. I sure wouldn't want to spend my time thinking about some superhuman, or perfect sort of person. Sure it would be nice if they were that way, but then, it takes average people to play the kind of music other people like.

Suzanne Brunson

★

Herman Teething?

To The One Who Writes The Articles About Herman:

What's wrong with you? Everytime I read an article about Herman I could just scream. You try to make him look like a baby — or like he is very moody and temperamental. But he isn't! You are too interested in the Beatles and the Stones to really realize what a great person Herman is.

In one issue of the BEAT you had a picture of him on the front with a sucker in his hand, and under the picture it read: "No more 'Little Boy' image for Herman. He's matured! Oh Yeah! What's in his right hand?"

But you should know he had his tooth (fang to you) knocked out and a new one is starting to come in. And if you have ever cut a tooth you will probably realize it helps a lot to chew on something hard. So quit cutting Herman down.

A truly devoted fan of, Herman's Hermits.

MANY TALENTS

O'Neill Career Very Colorful

By the Shindigger

"Hello everybody and welcome once again to Shindig."

No fans, that isn't the wondrous voice of yours truly, the Shindigger. That was tall, dark, 'n' handsome Jimmy O'Neill, who is the host of the swingingest show on TV.

Twice a Week

This week is kind of exciting because we are seeing Shindig not once, but twice a week from now on, so we thought we'd ask Jimmy to join us in our joy and chat with us for a few minutes. But alas, Jimmy had to be on stage just now. So instead, we can tell you all about him. (That's just as well, 'cause we all love to gossip, anyway!)

James Franklin O'Neill (that's what it says on his birth certificate) was born in Enid, Oklahoma January 8, 1940. At the ripe old age of ten years, he began singing with the Apollo Boy's Choir in Palm Beach, Florida, and became the featured soloist and pianist. At one time, he and the other members of the choir even performed for President Harry S. Truman at the White House.

His Voice Changed

In 1953, young master O'Neill faced his first big challenge — his voice changed! And so, Jimmy returned to his native Enid, and to native schooling as well!!

In 1955 while Jimmy was still in high school, he won first place in a University of Oklahoma State Radio Speaking contest, which eventually paved the road to a job with a radio station in Enid for Jimmy. By the time that he had graduated from high school, he had built his evening disc jockey show into the most popular nightly radio romp in all of northwestern Oklahoma.

He received an offer from the program director of the largest radio station in the state, and in no time at all his show was drawing the highest ratings in the history of the station.

This success brought him a new job at a station in Pittsburgh, Penn., where at the age of 18, Jimmy found himself suddenly the top radio personality in Pittsburgh. A year later, Jimmy was in Los Angeles working for the top radio station there, KRLA.

Teen Club

It was James F. O'Neill who pioneered the idea of a "teen age nightclub" and started a whole new trend in youthful entertainment with the opening of his "Pandora's Box" in Hollywood.

Nowadays, Jimmy spends his time with the Shindig family — both on TV and on the nationwide tours which bring live entertainment to teens across the country.

Yes, Virginia, there is a Jimmy O'Neill, and he's a great guy, too!

Next Week

Hey Shindiggers, y'know what? I've used up all my time again so I'll tell you about next week's show very quickly. Tune your tellies to Shindig this Thursday and Friday and you will see the Everly Brothers, The Byrds, Jerry Naylor, Chad and Jill Stuart, Ketty Lester, the Wellingtons, the McCoys — and lots more. It'll be a smashing session, so don't miss it.

Oh yes — Bobby Sherman should be back with us by next week so we'll be expecting you. Till then —

Shindiggers everywhere — ROCK ON!!!

DEAR SUSAN:

By Susan Frisch

Could you please tell me how old Donavan is, if he has a steady, and what kind of girls does he like?

Susan Hindson

Dear Susan:

Donavan just turned 19 last May. In answer to your question of the steady: No, he is not going steady nor does he have a steady girlfriend. I do not know exactly what you mean when you say what kind of girls does he like. But I do know he detests any kind of falseness in anybody, especially girls. He likes girls to wear whatever they want, not what the fashion trend is. In general he likes them to be themselves and individuals.

Can you tell me what Keith Richard's home address is and if he ever dates fans?

Sandra Walker

Dear Sandra:

I regret to tell you this but, I'm sorry, I can't publish his private residence. You must remember that the BEAT travels in England too, and if those girls over there saw his address poor Keith would never have a private minute in his life. I hope you understand! As to the other question: Good news, he does date fans.

Could you please give me some information on Donavan. Like, weight, height, hair and eye color, and most of all his love life?

Sandy Huckabey

Dear Sandy:

I am so happy that people have been writing me about 'Donny', because he is just the greatest! To begin with he is fairly tiny. He is 5'6¾", and if I remember correctly he weighs in at a mighty 133 pounds. He has brown, very wavy hair, and it isn't long and sloppy, and has brown eyes. As I stated before, he has no one girl!!

Could you please tell me the address of the Rolling Stones' biggest fan club, and where can I send them a fan letter?

Laura Smith

Dear Laura:

The best place to send the Stones a letter would be London Records Inc., 539 West 25th Street, New York, New York. They are sure to get all their letters there. Fan clubs are great, but — face it — they are not a post office, and things could happen to your letter and that would be bad especially if it was personal. Actually there is not one big fan club as there is for the Beatles. You could try the above address for one of the larger ones, because, to be honest with you, I don't know any of the bigger ones.

Is it true that P. J. Proby was married, or was that a misprint?

Jerrie Enfantino

Dear Jerrie:

It is true that P.J. was married once a few years ago, but as things happened it didn't work and so now he is divorced.

Could you please tell me what Herman's address is and a little about him?

Carmen Graham

Dear Carmen:

What address do you want? Fan club, office address, home, what? This is the kind of question I find difficult to answer because I am limited in space. If you would be kind enough to write me again and enclose a self-addressed stamped envelope I would be more than happy to ramble on about that cute Herman. I will be waiting for your next letter, so please write me and I will have your answer in the mail within 2 days!!!

What kind of make up does Marianne Faithfull use? And does Cher wear any; and if so how does she apply it?

Ali Kline

Dear Ali:

Marianne uses a brown cake eyeliner which is applied with a medium thickness across the eye lid. Sometimes she will either use a white or light beige eye shadow under the eyebrow, or she will use a brown eye shadow. Then she lightly strokes on dark brown mascara on her eye lashes. And one thing that people may not realize, but she never uses eyeliner on her bottom lid. YES, Cher wears eye makeup!! Cher uses a thick black line of eyeliner on her upper and lower lids. Then she uses thick black false eyelashes to highlight and make her eyes look bigger and better. Of course this is such a contrast to Marianne's, but then they are both two completely different people with different characteristics and everything else.

A Break Into The Big Time

(Continued from Page 5)

around the block right now. I'd like to teach him to sing rhythm and blues by the time he is six years old."

Well, okay Billy — whatever's right!!

Both boys are excited and enthusiastic about their work in the production of records as well as their own efforts in TV and movies. "We've just started producing our first records and we've formed a music publishing company. We've already signed three artists to our label. And we're gonna do a movie something like James Bond in October. Also, we're going to write and produce our next movie ourselves."

Fans All Important

Bill Medley and Bobby Hatfield are two of the most genuine individuals in the field of entertainment today. They are respectful of the feelings and opinions of others and grateful to those loyal fans who have placed them in their present position. They both insist: "Fans are important and almost all of them are good kids. No fan should be belittled. If anybody gets belittled, it should be us — we're getting paid!"

This season they will again appear on Shindig, as well as gracing the telly with visits to such shows as Hullabaloo, The Andy Williams Show, and The Danny Kaye Show.

When you try to sum up these two talented "brothers," there's only one thing to be said:

They're Righteous, Brother!!

...JIMMY O'NEILL

KRLA ARCHIVES

STONES TOP CHARTS

Well, they did it! The fantastic Rolling Stones made it to Number One this week with "Satisfaction." The song, released only about ten days, debuted last week at number three and this week had no trouble at all in moving into that number one spot and knocking Sonny & Cher down to number two.

The Walker Brothers, an American group who have moved to England and done tremendously well, jumped into the top ten this week at number four with "Make It Easy On Yourself."

Bob Dylan and his "Like A Rolling Stone" debuted last week at number seven and it looked as though he might have his second British chart topper (his first being "Subterranean Homesick Blues". However, this week he remained in that same number seven spot, so it is doubtful that he will reach that magic number one spot after all, especially since the Stones are so firmly entrenched in that top spot.

Cher and "All I Really Want To Do" has been chasing the Byrds for several weeks now. This week she is really breathing down their necks at number nine while the Byrds sweat it out at number eight.

The other new addition to the top ten this week is Tom Jones and his "What's New Pussycat?" It moved up from number 14 to number ten.

Sonny is not too far behind his Cher with "Laugh At Me" which took a big jump this week from number 22 to number 13.

The Hollies, just off their number one "I'm Alive," debuted this week at number 16 with "Look Through Any Window."

Looks like Herman is going to lose with his latest release, "Just A Little Bit Better." It came aboard last week at number 29 and took a drop this week, barely hanging on at number 30.

Herman, of course, is terribly popular here in the U.S. (following the Stones and Beatles) but he has been unable to duplicate that popularity in his own England.

British Top 10

1.	SATISFACTION	Rolling Stones
2.	I GOT YOU BABE	Sonny & Cher
3.	HELP	The Beatles
4.	MAKE IT EASY ON YOURSELF	The Walker Brothers
5.	A WALK IN THE BLACK FOREST	Horst Jankowski
6.	ZORBA'S DANCE	Marcello Minerbi
7.	LIKE A ROLLING STONE	Bob Dylan
8.	ALL I REALLY WANT TO DO	The Byrds
9.	ALL I REALLY WANT TO DO	Cher
10.	WHAT'S NEW PUSSYCAT?	Tom Jones

Pen Pals

All of these girls are between the ages of 12 and 14 years and all are Rolling Stones' fans.

Susan Lee
469 Edge Lane
Droysden, Manchester
Lancaster, England

Andrea Heal
19 Barlow Road
Stretford, Lancs
England

Janet Linda Shepard
34 Alexander Road
Horsforth, Heeds
Yorkshire, England

Marilyn Harris
23 Hogarths Road
Stifford Clays
Grays Essex

Yvonne Robinson
18 Lupton Drive
Greenhill, Sheffield, 8
England

Susan Hinton
18 Summer Lane
Royston N. Barnsley
Yorkshire, England

Jean Ward
45 Oakes Green
Attercliffe,
Sheffield 9, England

Jean Carter
5 Backway Road
Stratford Lanes,
England

Janice Cronshaw
156 Woodland Drive
Watford, Hertfordshire
England

Carol Hartlebery
50 Mungo Park Road
Rainham, Essex
England

Jean Discon
Beckhouses
Lambrigg, Nr. Kend
Westmoreland, England

Sondra Blount
'Larando'
297 Prince Charles Ave.
Mackworth Estate
Derby, England

Rosaleen Dack
57 Albert Street
Wisbech, Cambs.
England

Joan Oliver
54 Stothard Road
Streetford, Lancs.
England

Lynn Davis
53 Old Coach Road
Droitwich Spa,
Worcestershire,
England

ROY HEAD'S sensational performance before the National Association of Disc Jockeys not long ago moved Backbeat Records to release his first single, "Treat Her Right," even though Roy, far from a newcomer, had been leading his group, The Traits, in the Houston, Texas area the past seven years. The disc has become an overnight success.

Motown Chief Finds There's Really Magic

Do you believe in magic? Berry Gordy, president of Tamla-Motown Records does.

But the magic Berry believes in is not the necromancy of wands, newts eyes and potions. His proven magic is an elusive quality (others apparently cannot define it's secret) called the "Detroit Sound."

Star Sound

The "Detroit Sound", probably more than any other factor save the innate talent of Gordy's artists, is responsible for making stars out of such performers as The Supremes, The Four Tops and The Temptations. It has produced five Number One singles thus far and Gordy considers it the slam-bang formula for fortune.

So sold is Berry Gordy on his "Detroit Sound," in fact, he is now beginning to apply it to newly-signed singers in the Tamla-Motown stable. Convinced that it can do for other, more established stars whose record sales have not been exactly whooshing lately, he recently signed to recording contracts longtime pop favorites Billy Eckstine, Tony Martin and Connie Haines.

Reason Given

Gordy's vice president Barney Ales puts the reason for the acquisition of these artists this way:

"One of the reasons these artists haven't had hit product lately is that they haven't been recorded with an appeal to the record-buying public. We want to give them our sound."

It should go without saying that the stars in question are by no means reluctant to accept.

To start off on the right foot, in fact, Berry Gordy has already written a big beat tune for Connie Haines titled "Midnight Johnny." It's due for release soon.

Dick Clark Has Another TV Success

Dick Clark and his Midas touch have struck again!

Clark's latest network venture, "Where The Action Is," was originally scheduled as a summertime replacement show geared to capture the throngs of vacationing teens.

The on-location show was to vacate the air waves in the fall. However, due to over 25,000 letters imploring the ABC network to hold-over "Where The Action Is" the television officials have given Clark the go-ahead to continue "Action" through the entire season in a later time slot.

Big Break

It's a big break for Clark and also an unusual and rare occurence for the network.

For a long long time, TV officials did not wish to be bothered with teen-oriented shows. But now times have definitely changed.

KRLA ARCHIVES

BEHIND THE SCENES
WITH THE BEATLES

You had to be hip, but hip, babe, to keep up with the Beatles' behind-the-scenes happenings during their brief California vacation and concertizing.

But *BEAT* reporters, covering the entire Beatlescene like go-go-ing sandflies, ferreted out the gear mop-tops and brought back a sackful of soulful saga.

Did you know, for example, that:

They were asked at the press conference how they felt about those anti-Beatles Britishers who turned in their O.B.E.'s in protest when the M.B.E. was conferred on the Four. Replied flip-lipped John Lennon: "We got ours for entertaining people. Isn't that better than getting it for killing people?"

★ ★ ★

Asked if they've changed to any extent since the awards, Paul admitted, "We're more circumspect—and there are more conflicts." To a *BEAT* reporter's query on how he regards his personal life while on an international tour, Paul responded simply, "I like to be quiet."

In the course of the Capitol press confeernce, the boys were presented individually with gold discs symbolizing their million-selling "HELP!" album by Capitol president Alan Livingston. Noted Livingston: "Never in its history has Capitol experienced artists' success with such speed, depth and continuity."

★ ★ ★

The boys spent two-and-a-half hours visiting Elvis Presley and manager Colonel Parker. For a couple of hours they joined Elvis in a rock session on the carload of guitars provided by the Colonel. Ever candid, Paul told Elvis bluntly that he preferred the Tupelo lad's style in Elvis' early days when it was "wild."

★ ★ ★

Walter Shenson, producer of the Beatles' flicks, spoke about their behind-the-scenes attitude toward movie making. "The boys insist on a month's rehearsal before their next picture. They say, 'Whatever we do, let's make each picture different. Another reason, of course, is I can get worried about being typed as a 'Beatle picture producer,' because every Beatle picture will be differnt. Another reason, of course, is I can get very rich. Plus the fact I like it and the pictures are rewarding and a challenge. We work to make money—and to be gratified."

The boys also disclosed at their press conference that their next flick is to be a western. They already own the story, titled "A Talent For Loving," but the completed film may have a slightly different title—one more in keeping with "A Hard Day's Night" and "HELP!" In other words, an out-of-it title. Asked if the movie is to be filmed in Hollywood, they answered negatively. The entire production, except for some interior scenes, will be made in Spain where it's cheaper —cheapest, maybe.

★ ★ ★

John Lennon was asked to explain the now popular sport of "Beatle-baiting" in Britain— popular, that is, in the same crowd who were "insulted" when they were awarded the M.B.E. "I guess," answered John with more than a touch of Lancashire wisdom, "you can't expect everyone to luv us."

JOHN: BETTER THAN FOR KILLING PEOPLE...

A BEATLE ALPHABET

Christine May
Derbyshire, England

A is for Audience who all scream and shout.
B is for Beatles that everyone's mad about.
C is for Command Performance which they did so well.
D is for Drums that Ringo plays just swell.
E is for Entertainment which the Beatles bring.
F is for Fans who go crazy when the Beatles sing.
G is for George Harrison who sings into the mike.
H is for Haircuts, all of which are alike.
I is for Instruments which give a Mersey Sound.
J is for John Lennon who makes our poor hearts pound.
K is for Kids who dig the Mersey Beat.
L is for Liverpool where the Beatles used to meet.
M is for Mail which they get by the ton.
N is for Names—Ringo, Paul, George and John.
O is for Our favorite group and everything they've done.
P is for Paul McCartney—one of our favorite ones.
Q is for Queues of folk who wait to see their shows.
R is for Ringo Starr who's drumbeat makes you tap your toes.
S is for Stage shows where their fans make a din.
T is for Top Twenty which their discs are always in.
U is for Us, the Beatles we always see.
V is for Viewers who watch them on TV.
W is for Winning platters for their very own.
X is for Xcited fans who never, never moan.
Y is for Yeah, Yeah, Yeah that they always sing.
Z is for Zest, yes the Beatles really swing!

It's Happening...

It's settled — the Dave Clark Five will honor *Hullabaloo* with a number of visits this season.

Message to the Beatles Four: You need "Help!" from no one! The flick by the same name grossed $45,175 for its opening day at twenty-six N.Y. theatres.

Shades of Thrush at MGM these days. Our favorite superspies — Ilya and Napoleon — will find themselves temporarily shelved on Nov. 26 when Sean Connery host-narrates his special "The Incredible World of James Bond." Sorry, fellas — you'll just have to watch Sean on the telly.

Donovan will wing his way back to Uncle Samland Nov. 3 for a concert at Carnegie Hall Nov. 5. Sharing the marquee with the British folk singer will be our own Pete Seeger.

The Polish Artistic Booking Agency announced recently that the Animals will almost certainly put on a performance this fall. Quite a switch from Chopin, hmmm?

The Spokesmen — a new group out of Philadelphia — are *Happening* with their "answer record" of "Dawn of Correction."

The record, released by Decca, is getting back-to-back air play with the Barry McGuire single, "Eve Of Destruction," on Dunhill.

Although they were a little known group until the release of "Correction," the Spokesmen are now receiving bids for TV and personal appearances due to the success of this single.

Sam Rich, who is currently *Happening* big with his hit-disc of "Mohair Sam", has been signed by Smash Records for his future warbling. If the label Smash rings no bells for you, perhaps some of their other artistists will: Jerry Lee Lewis and Roger Miller are just two of the resident artists on this rising label.

OooH Baby   Tony Harris
FIRST RELEASE FOR Dee Gee RECORDS IS TOO-o-o-o-o MUCH!
"HONEY"
B/W "SCORPIE"

Dee Gee RECORDS
LOS ANGELES, CALIFORNIA

DISTINGUISHED ACTOR Sidney Poitier is about to receive a copy of The Supremes' LP, "A Bit of Liverpool," from the singing trio as the girls relax after taping the first **Hullabaloo** of the new season.
BEAT photo: Bud Fraker

KRLA ARCHIVES

THE BEAT GOES TO THE MOVIES

HALLELUJAH TRAIL

Do you like cowboys and Indians and the smell of the Old West? But are you tired of the old kind of oat-eaters?

Well, then United Artists has just the thing for you — a western (in the sense that it is set in the Old West) with a completely new and unique approach. It's the "Hallelujah Trail" and you shouldn't miss it.

The movie's plot concerns a very real problem: The miners of Denver are about to have a cold hard winter without the benefit of any liquid reinforcement — in other words, whiskey!

Now, how in the world can the miners face this draught? Well, they can't! So they order 700 cases of imported French champagne and 600 barrels of Philadelphia-brewed whiskey from Frank Wallingham (Brian Keith).

All this is fine and dandy — until word of the liquor-laden wagon train slips out. And then the fun begins!

The Indians (peaceful but always on the look-out for fire-water) make elaborate plans to way-lay the precious cargo.

The temperance ladies, lead on by Miss Cora Templeton Massingale (Lee Remick), and ably assisted by Louise Gearhart (Pamela Tiffin), and the ladies of the local U.S. fort decide to ride out and meet the train in order to destroy the hated hooch.

To add to all confusion, a detachment of U.S. soldiers, lead by young Captain Paul Slater (Jim Hutton) is sent out to escort the train, while another regiment of soldiers, headed by Colonel Thadeus Gearhart (Burt Lancaster) escorts the ladies!

Meanwhile, the Denver miners—worried about the safety of their liquor—also set out to meet the train and ensure its safety back to Denver.

Who reaches the liquor first? The Indians? The soldiers? The temperance ladies? Or the miners?

You'll have to go and see 'Hallelujah Trail' to find the answer—and even then you may have some trouble uncovering the truth!

TEMPERANCE MEETS THE DRINKER . . .

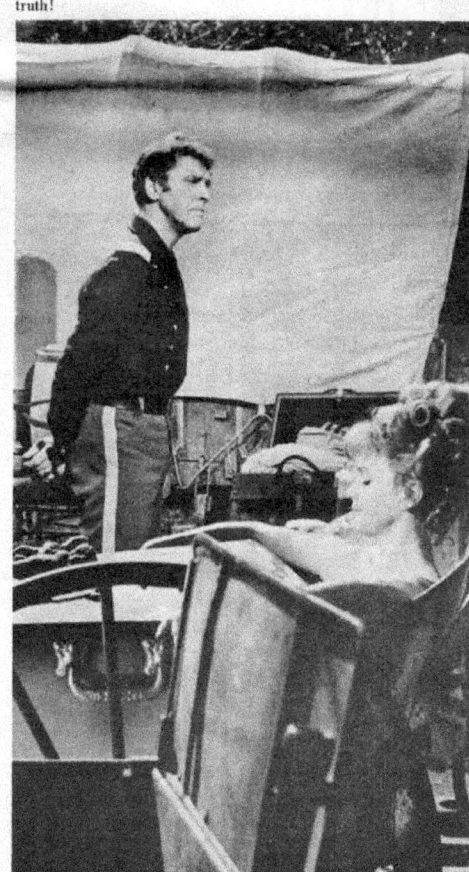

THE COLONEL MAPS HIS STRATEGY while the lady takes her bath. . . .

AND THE TEMPERANCE LADY SPEAKS HER MIND while the Colonel takes his daily and rinses his throat with a shot of whiskey.

KRLA ARCHIVES

KRLA Tunedex

EMPEROR HUDSON

CHARLIE O'DONNELL

CASEY KASEM

JOHNNY HAYES

BOB EUBANKS

DAVE HULL

DICK BIONDI

BILL SLATER

KRLA BEAT
6290 Sunset, No. 504
Hollywood, Cal. 90028

BULK RATE
U.S. Postage
PAID
Los Angeles, Calif.
Permit No. 25497

This Week	Last Week	Title	Artist
1	3	LIAR, LIAR	The Castaways
2	2	BABY I'M YOURS	Barbara Lewis
3	1	LIKE A ROLLING STONE	Bob Dylan
4	8	HELP/I'M DOWN	The Beatles
5	17	THE "IN" CROWD	Ramsey Lewis Trio
6	9	DO YOU BELIEVE IN MAGIC	Lovin' Spoonfull
7	6	UNCHAINED MELODY	Righteous Brothers
8	14	ROSES AND RAINBOWS	Danny Hutton
9	5	YOU WERE ON MY MIND	We Five
10	16	WE GOTTA GET OUT OF THIS PLACE	The Animals
11	4	EVE OF DESTRUCTION	Barry McGuire
12	27	TAKE ME FOR A LITTLE WHILE	Evie Sands
13	26	IN THE MIDNIGHT HOUR	Wilson Pickett
14	7	I GOT YOU BABE	Sonny & Cher
15	15	HEART FULL OF SOUL	The Yardbirds
16	21	DOWN IN THE BOONDOCKS	Billy Joe Royal
17	11	IT'S THE SAME OLD SONG	The Four Tops
18	30	MOHAIR SAM	Charlie Rich
19	10	SUMMER NIGHTS	Marianne Faithfull
20	20	LAUGH AT ME	Sonny Bono
21	22	THE TRACKS OF MY TEARS	The Miracles
22	13	NOTHING BUT HEARTACHES	The Supremes
23	12	IT AIN'T ME BABE	The Turtles
24	24	YOU'VE GOT YOUR TROUBLES	The Fortunes
25	31	AGENT OO-SOUL	Edwin Starr
26	28	HANG ON SLOOPY	The McCoys
27	29	SINCE I LOST MY BABY	The Temptations
28	23	CATCH US IF YOU CAN	Dave Clark Five
29	33	TREAT HER RIGHT	Roy Head
30	18	CALIFORNIA GIRLS	Beach Boys
31	42	DAWN OF CORRECTION	The Spokesmen
32	36	HOME OF THE BRAVE	Bonnie & The Treasures
33	34	HOME OF THE BRAVE	Jody Miller
34	39	GIRL FROM PEYTON PLACE	Dickie Lee
35	—	LOVER'S CONCERTO	The Toys
36	—	KEEP ON DANCING	The Gentrys
37	—	YOU'RE THE ONE	The Vogues
38	—	THE WAY OF LOVE	Kathy Kirby
39	—	WITH THESE HANDS	Tom Jones
40	—	I LIVE FOR THE SUN	The Sunrays

KRLA ARCHIVES

KRLA BEAT

Volume 1, Number 29   LOS ANGELES, CALIFORNIA   15 Cents   October 2, 1965

Was Yardbirds' Ordeal In Vain?

KRLA BEAT

Los Angeles, California — October 2, 1965

A BEAT EDITORIAL

UNWANTED VISITORS

Perhaps it took the unfortunate plight of a group of hurt, frustrated musicians to make some of us aware of the situation. If so, their shocking experiences will not have been entirely for naught.

The supposedly warm and friendly relationship between us and our English cousins has been strained to the danger point by the selfish, narrow-minded actions of some of our businessmen and labor officials, and the conduct of some British entertainers.

In this case a well-behaved, talented group known as the Yardbirds ("For Your Love," "Heart Full of Soul") flew to California recently with high hopes and friendly manners, excited and elated after finally realizing their life-long ambition to visit America.

Invited Here

They came over at the invitation of several television shows. After long negotiations they finally received permission from our musicians' union to perform on certain shows. The Yardbirds had booked reservations at a well-known Sunset Strip hotel and were looking forward to a visit to Disneyland as one of the highlights of their trip.

But then ugly things began happening. Upon hearing their English accents the hotel clerk curtly tore up their reservations and ordered them to leave. Later they tried to visit Disneyland. Here, too, they were refused admission when the man at the ticket counter noticed their English accents, the foreign haircuts and alien clothing. They were dressed neatly enough and their hair was combed, but that was not sufficient.

The final blow came from the musicians' union, the dictatorial organization which somehow has the power to decide who can appear on American television and seems to delight in turning away foreigners. The 19th century thinkers who make these decisions trapped them in a snarl of red tape and refused to allow the Englishmen to perform on Shindig, knowing full well they had travelled all the way from London to California for that purpose.

At this point the unwelcome entertainers must have been shocked by the display of our famous American hospitality. They must have wondered at a nation whose government spends billions for goodwill overseas while its citizens discriminate against foreign visitors.

Other Side of Story

True, not all British groups who come over here are as civilized or well-behaved as the Yardbirds.

Some of them look and act like a band of drunk Apaches on a raiding party. Naturally this has not set well with hotels whose facilities have been damaged by the barbaric behavior of certain English groups.

But they don't turn away customers wearing Masonic rings simply because the Shriners may have held a boisterous party. And they shouldn't refuse admission to all English entertainers because of the actions of some other group in the past.

One of the basic points of our democracy holds that a man is innocent until proven guilty. This also applies to those who are visiting our country. We can't take away any of their rights without giving up some of ours.

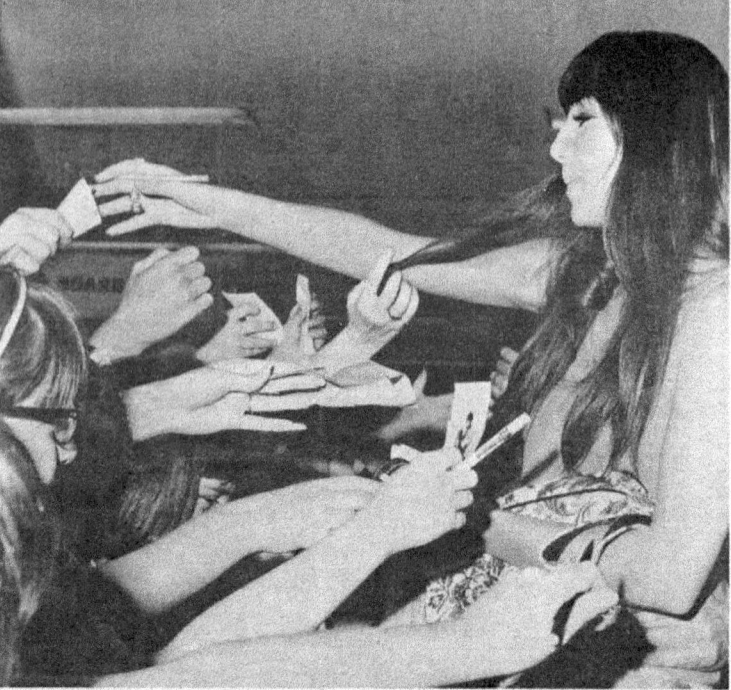

"LUV'S JUST FINE, BABE, but look out for the hair!" Cher could very well have that thought on her mind as one of many eager outstretched fans' hands reaches to caress her locks. But at the airport on her and Sonny's return from their triumphant appearances in Great Britain, Cher was much too happy just to be home again and to sign her fans' autographs. Three of their songs are in the British Top 10.
BEAT Photo: Chuck Boyd

EPSTEIN'S SURPRISE

Will Next Beatles Movie Sock Us With Sneak Shock?

What exactly are Brian Epstein and his everlovin' lads up to now? What's hidden behind those Beatle mops?

After months and months of aggravating "yes-we-will" and "no-we-won't," Epstein has finally *officially* announced the Beatles third movie venture as "A Talent For Loving."

The movie will be shot in England and on location in Spain. The Spanish location was, of course, chosen for economic reasons.

A Little Surprise

All of this has been strongly suspected but never officially confirmed up to now. However, Epstein did manage to squeeze in a little surprise when making his long-overdue confirmation.

He publicly revealed that Dick Lester, director of both "A Hard Day's Night" and "Help" will *not* take over the directing reins for "A Talent For Loving."

This presents an interesting and thoroughly thought-provoking question. Will Lester's replacement measure up to the sky-high standards of both of the Beatles' other movies?

No matter how good the actor, it *is* the director who is the actual creator of the final movie which you view on the screen.

Why The Switch?

Obviously, Dick Lester has done a fantastic job for the Beatles. So why the big switch?

Apparently the Beatles are looking for a new movie image and they felt that the easiest way to achieve a new image was to discard their old director.

Epstein hinted at this when he said of the new movie: "It will not necessarily be in the style of the previous ones."

Perhaps the Beatles are tired of playing themselves, perhaps they would like to be real movie actors and portray such historic figures as Napoleon or Caesar!

Is changing directors a good move? Or possibly a bad move? Only "A Talent For Loving" will tell for sure — *if* that is still the title when the picture is finished.

Inside the BEAT...

Stones' Secret Session	3
BEAT Visits Shindig	5
Donovan — Suddenly Hot	6
We Five Thank Dylan	6
Dylan Becomes A "Lion"	7
New Beatle Photos	11, 12
Leaves Not In Wind	9
Mick — Wedding Bells?	13
Dear Susan	13
Stones Stay on Top	14
New Hair Styles	15
Jan to Quit Singing	16
New KRLA Dragster	17
Sal's TV Show Shelved?	19
Munster vs. KRL"A"	20

The KRLA BEAT is published weekly by BEAT Publications; editorial and advertising offices at 6290 Sunset Boulevard, Suite 504, Hollywood, California 90028. Application to mail at second class postage rates is pending at Los Angeles, California, with additional entry privileges at San Francisco. Single copy price, 15 cents. Subscription price, U.S. and possessions, $3 per year or $5 for two years. Canada and foreign rates, $9 per year or $14 for two years. Exclusive distribution handled by Miller-Freeman Publications, 6328 Lewis Avenue, Long Beach, California.

TRYING TO SWIM TO BEATLES at Hollywood Bowl, two wet but still-hysterical fans are pulled from the pool in front of the stage at conclusion of KRLA Beatle concerts. John, Paul, George and Ringo stayed dry, dashing into an armored truck to escape after each show.
BEAT Photo: Chuck Boyd

KRLA ARCHIVES

A Beat Exclusive!
WE GO TO THE ROLLING STO

By Louise Criscione

The Rolling Stones were in the U. S. for just two short days. They flew all the way over here to cut some tracks at the RCA studios in Hollywood.

The session was closed — as closed as it could possibly be. No press and no photographers were allowed inside the studio — that is, no press *except* The *BEAT!*

Let's Go In

The Stones were nice enough to let The *BEAT* come in and capture a really exclusive-type exclusive. Anyway, since they were nice we thought we'd be nice and invite you all to come along with us. So, if you're ready — let's go.

Outside the studio throngs of the Stones' faithful fans are huddled around the door. It's cold (yeah, even in sunny California) but the fans don't care, they'll wait all night just to get a glimpse of the five Stones.

Inside Studio B the technicians are busy positioning the mikes and getting everything ready for the session. The Stones are all here.

Brian sits picking at his guitar. Mick parks himself on a stool surrounded by microphones and begins going over the words to the song which they will soon cut.

Charlie is seated at his drums but only his head is visible behind the partition which encloses the drums. Keith and Bill sit, guitars in their laps, going over the music. Bill is sick, his face roughly the color of a newly laundered sheet.

Dead On Feet

In fact, they're all tired — dead on their feet really. They've been on the go for so long now that they forget the last time they got a full night's sleep.

Mick and Charlie snap their ear phones into place. It's almost time to start. Andrew Oldham, Stones' record producer and co-manager, is (as usual) the A & R man on tonight's session.

Oldham seats himself in the control booth and asks to hear each of the Stones individually. "Can I hear you, Bill?" he asks and then promptly leaves the room.

Returning about five minutes later, Oldham repeats: "Can I hear you, Bill?"

Keith bursts out laughing: "He's been doing it for half an hour!"

"I've been out of the room," Oldham deadpans.

"Well, you should have told him," Keith grins.

Oldham ends the game with: "It's good practice!" And Bill plays it again.

Finally, Oldham gives them the go-ahead to take one. Keith starts counting: "1-2, 1-2-3-4."

Throbbing Sound

The throbbing Stone Sound vibrates through the studio. Mick sits at the mike with the words in one hand and a cigarette in the other. And he wails!

They do a complete take, but

BEAT photos: Robert W. Young

... THE FIRST PLAYBACK

... A MOMENT OF DOUBT IN THE STUDIO

KRLA ARCHIVES

Exclusive BEAT Photos: Robert W. Young

NES' SECRET RECORD DATE

the minute it is finished (without even waiting for the playback) Mick asks: "Can we take another one?" None of the Stones are satisfied, Oldham isn't satisfied.

They go into a huddle to find out exactly where the trouble lies. Mick thinks it's with him: "I'm hitting two wrong notes in there. I know it. I was doing it last night and I can't stop.

They get ready for take two and Keith's voice is heard again: "1-2, 1-2-3-4." They do another complete take and then all of them head for the speakers to hear the playback. But they're still not satisfied, so they do yet another take.

As the song ends this time, Mick holds up his hand and once again the Stones make it for the speakers. Mick and Charlie pace the floor. The others just sit and listen. Charlie speaks to Mick, he nods — they continue pacing. Mick walks with his head way down — listening, thinking.

Another Mike

The playback is still going on as Charlie runs out into the control booth and speaks to the engineer. He wants another mike placed near the drums. Mike in position — they try it once more.

This time they like it and another Stones' sound is in the can.

There is no fooling around; they go immediately into the next song and take one is called. Mick doesn't just sit this time — he moves! It's nothing like he does on stage, but that same old Jagger is there and it swings!

They run all the way through it. The tape screeches in rewind and the playback starts. And the pacing — it starts too. This time Mick, Keith and Charlie parade around dodging the empty coke bottles and cigarette butts while Bill sits motionless.

Bill Really Sick

He's really sick now. They're worried about him, worried enough to summon a doctor. Keith tires of pacing and sits down picking at his guitar strings as the playback continues.

Oldham has been listening intently at the speaker. He strolls into the control booth now and nods to the engineer: "Do it again."

Mick saunters over to the mike — coke in one hand, lyric sheet in the other. Keith starts the count but halfway through the song Oldham calls: "Cut it."

There is more discussion and then Keith begins the count again. This time the take is completed. Playback — and the crowd gathers around the speaker.

A guard, standing in the control booth, shakes his head, "No." Mick sees him out of the corner of his eye, grins widely, waves his hand and begins his pacing.

Doctor Arrives

The doctor arrives for Bill. And just in time. The boys had finished dates in England, hopped a plane, flew to L.A., checked into the hotel and then had driven immediately to the studio.

They recorded all night long, caught a few hours sleep and now they're back recording again. A couple of hours after tonight's session they'll catch another flight back to London because tomorrow they have an appearance to make. So who says being a pop star is easy?

The doctor finishes treating Bill for exhaustion and they get ready to take it again. They run through it once, listen to the playback and another one's in the bag.

Now it's time for a break. The Stones head for the cokes. Keith carries his guitar, it seems like he never leaves it. They fool around with their instruments for awhile and then Mick asks: "Andrew, can we run this down?" Oldham nods, "Yeah, we'll take it."

And Keith's voice comes over the mike: "1-2, 1-2-3-4." They take it all the way through, but a mistake is discovered. Another huddle and they're ready to go at it again.

Mick Tired, Too

Mick sits down at the mike: "This time right through." It's debatable whether Mick is encouraging himself or the other Stones. He's tired and it's beginning to show.

The take just gets started when another mistake rears it's ugly head — and they stop again. Some more discussion and it's time for take three. Mick signals to Charlie and they go all the way through it this time.

They take the short walk (which by this time has become a long walk) over to the speaker. Now Charlie paces alone — the rest of them sit it out. Oldham walks over to Mick, who is sitting with his head in his hand.

The playback ends — they've got it this time. Everybody's satisfied and all their material is now on tape. The only thing left to do now is some overdubbing.

We hate to leave, but we'd better not overstay our welcome. After all, we've been here for eight hours and we *were* the only press admitted to this VERY CLOSED session.

Say Goodbyes

So we say our goodbyes and exit. It's two o'clock in the morning. Outside there are still a few fans waiting — hoping. Some brought sandwiches and coffee, some brought pictures of the Stones which they hope they can get autographed, some brought only themselves.

They present a mixture of everything imaginable. Of course, the long-haired, bell bottomed girls are out in full force.

Then there are the really young fans, who have dressed up as if they were going to a party. They're the ones who clutch the autograph books and Stones' pictures.

And in the middle of the bell bottoms and party dresses stand a group of college coeds, attired in the traditional Ivy League sweatshirts.

It pictures perfectly the Rolling Stones' appeal to practically all of the "young" age groups — the just-barely teens, the middle-aged teens and the old college ladies!

Anyway — thanks, Stones, for letting us all come.

And a P.S. to all you Stone fans — just *wait* until you *hear* the sounds that session produced!

... YOU'RE SURE 'BOUT THAT ONE, MICK?

Rock Comes To York Univ.

Rock marches on in Great Britain.

As a matter of fact, rock — along with jazz — has marched right onto the super-respectable campus of ultra-scholarly York University in the capital of Yorkshire, England. From now on, according to university authorities, undergraduate students will be able to include rock and roll and jazz music in their degree studies. It marks the first time in the history of a British university that such courses have been included in the curriculum.

With Lancashire's Liverpool long acclaimed (or self-acclaimed, anyway) as home of the Big Beat in England, lately its rival city of Manchester has been contending for the limelight in its place. Now, from out of Yorkshire, in the east of England, comes yet another challenge to Liverpool. Will Liverpudlians take this lying down?

... A GOOD TAKE

KRLA ARCHIVES

The Shindigger

Howdy hi, Shindiggers. Welcome to the Sleepy Slooper's Sloppy Session of Shindig-by-Night. At this moment, it is about 10:30 at night here in the Shindig studios, and the cast and crew have just finished taping another fab show.

As you can all well see on our Super-Panavision Stereophonic column here, everyone is exhausted. Those two young men sipping coffee in the right hand corner are the Everly Brothers (Phil is the one with the black leather John Lennon cap) and sitting next to them on the floor is Gene Clark of the Byrds. Unfortunately, his five feathered friends have already flown the coop and are winging their way homeward. (Sorry 'bout that, Shindiggers, but I couldn't resist the pun!)

Bobby's Here

If you will look straight ahead, you will see a handsome young man with cool blue eyes heading in our direction. Yep, you guessed it—Bobby Sherman has made it at last. Hey Bobby, we were beginning to think that you were never going to join us for one of our little gab sessions. "Hi everyone. Sorry I'm late but I was delayed by a man-eating olive as I was leaving the studio commisary."

Bobby Sherman

Gee Bobby, that's too bad. (I don't know either, Shindiggers, but I think we'd better humor him) I hear you have a new record out, Bobby. Can you tell us something about it? "Yes, it's called 'Goody Galumpshus' and it's got a great beat; it really moves." Sounds great, Bobby; we'll be listening for it.

I think that the Wellingtons have a new single out, too. Oh— here comes Eddie now. Eddie, what about the new disc for you and the other two Wellingtons? "We've just released it, and it was written and produced by the Righteous Brothers. It's called 'Go Ahead and Cry."

(Aside to all female-type Shindiggers—hold onto your high-heeled sneakers, girls, 'cause here comes Jerry Naylor. Sigh!!) Greetings, Jerry. Before you sit down, you have to give the secret password. Do you have a new record? "Yes and I'm very proud of it. It's called 'City Lights.'" OK, Jerry—you'll qualify.

Protest Songs

By the way—what do you all think of Dylan and of all the protest songs which are so popular now? Gene, as the lone Byrd in our crowd tonight, what do you think? "I think Dylan is for now and for the future. I dig him. And protest songs—if they're well done, they're groovy. We have always looked for good lyrics and do even more so now."

Bobby, what do you think? "I think Dylan is a great writer, but I think that some of the protest songs are getting really rough now."

Hey everyone — there's Jackie deShannon. Jackie — c'mon over and tell us what you've been up to.

"Hi everyone. Well, I'm buying a jeep to go with a wild coat which I just bought. I'm trying to find an authentic army one, so if anybody has one — please let me know!

Writing Book

"Also, I'm writing a book which will be filled with stories and poems. It's real poetry — as much as I can write it. It'll be more for girls 'cause I like to talk about my values."

Jackie, can you tell us something about that little guitar you have with you? I've seen you play it on several shows now. "It's an eighty-year-old guitar. I had been looking for a small guitar with a great sound and I finally found this one in San Francisco. It's black ebony and mother-of-pearl." It really is a great looking instrument, Jackie.

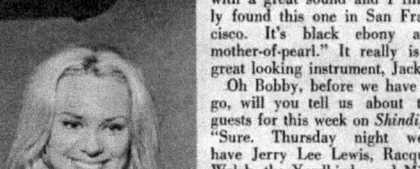
Jackie DeShannon

Oh Bobby, before we have to go, will you tell us about the guests for this week on *Shindig*? "Sure. Thursday night we'll have Jerry Lee Lewis, Racquel Welch, the Yardbirds, and Mike Clifford all joining the *Shindig* regulars. If you all tune in on Saturday you'll see a swingin' *Shindig* with Dick and Dee Dee, Jimmy Rodgers, Little Anthony and the Imperials, Donna Loren, Mary Wells, and Georgie Fame. It'll be a gas so be sure to join us for all the fun."

Thanks Bobby, and we'll see you again next week — and every week from now on — right here in the Shindig column.

Till next week then, maintain your soul, everyone; and no matter what *anybody* says, Shindiggers — ROCK ON!!!

THOSE GROOVY SUPREMES — (l. to r.) Diana Ross, Florence Ballard and Mary Wilson — have already opened wide the doorway to success with such fab discs as "Nothing But Heartaches." Now it's lunchtime and they prepare to swing wide the huge oaken door of the famous Brown Derby in Hollywood during a recent visit for TV appearances.

BY MAIL!
"OLDIES BUT GOODIES"
Original recordings of the **GREATEST ROCKIN' HITS** of all time!

Yes... **SEVEN GREAT L.P. ALBUMS**
84 OF THE GREATEST ROCK'N HITS OF ALL TIME!
MILLION-SELLERS!
RECORDED WITH **THE SAME ARTISTS** WHO DROVE THEM TO **THE TOP OF THE CHARTS!**
NO FAKING HERE! THESE ARE THE REAL THING ...JUST AS YOU REMEMBER

SEVEN GREAT L.P. ALBUMS

Each with 12 great rock'n hits, 12 great rock'n artists, and all different! Just read over the listing of the great rock'n songs and great rock'n artists shown. 84 wonderful tunes on 7 great L.P. albums to choose from. And remember... if you had bought any 12 tunes that are listed on each album of "OLDIES BUT GOODIES" when they were singles, you would have paid, not the low album price of $3.98, but more than $12.00! *JUST IMAGINE WHAT YOU WOULD HAVE PAID FOR ALL 85 SINGLES!*

Now... browse through the album listings and mail your order today. Satisfaction guaranteed or your money back.
OVER ONE MILLION "OLDIES BUT GOODIES" HAVE BEEN SOLD.
"OLDIES BUT GOODIES" are produced in the world's most modern record plant.

ALBUM No. 1
In The Still of The Night	5 Satins
Earth Angel	The Penguins
Eddie My Love	The Teen Queens
Tonite! Tonite!	The Mello Kings
Heaven And Paradise	Don Julian
The Letter	The Medallions
Let The Good Times Roll	Shirley and Lee
Confidential	Sonny Knight
Stranded In The Jungle	The Cadets
The Way You Look Tonight	Jaguars
Dance With Me Henry	Etta James
Convicted	Oscar McLollie

ALBUM No. 2
Devil Or Angel	The Clovers
A Thousand Miles Away	Heartbeats
Goodnight My Love	Jesse Belvin
Glory Of Love	Velvetones
Story Untold	Nutmegs
Deserie	The Charts
Shake Rattle And Roll	Joe Turner
Gee	The Crows
Nite Owl	Tony Allan
When You Dance	The Turbans
I Got Loaded	Peppermint Harris
Shake A Hand	Faye Adams

ALBUM No. 3
Lovers Never Say Goodbye	The Flamingos
You Cheated	The Shields
Oh What A Night	The Dells
For Your Precious Love	Jerry Butler
2 People In The World	Little Anthony & The Imperials
This Is My Story	Gene & Eunice
Come Go With Me	The Dell-Vikings
Don't You Just Know It	Huey (Piano) Smith
At My Front Door	The El Dorados
Sea Cruise	Frankie Ford
Bongo Rock	Preston Epps
Long Tall Sally	Little Richard

ALBUM No. 4
Silhouettes	The Rays
A Casual Look	The Six Teens
Could This Be Magic	The Dubs
Teenage Prayer	Gloria Mann
To The Aisle	The Five Satins
The Plea	The Chantels
Love Is Strange	Mickey & Sylvia
Whole Lot Of Shakin' Going On	Jerry Lee Lewis
Teen Beat	Sandy Nelson
Tell Me Why	Norman Fox & The Rob-Roys
Money	Barrett Strong
Blue Suede Shoes	Carl Perkins

ALBUM No. 5
Little Star	The Elegants
Angel Baby	Rosie & The Originals
Since I Don't Have You	The Paradons
Diamonds And Pearls	The Paradons
Daddy's Home	Shep & The Limelites
The Closer You Are	The Channels
Alley-Oop	The Hollywood Argyles
Stay	Maurice Williams
Sixty-Minute Man	The Dominoes
Rockin' Robin	Bobby Day
Bongo Bongo Bongo	Preston Epps
Hearts Of Stone	The Jewels

ALBUM No. 6
Those Oldies But Goodies	Little Caesar & The Romans
A Teenager In Love	Dion & The Belmonts
Every Beat Of My Heart	The Pips
Image Of A Girl	The Safaris
You Were Mine	The Fireflies
This I Swear	The Skyliners
Quarter To Three	Gary (U.S.) Bonds
Honky Tonk, Part I	Bill Doggett
Honky Tonk, Part II	Bill Doggett
Duke of Earl	Gene Chandler
Mashed Potato Time	Dee Dee Sharp
Raindrops	Dee Clark

ALBUM No. 7
It's All In The Game	Tommy Edwards
I Love How You Love Me	The Paris Sisters
Donna	Ritchie Valens
Teen Angel	Mark Dinning
Once In A While	The Chimes
He Will Break Your Heart	Jerry Butler
Handy Man	Jimmy Jones
New Orleans	Gary (U.S.) Bonds
Tequila	The Champs
Runaround Sue	Dion
I Know	Barbara George
Bumble Boogie	B. Bumble & The Stingers

STEREO $1.00 EXTRA EACH

Send check or money order:
1 ALBUM – $3.98
3 ALBUMS – $9.50
ALL 7 – $18.98
SAVE $10.00!

Mail to:
ORIGINAL SOUND
7120 Sunset Blvd.
Hollywood, Calif.
90046, U.S.A.

ORDER TODAY!
Please send the OLDIES BUT GOODIES albums circled, prepaid, insured. STEREO ☐
1 – 2 – 3 – 4 – 5 – 6 – 7 – All 7
Amt. enclosed $_____ (No C.O.D.'s)
Name _____
Address _____

KRLA ARCHIVES

WE (LEAPING) FIVE

We Five Thank Bob Dylan For Bringing Folk Feel To Pop

By Louise Criscione

They actually live on a houseboat which is anchored somewhere off Northern California. They're classified as a folk group, their hit record, "You Were On My Mind," is definitely a folk song — and yet they state with obvious conviction that they are *not* folk singers.

A paradox you say? No not at all — they are the We Five and today all five of them picked up the phone and called the *BEAT*.

It was a wild and wacky conversation (if you've ever tried talking to *five* people on *one* telephone you'll understand!) but surprisingly enough we did manage to uncover some rather pertinent information about the mystery-shrouded We Five.

Although the group now claims no particular affiliation with the world of folk, We Five did start out that way.

As Mike explains:

"This particular group has been together for a year and a half to two years. By limiting ourselves to folk music we found that we were fastly starving to death! So we did some jazz, some rock 'n' roll and some Broadway show tunes."

Only Girl

Beverly is the only girl in the group. How does she like being the lone female? "It's interesting to say the least! Really, though, we all get along just fine."

And what do the four boys think about having a girl amongst them? Bob answers this loaded question: "I think it's fine and it's good for us too. Also if we didn't have Beverly we wouldn't have a sound!"

Today the trend seems to be away from stage clothes, or at least away from traditional stage clothes. Although the We Five make all of their appearances in stage clothes of sorts (the boys wear velours and Beverly wears something which contrasts nicely with the boys' outfits) they have nothing against entertainers who prefer to dress in come-as-you-are attire.

Beverly says: "Their bag is to be free and uninhibited so they wear those type clothes."

No one will deny that folk music, thanks probably to Bob Dylan, is once again coming into its own in the pop market.

Folk Evolution

Jerry explains this folk evolution by saying: "What is happening is that some other groups are waking up to the fact that there is more than one form of music. And Bob Dylan is being discovered now because he bought an electric guitar."

The We Five all believe that a record does not necessarily have to contain a big message (such as "Eve Of Destruction" or "Laugh At Me") in order to be a number one record.

But they do believe that with some people lyrics *are* important. Beverly says: "Kids do listen to what Dylan is saying, so with Dylan listening to lyrics is important.

"There is a definite social change because these kids are more aware that there are problems in this world which have to be spoken out."

When the We Five walked through the recording studio door to cut "You Were On My Mind" none of them were strangers to a record session.

Peter does recall his first recording session vividly: "I felt crushed because I wasn't supposed to be there! It was about two years ago. I just walked into the studio — I didn't even know what to do. As a matter of fact, I didn't even know which key they were in!"

Peter has come a long way in two years and by listening to "You Were On My Mind" it is quite obvious that Peter has finally found the right key!

The We Five decided to live in that houseboat in order to insure themselves some peace and quiet. But if they continue to turn out records like "You Were On My Mind" I'm afraid that houseboat will lie vacant for quite awhile.

Beverly, Bob, Peter, Jerry and Mike won't have time to sit around in the sun — they'll be too busy performing!

Donovan As A Composer Hot As Pistol

Suddenly Donovan is hot as a pistol. No, we don't mean as a performer; we sort of knew *that* for some time, now. But the businessmen of music — the men who publish and sell the songs that make the hits — have now become truly aware of Donovan's bright talent as a writer of these songs.

Paul Barry, professional manager of the giant publishing firm of Peer-International, said in New York that his company is being flooded by requests, demands, pleas for anything new by Donovan. Many, if not most of these requests, Barry said, are coming from recording companies and disc artists anxious to jump on the Donovan bandwagon. They want to hurry onto record with his songs before even *he* gets to record them himself. This is an indication of Donovan's steadily growing popularity.

In addition to his demand as a songwriter, the list of his in-person appearances and tours continues to grow. He'll kick off his new American tour with an appearance at New York's Carnegie Hall Nov. 5, following this up with a string of college concerts and other appearances on top TV shows such as *Hullabaloo* and *Shindig* during the fall.

On The BEAT

By Louise Criscione

Spoke to Joey Paige right before he left for his 30 day stint with the Marines. He was a little worried about his hair, or rather the lack of it, because he had just had his long hair cut Marine-style!

However, he is really thrilled that his record, "Goodnight My Love", is doing so very well. And we at the *BEAT* are happy too 'cause Joey is, without a doubt, one of the nicest guys in the business.

If you'd like to drop Joey a little note while he's in the Marines, just send them to us and we will forward them on to Joey and give him a little something to do while he's peeling all those potatoes!

The *BEAT* sure had a nice surprise today — all five of the Yardbirds came up to see us!

They're really a great bunch of guys and they were looking forward so much to their first visit to America. But since their arrival they've been presented with nothing but obstacles.

... JOEY PAIGE

They flew all the way over here because they were booked on such television shows as "Shindig" and "Where The Action Is." But upon their arrival they were informed by labor union officials that they could not appear.

When their manager, Giorgio Gomelsky, asked the union officials for some kind of explanation, he was told: "We don't have to give any reasons."

It was a rotten thing to have happen and naturally the Yardbirds, as well as their many fans, are very upset about the whole thing.

It was a terrible disappointment for the boys because, as Keith Relf says: "We want to play for someone." So naturally, The *BEAT* heroically offered to let the Yardbirds play for us!

Guess we'd better shape up—all the pop groups visiting our country are getting the wrong idea about us.

A "Violent" Country

Both Keith Richard and Herman feel that America is violent. Keith says: "I wouldn't want to live in America. It's a violent country—all over the place you meet first generation citizens telling you to get out of THEIR country."

Herman was here during the L.A. riots so he naturally got the same impression as Keith did. He says: "I must say I was impressed with America—except for the constant violence. In comparison, nothing happens in England."

The Animals are negotiating for a possible movie. Their manager, Mike Jeffries, fills us in on the details: "It is a satirical war film with something to say and designed to shock.

"There will be acting parts for all the Animals. Several other well-known artists including Donovan have been invited to appear. We hope to go into production early next year."

Also set for a movie, of course, are the Rolling Stones. Mick gives us his views on the film: "I want it to say something. I don't want to do a slapstick thing where they make out we are all clowns. I want people to come out feeling they've seen something new. It should be an emotional film."

... RINGO

Attention all you Ringo fans: If you've been having a hard time deciding what kind of present to send to Ringo — I've just solved your problem for you. Ringo has taken to collecting antiques, especially swords and old guns.

He says: "I can't wait to find new pieces to buy. It all started a while back when somebody gave me this fantastic Roman oil lamp that dated back to 50 A.D. That was the start of the collection."

So Ringo lovers — better head for the nearest antique shop.

Brian Jones bought a piece of real estate in America. He explains: "I've just bought a house in Los Angeles. It's purely a business investment and neither I nor any of the others have plans to settle there."

KRLA ARCHIVES

DYLAN AT THE BOWL
"We Had Known A Lion"

BY SHIRLEY POSTON

Bob Dylan's concert at the Hollywood Bowl was much like its star.

Different, to say the least.

Where, oh, where was the fanfare that night? The drum rolls and flashing lights and secondary acts and endless introductions that invariably precede the featured performer.

Wherever the fanfare had gone to, it wasn't at Hollywood Bowl that Friday.

The concert was scheduled to begin at eight o'clock, but then, aren't they all? And the audience was still milling about when the show came in like a lamb.

Opening Number

The show being a smallish young man who sauntered unannounced onto the stage and plunged, without a word, into his opening number.

A welcome of applause came from those who had already laid their hot dogs aside, knowing to expect the unexpected. Others started visably at the first guitar chord and raced for their seats.

Others milled a bit longer, whispering "is it him?"

It was him all right.

For those close enough to view him clearly, the explosion of near-colorless hair and the thin sensitive face gave him away. So did the charcoal grey suit, the well-worn black boots, the shirt open at the collar, the defiant absence of necktie.

For those who could hear more than-see, the sound gave a name to the far away figure.

It was, unmistakably, Dylan.

One Man Show

For the first half of the performance, the show was one man. The equipment (drums, piano, organ, etc.) at the rear of the stage held the promise of noisier things to come, but for the present it was guitar, harmonica and Dylan.

His repertoire included hits from then and now. "Gates Of Eden", "Baby Blue", "Desolation Row", "Tambourine Man", more.

He sang a lot. But he sure didn't talk much.

He did venture forth with a "you know how it is" when the damp air made it next to impossible to keep his guitar in tune. And once, when an eager fan penetrated the applause with the rasp of a dime store trumpet, Dylan grinned.

"What *is* that thing," he wondered into the microphone. "I mean, what are you trying to *say*?"

That was about the extent of his spoken communication with the audience until his burst of conversation at intermission time.

"I'll be about fifteen minutes," he chatted.

He was about twenty. When Dylan returned to the stage, he was accompanied by a group of musicians. All trekked silently to the bandstand and plugged themselves in.

No Rock, No Roll

During this half of the show, Dylan did not rock. Nor did he roll. But the band did add a touch of the modern to his some familiar, some relatively unknown selections.

"Mr. Jones", a rambling, rangy number which often makes little sense and often makes far too much, proved to be the high point of this portion of the concert. To execute it properly, Dylan put down his electric guitar (which he'd been using to play rhythm, not lead) and ambled to the magic piano that sounds like anything but the average 88.

When the time came to honor the most-shouted request of the evening, Dylan searched momentarily for his C harmonica, couldn't find it, asked the audience for help and tuned up with a mouth harp that was helpfully hurled onto the stage by an unknown friend indeed.

He should have flung it back. Gently, of course. And returned to the piano.

The Main Moment

This was the moment the majority of his audience had been waiting for. Dylan, in the flesh and blood, singing the number one song that has made him the idol of millions instead of just thousands.

It was probably the moment he'd been waiting for, too.

He knew the song by heart. So did his audience. Unfortunately, the band did not. And the famous "Like A Rolling Stone" was minus the powerful, Dylan - composed background that helped catapult the song and the singer to international fame.

But Dylan made the best of it. There hadn't been time for the group to learn the intricate arrangement, so the band just more or less played on.

No one really minded that much. The words were still there. And Bob Dylan, the real Bob Dylan was standing there singing them.

How did it feel?

No More

It felt like more. For those of us who attended, it still does because that was all she wrote, there was no more.

At the close of the song, Dylan leaned toward the microphone. He said "thank you very much." Then, he left.

Oh, he did wave once on the way out.

Most of the audience stayed awhile. Some applauding. Some calling for an encore. Some just sitting. Teens and adults alike, just sitting. No rushing for autographs. No screaming. Just

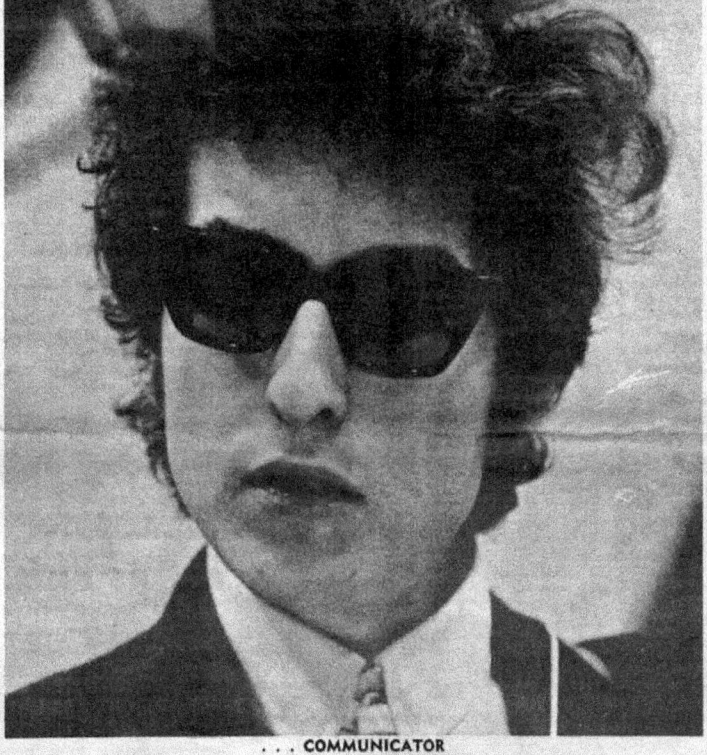

. . . COMMUNICATOR

sort of contemplating what had just finished happening.

Someone rather quiet, almost shy, had stood on a stage and communicated with music, not conversation.

The show that had crept in like a lamb had crept back out just as unceremoniously.

But, for an hour or two, we had known a lion.

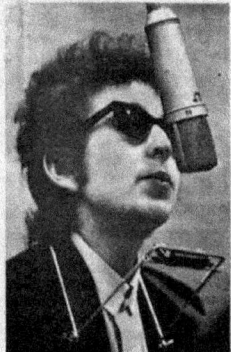

. . . PROTESTOR

How Do I Get To England, Please?

If you are interested in traveling to Merry Olde England you might be wondering about your chances of finding a job and how to attend a British College while you're there.

Your chances of finding a job in England depend upon many things, such as your age, the kind of work you do and how long you intend to stay. And in order to work in England as a non-citizen, your employer must be able to prove that no British citizen can fill the position he has made available to you.

Being accepted by a British college is next to impossible, but has been known to happen. You must have two years of higher education to your credit before you would have the slightest hope of being accepted, and must make all the necessary arrangements *before* leaving America.

In order to qualify for a "student visa" you will need a letter of acceptance from the British college in question when you go to apply for your travel credentials.

Anyone interested in staying in Britain to work or study should get in touch with the British Consulate in their area.

Thanks so much for your response to our English series. You aren't the only ones who want to take the next boat twice as bad now. So do we!

Hope we see you over there, old bean!

For Girls Only

By Shirley Poston

Sorry, boys. I'm not going to waste precious space this week, saying all sorts of clever things about the red-blooded American males who horn in on our weekly hen party.

Why this sudden change of heart? Because! (Because I can't think of anything clever to say, but don't go spreading it around.)

First of all, I'd like to thank the two latest contributors (don't look now, but I think I just made up that word) to my matchbook collection. Luv and thanks to Kathy Niles and Lynn Chittenden for helping with my hobby.

Enough Problems

In case you're wondering what I'm raving about, I collect matchbooks with restaurants on the front. Oh boy. There I go again, talking inside out and backwards. I mean *names* of restaurants. You'd know that if you were a regular reader of this column, and if you aren't, please send a five thousand word explanation of why you aren't. On second thought, don't tell me. I have enough problems!

Remember the column where I raved (I'm back on that word again so you can expect to see it about twenty thousand times in this column) (I'm also on an exaggerating kick) on about friendships that were wearing out, and how a boy can come between two girls who have been bosom buddies for practically centuries?

Well, did I get a letter and a half on this subject, from a girl in San Francisco. She and a long-time friend both have eyes for the same boy and their relationship is withering in the bargain.

"We haven't really talked it over," she told me. "Do you think we should? Maybe if we yell at each other a bit—this'll all clear up. I hate this competitive edge between us. We're all nerves."

In this particular case, the boy in question is out of town and isn't available to either girl. This sort of relieves a part of the problem, but in *any* case, I'd advise anyone in this predicament to talk it over but fast.

Secret Claws

I can't think of many things more depressing than secretly having your claws out for a close friend. You almost have to hold your breath when you're around the person, to keep from shrieking something you don't really mean.

Friendship should be a comfortable thing, and it can really be a nightmare when something charges the atmosphere with electricity, otherwise known as competition. Two people certainly aren't doing each other any favors by holding off on discussing the problem.

Really, which is worse. Letting off the steam by bringing the difficulty to the surface, or going around clenching your teeth when you're in each other's company?

Another thing. If two people are *really* friends, a situation like this will probably disappear in time, without it ever even being mentioned. But just think of all the fun you've missed during the cooling off period. Also remember that if you don't get it settled now, it just might happen again.

Since you share so many things with a friend, you often share the same taste in boys. To avoid these nerve-wracking situations, do your talking or arguing or screaming the *first* time it happens. If you do, you'll probably respect each other too much to let it happen again. Or find out you never really liked each other very much in the first place.

Less Depressing

Well, now that I have talked for approximately three hours on one subject and am getting nowhere fast, let's go on to something a little less depressing (that's one of my favorite words today, too).

You tell me. Is it barefoot, or barefooted? The other day my mother asked me to please put on some shoes and I said "But Mum (I always call her that and does *she* give me a look) I love to go barefooted."

"Barefoot," she corrected.

"Oh," I said.

Later that day I came into the living room wearing shoes and my dad looked at me real funny and then said "Hi, I didn't recognize you with your shoes on."

"So what's so bad about going barefoot?" I questioned.

"Barefooted," he corrected.

"Oh, well," I said.

Oh, good grief. Do you realize that I have just spent several paragraphs talking about *feet*? Of all the fascinating things to discuss. I think they're coming for me soon. I also think The *BEAT* will soon be looking for a columnist who can think of better things to discuss than *feet* for Pete's sake.

About Heels

Speaking of feet, let's talk for a moment about heels. Have you ever felt like one? Well, I have, and the previous discussion reminded me of that delightful (hah) memory.

One of the hardest things I've ever had to do in my whole life was break up with a boy who really liked me. Jeesh. Now I know why boys are so heartless when the situation is reversed. You almost have to be when you're trying to get out of an admiration society that has ceased to be mutual.

Anyway, the feeling used to be mutual in this particular instance, but slowly and surely things started to change. Pretty soon I just couldn't stand this boy. Being with him was bad enough, but when he'd kiss me goodnight, I'd run in the house and do everything but brush my teeth with Comet cleanser.

Well, I finally couldn't bear it another minute and told him I couldn't see him any more. He got all upset and wanted to know why, and I kept telling him all these gentle things like I had too much homework and my folks thought I was doing too much dating and several more of that kind of excuses.

Kept After Me

Nothing seemed to work and he just kept after me, wanting to know the real reason. About the time I'd exhausted my supply of reasons and was saying moronic things like I wanted to spend more time with my little brother (ARGH!!), I finally started getting mad because he wouldn't take no for an answer.

So the next time he said "WHY?" I shouted, "Because you make me ill." Then I took one glance at the shocked, hurt look on his face, burst into tears and ran into the house.

You know how it feels to be on the other side of a disastrous break-up. You wake up in the morning and for the first few seconds you see the sun shining and you think everything's fine. Then you remember what's happened and you all of a sudden can't breathe and your stomach feels as hollow as an elevator shaft.

Wanted To Crawl

Well, this is NOTHING compared with the way I felt the following day. I was so sorry for what I'd said, I wanted to crawl under the bed and die.

It was partly his own fault for refusing to give up and nagging me the way he did, but there's no excuse for anyone saying something like that to anyone. Most of the time, honesty is the best policy, but when someone's pride is at stake, a little white lie doesn't hurt, it helps.

Yeah, Well...

By Tammy Hitchcock

This week's "Yeah, Well" is dedicated entirely to that famous and unique duo: Sonny & Cher.

Sonny was recalling his recent trip to England: "We sang to a guy on a horse." Yeah, well that figures!

Has Own Style

A lot of people are beginning to imitate Cher, with the long hair and the bell bottoms. They may be way out of style because Cher says: "I don't worry about styles. I have my own." Yeah, well I'll say you do, Cher!

Is Sonny's long hair a sign of rebellion? "I'm not rebelling with clothes or my hair. I grew my hair like this three years ago because it was fun. Someday I may get it all cut off." Yeah, well listen, Sonny, I think you'd look kind of cute bald.

Ever since Sonny & Cher hit the big-time, people have been trying to put them in a category. Cher says: "We're not folk singers. We just give our own interpretation of folk and pop songs and try to put our own personalities into them, like the Beatles. Jazz is the only field of music I'm not interested in at all." Yeah, well jazz is a whole different bag of jazz, Cher.

Super-Fast Rise

Sonny & Cher's jet-like ride to the top came so fast that it has many puzzled. But Sonny's got it all figured out: "I think we owe just about everything to the kids and I want to give something back to them." Yeah, well listen, Sonny, this kid will take some money!

It is quite obvious that England liked Sonny & Cher, but how did Sonny & Cher like England? Cher says: "England is great because you can be a hit overnight there." Yeah, well when's the next plane leaving?

How does Sonny feel about being such a successful and popular songwriter? "It's nice when you can put out music you like — and it happens." Yeah, well that's nice, Sonny, now if you will only be so kind as to tell us *how* to make it happen.

...DIG BIKES, TOO? YEAH, WELL.

BEAT Photo: Robert W. Young

KRLA ARCHIVES

... THE LEAVES

'Leaves' Not Just Blowing In Wind

"The Leaves Are Happening!"

Oh no they're not — The Leaves have *happened!* And they have happened in a big way, too.

Not just "Blowin' In the Wind" are these Leaves, but a talented group of singers who are definitely here to stay.

All five members of the group are friendly, honest, appealing performers, but they are each interesting individuals in their own right, so let's meet them all now, Leaf by Leaf.

Leader Leaf

First, there is Bill Rinehart, the "Leader Leaf." He is 20 years old, tall, and the owner of two of the bluest eyes ever. He is a talented guitarist and plays lead on both the six and the twelve string. An accomplished song-writer, he claims that he gets his music "from cartoons."

The lyrics for Bill's music are provided by Leaf No. 2 — Jim Pons. Aside from being the group's lyricist-in-residence, Jim also holds the dubious distinction of being the Senior Leaf at 23 years of age. Jim plays bass guitar and supplies the upper-half of the harmony formed by Rinehart and Pons. He claims to love all kinds of music, but gets most enthusiastic at the slightest mention of Bob Dylan and the Rolling Stones.

Onward and upward to Leaf No. 3, Robert Lee Reiner. This 19 year old guitar player is credited with providing the "soul sound" of the Leaves.

Versatile John

Next in the line-up we find John Beck, who signs in as Leaf No. 4. He is 20 years old and instrumental (no pun intended!) in supplying the group with its image. The most versatile of the five Leaves, John plays harmonica, saxophone, tambourine, and maraccas, and is distinguished by his unique mouth harp and vocal style.

Finally, holding down position No. 5 we find the newest and youngest Leaf: an 18 year old drummer by the name of Tom Ray. However, the other Leaves have taken to calling Tom by his middle name, and so Tom is no longer Tom, but Ambrose.

Ambrose can be distinguished from his companions by his Tom Jones-style shirts decorated with huge lace cuffs.

Originally, Bill, Jim, and Bob and a fourth, now absent-member formed a rock and roll group at San Fernando Valley State College. They played at fraternity parties as a hobby for little or no pay. However, they were so successful wherever they played that the three original Leaves began seriously to develop their group and it's sound and soon Tom and John were added to the Leaves.

Booked Into Ciro's

Together the five ambitious young men developed a unique and distinctive sound all their own and succeeded in getting themselves booked into Ciro's Le Disc (now It's Boss) in Hollywood where they played to turn-away crowds for three history-making weeks.

Their first disc, "Too Many People," is a large request item and looks like a runaway hit on the charts.

Yes, it is certain that the Leaves have happened and from all prospects — they will go right on happening for a long, long while.

"POP JOURNALIST"
New York Writer 'Gives' Us Calif.

California doesn't know it, but it has just been unofficially presented to teen-agers.

Perhaps teens aren't aware of this unexpected gift either, but more and more they are becoming aware of a flop-haired writer for the New York Herald-Tribune, Tom Wolfe.

An Out Title

Wolfe visited California recently with the primary purpose of promoting his new book but he took time out to give utterance to some general remarks on contemporary culture and mores as well. His book — are you ready? — bears the out title, "The Kandy-Kolored Tangerine Flake Streamline Baby." It refers to the kind of restyled Detroit stock car you see so frequently in your boyfriend's backyard — and that doesn't have to be only in California either, as everybody knows.

Love That Machine

Wolfe, who is actually 34, is convinced "people are in love with the machine" and he reveres those teen-agers who are able to do so much, and make so much out of, say, a slightly superannuated Detroit stock car.

"Stock car racing," he declared, "is the new national sport. In 10 years every major sport will be a machine sport ... The stock car racer is the new America hero, the modern gladiator. People like the sense of combat," he went on feelingly. "When he's in his car a man feels all-powerful."

Baseball to Die

Just as the machine provokes our love, according to Wolfe, so by indirection is it killing off such sports as baseball. Wolfe feels baseball is doomed — not only because of the machine but because cities are getting more and more crowded, space in urban areas is getting more and more valuable. And to an ever greater degree the baseball diamond will have to give way to conversion to another kind of real estate probably closely linked to the machine and its products. The author, who says he played semi-pro baseball himself and is quite sympathetic to the sport in principle, cites as evidence of its coming decay the contention that too few people grow up involved with the sport.

Wolfe has been called "pop journalist" among other things. He takes no offense. How could he with a book to his byline called "The Kandy Kolored Tangerine Flake Streamline Baby"?

Person to Person

To John, Frank, Ozzie, John and Judd:

To know you is to luv you. I don't know you, but I still luv you!!

Thanks for making me an honorary member of your fan club. I'll try to live up to the title.

Sue

To Mark Volman:

So you think "It Ain't Me Babe?"

Sali

To Denise Longpre:

Thanks for the really gear birthday card. It was a little late, but better then than never. Keep digging the Beatles.

Bob, the Drummer

To Larry:

Thank you for everything you've done. I lost the piece of hair I cut from your beautiful head. Can I have another bunch? Please?

Be good and take care. Tell Randy, Jim Stanley, Jim Gee, Mike and Danny "Hi" for me. Good luck with the "Missing Links."

Nancy

Want English Pen Pals...

Linda Gregory
1986 Oceanside Drive
San Luis Obispo,
California U.S.A.

Ginger Lane
1411 Armigton Ave.
Hacienda Heights,
California U.S.A.

Linda O'Brien
994 Valencia, Apt. 1
Costa Mesa,
California U.S.A.

Nancy J. Griffin
15010 Lakewood Blvd.
Bellflower,
California U.S.A.

Jeanice Ruzicka
8956 Cimarron Street
Los Angeles,
California U.S.A.

Jackie Frazier
4612 Rockland Pl.
La Canada,
California U.S.A.

Margie Cabarhvias
2053 Bliss Street
Compton,
California U.S.A.

Beth Prendergast
14650 Leadwell Street
Van Nuys,
California U.S.A.

Pam Thompson
335 - 4th Avenue
Venice,
California U.S.A.

Lucia Underwood
3247 Hope Street
Huntington Park,
California U.S.A.

THE **MOTHERS** IS COMING...

Now Appearing!

Dee Gee Records*

PRESENTS

"THE FABULOUS ENTERTAINER"

The BLUE BOY
WITH HIS TRIO

at the

ROYAL LION

Ventura & Coldwater
Studio City

*Ask For Free Autographed Record

KRLA ARCHIVES

FETCHING BARBARA LEWIS' show business family encouraged her early in life in her songwriting ("Hello Stranger," "Puppy Love," "Think A Little Sugar") and singing careers. In both the pretty Detroiter has become the fabulous success we've become familiar with on her records for Atlantic.

Q: I have a very bad habit of biting my nails. What can I do to stop?
(Elaine R.)
A: First of all, determine when you do your nail biting. It might take you a few days to pin it down because nail biting is often an unconscious habit, something you do without realizing. You'll probably discover that it happens when your attentions are elsewhere, like when you're watching television, or when you're very nervous. Then either use a product, available at most drugstores, which makes your fingernails taste terrible, or wear gloves during the danger hours. Also, try having a professional manicure, even if your nails are bitten right down to the first knuckle. Once you see how nice you can look, it's less tempting to munch away.

Q: What can a girl do when she likes a boy who is too quiet and reserved to admit that he likes her too?
(Nola T.)
A: Be equally quiet and reserved about bringing up this subject, and maybe he won't stop.

Q: I'm from a small town in Minnesota and I picked up a copy of the BEAT (and ordered a subscription) when I was in California with my family this summer. While I was there, I didn't see one pair of anklets being worn. Are "bobby sox" completely out of style on the coast? If so, could you suggest something we might wear here in their place during the winter, so we can be "stylish" without freezing?
(Judy B.)
A: Anklets have been a thing of the past for several years here in the West. When it's below-zero time in your part of the country, we suggest full length knit socks in all sorts of zany colors and patterns, and also the knee socks that are such a big deal fashion-wise this year. That should keep you in high style without danger of frostbite! If the stores in your area don't sell socks like we've just mentioned, please let us know and we'll try to help you and your friends order them by mail.

Q: I received a birthday present from the members of a club I belong to. There are twenty of them and everyone chipped in for the gift, which was really great. Am I supposed to send all of them thank you cards, or would one addressed to all the club members do? Please print this right away because I have to do something soon.
(Gerri F.)
A: One card addressed to the entire club will do nicely. If you want to go to all the trouble of sending separate cards, go ahead, but it isn't really necessary. If the donors weren't all members of a club or some such, it would be necessary to send separate cards, but this time you lucked out!

Q: I have heard from a friend that you can get a good tan by mixing salad or cooking oil and iodine, then smearing it on before you go out in the sun. Is this true?
A: A mixture of this type does seem to help, but use baby oil, not the edible sort. And keep your sunning down to small doses so you won't burn and ruin everything.

HINT OF THE WEEK
If you feel like you need to lose a couple of pounds real fast, and don't feel you have the will power to do so, listen to this. Start a fan club and get it listed in The BEAT.
If you have a question you'd like answered, or a hint you'd like to share, drop a line to The BEAT.

THESE GREAT SMASH LPs AVAILABLE WHEREVER YOU BUY RECORDS

MONO 27040 — STEREO 67040

MONO 27056 — STEREO 67056

MONO 27063 — STEREO 67063

Jerry Lee Lewis - A LEGEND

IF YOU HAVE EVER SEEN HIM PERFORM, THESE GREAT ALBUMS WILL RECAPTURE THE MEMORY

IF YOU HAVE NEVER SEEN THE FABULOUS JERRY LEE LEWIS YOU'LL DISCOVER WHAT A ROCKING EXPERIENCE YOU MISSED.

EITHER WAY - HIS ALBUMS ARE A MUST!

KRLA ARCHIVES

KRLA + BEATLES = WOW!

BOB EUBANKS PLAYS STRAIGHT MAN for RINGO

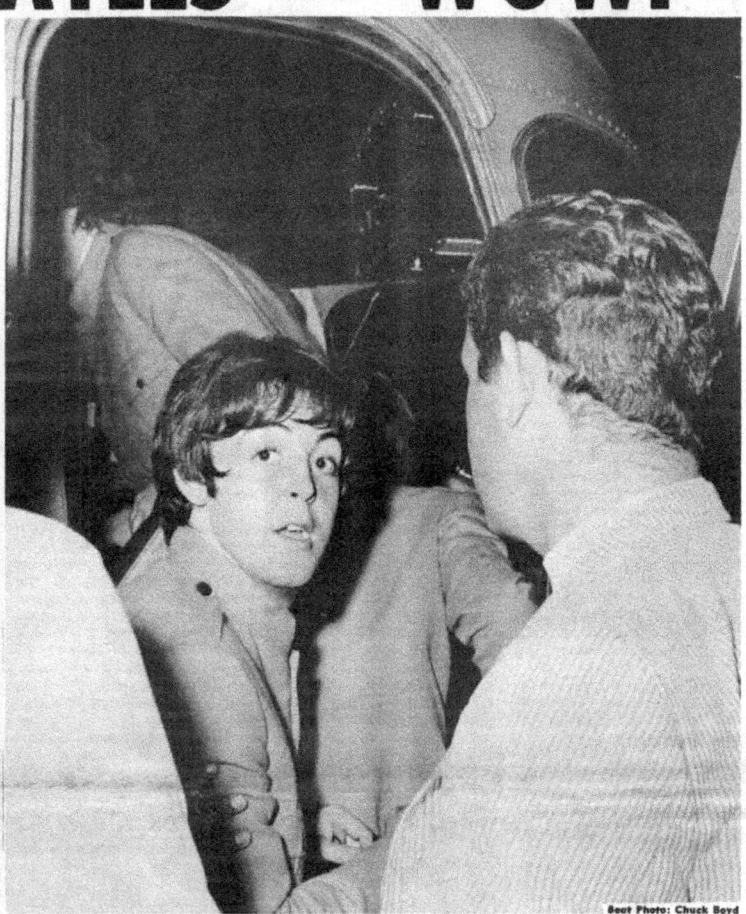

KRLA'S JIM STECK HELPS BEATLES INTO ARMORED CAR FOR GETAWAY

FLANKED BY BRIAN EPSTEIN, BOB EUBANKS AND TONY BARROW, BEATLES LAUGH AT DAVE HULL DURING THEIR PRESS CONFERENCE.

KRLA ARCHIVES

HOLLYWOOD BOWL PRESENTED AN IMPRESSIVE SIGHT FOR THE BEATLE CONCERTS. CROWDS PACKED IT BOTH NIGHTS.

THE BEATLES PUT ON TWO FABULOUS SHOWS — AND SOMETIMES YOU COULD EVEN HEAR THEM SINGING.

KRLA ARCHIVES

By Susan Frisch

Dear BEAT People. I am going to start my column off a little differently than I usually do, because I have some news of importance I want to share with you.

Last week I wrote that the Beatles would not be back, and that I thought there was little chance of we fans trying to persuade Brian Epstein. Well, Beatle People, good news! They will be back again for a 1966 tour of the United States and will quite possibly be staying in California for a vacation such as they had this year. Without doubt they will be back, even if it is for a vacation alone, for I happen to know that California is their favorite state in the U.S. So, all you Beatle fans, start saving your money for next year's concert, 'cause it should be even better than the last two they gave, if that's possible! Now to resume.

☆ ☆ ☆

Dear Susan:
Could you please tell me what kind of cigarettes George smoked on his recent visit to Los Angeles?   Dillon Scott

Dear Dillon,
George smoked Kent cigarettes this trip. At least everytime I saw him that was the brand he was smoking. Just for the record I noticed Paul, who usually smoked Marlboro, was smoking Players. You've heard of those, haven't you?

Dear Susan:
I recently saw a group on television called The Liverpool Five. I haven't heard much about them since. Could you give me some information about them?   Carol King

Dear Carol,
I can only say that I hope your letter is one of the many thousands I will be getting in the near future about this particular group. I would LUV to tell you about them! To begin with there is Steve Laine, lead singer, Ron Henley, on the electric piano, Dave Burgess, bass guitar, Ken Cox, rhythm guitar, and Jimmy May, drums. They were all born in England, but met in Liverpool, hence the name, Liverpool Five. Their first record, "Everything's All Right", made the charts back east, but was never released in California, so we weren't lucky enough to hear it. Their latest record, which they have sung on *Where The Action Is* and *American Bandstand*, is titled, "If You Gotta Go, Go Now," a Bob Dylan composition. The "B" side "Too Far Out", written by Jackie DeShannon, is a complete gas.

Dear Susan:
Would you please tell me whether Elvis asked the Beatles to meet him, or if the Beatles asked Elvis whether they could meet him?   Susan Drawf

Dear Susan,
It was sort of strange how it happened. Actually a man connected with the Beatles, while in California, had tried to arrange a meeting of the five boys through Elvis's manager, Colonel Parker, not Elvis or the Beatles themselves. The Beatles, however had wanted to meet Elvis very, very much and were quite happy when they found out they would be able to. Likewise was Elvis, I'm sure. The Beatles were the ones who had suggested a meeting between them and Elvis, but they were not the ones who had set it up.

Dear Susan:
The last few days, though they seem like years, the most wonderful things have happened to me. Not only seeing the Beatles perform, but actually I feel something better. I have heard Paul McCartney's new song, "Yesterday," on the radio. PLEASE tell me all you know about it. It is just fantastic, I cry every time I hear it!   Lucy Crosbey

Dear Lucy,
There is nothing more I can say except to agree with you and all the other millions of people who are experiencing this new phenomenon. You see I don't even call it a song, for I feel this is above the usual record that is *just* recorded. The night that it was released here, actually the night of the Monday morning I spoke to Paul McCartney himself, and I asked him a few questions about the record, and from the answers he gave me, I'll tell you all I know about it. It was written by Paul himself; no one, not even John, helped him. He is the only Beatle on it. He also said that on the British album, "HELP!", where "Yesterday" is waxed, McCartney-Lennon are credited as being the writers, but this isn't so. Usually whether Paul or John writes a song it is always credited as Lennon-McCartney, or vice-versa. The instruments used in this "masterpiece" — and I are violin, viola, bass.

Dear Susan:
Last week I went to see "HELP!". I was wondering if Jane Asher was in it at all, because there was one part, while skiing, and I could have sworn Jane was one of the girls at the ski lodge. She was dressed all in white with black boots. Was it?   "Patti Boyd"

Dear Patti? (How's George by the way?!!)
Yes! That pretty red head was Jane Asher, and no one else! Some girls have all the luck don't they? But I don't feel sorry for you. . . "Patti."

DANNY HUTTON

Hit Writer Of 'Roses' Is Reluctant Singer

The BEAT, being our usual efficient selves, finally discovered who the mystery man, Danny Hutton, is. For the longest time no one knew, but the BEAT snooped (oops, we mean looked) around until we uncovered the truth.

Danny is a 22-year-old Irish-born young man whose very first record, "Roses and Rainbows," is a huge hit.

Elated Over Success

Danny wrote the song himself but declares that it is not his favorite, although he is naturally elated over the record's tremendous success.

Danny had no intention of becoming a singer. He actually prefers A&R work, but the fates brought Danny and Larry Goldberg of Hanna-Barbera Records together — and the pop world was duly blessed with "Roses and Rainbows."

Added Moustache

Danny stands 6'1" and wears his black hair rather long. Since our picture of Danny was taken, he has added something new to his appearance — a mustache!

Everyone is besieging Danny to have the hairy thing cut off, but he steadfastly refuses saying: "It may catch on."

And it just may! At least, his record sure did!

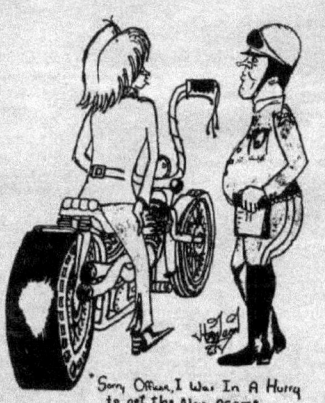

"Sorry Officer, I Was In A Hurry to get the New BEAT"

ERICH HANSON, *Whittier, Calif.*

Forget Those Mick-Chrissie Wedding Bells

You can forget all of those Mick Jagger-Chrissie Shrimpton marriage/engagement rumors. Mick says that he is not about to marry Chrissie 'cause "she's too young."

In fact, the whole idea of marriage kind of scares Mick — to be honest, it *panics* him!

Mick was recently in the wedding party when photographer David Bailey took the long walk. Poor Mick was so nervous he almost didn't make it down the aisle — and he wasn't even the one getting married!

One helpful hint to all you Jagger-lovers who are planning on capturing Mick for your very own: he dislikes girls who are "too pushy."

It's Happening . . .

"Eve of Destruction" has broken in England, so singer Barry McGuire and singer-composer P. F. Sloan are off to Jolly Olde for a short trip. Hey — wait for me, fellas!

☆ ☆ ☆

Look for pretty Shindig dancer Carole Shelyne (the girl with the horn-rimmed glasses) to star in an upcoming segment of the Patty Duke show, entitled "Patty's Private Pygmalion."

☆ ☆ ☆

Sid Bernstein has made an offer of $500,000 as against 60% of the gross for two performances in Shea Stadium to the Beatles and their manager Brian Epstein, boy millionaire . . . Bernstein wants to bring the Beatles over for two concerts early in June, and he intends to charge a maximum of $12.50 per ticket . . . Well—I guess the teenagers in New York really *are* richer than the rest of us!

☆ ☆ ☆

Roger Williams has received a gold album for his hit waxing of "The Return of Roger Miller."

☆ ☆ ☆

Big honor in store for our gals the Supremes. The three talented singers from Detroit will represent these United States at Holland's annual pop song festival in Amsterdam on October 3.

☆ ☆ ☆

Herman and his Hermits are in L.A. Town now completing work on their first motion picture, "There's No Place Like Space". . . The boys will vocalize nine new tunes for the upcoming flick, including the title tune, all of which will be released in an album.

KRLA ARCHIVES

OH, YOU ZEKE!
Secret Of Success – Is It Sloppy Dress?

Is there a secret of success in pop music or is it all just a matter of blind luck?

The Preachers believe there may be some truth to the blind luck bit, but they also believe in seeking a secret, too. At least Zeke, one of the Preachers, does and he has this story to back him up.

Not long ago, says Zeke, the group was appearing at the Teen Age Fair in San Diego. One of the big features of the Fair is a competition between some 20 amateur bands for various prizes.

The leader of one of these amateur bands, according to Zeke, drew him aside and confidentally asked him what Zeke thought the chances of his amateur group would be in winning one of the prizes.

Zeke, not one to give a hasty opinion, carefully looked his questioner over, noting the natty costume of blue cardigan with white shirt and tie. He himself had not yet put on the Preacher uniform.

"Your boys play pretty well," replied Zeke, "but you dress too sharp. Those cardigans look too good; you've got to dress grubby before you can make it."

The amateur's leader thought for a moment, then said: "I think you're right. I got a pair of torn pants at home and a dirty shirt and so do the others. That's how we'll dress tomorrow for the contest. We should have a better chance of winning."

Zeke has a P.S. to the story: They lost.

John And Paul Sign Up George

It took George Harrison a little longer than John and Paul, but he has finally arrived in the songwriting business in a very big way.

Of course, George has been contributing more and more to the Beatle's original recordings — his latest effort being "I Need You" from their movie, "Help."

So naturally, being enterprising young businessmen, John and Paul have enticed George to sign an exclusive songwriting contract for their publishing company, Northern Songs, Ltd.

Smart bunch of boys, those Beatles!

Breaks Own Record

Breaking records — his own included — is nothing new for Harry Belafonte, a performer whose fab appeal continues to amaze admirers of all ages.

During a recent California stand, the entertainer repeated his record-breaking habit. During a month at the Greek Theater, for example, not only did he break all existing records there, he also broke his own all-timer set in four weeks there in 1963.

PORTMAN'S PLATTERPOOP
By Julian Portman

Beautiful *Deborah Walley*, AIP's delightful-to-look-at bikini doll and star of "Sgt. Deadhead", has been huddling with record producer *Hank Levine* regarding her first platter for Dee Gee records . . . *The McGuire Sisters* slipped away from Reprise and dotted with ABC-Paramount. Don't know if I'm letting the cat out of the bag, but ABC-Paramount has been doing a little artist raiding and have also snared *George Hamilton* from MGM. They're readying his first album, titled "By George".

Barry McGuire, prior to his hit single, recorded for two other labels, so naturally, both are releasing singles. Mira Records have already placed on sale McGuire's "Green Back Dollars" with other singles being prepared for future release . . . Keep an ear peeled for *Keeley Smith's* new release of "That Old Black Magic". It's styled in the sounds of her ex-hubby, Louie the Prima, with a rock 'n roll touch added . . . *Joe & Eddie's* newest effort for Crescendo is "I Got You" b/w "Petticoat White", number one on the nurse corps hit parade.

Ed Sullivan, still raiding the teen-star market, invited *The Supremes* to come back for eight more appearances. He's also seeking Capitol records and the Los Angeles Rams footballing *Fearsome Foursome* to come onto one of "Smiley's" shows when it originates from H'wood. It'll have to be arranged between two home games, and if his luck is not better than *Lloyd Thaxton's*, he may have to take his cameras onto the gridiron . . . *Sherri Knight*, a dainty 16 year old vocalist, pacted with Playa del Rey records and her first release is "Too Young to Know".

It's A Fact: A recent 30 minute TV appearance by *The Beatles* on a Los Angeles station did not bring the desired number one ratings for that harassed station manager. They were beaten-out (are you ready for this) by *Lawrence Welk* and his magic . . . Have you glanced at the name attractions "It's Boss", the teen age nightclub, is bringing into its Sunset Blvd. club? Two that particularly interest everybody, according to early reservations pouring in, are *Petula Clark* and *Sonny & Cher*. Oh *Paul Raffles*, don't forget mine! Reserve early, or too late will be tooooo late!

MGM is releasing the soundtrack from "When the Boys Meet The Girls", with the following artists performing specialties: *Connie Francis*, *Louis Armstrong*, *Herman's Hermits* and *Sam the Sham* and *The Portmans* . . . *Denny Belline and The Dwellers* are gleeful with their first release on RCA titled "It Happened That Way" . . . According to the delightful *Dick (Shindig) Howard*, *Sonny & Cher* perform a November 11 concert in New York's dignified Lincoln Center. The city fathers must be trembling!

Destined for Hitsville: "Little Miss Sad" by *The 5 Emprees* on Freeport . . . and "Honey" by *Tony Harris* on Dee Gee records. "Honey" has already been on "Hollywood A Go Go" and "Where The Action Is" and it's only been in record stores in recent weeks.

Merrill Sparks & The Exiles single on Golden World "Can't We Get Along" and *Gene McDaniels'* rush Liberty Records release "Hang On A Little Longer" are the handicraft of talented writer *Larry Mannering* . . . Deem Records' "God, Country and My Baby", featuring the handsome young movie star, *Brad Berwick*, is the talk of platter spinners across the country. It's a reply to the numerous protest songs and a good one . . . *Bobby Goldsboro's* newest for United Arists is "If You Wait for Love". . . *The Checkmates* scribbled their signature to a Columbia contract, almost the same time *Chris Montez* did likewise for *Jerry Moss* at the hottest little label, A & M Records.

. . . Dee Gee records *The Blue Boy* opened a month's engagement at Studio City's "Red Lion" . . . *Sam Dubreville* joined *Spanky McFarland's* Deem Records and became the boss . . . and *Art Laboe*, the genius behind the Original Sound label, called and *asked*, "Can *Sig Sakowicz* sing, if so, I have a contract ready!" . . . later baby!

Stones Stay On Top

The Rolling Stones have managed to hold on to that number one spot again this week with "Satisfaction." There was some speculation on just how high the record would go because the pirate radio stations got ahold of "Satisfaction" way before the English release date. The pirates played it and played it and it was felt that perhaps this early exposure would cause the record to lose sales when it was finally released.

But, as it went straight to the top, obviously the exposure helped rather than hindered "Satisfaction."

Bob Dylan and "Like A Rolling Stone" surprised many and moved up this week to number three. Since it had remained stationary for the last two weeks, it was highly probable that the record would drop instead of climbing. But then Bob Dylan is a man of surprises—so . . .

The Hollies are making tremendous jumps on the charts. They debuted last week at number 16 and this week "Look Through Any Window" leaped into the top ten at number eight.

Cher finally made it—she beat out the Byrds with "All I Really Want To Do." She's been chasing them for weeks and weeks now.

Cher's everlovin' Sonny also made his way into the top ten this week at number ten with "Laugh At Me." So between them they now have three records in the British top ten! Quite an achievement, isn't it?

Here in the U.S., Donovan released his "Universal Soldier" as a single, but in England it is a track on an E.P. However, the record is selling just like a single and this week finds it at number 15.

British Top 10

1.	SATISFACTION	Rolling Stones
2.	I GOT YOU BABE	Sonny & Cher
3.	LIKE A ROLLING STONE	Bob Dylan
4.	MAKE IT EASY ON YOURSELF	Walker Brothers
5.	HELP	The Beatles
6.	A WALK IN THE BLACK FOREST	Horst Jankowski
7.	ZORBA'S DANCE	Marcello Minerbi
8.	LOOK THROUGH ANY WINDOW	The Hollies
9.	ALL I REALLY WANT TO DO	Cher
10.	LAUGH AT ME	Sonny

UPBEAT OF THE WEEK

It's definite now — there are *three* big B's in the world of music: Beethoven, Bach, and . . . The Beatles!!

That's right, The Beatles, and if you have heard their new record "Yesterday" with Paul McCartney in the solo spotlight, you can understand just what we mean.

Certainly one of the most beautiful records to be released in a long while, Paul's tender crooning is accompanied by a string quartet of cello, viola, violin, and bass.

By Paul Alone

The song itself was written by Paul — and it is performed in a two-part counterpoint. The preceding term might sound like Greek goulash if you don't happen to be of a musical mentality, however by way of simple explanation and identification — it is the sort of thing one J. S. Bach was doing a few years back.

"Yesterday" is included in the selections on the British LP of "Help!" but Beatlemaniacs in Uncle Samland will have to be content to obtain it on a single 45 for now.

This soulful disc is already reaping glowing critical acclaim as it heads for the top spot on charts all across the nation.

KRLA ARCHIVES

HEADLINERS' HAIR BEAT

'Cool It' If You Iron Your Hair

By Robert Esserman and Frank DeSanctis

HOLLYWOOD—Hot irons—hot irons everywhere! What are all the girls doing to their hair?

"I wish my hair looked like hers, it's so shiny and straight." Sound familiar?

The BEAT has been asked by many of our readers to solve this problem and many other questions concerning girls and their hair. Providing the answers are Robert Esserman and Frank DeSanctis, who operate the famed "Headliners" in Beverly Hills, where many of the top movie and television stars are regular patrons.

To begin with, girls, ironing your hair can be done successfully providing you don't make the mistake of using a *hot* iron. So cool it!

Any hot metal object put to your hair can result in breaking it and may frizz it or dry it out. Through our experience we have found the best way to achieve the straight look is to use an electric air comb, a fairly simple process.

First we wash your hair, then towel dry it. Third, comb out the tangles. After this we take the electric air comb, start from the top of the head and comb the hair straight to the ends.

While we comb through your hair the hot air blows the hair dry and the comb straightens it. This method can be used as often as necessary. Unfortunately, you cannot use the hot iron method so often without severely damaging the hair.

Shiny and Healthy

We feel straight hair is attractive but you've got to remember your hair must always be conditioned. The most beautiful thing about long, straight hair is having it shiny and healthy looking.

Face it, girls, no matter how long the hair, split ends, dryness and stringiness *won't* make the guys' heads turn your way!

We find that the best method of conditioning hair is to apply a liquid conditioner to the hair with cotton. This is followed by wrapping the head in a towel, causing the heat from the scalp to drive the conditioner into the interior of the hair.

The process takes only 20 minutes for all the magic ingredients in the conditioner to really sink in—magic because after rinsing and drying the results can be really beautiful.

Quickie Method

For girls who are late for their dates, we have a quicker method, a conditioner that can be just poured over the head then set immediately. The results of both are "Like, Wow!" But, of course, the conditioner washes out with the next shampoo.

Long hair is groovy all right, but it requires constant trimming. The hair splits from excessive brushing, combing and weather conditions. Always try to keep the ends of your hair even and trimmed, trimming about once every four weeks.

The latest cut that requires little attention is the Headliners' popular "Guy Cut." The "Guy" is a short cut that needs little setting during the week because the line of the hair cut is trimmed around the contours of your head. We can honestly claim we haven't sheared one girl yet who didn't dig her new "Guy Cut."

Short hair *is* very feminine, if any of you gals have any doubts. Short hair can be styled in many different ways, each cut individualized to accent your best features.

Many girls are more conscious than ever before of short Do's, since there are so many extremes today in haircuts. Many new styles have come about as imitations of the Beatles' haircuts and those of Sonny & Cher.

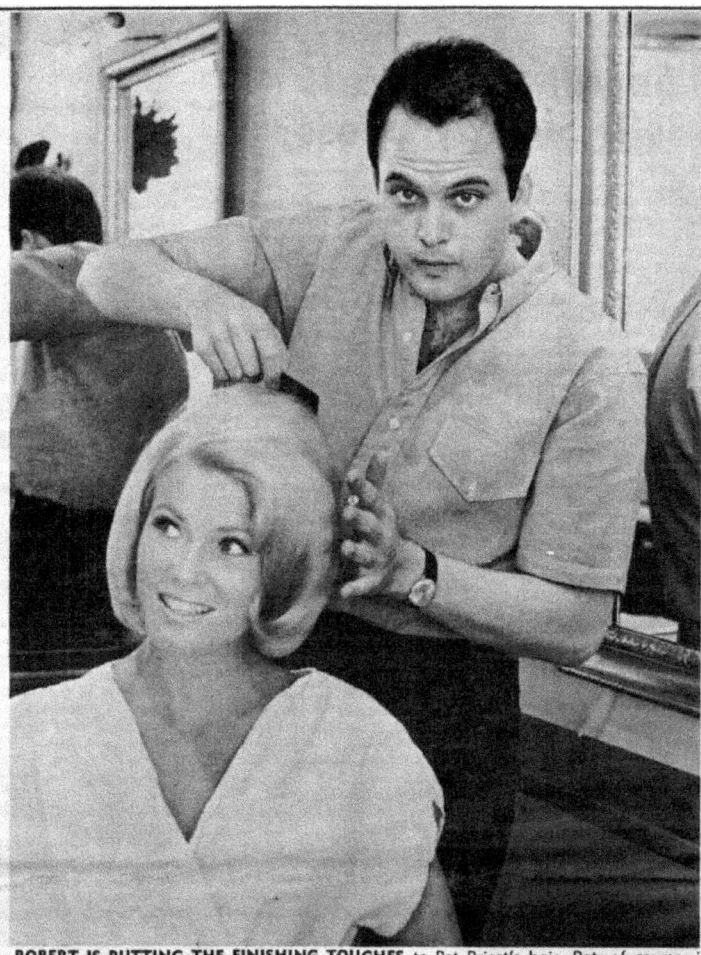

ROBERT IS PUTTING THE FINISHING TOUCHES to Pat Priest's hair. Pat, of course, is seen regularly on "The Munsters" television show.

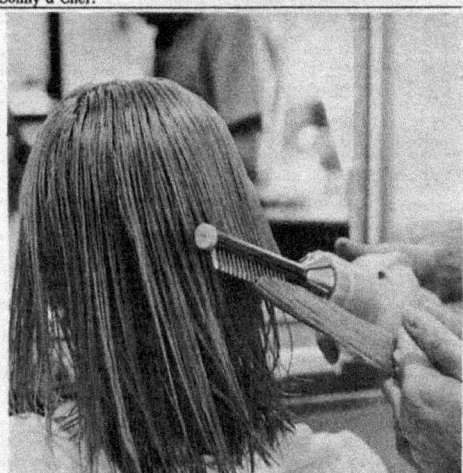

HERE IT IS — the electric air comb in action.

FRANK IS PICTURED HERE busily working on one of the Headliners' regular customers.

KRLA ARCHIVES

Jan Says He'll Quit Song To Become A Doc
By Eden

A few short weeks ago, a young man named Jan Berry spent a few days in the hospital with a broken leg, the result of an accident which occured on the set of a film which he was making with partner Dean Torrance.

For some strange reason however, Jan wasn't too overly thrilled with his new surroundings, and just as soon as he could get a hold of his new gold-plated crutches, he hobbled aboard his twin-engine, jet powered skateboard and split for home.

Crucial Question

Just before he left the hospital, your ever-present BEAT reporter was on the scene to ask Jan the crucial question of the day: Although it will never replace sidewalk surfing, have you tried hanging ten off of the mattress yet? To which Jan gravely replied in his most serious tones: "Yes, but now I hang my socks out on the line!"

With that bit of philosophy clearly defined, your trusty reporter made a pilgrimage to the mountain-top hideaway of Jan Berry high in the hills of Hollywood for this exclusive, after-the-hospital interview.

Everyone — but *everyone* — has a first record. In discussing the very first record he ever made, with a chap by the name of Dean Torrance, Jan candidly confided:

"I had an old piano in my garage and I bought a tape recorder. This was when we were still in high school. So, Dean would come up all the time and we would fool around singing. And we had a group in high school of about five guys.

Strip Show

"We went down to Sixth and Main with a bunch of guys one day to see the strip show (Ed. note: the preceding line is censored for all those readers under the age of 34¼), and we saw Jenny Lee. After the show, she passed out her "Bomp Bomp" cards and we took them all home and wrote a song that night about Jenny Lee.'"

Jan is a tall, handsome blond person who bears a close resemblance to some Greek-god type (please insert Greek-sounding name here).

He is also frequently mistaken for a surfer (hallowed by the name!). But hark! — on the subject of surfing, and surfing music, Mr. Berry adamantly proclaims: "There is no real 'surf music,' or 'surf sound.' There is just the 'sound' of the individual artists. We don't have a surf sound.'"

Yes sir, Mr. Berry sir!!

Little Old Lady

Undoubtedly you are all acquainted with "The Little Old Lady From Pasadena." (No Mergatroyd, *not* your grandmother; the hit record by Jan and Dean) But how would you like to be re-introduced to the little lady in the form of a symphonic production? Well, hold onto your hot rods while your faithful BEAT reporter lays this next line of info on your eager ears: Jan Berry has conducted a symphonic orchestra and recorded an album entitled "The Jan and Dean Symphony Number One — in Twelve Movements!" Inside the album (if you can recognize them!) you will find all of Jan and Dean's hits, including Pasadena's favorite Senior Citizen, all with a symphonic arrangement.

Here is another side of Jan Berry: he hopes to perform the selections on the album at the Music Center in Los Angeles and then to use the proceeds to build a children's hospital and research foundation. He says, "After all, the kids paid for it. They're the ones who went to see our concerts and who bought our records. Why *not* build it for them?"

Grateful to Fans

Yes, Jan is genuinely grateful to his fans for what they have done for him and he seriously hopes to reciprocate when and where he can.

JAN: NO REAL SURF MUSIC

Then there is the question of Jan's *second* career — in medicine. Of his immediate plans for the near future, Dr. Berry-to-be prescribes the following for himself: "I am returning to California College of Medicine in the fall. I have already completed one year there. Otherwise — I plan to manage Dean's career as a single."

To Practice Medicine

"I plan to continue, as I have been doing, with my schooling in medicine. I want to practice when I receive my M.D. degree; it isn't just something to fall back on."

The movie Jan was making when the accident occurred has been temporarily postponed, but will be resumed in the Spring.

But what of Jan's future plans? Does he have any ambitions for his personal career for the future?

"Not for the next six months!!"

Oh well, we'll call you back then, Jan!

MAIL BOX

Dear BEAT:

Although I agree with suggestions to create your own message from Dylan's many ideas, I think there is more to his lyrics than that.

To many people Dylan's songs don't make sense. They are confused because they don't know how to explain the lyrics in concrete terms. I don't think they should try to explain them because his lyrics are something to sense and identify with, not to classify. Dylan's songs come the closest to expressing emotions in words than anything I have ever read or heard.

When I say emotions I don't mean just hate, love, or fear, but the feelings one experiences that are all, none or a combination.

The beauty of Dylan's songs lies in his lyrics and in his stylization. This is true whether he uses the traditional folk sound or the electric guitars. This is greatness and I'm all for it.

Helen Roberts

Dear Editor:

I've heard and read some comments about how the British pop papers are so superior to the American ones. They should only see The BEAT! I've read their papers and have found The BEAT to be ahead of them *all*.

How about a story on the fabulous Beau Brummels. You could mention their upcoming tour of England and that they'll be on The Flintsones — yes, The Flintsones — (as cartoon characters) later in the year. Congratulations on your wonderful paper.

Marian Pearlman

Dear BEAT:

I think The BEAT is a great paper and I would especially like to thank you for all your articles on the two wonderful talented people — Sonny and Cher.

You have excellent articles and stories on them and all the other top entertainers.

Paula Nechak

To the Editor:

I have just started receiving The BEAT and want to tell you I think it is really the greatest. Our radio stations here in York, Pennsylvania, are rather behind so most of us listen to out-of-town stations. Your paper is a good way to keep up to date.

I happen to be a Beatle fan and your Beatle features are Tops! I saw them at Shea.

Judi Grove

Dear BEAT:

When I was in California for the summer I picked up a copy of The BEAT at a record store. It was even better than advertized.

Thank you and please rush my weekly copies to the East coast.

Monica Staar

KRLA ARCHIVES

AFTER AN INSTRUMENTAL STROLL down "Whittier Blvd." with Thee Midniters on his **Shebang** TV show, KRLA's Casey Kasem (center) interviews San Diego television personality Bob Hower. Midniters are (l. to r.) Willie Garcia, lead singer; Romeo Prado, trombone; Larry Rendon, saxophone; George Dominguez, lead giutar; George Salazar, drums; Jimmy Espinoza, bass; and Roy Marquez, rhythm guitar. Organist Ronnie Figueroa, not seen here, is hidden behind guest Hower.

DRAG RACERS' DREAM
KRLA's Streamlined Dragster Is Talk of L.A. County Fair

KRLA's twin candidates for the Automotive Hall of Fame are the talk of the county fair.

Both the handsome KRL"A" and its streamlined stablemate, the lightning-fast Horsepower Engineering Dragster, are the center of attention at the annual Los Angeles County Fair, on the Pomona Fair Grounds.

The souped-up, highly customized, beautifully - restored "A" is being displayed in the KRLA booth on weekends for the duration of the fair, which runs until Oct. 10.

On weekdays the "A" moves out and the KRLA Match Competition Dragster is displayed in the same booth.

Dragster Fame

While KRLA's Corvette engine-powered Model-A has gained fame through daily appearances throughout Southern California, the sleek, needle-nosed dragster is gaining equal fame on the drag strips.

Built by Doug Robinson, who is owner of Horsepower Engineering and one of the most successful drag racers in the country, the Dragster is a dream to behold — one of the fastest machines ever to scream down a drag strip.

For those concerned with mechanical specifications, we'll leave the description to Rod & Custom Magazine, which featured the Horsepower Engineering Chrysler-powered rail in its August issue:

"Torrid '57 Chrysler runs stock at 392 cubic inches, with Herbert push rods, while C&T helps out with a modified crankshaft. Herbert rustles lifter action with a specially ground roller cam. M/T pistons are aluminum, circled with Ramco rings. Aluminum rods are also M/T items.

Into Orbit

"Chrysler heads compress 6.5:1 and were modified by Tims Precision Engines. Cragar intake manifold boasts modified GMC 6-71 puffer and Hilborn low-profile injectors for some furious co-ordinated activity when 75 percent nitro is pumped and the Schiefer magneto is lit.

"All power is directed through the torque tube and rear end out to Halibrand mags lighting up M&H skins. Activity stops in less than eight seconds from blast off with help of a 12-foot Diest ribbon chute and dual Airheart dics binders. Speed at re-entry tops 201 mph. Cockpit offers all the comforts of dragging — black naugahyde, plushly presented by Ron's Top Shop of Monrovia. Yellow enamel covers streamlined beauty right out to the nose where torsion bars, Speed Sport spokes and Pirelli tires hold up the front. The 1½ inch diameter .049 thick tube chassis was built by Horsepower Engineering and has wheelbase of 150 inches."

Watching from the grandstand while the big boys fire up doesn't impress Doug and his crew. Their first entry into big league A/A fuel racing takes a back seat to nothing else on wheels.

More About "A"

Perhaps only rodders are still with us at this point, following the exacting description above, but here are couple of other items concerning the splendid old KRL"A", which draws more oohs and ahhs now than it did back when it was first introduced as the pride of Henry Ford in 1929.

In last week's story we accidentally left out the name of the man who is chiefly responsible for originating the mechanical and styling concept of the KRL"A" and who has been responsible for restoring it to its present beauty. That achievement belong to Warren Hall, who has worked tirelessly at the project.

Warren, incidentally, is the brother of KRLA Program Director Mel Hall. Mell, who lives next door to a supermarket parking lot, furnished the hubcaps and several other accessories.

A reminder: when you see the "A" at the fair, be sure to ask for your free KRLA/Bardahl Maltese Cross racing decal.

just letters

Dear BEAT:

I would like to direct this letter to the English girl (Mail Box Aug. 28) who was so baffled by the "frantic desire" of American girls to go to England. Perhaps I can clarify her confusion.

For the past two years I, too, have longed for the day when I will set foot on England's shores, but to afford myself a better chance to meet the "stars" is the very least of my reasons. In these past two years, I have had the wonderful experience of writing to twenty-one English pen pals, and I have drawn the conclusion that the English are the friendliest people in the world. I am fascinated by their generosity, politeness and their attachment to tradition. In England, people take time to live; progress and "fast, big business" is of minor importance.

Even though I have never experienced the "glorious weather and climate" of California (I am a Pennsylvanian), I would eagerly welcome the rain and fog of England as a novelty, if nothing else.

So you see, when we Anglomaniacs seem so determined to go to your homeland, it is for more sincere and deeper reasons than mentioned in your letter.

Thank you,
Roberta Manbeck

P.S. Thanks for the greatest pop magazine or newspaper in *all* 50 states!

PERSONALS

To Pat Dutton of Sconthorpe, Lincolnshire England:

Remember when I told you to stick with me and you'd see your name in print? Well, what's better than seeing it in the fab *BEAT*?

Pauly of Fullerton
☆

To Cathy Davies of Manchester, England:

This is the highest honor ever bestowed upon a pen pal, their name in the fantabulous *BEAT*. Gene Pitney, The Kinks, and Joey Paige rule — right?

Chriss
★

To KRLA:

This is just a small and late note to publicly thank KRLA for helping me to see "Help!" It was just great, and I let everybody know that I saw it with the help of KRLA. Thanks.

Susan Qualici
☆

To Rachael Lara:

So you knew Bob (wonderful) Eubanks was playing my Teen Topper.... Well, why didn't you let me know instead of Susan. I had no idea and when he said, "Hi Pat," I nearly fainted. I didn't know what to say and I ended up with, "Oh, I didn't know. I was watching television." Thanks loads. Oh well, that's what you get for having a secret crush on a disc jockey. Hi Bob.

Luv, Pat H.
★

To Cathy De Vaney of La Habra:

Please write to me because I forgot your address! I've got some very important news from Peter and Gordon.

Rosalie of San Pedro.
☆

Dear BEAT,

I've noticed most rock 'n' roll groups that hit big are male groups, like the Rolling Stones, Beatles, DC5, Herman's Hermits, etc.

Girls have all those men to swoon over and even the younger girls have Dino, Desi and Billy.

Now, all you talented girls, us *boys* need some girl bands to swoon over and collect pin-ups since we're too young to buy *Playboy*!

So how about some female Hermits?

Simi Sam

... EQUAL FAME ON THE STRIPS

KRLA ARCHIVES

Fan Clubs

(For information from any of the listed fan clubs enclose a self-addressed, stamped envelope.)

SOUL INC
c/o Dewey Reeves
1616 N. Argyle Ave.,
Hollywood, Calif.

ROLLING STONES
Tina Zink
130 E. Greenwood
La Habra, Calif.

MISSING LINKS
Laura Best
2125 S. Crescent Heights
L. A. 34, Calif.

BARBARIANS
Kathy Doyle and
Juliet Butterworth
400 John St.,
Manhattan Beach, Calif.

JOEY PAIGE
Mary Lutes
7311½ Seashore
Newport Beach, Calif.

SAL VALENTINO
Patti Uliana
7629 23rd St.,
Sacramento, Calif. 95832

PAUL REVERE and THE RAIDERS
Kylie Schribner
7216 S. E. 30th
Portland, Oregon

DUSTY SPRINGFIELD
Peter Jones
200 W. 57th St.
Suite 1204
New York, N.Y.

EVERLY BROS.
Catherine Jennings
95 S. Burritt St.,
New Britain, Conn.

WAYNE NEWTON
Robin Blair
347 Steele St.,
New Britain, Conn.

BILLY J. KRAMER and THE DAKOTAS
Susan Caughron
2334 South Kella Ave.,
Whittier, Calif. 90601

HERMAN'S HERMITS
16537 Sunset Blvd.
Pacific Palisades, Calif.

SONNY & CHER
4705 W. 191 St.
Torrance, Calif. 90503

DINO, DESI AND BILLY
Debbie Kent
6514 Oakdale Avenue
Woodland Hills, Calif. 91364

The above information is provided as a service to our readers. Accuracy of the information you receive is the responsibility of the officials of each club.

DANCING 7 NIGHTS A WEEK
PANDORA'S BOX
8118 SUNSET STRIP

Even ordinary spys listen to extraordinary KRLA

CASEY'S QUIZ

By CASEY KASEM

A number of years ago, a family in Beaver Dam, Wisconsin came to a decision. For some time they'd been wondering whether it would be wise to fulfill a long-time ambition and move to Southern California, and they finally decided to take the big step, hoping everything would work out. One of the family members was a small boy who later went on to become president of his high school, a prominent area athlete and a member of one of the most successful vocal duos in record history. And he still turns a little pale every time he remembers the day they almost decided not to go West!

Answer: Bobby Hatfield of the Righteous Bros.

Back issues of the KRLA BEAT are still available, for a limited time. If you've missed an issue of particular interest to you, send 15 cents for each copy wanted, along with a self-addressed stamped envelope to:

KRLA BEAT   Suite 504   6290 Sunset Blvd.
Hollywood, California 90028

ISSUES AVAILABLE
- 3/31 — BEATLE TITLE CHOSEN
- 4/14 — INTERVIEW WITH JOHN LENNON
- 4/21 — INTERVIEW WITH PAUL McCARTNEY
- 4/28 — CHIMP EXCITES TEEN FAIR
- 5/5 — HERMANIA SPREADS
- 5/12 — HERE COME THE BEATLES
- 5/19 — VISIT WITH BEATLES
- 5/26 — FAB NEW BEATLE QUIZ
- 6/9 — BEATLES
- 6/16 — BATTLE OF THE BEAT
- 6/30 — PROBY FIRED
- 7/24 — BEATLES TOP STONES
- 8/7 — DYLAN
- 8/14 — HERMAN
- 8/21 — STONES TESTIFY
- 8/28 — KRLA PRESENTS THE BEATLES
- 9/4 — BEATLES . . . . IN PERSON NOW!
- 9/11 — THE THREE FACES OF BOB DYLAN
- 9/18 — PROTESTOR BARRY McGUIRE
- 9/25 — SONNY

HELP! . . . HELP! . . .

Sue in San Diego
HELP!
I need somebody! That somebody is a girl named Sue who lives in San Diego and joined my fan club for Herman's Hermits, but forgot to put her last name and address. Please help me! Write to: Greer Eagleson, 9191 Randall Avenue, Whittier, California.

Beatle Cards
HELP!
I'm making a vest made of Beatle cards but ran out. If any BEAT reader has any extra Beatle cards please send them to: Robert Julius, 12117 Havana Avenue, Sylmar, California.

HELP!
We need teens between 14-17 to join our newly formed Teen Amateur Movie Group. All we require is that you live in the vicinity of Alhambra. We need a stage crew badly. If you are interested call Mike at 284-8966.

HELP!
Female drummer-vocalist wanted. Ages 14 to 15 in the Upland Ontario-Alta Loma area. Please contact Gloria Hamblin, YUkon 2-1929.

Pictures To Trade
HELP!
I have a lot of pictures of all British and American entertainers that I will trade for any pictures of the Beatles or Rolling Stones. Be sure to list three choices for each trade. This includes Beatle Cards. Please enclose stamped, self-addressed envelopes for picture swaps. Please do not fold pictures. Send to Pat Enos, 677 Larimore, La Puente, Calif., 91744.

L. P.'s To Trade
HELP!
I have three L.P.'s that I want to trade for anything by Chuck Berry, The Supremes, The Righteous Brothers, James Brown or Dionne Warwick. I have "Jan and Dean—Command Performance," "The Kinks," and "Kinks-Size." Please write to Fran Dorfman, 1206 N. Amalfi Drive, Pacific Palisades, Calif., 90272.

Snare Drums For Sale
HELP!
Must sell snare drum, symbols. Sixteen inch, eight inch snare drum is a St. George, blue sparkle finish. Please write Jack Krevoy, 2812 Anchor Ave., Los Angeles, Calif., 90064.

KRLA BEAT SUBSCRIPTION

you will SAVE 60% of the regular price!
AN INTRODUCTORY SPECIAL . . . if you subscribe now . . .

☐ 1 YEAR — 52 Issues — $3.00   ☐ 2 YEARS — $5.00

Enclosed is $..........................

Send to:.. Age:............

Address:..

City:... State:......................... Zip:...............

MAIL YOUR ORDER TO: KRLA BEAT
1401 South Oak Knoll Avenue
Pasadena, California 91106

Outside U.S.: $9.00 — 52 Issues

KRLA ARCHIVES

THE ROLLING STONES, in town for a recording session at RCA, stage a reunion with the KRLA disc jockeys. From left: Bob Eubanks, Bill Slater, Charley O'Donnell, Charlie Watts, Keith Richard, Dick Biondi, Brian Jones, Dave Hull, Bill Wyman, Mick Jagger.

SAL MINEO IN CHAT WITH KRLA's DICK BIONDI, CHARLIE O'DONNELL

TV Execs Produce Big New Pop Show, Then Shelve It

A new rock TV series described by insiders as rivalling *Hullaballoo* and *Shindig* in quality and produced by an award-winning staff may just wind up a might-have-been, The BEAT has learned.

With movie star Sal Mineo as regular weekly host, the projected series of weekly showcases for the best in pop and rock is titled *TJ's*. A first sample program, or pilot, has already been filmed but is sitting on the shelf at ABC-TV. It had been scheduled originally for a time slot on the network in the fall of 1966.

Stars of the pilot show are the Dave Clark Five. The BEAT learned, in keeping with the program's intended policy to feature one young star or group each week. Produced by Emmy award-winning Jimmie Baker, *TJ's* is directed by Steve Binder from the *Danny Kaye Show*. Both Baker and Binder have deep and varied experience in musical productions on television.

First seen as a natural twin to *Shindig* on ABC-TV, the new series later suffered the fate of many programs in television — a change of heart and mind by the highly placed executives.

"It should have got on the air," an informed source told The BEAT, "but now the only way it will is if something else, some other program falls off. Then it could fill the opening. What a shame — it was much better than either *Shindig* or *Hullabaloo*."

READER CALLS FOR ACTION
Protest Songs Fine, If They Offer Hope

The BEAT received a rather interesting and thought-provoking letter recently which we felt we would like to share with you. It was written by one of our readers, Paul Shactee.

Dear BEAT:

P.F. Sloan's "Eve Of Destruction" seems to be a very hopeless and pessimistic song with regards to ever finding solutions to the problems which are bugging and terrifying so many of us today.

Over all, it is written as though the person was looking at the world with only one eye. He just sees everything ugly.

Sure, these ugly things do exist but I'm fed up with protest songs that just state truths which are only part (and a small part too) of the big reality of life.

If Sloan is trying to be as truthful as Bob Dylan he is doing a poor job. Dylan feels that there is much hope in the world by penning such songs as "Blowin' In The Wind" and "Chimes Of Freedom."

Admittedly, Dylan does sometimes get depressing with his thoughts of despair but he still knows that there *is* hope.

For a great protest song one would have to look around at the freedom chants of the American Negro which definitely state that they have so much hardship, yet still they are sure that they will ride at the front of the bus and "overcome."

Protest songs are good for pointing out injustice, wrongs, problems and causes for things but they should be completed with the thought of overcoming the wrongs.

When people stop and listen to a song that says there's no hope, "We're on the eve of destruction," they get driven to the depths of despair and darkness.

The Indians have had a long string of injustices done them and can now find voices with the tongues of Peter La Farge ("Ballad of Ira Hayes"), Buffy Saint-Marie ("Now That The Buffalo's Gone") and Johnny Cash. All of them are Indians.

As of yet, the Spanish-Americans remain silent, yet they are often treated miserably. They and other Latin minorities are being drowned in the Negro tide. The Negro also has long awaited attention and concern and final action in response to his ceaseless struggles.

So what I'm trying to say is that if you really want peace and security you have to do something about it. Don't just listen. You must sing out too!

Buy a record and make it number one but if you really want change, you have to push for it. And to get into the feeling of doing something one has to know that there is hope. He mustn't let songs saying "Forget it, you're bound to die" turn him around.

KRLA ARCHIVES

BE A DREAMER
Road to Success Paved in Dreams

by "Elinore"

Fellows and gals, have your folks and your teachers told you to quit that dreaming? If so, don't listen to them — go right ahead and dream!

Some of our outstanding successes in show biz were dreamers, but adults are funny, so don't mention this to them. Mention Edison, who tested thousands of filaments to light his lamp, and through these tedious experiments kept right on dreaming that it could be done. Da Vinci sketched jets and subs hundreds of years before anyone else could believe that such miracles would be possible.

Walt Disney has said, "You don't work for a dollar. You work to create and have fun." His special joy is Disneyland because he can keep adding and perfecting, while movies are finished and unchangeable.

Great Dreamer

Now to get back to show biz — where many BEAT readers would like to be, let me mention one of the greatest dreamers on the scene — Roy Orbison. Not only because of the collection of dreams in his "In Dreams" LP, but because of the wonderful inspiration woven into the fabric of his songs.

Characters in his songs often have humble beginnings, just as you and I, and we get a personal life from their optimism or success. In "Blue Bayou" when Roy sings about "saving nickles, saving dimes; working 'til the sun don't shine", he becomes one of us. In "Uptown" we wish along with him, "One of these days I'm gonna have money . . . a big car . . . fine clothes . . ."; and in *Working for the Man*, when he declares, "I'm gonna BE the man!," we decide we WILL be, too.

For we see what dreams can do. Roy not only has five cars and wears fine threads — Italian style. He has a million dollar contract with MGM; record sales on Monument of over *20 million discs,* (4 million of *"Oh, Pretty Woman"*); six tours of the United Kingdom where his fan club membership is well over a thousand; and he's composed close to 200 songs, many published by Acuff-Rose. How's *that* for a success story?

Hard Day's Night

The Beatles were dreamers too, and for those who still believe success just fell into their laps, more should be said about their early struggles. How Ringo pounded the skins 12 hours a night, working with almost every group on the stand. How the Nurk Twins — John and Paul — wouldn't give up without a final try when luck was down. How George progressed from simple chords to his terrific lead of today by practicing tirelessly on his dozen guitars.

Now you may wonder what all this has to do with you? You don't visualize like Da-Vinci or Disney. You don't have the persistance of Edison, the fantastic voice and mind of Orbison, or the unique background of a Beatle.

But you do have a mind with not only an INTELLIGENCE LEVEL but a CREATIVE LEVEL as well. You need only recognize it and develop it.

Here is how you will do it:
(1) Dream
(2) Visualize
(3) Create

Do Something

The secret of success of course — and here is where your parents and teachers will agree — is to do something about your dreams. If music is your desire — wonderful! You know the left side of your brain controls the right side of your body, and vice versa. Practice a piano and you will learn to use *both sides of your brain at once.* I feel the same is true of many other musical instruments. Tell this to Mom if she objects to you having a drum kit in your room! If you want your parents to sponsor an instrument or a typewriter, tell them it's to develop manual dexterity — an indispensable job skill you'll be needing.

If you're still not able to promote an instrument, use your voice to sing. (That may be just the move to prod your family into action.) Let's say you don't have the swingin' style of Elvis, or the fantastic vocal range of Roy. But you remember lyrics and sing more or less in tune, on key, not too flat. So now you can practice your breathing and phrasing, and work on tonal quality, depending on the type of music you are singing. Now you may need a tambourine to shake and you're in. Sing with a group and earn the bread to buy that Electric Guitar and Amplifier you've been dreaming of. Gals, you don't even need the tambourine. Just learn to express yourself with your hands as well as your voice.

In addition to developing your talent — music, gardening, handicraft, cooking, or whatever, keep in mind the positive approach with things you *don't* do well. Instead of saying "I can't", say "I'll try".

DANCING 7 NIGHTS A WEEK
PANDORA'S BOX
8118 SUNSET STRIP

Which Car Wins - 'Shocks' or 'Jocks'?

HERMAN MUNSTER GIVES DAVE HULL a hypnotic argument that his "Munstermobile" is still king of the road. Bob Eubanks and Emperor Hudson laughingly insist that he's dead wrong. Herman drove by the KRLA studios to take the boys for a scenic drive through the cemetery, only to discover that his Munster Roadster was no longer in style.

WITH ASSISTANCE FROM DICK BONDI, Dave proudly prepares for a spin in the most regal coach in existence—the KRL"A".

BYRDS' GENE CLARK (right) describes their visits with Beatles—both in England and Southern California—to BEAT Reporter Louise Criscione and KRLA Deejay Bill Slater.

KRLA ARCHIVES

KRLA Tunedex

EMPEROR HUDSON

CHARLIE O'DONNELL

CASEY KASEM

JOHNNY HAYES

BOB EUBANKS

DAVE HULL

DICK BIONDI

BILL SLATER

KRLA BEAT
6290 Sunset, No. 504
Hollywood, Cal. 90028

BULK RATE
U.S. Postage
PAID
Los Angeles, Calif.
Permit No. 25497

This Week	Last Week	Title	Artist
1	1	LIAR, LIAR	The Castaways
2	2	BABY I'M YOURS	Barbara Lewis
3	5	THE "IN" CROWD	Ramsey Lewis Trio
4	4	HELP/I'M DOWN	The Beatles
5	6	DO YOU BELIEVE IN MAGIC	Lovin' Spoonfull
6	13	IN THE MIDNIGHT HOUR	Wilson Pickett
7	7	UNCHAINED MELODY	Righteous Brothers
8	11	EVE OF DESTRUCTION	Barry McGuire
9	12	TAKE ME FOR A LITTLE WHILE	Evie Sands
10	3	LIKE A ROLLING STONE	Bob Dylan
11	10	WE GOTTA GET OUT OF THIS PLACE	The Animals
12	9	YOU WERE ON MY MIND	We Five
13	26	HANG ON SLOOPY	The McCoys
14	29	TREAT HER RIGHT	Roy Head
15	18	MOHAIR SAM	Charlie Rich
16	8	ROSES AND RAINBOWS	Danny Hutton
17	21	THE TRACKS OF MY TEARS	The Miracles
18	35	LOVER'S CONCERTO	The Toys
19	24	YOU'VE GOT YOUR TROUBLES	The Fortunes
20	25	AGENT OO-SOUL	Edwin Starr
21	19	SUMMER NIGHTS	Marianne Faithfull
22	28	CATCH US IF YOU CAN	Dave Clark Five
23	15	HEART FULL OF SOUL	The Yardbirds
24	16	DOWN IN THE BOONDOCKS	Billy Joe Royal
25	27	SINCE I LOST MY BABY	The Temptations
26	36	KEEP ON DANCING	The Gentrys
27	31	DAWN OF CORRECTION	The Spokesmen
28	—	DRUMS A GO GO	Hollywood Persuaders
29	—	UNIVERSAL SOLDIER	Donovan
30	—	EVERYONE'S GONE TO THE MOON	Jonathan King
31	32	HOME OF THE BRAVE	Bonnie & The Treasures
32	34	GIRL FROM PEYTON PLACE	Dickie Lee
33	38	THE WAY OF LOVE	Kathy Kirby
34	33	HOME OF THE BRAVE	Jody Miller
35	39	WITH THESE HANDS	Tom Jones
36	37	YOU'RE THE ONE	The Vogues
37	40	I LIVE FOR THE SUN	The Sunrays
38	—	EVERYBODY LOVES A CLOWN	Gary Lewis & The Playboys
39	—	JUST A LITTLE BIT BETTER	Herman's Hermits
40	—	I KNEW YOU WHEN	Billy Joe Royal

KRLA ARCHIVES

KRLA *Edition* BEAT

Volume 1, Number 30 — LOS ANGELES CALIFORNIA — 15 Cents — October 9, 1965

BEAT Photo: Chuck Boyd

Why Are Paul & Ringo Now Soloing? (Story Inside)

KRLA ARCHIVES

KRLA BEAT

Los Angeles, California — October 9, 1965

Beatles All Pretending They're Single Artists

The Beatles have never been able to stand still—musically, personally or any other way. They're always on the go, always moving and coming up with something just a little different and unique.

After conquering the world as a quartet—becoming more popular in more countries than any other entertainers in history—they have now proven themselves as top singing stars individually.

All four have recently become equally renowned as soloists, and it looks like this may be just the beginning.

It is reflected in their albums and the singles which are released from their albums. Instead of John and Paul doing almost all the singing together we now have Ringo warbling "Act Naturally,"—and singing the western tune as naturally as a hillbilly singer from Tennessee—and Paul with his warmly intimate style reminiscing about "Yesterday."

Those two numbers, on the same 45 r.p.m. disc, have made it the hottest single record on the market.

John again displays his delightful ability as a soloist with a record of his own, "You've Got to Hide Your Love Away." George, who recently signed a separate solo contract with the McCartney-Lennon music publishing firm, turns in a great single performance on "I Need You."

Of course each of these solo efforts still has the great Beatle musical backing but their fans are

JOHN – ALSO A SINGLE

GEORGE – SOLO CONTRACT

HERMAN THE CUTE CUT-UP BECOMES HERMAN THE SHARP-TONGUED CRITIC

OOOH—WHAT HE SAID!

Herman Blasts Byrds, 'B's

There's one thing about Herman and his "little boy" image—he can turn it on and off at will.

And there was no better example than a few days ago when wondering about the significance of this new trend.

Are they doing it for amusement?...as a challenge?...or perhaps just to help lead the pop trend away from the old "one lead singer and the rest of the group in the background" concept. It may even be a combination of these reasons, but whatever their motive there is no talk or even speculation that any of them is considering leaving the group.

And regardless of motive, it also seems like a very healthy development. It adds a touch of variety which seems certain to keep the group scene alive and interesting for years to come.

he suddenly dropped his sweet kid role and began sounding off with some comments that scorched the hair on quite a few people's necks.

The very first thing which Herman wanted to scream about was the condition of the British pop scene.

"All our good groups are leaving the country because it's such a sick scene. In England to earn 300 pounds a night you have to travel miles around. But in America I have earned 8,000 pounds in one night. So why not go to America for a few weeks. Nothing's happening in England.

Kinks Fade

"Look at the Kinks—they started fantastically well but they are just another group now with a 100-yard sprint to catch up with the Big Two, the Stones and the Beatles.

"We're just a group, so why shouldn't we go to America where we are an English group?

"In America I really work on the 'little-boy-lost' image. But it's true—I really am thick!"

That was a mouthful and Herman began to feel just a little bit better but he wasn't quite through yet—he still had some more to say.

In fact, he had a solution for Britain's "sick scene." "We need something new, something as big as the Beatles or the Stones. They are the kings of the theatres and Georgie Fame is king of the clubs.

Knocks Byrds

"As for the Byrds—we've got five million groups as good as the Byrds. They're just a second-hand Rolling Stones.

Next on Herman's agenda was a little mud-slinging in the direction of one of England's top teenage shows, "Ready Steady Go."

"'Ready Steady Go' does more harm than good. The only excitement you get on the show is a shot of a girl's skirt and you say 'how disgusting' and talk about it for hours."

And with that parting shot Herman got down from his soapbox, put on his sweet little boy smile, and went happily off to play the Hermits' next date.

What Causes Beatlemania?

By Eden

You've seen it hundreds of times before—in mob scenes at airports, in screaming crowds of fans at concerts, even in one's and two's sitting 'round the television set when "they" were on.

Yes, you've seen it all before. The girls who scream, the girls who faint—the girls who cry.

Why Do They Cry?

Time and again parents and teachers and other concerned adults ask the same old question—why? Why do they act this way? Why do they cry?

The most obvious and most frequently seen example of this teary problem is to be found in anything even remotely connected with the Beatles.

Beatlemania, as it were, has indeed taken over the world. Members of every age group have found themselves succumbing to this delightful disease, and the main symptom is sheer happiness!

But, what of the young—and not-so-young—girls who scream, faint, and cry at the slightest mention of the Four Fabulous Fellows from Blightyland?

Intensive Research

Psychiatrists, psychologists, and sociologists the world over are among many who have done, and are still doing, intensive research in this area in order to answer this question. As yet, there seems to be no one who has been able to find the answer; perhaps no one ever will.

This reporter does not profess to be a psychiatrist or even an expert in the field of human behavior. But I am a female and I am a Beatlemaniac—and very proud of it. Beatlemania is one of the happiest states of mind conceivable and there is no greater group of people in all the globe as the one we label "Beatlemaniacs."

Through my own personal encounters and experiences with Beatlemania, I have been able to draw some conclusions and form a few answers of my own. Per-

Turn to page 11

Inside the BEAT

Star Loses His Hair	4
On the Beat	4
Adult Music Myth	4
The Emperor	5
Readers' Opinions	6
Dave Hull Antics	10
Susan's Answers	11
Report From the Cavern	12
The Shindigger	15
Tips to Teens	16
British Top 10	16
KRLA Tunedex	Back Cover

The KRLA BEAT is published weekly by BEAT Publications; editorial and advertising offices at 6290 Sunset Boulevard, Suite 504, Hollywood, California 90028.

Single copy price, 15 cents. Subscription price, U.S. and possessions, $3 per year or $5 for two years. Canada and foreign rates, $9 per year or $14 for two years.

Exclusive distribution handled by Miller-Freeman Publications, 6328 Lewis Avenue, Long Beach, California. Inquiries should be directed to the attention of David Thomas.

BEATLES-EYE VIEW OF BEATLEMANIA — NATURE PROVIDES A SAFEGUARD

KRLA ARCHIVES

YARDBIRDS WAIL!
Britishers Play For BEAT At A Party

By Louise Criscione

BEAT Photos: Chuck Boyd
..(l. to r.) Beck, Relf, Samwell-Smith, McCarty, Dreja

So desperate were the Yardbirds to play their music for someone that they decided to throw a party.

They figured this way they could kill two birds (not Yardbirds, of course!) with one stone—they could give us a demonstration of the Yardbird sound and they could, at the same time, show their appreciation to those people who had been nice to them on their first visit to America.

And what a party they threw! Kim Fowley was kind enough to donate his way-out house, located high (and I do mean high!) in the hills for this historic occasion.

You see, this was the first time that the Yardbirds had been able to play "live" since they arrived in the U.S.

Going Strong

By the time The BEAT made the scene at 11 o'clock the party was already going strong. Two of the Yardbirds, Chris and Sam, were already there and the tri-level house was packed with an assortment of *everything*. You name it—and it was there!

Such notables as the Byrds, Peter & Gordon, Jackie DeShannon, Phil Spector and Danny Hutton dropped in to give the Yardbirds a listen.

A brand new group, the Brin Smythe, provided the music until we could drive over to the hotel and fetch the other three Yardbirds.

With all five Yardbirds on the scene, equipment was set up and the boys from England gave us an hour of the most fantastic sound you've *ever* heard!

Kim's Pad

Kim's modern house (oops, I mean "pad") provided a perfect backdrop for the Yardbirds' modern sound, a sound which is all their own and which seems to combine rock 'n' roll, rhythm and blues and jazz. Throw it all together, add a touch of Yardbirds, and does it swing!

...Chris Dreja

Seriously, if you think you've seen and heard all there is in the way of English groups—you haven't seen ANYTHING until you see the Yardbirds move and hear them wail!

They didn't touch either one of their big American hits, "For Your Love" and "Heart Full of Soul." Instead they concentrated on long and fantastically good versions of such songs as "Smokestack" and "Hang on Sloopy."

...Jeff Beck

One of the Yardbirds' unique points is the fact that they use each of their instruments to full advantage. Many times in a group the only instruments heard above the voice of the singer are the lead guitar and the drums.

Instruments Utilized

Not so with the Yardbirds. Each instrument is utilized to its fullest capacity, probably because the boys feel that the instrumental part of a song is much more important than the vocal.

Standing out in the Yardbirds' instrumental line-up is the tremendous lead guitar of Jeff Beck. Talk about working a guitar—well, Jeff *slaves* his!

He moves right up to the amplifier to catch the "reverb" and produce that driving sound. The Yardbirds had used the Smythe's amplifiers and since Jeff's process of catching the "reverb" sometimes results in blowing up the amplifier—was the owner of that particular amp scared!

But he needn't have worried—the driving Yardbird sound *was* produced and the amplifier survived the ordeal and is still around.

Keith Relf, of the long blond hair, handles all of the lead vocals as well as harmonica, tambourine and bongos. He wails in the very best tradition of top people in the pop field.

Shade of Burgundy

In fact, Keith was working his poor harmonica so hard that his face became about the shade of burgundy wine!

Chris Dreja lays down the rhythm for the group. He stands sort of off by himself in the corner. He doesn't say much, he doesn't move around much—but he picks his guitar for all he's worth.

Then there is Paul "Sam" Samwell-Smith, known to all as just plain Sam. Sam plays the bass guitar, which in a group is usually a pretty thankless job as far as the audience is concerned, for the bass is rarely heard and is *never* singled out.

But again it's not so with the Yardbirds. You can actually *hear* Sam—he doesn't try to overtake Jeff's lead but you *can* hear him just the same.

The last member of the group provides the Yardbirds' beat. He's Jim McCarty—and can he lay down that time!

Take the person whom you consider to be the best drummer on the pop scene today and then set Jim on a level just above him. And that's how good he is!

You blend these five together—Jeff, Keith, Chris, Sam and Jim—and you have the Yardbird's sound. Of course, to really judge them you've got to see them perform "live" as we did. As good as they are on their records, they are much better in person, as is the case with so many *groups*.

...Jim McCarty

Their manager, Giorgio Gomelsky, explained to The BEAT why: "We try to make our records commercial. But when we perform in a club we like a lot of atmosphere."

After telling Giorgio how fantastic we though the Yardbirds were, he replied: "Well, actually tonight they were a little nervous and, of course, they didn't have their own equipment or amplifiers. You should see them when they're in a regular club or ballroom."

e went on to give *us* a complete *rundown* on Yardbird history—and on part of his *own*, too.

Experience in clubs is one thing of which the group has had plenty. When the Stones left the Crawdaddy Club in Richmond, their place was taken by the Yardbirds.

Tough Going

At first it was tough going because, as you well know, Stones' fans are not too keen on other groups attempting to take the Stones' place.

However, after seeing the Yardbirds perform, the club's patronage decided that they weren't so bad after all—were, in fact, quite good.

Theirs is really a kind of Cinderella success story. Soon the Yardbirds were packing the Crawdaddy in the same way in which the Stones had previously jammed the club.

That's also how the bearded Giorgio came into the picture. He was the man responsible for booking the Crawdaddy's talent. He had seen the potential in the Stones, so had booked them and for awhile had been their manager, too.

But the Stones took off so fast that Giorgio was not quite ready to go with them, therefore, the Stones signed with Andrew Oldham.

Ready To Fly

When Giorgio set eyes on the Yardbirds again he smelled the potential and this time he was ready to fly! Opportunity does not usually knock twice at the same door so Giorgio quickly joined forces with the Yardbirds and became their manager.

The boys hit the market with a couple of singles which went nowhere fast. They were strictly rhythm 'n' blues—of the way-out variety. But that's all changed now. Keith explains: "For Your Love" was definitely a swing away from R&B. The market was saturated and now the interest is dwindling. We've seen the signs."

However, the Yardbirds' former lead guitar player, Eric Clapton, evidently did not see the same signs for he refused to play any-

...Keith Relf

thing but pure R&B. His steadfast stand, needless to say, caused the rift which was finally remedied by Eric's departure from the group and his replacement by Jeff Beck.

But this presented another problem. "Eric was very popular," explains Jeff. "Now I honestly find I can't look directly at audiences. I've got this feeling, you know, that they're all there just waiting for me to make a mistake, so they can stand shouting out to get Eric back in the group."

For Authenticity

Sam told Jeff that he was worried about nothing and went on to say: "Eric helped us a lot. Fine. But we couldn't get him to bend his approach at all. He was all for authenticity. We all were... once. But it's useless having a tiny band of fans and failing to get through to the mass audience. Eric hated our hit single, 'For Your Love.' But look at the way it sold."

...Paul Samwell-Smith

Giorgio continued: "This labeling of groups is pure suicide. Groups have to realize that they are entertainers—not merely trend-setters. If everything could just be called "music" we'd all be a lot happier. Why complicate something which is basically so simple."

Of course, the Yardbirds still dig R&B and it is very apparent in their sound. However, they do feel that a group should be versatile enough to change with the times.

Don't think for one minute that the Yardbirds are not completely original. They'll give the public what it wants, but they'll give it to them with a Yardbird sound firmly affixed to it!

And the Yardbird sound is a pretty good sound to give to anybody!

KRLA ARCHIVES

Singer's Stylish Locks Sheared for Uncle Sam

You'll recognize the handsome fellow on the right as Joey Paige, the talented California singer who pals around with the Rolling Stones and favors the long hair popularized by the Stones, Beatles and other English groups.

But Joey recently left for a 30-day stint in the Marine Corps, and the Marines just don't dig long hair. So with heavy heart the popular singer visited his hairdresser and told him to whack it off. A BEAT photographer suffered through the ordeal with him (bottom left) and then snapped the first public photo of the "new" Joey (bottom right) when the clipping was done. Note the bulging ash tray on Joey's lap—he was so nervous that he smoked the entire pack while the hairdresser cut away!

Joey looks "peeled" by comparison, but we have the sad feeling that Marine barbers still won't be satisfied with the results. Did you ever see a leatherneck wearing bangs?

JOEY PAIGE—BEFORE

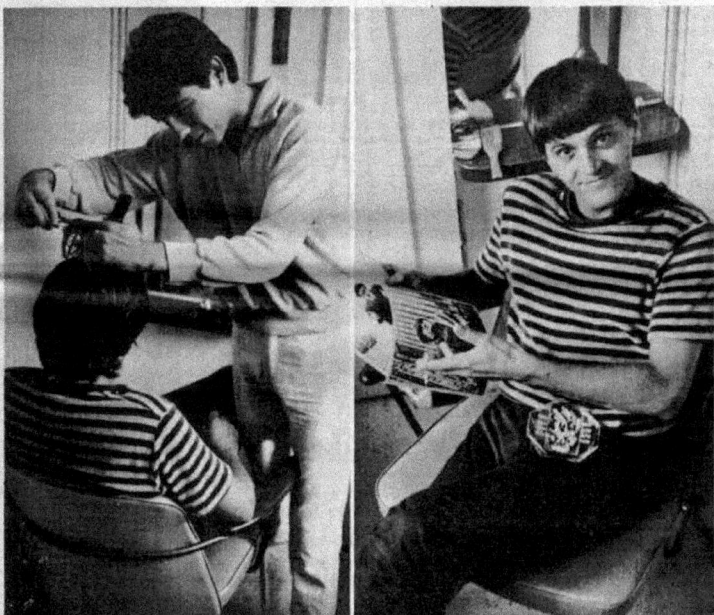
SCISSORS CHANGE "PAIGE BOY" CUT ... TO "DOUGHBOY" CUT

On the BEAT

By Louise Criscione

While the Stones played some dates in Ireland a "hip" camera crew traveled with them shooting the Stones in all kinds of places where you'd *never* expect to find them.

Stones' co-manager, Andrew Oldham, says: "We'll give the film to TV companies to use with our new records and won't charge them. I feel this is all part of the exploitation of a record and must be a part of the business which will grow."

Fontana Leaving

Wayne Fontana is seriously considering leaving the Mindbenders, the group with which he has been for two and a half years. He reveals: "I've been thinking of making a move for some time and had, in fact, decided to sever all professional links with the Mindbenders."

QUICK ONES: Barry McGuire's name has been mentioned as a possible for Herman's Hermits-Fortunes tour of Britain which begins on November 3 ... Shades of the Beatles—three thousand Rolling Stones' fans camped all night outside a Manchester theater to make sure they got tickets for the group's upcoming appearance ... Bob Dylan attended Sonny's & Sher's recording session in New York where they cut "They're Looking In," another Sonny Bono composition ... Donovan has decided *not* to make a popa life-long career. He says: "I don't intend staying too long in this business as I'm not knocked out by it." But when he does leave "this business" he will not desert singing, rather he will spend his time traveling, writing, playing guitar and singing.

Marsden To Wed

It's really official now. Gerry Marsden and his former fan club secretary, Pauline Behan, will tie the knot in their native Liverpool on October 11.

Gary Lewis and his Playboys have thus far failed to even dent the British charts, so they're flying over there this month to see if they can't get something going.

Animals Next Record

While the Animals are in America for their cross-country tour, they will take time off in Los Angeles to cut their next record. The record will be cut at the MGM studios but, unlike the Stones, the Animals do not intend to record exclusively in the U.S. Lead guitarist, Hilton Valentine, explains: "This is the only time we have to record between now and October 22 when the disc is scheduled for release. Our recording manager, Mickie Most, will be joining us for the session."

Enter Zak Starr

Congratulations to the Ringo Starrs on the birth of their son, Zak. Ringo has already given the idea of being a father plenty of thought and he has decided: "I will never send my child to boarding school. And I'll never push him. If he passes tests and gets diplomas and everything, all well and good, but I'll never say, 'You won't get this bike unless you go to college.' And I'll let him decide as he grows up, what he wants to be."

Mick Jagger recently purchased a pair of really far-out pants. They're checked—and I do mean checked—and since he wore them on stage his faithful followers have been flocking to their clothing stores searching for a similar pair. Who knows, maybe Mick will start a whole new trend—with checks, checks everywhere!

QUESTION OF THE WEEK: Will the old Chad and Jeremy be replaced by the new Chad and Jill? It kind of looks that way, what with Jeremy off in Londong doing "Passion Flower Hotel" and Chad and Jill (Chad's wife) busily doing such shows as "Shindig" and "Hullabaloo."

Guess only time will tell about this one.

It's Happening...

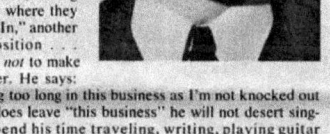

This week, Beaters, we're going to take a short trip to the pop fashion capitol of the world, the place whee "it's all happening, baby"—Merrie Olde England.

In brief notes 'round the Foggy Town, here are what some of Britain's young stars are wearing.

Herman (of the Hermitic fame) has purchased a black suede jacket, designed battledress style. But here's the big surprise: Peter's new coat was purchased right here in the U.S. on a recent American tour!

Beatle Paul McCartney has been sporting a brand new timepiece since his birthday back on June 18. The watch was a gift from manager Brian Epstein, and is made of white gold with a black leather strap. It is long and oblong in shape and it has sort of a modern look to it.

Guess you'll be on time now, huh Paul?

Sweet Cilla Black paid a visit to London's famous Regent Street and plunked down a few of her hard-earned shillings in one of the many small shops for a midnight-blue bikini embroidered with white daisies. Cilla also selected a pair of little round sun shades trimmed with shells.

It all sounds very nice, Cilla, but in Chillie Olde, yet??!

Tom Jones has a passion for jeans with an extra tight fit. In fact, he swears that his are fitted with a shoe horn!!

Really, Mr. Jones!

Chris Curtis of the Searchers seems to be an understudy of one Mr. R. Starkey. Seems that Chris is a 'bug' for antique rings. He collects them wherever he goes and hopes to find some new ones when he returns to America this year.

Gordon Waller, Peter Asher's other half, is also a collector of sorts. Mr. W. boasts a collection of over one hundred hand-made shirts.

And that's what's Happening, this week. Cheerio for now, luvs.

KRLA ARCHIVES

BEAT Photos: Lex Diamond

THE LOVIN' SPOONFUL SHOW WHY THEY'RE IN SUCH DEMAND — THEIR SHOWS ARE A TREAT TO THE EYE AS WELL AS THE EAR.
Enthusiasm is evident as Steve Boone and Zal Yanovsky harmonize to the accompaniment of Joe Butler, drums, and John Sebastian, harmonica.

KRLA ARCHIVES

Readers' Opinions
Destruction or Construction?

Free Choice

Dear *BEAT*:

I saw your great, fabulous and marvy article on "Do Clothes Make the Man?" in a recent issue of your fast-rising teen paper. It was a very good article—well done and explained. I agree with you.

To get to the point. I'm about the greatest fan Sonny and Cher have. My walls are covered with 126 photos of them and 12 articles including your latest on them. To me Sonny and Cher will always be tops over the Beatles or *any* other group or singer. They have a new style (not English) and are loaded with talent. I think their main reason for success is love for each other and their work.

I just bought Cher's fantastic album and there is nothing like it. In the song "See See Rider" there is a part I have a question on. She sings, "Well, I'm going to the Hilton and I know I won't get in, etc." Are these words any relation to their incident at the London Hilton?

I think that any person may wear what he wants anytime-anywhere. If a person only looks at the outside to judge someone, the on-looker must have a questioning pesonality. Let any man choose his clothes, life, love and religion.

Mary Andrews

Another Viewpoint

Dear Editor:

After reading the editorial in *The BEAT* entitled "Tolerance" I would like to say my piece. Beginning with this question: Do you actually think this world is in such a mess?

P. F. Sloan's song, "Eve of Destruction," does bring about many true points, but I agree more with the opposite side. The record "Dawn of Correction" recorded by the Spokesmen is more of the truth, in my opinion.

You can't just look at one side of any argument. If you just open your eyes more, you can easily see that there are as many and *more* improvements in the world than there are "bad" things.

True, this world is in much of a mess, and it will be in more of a mess if people never see all the good! We can't and must not neglect all that is good. We also must realize what is bad so that we can improve it. And we are improving all the time!! We have to work at it though! Nothing comes to any good if we only sit back and point out what is no good or wrong.

Love is as powerful as hate. There is more love around than you know.

Our world is not on the eve of destruction but we are on the dawn of correction!

Denise Davies

Defends Teens

Dear Editors *BEAT*:

In a recent issue of our local paper a "Question Answerer" named Abby wrote an answer to a man who had asked: Why are today's teenagers such an unruly lot?

Abby's answer was, "Our youth now love luxury. They have bad manners, contempt for authority. They show disrespect for their elders, and love chatter in place of exercise. They no longer rise when others enter the room. They contradict their parents, chatter before company, gobble their food and tyrannize their teachers"...

Abby is not the only one who thinks that. When I enter a room with adults in it, I rarely leave the room without later hearing the same adults talking about how today's teenagers are lazy slobs.

As for contradicting parents, well all I can say is that they think that everything should be served on a platter.

Well, we have duties, too. We can't give them anything and everything they want. We aren't completely mature. We're in between. But, is that any reason for us to be put down? Is that any reason for them to treat us like dirt? NO!! I don't think it is.

If you don't agree or have some comment, I'd like to know.

Sue Williams

Dear *BEAT*:

A lot has been said for and against Barry McGuire's hit record "The Eve of Destruction;" so much in fact that I will not go into my personal views on the song, except to say that I like it.

What I don't like however, is what happens every time the song is played on the radio. I do not feel that the song need always be preceeded by a three minute editorial.

Just because a song deals with topics remotely related to world politics, instead of Moon, June, Goon, does it have to be explained and apologized for before it can be played?

To my way of thinking, "Eve of Destruction" simply says: There are still a lot of things wrong that need fixing—right here at home—so don't put your head in the sand, ostrich-style, and say you can't see it. If you won't do anything about it, at least recognize that it's true.

"Dawn of Correction" says: Be an ostrich. There are a few good things happening here and there, so think about them and maybe the bad things will go away.

In my opinion "Eve of Destruction" is the far more realistic and optimistic of the songs. In stating what is wrong it at least points a direction for action.

"Eve of Destruction" is an interesting song sung by a good singer, and as such deserves no apologies or explanations, but should be simply played as the song that it is.

Lori Spring

Lovin' Spoonful

Dear *BEAT*:

The story about the Lovin' Spoonful a few issues back was really fabulous! Maybe that's because the Lovin' Spoonful are really fabulous! Please do some more articles on them as soon as possible. I just can't seem to get enough of them.

Thanks for the best newspaper in print.

Pam DeMenno

THE TURTLES GET READY . . . to follow the signs to San Francisco's Whiskey A-Go Go. The boys just finished a Caravan of Stars tour and will next head out on the Kingsmen's tour. Between tours the Turtles took time off to record their first album which is titled after their smash single, "It Ain't Me Babe."

Luvves Feeling Of 'Being With' Beatles

Dear *BEAT*:

A few issues ago, I read where the *BEAT* staff attended the opening of The Beatles' "Help", and I enjoyed your comments about the film.

My friends and I went to see it tonight and liked it so much we sat through it twice. After I got home, I wrote down some of our comments about the parts we particularly liked. I'm sending them along so we can kind of compare notes.

1. One of our favorite parts was when the Beatles were being chased by that tank and John fell down. The other three said something like "Get up, Johnny—you can walk, Johnny—do it for us, baby." That was really wild. Don't know exactly why. Maybe it was hearing him called Johnny for the first time or something like that. Anyway, we just luved that part.

"Hey, Beatle!"

2. To us, one of the funniest things about the movie was the time that ghastly man (the one leading the chase) came up to one of the boys and said "Hey, Beatle!" It was the way he pronounced the name, as though it rhymed with Seattle. We've been calling them the Be-at-les ever since!

3. We about flipped when George opened the trunk of that car and found Ringo all cuddled up in that orange blanket. The way he looked and the way he said "Hello" so nonchalantly just made us want to hug him!

4. We'll never forget that wild apartment with its separate entrances. It was really fabulous. Especially John's sunken bed and him lying around reading copies of his own book.

5. There were several extra touches that you didn't really have to understand to get what was going on, but it made things all the funnier if you did. Like when they were recording out in the middle of nowhere and a shot of Stonehenge, the centuries-old Druid ruin flashed on the screen. And when the bad guys thought they'd blown up the Beatles' tank and were shooting off their cannons to celebrate the victory. The music behind this was a very famous song called the "1812 Overture" and we about died. (Guess that should show everyone that straight A students like the Beatles, too!) (You'd better believe it!)

Just Sitting

6. Another special favorite was the scene in their flat or apartment where John was singing "You've Got To Hide Your Love Away" and Ringo was sitting in the stepdown "bedroom" playing the tambourine. This was one of the few times the group stood still long enough for us to really get a close look at them. And it gave you a nice feeling for them to be just sitting around, singing for the heck of it.

7. Several of Paul's antics still have us in stitches. When he grabbed that Spearmint wrapper just in time, for instance, and when he was sort of flirting with that weird girl who kept rescuing them. Also when he kept trying to make John quit acting up in front of the camera—that seemed so natural we wondered if it was in the script. Paul is too cute for words, and he's also a very good actor.

8. Another high spot was the scene where John, George and Paul were trying to convince Ringo to cut off his finger. That card game was really a riot, and one of the reasons we sat through the movie two times. We just had to see it again.

Riding Bikes

9. My special favorite was the sequence where the Beatles were riding bicycles. You don't often get to see the Beatles doing an ordinary every-day thing, and when they do, it gives me the shivers for some reason. Every time I think of that scene I imagine what they must have looked like, pedaling around Liverpool about ten years ago. What I wouldn't have given to know them then, and what I wouldn't give to know them now! Isn't it strange how some very natural thing can be more appealing than something that was planned to sort of get the audience going?

10. The end of the movie was another reason we stayed through it twice. When someone put a knife to the head bad guy's throat and the Beatles' voices came over the sound track singing "Help", that was really hilarious! And we also loved that kooky way they featured the titles, with the Beatles kidding around in front of that crazy camera lens of whatever it was.

Really A Blast

All in all, the movie was really a blast. There was only one thing I didn't like about it. For the next few days, even when I was doing something I liked, or in a really good mood, I'd get this funny feeling. It was almost like I was lonely for the Beatles and wanted to run all the way back to the theater and sit through the movies about a hundred more times.

I guess what I really wanted to do was be with them in that wild flat of theirs. Or skiing with them in the Alps.

On second thought, I'm not really telling the truth when I say I don't like that feeling. It may make you a little sad once in a while, but it sure is fun!

If you want to have more fun, or be more fun, see "Help"! It helps!

Annette Costello

KRLA ARCHIVES

KRLA ARCHIVES

Donovan... What's He Up To?
By Susan Frisch

Q—How did you start in this business?
A—I just went to London and did some tapes. That was in January of 1965.
Q—When did you start professionally?
A—I started in January of 1965.
Q—What is your real name?
A—My real name is Donavan Phillips Leitch.
Q—Who are your favorite groups?
A—My favorite groups are: The Byrds, Beatles, Rolling Stones, The Who, The Loving Spoonful, Sonny and Cher, and the Moody Blues.
Q—What do you have to say about the way people say you copy Bob Dylan?
A—It doesn't bother me much. I have better things to think about.
Q—Have you ever met Dylan?
A—Yes.
Q—What do you think of him?
A—I don't. I guess he's like any other pe any other person.
Q—Why do you have long hair?
A—I've always had it. For about three or four years now, anyway.
Q—How do American girls compare with English girls?
A—There's no difference. It's difficult to say; they're the same all over.

Teen Drinking
Q—What do you think of teenage drinking problems we have?
A—Look, people have been drinking all the time. I don't know why they make such a big thing about it now.
Q—Of all the places you have been to, where do you like it the best?
A—I suppose Cornwall, England. It's a rugged, bleak coastline with screaming gulls.
Q—What was your first record?
A—"Catch the Wind."
Q—What label do you record for?
A—I record under PYE, and out here I record under HICKORY.
Q—What is the most attractive quality you find in girls?
A—I wish I could narrow it down to one but I can't. You can just tell.
Q—What is happiness for you?

Peace of Mind
A—Peace of mind through slowness.
Q—Pick one thing you hate more than anything else.
A—I don't hate anything really, but at the moment I hate the way my ear filled up when I took my earring out.
Q—Would you ever date a fan?
A—NO!!!!!
Q—Why?
A—'Cause I don't want to take on the complexes that go with it.
Q—Do you have a girl friend, or are you going steady?
A—No.
Q—What did you do before you became a singer?

Art Student
A—I went to art school.
Q—Is it true that you've had only one suit at the age of 16, and you threw it away, and have never worn one since?

A—Yes. I threw it away because I didn't want to wear it.
Q—Whey do you dress the way you do?
A—Because I don't feel I have to put on any fronts or anything for anything.
Q—Have you yourself felt that you have changed at all since you've become what you are?
A—Yeh, I've had loads of changes but not in ideals. I've gotten quite a few things straight though.
Q—What are (or is) your favorite record?

Indian Music
A—An album of Indian Ragas by Ravi Shankar.
Q—What is the favorite record you've recorded?
A—"Candy Man."
Q—How long did it take you before things really started happening good for you?
A—About one week.
Q—What do you think of the problems the English groups are having trying to attain work permits?
A—I had no trouble—I suppose because I didn't worry about it. I don't think about it though, it doesn't bother me.
Q—What are your personal plans for the future?

Might Quit Soon
A—I plan to write a lot and live on the money I've made now, being this pop artist. It's just a novelty and I might quit soon instead of me just dying down. If I need money I might sell my writings.
Q—What are your future plans in line of tours?
A—Not many, but I might go to Australia.
Q—What is the story behind your earring that you wear?
A—It was given to me by a very legendary folk singer of Ameica whose name was Deroll Addams, a beautiful cat. Beautiful things happened between us—he taught me a lot of beautiful things. Gypsy Dave pierced my ear for me. He wears one too. You might know him as Gypsy Boots as Bobby Dylan so beautifully likes to put it.
Q—I understand you don't like Hollywood. If this is true why did you come back?

Pace Too Fast
A—I like the people, it's the television commercials and the fast pace I don't like. It's too fast for me.

Q—On your guitar there's a sign that says, "This machine kills" well, what does it kill?!
A—It kills war among us.
Q—Why do you have it there?
A—Woody Guthrie had it on his guitar, so I wanted it on mine.

...Donovan chats while BEAT Reporter Susan Frisch takes notes *BEAT Photo: Chuck Boyd*

CLOSING IN on the world famous statue, The Thinker, the Beau Brummels can only be thinking — and hoping — that their new release, "Don't Talk To Strangers," will be a fab success.

A BEAT EDITORIAL
Our Music

Hmmmmm...
That may be a strange way to begin an editorial, but it expresses exactly how we feel at the moment.
About what? Well, it's like this.
You know how some people (who secretly wish they were still teenagers) love to sort of pick on the people who still are.
Our music is a favorite topic for discussion. A discussion that might go something like this.
Whew, that stuff is *ghastly!* How does this *noise* become *popular*, anyway?
Simple! One of three ways.
They can dance to it (if you call that *dancing*). Or the melody and lyrics are *cute* (if you're about *seven*) and they can sing along. Or some group they're fainting over records two or three minutes of *sheer rubbish* and they buy it out of blind (or is it *deaf?*) devotion.
Another thing about that *new sound* of theirs. They don't even know where it *came* from. *They* think it was imported from *England!*
Go ahead, ask one of them if they have any *idea* where and how this all started? Know what they'll say in return?
HUH? That's what. And what's more, they don't even care to *find out!*
Makes you wonder, doesn't it? Wonder about a song called "The Bo Diddley Story".
You can't dance to it. There isn't any tune to sing along with. Hardly anyone faints over the Animals. We're too busy listening.
All the song does is re-trace the history of our music, and pay a debt of gratitude to a man whose contribution will never be forgotten. How *dull!*
Guess that's why this portion of the Animals' stage repertoire, which later became a part of their latest album, is now tearing the charts apart as a single.
We hope we're invited to the next discussion. We'd sure like to hear them explain that one.
Like we said before. Hmmmmm...

KRLA ARCHIVES

Guess Who Beatles Were Listening To?

KRLA was pleasantly surprised to receive the following letter shortly after the Beatles completed their Hollywood Bowl performances:

"As a personal friend of the Beatles and their management, I spent much time with them in New York City; backstage at Shea Stadium and in the center of the field at the stage. I attended the press conference and all their parties and assisted their press officer, Tony Barrow, and Road Managers, Malcolm Evans, Neil Aspanell and Alf Bicknell, in addition to the DJs who toured the country with them.

"In California, I was taken to the Hollywood Bowl concerts and accompanied them to the concert in San Diego. I attended the Capitol Records press conferences, and spent most of the days at the beautiful house in Benedict Canyon.

"So who am I? Just an ordinary secretary who works for NBC's "Hullabaloo".

"Actually, the reason for my telling all this is that I think it may be of special interest to you to know that during their stay at the house in Benedict Canyon, the only sound heard all day was that of KRLA's, from George Harrison's transistor radio. This was my first trip to California, and I want to express my appreciation as well, for KRLA's powerful lineup of entertainment.

"I hope to return to California soon, this time for a longer period, but until then let me just say that I wish they could change the "K" to a "W" and bring the whole KRLA staff and sound to New York City!

"P.S. I would appreciate it if you would advise me of the subscription rate for the KRLA BEAT."

We will not include the young lady's name, since she may not care to be publically identified with such an endorsement due to her position with "Hullabaloo." But we appreciate her thoughtfulness in sending us the above information, as well as the unsolicited compliments.

Personals

To BEAT Readers:
I would like to publicly thank Dell Kennedy for what she did for me in Chicago in regard to Peter Asher. I'll never forget it, Dell, and I appreciate it more than I could ever say. Give my best to Deb and ML and the whole gang. And PETER FOREVER!
— Diana
La Habra

★ ★ ★

To the fab Johnny Hayes:
To Sandy, Russ, & Tom of Norwalk:
Finally got England's newest hit makers. Also Bob Dylan's groove. See you Christmas.
— Sheridan Tahleguah

★ ★ ★

To Juel:
Hope you are enjoying your BEAT in New York and are sharing it with all of your friends.
— Judy

★ ★ ★

To the ETCS:
Confusius say—He who stow away on plane end up in hot water! Right Dave?!

DANCING 7 NIGHTS A WEEK — PANDORA'S BOX

Back issues of the KRLA BEAT are still available, for a limited time. If you've missed an issue of particular interest to you, send 15 cents for each copy wanted, along with a self-addressed stamped envelope to:

KRLA BEAT
Suite 504
6290 Sunset Blvd.
Hollywood, California 90028

ISSUES AVAILABLE
3/31 — BEATLE TITLE CHOSEN
4/14 — INTERVIEW WITH JOHN LENNON
4/21 — INTERVIEW WITH PAUL McCARTNEY
5/5 — HERMANIA SPREADS
5/12 — HERE COME THE BEATLES
5/19 — VISIT WITH BEATLES
5/26 — FAB NEW BEATLE QUIZ
6/9 — BEATLES
6/16 — BATTLE OF THE BEAT
6/30 — PROBY FIRED
7/24 — BEATLES TOP STONES
8/7 — DYLAN
8/14 — HERMAN
8/21 — STONES TESTIFY
8/28 — KRLA PRESENTS THE BEATLES
9/4 — BEATLES... IN PERSON NOW!
9/11 — THE THREE FACES OF BOB DYLAN
9/18 — PROTESTOR BARRY McGUIRE
9/25 — SONNY — HE & CHER HAVE 5 HITS
10/2 — WAS YARDBIRDS' ORDEAL IN VAIN?

"Because there's something about a KRLA Man!!!" — by Mood

THIS WEEK'S BEST BEAT CARTOON was submitted by Mood Sivik of Derry, New Hampshire.

CASEY'S QUIZ
By CASEY KASEM

This famous singer's voice was first heard on records over two years ago, as part of the background on a number of Phil Spector recordings, but it wasn't until 1964 that he came into the foreground and stayed! He was born in Detroit, one of the birthplaces of today's sound, and came to California immediately after finishing school. Singing isn't his only forte. He's also well known as a song-writer, and composed one of the early Righteous Brothers' first two hits. He's also famous for being especially wonderful to his countless fans.

ANSWER: Sonny Bono

KRLA Jingles Becoming Hits

KRLA's new jingle package has turned out to be a smash hit.

Since the station songs were first introduced at the Hollywood Bowl Beatle performances they have been receiving as much fan mail as some of the current hits.

The catchy tunes were produced by KRLA Program Director Mel Hall in conjunction with some of Hollywood's top names.

KRLA BEAT SUBSCRIPTION
you will SAVE 60% of the regular price!
AN INTRODUCTORY SPECIAL... if you subscribe now...

☐ 1 YEAR — 52 Issues — $3.00   ☐ 2 YEARS — $5.00

Enclosed is $..................

Send to:...Age:...........

Address:...

City:.........................State:.................Zip:..........

MAIL YOUR ORDER TO: KRLA BEAT
1401 South Oak Knoll Avenue
Pasadena, California 91106

Outside U.S.: $9.00 — 52 Issues

KRLA ARCHIVES

Dave Hull—Serious, Dedicated...

Pen Pals

Dorienne Doyle
400 John Street
Manhattan Beach, Calif.
90266

Cindy Blackwell
1032 N. Magnolia
Rockport, Texas 73882

Meg Olds
512 Verano Dr.
Santa Barbara, Calif.

Anne Borecki
124 E. Magna Vista
Arcadia, Calif.

Carol Lurran
54 Pitkerro Rd.
Linlather
Dundee, Scotland

Candi Purcell
5302 Yale Ave.
Westminster, Calif. 92683

Chip Wende
900 Geneva St.
Glendale, Calif.

Jan Gothard
925½ S. Wilton Place
Los Angeles, Calif. 90019

Claire Misaki
1453 70th Ave.
Oakland, Calif. 94621

Ann Maher
6 Baird St.
Wilston, Brisbane
Queensland, Australia

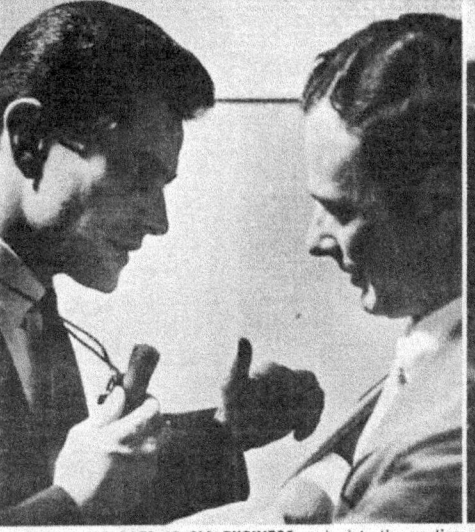

THE HULLABALOOER IS ALL BUSINESS as he intently questions Beatle Manager Brian Epstein (left) verifying a point with KRLA Teen Topper Vaughn Filkins as he pursues an answer.

...But a Devil Around the Ladies!

Help!

HELP!
Four half-breed kittens (Siamese mother) born August 19 and to be given away at age six to eight weeks to good homes. First come—first served. For details, call 363-3286 or write to Sara Jane Turner 17938 Lahey Street, Granada Hills, California 91344.

HELP!
We need you if you are a drummer or a bass guitar player - boy or girl. Qualifications include being between 13 and 15 years old and living near El Monte. Contact Dave Novak, 10724 Asher Street, El Monte, California.

HELP!
I'd like to start a fan club for Paul Revere and the Raiders. I luv 'em! I need some people to HELP me. If interested please write to Donna Stewart, 678 Gleneagles Avenue, Pomona, California.

HELP!
A Japanese girl I know would like to have some American pen pals. She is 17 years old and has black hair and brown eyes. She would like to learn about surfing, the Beatles, the Rolling Stones and other interests of American teens. She will be grateful for your letters. Write to Keiko Schichino, 1607 Obatsuji Fuse-city, Osaka, Japan.

HE TURNS ON THE CHARM when the ladies are around—but they don't seem to complain.

KRLA ARCHIVES

By Susan Frisch

Could you please tell me what George Harrison's favorite TV shows are, and whether he prefers red wine, dry white wine, or sweet white wine?
Marianne Ross

Dear Marianne:
George's favorite shows are all the ones in the line of *Shindig, Ready Steady Go*, etc. As for his preference of wines, I am sorry, I was not able to find this out. However, if it means anything, he luvs light Scotch and Coke, with a touch of lemon.

Has the new Herman movie been released yet? If so, where is it playing, or where will it be playing?
Chris Buckner

Dear Chris:
The new Hermits movie will not be released until Christmas. When it does come out it will be playing at all the local theatres and drive-ins in your neighborhood.

Could you please tell me who sings background of Mick Jagger on the Stones records? Sometimes it is really high pitched and sometimes it sounds like Mick.
Linda Manuel

Dear Linda:
The people who you hear in the background are Keith and Bill. In quite a few of the cases it is Keith that really sings those high notes. For an example, in the song, "Everybody Needs Somebody", the high pitched voice you hear is Keith's.

Could you please tell me the full names and ages of Paul Revere and the Raiders?
Janice Zamzon

Dear Janice:
To begin with there is, naturally, Paul Revere. Then comes Mark Lindsay who is 24, Drake Levin who is 18, Mike Smith, not of DC5 fame, who has 21 years behind him, and next, but not least, Phillip Volk, who is 19. Paul, by the way, is 24, making him not only the leader of the group, but the old man too!!

Do you have any knowledge of the book, "Ode to a High Flying Bird," by Charlie Watts? I want to know where I can buy a copy of it.
Julie Dewitt

Dear Julie:
You should be able to get this book at any of the larger book stores around you. If you have tried and have failed, why not write a letter to Simon & Shuster, 630 5th Avenue, Manhattan, and ask them about the various locations where it may be purchased.

I would like to know if Herman and the Hermits, and the Beatles ever read their fan mail. If so, what address can I send a letter to insure their attention? Don't tell me to write to a fan club because I know it would never get to them.
Terri Murphy

Dear Terri:
Of course they read their letters! If they don't who do you think does?!!! To insure positive reading concerning Herman and the Hermits, you can write a letter to them c/o 20 Manchester Square, London W.1., Eng. This is not a fan club, so don't worry. As for the Beatles, I cannot give out any private addresses, but there is one place that you can write and be sure that they will read it. It is a sort of fan club, and yet it isn't. Regardless, it *will* see your letter through to the boys. Just write to, Beatles U.S.A. Limited, P.O. Box 505, Radio City Station, New York, New York 10019. I promise you that this address does give all the Beatles their mail!

Could you please tell me what Donovan's real name is and his age? Also, is he coming back to America, and if so, when?
Louise Alberti

Dear Louise:
Donovan's full name is, Donovan Phillip Leitch. He was 19 last May. And guess what? I have good news! Donny will be back here in California towards the end of this year.

Would you please tell me where I can write to Barry McGuire?
Name Withheld

Dear "Name Withheld":
You can write to Barry in care of, Dunhill Productions, 321 S. Beverly Drive, Beverly Hills, California.

Will Bobby Sherman be doing any other TV shows besides Shindig this fall?
Cari Hanover

Dear Cari:
It looks as though our Bobby will be quite busy this fall. Besides his regular appearances on *Shindig* he will be appearing on *Ben Casey*, and *Honey West*. A few other TV programs are in mind, but these are nothing definite yet. Also in case you are interested, Bobby has just cut a new record and it should be out shortly. To find out more about it, read *The BEAT*. One of our other reporters is going to be covering it in her column.

Could you please tell me if Barry McGuire was ever in The New Christy Minstrels? And if he was, why, and when did he quit?
Lynda M.

Dear Lynda:
Barry was in the group, and the reason for leaving was because he wanted to become a solo singer. He made his departure in February, 1965.

Do Sonny and Cher buy, or have their clothes made?
"A Fan"

Dear "Fan":
Sonny and Cher have all their GROOVY clothes made up by two dressmakers.

I would like to know the hates and loves, or likes and dislikes, of Paul Revere and the Raiders.
"Me"

Dear "Me":
Here goes: Paul Likes: home life and music; dislikes: phonies. Mark likes: blonde girls and sun; dislikes: phonies. Mike likes: staying up late; dislikes: nothing. Drake likes: girls, dislikes: dishonesty. Phil likes: music and the outdoors, dislikes: nothing yet . . . "I'm too young for prejudice." (Phil will be 20 this Oct. 25.)

Can you please give me George Harrison's address in England?
Judy Bogan

Dear Judy:
George's address is, Fair-Mile Estate, Wall Bungalow, Claremont Esher, Surry, England. He no longer lives in Liverpool.

Could you please tell me what the initials M.B.E. (medals) and I.C.B.M. stand for?
"Stupid"

Dear "Stupid":
M.B.E. stands for, Member of the British Empire. As for I.C.B.M., it stands for, Inter-Continental Ballistic Missile.
About George Harrison. I was wondering if there was in existence a fan club for him alone? If not we would like to hear from anyone interested in starting one.
Marsha Thompson

Dear Marsha:
Looking through our files on fan clubs, I see no particular one for George. However, I will print your address so if any of *The BEAT* readers would like to start one, they may. 1828 39th Street, San Diego, Calif. 92105
Where can I write to Sonny and Cher? I have tried ATCO records but have failed. Please give me an address to write to them where they will read my letter.
Sue Montana

Dear Sue:
I am sorry that your letter did not get through. Try writing to, Greene/Stone Productions Inc., 7715 W. Sunset Blvd., Hollywood, Calif. Good Luck!

WHY IS TRINI LOPEZ SMILING? — Easy. The rocking vocalist just got word from Bullets Durgom, his manager, that his Reprise LP, "Rhythm & Blues," sold over 100,000 copies in first two weeks.

What Causes Beatlemania?

(Continued from page 2)
haps one of these will satisfy this question for someone else.

In America, during the summer of 1964, Beatlemania grew to a mighty peak. For months beforehand, the radio and television stations were flooded with Beatle music and Beatle programs, and every publication of any import in the nation carried news and pictures of the four lads from Liverpool.

Not Close Enough

But all during those preliminary months, the closest source of communication which the Beatlemaniacs in Uncle Samland had with their idols were the radios, television and magazines, and that just wasn't close enough.

Then suddenly—the Beatles had arrived. They were actually *here* on American soil. For the very first time after all those months of waiting, they were close enough to touch, to reach out and touch; they were no longer ten thousand miles away.

And then, the big night of the Beatle concert—a scene which was to be repeated in cities all across the nation. Hundreds and thousands of loyal Beatlemaniacs poured into theatres, stadiums, and amphitheatres around the country for their very first, live Beatle performance. It was an evening which would never be forgotten.

The lights went up, the introductions were made, and then—there they were: THE BEATLES!

The Waiting Girls

And in front of the Beatles were the girls; the girls who had waited for countless days, and weeks, and months. What were they to do now? Their beloved Beatles were now within feet, within *inches* of their grasp, and yet—they could not touch. The Beatles were there—and yet they weren't. For the moment, they were live, in person, ringing their hearts out to their many screaming fans. For that one brief moment—they were *real*. They were no longer a dream. But all too soon that newly-found reality would be shattered. The Beatles would finish their performance and leave, and once again would be but a beautiful fantasy from a far-off land.

And so—happy to see them in reality at long, long last, and yet sad in the knowledge that all too soon they would be gone again—thousands of girls cried. They *wanted* to smile; they wanted to laugh, and smile, and shout, and scream, and cry. They wanted to do *all* of these things at once, because they *felt* all of these things at once. But in their confusion, they could do nothing but cry.

A Good Cry

Whenever the emotions are confused, whenever tension has been built up inside until it reaches the bursting point—the natural reaction is to cry. This is one of Nature's greatest safeguards for the human being who is the product of his own emotions.

Yes, they cry. The foregoing is just one of the many reasons for these tears, but it is also one of the most important.

Beatlemaniacs aren't really so very odd — they are just very human.

**The Mothers
—Soon**

KRLA ARCHIVES

Liverpuddles

By Rob McGrae
Manager, The Cavern

...Earl Preston's REALMS.
BEAT Photo: Neville W. Peyton

This week I would like to tell you about one of the Liverpool groups who have yet to make a big hit record—but I am certain that they will do so very soon. Their name: Earl Preston's REALMS. They have been on the Liverpool scene for quite some time, now.

Earl Preston, the singer and leader of the group, been singing in the Liverpool clubs such as the Cavern for five years now, his first group being the T.T.'s. The REALMS have been together for about three years.

"Good Looks" First

When forming the group Earl Preston decided—or so he says—to pick a group with good looks first and musical ability second. However, all has worked out well, for not only are the boys good-looking but they are also first-class musicians. They have during the past three years built up a very large fan following.

The members of the group:

On drums, Tommy Kelly, 19-years-old; he also takes the lead in some of the vocals. Tommy told me when I spoke with him recently that his hobby is Girls-Girls-Girls, and from what I have seen, the girls love him.

Bass guitarist and vocalist is John Caulfield, 21. John has wonderful blond hair and amongst his hobbies rates horse riding as his favorite.

The lead guitarist is Tony Priestly, 22, and a great fan of Gene McDaniels. On organ is Dave Tynan, 22.

A Character

The newest member of the group is saxophonist Tommy Huskey who has been with the group 18 months and is 23 years old. Tommy is quite a "character" and a great musician who has ever been found "busking" *(Ed. note: "Busking" is Liverpudlian for ad libbing without any music)* outside theatres to earn extra money for himself.

All members of the REALMS are great comedians in true Liverpool style and you will be able to see and hear them in a documentary film, "Liverpool Au-Go-Go," to be networked on American TV. The boys are looking forward hopefully to October 8, when their third record is due for release in England. It is called, "Memory of Our Love," and was in fact written for Elvis Presley. It was given to the REALMS by Herman's manager. The record is to be released in the U.S. later in the year.

By the way, if you would like to write to the REALMS you may do so by writing them c/o The Cavern. I have been assured by them that they will answer all your letters as they would love to hear from you.

Cavern Competition

I am sure that a lot of you would like to have a souvenier from The Cavern, so I have decided to hold a competition. The prizes will be for the two correct answers to the following question:

HOW MANY APPEARANCES DID THE BEATLES MAKE AT THE CAVERN?

The prizes will be:
1. A piece of the actual stage on which The Beatles performed;
2. A genuine five-feet by four-feet Cavern poster;
3. A Cavern book which tells you all that you might wish to know about this famous location;
4. A Cavern pen.

The first two correct entries will each get these prizes . . . PLUS: an autographed photo of Earl Preston's REALMS. In addition to this there will also be 20 consolation prizes of Cavern pens. So get busy sending your answers to: 17 Heydean Road, Allerton, Liverpool 18, England.

'Trimming' – 10 Easy Lessons
By SHIRLEY POSTON

Fads may come and fads may go, but here's one that's bound to be going great guns for a long time to come.

It's called "Trimming", it originated just recently in California, and watch it catch on all over the country!

It all began when a group of high school seniors in Los Angeles decided to do something about one of the problems that seems to happen at the start of every school year.

Students return to school in great shape because of all the activity of the summer, but when they get back to sitting in a classroom most of every day, their horizons aren't all that begin to broaden.

Fun To Do

"Trimming" is, in a word, exercising. But the kind of exercise that's as much fun to do as it is *easy* to do. It doesn't require going off into a dark corner by yourself or take up one extra ounce of the time you have so little of what with homework and all that. "Trimming" is incorporated into the things you do every day, and here are ten ways to join the fad and the fun.

1. While dancing, touch your toes at least five times during each number, in time to the music. Any song will do fine as long as it has a lively background beat. (Bet it won't be long before some crafty soul writes a song and a dance especially for "Trimmers".)

2. When you're sitting around watching your favorite show on the telly, putting on extra pounds by snacking away on peanuts or popcorn, sit cross-legged on the floor or couch, placing the bowl of goodies directly in front of you, just slightly out of reach. Then bend in the middle and grab one peanut or kernel at a time. Place the bowl to either side for variation.

Give A Yawn

3. Add a little "Trimming" to your homework sessions by simulating a yawn every so often. (Don't really yawn or you'll make yourself sleepy. Just pretend to.) This is great for the facial muscles and people won't point even if you do this in study hall. They'll just think you're terribly bored by it all.

4. When you're cleaning your room, picking up clothes, records, etc., plant both feet firmly on the floor and bend from the waist. When you're putting things on the top shelves of your closet, don't take the easy way out and stand on a chair. Reach, while standing rigid on your tiptoes.

5. Stop sauntering up the stairs at home or school. Sort of bounce instead. The more bounce the better as this awakens a lot of lazy muscles.

6. When you're walking home from a friend's house, or from classes, run don't walk. Well, not *run* actually. March is a better word for it. If you don't have a transistor radio to accompany your stalking about, hum "Anchors Aweigh" or some such and march off into the sunset. Marching activates more muscles than just walking, and burns more calories. It also enables you to walk almost as fast as you could run.

Turn Head, Too

7. Looking from left to right is more or less an automatic reflex when you're driving a car. Add a little power to the motion and this becomes a method of "Trimming". Don't just turn your head at corners. Bend each way *from the waist*.

8. When you're putting your books away in your locker, don't just toss them in. Put them on the floor and pick them up one at a time.

9. Talking on the telephone is a perfect background for this "Trimming" exercise. While you're gabbing, lie flat on the floor or couch or what have you. With your ankles together, raise your legs as high as they'll go and then lower them as slowly as possible. This will be a little uncomfortable at first, but you'll get used to it and be glad you did!

10. When you set your hair, sit in a straight chair, keeping your back firmly pressed against the chair. This is great for posture. Then, each time you put in a roller, reach both arms high before starting the next curl.

These are only ten of the unlimited possibilities for "Trimming." Let us know if you can think of any others and we'll print them here in *The BEAT.* We'll try them, too!

Sullivan's Last Beatle Program Is Still a Thrill

An entire nation of Beatlemanics still hasn't recovered from viewing John, Paul, George and Ringo on "Sullivan Show."

And who wants to recover? The foursome, clad Sullivan-show-style in conservative dark suits and ties, treated us to six live numbers and seemed in the liveliest of moods.

Paul was especially bouncy, and turned serious only during his soulful "Yesterday" solo, a song destined to be the Beatles' next number one disc.

Ringo's big moment was prefaced by a quip from Paul, who announced that the next number would be done by someone who "doesn't get to sing much except every night." Our favorite drummer boy then launched into his "Act Naturally" with Paul helping on the harmony.

John did a great job of playing the electric piano with his elbow in "I'm Down."

Hard-working George handled his lead guitar cores with ease, as always, and added the Harrison touch to several of the vocals.

The Beatles closed their miniature concert with "Help", the song that's still riding high on the charts.

Sullivan paid the group a *really big* compliment by stating it was an honor to have them back on the *shew.*

Took the words right out of our mouths, he did.

KRLA ARCHIVES

DO YOU RECOGNIZE THE NEW JERRY NAYLOR? Jerry's changed his look a little bit by wearing his hair combed forward and his clothes more casual. He looked good before — but now he looks even better! He's also doing big business since going solo. He recently opened Les Poupees club in San Jose where his back-up group was the Sinners instead of his famous Crickets. Jerry packed the place every night and no wonder — this guy has talent!

Ventures Will Offer More Guitar Lessons

If you were one of those who filled out the questionaire that went along with the Ventures' album, "Play Guitar with the Ventures," some months ago, you may really have started something.

As a result of the replies to its questionaire card enclosed with the LP, reported Don Blocker who helped create the package, Dolton Records is now ready with follow-up album ideas along the same lines as the first.

The idea was kind of cute, remember? It was designed to teach you to play guitar using what the company called the "Guitar-Phonics" system. In the questionaire you were asked what styles of guitar you would like to learn and what tunes from the Ventures' repertoire you would dig playing, among other similar questions.

Dolton reports selling more than 52,000 copies of that first album; now, according to Blocker, the second package using the "Guitar-Phonics" system is due for release in November.

Because of the success of the questionaire placed in only 1,000 albums of the first release, says Blocker, the next such one will be based entirely on information taken from the cards.

The "Guitar-Phonics" system provides students diagrams for placing the fingers on the fingerboard to get the correct chords. In addition, the LP teaches lead, rhythm and bass guitar.

Record Quiz

Many of today's hit records have something in common. A certain word that continues to crop up in the title of disc after disc.

Next time you have a few minutes to spare, put on your thinking cap and see if you can come up with the word, and match the names of the artists with the five hits listed.

It won't win you any prizes or awards, but you'll find it a marvelous waste of time when there isn't anything better to do.

The songs (minus that certain word) are listed below, as are their singers. You'll find only four artists listed for five songs because one of the songbirds in question recorded not one but two of the tunes mentioned.

1. "Make Me Your _____"
2. "Since I Lost My _____"
3. "_____ I'm Yours"
4. "I Don't Wanna Lose You _____"
5. "_____ Don't Go"

A. Sonny & Cher
B. Chad & Jeremy
C. The Temptations
D. Barbara Lewis

ANSWERS (AND STOP READING THEM UPSIDE DOWN): The word is baby and the match-'em-up answers are (1) D, (2) C, (3) D, (4) B, and (5) A.

For Girls Only

By SHIRLEY POSTON

I'm in the kookiest mood today. I'm not even going to discourage the sneaky boys who are reading this column again. So let them!

Why am I in such rare good humor? Well, you know how you're always reading about really nutty things that happen to other people but never to you or anyone you know?

Times must be changing because I've had two of the wildest experiences lately, and you might just as well prepare yourselves because I'm about to rave on about both. (Don't fret, you need the sleep.)

Battered Car

First of all, about three years ago, I read the funniest thing about this boy who had kind of a battered car. He took a girl to a drive-in restaurant and when the waitress put the tray on the car door, the door fell off right in the middle of the parking lot.

My experience wasn't quite that hysterical, but almost. My little brother (little above the eyebrows only — he's sixteen and six feet tall) decided he was going to take the hundred dollars he earned this summer and buy a car.

He was trying out this really junky looking heap and threatened me into going for a ride with him. Every time we went over a pebble in the road I about bounced into next week, but I kept quiet (meaning I didn't laugh out loud) until we pulled up in front of the house.

Then he swaggered out and, playing the big man, decided to open the car door for me. Well, it fell off right in his hand! Not the handle, either. The whole door!

I thought I was going to die laughing (out loud this time) (very). I don't know what I'd have done if this had happened on a date. I suppose it would be horribly embarrassing for the boy. Especially if his date was unable to keep her inner merriment from becoming outer.

Hmmmm. That poses a question I've never really thought about. Wonder what a girl is supposed to do when she's on a date and something really hilarious (but embarrassing to the boy) happens? Hope someone reading this can answer that one, because I can't!

A Real Stinker

I must have said something in a past column about dropping cute little notes to boys because I received a letter on this subject. The girl who wrote seemed to think I was against this, and come to think of it, I guess I am.

It is a lot better than calling a boy, but it can sort of turn him off in your direction. When a boy receives one of those "cute little notes" in the mail, every member of his family just *has* to know what's in it.

If the boy is one of "those", he probably shows them, too! And if he's a real stinker, he shows all his friends also. On the other hand, if he isn't the blabbing sort, he probably gets all red in the face and then *really* gets teased by his family.

But I am all for sending a "not-so-cute" note to a boy who suddenly decides not to call you for about ten years. You know, when you want it to be perfectly clear in his mind that you couldn't care less.

I just foam at the thought of some boy going around thinking I'm languishing over him. I told you about the girl who sent that "BYE" note to my brother and had him talking to himself for days!

Onward to other subjects before I run out of room again.

Clothes Habit

Don't you just love this time of year? September is synonymous with buying clothes in my book. Guess that comes from so many years of going back to school this particular month.

I'll probably never get out of the habit. Can't you just see me about fifty years from now, wobbling into a department store to buy a back-to-school wardrobe? The clerks will probably call the men in the white coats.

Speaking of men in white coats, I think someone should call them to rescue the person who dreamed up those odder-than-odd boots with holes in the toes. I mean, get serious! Someone has to be kidding, only they aren't!

Well, I've done it again. It's time to go. But before I do, have you seen Wanda The Witch's latest TV commercial? (Wanda The Witch — GOOD GRIEF!) Anyway, this girl is standing out by a touring bus, shrieking at her male-type companion about her hair not combing.

Surely that commercial isn't trying to lead us to believe that she's going to stay out there in the woods if her hair doesn't shape up. I don't know about you, but if I ever acted like that around any of the boys I know, they'd never speak to me again. They'd also punch me right square in the nose, I hope.

Down, girl. Say goodbye this instant!

So goodbye, keep your letters coming and I'll see you next *Beat*!

Sonny & Cher Now Lecturing College Course

There will be animal skins in the college classroom this fall — and by invitation of the University of California, Los Angeles.

Behind the skins, of course, will be the cheerful self of Sonny Bono who, with Cher and other guests of UCLA, will take part in a most successful annual feature of the university adult extension division — Walter E. Hurst's special fall course, The Music Industry — It's Structure and Economy.

From the title of the course, it all sounds dry and dull. But we'll bet things liven up more than a little when Sonny and Cher get up in front of the class to explain their phenomenal success in making hit records (last time we checked they had five hits going at once).

Other guests invited to speak to the students include Freddie Cannon; *Shindig* producer Leon Mirell; Richard Burns and selected A&R men from various record companies.

WHY SO SERIOUS? That's Sonny Bono's teacher-face he's wearing for his class at UCLA.

KRLA ARCHIVES

PORTMAN'S PLATTERPOOP

HOLLYWOOD—A flying trip to Chicago proved that *The BEAT* is read all over, at least by people who appreciate today's music. The program director of WLS in Chicago was intently reading *The BEAT* to find out what's happening in Los Angeles and San Francisco when I burst into his office..."That's All" is the title of the single being pulled from *Three Midniters* new Chattahoochee album. The requests have been overwhelming!

Gemcor records *The Beckett Quintet*'s Dylan-tune "It's All Over Now Baby Blue" is going across the country. It's tuneful!...*The Righteous Bros.* new single "Gotta Tell You How I Feel" and a January pact for a Las Vegas appearance, with *Sinatra the Elder*, arrived at the same time...Tower records released *Jerry Naylor*'s new single "City Lights" and it should brighten up the record markets.

Lloyd Thaxton, the "Big Daddy" of the dance shows, has entered his third year of presenting this type of program on tv...*The Bea's*, a lovely teen-gal vocal group on Chattahoochee, new single is "Nothing Can Go Wrong"...*Dick Howard*, Shindig's most popular talent buyer, popped for lunch and mentioned that *Jimmy O'Neill* will apply for his 100,000 mile airline club before he begins his 40 city tour with the "Shindig Show". He'll be commuting each week to arrive on Wednesday to tape, then depart for the next locale. What a way to meet thos lovely airline hostesses.

Press Release received by your glaring editor: "As a result of their recent appearance on CBS-TV's Talent Scouts, *The Legiondaires* will be among the first "unknowns" to appear on Scopitone"...Editor's reply: Evidently the person who created this release has never watched the one-eyed juke box, for most of the artists are newcomers to the American public. And then, who wants to invest 25c to view two-and-a-half minutes of music, when you can get 3 for 25c on the normal-type juke machine.

Burt Bacharach, the man who's writing all the teen hits today—oops, sorry *Mr. Dylan*—will write the special song material for Colpix's next effort for *Vince Edwards*. Vince claims it's the music that hasn't given him a hit record, nothing else?

Buddy Greco has developed a fanatic teen-following. His Sept. 28 appearance at H'wood's famed Cocoanut Grove brought out his fans in huge numbers. The boss man of the room hoped they would come inside, but at those prices it was best to wait for their "idol" at the door...Sensational-looking *Deborah Walley* sliced a *Gene Page* arrangement for her first Dee Gee Records effort... Perennial teen-ager *Jack Benny* lifted his pen and scribbled the liner notes for the *Smothers Bros.* new Mercury album, "Mom Always Liked You Best"... *Gene Barry*, my favorite Bond-type character, does his second album for RCA Victor "Love in 5 Towns". Could he be including Chicago?

The Beatles' new single—as if I had to tell you— "Act Naturally"/"Yesterday" is selling in mass quantities...Congratulations to *Ringo* on the birth of his offspring, and pleeze *Ringo*, "You don't have to name it after me"...BBC, the British Broadcasting Company, banned the *McGuire* tune, "Eve of Destruction." With each ban, the record becomes larger. I understand it's the hit of our GI's in Vietnam!

Shelly Fabares, a talented and wonderful human being, signed to appear in *Herman's Hermits'* motion picture. Shelly needs another hit record, so perhaps Herman's magic will rub off...*Leon Mirell*, the boss of Shindig, returned from England and declared that single performers are the vogue in the Jolly Country. He predicts that within six months we'll feel the same way in the U.S. Gee dad, what's going to happen to our *Fearsome Foursome*? Must check to see how the *Los Angeles Rams* are doing!

BEAT Cartoon: Judy Moncz

THE NEW BABY looks strangely familiar, luv.

French Spurn Beatles

If there's anywhere in the world that the Beatles need help, it's in France only.

In spite of their return tour of this country, the Beatles have not been able to crack the almost impenetrable French charts.

Their "Help!" disc has been a powerful international hit elsewhere. At present it has claimed top honors in both America and Britain, and also been at the head of the sales list in Canada, Ireland, Hong Kong, New Zealand, Australia and South Africa.

The Beatles have also registered on the charts of late in Argentina and Singapore, but the only two foreign groups to win recent slots in France are the Rolling Stones ("Satisfaction") and Sam The Sham & The Pharoahs ("Wooly Bully").

Could it be that the French just don't parlez-vous where the Beatles are concerned? It's beginning to look that way.

Just goes to show that fifty million Frenchman *can* be wrong after all.

---

we five » you were on my mind

A&M RECORDS

You won't believe your ears !!!

KRLA ARCHIVES

The Shindigger

Howdy hi, Shindiggers! We're back for another gear gab session and have we ever got a lot of people to speak with today.

Right now I'm sitting on the steps of the famous *Shindig* stage and there are at least thirteen million, five hundred thousand and ninety-four people standing around me — so, let's get started!

There is a man standing over there by the piano who should be very familiar to anyone who is a fan of rock 'n' roll. It's Jerry Lee Lewis. Welcome to Shindig, Jerry Lee — it's good to have you back. C'mon over and tell us what you've been doing. Have you done many personal appearances lately?

"All the time. I play more one-nighters than any other artist in the business. I play twenty-five a month – *every* month!"

Wow! That's a whole lotta concerts, Jerry Lee! Tell me, what do you think of the Beatles and the British sound?

Not British Sound

"The Beatles are original in their style. I like somebody with style. I like 'em 'cause they sing rock 'n' roll. We originated the sound – nobody can say it's the British sound. I can appreciate the Beatles and I like them."

Alright fellas — our next guest is all for you. May I introduce to you beautiful Miss Raquel Welch. H'lo Raquel. Hey — I was really surprised to find out that you were going to sing on the show. What gives? "I've always sung, but I'm an actress. I sing and dance. I get a kick out of a show like this. I'd like to cut records but I don't have time." Thank you, Raquel. Alright all you Miserable Males, you — back to your seats!!

...Billy Preston

"Howdy hi, everybody." Hey gang, look who's here – it's Jimmy O'Neill. Hi Jimmy, what's up?

"Hey, I'm very excited because I've just returned from a very successful whirlwind tour of the country. I really love to travel 'cause it's the most fun I get out of doing *Shindig*: meeting the kids and finding out what they like. By the way, I just did something that was a lot of fun. I am going to be a character in a segment of *The Flintstones* and I've just finished doing the voice for it. The show will be called 'Shinrock!'" Well, you've certainly been keeping yourself busy, Mr. O'Neill.

There is a young man here who is completely in charge of the "Soul Dept." on Shindig and his name is Billy Preston. Billy, will you please clue us in – like, uh, *where* did you get all your "soul?"

"In church!" Oh. Well, what kind of music do you prefer to sing? "Soul music, of course!!"

Ah me — I should have known better than to try and get a straight answer from you! At least tell us a little something about yourself then.

"Well, I like dancing a lot and I do an imitation of James Brown. I'd like to end up like the Beatles – rich!! I play the organ, the piano, and the guitar, and someday I'd like to branch out into all areas of show business. Some of my favorite artists are James Brown, Marvin Gaye, Earl Grant, and my No. One favorite is Ray Charles."

Thank you, Mr. Soul.

Message Dept.

By the way, Shindiggers, I have a couple of messages for you. First of all, Bobby Sherman called and asked me to say hello to everyone 'cause he had to leave for the mid-west. But fear not – Robert will return next week and maybe he'll even sing a few bars of his latest record, "Goody Galum-shus" for us. Secondly, to Jane Nelson and her three friends: keep your orbs glued to this column next week, girls, 'cause the ol' Shindigger will be bringing in your fave raves – Joey Cooper and Delaney Bramlett – to say a few words 'specially for you!

Also, joining us next week will be Jimmy Rodgers, Mike Clifford, Donna Loren, Little Anthony and the Imperials, and Billy Joe Royal so be sure that you fall by, too.

...Donna Loren

This Thursday and Saturday will find loads of excitement aboard Shindig, with exciting guests like the Turtles, Leslie Gore, Donovan, the Dave Clark Five, the Hollies, the Shindogs, Ray Peterson, Billy Joe Royal, the Who, Gerry and the Pacemakers, the Four Tops, and many, many more.

Keep your questions coming in to the Shindigger 'cause they keep me company when I'm all alone and blue. (Not to even *mention* violet!)

Till next week then, remember Shindiggers – no matter what *any*one says: ROCK ON!!!

THE BEAT'S Restless Reporter Asks...

The Question of the Week

WHAT WOULD YOU DO IF YOUR BOYFRIEND SHOWED UP FOR A DATE DRESSED IN ANIMAL SKINS LIKE SONNY BONO?

Answers:

"If it was David McCallum, I'd let him come in. Otherwise I'd get a leash and take it for a walk."
— Darlene Dunn

* * *

"I'd go out with him, of course!"
— Rosie Mata

* * *

"Call the zoo and tell them one of their animals escaped."
— Laurie Eisenberg

* * *

"What else could I do but play like Cher!"
— Dinah Clark

* * *

"Enter him in a dog show."
— Cathy Moran

* * *

"What boyfriend?!"
— Judee Schumacher

* * *

Readers of The BEAT are invited to send in answers to the Restless Reporter's next QUESTION OF THE WEEK, which is:

If actor Robert (Napoleon Solo) Vaughn were a candidate for the office of Governor of California, why would you urge adults to vote for him?

Please keep your answers **short**. Please mail your answers in right away — no later than Wednesday. Remember, the Early Birds catch the free LP records. (All entries become the property of The BEAT.) Mail your entry now to THE QUESTION OF THE WEEK, The BEAT.

Our QUESTION OF THE WEEK has had a great response from you gals — and even from some of you guys. Sorry we can't print all the answers, but these are a few chosen from the mailbags. Each one whose answer is printed will receive in the mail an LP record album.

WELL, BOYS, THEY'VE FINALLY DONE IT — Formed an all-girl group for you guys to drool over. They're simply "The Girls" and, believe it or not, they **are** actually sisters. The group consists of (l. to r.) Diane, who plays rhythm guitar; Rosemary, who plays lead guitar and sings; Margaret, who plays drums; and Sylvia, who plays bass guitar and sings. The Girls are terrific performers who have acquired plenty of avid fans, and leading the pack of admirers is the one and only Bob Dylan.

KRLA ARCHIVES

KRLA Tunedex

EMPEROR HUDSON

CHARLIE O'DONNELL

CASEY KASEM

JOHNNY HAYES

BOB EUBANKS

DAVE HULL

DICK BIONDI

BILL SLATER

KRLA BEAT
6290 Sunset, No. 504
Hollywood, Cal. 90028

This Week	Last Week	Title	Artist
1	1	LIAR, LIAR	The Castaways
2	3	THE "IN" CROWD	Ramsey Lewis Trio
3	18	A LOVER'S CONCERTO	The Toys
4	5	DO YOU BELIEVE IN MAGIC	The Lovin' Spoonful
5	4	HELP!/I'M DOWN	The Beatles
6	2	BABY, I'M YOURS	Barbara Lewis
7	42	YESTERDAY/ACT NATURALLY	The Beatles
8	13	HANG ON SLOOPY	The McCoys
9	6	IN THE MIDNIGHT HOUR	Wilson Pickett
10	11	WE GOTTA GET OUT OF THIS PLACE	The Animals
11	8	EVE OF DESTRUCTION	Barry McGuire
12	14	TREAT HER RIGHT	Roy Head & Traits
13	9	TAKE ME FOR A LITTLE WHILE	Evie Sands
14	15	MOHAIR SAM	Charlie Rich
15	29	UNIVERSAL SOLDIER	Donovan
16	7	UNCHAINED MELODY	The Righteous Brothers
17	30	EVERYONE'S GONE TO THE MOON	Jonathan King
18	10	LIKE A ROLLING STONE	Bob Dylan
19	20	AGENT DOUBLE-O-SOUL	Edwin Starr
20	19	YOU'VE GOT YOUR TROUBLES	The Fortunes
21	27	THE DAWN OF CORRECTION	The Spokesmen
22	22	CATCH US IF YOU CAN	The Dave Clark Five
23	16	ROSES AND RAINBOWS	Danny Hutton
24	17	THE TRACKS OF MY TEARS	The Miracles
25	26	KEEP ON DANCING	The Gentrys
26	33	THE WAY OF LOVE	Kathy Kirby
27	38	EVERYBODY LOVES A CLOWN	Gary Lewis & The Playboys
28	39	JUST A LITTLE BIT BETTER	Herman's Hermits
29	43	CRAWL OUT YOUR WINDOW	Bob Dylan
30	44	THERE BUT FOR FORTUNE	Joan Baez
31	36	YOU'RE THE ONE	The Vogues
32	37	I LIVE FOR THE SUN	The Sunrays
33	40	I KNEW YOU WHEN	Billy Joe Royal
34	47	I'M YOURS	Elvis Presley
35	45	NOT THE LOVIN' KIND	Dino, Desi & Billy
36	41	GOODNIGHT MY LOVE	Joey Paige
37	46	WHAT COLOR (IS A MAN)	Bobby Vinton
38	—	POSITIVELY 4th STREET	Bob Dylan
39	—	MAKE ME YOUR BABY	Barbara Lewis
40	—	LIFETIME OF LONELINESS	Jackie De Shannon

KRLA ARCHIVES

KRLA *Edition* BEAT
MFP

Volume 1, Number 31   LOS ANGELES CALIFORNIA   15 Cents   October 16, 1965

Portrait by June Kelly

Elvis–Ten More Years as King of Pop?

KRLA BEAT

Los Angeles, California — October 16, 1965

EX-BEATLE CHARGES LIBEL

Here's Real Story Behind Best's Suit

A ghost from their past has risen to haunt the Beatles and manager Brian Epstein.

His name is Pete Best, and he's involved them in a $45 million lawsuit that may cause nightmares.

...Best Claims Worst

Pete was once the Beatles' drummer—before Ringo Starr—but after coming to a bitter parting of the ways with John, Paul and George over four years ago he sank into obscurity.

Now the handsome ex-Beatle has filed a huge lawsuit against Brian Epstein, Ringo "and others" both in London and New York Superior Court. Pete accuses Ringo of libel and slander and demands $45 million in damages.

The BEAT learned further that Best claims ownership to original record masters of the Beatles cut in Hamburg, Germany, in 1961 (while they were playing at the "Top Ten" Club) and is releasing two albums of these sides both in the U.S. and Great Britain.

The first single, already released, is titled "Best of the Beatles." The following album will be called "The Young Savage Beatles." Neither title is apt to help the digestion of John, Paul, George and Ringo. *Turn to page 14*

Pop Music World Hails King Elvis!

By John Tynan Managing Editor

Wonders abound in the world of pop recording. But as wondrous as many groups and performers may seem today, all too often they quickly become tomorrow's forgotten as they slip from the hit record charts, as their fortunes wane in the public eye.

Today The Beatles rule. Tomorrow? Hope as we most certainly do that the fortunes of The Beatles will never fade, we are reminded of those many performers whose careers turned out to be short-lived.

We Giggled

Probably the most notable exception in today's pop music and movies is a young man originally from the rustic town of Tupelo, Miss. When we first heard his name we giggled. He wiggled. We wriggled—in delight at his dancing and singing. And at his looks, of course.

We bought his records—singles and albums—in numbers so vast it is estimated that RCA Victor Records grossed $150 million on their sales.

We went to his movies so consistently and in numbers so numerous that we made of him one of the most valuable "properties" any manager (the well-known Col. Tom Parker) and any movie producer (Hal Wallis) could wish for.

The lad is, of course, Elvis Presley. He burst onto the pop music scene in the mid-1950s like the horde of Genghis Kahn out of Mongolia. (In fact, some of our parents at that time liked to compare Elvis to Genghis Kahn in terms of the "damage" they said he was doing to the morals of the nation's young people.)

The impact of the Presley coming was so powerful it was a bit hard to believe. So hard, in fact, that a great many adults became fond of predicting his demise approximately every twelve-month.

New Contracts

So far from extinction in the public eye—and ear—is Elvis, in fact, that it came as no surprise at all to The BEAT recently when it was "leaked" to the press that RCA Victor had signed him up

Turn to page 8

...Elvis Still Reigns

TV Men Admit: Shorter Rock Shows Are Zippier

Hullabaloo producer Gary Smith is not very happy over his show's getting cut from an hour to 30 minutes.

Smith said that the shorter version does make for a zippier paced show but "it doesn't give us enough time to really develop ideas when we put acts together to create a certain idea."

"The show is faster because it's shorter," he added. "It's frustrating creatively, but probably commercially will be more successful.

Leon Mirell, Executive producer of *Shindig*, agrees with Smith about a half hour show being more quickly paced but says he prefers the shorter show because it is faster. *Shindig* has now been cut to a half hour also, but is seen twice a week.

"It does make for a different show," Mirell said. "In an hour you get a chance to develop a theme. But in half-hour it is over before you know it and you don't get a chance to build."

"The current sound is folk music with an r&r beat. It's California-originated basically," said Smith, explaining the trip to the Coast.

The cut in time means that *Hullabaloo* will only be able to use four to five guests per show instead of eight to nine.

GEORGIE PORGIE KEY FIGURE

Battle On Bangs

This school year will long be noted for the "battle of the bangs."

Major conflicts are underway in virtually every school district in the land as school administrators enforce strict rules against boys who wear their hair long.

It is even the subject of a popular song, Jody Miller's "Land of the Brave, Home of the Free." Generally the blacklisted long-hairs are finding popular support among the student body, and in some cases they have replaced the football stars as popular heroes.

The girls, too, are having their problems as they encounter bans against short skirts, long "granny" skirts and high boots.

"Distracting"

School officials refuse to allow non-conformists of either sex to attend classes on the grounds that their appearance would be distracting to other students.

But in many cases these school policies are being appealed to the courts, resulting in some eloquent arguments on both sides.

A long-haired teen orchestra leader who has been banned in Boston, George (Georgie Porgie) Leonard, may well decide the fate of thousands of other similar cases.

Georgie Porgie, a senior at Attleboro High School, has been barred from attending classes until his Beatle-like haircut is clipped. Georgie has refused on the grounds that his long hair is necessary for his musical career. He says he'll lose his musical following if he cuts his hair.

Court Hearing

The Massachusetts Supreme Court has agreed to hear the case.

Attorneys for Georgie Porgie have filed a legal brief saying, "Surely a long haircut in the days of Beethoven, Liszt, George Washington and General Custer or bangs as worn by General Ben Butler did not carry with it a presumption of uncleanliness. These were all fashions of the times."

Pointing to Albert Einstein's hair style, the legal brief said, "It is not in the best interest of the public to restrict the freedom of men's minds by making them conform to what other people like.

"The times are fraught with momentous problems of great complexity, among the foremost is that of civil rights with which Congress and the courts are wrestling...

"Times are changing and we must accept these changes...

"School authorities, as against the wishes of parents, have no power to dictate how students should wear their hair or to what length it shall be cut," the brief said.

Long hair fanciers everywhere are keeping an eye on the Massachusetts Supreme Court as it deliberates the issue of whether Georgie Porgie Leonard and Albert Einstein have anything in common.

Inside the BEAT

Lettermen Reveal Secret	3
Byrds Love English "Cats"	4
Shindig Personalities	5
Report from Liverpool	7
"Bandwagons"—an Editorial	8
Jerry & Gary Lewis	8
Dave Hull Tells All	9
New Styles for Girls	11
Barry McGuire Interview	12
Dear Susan	14
British Top Ten	16
KRLA Tunedex	Back Cover

The KRLA BEAT is published weekly by BEAT Publications; editorial and advertising offices at 6290 Sunset Boulevard, Suite 504, Hollywood, California 90028.

Single copy price, 15 cents. Subscription price, U.S. and possessions, $3 per year or $5 for two years. Canada and foreign rates, $9 per year or $14 for two years. Application to mail at second class postage rates is pending at Los Angeles, California, with additional entry privileges at San Francisco.

Exclusive distribution handled by Miller-Freeman Publications, 6328 Lewis Avenue, Long Beach, California. Inquiries should be directed to the attention of David Thomas.

KRLA ARCHIVES

Lettermen Relate Secret Of Success

Top Pop Group For Five Years

By Louise Criscione

The Lettermen have accomplished the impossible—they have managed not only to remain active on the pop scene but also to maintain their popularity for *five* years!

They made their debut in 1961 with such hits as "When I Fall In Love" and "The Way You Look Tonight."

Since the Lettermen's initial appearance on the pop scene they've had hit after hit with both singles and albums. And to top the whole thing off, they're in such demand on our college campuses that the group stays so busy playing American colleges that they don't even have time to go globe-trotting!

Change With Times

As far as the Lettermen are concerned there is a definite reason for their success—they change with the times. They don't stagnate—they move.

The Lettermen are best known for their renditions of old songs, which they try to sing as the composer would have liked them sung.

"We don't mean that you should use a 20-year-old arrangement," Tony explained, "but that the composer wrote words which carry some kind of message and if you drown out the lyrics then you can't possibly get the message."

"We don't use any gimmicks," grinned Bob. "You know, we're straight from the shoulder."

Since the Lettermen play mostly for college audiences, do they aim their material strictly for a college-type audience?

"It depends on who we're playing for. If we're playing a college, naturally we gear our material for them," said Tony.

Average Ears

"We really aim our material for average-type ears!" Bob put in. "Ninety per cent of our work is done for college audiences. We play very few high schools, only about 10 or 15 a year, simply because they don't have the budget to hire an act such as ours."

(We really ought to inject a little note here in case you're confused. There *are* three Lettermen but only Tony and Bob showed up for the interview because Jim was stuck somewhere with their bus which had broken down!)

Obviously, the tremendous popularity of the English groups has hurt some American groups but apparently it has had the opposite effect on the Lettermen.

"No, in fact, it has helped us!" said Tony. "Since the Beatles are also on Capitol we find it easier to get our records played because the Capitol man walks into a radio station and the program director sees that it's a Capitol record and he is more inclined to play it since such people as the Beatles and Beach Boys are on the same label."

Very Bitter

Many American groups have not been as fortunate as the Lettermen and have felt the sting of Britishers' popularity. These groups (such as Jay and the Americans) are very bitter about the success of the English groups.

"How can you blame the English groups?" asked Tony. "They're not being pushed down our throats. If the kids didn't like them, they wouldn't buy their records."

"Bitterness is a bad idea anyway you look at it," added Bob. "Tony's right. If the kids didn't want the English groups over here we wouldn't have them. They certainly haven't hurt the American record scene."

The Lettermen make it a policy to give the audience what it wants.

Grew With Rock

"The college kids today grew up with rock 'n' roll. It used to be that they wanted folk, but now folk is dying. In the colleges today they still appreciate a good beat. So we're trying to adapt by putting more rock into our act," Tony explained.

"We want to create variety," said Bob. "For instance, we started out with the letter sweaters. Now we wear velours and high collars and we even have an 'English Outfit.'"

Thinking about it further, Bob added: "We don't want to be outdated and have the kids look at us and say: 'They're old—they're out of the scene.'"

LETTERMEN (l. to r.) Jim Pike, Tony Butala, Bob Engemann.

The Lettermen present a rather conservative picture on stage—what do they think of artists' who wear far-out stage suits?

"If they make money," Bob grinned, "then it's okay."

"Teenagers don't take life as seriously as adults do," Tony added. "If someone wants to dress a little far-out, teenagers feel that it's their right and they accept it."

"These far-out clothes are all right—they don't hurt anyone," Bob said. "As long as they're not dirty. But when they get dirty is when I don't like them. But as long as they're clean they're fine."

Will Protest Last?

Protest songs seem to be the "in" thing of today—will they last?

"I think it's just a fad," said Tony, "which people are beginning to capitalize on. I don't think that the composers of these songs are really trying to get any message across. They're just out to make some money."

"I don't think they're going to be big for long. But, of course we made another prediction," Bob said grinning widely in Tony's direction. "It was about two years ago, right before the Beatles really took off here. We were being interviewed and the reporter asked us if we thought the Beatles would make it.

"Well, I'm sure you've guessed that we came out with the great prediction that they wouldn't! I really didn't think they would be so big because so many record labels were releasing their songs that I felt they would burn themselves out by overexposure.

Miscalculation

"Looks like we made a slight miscalculation on that one," Tony laughed.

It also looks as if the Lettermen will *not* burn themselves out by overexposure. In one year they travel roughly 100,000 miles hitting approximately 200 colleges.

They travel in a huge bus which houses them, their back-up trio and their equipment. They do anywhere from five to seven shows a week, but says Bob: "Never on Sunday."

"Our reruns average about 10% a year. We were afraid that the kids wouldn't like to see us again in the same year because, although we do change some of our numbers, we can't change the whole show.

"We did a concert once, I think it was in Nashville, and three months later they asked us back. We were really worried about what they expected.

Kids Dug It

"So we talked to the activities chairmen of the college to find out if the kids expected an entirely new show;" Bob explained. "He said: 'No, the kids liked your show the way it was. Why do you think we asked you back?'"

Since the Lettermen travel around the U.S. so much, I asked them if they found any differences in audiences.

"Well, the audiences in different areas express themselves in slightly different ways," said Bob. "For instance, the kids in the South express themselves by hooting and hollering whereas someplace else they may just sit and clap."

"We play a little game—we count the number of standing ovations we get. Usually we average about 40 standing ovations out of 45 shows," Tony continued.

Not a bad average, is it?

(Turn to page 7)

PERT JOY TOBIN, former "Miss Georgia," muses on her coming debut as an actress in the picture, "The Seventh Sun." Only 20, she will also make pop records.

KRLA ARCHIVES

TURNING ON THE CHARM for fans are Byrds (l. to r.) David Crosby, Chris Hillman, Gene Clark, Jim McGuinn and Mike Clarke.

BEAT Photos: Chuck Boyd

Byrds Report On British Scene; Say English Dug Dylan First

By Michelle Straubing

The Byrds had just returned from their very successful tour of America and England when I spoke to them in the office of their press agent, Derek Taylor. After the introductions were made, we began talking about their tour and the people they met.

On this particular trip they covered these cities: London, Ipswich, Brighton, Portsmouth, Bristol, Manchester, and Lancaster. They noticed that their fans were more receptive to the Dylan tunes than they are here in America. But Jim McGuinn, lead guitarist, had an explanation for it.

Dylan Big There

"Dylan is big over there", Jim explained. "He's big now over here, but the time before we went there, he wasn't as big here as he is now. Over there he was, so they dug Dylan and his songs. They were tuned in on him. They could sing the songs even if they didn't know the lyrics. They could pick them up right away. They reacted very strongly to it."

The Byrds think the reason for Dylan's bigger acceptance in England is that he's from the U.S. They feel it's more difficult to make it in your own country than somewhere else.

Not only did they do concerts on their tour of England, but they played several jazz clubs. Mike Clarke, drummer, recalled one place in particular called The Flame.

"It was very hot", he said. "For instance, The Animals played there recently and collapsed after twenty minutes because it was so hot. You can hardly stand to be on the stage for more than ten minutes. It's like being on the equator."

Met The Beatles

Another club that stands out in their memory is The Blazes, where they met The Beatles. David Crosby, rhythm guitarist, describes the club as being like a "steamheated closet," but Jim gives a more detailed explanation.

"They had about three hundred people there and it only holds about one hundred. It was about 120 degrees. There was a lot of steam in the air. Anyway, The Beatles came up to our dressing room after our performance. They talked to us and opened a bottle of wine. Then we all went over to Brian Jones' house and hung out all night. It was a good party and we had a great time."

The Byrds met several other artists while on their tour including The Moody Blues and The Animals, both groups David described as being "good cats." They met some whom they already knew such as The Rolling Stones and Donovan. They also met Lionel Hart, author of "Oliver" and many other current musicals.

Many TV Shows

They also appeared on many TV shows such as *Ready Steady Go*, *Top of The Pops*, *Thank Your Lucky Stars*, and *Gadzooks*. They feel that these shows are different from the American pop TV shows because they're livelier.

"*Ready Steady Go*, for example", said David, "seems to be closer to reality because they let the kids dance more. It's a freer and more relaxed atmosphere than the shows here. There the pressure is probably about the same, but they don't show it."

I asked about the conflict they had with the English group called The Birds. David told me what happened when "The Birds" wanted to sue "The Byrds" for allegedly causing them employment problems.

(Continued on Page 16)

...JIM MC GUINN

...GENE CLARK

KRLA ARCHIVES

The Shindigger

Howdy hi, Shindiggers, and welcome once again to our weekly gab festival. By the way, we have a whole lotta gabbin' going on this week, so let's get things moving right away with our first in-person guest—Billy Joe Royal. Billy was talking about songs and lyrics when you came in, and I think we ought to let him continue. Billy—

"I like to record songs with a lot of feeling. I like a song with good lyrics—they mean a lot to me. Dylan? As a writer, I think he's great. I don't go along with the protest movement at all, though. My feeling is that the country is doing what it has to and we ought to go along with it, and support it. I like the Beatles a lot and I think the British sound is great, although it hasn't influenced me. Y'know—I'm gonna record 'Down in the Boondocks' in German and Italian."

Billy Joe ...

Hey Billy, that's great. And thank you for stopping by.

Well, if it isn't Jimmie Rodgers falling by to say hello. Howdy Jimmie, c'mon over. You've been a great favorite for a long time Jimmie. Do you think your 'sound' has changed much in the last five years?

"Oh yeah—my voice has gotten lower, but basically my interests are the same. I still prefer ballads."

What do you think of the British sound in comparison?

"Some of it I like and some of it I don't care for. I'm strictly against the sloppy-dress type. As far as professionalism is concerned, the Beatles are good representatives. They've set a different trend—this is the thing I dig about the Beatles—they're always coming up with new things."

One of the nicest people this side of Emerald City is the young man who just sat down next to me—Little Anthony. Anthony, you and the Imperials have been responsible for many beautiful records over the last few years. What do you think of the protest songs which are so popular now?

"Well, if you notice—whenever there has been conflict in the world, there has been 'action' music. Everyone likes to express himself and to hide his fear. I think it's good because it brings out the truth."

Here's Ray

Another new addition to our gathering is the handsome young man who just sat down in the chair next to me. Ladies and gentlemen, may I introduce you to Mr. Peterson?

Ray, how do you feel about Dylan and the protest movement?

"Some of it is all right. If it fits me, I'd sing it. If I found the right song, I think I would like to record Dylan's work.

"I like to sing all types of music. I think ballads are my favorite."

Wait a minute everyone, I think I see Bobby Sherman sneaking in the back way. All right, Robert—how come you're so late?

"Well . . ." I'm sorry, Bobby—there's no excuse! Now, what are you going to do to make up for all of this? "I promise that the very next song I sing on the show will be 'specially dedicated to all of the female readers of The BEAT, 'cause I dig Shindiggers!"

Is that all, Bobby?

"Well, I dig girls!"

That's the understatement of the year! Just what kind of a girl do you like, Bobby?

"I like intelligent, attractive girls; I like an air of innocence—but knowing!"

Upcoming Shows

All right, Sherman, that'll be enough out of you! Now why don't you make yourself useful and tell us about next week's shows?

"OK—next Thursday, Dee Dee Sharp, Evie Sands, Charlie Rich, the Shindogs, the Wellingtons, the Blossoms, and yours truly will all be here, and on Saturday we'll be grooving with the Animals, Millie Small, Donna Loren, Willy Nelson, Jimmy Wetherly, and all the Shindig regulars. I'll see you all then."

Uh-uh—not so fast, Bobby. You promised that you'd split a cumquat with me for lunch in the commissary, so wait just a minute till we say good-bye to everyone.

In the way of last minute messages this week, we have this hot flash from George Patterson of the Wellingtons: United Artists is currently developing a television series around the three boys, and in the meantime, we are all excited about their new record release which we will talk about next week.

... Wellingtons

THE "IN" CROWD ... The Ramsey Lewis Trio play music for the "in" crowd and they play it well enough to push their record way way up there on both local and national charts. The "in" crowd men are (left to right) Eldee Young, Ramsey Lewis and Red Holt.

You Don't Have To Be Irish — But It Helps!

America's Newest *Imported* Sound

The FENIANS

(Translated From the Gaelic — We're Rebels!)

Presenting Their First American Disc Success

"Got A Feeling"

Dee Gee Records

For Genuine, Free Shamrock Write To:
Fenian Fan Club,
1953 Pontius,
Los Angeles 90025

KRLA ARCHIVES

THE SIGN SAYS "JOIN THE MARINES" and that's exactly what (l. to r.) Phil Everly, Marshall Lieb and Joey Paige have done! The three new PFCs read recruiting material over Sgt. John Standish's shoulder at Twenty Nine Palms Marine Base.

Join the Marines – They May Barely Cut Your Hair

It looks as if the stars have taken over the "L" Battery, 4th Battalion, 11th Marines! And not the kind that hang in the sky, either.

Joey Paige, Phil Everly and Marshall Lieb (composer of "You Were On My Mind") have all joined the reserves and are all currently serving four weeks in the Marine Corps at Twenty Nine Palms, California.

Hair Still Long

In the picture you can see that the Marine Corps relented and let all three of their "stars" keep their hair much longer than regulations really call for.

Joey flew into our office last week to report that the Marines are treating him very well and that it's not so bad after all.

He also had some good news to tell us – he will be appearing on "Shindig" in the very near future, so you all had better watch for him and view his new haircut for yourself. We at The BEAT have decided that we like it even better than his old cut. What do you think?

Heading For London

As soon as Phil finishes his stint with the Marines he and his brother, Don, will head for London for several appearances and then on to other parts of Europe.

During their short stay, the three boys put on a giant spectacular for the troops in the base theater which, of course, was a huge success.

Wish we could have been there but it won't be long before Joey, Phil and Marshall come marching home and back to the long(er)-haired fraternity.

Upbeat of the Week
By Eden

There is a lot of excitement on the Upbeat in the world of music this week, and much of it seems to be centered around the new "message song" trend.

Out in front of the pack is "The Leader" himself – Bob Dylan – with his brand new album on Columbia, "Highway 61 Revisited." If nothing else, this disc is outstanding for its remarkably long selections, including the six minute cut of the super hit "Like a Rolling Stone," and an epic eleven minute version of "Desolation Row."

New Sloan

In the same popular folk-rock vein, P.F. Sloan – one of the most talented of the new composer-singers – has a strong candidate for that chart-topping position with his new LP, entitled "P.F. Sloan: Songs of Our Time."

The talented young author has included twelve of his own compositions on this fine album, and it is definitely one of the most important and outstanding of the new crop of releases.

On the single side, a brand new group called the Beckett Quintet have one of the most excellent recordings to date of Dylan's "Baby Blue." It looks like a future hit for the Five.

Sherman's Latest

Bobby Sherman – of Shindig fame – introduces his latest contribution to the race of 45 RPM with his "Goody Galum-shus." And same show, new faces – the Wellingtons are smiling proudly over their latest discing, "Go Ahead and Cry." This one's a real beauty.

RECORD QUIZ

Have you noticed how the hit record charts are starting to read like one of Doc Kildare's files?

You haven't? Well, now's as good a time as any to start! And also to do this quiz!

See if you can match the song titles in the left hand column with the portions of the "anatomy" listed in the right hand column.

1. "You Were On My _____" (We Five) — a. heart
2. "Heart Full Of _____" (Yardbirds) — b. heel
3. "Shake And _____ pop" (Walker All Stars) — c. eyes
4. "Save Your _____ For Me" (Gary Lewis) — d. hands
5. "Through The _____ Of Love" (Gene Pitney) — e. mind
6. "Ju Ju _____" (Sam The Sham) — f. finger
7. "High _____ Sneakers" (Stevie Wonder) — g. hand
8. "With These _____" (Tom Jones) — h. soul

ANSWERS (AND STOP THAT PEEKING): 1-e, 2-h, 3-f, 4-a, 5-c, 6-g, 7-b, 8-d.

On the BEAT
By Louise Criscione

Ever wonder how the McCoys came up with their name? You know that old story about the two hillbilly families, the McCoys and the Hatfields, and their famous feud? Well, if you don't the McCoys do and that's how they got their name!

Another little sidenote on the McCoys: If you've ever seen them perform you've probably noticed that the drummer, Randy Zehringer, always stands. There is a definite reason for his standing position – when he began playing the drums he was too short to reach the bass pedal and now that he's older and taller he can't seem to adjust to sitting down while pounding out the McCoy beat!

Cher's Boutique

Sonny & Cher may have found the ideal location for their first boutique. Cher reveals: "It's right next door to Dino's on the Sunset Strip – they have a vacant lot right next door."

Wayne Fontana has apparently changed his mind and now declares that he and the Mindbenders will not split up. He admits that they did have some trouble but it's all been worked out now and he predicts that the group will be together for at least the next two years.

The Rolling Stones have just completed a European tour and it will probably be some time before they forget the wild crowds which turned out to greet them at every stop.

...CHARMIN' CHER

In Berlin the crowd went so out of control authorities had to call in about 400 policemen to keep the audience from reaching the Stones! And even that was not enough because the show turned into a full scale riot with the auditorium sustaining severe damage and the Stones barely escaping with all their hair!

Then as the Stones arrived in Dusseldorf the German police were forced to turn fire hoses on the crowds to keep the overly-enthusiastic fans from devouring the group.

All shows were sell-outs far in advance and it just goes to show that the Stones have a vast and particularly zealous band of followers.

Where's Mick

The Kinks were forced to fly to Iceland minus their drummer, Mick Avory, 'cause Mick vanished into thin air somewhere in Copenhagen! I'm sure he'll turn up – but when and where is anybody's guess.

Donovan is reported to be seriously considering releasing no more singles! Instead he intends to concentrate on becoming an album and EP artist.

Mick Jagger put down any rumors about leaving the Stones to become a solo performer when he said: "Why should I? I'm happy to be a member of the Stones and I've no intention of going solo. We get on very well, always have, so why split a successful partnership?"

Mick's plans for a movie with friend, David Bailey, are coming along and Mick says they're hoping to begin filming a little later on in the year.

Zany Comedy

He also revealed that it would be a zany comedy, that it will be a short and that none of the other Stones will appear in it.

But Mick's not going solo? Well, at least as far as singing is concerned he's not!

As you no doubt know, Tom Jones has been touring America for what seems like years! Anyway, during the entire tour the thing which Tom feels has been his greatest achievement (and there have been many!) is in "breaking through to colored audiences."

Tom tells a funny story about one of his appearances down South. "All the church people turned up one day to watch me. I came on and started leaping about and two parents came in and took their children out of the audience!"

I only have one thing to say to those parents – they should see P.J. Proby in action! They'd think Tom was a pussycat!

...TOM JONES

KRLA ARCHIVES

Liverpuddles

By Rob McGrae
Manager, The Cavern

The Masterminds

The Cavern has really been in the news recently with the startling dicovery that the owner, Raymond McFall, is in debt. The fantastic hold which the Cavern has over people, however, has been shown by the donations that have been received from many people in order to help McFall.

Even more incredible was the fact that 24 of the local groups including the Clayton Squares, Earl Preston's Realms, the Hideaways and the Masterminds offered their services free for a Marathon Session from 12 p.m. to 12 a.m. on Monday a few weeks ago. A great many people attended the session.

Talking about the Masterminds, what a terrific group they are—they had their first record released this month. It's already doing very well and it looks as though they will be the next Liverpool group to make it big in England. Their record features a Bob Dylan song, "She Belongs to Me" and a number they wrote themselves, "Take My Love." Like Herman's Hermits, the average age of the group is very young, in fact they are all only about 17 years old.

A great guy on the Liverpool scene is Billy "Spin-A-Disc" Butler, the disc jockey at the Cavern. Billy appeared on a television show for 26 weeks reviewing the latest records. Like all Liverpudlians, Billy has a zany sense of humor. He also has a wonderful knowledge of records. In fact, I am sure that there are very few people who could better his knowledge about the music scene. An interesting point about Billy is that before he became a D.J. he was a vocalist and used to front groups. He was the singer with the Merseybeats before he left them to form his own group known as the Tuxedos.

Billy's favorite singer is still Buddy Holly, whom he considers has had an incredible influence on pop music. Among the many artists who are said to have been influenced by Buddy Holly are George Harrison of the Beatles and Ray Davies of the Kinks. Billy also considers that a majority of the older records of the rock and roll era are better than the ones of today, and he has a very large selection of old records which he plays along with the new releases. This is a very popular part of the show and Billy has asked me to say that if any of the readers have any old records which they do not want, he will be very pleased if they would be willing to send them to him at 17 Heydean Road, Allerton, Liverpool 18; England. So don't forget, if you do have any old records which you no longer play, send them to Billy and he will play them at the Cavern.

OUR ROVING REPORTER
Cherry Lane Is Chic In Paris

The BEAT is fortunate enough to have a roving reporter who is currently roving around Europe. Her name is Sharon Held and from now until her travels end Sharon will be sending us reports on what's happening on the Continent.

Sharon's first stop was Paris and here she shows us a French discotheque as seen through an American teenager's eyes.

By Sharon Held

If you are ever in Paris one evening and you are cold from walking down Boulevard Saint Germain, why not duck into Rue des Ciseaux and stop at Cherry Lane.

True To Life

Cherry Lane is a real honest-to-goodness, true-to-life French discotheque. (After all, they began in France.)

Once inside you have no more fear of being cold. Because now, you have just stepped into the likeness of a freindly Turkish bath. Hot and sticky yet delightful are the words to describe the inside. The actual space available is tiny. When mobs of young people gather around, the climate becomes somewhat thick.

At a true discotheque (because that's what the word means) records are the only music played. Dancing is usually in one room but there are several rooms all connected for seating. Some discotheques are just like caves. Candles are on the tables. Everyone is speaking French but if you try hard enough, you may hear some English from around the corner.

The Beatles, Too

While all the French is being spoken, you can hear Them doing "Gloria" or Shirley Ellis singing "The Name Game." Oh, and yes, the Beatles are heard, too.

Drinks range from seven francs ($1.50) to 10 francs ($2.00). There are no cocktails, but a coke costs that seven francs!

Being very fashionable young men and ladies, the clothes worn are in style and neat. You won't find wild shirts or way-out faddish dresses.

The air becomes really heavy, but the atmosphere is so exciting that you will be dancing away just like the rest. There is no need to be shy, because everyone is exceedingly polite and friendly.

Smooth Effect

The French way of dancing has most of the basic arm movements as in America. However, they don't move their feet nearly as much. The weight is shifted from one leg to the other with a sort of up and down movement. The whole effect is smooth. It is not as restrictive as you may think. Just watch a while and you will see plenty of action.

One thing you will notice is that no one seems to be doing the jerk. And, if you ask, you will find that they don't even seem to know what it is. These kids sure can frug, monkey and swim, though.

Before leaving with the crowd, check your watch, because you will find that the time is around 6:00 a.m.—or even later. The action begins around midnight and ends when everyone leaves. (One time the whole dealie folded up at 10:30 a.m.) This sort of evening is not advisable on the night before a school day.

Visit the Louvre

Don't spend all of your time in Paris covering the discotheques. Spend at least two days in the Louvre. You will find it one of the most rewarding experiences of a lifetime.

LETTERMEN
(Continued from Page 3)

The Lettermen have been on the pop scene for a long time, do they find that audiences have changed much in that time?

Not Much

"The audiences themselves haven't changed much. At least, their reaction to us hasn't changed but their tastes have definitely changed," Tony replied.

"As we said before, folk used to be very popular. So in our act we used to do a lot of Peter, Paul and Mary material.

"But about six months ago we made the big break and started including rock and folk-rock in our act because that's what they want to hear now."

So the Lettermen will continue bending with the times and their audiences will continue demanding return engagements for the boys who started out five years ago and who still find themselves on top.

KRLA ARCHIVES

For Girls Only

By SHIRLEY POSTON

Stick around, boys. For the moment anyway, because I'm about to clear up a mystery.

I've received so many letters in the past few weeks, asking why I seem to have a surplus of names. Like, the name at the top of my column changes, but I don't, which seems a bit kooky.

Well, it's like this. *None* of the names that have appeared are my real name. Now, I know this is going to sound utterly ridiculous, but bear with me. It's just that I *can't* use my real name yet.

Well Known Relative

You see, I have a sort of well known relative, but I wanted to do this column on my own and see if it would be interesting *without* my using a name that would be familiar to some of you. You know what I mean. Like if I were Ringo's sister (I'm not—darn—just think how well I could get to know George Harrison if I were—double darn), I'd want to write this column under another name so I wouldn't be "cashing in" on someone else's popularity.

Like I said, it probably sounds ridiculous, but that's the way I am (ridiculous). That's why I've gone through a series of pen-names, finally ending up with Shirley Poston, which is going to have to do for a while longer.

Enough about that for the moment. (Boys, you can go away now. Or else.) And on to more important topics.

Remember when I said that in spite of the fact that George Harrison is my number one, I also like Donovan? Well, I received a letter from a girl who shares my sentiments, only Donovan has taken George's place with her! Well, that's never going to happen with me (G. H. Rules) but I do agree with her that George and Donovan are somewhat similar, and almost look alike when you think about it.

Donovan Dream

The reason I brought this up is because I want to tell you (briefly, I hope) about this dream I had about Donovan.

I wrote a song while I was on tour with a rock and roll caravan (in my dream, that is—I dream big) and Donovan came up to me and asked me to explain what I was trying to say in one of the verses. Instead of giving him a sensible answer, I looked up at him and breathed "I was afraid I'd be taller than you are." (I'm rather enormous.) (9'3") (Well, it *feels* like it.)

Then he looked down at me and grinned. *Then* he picked me up and sort of swung me around and said in this real *delicious* voice: You're just fine, luv."

I was about to faint from sheer joy when I, of *all* things, woke up. I have never spoken to that alarm clock since!

Favorite Someone

Isn't is just fabulous when you have a dream about a favorite someone? I always walk around with my head in the clouds for days, and every time I have a chance to sit still for a moment, I always reconstruct the dream from beginning to end. You know, just like the ones I *don't* dream, but make up instead.

Fortunately, I've discovered that I'm not the only one who goes in for this sort of thing. When I asked the readers of this column to please write and tell me if you lie awake nights planning conversations with your favorite sar, you did exactly that. And I can't thank you enough! Here I was going around thinking I was nutty or something!

A Hobby Corner

Hey! I've just had another of my brilliant (oh, well) ideas. Why don't we start a Hobby Corner type thing in *The BEAT* where everyone lists their particular hobby so other readers can pitch in and help? What an idea! Let's start it off by sending a letter to the Hobby Corner, c/o *The BEAT*, and when we have enough of them to make up a column, we'll print them. So hurry!

Well, I'm raving off at the typewriter, and had better hurry and start talking about something besides myself.

Oh, wait. I just had another idea (this must be my day.) Another thing I think we should have in *The BEAT* is a list of foreign students in California. You know, kids away from home who would probably like to get acquainted a bit more. If you know of anyone, please drop me a line and I'll print his or her name and address in this column. Write special delivery if it happens to be a boy from England. Wow! (I'm still going through *that* phase.) (Also praying I never *stop* going through it.)

Mad Money

How do you feel about money Vs dates? I don't mean about spending money on boys. I mean about taking money *with* you on a date, just in case. Most of the girls I know don't even think twice about this, but I picked up the mad money habit from a close friend who had quite an experience.

She and her date were on the way home from a football game in another town and something ghastly happened to his car. He'd spent every cent of his money on her, and neither of them had a dime to call for help. Her date finally had to *leave his wrist watch* with a gas station attendant, in order to borrow a dime. I'm not kidding! (What's wrong with some gas station attendants, anyway?)

After that, I started taking at least some money with me on a date, and now I'm really hooked on the habit. It's come in handy so many times and I advise everyone to tuck a dollar or two into your purse before going out for an evening. Either that or an extra wrist watch.

I don't have room this issue, but sometime soon I'll tell you about an "Emergency Kit" a friend of mine carries *everywhere* she goes. It's really wild, but I've talked so much now, there isn't room to go into detail.

In fact, all there *is* room to do is say keep your letters coming and I'll see you next *BEAT*!

Elvis Still King

(Continued from page 2)
for another 10 years with the record company.

Nor were we fazed by the news, announced at the same time, that Producer Wallis also had extended their longtime association.

Elvis is now completing his eighth movie for Wallis – "Paradise Hawaiian Style" – and he also has two more pictures on schedule at MGM at a later date.

A decade ago we snorted at notions that Elvis wouldn't "last." We're not saying "We told you so," or anything. It just figured.

Donna To Do Third Picture

Shindig's own Donna Loren has just been signed to star in her third movie.

She'll star in "Slumber Party in Horror House," her third movie with American International Pictures.

Production will begin next month with Don Weis directing. The movie was written by Louis M. Heyward and is being produced by James H. Nicholson and Samuel Z. Arkoff.

Miss Loren previously appeared in "Sergeant Deadhead" and "Beach Blanket Bingo."

A BEAT EDITORIAL
BANDWAGONS

A bandwagon is different things to different people.

To everyone, it's a symbol of success. But to some, it's a vehicle that has to be pushed all the way to the top, under your own steam. To others, it's a free ride where everyone else does the work.

A lot of would-be "stars" fall into that latter category. Because they are only cheap imitations of the talented people who took the time and trouble to be original.

Every singer who makes it to the very pinnacle of success has this view to look back on when he finally gets there...a host of "climbers" following clumsily in his footsteps.

The bigger the star, the bigger the number of attempts at mimicry. Elvis has battled off an army of imitators for ten years. The Beatles have been subjected to the same warfare.

Open season has now been declared on Bob Dylan.

Too many songwriters are putting meaningless phrases together in "pretty patterns", hoping to ride in on the Dylan bandwagon.

Too many singers are inadequately aping every tone and moan of the Dylan style.

We have only one suggestion for those who are trying so hard to sound like Bob Dylan. Why leave it at that? Why not *BE* like him? All you have to do is get off the bandwagon and get out and push. Like he did.

FATHER AND SON—Gary (l.) and Jerry Lewis got together recently on **Hullaballoo** to exchange experiences — and laughs as seen here — on their show business adventures. In this photo Jerry is the one who seems to be making with the wisecracks while Gary listens meekly. Actually, Gary has quite a store of stories to tell since returning from his and the Playboys' trip to Great Britain where they made a couple of important TV appearances and were well received by the British who seem to dig their rising hit record, "Everybody Loves A Clown" quite as much as we do on this side of the Big Pond.

KRLA ARCHIVES

THE DAVE HULL STORY
Hullabalooer Tells All: Has No Hi-Fi At Home

Hey Beaters—are you ready for this? In answer to thousands and thousands of your requests . . . well, lots and lots of requests, anyway . . . we are starting a series of interviews with the fantabulous KRLA DJ's this week. And just to get everything off to a rip-roaring start, we have the Hullabalooer himself here to blow his own horn and say a few words to you.

So, if you're all ready, let's get the show on the road!

By Eden

"Hiya, Hullabalooers! How're ya doing?"

Yep, it's the one and only Hullabalooer, *BEAT* fans, and the Scuzzy One himself has stopped in this week to start off our brand new series on the fab *KRLA* DJ's by telling us a little bit about himself and his activities.

Alright Dr. Hull: sponge, scalpel, horn-in-hand—I think we're just about ready to begin . . .

Toot Ta Toot!!!

"I was born January 20, 1937 in Alhambra, California and I went to high school at Alhambra high. I went into the service right after high school—into the Air Force—for four years and I was trained for radio with the Armed Forces Radio in Frankfurt, Germany with the Armed Forces Network. I stayed two years in North Africa, working for the North African Network, and that was where I got my radio experience."

"I like surfing very much; I don't have the time to do it anymore. I used to when I was younger. But that's about the only hobby I have because I don't have time for hobbies anymore. I don't even have time to build little models or anything that people do when they have hobbies—"

Awwww—poor baby! Listen Dave, we'll build some *for* you! . . .

Considering the fact that you are a world-renowned maestro on all the many instruments you play so well (??), David, what kind of music do you like to listen to at home? That is, of course, after you have tucked in your little horn for the evening?

"I like popular music very much, but I don't own a hi-fi set. It's just like a doctor working at an operating table and then rushing right home to operate on his family. I don't like to listen to music at home and I very rarely do—although I'm very interested in popular music. But I don't listen to music at home—I don't own any albums. I've had plenty given to me, but I always give them away to underprivileged children and I don't own a record to my name!"

Name Dropping

Speaking of names, let's start dropping a few and see what we can pick up. Like *Dylan*, for example. Would you care to make a statement for our Beatavision cameras, Mr. Hull?

"Well, first of all—the man is a poet. He is a phenomenon in the business. His lyrics are just unbelievable and we'll never see another one like him."

Have you considered letting your hair grow, Hullabalooer? . . .

Toooooottt!!!

Okay—Sorry I asked! Here's another name for you, then—Paul Beatle, MBE. What do you think of Paul's new solo disc, "Yesterday?"

"Oh, I don't *believe* Paul's new song! This is really not *all* Paul; it's some John, but it's mostly Paul. He called upon John to write the middle eight bars, I understand. But it borders on genius because it's been a long

THE BEAT thanks Marli Cooper, Woodland Hills, Calif.

time since we've had anything sung in pop music like this. "There's a guitar part just before he starts singing and he does that himself. Then, after that, he doesn't play any more—he just sings. Now, I think it's gonna start a new trend. Because they don't—they're trend-*setters*. I think that this is going to set a new trend for popular music, and I think it's going to be a turn for the better, I really do. I think you're going to find that a lot of the more popular artists are going to go this way. It's just like their whole British sound has brought in a whole influx of British artists in sound and I think that this will start a new trend. Music is going to be lighter and fresher, and it's going to be quieter."

Oh dear—does that go for your Famous Horn, too, Hullabalooer?

Tooot Toooot!!

Thank you, Hullabalooer, I feel better already!

Y'know Dave, you make so many "sounds" yourself that you must be an expert on the subject by now. Do you have any little expert ideas on the Beatles sound which you care to share with us?

"Well, as you've noticed—they've changed a great deal since last year. Well, they've gotten away from that now; John is recording things in a Dylan-type folk manner with "You've Got to Hide Your Love Away." They've got great respect for Dylan and "Hide Your Love Away" is a folk-type thing. But even "Help!" and "A Ticket To Ride"—which are some of my favorite things—and "A Hard Day's Night" they've changed a great deal from just last year. They're changing all the time. That's why I say they're setting trends all the time; every tune is different. And I think that their repertoire is very, very diversified. I think they're great! Especially Paul. Paul has been *so* good to me. He and I have had more fun together than all the others combined."

(At this point, Hullabalooers, we must make a familiar pause—for station identification. With horn honking and heart warm, we invite you to join us next week in this BEAT spot for the conclusion of The Dave Hull Story.)

SORRY ABOUT THAT, MICK . . .

KRLA BEAT SUBSCRIPTION
you will SAVE 60% of the regular price!
AN INTRODUCTORY SPECIAL . . . if you subscribe now . . .

☐ 1 YEAR—52 Issues—$3.00   ☐ 2 YEARS—$5.00

Enclosed is $..............

Send to:..Age:..........

Address:..

City:........................... State:.............. Zip:..........

MAIL YOUR ORDER TO: **KRLA BEAT**
1401 South Oak Knoll Avenue
Pasadena, California 91106

Outside U.S.: $9.00—52 Issues

Back issues of the KRLA BEAT are still available, for a limited time. If you've missed an issue of particular interest to you, send 15 cents for each copy wanted, along with a self-addressed stamped envelope to:

KRLA BEAT
Suite 504
6290 Sunset Blvd.
Hollywood, California 90028

ISSUES AVAILABLE
3/31 — BEATLE TITLE CHOSEN
4/14 — INTERVIEW WITH JOHN LENNON
4/21 — INTERVIEW WITH PAUL McCARTNEY
5/5 — HERMANIA SPREADS
5/12 — HERE COME THE BEATLES
5/19 — VISIT WITH BEATLES
5/26 — FAB NEW BEATLE QUIZ
6/9 — BEATLES
6/16 — BATTLE OF THE BEAT
6/30 — PROBY FIRED
8/7 — DYLAN
8/14 — HERMAN
8/21 — STONES TESTIFY
8/28 — KRLA PRESENTS THE BEATLES
9/4 — BEATLES . . . IN PERSON NOW!
9/11 — THE THREE FACES OF BOB DYLAN
9/18 — PROTESTOR BARRY McGUIRE
9/25 — SONNY — HE & CHER HAVE 5 HITS
10/2 — WAS YARDBIRDS' ORDEAL IN VAIN?

KRLA ARCHIVES

BOB EUBANKS Premiers His New Celebrity TV Show, "Hit or Miss" (Friday, 8 p.m., Channel 5). Here Bob Plays New Records as Molly Bee, Chad Stuart, Kathy Nolan and Roger Miller Vote.

Chad Listens Thoughtfully to New Release Before Voting on "Hit or Miss."

Kathy Nolan Listens Thoughtfully as Bob Introduces New Record, But Roger Seems to Think It's a "Miss."

CASEY'S QUIZ

By CASEY KASEM

This singer is being heralded as one of the brightest newcomers of the year, and incorrectly so. Bright he is. Newcomer he isn't. Two years ago, his voice was heard in the solo portions of one of the biggest hit records of that or any other year. At that time, he was singing with a famous group, one he later left to go out into the music world as a single. His first disc was even more popular than his previous hit with the group, sailing all the way to the number-one-in-the-country slot. Newcomer or old-timer, it appears as though he's here to stay.

ANSWER: Barry McGuire, former New Christy Minstrel whose voice we heard on "Green Green".

Helllllp!

HELP!
I'd like a buyer for a used monkey. It doesn't eat much, except a tube of toothpaste every morning and loves to eat soap suds. It just loves whipped cream (the soap suds are mistaken for the whipped cream). For further information call Linda Werley at 365-1931.

HELP!
Very few of my Hollywood Bowl Beatle performance photos came out. I'll pay for all prints. Please send information to Sue Malins, 1302 Linda Way, Arcadia, California 91006.

HELP!
I am a super gigantic fan of Luke Halpin who stars in "Flipper"—he plays "Sandy". If anyone has any pictures, articles or just any news on him I would certainly appreciate it if they would send them to Janet Segal, 11853 So. Atkinson Avenue, Inglewood, Calif. 90303.

HELP!
I just started putting together my scrapbook of Sonny & Cher. I'd appreciate any articles and pictures of them you might have. Cher Williams, 638 West 168th Place, Gardena, California.

HELP!
Four boys and one girl needed to organize a band with me. Ron Wynne, 8421 Leroy Street, San Gabriel, California 91775.

KRLA ARCHIVES

HEADLINERS' HAIR BEAT
Gals Get Guy Cut; Wispiness Prevails

By Robert Esserman and Frank DeSanctis

For every girl—there is a correct hair style, and one of the newest and most famous hair cuts is "The Guy," which was introduced right here in *The BEAT* last week. Although this is only one of many new styles, it has already proven itself to be one of the most popular. It can be worn both as a "whispy-do," or as a short hairdo with a lot of length on top.

Displaying Ears

Although some girls feel funny when their ears show, don't be afraid to display them if they lie flat against the head; especially now when earrings have become so very popular.

Bangs, too, are very big now, and some girls wear them below the eyebrows. However, the eyebrow should be the limit. To set or not to set will depend on the curl or wave which your bangs take.

Cheek curls—worn both forward and back—are also in, if worn *below* the ear lobe.

Hair Color

Hair coloring can be a very touchy subject—especially when there are parents involved in the discussion! But contrary to some popular opinion—hair color is *not* a luxury to be reserved exclusively for adults.

Nature can be a fabulous friend, but nevertheless, she *does* occasionally jilt someone along the way. Therefore, we offer these helpful color hints to you.

The most popular color trends include two-toning, frosting, and highlighting your own color.

Two methods can be used to achieve the two-toned affect. In the first, we take the front portion of your hair (ear forward), bleach the entire section, then tone the front section a contrasting color so that it will blend with the rear portion of the hair which was left in its natural color.

Second Method

The second method is used when the rear portion of the hair is not a satisfactory color to contrast with. In this situation, the entire head is bleached out and the back is then toned slightly darke than the front.

The frosting is a very popular style because it only colors a fraction of the head. For this style, a frosting cap with many holes in it is used in combination with a hooked needle. The small strands of hair are pulled through these holes and are then bleached. In this way, the bleach never touches the scalp. The final step is the application of a toner.

An extra attraction is added for the girl who can't seem to get her hair shiny or vibrant, in hair coloring as it brings a brilliant glow to her hair—and often, a flowing reassurance to her personality!

Headaches Section

Q. *In your last article you said that using a hot iron would damage the hair. I've been using a hot iron for six months and nothing has happened.*

A. Lots of luck! Three months from now don't be surprised, though, if a wig is necessary! No joke, take a good look at your hair strands and you will see that they're fried by now.

Q. *Where can I buy an electric comb?*

A. In a beauty supply store, but first try it in a shop. The price is between $35.00 and $45.00 and by the time you received yours (They are available by special order only), changes in hair styles may make the comb of no interest to you.

Q. *My hairdresser never knows how to do my hair the way I like it. I bring him pictures and he never does it the same way. Why?*

A. Tear up the pictures and let him groove! If still no results—try another hairdresser. No offense—but it might be your fault because you may not be ready for what is "in" in popular styles.

That's the poop for the Headliners this week girls, but please keep your questions coming in for the future columns. Address all questions in care of *The BEAT*.

PICTURED HERE is a front view of the popular "Guy Cut." The bangs are left straight and allowed to fall slightly below eyebrows. Section of hair above the bangs is shaded darker for two-tone color effect.

PRETTY BARBARA EDEN shows off version of "Guy Cut" which she prefers to wear in a lovely whispy-do.

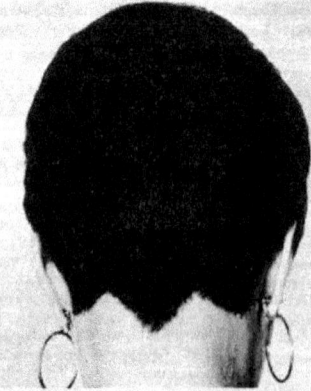

IN THIS BACK-VIEW of the "Guy Cut" notice the interesting symmetrical effect achieved with the unique shaping at nape of the neck.

KRLA ARCHIVES

Tips to Teens

Q. Is there any way I can keep clear nail polish from turning yellow every time I help my mother with the dishes?
(Linda H.)

A. Yes, and there's also a way to keep your hands looking prettier years longer. And there's no time like the present to start using this method. All you have to do to protect your polish, hands, etc. is wear rubber gloves when your hands are in water. They'll feel sort of funny the first couple of times, but you'll get used to them, and be glad you did!

Q. I just spent my entire life's savings on a suede coat. Can you give me any pointers on how to take care of it?
(Melanie M.)

A. Be careful not to wear it on rainy days, for one thing. If your coat ever does get rain-spotted, let it dry and then brush it with a suede brush. When it's time to have your coat cleaned, do NOT take it to your regular cleaners UNLESS they specialize in leather and suede. Look in the yellow pages for a company which does offer this special service.

Q. About a month ago I put peroxide on my hair and I've been sorry every since. What would be the fastest and least horrible (I can't just let it grow back out—ugh!) way to go back to my natural color?
(Cindee Y.)

A. Find a rinse that is the same tone (or very close) to your own shade. After you've used the rinse, no one will even know when your natural color begins to grow back out.

Q. A girl at school received a "diamond engagement ring" from her boyfriend in the service. It's about as big as a boulder, and twice as phony. I'm afraid she thinks it's real, although it's zircon all the way, and she's making an awful fool of herself telling everyone how it must have cost him a fortune. Shouldn't someone tell her the sad news?
(Margaret W.)

A. That's a rough question to answer. Yes, someone certainly should. Chances are her boyfriend never dreamed she'd think it was a real diamond, or make such a fuss about it. She needs to know the facts before she makes an even larger fool of herself, and of him. But who should do the telling? That is the question. Since you don't sound like a close friend of hers, I'd drop a gentle hint to someone who is. It would be a bit easier to take, coming from someone she knows well.

Q. I'm in a real fix. About a week ago I was in a store looking at cardigan sweaters. I had my own with me (I was just carrying it, not wearing it) and when I left the store I discovered I'd picked up a new sweater the same color as mine and left the old one lying on the counter. I suppose I should just keep it and forget the whole thing, but it's bothering me. I want to take it back, but I'm afraid the store manager will get the wrong idea. You know how some people are about teenagers. I'm even embarrassed to tell my folks. They're always teasing me about being absent-minded as it is. Help!
(Allen C.)

A. Tell your folks in one large hurry, and have them go with you when you return the sweater. Don't go alone! It was an honest mistake, but it could be misconstrued if the manager happens to be "that type." And be glad it "bothers you." An active conscience comes in very handy.

Q. My teeth are slightly crooked (I'm 14), but not to the point where I look creepy or anything. However, the school nurse said they might get worse if I don't have braces now. I hate to tell my parents because they don't have a lot of money to spend on something like this. I have an after-school job, and would like to know how long it would take to pay for braces myself.
(Janet P.)

A. Your parents are fortunate to have such a thoughtful daughter, but this is one time you're going to have to think of yourself first. Your smile has to last a lifetime, so don't take the chance of allowing it to be anything but pretty. Tell your folks what the nurse told you, then offer to use part of your after-school money to help pay for the braces.

HINT OF THE WEEK

I read somewhere in *The BEAT* about a girl who wanted to liven up her room without having to spend any money. She found several drips and drabs of paint in the garage and painted her venetian blinds stripe-fashion. Well, I did almost the same thing with my door. I found about ten different remnants of leftover material (cloth, I mean. My mom sews a lot), cut them into strips with pinking shears, pasted them on paper strips and then glued them on the door of my room (inside.) Boy, does it look great! The whole room has a carousel look now, and it didn't cost me a penny. Try it if redecorating just isn't included in your budget!

If you have a question you'd like answered or a hint you'd like to share, drop a line to Tips To Teens, in care of The BEAT. Our address appears in each issue.

The Mothers —Soon

Hail Barry McGuire As New-Born Star

By Eden

In the Western world,
A star is growin',
Excitement's flarin',
And minds are blowin'.
He's causing such a stir,
And such commotion—
That everyone is saying:
He's in motion.
And we'll tell you—
Over and over and over again,
He's happening, he's great—
He's Barry McGuire!

The world of entertainment is on the eve of something great right now. His name is Barry McGuire. Although this exciting, dynamic young man sings of the "Eve of Destruction," his future is filled with the brightest promise possible. This man is on the Eve of Construction.

Barry McGuire Onstage

He is captivating, exciting, dynamic, and overwhelming; Barry McGuire is a *great* entertainer.

From the moment he first enters the room, until the last resounding note of applause has finally died—there is never a lull in the constant feeling of excitement and electricity which he creates for his audience with his mere presence.

Barry doesn't make a stage entrance, nor does he dramatically appear in a carefully designed setting of lights and flowery scenery. Suddenly he is just there—as though he always had been—singing with all his heart and soul. Singing wild versions of "Hang On Sloopy," Dylan's soulful ballad "Baby Blue" and demanding "Don't You Complain, Babe." His repertoire ranges from the controversial smash "Eve of Destruction," to a sensitive rendition of the soft ballad "Try to Remember."

Vital and Vibrant

Barry has a very vital and vibrant stage presence which literally commands the attention of all those within earshot. He is somehow miraculously capable of totally immersing himself within the songs he is singing, and the result is an exciting and effervescent performance by one of the most compelling entertainers of our time. For Barry—it is a never-ending love affair with his audience.

Barry brings with him to the stage a powerful voice, capable of rendering both tender ballad or rough-edged rocker to match his own sandpapery voice. He brings a dynamic and forceful personality which completely captivates his audience, and a zany sense of humor replete with the most infectious laugh to be heard on this planet. And one thing more: Talent. Barry McGuire brings with him enormous talent, both *for* entertaining, and *as* a great entertainer.

If the age-old expression "Seeing is believing" is indeed a truism, then you won't believe Barry McGuire until you have seen him in person for yourself.

Because—Barry McGuire is *unbelievably* great!!!!

... Reflection
BEAT Photo: R. Custer

Animals To MGM

The animals have migrated.

They've been lured away from their independent producer Mickey Most and are signing with MGM in the United States and Canada and British Decca for the rest of the world.

The actual change in producers won't take place until next February when Most's contract with the popular British group expires.

Most recently flew to New York to accompany the Animals to California where they appeared at Melodyland. The group was reported to have agreed to cut their last record with Most during their stay on the coast.

Most first signed with the Animals in 1964, shortly before their second recording, "House of the Rising Sun," made it to number one both in America and England and sold over a million copies.

The Animals will receive a guaranteed $280,000 from Decca and an additional $250,000 from MGM.

The change gives the group the exact same release arrangement as the one recently signed by Roy Orbison.

Barry in action . . .
BEAT Photo: Robert R. Custer

KRLA ARCHIVES

Yeah, Well Herman...

By Tammy Hitchcock

Yeah, well...Herman is the occupant of our "Yeah, Well Hot Seat" this week, so turn on the fire and here we go.

The toothed wonder is currently making his second motion picture in his first starring role. Herman confidently predicts: "I think I can become a better actor than Elvis." Yeah, well never mind the acting bit, do you think you can make as much money as the old El does?

Huge Success Here

Herman, of course, is a huge success here in America but in his native England he has not had the same kind of luck. He says: "We would really love to be as big a success here (Britain) as we have been in the States." Yeah, well listen, Herman, Londoners reveal that they would like you much better if you, a Manchester man, would drop the phony Cockney accent which you use in such ditties as "Mrs. Brown" and "Henry The VIII."

Herman is very much interested in money, though he says he's not in the entertainment business solely for money, rather, "It's just personal satisfaction." Yeah, well I guess you've sure acquired a lot of that personal satisfaction here in the good old U.S., haven't you, Herman?

Once again on the subject of money: "I admit I was a fool at first with money and so on. I bought a car and smashed it and spent money on all sorts of mad things." Yeah, well if you spent a lot of money on mad things, how come you didn't spend any on me?

More Careful With Money

Herman's whole outlook on money has undergone a big change: "Now I'm much more careful with money. I take a great deal of interest in percentages, investments, the bank rate and so on." Yeah, well in that case I think I'll put you to work on *my* bank rate. I just can't figure out why my bank account is so low and my bank rate is so high!

Besides filming "There's No Place Like Space" for MGM Herman says: "I'll also be taking dancing lessons." Yeah, well listen, Herman, if you ever need a dancing partner, I'm available!

Herman has a philosophy of life, you know, just like Plato and Aristotle and all those. Only Herman's philosophy is much simpler: "After all, life's just a big giggle." Yeah, well I don't know how much of a giggle it is but it's sure one big laugh.

Spend Time At Home, Boy

Many of Herman's fellow Britishers don't think that Herman spends enough time in England and that he spends entirely too much time in America. Herman answers: "I don't think we spend too much time there." Yeah, well personally I don't think you spend enough time here—and I know you don't spend *nearly* enough time with me! Matter of fact, you don't spend *any* time with me. Why is that, Herman?

A Lolly? Yeah, Well...

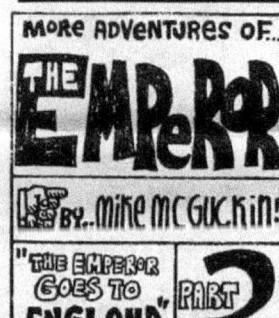

KRLA ARCHIVES

AN HISTORIC MEETING takes place between two of the pop world's chart-toppers as Roy Head (r.) tells Billy Joe Royal: "I'm always glad to meet a fellow from 'Down in the Boondocks'." BEAT Photo: R. R. Custer

Barbarians Mock Own Long Tresses

Former Beatle Drummer Yells Libel, Slander

(Continued from Page 2)

The legal trouble rose from an interview with the Beatles that appeared in the February 1965 issue of Playboy magazine, in the course of which Ringo was asked about Pete Best. Ringo reportedly replied to the question by saying, among other remarks, that Best "took little pills to make him ill." Best apparently felt this remark to be more than merely offensive. He called his lawyer.

A few months ago, broke and disillusioned, Best disbanded his musical group, the Pete BestCombo, explaining to British reporters that he was simply unable to find enough work to keep going. But now he is touring America with his new group, which he apparently calls "Best of the Beatles." And he's apparently having no problem finding work.

Before his stormy departure from the Beatles Best had recorded three sides with them which later became hits—"Love Me Do," "P.S. I Love You" and "Please Mr. Postman." He also recorded dozens of others with them, but during their "hunger" days many of these were sold outright for a few dollars each.

Legal Storm

Release of Beatles records on Mr. Maestro Records is almost certain to kick up another legal storm among the record companies. Capitol Records and Vee-Jay Records went to court against one another over a contest about who had the right to distribute the discs. The squabble lasted a long time and even now the wounds of the struggle have not entirely healed.

Four young men from Massachusetts are currently on their way to success with a record making fun of their own long hair.

The Barbarians record "Are You A Boy Or Are You A Girl?" really hits at guys who wear long hair and tight pants with lines like "You may be a boy but you look like a girl." The members of the group are Moulty Moulton, Jerry Causi, Bruce Benson and Geoff Morris.

Jerry is the lead singer and plays banjo. He's from Provincetown, Mass., started playing the bass guitar when he was 16 and played with many different bands before joining the Barbarians. He is 24 years old.

Rocket Exploded

Moulty is 20 and started singing and playing guitar when he was in grade school. At the age of 14 he tried to build a rocket but it exploded and cost him his hand. This ended his career as a guitarist but when he was 16 he took up drums and now, with one stick handily notched for his hook, is pretty wild on the skins.

Bruce plays lead guitar and sometimes doubles on the trumpet. He was recently accepted at the University of Massachusetts but has decided to put off his college work because of the group's success.

Geoff started playing the guitar when he was eight and has worked with several New England bands. He spent a year and a half as a Business Administration major at Boston University before joining the Barbarians.

What will happen when Best's reported 48 original Beatle sides hit the record stores is anybody's guess. Except for two things: (1) They're bound to sell like popsicles in the Congo; (2) Pete will not become the Beatles' *Best* friend.

Dear Susan

By Susan Frisch

What kind of house does Sonny and Cher live in, and where do they live? Also, is it possible for me to buy any of Cher's clothes in the stores?
"A Sonny and Cher Fan"

Dear Fan:
They live in a beautiful house in the hills. At the front is the garage. There is a long and steep stairway leading to the front door. In the living room they have an enormous picture window with the most fantastic view of the city. Little by little they are furnishing it with Spanish furniture. As to the purchasing of Cher's clothes—No, you can not buy them in any stores. Sonny and Cher both have their clothes made up especially by their own dressmaker, who does original work for them alone.

Can you tell me where I can write to Dick Clark and insure his reading my letter personally?
Paul Rubell

Dear Paul:
You can write to Dick at Dick Clark Productions, 9125 Sunset Blvd., Los Angeles, Calif.

Could you please tell me if Patti Boyd was in the movie, "HELP?" If so, what scenes of the movie could she be seen in?
Peggy Kravitz

Dear Peggy:
Patti was not in the movie. However, Jane Asher was shown in the scene up at the skiing lodge. She was only shown for about twenty seconds so you would have to look closely.

I would like to know why they don't have night clubs for the 13 to 16 year olds. We like to dance and have fun too.
"Confused"

Dear "Confused:"
In answer to your question, I really don't know. Maybe it is because they feel the kids at that age shouldn't be in places without parental supervision.

Does Peter Asher live with his parents? If so, where does he live? Also, how much does he weigh?
Janice Borth

Dear Janice:
Peter lives at home with his two sisters, his mother, and his doctor father. The house is on the famous Wimpole Street in the heart of London.

Where is Bob Dylan's regular home? And is there any truth in the romance between him and Joan Baez?
Caren Cotman

Dear Caren:
Bob doesn't really have a 'regular' home. I suppose if you had to narrow it down, I would say Minnesota. When you asked me whether the rumor was true about him and Joan, all I have to say is that is exactly what it is, a rumor. Joan and Bob are very dear, close friends. Nothing more than that.

What are the selections from the British L.P., "Help"?
Steve Brown

Dear Steve:
It is the same as the American version, but it also includes, "Yesterday," "Act Naturally," "I've Just Seen A Face," "You Like Me Too Much," "It's Only Love," "Tell Me What You See," and "Dizzy Miss Lizzy."

I read in a magazine that the Stones won't be coming to America any more to make records. If this is so, then will they continue to make them anyway?
A Stone Fan

Dear Fan:
Don't worry... the Stones will be coming back here many, many times again, and they will, too, be making many more records.

Can you please tell me Bob Dylan's height, weight, coloring, marital status, and where I can write to join a fan club of his?
Sue Paige Harrison

Dear Sue:
Bob is approximately 5 feet 9 inches, weighing 140 pounds. He is medium in skin coloring, and has brown curly hair, and brown eyes. He is single. Why don't you drop a letter to Bob Dylan, c/o Bob Dylan Fellowship, 758 33rd Ave., San Francisco, Calif.

Is the rumor true that John Lennon and Bob Dylan are the same person?
Puzzled

Dear Puzzled:
Be serious... NO, NO, NO! There is some resemblance between Bob and Ringo. Don't you think so?

Where can I write to Billy Joe Royal?
Alice Leong

Dear Alice:
You may write to Billy at Columbia Records at the address above.

Can you please give me Joey Paige's home address? I met him recently and I forgot to ask him for it.
Arlene Santal Cruz

Dear Arlene:
I am sorry, but I do not supply home addresses of the stars, unless they have already been published.

Can you please tell me where the Supremes were born, and where I can write to them personally?
Tom Shepard

Dear Tom:
All the Supremes were born in Detroit, where they practically grew up together. You can write to them at, Motown-Tamla Records, 6290 Sunset Blvd., Hollywood, Calif.

Can you please tell me when the Rolling Stones will be in San Jose?
Laura Partea

Dear Laura:
I do not know whether their next tour will include San Jose. This is something that their manager sets up, and I don't know if he included San Jose this time.

Can you please tell me where I can get the correct lyrics to the song, "Like a Rolling Stone," by Bob Dylan?
Kathy Deiss

Dear Kathy:
Try going to your local record store and ask if they have the sheet music to that song. I am quite sure they do.

Can you please tell me if Cynthia still paints and draws, and if she sells her works? Also, does George live entirely alone at his new house in England?
Janet Engelbrecht

Dear Janet:
Cynthia Lennon still paints and draws, but only as a hobby, and when time permits. George lives alone in his new home, but he quite frequently has special guests that stay there.

Does Paul have any intentions of marrying in the near future, or right now? Also, how old is John's boy?
Lynne P.

Dear Lynne:
I cannot answer your question regarding Paul getting married. How can anyone know? I doubt that Paul himself even knows. John Jr. is about 2 years, 8 months old.

Where can I write to Mick Jagger, and where can I write to join his fan club?
A Mick Jagger Fan

Dear Fan:
You can write to Mick, and to the fan club at P.O. Box 1525, Brooklyn, New York.

Can you please tell me exactly who is Twinkle and where did Herman meet her?
A Herman Fan

Dear Fan:
Twinkle used to be the girl that Herman dated before he rose to his present popularity. There is nothing romantic between them now. He met her in England while doing a show. She is a singer, too.

KRLA ARCHIVES

...**WAILING** (l. to r.) Steve Nagle, Tommy Munirief, Norm Reccius, Tim Taylor and Barry Dunkeson.

CINDERELLA STORY

Becket 5 Defeat Wicked Manager

Talk about a Cinderella story—well, the Becket Quintet have a real one. They have succeeded in overcoming odds almost as great as the ones which faced Cinderella.

Only instead of a wicked stepmother the Becket Quintet had a wicked manager and instead of a horse-driven coach the Quintet used a '63 Chevy Nova to transport them from the wilds of New Mexico to the neon lights of Hollywood.

The five boys—Tim, Steve, Norm, Barry and Tommy—met at Eastern New Mexico University about eight months ago.

Equipment Poor

As far as equipment was concerned, the Quintet's equipment was as poor and as haphazard as Cinderella's rag torn dress.

They laugh about it now—they probably laughed about it then—but it's really not that funny when you stop to think about it.

They recall one dance where they had two poorly constructed amplifiers for three guitars, no microphones and Steve's drums were in such bad shape that he was forced to follow them all around the stage!

Since they had no mikes when it was time for the guitar break, one of the guys would yell at Tommy and he'd quit singing, and then when Tommy was finished singing he would give the rest of the group the high-sign and they would automatically stop playing!

Slightly Hilarious

No doubt they presented a slightly hilarious sight what with Steve playing his drums wherever they happened to land and tracking down his cymbals as they fell off of their stands.

But as funny as they may have looked, the audiences always liked them because despite their poor equipment these boys were good!

They remember another night when they arrived at a competition dance an hour and a half late and again armed with their faulty equipment.

The Quintet was sure that they hadn't won and they didn't particularly fancy being laughed at so as the winners were being announced the boys were half-way out the door when they heard *their* names called as the first place winners!

Again they had proven that with all their handicaps they were good.

First Autographs

Soon thereafter the Becket Quintet became known as the best group in New Mexico and it was not too long before they were asked for their autographs for the very first time.

This historic event took place at a dance which the boys will probably never forget. The group had driven all the way out to Zuni, New Mexico; and as they pulled into town they got the shock of their lives—there *was* no town to speak of, only a bunch of old Indian huts!

They don't give up easily so they kept on driving and eventually they came to the high school where the dance was to be held. And there they *really* got a surprise, for the auditorium had been so beautifully decorated that the boys could hardly believe their eyes.

"The Indians were so sincere and so nice to us", recalled Tommy. "And when we went to leave the lady who was signing our check had tears in her eyes! Then one of them came up and asked us for our autographs. No one had ever done that before and I don't think we'll ever forget that dance or those Indians."

The Becket Quintet was not satisfied with being the top group in New Mexico, they wanted to come to Hollywood and crash into the big time.

It's an old dream—practically everyone has had it at one time or another. But the Becket Quintet aimed to *do* something about their dream to make it a reality.

So they made big plans, they saved their money and they had a ritual. Everytime they were feeling low and it looked as if they would never make it they would face the West and have what they called their special ritual!

Hollywood Ahead

Along the way they acquired a manager but, unfortunately, he soon took on the character of Cinderella's wicked stepmother. The boys finally saved enough money to come to Hollywood but just as they were about to leave for the promised land the money mysteriously disappeared.

But nothing, absolutely nothing, was going to hold the Quintet back, so with $20 between the five of them they climbed into the '63 Chevy which Barry's parents had so graciously allowed the boys to use, they loaded their equipment (such as it was) and they were on their way!

Down To $5

By the time they actually arrived in Hollywood they had but $5 to their name. They moved in with Steve's friend and slept on the floor. They became so accustomed to hard floors that now they say they have a hard time sleeping in beds!

The boys existed on one peanut butter sandwich a day. They looked for work but only two members of the group were able to find any.

Meanwhile, they got hungrier and hungrier and, in fact, two of them finally passed out from malnutrition! But they kept on going.

Can Hardly Wait

They have stacks and stacks of their own original material, written by Tim, and they can hardly wait until they can put out an album and show it off!

The Quintet is all for sincerity, originality (they want their sound to be just "us") and for the audience to really like their music.

They all five trouped up to our offices the other day and they are as fresh, original, exciting and nice as any five guys can be.

And you know what? They'll make it yet—they came all this way, surmounted all those obstacles (they're now eating macaroni with their peanut butter sandwiches!) and with their steadfast determination they've just *got* to make it big!

BEAT CARTOON by Charmaine Ervin, San Jose, Calif.

KRLA ARCHIVES

PORTMAN'S PLATTERPOOP
By Julian Portman

HOLLYWOOD — The **Byrds** have recorded their third single for Columbia, "The Times, They Are A' Changing". Certainly it's a Dylan-penned tune — they can't sing anyone else's! ... I wonder if **Jerry Lewis'** (Sept. 20) appearance on Hullabaloo had anything to do with the show being chopped 30 minutes. He has all the luck! Didja notice, he's trying to sing again for the Dot label! ... **Liza Minnelli** is receiving the star promotional treatment at Capitol records. She's been signed for that "Little Red Riding Hood" TV-special, with **Vic Damone** co-starring. This proves the point: you gotta know somebody!

The sensational folk-rock **We Five** were introduced to the Hollywood press with a smashing party hosted by A & M Records' **Jerry Moss** and **Herb Alpert**. If you have not seem them perform, do so! They're delightfully talented, and a fine looking group ... **Deem** records is seeking new young artists and musical groups. Those interested, with talent, contact **Sam Dubreville** or **Bill McFarland** at 877-5133 ... Warner Bros. **Freddie Cannon** is now sipping cokes since he sang a commercial for them.

Mira Records' **The Leaves** drifted into Bido Lido's nitery for a long stay ... **The Blue Boy** appearing at the Royal Lion in Studio City has all Ventura dancing to his music ... **Steve Lawrence** signed *The Wild Ones* for his tv show. This is the group headed by **Jordan Christopher**, now married to Sybil Burton. Sybil will not appear with them.

Era records topper **Herb Newman** released "The Barber's March" by *The Clippers* ... **Tommy Sands**, formerly of the Sinatra family, unveils his new Liberty sound on the Nov. 17 *Dean* (Clan-member) *Martin Show* ... **Sonny & Cher**, whose rise in the recording industry is just short of phenomenal, were so sensational at *It's Boss* that the owners of the new nitery *The Trip* rushed over with a contract and a fresh pen to sign the duo.

The **Supremes** do a 9 day stand in San Juan, Puerto Rico, on January 31. Motown is thinking about cutting them at that time, something like "The Supremes Go Latin, Baby" ... **Barry McGuire's** opening at *The Trip* overflowed onto Sunset Blvd. I guess lots of people got his message ... **Lesley Gore** signed a multi-picture pact with Paramount... "Moonlight & Roses" seems destined to be **Vic Dana's** next song hit. If Vic continues to breathe fresh life into old tunes, I guess his next will be "When You and I Were Young Maggie"? ... **Connie Francis** sings the love theme from the new motion picture "Phoenix" in six languages. Wonder if she'll try American, baby?

Lloyd Thaxton enshrined in the H'wood Wax Museum has the place of honor next to the wax image of **The Beatles** ... *The Beatles* are encased in glass so that fans' lipstick won't smudge their suits as they do the glass. This should happen to Frankenstein that's near by ... **Patty Duke**, as pretty as ever, minus an appendix, is up and about and preparing to cut her next hit for United Artists.

A record company should look into **Art Benson's** protege **Tommy Cooper**. His recent rave tour of the Far East was nothing less than sensational and Las Vegas is hollering for appearances ... To all those who have inquired, **The Mothers** are a rock 'n roll aggregation headed by handsome **Frank Zappa**. They are as good as their name implies ... **Ike Cole**, he's the late Nat's talented brother, has penned a long-termer with Dee Gee records ... Chicago radio personality **Sig Sakowicz** claims he can become a bigger talent than his late illustrious brother.

Dick *(Shindig)* **Howard** has become the "big daddy" to all the female vocalists that come on the show. They all think he's cute? ... Dee Gee records is packaging a musical group to tour the Los Angeles and San Francisco areas during Thanksgiving Holidays. They'll be combining the talents of *Freddie Cannon, Martha and the Vandellas, The Marvelettes, Junior Walker* and his all-stars, *H. B. Barnum, Jean Haywood*, and *The Fenians*, a true Irish rock group from the land of our managing editor, "The Olde Sod", Ireland. It'll be the first appearance on the west coast for the Tamla-Motown aggregation... Later, baby!

AND The Beat's JUST "MOD" about Adrienne Jacoby of 4528 Van Nood, North Hollywood for submitting her clever cartoon of the typical BEAT reader in her typically "mod" outfit. Of course, not all of our readers wear those "mod" clothes — some of them wear tiger skins!

Dodd Downs Stones

Ken Dodd has succeeded in knocking the Rolling Stones out of that first place position which they have held down for the past three weeks! "Tears" jumped up from number five to capture the number one spot this week while "Satisfaction" took a drop to the number two position.

The Walker Brothers and "Make It Easy On Yourself" remained stationary this week hanging in at number three. These transplanted American boys have really made it big in England and practically every one of their personal appearances have ended in enthusiastic fans rushing the stage!

The Hollies, a very popular English group who would like to visit the U.S. but can't because of immigration difficulties (you know, that same old story), moved up from number six to land in the number four spot this week with "Look Through Any Window."

Sonny & Cher's visit to Britain sure paid off handsomely for the California duo as their record sales have been soaring ever since!

For the past several weeks, Sonny & Cher have had three records on the British top 30, "I Got You Babe," "Laugh At Me" and "All I Really Want To Do."

Barry McGuire's "Eve of Destruction" continues to make big strides, this week jumping from number 13 into the top ten at number eight.

Barry's popularity will probably be heightened by his upcoming visit to the British shores — so look for "Eve Of Destruction" to climb much higher in the following weeks.

British Top 10

1. TEARS — Ken Dodd
2. SATISFACTION — Rolling Stones
3. MAKE IT EASY ON YOURSELF — The Walker Brothers
4. LOOK THROUGH ANY WINDOW — The Hollies
5. I GOT YOU BABE — Sonny & Cher
6. LIKE A ROLLING STONE — Bob Dylan
7. IF YOU GOTTA GO, GO NOW — Manfred Mann
8. EVE OF DESTRUCTION — Barry McGuire
9. A WALK IN THE BLACK FOREST — Horst Jankowski
10. IL SILENZIO — Nini Rosso

Byrds Return; What's Ahead?
(Continued from page 4)

"The whole thing was absurd", he contined, "There never was any possibility of a case because we spell it differently. They knew that and we knew that. Everybody knew that. They just did it to get publicity."

Fashion Conscious

The Byrds are fashion conscious, and I asked if English fashions for girls were changing in any way. Here is the latest tip from this quintet on what the best dressed English mod is wearing:

"These chicks were wearing dresses with holes in them", David recalled. "They're really groovy. They were showing them on all the TV shows. They have great holes over their stomachs or over their sides, or their backs. They're beautiful. They cut big holes in their dresses and they match them. It's just weird."

The Byrds expect to be in California for just a few weeks. In that time they will cut their new single and album. Then they go on a concert-dance tour. They're not sure what the future holds for them.

David said, "We're going to go back to work is what will happen. But we don't know where. They've got a bunch of different stuff planned."

To which Mike added as Gene and Chris, engrossed, turned a page in *The BEAT*, "It's not that we're not working here. I mean it's no holiday. We'll be going back to the *real* work."

KRLA ARCHIVES

KRLA Tunedex

EMPEROR HUDSON

CHARLIE O'DONNELL

CASEY KASEM

JOHNNY HAYES

BOB EUBANKS

DAVE HULL

DICK BIONDI

BILL SLATER

KRLA BEAT
6290 Sunset, No. 504
Hollywood, Cal. 90028

This Week	Last Week	Title	Artist
1	7	YESTERDAY/ACT NATURALLY	The Beatles
2	3	LOVER'S CONCERTO	The Toys
3	2	THE "IN" CROWD	Ramsey Lewis Trio
4	1	LIAR, LIAR	The Castaways
5	5	HELP/I'M DOWN	The Beatles
6	8	HANG ON SLOOPY	The McCoys
7	12	TREAT HER RIGHT	Roy Head
8	4	DO YOU BELIEVE IN MAGIC	The Lovin' Spoonful
9	10	WE GOTTA GET OUT OF THIS PLACE	The Animals
10	14	MOHAIR SAM	Charlie Rich
11	6	BABY I'M YOURS	Barbara Lewis
12	9	IN THE MIDNIGHT HOUR	Wilson Pickett
13	11	EVE OF DESTRUCTION	Barry McGuire
14	13	TAKE ME FOR A LITTLE WHILE	Evie Sands
15	15	UNIVERSAL SOLDIER	Donovan
16	26	THE WAY OF LOVE	Kathy Kirby
17	17	EVERYONE'S GONE TO THE MOON	Jonathan King
18	19	AGENT DOUBLE OO SOUL	Edwin Starr
19	27	EVERYBODY LOVES A CLOWN	Gary Lewis & The Playboys
20	25	KEEP ON DANCING	The Gentrys
21	28	JUST A LITTLE BIT BETTER	Herman's Hermits
22	38	POSITIVELY 4TH STREET	Bob Dylan
23	32	I LIVE FOR THE SUN	The Sunrays
24	20	YOU'VE GOT YOUR TROUBLES	The Fortunes
25	30	THERE BUT FOR FORTUNE	Joan Baez
26	33	I KNEW YOU WHEN	Billy Joe Royal
27	31	YOU'RE THE ONE	The Vogues
28	39	MAKE ME YOUR BABY	Barbara Lewis
29	—	RESPECT	Otis Redding
30	40	LIFETIME OF LONELINESS	Jackie DeShannon
31	—	FOR YOUR LOVE	Sam & Bill
32	—	RIDE AWAY	Roy Orbison
33	34	I'M YOURS	Elvis Presley
34	—	ALL NIGHT LONG	Palace Guards
35	36	GOODNIGHT MY LOVE	Joey Paige
36	35	NOT THE LOVIN' KIND	Dino, Desi & Billy
37	37	WHAT COLOR (IS A MAN)	Bobby Vinton
38	—	BUT YOU'RE MINE	Sonny & Cher
39	—	ROUND EVERY CORNER	Petula Clark
40	—	RESCUE ME	Fontella Bass

KRLA ARCHIVES

KRLA Edition BEAT
MFP

Volume 1, Number 32 LOS ANGELES, CALIFORNIA 15 Cents October 23, 1965

Beverly Bivens — <u>Wee One</u> of the We Five

Win $1,110 in Football Contest-Entry Form Inside

KRLA BEAT

Los Angeles, California — October 23, 1965

Voting Starts On Pop Awards

BEAT Photos: Darryl Kniss

SONNY AND CHER, in their night club dressing room, talk by long-distance telephone to a girl who sent them a telegram saying she intended to kill herself. BEAT Photographer Darryl Kniss was with them, capturing this candid photograph as they successfully persuaded her to change her mind.

BEAT REPORTERS' DIARY
Sonny & Cher in Orbit

By Bob Feigel & Jeannie Castle

HOLLYWOOD — Following Sonny and Cher is like going *up* the "*down*" escalator during a basement sale. You don't have to be an astronaut to follow these stars, but a rocket would come in handy.

We recently followed them around for a couple of days, during which:

(1) One of us received a broken ankle
(2) We were surprised by a policeman's remarks
(3) They may have saved a girl's life by long-distance telephone
(4) We chased them on a secret flight to visit a world-famous lady.

Pre-Flight Briefing
The briefing took place in the plush office of their managers, Charlie Greene and Brian Stone (of Greene & Stone Productions). Despite their hectic schedule their managers rolled out the red carpet while Sonny and Cher gave The BEAT an exclusive interview that was both delightful and fantastic.

Sonny helped me set up the tape recorder while Cher discussed less mechanical things with Jeannie. The atmosphere was casual and friendly, as you'll gather:

BEAT: What is your pet peeve?
SONNY: Cher doesn't like to make coffee for me in the morning.
CHER: I hate to make coffee for anyone in the morning.
BEAT: Both of you have recorded solo discs. Why?
SONNY: I like to hear Cher's voice.
CHER: Then why don't you let me sing around the house?
SONNY: (Laughs) I like to hear you sing in a recording studio with guitars and violins in the background.
CHER: But not at home?
SONNY: Not in the living room... while I'm watching a good show on TV.
CHER: Oh! (Laughs)
SONNY: Or while I'm on the phone... That's when she always sings. When I'm on the phone.
(Looking at each other, they both break out laughing.)
BEAT: *This is a rather deep question, so you can take your time in answering it. What do you see when you look in a mirror?*
SONNY & CHER: (simultaneously) Hair! Lots of hair.
When we all stopped laughing, they told us about the time they escaped from an over-enthusiastic crowd by running through a Billy Graham crusade. And Cher recalled a show they did when 18
(*Turn to page 15*)

Inside the BEAT
Freddy Cannon's Story 3
Tom Jones Talks 4
News From U.N.C.L.E. 5
"Miss Teen" Expands 6
Dear Susan 7
For Girls Only 8
Rack Robbers — Editorial 13
Beatles Running, Running 11
It's Happening 14
Movies: Love and Kisses 16

The KRLA BEAT is published weekly by BEAT Publications; editorial and advertising offices at 6290 Sunset Boulevard, Suite 504, Hollywood, California 90028. Single copy price, 15 cents. Subscription price, U.S. and possessions, $3 per year or $5 for two years. Canada and foreign rates, $9 per year or $14 for two years. Application to mail at second class postage rates is pending at Los Angeles, California, with additional entry privileges at San Francisco.

Exclusive distribution handled by Miller-Freeman Publications, 6338 Lewis Avenue, Long Beach, California. Inquiries should be directed to the attention of David Thomas.

Pop music is just what the name implies — music which enjoys the widest popularity with the public.

Yet, aside from buying their records, there is no way for the public to show its appreciation for outstanding accomplishment by the many talented pop music artists and composers who daily provide delightful entertainment for millions.

In an effort to correct this oversight, KRLA and The BEAT are founding the first annual International Pop Music Awards.

Through an official poll BEAT readers will select those who have contributed most to popular music entertainment in 1965. Then KRLA will serve as host for the entire recording industry as the winners are honored with International Pop Music Awards.

With the world's top music stars attending, the glittering, star-studded formal presentation ceremonies should be comparable to the Oscar and Emmy awards presentations in the movie and television industries. The ceremonies will be covered by press, radio and TV.

Public Choice
Winners of these awards will enjoy one major distinction. The Oscar and Emmy winners are selected by only those in the industry. The BEAT International Pop Music Awards will be selected by you, the public.

With BEAT subscribers in all 50 states, plus most of the English-speaking foreign countries, the poll will have a truly international flavor. And entertainers from throughout the world are eligible for the awards.

Separate categories will include Best Male and Female Vocalist, Best *New* Male and Female Vocalist, Best Vocal Group, Best Duo, Best Instrumental Group, Best Vocal Record, Best Intrumental Record, Best Vocal Album and Best Instrumental Album.

There will also be special categories for others in the recording industry who have contributed most to popular music during 1965. These will include: Outstanding Record Company, Best Producer and Best Composer.

Here's how the balloting will work:

Each week a list of nominees in two or more categories will be printed on a special ballot in The BEAT. Spaces will also be provided for write-in votes. BEAT readers will select up to ten names in each category.

After the results are tabulated the field will be narrowed to ten names in each category and then a complete ballot will be printed in one issue of The BEAT and you can vote on your top choice among the finalists.

This Week
This week's preliminary ballot is for the Best Pop Male Vocalist of 1965. You will notice several artists are listed in *both* categories.

This is because all male singers are eligible for the Pop Male Vocalist award, but only those who have introduced their first hit record during the past year are included on the second list.

Thus you'll notice a few oddities such as Bob Dylan being listed as a new pop vocalist, even though he has been recording for a number of years and his albums sold well in he folk field. But pop records — whether they have a rock, folk, western or blues sound — are those which enjoy mass popularity with a broad, cross-section of the public. Dylan's spectacular arrival as a pop star came only this year.

One other word of explanation— many of the world's top vocalists are not included in either category this week because they record as a group. For instance, even though John, Paul, George and Ringo often sing individually, they record only as "The Beatles." The same holds true for such stars as Herman, Freddie, Bobby Hatfield and Bill Medley of the Righteous Brothers, Gary Lewis, Mick Jagger and several others.

Both Categories
On the other hand, some vocalists such as Sonny and Cher record not only as a duo, but also individually with only one name appearing on the record label. Thus, they are eligible as individuals and also as a duo.

So much for explanations. Look over the list now and send us your nominees for the outstanding male vocalists of 1965. So that overly-enthusiastic fans cannot provide anyone with an unfair advantage, only those ballots submitted on the official BEAT entry blank will be counted.

(*Ballot On Page 13*)

Win $1,110

Win $1,110 in the KRLA BEAT 11-10 football sweepstakes!

Weekly Award
In keeping with its expanded coverage of all high school football scores, KRLA will award $1,110 each week to everyone who correctly predicts the actual scores of 10 out of 11 games on Friday night.

It costs nothing to enter. Everyone can play — anyone can win! There's no one to beat, and you can send in as many entries as you like.

In each weekly edition of The BEAT you'll find a list of 11 high school football games to be played.

Fill In All 11
Fill in all 11 of them, because you can miss one and still win $1,110 if you guess right on the others!

You'll find a list of the games, contest rules and an entry form on page 10 of this issue.

KRLA ARCHIVES

TALK WITH A STAR

Freddy Cannon Success Is Simple: He Stays Himself

...FREDDY CANNON
BEAT Photo: Joan Reeves

By Louise Criscione

A tornado of talent just hit our offices in the person of one Mr. Freddy Cannon! Freddy is a phenomenon of our times because he has been *successful* on the pop scene for the past *six* years! He has seen artists come and go and go and come but he's still here—one of the few remaining holdouts.

And what is really amazing is that Freddy has accomplished this feat by simply remaining the same. His songs and his styles are unmistakably Freddy Cannon.

Freddy himself can't really explain his success but he has given the subject plenty of thought. "My style is always a beat and a driving sound because the kids love to dance—*I* love to dance.

"The people who were popular when I first came on the scene—Frankie Avalon and Bobby Rydell—haven't lasted because their sound was a sound which couldn't last through the years."

The Record Industry

Since Freddy has been on the scene for so long, naturally our conversation turned to the record industry and specifically to the changes in the scene during the past six years.

"I don't see too big a difference." he said. "All I see is that the English are here now. Of course, the actual music itself has changed. Before, you had maybe two chord changes, now if you don't have at least 10 or 12 chord changes you don't sell."

No one can deny the fact that the English have had tremendous success here in America. I asked Freddy why he thought that was.

"The Beatles are great, they write great songs but I think the reason for their success is that their records, and all the English records, are 'hot.' Do you know what I mean? When you put one of their records on the record player you have to turn the sound down. This was new—it was different. When you put an American record on, you had to turn the volume *up* to hear it.

Little Reasons

"Really, there are a lot of little reasons. I don't think my music has changed, will ever change, as long as it's happy. I think there is always room for my kind of music—a happy song with a driving sound.

"The English really are just singing American songs. Take the Everly Brothers. These guys haven't had a hit in three years and they deserve a hit. Just listen to the Beatles and you hear the Everly Brothers.

"I think maybe that's another reason why I have lasted. No one has ever tried to copy me. You never hear an English group singing my kind of music."

Freddy has always been known for his fast and exciting sound. Did he ever try anything slow?

Tried To Change

"I tried to change my sound once. But the kids wanted to hear the old Freddy Cannon—they wanted that driving sound. I gotta hear that jumping stuff.

"You know, people say to put on slow music because it puts you in a mood. Well, it puts me in nothing! I gotta have fast, driving music. People like to get up and sing and dance and I've got to have this."

Although Freddy likes happy music, it appears that more and more of our music today is turning toward the sad protesting vein. I asked Freddy why he thought this type of music is so popular today. Why not yesterday or the day before? *(Turn to page 8)*

KRLA ARCHIVES

WELSH PUSSYCAT
'Ideal Girl' Doesn't Exist--Tom Jones

Well, that pussycat of a tiger, Tom Jones, blew into our town and straight to our office for a short visit. The extremely handsome Welshman from Printypodd, Wales has been touring the U.S. for months now and has made a definite decision on the merits of the country.

"I like it very much. The people are great, everywhere I've been accepted very well. So everything is great as far as I'm concerned," Tom enthused.

Since "Tom Jones" is also the name of a rather famous character from a famous book, Tom is frequently asked if his moniker is real. "Yes, actually it's my two Christian names. My full name is Tom Jones Woodward—we just left off the Woodward."

Of course, every man has at one time or another dreamed up his ideal girl. Maybe Tom did at one time too but now he's given up the idea. He says: "I don't think there *is* an "ideal girl"—it's all according to what kind of a fellow you are."

A New Trend

Practically every week brings a possible new trend into the record business, does Tom think there is a new trend going today?

"The thing now is folk-rock," Tom explained. "That's the biggest thing I can think of now. It's very big in England too with Bob Dylan."

Tom has one of the most fantastic singing voices around. In fact, before people actually see him they are invariably convinced that he is Negro. It's only natural then to wonder if Tom was particularly influenced by the great Negro blues singers.

Early Influences

"I was influenced a lot," Tom revealed, "by Jerry Lee Lewis, Elvis Presley and those early rock 'n' roll singers and a lot by colored singers such as Soloman Burke."

Since the tremendous influx of British artists, American teenagers have been extremely curious about the English teenagers—what they do, where they go, who they like, and most important of all—where do they go on dates?

"They're generally in coffee bars or the movies, as you call them, and things like that—dances," Tom recalled.

Fan reaction—the screaming, fainting and sobbing—bothers some performers. Is Tom among this number?

Teens Great, Too

"I like it because if I didn't get it, it would be time to worry," Tom grinned. "I think the teenagers of America are great!"

Tom has travelled the world rather extensively since becoming such a popular entertainer. Does he find that teenagers around the world are much different?

"I think teenagers are the same the world over," he philosophised. "They change from time to time just as times change all the time. The only trouble is that when you grow older and look back, you don't see it the same way they do."

With all this protesting going on today, all this talk of destruction and other morbidity, is the world really in such a bad shape?

Opportunity

"I think there is plenty of opportunity to learn and to do what they (teenagers) want to do—more than at any other time." Tom said with conviction.

Just as "The Tiger" stalked out he offered this parting word of advice to all you teenagers: "I think whatever you want to do go all out for it. I wanted to be a singer and if I knew then what I know now, I would've started earlier. They should talk it over with their parents, get it worked out and then go ahead."

And then Tom was gone—out of the door and into a blue Stingray. But through the trail of exhaust one could hear the powerful notes of "It's Not Unusual." Well, maybe *it's* not unusual but Tom Jones sure is. He's a tiger!

Grrrrrrrrrr!!

Trini Plays Himself In U.N. Movie

Trini Lopez will play himself in a United Nations anti-dope film entitled "Poppies Are Also Flowers."

The film, produced by the Telson Foundation of the UN, will include a night club sequence featuring Trini as himself.

Special guest stars in the film also include Trevor Howard, Rita Hayworth, Marcello Mastroianni, Gilbert Roland, E.G. Marshall, Angie Dickinson, Sterling Hayden, Barry Sullivan and Alberto Sordi.

OUR ROVING REPORTER
Germans Adore Rolling Stones

Our roving reporter, Sharon Held, is having a bit of trouble—all her suitcases were lost in transit from Paris to Munich! Being a true reporter Sharon is now in Munich with only the clothes she wears on her back—but she's there! And did she come up with an exclusive! But we'll let her tell you all about it.

By Sharon Held

I send you greetings from Munich.

Before I left the States I didn't think that my mentioning I worked for *The BEAT* would have any effect on the Europeans.

Well, guess what? It does have an effect—a big one!

Goes To Concert

The Rolling Stones were here in Munich on tour. With a German-speaking American girl I went to the auditorium where the concert was being held and she told the German police that I was a reportword with the police was California—but not with the Stones.

After getting inside and hanging around for about an hour, the right person finally asked me what I wanted. I told him I worked for *The BEAT* and he let me right in!

The Stones were glad to see that *The BEAT* had made it to Munich. I say this in all awe because apparently the auditorium officials were being very selective about who came for interviews. In fact, the German press managed to get only about a two-minute interview while the Stones were nice enough to talk to me for 20 minutes!

The first thing I asked them was how they like German fans and what strikes them the most about German audiences.

Keith Richard immediately quipped: "The boys."

Mick agreed: "Yeah, the boys. I'd say that from 60 to 70 per cent of the people are boys."

And not to be left out, Charlie and Bill chimed: "Boys—lots of boys."

Mick further commented that in America and in England the fans are mainly made up of girls but that in the rest of Europe it was quite the opposite. "The audiences are made up of kids mainly 12 to 20," said Mick, "and girls just aren't allowed to go out at night like they are in America."

Audience Reaction

My next question concerned the difference in audience reaction say between Germany and California.

"The big difference," Mick replied, "is that here the boys yell at the end of each number, whereas in America the girls scream all the time. And also the boys whistle a lot."

I wondered how the security was in Germany.

"Great," he enthused. "There are more policemen downstairs than there are people! When we arrived they had to bring out the fire hoses and police dogs as well as all the police."

There is nothing more marvelous than a rock 'n' roll concert in Munich. First of all, there ARE about 75 per cent boys (and I believe that is a conservative estimate!). They are all orderly and don't get out of their seats.

Better Than U.S.

They are completely enthusiastic and appreciate the beat and the music far more than I found in the U.S. They do yell at the end of the songs and as soon as they recognize the next. Also they whistle quite loudly.

But the whole magic of the audience is that they all seem to do the same thing at the same time so as to have the effect of being entirely united.

There is really no limit to the number of songs which the three acts preceeding the Stones could do. After about five songs the group would sort of look at the audience for the signal. And that signal was literally a thumbs up.

When people sat in their seats and put both thumbs up in the air it meant to keep going. Each group was received enthusiastically and complete attention was given to them rather than an attitude of come on and get off so we can see the Stones.

Exciting Noise

Of course, when the Stones did come on the noise was really exciting! Most of the audience (mainly boys) sat in their seats clapping their hands and/or swaying back and forth with the beat. I was completely impressed with the whole thing.

As for the Rolling Stones, they have a new fan—me! I'm still captivated by the Beatles and am a dedicated fan—but the Stones have impressed me.

They were extremely polite and considerate when I was interviewing them. They didn't seem to be bored or to wish that I would leave.

And they didn't appear grubby as many of their pictures would have you believe. Of course, when Mick Jagger gave me a wink as I was leaving he hit upon a girl's weak side!

Well, that's it from Munich and the Rolling Stones. Talk to you later and bye for now.

... PUSSYCAT TIGER TOM

KRLA ARCHIVES

The Shindigger

Howdy Hi, Shindiggers. Welcome to the Shindig Shadows segment of our column.

This week, we're all going to put on our Super-Spy costumes and do a little Super-Snooping. After all — a little eavesdropping is good for what ails you. Right? OK then — let's go!!

Here Comes Charlie

Ah-Hah! There's Charlie Rich telling his life story to one of the Shindig dancers now. Let's listen.

"I started playing piano in the third grade and the sax about the ninth grade. I started my career by writing and playing on sessions for others, like Elvis, Johnny Cash, and Bobby Bear.

"Yeah, I hope we have a sound of our own — I think it's kind of rhythm and blues with a rock beat."

Careful not to breathe too loudly, Shindiggers, 'cause if we get caught — it'll be the firing squad at sunrise for us!

Attention for red-blooded American males in the crowd: directly to our right is a talented and pretty little girl by the name of Evie Sands. Now, if you can all sneak around behind her and hide yourselves behind that guitar pick, perhaps we can hear what she's saying to Jimmy O'Neill.

... CHARLIE RICH

"Music is my life; I could listen to music twenty-four hours a day. And I love to sing. Actually, I have a much bigger singing voice than my speaking voice; it's like a soul sound."

(Yep Shindiggers — 'round these here parts we call her "Soulful Sands!")

"Protest songs? These songs should make people *think*, but not be rebellious.

"I feel that it's healthy for people to express their feelings if they mean what they say and it's not dangerous."

Zany Zal

EEEEEEEEYYOOOWWWWWWW!!

And that, my friends, was a certain zany young man by the name of Zal Yanovsky who just ran screaming across the stage with a lime-green hat decorated with a magenta flower. Zal is the lead guitarist for the Lovin' Spoonful, and the hat was a gift from a fan. I think that the scream was a gift from his parents, however!

Zal is also the biggest practical joker between here and Transylvania, and when he's not actually *pulling* a joke on someone, he is usually *bragging* about the times he has! In fact, he is telling Kirby, of the Wellingtons about some of the stunts he has pulled off on John Sebastian — the group's lead singer — right now. C'mon — let's listen in.

"Oh — sometimes I'll send John down to get something he doesn't need — and he doesn't know he doesn't need it!! Or, I cut John's strings with a wirecutter on stage in the middle of our act one night. Another time, I hit a friend of ours in the face with a cream pie while he was in the middle of singing a song in a nightclub. And I'm always taking John's glasses and fogging them up so he can't see. He's blind without them!!"

Uh, let's go, Shindiggers — I'm suddenly beginning to get just a little worried about staying too close to our good friend, Zal! Let's just quietly sneak out of — "BOO!!"

Bobby's Boo

Hey — Bobby Sherman! What's the big idea of sneaking up behind us and screaming Boo??!

"All's fair in love and war, and if *you* can snoop around, so can I!! I mean — they don't call me Agent OO 'Soul' for nothing, y'know!"

Alright James Bond, put away your Zap-gun now and tell us about next week's guests.

"Aw — allright. We're gonna have some great guests next week, including Jimmy Witherspoon, Ray Peterson, the Lovin' Spoonful, Kelly Garrett, the Shindogs, Glenn Campbell, the Wellingtons, the Blossoms, the Animals, the MFQ, Millie Small, Willy Nelson, Donna Loren, and Jimmy Wetherly. Hope you'll all be around for the fun."

... EVIE SANDS

We will, Bobby. And till we see you all again next week, maintain your soul, Shindiggers, and remember: no matter what *anybody* says — ROCK ON!!!!!

EARPHONES AND TRIGGER-FINGER ITCHY, The Byrds' Gene Clark during their recent record date takes careful aim at the group's a&r man, Terry Melcher, while fellow-Byrd Chris Hillman pretends he doesn't notice a thing. (Relax ... we're only kidding ... it's a toy pistol ... Gene LIKES Terry ... Honest!)

SPECIAL U.N.C.L.E. SHOW
Illya And Solo May Star With The Beatles

David McCallum fans and Beatle Fans of the world — unite! You may get to see your idols together.

The ever-clever people who produce "The Men From U.N.C.L.E." have come up with a script idea that would involve both the Beatles, and the two U.N.C.L.E. men, David McCallum and Robert Vaughn.

Ardent Fans

The story revolves around a rock and roll group that has some ardent fans. It seems the big wigs from U.N.C.L.E. are watching a film of the group on a public appearance tour and notice that there are always THRUSH (the bad blondes who are always giving our boys a rough time) agents in the crowd.

The big wigs get worried about why the enemy agents are always present and send Napolean and Illya to check up on them. They discover that the singing group has a fan club made up of five girls who's fathers are United Nations diplomats and the THRUSH agents are planning to kidnap the girls. (There are more dangers to being a fan than just getting trampled by the millions of other fans.)

David Victor, supervising producer of the show, doesn't believe in thinking small so he's going to try to get the Beatles themselves for the part.

Script Not Ready

"The script's not even ready yet, so I can't get really started on getting guest stars," said Victor. "However, if I can't get the Beatles, I'm going to try for another big name group."

Another episode in store for our heros from U.N.C.L.E. involves camels and Bedouins and lots of sand.

In this one Illya is captured by a band of Bedouins while he's chasing THRUSH agents. Illya really loses out this time because one of the Arabian girls wants to trade him in for a camel (the animal variety). Now who would want to trade Illya for anything?

Illya Escapes

Anyway Illya, with his usual cleverness, escapes by telling them he is the son of Lawrence of Arabia.

... ROBERT VAUGHN

... DAVID McCALLUM

Kids Barred From 'HELP!'

A California movie theater recently gave adults a chance to do something most of them thought was impossible — see the Beatles' movie, "HELP!", without a horde of excited youngsters present.

The theater decided to give more mature movie goers a chance to see what all the excitement's about without having to sit in the middle of the excitement.

So for two nights one week, no one under the age of 16 was allowed in the theater.

"You see," explained Mrs. Trudy Clark, operator of the theater, "Young kids, especially 13 and 14-year-old girls, make so much noise that nobody can hear what's going on on the screen."

KRLA ARCHIVES

INTERNATIONAL CONTEST
'Shindig' to Feature 'Miss Teen U.S.A.'

Hey girls, guess what the Teen-Age Fair is going to do this year? They're going international and they're going on television.

This year the Miss Teen U.S.A. Pageant will be expanded to the Miss Teen International contest with contestants from 13 regions of the U.S. and at least 13 foreign nations.

The finals of the Miss Teen U.S.A. Pageant will be held during the 5th annual Teen-Age Fair at the Hollywood Palladium and Moulin Rouge April 1 through 10, 1966.

Winners On TV
Thirteen regional winners will be introduced on nationwide television starting January 1966 on the *Shindig* Show through the co-operation of the Teen-Age Fair and Selmur Productions. These 13 girls will then enter the Miss Teen International contest which will also be televised live on *Shindig* on April 9, 1966.

Contestants in both pageants must be between 14 and 18 years of age and must not reach their 19th birthday before April 10, 1966. They will be judged on general appearance, scholastic achievement and accomplishments, poise and beauty and the ability to communicate ideas by talking before people.

The girls will be judged by personal interview and in long formals and bathing suits during the actual competition during Easter vacation. They will also have to speak for less than one minute on their favorite sport, hobby or ambition. Their speeches will be judged on creativity, originality and choice of subject.

Travel By Air
All contestants in the pageant will receive round-trip air transportation, hotel accommodations and expense accounts.

Final arrangement for the televised special have been made by Leon I. Mirell, executive producer of *Shindig* and vice president of Selmur Productions; Al Burton, president of Teen-Age Fair Inc., and Bernard Schwartz, president of Joseph M. Schenck Enterprises.

British Top 10
1. TEARS — Ken Dodd
2. MAKE IT EASY ON YOURSELF — The Walker Brothers
3. IF YOU GOTTA GO, GO NOW — The Manfred Mann
4. LOOK THROUGH ANY WINDOW — The Hollies
5. SATISFACTION — Rolling Stones
6. EVE OF DESTRUCTION — Barry McGuire
7. HANG ON SLOOPY — The McCoys
8. ALMOST THERE — Andy Williams
9. IL SILENZIO — Nini Rosso
10. JUST A LITTLE BIT BETTER — Herman's Hermits

'Tears' Tops

Ken Dodd is still shedding his "Tears" in the number one spot on the British charts. This is the second straight week for Dodd as the chart-topper. We at *The BEAT* received a copy of "Tears" and although it is a very pretty record we doubt if it will ever duplicate it's British success here in America.

A record which no doubt *will* achieve as much success here in America as it has in Britain is "Make It Easy On Yourself" by the Walker Brothers. This week finds it at number two on the British charts and possibly next week will find it Number One.

As you may know, the BBC has banned Barry McGuire's "Eve Of Destruction" and as you have probably guessed when a record is banned its sales increase a hundredfold. And Barry's record is proving no exception by moving up this week from number eight spot into number six spot.

The McCoys' "Hang On Sloopy" took a nice seven place jump this week to land at number seven. Andrew Oldham, Stones' co-manager, is elated over the McCoys' success because in England the record is released on Oldham's new label, Immediate Records.

Another big jumper this week is Andy Williams and his "Almost There." It flew up 10 places to number eight and again it goes to show how different British record buyers tastes are from their American counterparts. Here it is extremely doubtful if the teenagers would ever buy enough Andy Williams records to send him spiraling to the top!

It looks as if Herman just might have that big record which he has been waiting for for so long. Of course, he's had several huge smashes here in the U.S. but in his native England he has so far failed to make a really tremendous dent in the charts. But after a very slow start "Just A Little Bit Better" is beginning to make terrific strides and this week ended up in the number 10 spot. So, maybe this is the one?

The highest debuter of the week belongs to that barefooted gal, Sandie Shaw. Her "Message Understood" came aboard the charts at number 17 so watch for it to go in a very big way!

The second highest debut sound comes from Wayne Fontana and the Mindbenders and "She Needs Love." Wayne debuted at number 23 and from indications it seems as if he just might have another "Game Of Love" on his hands which, of course, would make Wane and the Mindbenders a bunch of pretty happy guys!

Upbeat Of The Week
By Elinore

"There Is Only One Roy Orbison" . . . Yes, this is the title of Roy's first LP on MGM. On the cover appears an exciting photo of Roy, in a reflective mood, pictured against a background of beautiful blue sky.

This album is surely one for listening! When you weary of the rhythm of dance music and singalongs, the incessant beat of Rock, and the monotonous repetition of protest—seek a quiet corner and relax with this one!

World Famed
Roy's creative voice and songwriting talents are world famed; now that he's his own A & R man he has further outlets for expression, and fabulous new sounds are the result. His personal message on the album explains this new freedom of expression far better than I can.

The sound and the story of "Ride Away" are now familiar to all, but have you noticed a new depth in Roy's voice—a full rich baritone. For contrast, there are those high notes in "Wondering". As Bobby Mitchell says, he reaches "way up there where the air is rare."

Vocal Harmony
Other highlights are the unbelievable vocal harmony in "You Fool, You", and out-of-this-world instrumental effects on "Sugar and Honey".

It is significant that Roy is now sharing the lively and charming "Claudette" with us. During the 8 years he was married to Claudette, I don't believe this song was available. Next to "Ride Away" and "You Fool, You", it is my personal favorite, but every one of the 12 cuts has something special to offer.

On the BEAT
By Louise Criscione

John Lennon had a rather profound statement to make about the Beatles' recent American tour: "The weather's too hot and someone's pinched three of my shirts." George promptly blamed Ringo for John's misfortune but Ringo deadpanned: "Don't look at me! I've got nothing to do with the weather!"

Some more Beatle news—the four boys will cut a new record in November for pre-Christmas release and then, of course, around the Christmas holidays they will begin another one of their fabulous Christmas shows. There was some talk of close-circuiting the show so that people in other parts of England (and possibly the U.S.) could also view the Beatles' show but nothing further has been said so I guess we lose!

Dig Khaki Ties
Have you noticed that all of the Beatles have suddenly taken to wearing khaki army ties? Well, there is a very good explanation for this. While they were filming "Help" on Salisbury Plain, Paul happened to mention to an army colonel how much he liked the tie the Colonel was wearing and sure enough the next day the Colonel showed up loaded down with ties for all of the Beatles!

Mick Jagger revealed to a London newspaperman: "When there are thousands of people out there rioting—I don't mind telling you I get pretty scared."

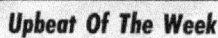
. . . JOHN LENNON

Well, I guess so! In fact, after what happened in Germany it is a real wonder that Mick and the rest of the Stones even get up there on the stage at all. On that German tour 20,000 seats were broken to the tune of $120,000. That's a lot of broken seats, isn't it? And it's also a heck of a lot of rioting!

QUICK ONES: Barry McGuire shelved plans to go on the Herman's Hermits' tour of England, instead he will make his own ten day promotional visit to England . . . Accompanying Barry will be P. F. Sloan who wrote "Eve Of Destruction" and whose "Sins Of The Family" has been covered by a new Manchester group, Ivan's Meads . . . Tom Jones will sing the title song of the latest James Bond thriller, "Thunderball." Tom may also record the song for possible release as a single . . . Well, the Hollies (after numerous delays and postponements) finally made it to the U.S. and they declare our country, "Great!"

Something's gotta stop or the world is going to have three dead Walker Brothers on her hands! Every single one of the Brothers' personal appearances has been marked by rioting, fans crashing on stage and Walker Brothers being roughed up something awful!

Feared Broken Back
Recently, Scott took such a beating that it was feared he had broken his back. Luckily, this first diagnosis was wrong—but as far as Scott is concerned it was much too close for comfort!

The Yardbirds have departed but not before Epic Records threw a huge party for the boys at New York's Rolling Stone Discotheque. At first, the Yardbirds' tour looked very bleak for the boys because of immigration difficulties but evidently things got straightened out and they were able to appear on both *"Shindig"* and *"Hullabaloo"* (the "Hullabaloo" show will air during Thanksgiving week).

The Supremes are without a doubt the most popular female group in the world and they continue to earn honors as if they were going out of style. Their latest honor was in being named the official representative at Holland's Annual Popular Song Festival in Amsterdam.

Stones' notes: Charlie considers the pop art craze "a load of rubbush" . . . Mick is temporarily off dancing now, says that one two minute dance a night is plenty for him . . . Bill has taken up photography and he and his wife, Diane,

. . . KEITH RICHARD

are now home-movie addicts . . . When they were in Scotland, Mick and Brian took off at 3 a.m. to go hunting for birds' nests! 'Course, they're not true "hunters" because Brian toted along a huge umbrella to keep the two "hunters" dry . . . Keith reveals that the Stones really do answer their fan mail — at least, as much of it as they can!

KRLA ARCHIVES

MIKE CLIFFORD SERENADES a bevy of beauties in a scene from "Village Of The Giants." The movie is a Paramount release which begins its theater run on Halloween night. Mike himself will spend practically the whole month of October doing cross-country promotion for the movie—so it ought to be one heck of a box office smash!.

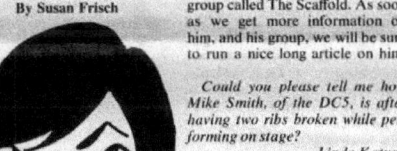

By Susan Frisch

Dear BEAT People,
I want to thank you all so very much for the wonderful letters I have received, but ever since I mentioned that all of you could receive personal replies I have been "flooded." Because of this, I'm afraid, I will have to retract this. Please, no more personal replies from me concerning my column. I hate to say this, but there have been just so many of your letters, and I just can't answer them all. Your questions will get answered much faster if I print them in *Dear Susan*. Thank you all so much anyway for your thoughtfulness in writing to me.

There is one more thing. I have received quite a few asking me the same question, so will now answer it for all of you. The question involved Paul marrying Jane Asher. This is the story: Jane announced on British Television that SHE would marry Paul. At their recent press conference here Paul told The BEAT staff that he had no, I repeat, NO, intention of marrying her. He apparently was unaware of her statement, and when he found out he was not overjoyed about it. So the answer to the question still remains the same: They are NOT married.

★ ★ ★

Could you please tell me if the Beatles wear wigs?
Cathy Schnur

Dear Cathy,
What do you mean?!!! No, No, No! The Beatles do not, have not, and will most likely never wear wigs in their lives!

Will you please tell me all you know about Mike McGear, Paul McCartney's brother?
Carolyn Bell

Dear Carolyn,
Mike is 5 ft. 11½ inches tall. He has brown hair and hazel eyes. He got the name "McGear" from the first two letters of his own name, and "gear" from the word gear. He is an actor who plays mostly to stage and nightclub audiences. Right now he plays with his own group called The Scaffold. As soon as we get more information on him, and his group, we will be sure to run a nice long article on him.

Could you please tell me how Mike Smith, of the DC5, is after having two ribs broken while performing on stage?
Linda Katuna

Dear Linda,
Don't worry any longer. Mike is fine.

Help! Pleazzzze can you tell me where I can buy a John Lennon hat?
Charlii Volt

Dear Charlii,
Have you tried all the big department stores around your neighborhood? If this has failed I might suggest you try some record stores. If any of The BEAT readers know maybe they can help you out. I will print your address in case they can. 501 East 14th Street, Beaumont, California.

I would like to know why Paul didn't wear his I.D. bracelet in "HELP!" I thought he never went anywhere without it.
Dingletoes Dunlap

Dear Dingletoes??
I really don't know. Nothing was ever said or printed about it so I guess we'll all have to wait till we can ask Paul ourselves.

Where can I write to a Donovan Fan Club?
Kris Britin

Dear Kris,
Sorry to say this, but I find no fan club available for him. If you, or any other BEAT readers would be interested in starting one, just drop us a line, and we'll print it.

How old is Herman, and when is his birthday?
Georgia Junkins

Dear Georgia,
Herman is 17 years old. His birthday is November 5, 1947.

How long were the Animals in California, on their most recent visit?
Barbara Greene

Dear Barbara,
Those "Animals" were here for five whole days.

How old is Cher, and what is her last name?
Kathi Rose

Dear Kathi,
Cher is 19 years old, and her last name is Bono. Her maiden name was LaPierre.

Are Bobby Sherman and Donna Loren going steady, or are they just dating?
Sylvia Cox

Dear Sylvia,
Bobby and Donna are nothing more but very good and close friends. They are not going steady or anything like that.

Will you please tell me if the Stones will be back for another tour of California?
Laren Wyman

Dear Laren,
The Stones are due back for another tour at the end of this month, or the beginning of November.

Where can I write to the Leaves?
Sally Ministo

Dear Sally,
You can write to the Leaves in care of Penthouse Recordings, 9025 Wilshire Blvd., Beverly Hills, California.

Can you please tell me if Dino, Desi, and Billy have any girlfriends?
Donna Wright

Dear Donna,
None of the boys have any girlfriends or steady girlfriends, or anything! After all, they are pretty young to date, aren't they???

Q: My hair looks awful if I don't comb it every half hour or so, and to make things worse, I have to use a brush instead of a comb. I don't always carry a purse, and when I don't I have to run around carrying a hair brush. This looks silly, I know, but a lot of girls do the same thing. Any brilliant ideas as to how I can stop being so "obvious?"
(Matsy P.)

A: Buy a small teasing comb which will be easier to tuck into a pocket. Teasing combs are almost as good as brushes when it comes to touch-ups, because the teeth don't completely penetrate the hair style. This may sound weird, but we know of one girl who tapes a teasing comb (with masking tape) inside her blouse or the bell-bottom part of her slacks when she doesn't want to carry a purse! At any rate, anything's better than carrying a hair brush around.

Q: I want to buy a pair of false eye lashes. Can you give me some advice on what kind to buy and how much I'll have to pay for lashes that will last?
(Arlene T.)

A: Good false lashes are either made from real hair or fur. The hair type usually costs about $5, the fur about $10. Both of these types last long enough to be worth the money spent. Many girls prefer hair lashes because they seem to have a more natural look. Max Factor and Elizabeth Arden are two good brands you can count on. You can also buy synthetic lashes for $1, but if you wear them often, they will probably have to be replaced before long. Also, low-priced lashes don't have a very genuine look.

Q: My skin always gets funny in the summer, probably from being out in the sun too much. I used my mother's scented bath oil, but it just made me feel more parched than ever. Do you know of some product that doesn't have perfume in it?
(Gaby W.)

A: Try Polyderm, a scent-free bath oil for dryness. It's by Prince Matchabelli, costs around $2.50 and one bottle should clear up your condition. When sun tan time rolls around next summer, start using this product again and you probably won't have your annual problem.

Q: Is it true that you can really wash wool skirts with the new cold water soaps?
(Doreen A.)

A: They say it's true, but we suggest you try this method on an old skirt that's seen its best days, just to be safe.

Q: I used some old cold cream to remove my makeup and the next day I was all broken out. This isn't like me and I want to know if you have any idea why this happened.
(Sherry L.)

A: Nearly all cosmetics lose their strength if they sit around too long, and some of them reach the point where they do more harm than good. You didn't say how old the cream was, but if you've had it over a year, this probably caused the break out. Either that or you may have developed an allergy to one of the chemicals in the product. Just throw it away and do the same to any cosmetic that may be all worn out.

HINT OF THE WEEK

I was always having a problem making extra money to buy records and all that. Then I got one of the new $20 Polaroid Swinger cameras for my birthday. It makes finished pictures in just seconds and when I go to a rock and roll concert, I take it along and sell the pix (for a reasonable price). Sometimes my friends even have me take their pictures and buy them. Try it, it's a great way to earn extra dollars!
(Melody B.)

If you have a question you'd like answered, or a hint you'd like to share, drop a line to Tips To Teens, c/o The BEAT!

KRLA ARCHIVES

For Girls Only

By Shirley Poston

Hi, everyone! Including the boys who are craftily reading this column! I'm in such a good mood today, even *you* are invited to this week's gab fest.

So what am I so riotously happy about? No, I haven't been at the cooking Sherry. No, my little brother was not kidnapped by a roving band of gypsies (unfortunately).

Spring Cleaning

It's like this. Last night I cleaned out my closet. Spring housecleaning, you know. I know spring has sprung and it's fall and all that ... oh, did you know that they don't say *fall* in England—they say *autumn*.

What on earth was I saying before I got off the track (me and my English phase)? Oh yes, I was doing my spring housecleaning a little late (which figures) and throwing out a bunch of really cruddy looking old purses that have been sitting around collecting dust for years.

And you'll never guess what I found in one of them! I found *George!*

Don't get me wrong now. I don't mean George Harrison (sigh, gasp), although I sure wish I did (shiver, shudder).

The Other George

I found another sort of George. George Washington. Ten of him, in fact.

I suppose by now you're thinking I've finally flipped and that the men in white are zooming over to my abode this very minute (with large nets).

Well, you're wrong (I hope). The George Washingtons I found were green, wrinkled ones! Like, MONEY!

Really, I did about flip because crammed into the bottom of this really *sick* purse were ten grimy one dollar bills.

Where From?

After I'd turned a few cartwheels I started trying to remember where they came from. Finally did. I hid the loot Christmas before last, to buy a present for a boy I was nuts about at the time.

Unfortunately, he moved to West Virginia early that December (wait – now that I think of it, make that *fortunately*) and I forgot all about my buried treasure.

Wild, huh? Now I have ten whole unexpected dollars to spend on something I don't need! And I think I'm going to have a lot of trouble deciding what. I want something to wear, but there are so many cute things to choose from these days.

That Grammer!

Ain't that the truth (pardon my grammer) (well, my gramper likes her)! I haven't exactly been around for forty years or anything, but I've NEVER seen such adorable fashions as we have today. Things sure have changed, haven't they? Even five years ago clothes were nothing like this.

Are George and I going to have fun shopping around!

Oh, guess what esle I found. I found *my* George, too. Dolt that I am, I bought a "Hard Day's Night" album over a year ago and lost it before I could even play it one time. Well, it turned up in my closet type spree. Now what am I going to do with two "Hard Day's Night" albums? Contrary to popular rumor, I don't really have two heads, you know.

Ahah! Now it dawns on me. I'll give the album to one of my faithful (or else) readers! Tell you what. I'll send the real George (faint, faint) to the first Harrison fan who writes and tells me they don't have this album. Just drop a line c/o this column!

So Wonderful

Now that I have spent pages talking about myself again (I'm so wonderful I think I'll meet myself later) (I'm kidding, I'm kidding), let's go on to something a bit more interesting.

Remember when I told you I was going to tell you about the Emergency Kit this girl friend of mine carries wherever she goes? She got the idea from reading an article in *The BEAT* that suggested giving some kind of a kit to a visiting star.

Anyway, she took a small make-up bag, the kind that fits in your purse, and here's what she has crammed into it.

Needle and thread, a dollar bill for boys who run out of gas, a cloret in case she meets a fab boy just after she's devoured a hamburger-with, a 50 cent engagement ring (in case she decides the boy isn't so fab after all and has to give him the brush but quick), safety and bobby pins, a combination pen and flashlight, two false fingernails and a tiny tube of glue in case she breaks one at the prom or something, and about a jillion more kooky things that would really come in handy in an emergency.

An Emergency

Good idea, huh? Think I'll try it. My makeup bag looks more like an emergency than it does an emergency kit.

Oh, she also has, carefully wrapped in wax paper, this tiny lock of hair that she swears came from the heavenly head of John Lennon himself. But I wonder about that one. Well, maybe it's a *coincidence* that "John's hair" is the exact same color as her dog's.

It is now plug time. I've come across a product that's really great and want to clue you in if you don't already know about it. It's a tube lip gloss by Clairol that's really the gear (sorry mates, got carried off, I did). It's colorless and can be used with or without other liptstick. I like it all by itself. Oh, it's called "Flicker Stick." Cute name, too.

Oh, Don't Go

It is now time to start winding up this week's ravings, but before I go, one more thing.

I saw another of "those" commercials. In this one, some girl is fretting about not knowing her lines for the school play. Suddenly her mother and her teacher are telling her to use Colgate toothpaste.

I have yet to figure out what toothpaste has to do with the school play, but that's beside the point. What I know I'll NEVER figure out is why adults are wacky enough to think that parents, teachers and students gather ANYWHERE (much less backstage) to discuss TEETH!

I mean, come off it! They've got to be kidding. Have you ever had a teacher who stayed up nights worrying about your dental problems?

Off the Soapbox

Oh, get off your soap box, my old. Teenagers aren't that soft, and every teenager knows that, but it looks like the rest of the world is going to have to wait until WE'RE adults before they'll ever find out how things really are.

Don't know about you, but I'm in no hurry for that day to come. Being young is too much fun to really want to be anything else.

Now, if you'll excuse me, I have to go reassure several teachers that I brush after every meal.

Don't forget to let me know if you want my extra album, and I'll see you next *BEAT!*

BUSY, BUSY BARRY

Busy is the word for Barry McGuire. Since "Eve of Destruction" became a hit, the blond singer is off and running in his career. The latest development, *The BEAT* learned, is that he is being offered to star in a projected ABC-TV series, titled for the time being, "Folk & Roll."

TRIUMPH FOR JERRY NAYLOR! Since Jerry has been playing the Les Poupees Club in San Jose he has outdrawn the Supremes both audience-wise and money-wise! That's quite an achievement.

Cannon's Career

(Continued from page 3)

"Because of all the junk that's gone on in the last six months—the racial riots and stuff. I think that people like Bob Dylan and Barry McGuire are putting out truthful records. I mean, if you listen to the lyrics of these records you know they're true.

Kids Want Truth

"I'm not saying that we're on the 'Eve Of Destruction', but I am saying that maybe the kids today want to hear the truth for a change instead of trying to hide it."

The teenagers who first got excited over Freddy Cannon are now for the most part married and have children of their own and a new set of teens have taken over. Freddy's seen them both, does he think they differ?

"In a way," he reflected. "You can tell by the music they like today. They still like to listen and hear records they can reminisce to, but they're growing up a little faster. They're hipper. They've heard a lot about the record business and they know the insides of the business – things which the teenagers before didn't know.

"One thing I hate is when an adult says 'why do kids buy that trash? First of all, it *isn't* trash and kids buy it because they like it. They go into a record store just full of records but do you think they buy every one of them? No, they only have 98 cents or a dollar or whatever a record costs – and they buy what they like, what sounds good to them."

Teen Tastes

Many people have voiced the opinion that teens like only what adults do not like and that this acceptance of what adults reject is a form of rebellion. I asked Freddy if he agreed with this view.

"No. There's something in every act that excites somebody – that they send a message to. Just something that people like. It can just be being nice. I think 50% of my popularity is because of that.

If a kid walked in here right now I'd think he was just as good as I am. I try to make a lot of friends and I think every kid is equal. Once you start thinking you're something you're not, then you're in trouble."

Freddy is one busy boy. He's just finished a movie, "Village Of The Giants," in which he sings but not acts. Freddy says he did do some acting once in "No Time For Sergeants."

Went Off Air

"But that show went off the air! Acting is a tough business – getting up at that hour of the morning! But if someone offered me a role I'd probably take it – I'd try anything once!" Freddy grinned.

Besides his movie Freddy has two new albums coming out on Warner Bros. Records – an "Action" album and an "Oldies" album which will contain all of the old Cannon hits like "Tallahassee Lassie."

Freddy also has a new record coming out shortly which he brought up to the office for *The BEAT* staff to hear and decide which side we liked the best. I'll tell you right now – *both* sides are great!

And so is Freddy Cannon and I'll lay you any kind of odds that six years from now Freddy will still be turning out those hits. 'Cause with a sound like this – he just can't lose!

KRLA ARCHIVES

THE DAVE HULL STORY, PT. 2
Monarch of Toot Honks Horn Again

Hiya Hullabalooers. Well, we're back again and ready to start the second installment of our Dave Hull Story.
Now if you recall, when we left you last week we were speaking of the Beatles. As we pick up our story this week, we find that we are—still talking about the Beatles!!! Well, what are we waiting for? Let's go!! TTOOOOTTT!!

Stop, stop—I'm turning *green* with jealousy, Hullabalooer! Sigh! Oh, well, What do you think of John and Paul as songwriters?

"Oh, I think they're *fantastic*! They plan on writing—they haven't publicly said so—but I would look for the Beatles to do some show tunes; to do a musical, write it. And I think they could do a magnificent job of it. I think the tunes in it would become automatic smash hits, and I think this is forthcoming. I don't think it will come in the next three years, but I think someday in the next ten years it will come. Lennon and McCartney will become one of the greatest songwriting teams the world has ever seen!"

Amen!! Hullabalooer, as the Clown Prince of the Air Waves, you have been involved in a good many funny situations. Were there any particularly humorous incidents which occurred while you were with the Beatles?

"Yes—one was stealing on the plane, as you know, to Denver and the Beatles not knowing how in the heck I got there so fast. That still stumps Paul; he's still amazed."

Aww, c'mon Hullabalooer—do you mean to tell us that he *still* doesn't know?

"Well, yeah, he does *now*—but at the time he didn't because I told him I took a jet. I was putting him on, and he *believed it!!* He couldn't understand. Boy! He thought that was just amazing the way I could just hire a jet and just fly out there and beat them!!

That's all right, Hullabalooer—we all know the *real* truth now; underneath your handy-dandy mild-mannered DJ disguise you're really Super Scuzz, able to leap tall daisies at a single bounce!!

Ta Tweet Toot!!

Oh, you're in good form today, David!!

And speaking of form, it seems that your *format* has acquired an imitator, Hullabalooer. Oh well, it *is* the sincerest form of flattery, y'know. Can you tell us anything about him?

"Oh, I'll tell you about *him!* One day about two years ago when I was here about six months, this fellow came from KENO and asked if he could come in and watch the show; he'd heard me on the air. I said it was fine. So, I was nice enough to let him come in—which I *wasn't supposed to* do—and let him watch for about a half an hour. He looked at the horn I was using and my voice and my phone—the whole bit; calling myself the Hullabalooer and all the people that listen to me. And then he took it out of here and ran back to this station he was working for and did the *same thing!* Now I understand he's saying to press and magazines that he taught *me* everything I knew, which is rather disgusting to me. Since I heard that, he's done stories saying he invented the word 'scuzzy' and invented all these different things. I sent him a wire and told him to grow up!"

A Lot of Growing

You've got a lot of growing up yourself, David. At least, we *think* you have! So just to clear up matters for everyone, why don't you tell us the fascinating facts about the Hullabalooer as a child? What sort of hopes and ambitions did you have as a small boy—other than learning how to blow your own horn. (Sorry about that.)

"First of all, when I was very young, I went to an old radio show here in town, and the announcer who came out and warmed-up the audience got them to laughing just seconds before the show was started, and I thought that was amazing. I told my mother at the time—I was about seven years old I think—I wanted to be a radio announcer. And she told me 'Shut up and watch the show!' because she thought I was just putting her on! Then, when I was in high school, I wanted to be a Secret Service man and protect the life of the President, so it was either one way or the other. So I had these two ideas, and I found out how much money a Secret Service man makes and that he has to work twenty-four hours a day—then I found out how much a disc jockey makes and how many hours *we* have to work—so I decided I'd be a disc jockey!!"

And there you have it folks, the success story of the year—a young man and his horn!...

Tooot Ta Toooot!

Thank you, Hullabalooer; you never sounded better! And now, Mr. Hull—have you any parting words of wisdom for all of your faithful fans?

"I'd just like to say that the kids have been *so* great to me and I really don't deserve it, I really don't. And I want them to understand that. I could never, *ever* thank them for everything they've given me by being fans of mine. I just want to say that I appreciate that very much."

Hullabalooer—I am certain that I speak for all of the many KRLA listeners who are devoted fans of yours when I say: the pleasure has been all ours!!

...HULLABALOOER AT WORK

...BLOW, DAVE

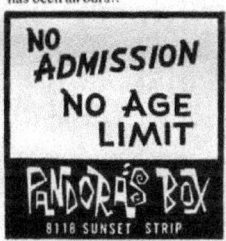
NO ADMISSION
NO AGE LIMIT
PANDORA'S BOX
8118 SUNSET STRIP

KRLA BEAT SUBSCRIPTION
you will SAVE 60% of the regular price!
AN INTRODUCTORY SPECIAL... if you subscribe now...

☐ 1 YEAR—52 Issues—$3.00   ☐ 2 YEARS—$5.00

Enclosed is $..................

Send to:..Age:..........

Address:..

City:....................................State:..............Zip:..........

MAIL YOUR ORDER TO: KRLA BEAT
1401 South Oak Knoll Avenue
Pasadena, California 91106
Outside U.S. $9.00—52 issues

BEAT BACK ISSUES

YOU DON'T HAVE TO MISS OUT...
on any great pictures, fab interviews or newsy items appearing in any of the following KRLA *BEATS* which you might have missed. For a limited time only, these *BEATS* are still available.

ISSUES AVAILABLE
- 3/31 — BEATLE TITLE CHOSEN
- 4/14 — INTERVIEW WITH JOHN LENNON
- 4/21 — INTERVIEW WITH PAUL McCARTNEY
- 5/5 — HERMANIA SPREADS
- 5/12 — HERE COME THE BEATLES
- 5/19 — VISIT WITH BEATLES
- 6/9 — BEATLES
- 6/16 — BATTLE OF THE BEAT
- 6/30 — PROBY FIRED
- 8/7 — DYLAN
- 8/14 — HERMAN
- 8/21 — STONES TESTIFY
- 8/28 — KRLA PRESENTS THE BEATLES
- 9/4 — BEATLES... IN PERSON NOW!
- 9/11 — THE THREE FACES OF BOB DYLAN
- 9/18 — PROTESTOR BARRY McGUIRE
- 9/25 — SONNY—HE & CHER HAVE 5 HITS
- 10/2 — WAS YARDBIRDS' ORDEAL IN VAIN?
- 10/9 — PAUL & RINGO—NOW SOLOING
- 10/16 — ELVIS—KING OF POP?

To order a back issue, send 25¢ (15¢ plus 10¢ postage and handling charge) to: KRLA BEAT, Suite 504, 6290 Sunset Blvd., Hollywood, Calif. 90028. IT IS NO LONGER NECESSARY TO SEND STAMPS OR SELF-ADDRESSED ENVELOPES

KRLA ARCHIVES

KRLA $11-10 Football Sweepstakes

The KRLA BEAT will award $1,110.00 to everyone accurately predicting the scores of 10 of the 11 games listed below (games to be played Friday, Oct. 22). This contest will be repeated each week for the remainder of the high school football season.

ENTRY BLANK

1. Bell_____ Wilson_____
2. South Gate_____ Garfield_____
3. Narbonne_____ Gardena_____
4. Carson_____ San Pedro_____
5. Marshall_____ Verdugo Hills_____
6. Lincoln_____ Franklin_____
7. Dorsey_____ Jefferson_____
8. Fremont_____ Los Angeles_____
9. Hollywood_____ Hamilton_____
10. Venice_____ Westchester_____
11. No. Hollywood_____ Van Nuys_____

Weekly Contest No. 1

Name_____ Telephone_____
Address_____
City_____ State_____ Zip_____

$11-10 CONTEST RULES

1. Scores for all 11 games must be filled in. Everyone correctly guessing the scores of any 10 of these varsity games will win the jackpot of $1,110.00.
2. Entries should be addressed to: KRLA BEAT 11-10 Contest, 1401 S. Oak Knoll, Pasadena, Calif.
3. Entries for this week's contest must be postmarked no later than 12 p.m. Wednesday, Oct. 20, 1965.
4. Enter as many times as you like. Each entry must be made on a BEAT official contest blank or on a hand-drawn facsimile.
5. Employees of KRLA and The BEAT, and members of the families of employees, are not eligible to compete.

Hear the scores of all varsity football games every week on the KRLA-Herald Examiner Sports Line. Listen for Danny Baxter's Weekly Predictions on KRLA — "The Station That Knows The Score!"

TEXAS SINGER ROY HEAD'S fashion-wise appearance is new to our music scene but it doesn't seem to faze KRLA's and Shebang's Casey Kasem who here points out this latest trend in men's fashions — no pocket but rather a bound strip of the jacket loose for insertion of a silk necktie-matching handkerchief. Roy recently visited Casey on Shebang hosted by him daily at 5 p.m. on Channel 5.

CASEY'S QUIZ
By CASEY KASEM

This group, besides having a hit disc, boasts of several additional talents. One member insists he is equally famous for his ability to simulate (on his guitar) the sound of a chicken chasing a steam roller. Another is an expert at faking work holes in antique furniture. Still another proudly states that drums are not his only musical feat — he also plays tin cans and bath stoppers. Put them all together, add two more and you have a group whose sense of humor is as fantastic as their sound!

ANSWER: The Yardbirds

Hellllp!

HELP!
We are in need of a female rhythm guitarist, bass guitarist and drummer. They must be ages 14-16 years old and live in the Santa Maria-Lompoc area. Please contact Genni Paschal, 283 Orion Ave., Lompoc, California.

HELP!
I am 16 years old and would like an English pen pal. I luv the Beatles, Byrds and Sonny and Cher. I will answer every letter. Write to Barbara Rioza, 441 South McBride Avenue, Los Angeles, Calif.

HELP!
I'm a 13 year old piano and harmonica player. I've had group experience and started playing in 1959. I'm searching for an experienced guitarist about 12, 13 or 14 years old who is musically inclined. It's just for fun, not profit. Should live in or near West Los Angeles area. Write Alan Levin, 12123 Ivy Place, Los Angeles.

HELP!
I am starting a Rolling Stone Fan Club. Anyone wishing to join write to Tina Zink, 130 E. Greenwood, La Habra, California.

HELP!
Anyone who is interested in promoting a great new singing group, please get in touch with me. Don't apply unless you are willing to work hard. Write to Randy Garrison, 14930 Magnolia Blvd., Apt. 6, Sherman Oaks, California.

HELP!
I lost my binoculars at the Beatle concert the night of August 30. They are opera glass style, clamp open and are red in color. They were dropped in Section F. If found please call 635-4045 and ask for Jeanne. P.S. The serial number is 2 5 X.

HELP!
I lost my ticket stub at the Sunday night Beatle concert. It means a lot to me. It was Section S, Row 14, Seat 28. If you found it, please return. Also, Monday night at the concert I found the stub of Seat 105, Section K, Row 22. If you lost it, write me and I will return. Kathy Ellsberry, 4402 Lomina, Lakewood, California.

CENTENNIAL, TAFT WIN KRLA GRID SALUTE

KRLA Sports Director Danny Baxter has selected Centennial High and Taft High as "Team of the Week" during the second week of play in prep school football.

In the Southern Section, Centennial pulled a 32-20 upset over top-rated Muir. In the City Section, Taft defeated Cleveland 12-6 in a big season-opener in the West Valley League.

During the previous week El Rancho of Pico Rivera drew the KRLA salute as Team of the Week in the Southern Section and Gardena in the Los Angeles City division.

****
Great Western
Exhibit Center
"Battle of the Bands"
Nov. 17 - 20
For Info: RA 3-3618
****

The MOTHERS —
A Musical Group That's A
'Must Have' at Your Club or
Next Party... Call

Frank Zapa
383-7063

KRLA ARCHIVES

Beatles Running; Running; Running

By Jamie McCluskey III

Running, running — at a dizzying pace; *running* are the Beatles, faster than the speed of light.

Running to their many concerts, *running from* their screaming fans. *Running* 'round the world in waxen circles of chart-topping records, and *running* circles 'round the world!

Until now, the Beatles had always run together: a relay team of four. But lately there have been some changes in the running line-up, and some of the boys have been venturing forth on solo trots all their own.

Beatle Paul contemplates his tears in mournful solitude.

M. Starkey, MBE, has decided to be himself and in a rare solo performance by The Nose, Ringo bravely sets forth to "Act Naturally."

Of course, it is left to Mr. Lennon — John-John by name — to be the sneaky one, as he deviously demands that "You've Got to Hide Your Love Away."

Yes, it is true that the Beatles are doing more and more individually in the records which they are producing now. However, they have said from the very first that the act was "a whole, and each one of us takes one quarter of the whole."

Among the many countless reasons behind their phenomenal success lies the fact that each Beatle is a very talented individual in his own right. We are all well-acquainted with the works of the talented team of songwriters — Lennon and McCartney — and the genius of John Lennon as author in *"his own write"* is far from secret. In the music industry itself, Ringo Starr has a fine reputation as being one of the best natural drummers in his field, and George Harrison is adding to his own excellent reputation as a great guitarist by writing songs of his own for the group.

But concern has been voiced because John and Paul have gone into record production for one or two other groups outside of their own, and over the now widely-known solo writing and performing efforts of Paul on his beautiful new record, "Yesterday."

The truth is that all four of the boys have always worked on little projects of their own, independent of other members of the group. But just as they have said of themselves, there are four unique individuals in this group and each member is an important entity in himself even before he has joined with the other three to form the perfect foursome.

Yes, the Beatles are *running* — only running far ahead of everyone else on the track. And Paul? Well, he's just leading the pack!!

...PAUL LEADS PACK

BEAT Photo: Chuck Boyd

A TWIN HIT

San Francisco Sez So!

AND SO DOES... WASHINGTON, D.C. (Johnsonville, U.S.A.), BOSTON...PHOENIX...and now — LOS ANGELES!

Mira Records

9145 SUNSET BLVD. ★ ★ (213) CR 8-1125 ★ ★ LOS ANGELES, CALIF.

KRLA ARCHIVES

Liverpuddles

By Rob McGrae
Manager, The Cavern

The Richmond Group

PORTMAN'S PLATTERPOOP

By Julian Portman

HOLLYWOOD ... **The King Family** of singers will record for the teen-market under the title; **King Cousins.** Who cares? ... "The Teen-Age Revolution," an A.B.C.-TV documentary will be viewed October 29. Should be a must for all teens!

Sonny & Cher will vocalize at the Hollywood Palace October 23 following the presentation of their first "gold" record for selling one million copies of "Look at Us" ... **Eddie Hodges,** a nice guy, has another groovy single on Aurora titled "The Old Rag Man" ... Didja ketch **Hullabaloo's** October 11th tribute to **Bob Dylan** with **George Maharias** trying to act as host. 'Nuff said! ... **David McCallum** has a single titled "Agent OO Soul." It came off during his appearance on a TV show ... **Roger Miller** signed to do a bit of acting in the "Tammy" TV series. Certainly he'll sing "Bottle Baby." That's why they asked him on in the first place.

Demand For Shamrock

Dee Gee records is being swamped with requests for the Irish shamrock they offered in last week's BEAT ad in introducing their imported Irish folk-rock group **The Fenians** ... "For Your Love" is the new **Righteous Bros.** single that was lifted-out of their hit album "Some Blue-Eyed Soul"... **Herman's Hermits** found only one thing left over from **The Beatles** when they moved into the same diggings on Benedict Canyon, the fans! They encamped all over the place ... **Dick Clark's** "Where The Action Is" TV show visits the H'wood Wax Museum for Halloween. Need any more ghouls?

Les Crane goes teen-age. He's thinking of bringing lots of teen groups on his late night interview show. He feels teens are still awake; why not give them a treat ... **Dick Howard,** my man of information from the **Shindig** offices, heard that **Mike Henry,** the former SC footballer will be singing in his next **Tarzan** roll. Author **Edgar Rice Burroughs** must be turning over in his permanent shelter, for at one time **Tarzan** swung, at least through the trees ... Capitol records **The Lettermen** are the only singing group in the Top 20 who wear short hair ... and **Walter Winchell** reads *The BEAT,* and I read his column. There, we're even!

Bigger Than Beatles

The Walker Bros., virtual unknowns in the U.S., but bigger—are you ready for this?—than **The A** teenager (like those who scream during a Beatles appearance) who grew into a lovely successful bus-Beatles in Britain, were born right here in Los Angeles. Their new "hot" disc is "Make It Easy On Yourself" ... **Norm Ratner,** the creator of **The Leaves** masterpiece for Mira records, "Too Many People", has signed to do their first album. Can't wait! ... **Robert Horton,** hero of TV westerns, flopperoo as night club performer, goes the Nashville Sound route in his next Columbia album ... **The Rolling Stones** and **Cilla Black** have signed to appear in a British TV series, The Baron ... **Chad & Jeremy,** disregarding all breaking-up rumors, have a new single released. It's titled "Should I"! If you must, go right ahead!

Sonny & Cher, a nice way to begin another paragraph, went the big route when they performed for **Jackie Kennedy** and friends. Amid the friends were **Paul Raffles** and his favorite date, luscious **Stella Stevens.** To do this scene, "S & C" appearing at **It's Boss** in H'wood had to get permission of its owner. The gentleman, being a man of honor, said fine and due to the late notice shuttered **It's Boss** for this one night so that "S & C" could leave for New York. The boss who's so nice is **Paul Raffles,** the same one who led the cheers.

Handsome Hero

Jim Stacy, one of the heroes in "A Swinging Summer" has signed with Domino records ... **John Ashley,** handsome hero of teen movies, and the husband of **Deborah Walley,** has two labels seeking his musical services. His wife **Deborah,** the pixie of Gidget that went Hawaiian and now of the Bikini-type movies, has a **Marianne Faithfull**-type voice. She's readied a socko single for release by Dee Gee records ... Do yourself a favor, pick-up an **Ed Ames** single on RCA Victor!

Gary Owens, the radio personality with that deep, deep, deep sounding voice, has a large role in one of **The Munsters** segments. His audience is the teen of yesterday who has grown into the type called today's mothers ... **Freddy Cannon** goes the one niters route. Guess he can't get sleep at night! ... **Chad Stuart,** without **Jeremy** or **Jill,** appears in a **Walt Disney** epic ... er, rather his voice will be heard playing the part of a Vulture.

The Byrds are hungry for another hit. Can't live off one record, men? ... Out of nowhere has come **Charlie Rich's** "Mohair Sam." It's very listenable ... iness woman in a field normally reserved for tough-minded men, will be the theme of an article to appear in **Vogue** magazine. The story is on **Doris Gilbert,** prexy of Dee Gee records, and should be a model for all our female teen readers ... **Sig Sakowicz** sends along this quote: "Know how to tell girl pancakes from boy pancakes? By the way they're stacked!" Later baby!

LIVERPOOL, England—Liverpool groups are starting to make another assault on the record scene here in England.

The Masterminds already have a record in release which looks as though it is going to be a big hit. Hot on their heels are the Clayton Squares and Earl Preston's Realms, who both released records on Oct. 8. The Hideaways also have a record being released in October. And now I have just heard of another—the Richmond Group. The man who's going to record them is none other than Andrew Loog Oldham, the manager of the Rolling Stones. Oldham thinks the Richmond Group are a very exciting act which is sure to make a hit.

Liverpool Still Swings

All this tends to show that, contrary to many people's beliefs, Liverpool is not finished as the Big Beat center. In fact, it looks as though it is going to be the town to produce a new sound, because all the new groups from Liverpool have a far bigger sound than their better known townmen such as the Beatles.

However, getting back to the Richmond Group (and I know a lot of girls would never leave them if they got the chance to meet them) they have a really tremendous act which features two vocalists, thus enabling them to do close harmony numbers.

The vocalists in the group are Dave Kerry and Eddie Cave. Dave really goes wild on some numbers, driving the girls to screams. The comedians of the group are Howie Jones, the bass player, and Barry Wheldon, the rhythm guitarist. On lead guitar is Barry David while Pete Taylor is the drummer. Their average age is about 19.

Forgot Closing Time

While the group was appearing at the Waterloo Winter Gardens in Liverpool they had a really funny experience. They went on stage at 10 p.m. and were due off stage at 11 p.m. but they got so involved in their act, and were having such a good time, that they played way past the scheduled closing time of the hall. In an attempt to get the boys off the stage the stage hands put the lights out and even went to the extent of pulling the curtains across. However, the group continued to play. It was only after the stage hand switched off the electric current to their equipment that the boys were forced to stop playing.

Eddie remarked later, "The crowd was so great that we just didn't want to stop playing to them and from what we could see they wanted us to continue playing."

The Richmond Group love to hear from their fans. They'd like to hear from some of you in America too. You can write to them at Dept. R., 8/12 Mathew St., Liverpool 2.

Walker Bros. Expected

That fab trio from America, the Walker Brothers, are to appear in Liverpool shortly with several of the top Liverpool groups. The Walkers have been looking forward to this because it is their first appearance in Liverpool and they will be appearing for the first time with the Masterminds. Their admiration for the Masterminds grew when they heard the "B" side of a Masterminds record which they wrote themselves and would like to have recorded. Next week I hope to report on this fab show.

Now let me thank all you wonderful people who have written to me. I love to hear from you and hope that you will continue to write. I also want to let you know that the letters which I have already received will be answered as soon as possible.

Well, that's all for now. I'll be writing for you again next week. So until then, look after yourselves and tarra for now.

BEAT Photo: Denny DeWinter

REMEMBER THIS PHOTO because you are looking at a star of the future shown here with Herman, a star of the first magnitude of the present. Her name is Jade East; she is a student at Granada Hills, Calif., High School; her age is 16. Blonde, green-eyed Jade, who came to California from Cleveland, Ohio, at the age of nine is a singer and dancer of great promise and a BEAT bet for stardom.

KRLA ARCHIVES

BEAT Pop Music Awards Poll
CATEGORY I: OUTSTANDING MALE VOCALIST

(Please Check 10)

- AKINS, JEWEL
- BARRY, LEN
- BENNETT, TONY
- BENTON, BROOK
- BERRY, CHUCK
- BLACK, TERRY
- BONO, SONNY
- BROWN, JAMES
- BURKE, SOLOMON
- CAMPBELL, GLENN
- CANNON, FREDDY
- CARTER, MEL
- CHARLES, RAY
- CHANDLER, GENE
- CLARK, TONY
- CLIFFORD, MIKE
- DANA, VIC
- DARIN, BOBBY
- DAVIS JR., SAMMY
- DONOVAN
- DORSEY, LEE
- DYLAN, BOB
- DOVE, RONNIE
- FAME, GEORGIE
- GAYE, MARVIN
- GOLDSBORO, BOBBY
- GRAY, DOBIE
- HEAD, ROY
- HUGHES, FRED
- HUTTON, DANNY
- JONES, JACK
- JONES, TOM
- JOY, RODDIE
- KING, JONATHAN
- KRAMER, BILLY J.
- LEE, DICKIE
- LEWIS, JERRY LEE
- LITTLE CAESAR
- LOPEZ, TRINI
- MARTIN, DEAN
- MATHIS, JOHNNY
- McGUIRE, BARRY
- MILLER, ROGER
- ORBISON, ROY
- OWENS, BUCK
- PAIGE, JOEY
- PETERSON, RAY
- PICKETT, WILSON
- PITNEY, GENE
- PRESLEY, ELVIS
- PROBY, P. J.
- REDDING, OTIS
- REED, JIMMY
- RICH, CHARLIE
- RICHARD, CLIFF
- RIVERS, JOHNNY
- ROUND ROBIN
- ROYAL, BILLY JOE
- RYDELL, BOBBY
- SEDAKA, NEIL
- SHANNON, DEL
- SHERMAN, BOBBY
- SINATRA, FRANK
- STARR, EDWIN
- STEWART, BILLY
- TILLOTSON, JOHNNY
- TEX, JOE
- VINTON, BOBBY
- WHITCOMB, IAN
- WILLIAMS, ANDY
- YARBROUGH, GLENN
- WRITE-IN: _____
- WRITE-IN: _____
- WRITE-IN: _____
- WRITE-IN: _____
- WRITE-IN: _____

NEW MALE POP VOCALIST
(Please Check 5)

- AKINS, JEWEL
- BARRY, LEN
- BLACK, TERRY
- BONO, SONNY
- CAMPBELL, GLENN
- CARTER, MEL
- CLARK, TONY
- DONOVAN
- DYLAN, BOB
- DOVE, RONNIE
- FAME, GEORGIE
- GOLDSBORO, BOBBY
- GRAY, DOBIE
- HEAD, ROY
- HUGHES, FRED
- HUTTON, DANNY
- JONES, TOM
- JOY, RODDY
- KING, JONATHAN
- LEE, DICKIE
- McGUIRE, BARRY
- PAIGE, JOEY
- PICKETT, WILSON
- PROBY, P. J.
- REDDING, OTIS
- RICH, CHARLIE
- ROYAL, BILLY JOE
- SHERMAN, BOBBY
- STARR, EDWIN
- STEWART, BILLY
- TEX, JOE
- WHITCOMB, IAN
- YARBROUGH, GLENN
- WRITE-IN: _____
- WRITE-IN: _____
- WRITE-IN: _____

A BEAT EDITORIAL
Rack Robbers

The recording business is really booming these days. Which is great! But, all explosions make waves. Some of which aren't so great. Like the one we're about to mention.

With the interest in records and record stars at an all time high, a few con-by-day fly-by-night companies have decided to lower the boom *on* the boom. By producing records that just aren't what they're cracked up to be.

The records we speak of are usually albums. "Bargains" which sell at a very low price (usually 99c or less), claiming to be by top artists and turning out to be just the opposite.

You won't find them in record stores where demonstration discs are available. There you have the opportunity to hear what you're getting yourself into.

You'll find them on racks in unsuspecting markets, drug stores, etc. Places where you buy a recording on sight, not sound.

All "bargains" aren't this sort. Most are just what they claim to be. But some *are* this sort, manufactured by people who would go to *any* length to cash in on the powerful teenage dollar.

Don't let them (or *anyone*) take advantage of you. If you come across a "bargain" that's just too good to be true, find out whether it is or isn't. Contact a reputable record shop and ask if the album is a legitimate release.

Any shop should be more than willing to help you because they're just as furious about all this as we are.

If that's possible!

'Wooly Bully' Wailing All Over The World

After earning a gold record in the United States for their recording of "Wooly Bully," Sam the Sham and the Pharaohs are now trying to conquer the world.

Their record is currently number one in Mexico where it translates to "Bule Bule" and it's in the top ten in Argentina, Belgium and France.

To date the song has sold over 100,000 thousand in Germany, Japan and England and over 25,000 in Holland, Belgium, Mexico, Canada, France and Scandinavia.

Toys Hit On Bach Kick

Three girls from New York currently have a fast selling record out that was originally written by J. S. Bach!

"Lover's Concerto" is the first release by the Toys, three girls who just met a few months ago. Bach set down the original notes over 200 years ago.

The girls are Barbara Harris, June Montiero and Barbara Parritt, all from Jamaica, New York.

Barbara Harris, the group's lead singer, known affectionately as Genius Inc., decided after the group had rehearsed a little that it was time someone heard them.

She made an appointment with Vince Marc, who liked what he heard and called in Denny Randell and Sandy Linzer. Randell and Linzer produced the record for the girls and the rest is history.

Maybe a group doesn't have to have a Lennon-McCartney or Jagger-Richards writing combination behind it to be successful in this business. Maybe Bach doesn't *hurt* either.

PRETTY JODY MILLER, who sings both western and pop music, carries the banner of protesting teens everywhere with her recording of "Home of the Brave, Land of the Free"—the story of a boy who was expelled from school for wearing long hair.

FAB! FAB! FAB!

Dylan's Greatest Song

"Love Minus Zero"

by

Eddie Hodges

AURORA RECORDS
LOS ANGELES, CALIF.

KRLA ARCHIVES

Have A Blast On Fave's Birthday

By Shirley Poston

This isn't going to be easy to believe, but did you know that *some* people think it's *utterly ridiculous* to celebrate the birthday of a favorite star?

Well! If there's anything ridiculous around here, it's *some* people. (Huh?)

Line It Up

Why, there's nothing more fun, fab and/or gear in this whole *world* than getting together with all your friends and living it up on the day you-know-who was born!

It not only gives you the chance to honor your fave. It also gives you a reason to get together and be ridiculous! (Which, as everyone knows, is good for the soul.)

In case you've about run out of ways to live it up on that special day (without having to live it down later), here are ten great methods of having more fun on your rave's birthday than he's having!

Ways and Means

1. About a week before his birthday, threaten all your friends into circulating petitions requesting that school be let out early (or better yet, ask for the day off) on B-Day. It won't work (unless your principal needs medical attention), but think of all the fun you'll have getting signers! Then, when B-Day arrives, cram all the petitions into a birthday card and mail them off to the star. He'll flip!

2. There are a trillion different kinds of birthday parties you can have on B-Day. One of the most fun is the kind where each guest brings his or her favorite record sung by the star and pantomines the record! This is really a blast. In fact, it's a blast in more ways than one, so lay in a large supply of cotton for your folks' ears.

3. Have a B-Day parade (I love a parade, don't you?)! All you have to do is threaten those same friends into helping you make big placards that say happy birthday or something equally original. Then with B-Day arrival, re-threaten your friends into joining a merry march around the neighborhood, or, if you feel energetic, the entire town! Marching music can be supplied by transistor radios. But turn them all to the same station, *please*. (Hint, hint.)

A Marathon

4. Another great party idea is a B-Day marathon. If your fave is a record star, that means playing his discs all day long (for all twenty-four hours if possible, which means you'll have to turn it into a slumber party, too.). Your parents will be more than happy to let you have a B-Day marathon, providing they are visiting friends in Calcutta at the time. If your fave is an actor, see how many times you and your friends can sit through one of his films (before the theater owner calls the man with the net).

5. This may sound crazy, but why not celebrate B-Day by doing something you've been meaning to do? Like getting everyone together and going to an amusement park or going on a bike hike or something fun? This would be a ball in itself, and even more so if you all wear B-Day buttons announcing whose B-Day it happens to be!

6. If circulating petitions isn't quite your cup of tea, celebrate by making a huge birthday card out of art construction paper and having everyone in the entire world sign it. Again, your fave will flip when he sees how many fans wish him a happy B-Day.

A Cake Party

7. If you try this one, your mother may never speak to *The BEAT* again for even *suggesting* something this ridiculous, *but*, here it is anyway. Have a B-Day cake party! Each guest brings a cake mix and one or two layer cake pans (have some of the guests bring prepared frosting instead). Then you bake up a storm and see just how high a cake you can make. When you're finished (and how), take a pic of the cake and then devour it! (The cake, not the pic.) Send the pic and a small piece of the masterpiece to your fave. (He won't eat it, but maybe he can throw it at someone he doesn't like.) By the way, clean up the kitchen afterwards or your mother may never speak to *you* again (either).

8. Don't make him a cake, make him a present! You know, something really wild. Like all of you could knit a square (different colors of yarn) and then sew them together and tell him it's a blanket (or, if you have an awful lot of friends, a tent). Or make a big scrapbook with clippings and stories he may not have seen. This is as much fun to give as it will be to receive!

9. This method makes sense only if you and your friends all have formal type dresses, preferably long, which are just hanging around in the closet feeling left out. If you do possess such items, have a formal B-Day party! Each girl invites some lucky boy to take her out to dinner. This is even more of a blast if you *don't* go somewhere swanky for din-dins and go to Bob's Big Boy or some such. Can't you just imagine everyone peering at all of you? They'll peer extra suspiciously if you wear the aforementioned B-Day buttons!

Make Posters

10. If you're long on devotion but short on allowance and can't quite manage a party of any kind, scrounge up friends, paper, crayons, paints, etc. Then make posters until you can't see straight. Posters which, of course, proclaim whose B-Day it is and just how impressive an international event this happens to be! Then, on B-Day, plaster those posters all over everything and everyone in sight!

If you have any additional kooky ideas to go along with this list, just let us know! And happy celebrating!

P.S. *Whatever* you do on your fave's special day, don't forget to let *him* know about it. And don't forget to send a card. Don't think it won't be appreciated, because it will!

THANKS FROM THE BEAT to Shirley Amoroso, San Mateo, Calif., for the Cartoon of the Week.

It's Happening...

By Eden

The Rolling Stones are definitely "What's Happening, baby!" and this week the Stones have decided to tell *BEAT* readers what they think is happening.

America:

"It's a country where you do ten times more work than anywhere else in the world. But, of course, you do get ten times more money. The only problem: it's difficult to relax; much too fast. Los Angeles was about the only place we could let off steam. Audiences? Wild and enthusiastic."

Fans:

"We always sign autographs and pose for pictures for fans. We regard them as V.I.P.'s. But if someone gets to be a bit of a pest, we never tell them to go away. We just drop gentle hints and hope they get the message."

The future:

"We don't think about the future much. It's really not worth worrying about. How can you see what you are going to do ahead? Of course, our present life can't go on. You know, the great feeling of having the best of everything, fantastic service in hotels, police escorts. But we're just happy to take it as it comes."

Their upcoming film:

"It's going to be weird, and full of suspense. It'll surprise you, too. I can't say much about the story now but it's so strange. The sort of thing where everyone dies in the middle. It's going to be great—better than anyone will expect from US! Keith and I are writing the songs for it, and we're even lending a hand on the script!"

Police:

"They can take jokes, and they don't find it beneath them to come in and ask for autographs."

From the Stones to you, then, that's what's Happening!

It just goes to show you that kids aren't all bad; at least—Herman and his Hermits aren't, anyway.

The popular quintet had been on the road and working hard for a long while, and it had been some time since they had been able to get home and spend some time with their parents and families. Solution? Simple; all five of the Hermits—including Herman—sent tickets to their parents and treated them to a vacation in California while the boys were working on the film, "There's No Place Like Space." It was the first trip Stateside for all of the proud parents.

* * *

Dept. of Arrivals and Departures:

Herman winged his way homeward on the 19th of October. Intended plans for the near future include nothing but a long, and well-deserved rest.

Tom Jones arrived in the land of the Stars and Stripes this month for a series of appearances, including some guest shots on *Hullabaloo* and *Shindig*.

The Liverpool Five arrived in the City of the Angels on the eleventh of October, and immediately began work on a new LP.

Watch out for this handsome quintet of Liverpudlians, 'cause they're headed for the top.

* * *

What's all this about Chad Stuart becoming a bloomin' American citizen? Well, it just ain't so, and that information comes to us durectly from Mr. Stuart himself.

This reporter spoke to the charming Britisher for some time the other eve, and it seems that the AFM (musicians union) is insisting that Chad become a citizen so he can continue working in this country. "But I've got a lawyer in Washington fighting it right now," proclaims the talented young Londoner defiantly.

Cat "Tale": Chad Stuart proudly announced to *BEAT* readers that he and wife Jill are now proud parents to two, tiny soft kittens. However, the two new additions to the household didn't arrive at the Stuart's by the conventional stork-route.

Actually, they were acquired accidentally while Chad and Jill were attending a Sonny and Cher opening at a Hollywood night club. "They romp around, and run and play, and they're very cute," says Papa Chad. Well, *The BEAT* sends its best wishes and a warm welcome to the two-newcomers. Hmmm—wonder if *they* can sing, too?!!

And that's what's Happenin', baby!

U. A. Signs Crystals

The Crystals, who started their career with the hit "Uptown," have just been signed to a long-term contract by United Artists effective immediately.

The group, discovered by Phil Spector, is composed of Frances Collins, De De Henry and Delores Broosk. Their hits have included "He's a Rebel," "He's Sure the Boy I Love," "Da Doo Ron Ron" and "Then He Kissed Me."

KRLA ARCHIVES

Sonny & Cher in Orbit

(Continued from page 2)
people in the audience fainted:
CHER: The auditorium held 1,500 people so they knocked out a wall to make room for 2,000 and 5,000 people showed up. It must have been 105 degrees in there.
SONNY: Cher and I came onto the stage and the audience mobbed us.
CHER: I fainted.
SONNY: Yeah, Cher was at the bottom of this heap of people and I guess she sort of passed out cold. But we came out and did the show 15 minutes later—after we made a fast retreat to the dressing room and straightened up.
CHER: Eighteen people fainted during the show—and one of them was a boy.
SONNY: It sure was hot!
CHER: I think that's the most terrible thing that can happen to a performer. You're up on the stage singing, and all the time they're carrying limp bodies out right in front of you. I don't like it at all. (Pause) Sonny, do you remember that show in the Mid-West where they took your shoes and socks?
SONNY: Both shoes and one sock.
CHER: He keeps his money in the other sock.
BEAT: What do you think about beforegoing on stage?
CHER: I worry about Sonny.
SONNY: I worry about Cher worrying about me.

As the interview ended Sonny and Cher invited us to join them for their opening night at a local young-adult nightclub.

One Hour Till Blastoff

We arrived at the club early, but already a crowd of several hundred stretched out front for several blocks waiting to get in. Sonny and Cher's influence on clothing styles was evident in the sidewalk scene. One passer-by (dressed in walking shorts and an Aloha shirt) asked sarcastically if this was a convention of sheep herders.

Before I could answer, a voice from the crowd spoke up, "No, friend, we're just having fun." With a sneer, and muttering something about atomic bombs and communists, the hairy-legged passer-by walked off.

Just then a policeman who had been directing traffic asked me if he could say something. I held out the tape recorder microphone and was pleasantly surprised to hear the following statement:

"These kids are great, and they love Sonny and Cher. That's my daughter back there in line (pointing to a beautiful girl dressed in bell-bottoms). And I think it's wonderful that these kids are learning to take a person for what he is, instead of how he dresses. I have four teenage kids and they seem to take the time to learn about people from the inside, if you know what I mean."

He continued, "If they (Sonny and Cher) can teach that to just one person each night, it's worth a great deal, if you know what I mean."

Yes, we know what you mean. It's too bad there are so many people who don't.

Sonny and Cher's dressing room overflowed with opening night gifts, but unlike the usual flowers and telegrams, these gifts came in person. One of their friends had travelled all the way from England just to say "good luck."

Jeannie and I were having a great time, and met some wonderful people. But the most outstanding moment came when we were introduced to Cher's beautiful mother, Ginger La Piere. You can't beat a mother-daughter combination like that.

Blast-Off

The performance was fantastic, and the audience reaction was one of the most enthusiastic we had ever witnessed.

Jeannie was so carried away by it that she seemed to have forgotten her throbbing, swollen ankle. Earlier in the evening her high heels broke off and she had taken a bad fall. After the final number she still insisted on getting more information for *The BEAT*, and wound up with the last scoop of the evening: Andy Williams went to their dressing room and congratulated Sonny and Cher on their performance.

(Seems like *BEAT* reporters will go through anything to get our readers a story. Jeannie had broken her ankle in two places.)

First Stage

Two nights later, with Jeannie confined to her home while her ankle mended, photographer Darryl Kniss and I returned to the club to get some exclusive pictures for *The BEAT*. Sonny and Cher met us outside the club and took us up to the dressing room. Refreshments were served and while we were setting up the cameras Charlie Greene rushed into the room with an urgent message.

A girl in New York had sent a telegram and had made a long distance phone call threatening to kill herself unless Sonny and Cher

Without hesitating, Sonny picked up the telephone and placed a call to the number on the telegram. He spoke to the girl in soft, reassuring tones for a while and then handed the phone to Cher.

Cher told the girl, "You shouldn't even think of doing something like that. You had Sonny and me scared to death."

Fifteen minutes later, satisfied that the girl had given up any suicide plans, Sonny (see picture) and Cher told her goodbye.

We'll probably never know whether the girl was serious in her threats, but it's nice to know two people who wouldn't take a chance.

Second Stage

The performance Monday night was just as exciting and successful as opening night, but there was one big difference.

After completing their show and shaking all the outstretched hands as they made their way backstage, Sonny and Cher took off like bullets.

As Sonny and Cher hurriedly packed their instruments and grabbed already-packed overnight bags, Brian Stone paused in his last-minute instructions to the musicians to inform me they were leaving by car in less than five minutes.

Accepting his invitation to follow them, photographer Kniss and I trailed "Big Bertha" (Greene and Stone's $20,000 custom limousine) through traffic. Half an hour later we wound up at the TWO terminal at International Airport and learned the group had reservations aboard a plane that was due to leave in ten minutes.

Sonny went directly to a waiting "power buggy." Cher made a quick phone call as Green got the musicians together (they had arrived in a separate car) while Stone picked up the tickets.

When Cher climbed into the "power buggy" with Sonny, *The BEAT* photographer took a shot of them an instant before the batteries went dead in his automatic flash pack.

As their electric cart pulled out in the direction of the boarding ramp Darryl and I made a frantic dash over to the candy counter and asked for four flashlight batteries. The clerk behind the counter picked up the batteries and leisurely inspected them, trying to find the price. After vainly looking through her price book she picked up the phone to check with the office. By this time Sonny and Cher were half-way to the boarding ramp.

I snatched up the batteries and threw a $5 bill on the counter, sprinting off with the photographer to catch the "power buggy."

We reached them a few yards from the exit. As the photographer took more pictures I tried to reassure Cher (she hates airplanes) and they finally told me their destination—a big party in New York—but asked me not to reveal the identity of the guest of honor.

It wasn't until some time later that the daily newspapers picked up the story of the party given in New York for Jacqueline Kennedy.

Down to Earth

As I was leaving the terminal a woman rushed up to me waving money in her hand. She was the

BEAT REPORTER BOB FEIGEL BACKSTAGE WITH SONNY & CHER
BEAT Photos: Darryl Kniss

clerk, tracking me down to give me back the change for the batteries.

She asked if I was always in such a hurry. When I answered, "Only when I'm chasing a comet's tail," she gave me a funny look.

But I really don't care, because I had a lot of fun sharing in the excitement that is a daily routine for Sonny and Cher.

Don't Let Your Parents Hear This Album!
(unless you want them to become swingers)

Thee Midniters —
Terrors Of
Whittier Boulevard

9165 SUNSET BLVD. ▼▼▼▼▼▼▼ 213-CR 5-5021 ▼▼▼▼▼▼▼ LOS ANGELES, CALIF.

KRLA ARCHIVES

THE BEAT GOES TO THE MOVIES
'LOVE AND KISSES'

By Jim Hamblin

THE ADVENTURES OF OZZIE AND HARRIET is one of the longest running shows in America. First on radio, now TV, the perennial favorite has pretty much made the Nelson family a part of everyone else's family.

Today's post-teens grew up with Ricky Nelson, and now he's a star all his own. And married, even.

Now, Daddy Nelson has produced a motion picture, starring the self-same Ricky. (Who has added back on the "y" after a spell of *insisting* on being known as RICK Nelson).

Judging from the "niceties" with which the Nelson Family usually deals, the film is rather frank about many of the things you're not supposed to put in a family movie. Suffering under a rather un-inspired title, the movie clicks along pretty well, and doles out a few Facts of Life worth paying attention to, IF you happen to be in the same situation, or heading in its direction.

Director Ozzie, who also finalized the screenplay (the script) runs his actors around on the stage picking up their line cues too much like a theatre stage production, but still including enough actions and very un-Nelson behavior, like saying "d---" and "h---", to make the whole thing very entertaining. He's even thrown in a *strip show* as part of a dream sequence, in which Rick-back-with-a-Y gets in some neat Karate chops and slugs his way through a beaut of a fight.

From the pictures we have scattered around this page, you'll be able to get an idea of the movie, and a delightful view of sportscaster Tom Harmon's daughter, who also happens to be the real Mrs. Ricky Nelson. Her name is Kristin.

Naturally there's a happy ending.

LOVE AND KISSES, all!

WHY DO YOUR FOLKS HAVE TO BE SO DIFFICULT? . . . Kristine bursts into tears while Ricky explains to his parents that despite wandering rabbits, strip shows and the fact that they are only 18 years old, that they have just eloped. Wonder what her folks will have to say?

RICKY HAS SOME WILD DREAMS . . . In this dream sequence he sees his wife as part of a strip show. She's not really stepping out on him. She's just stepping out of her clothes.

LOVE AND A BUNNY RABBIT conquer all and Ricky and Kristine solve all their problems in the new Universal picture "Love and Kisses." The solution to their problems has something to do with the bunny sleeping in the top bunk from now on. Don't they make a lovely family?

KRLA ARCHIVES

KRLA Tunedex

EMPEROR HUDSON

CHARLIE O'DONNELL

CASEY KASEM

JOHNNY HAYES

BOB EUBANKS

DAVE HULL

DICK BIONDI

BILL SLATER

KRLA BEAT
6290 Sunset, No. 504
Hollywood, Cal. 90028

This Week	Last Week	Title	Artist
1	1	YESTERDAY/ACT NATURALLY	The Beatles
2	2	A LOVER'S CONCERTO	The Toys
3	3	THE "IN" CROWD	Ramsey Lewis Trio
4	5	HELP	The Beatles
5	6	HANG ON SLOOPY	The McCoys
6	4	LIAR, LIAR	The Castaways
7	20	KEEP ON DANCING	The Gentrys
8	10	MOHAIR SAM	Charlie Rich
9	19	EVERYBODY LOVES A CLOWN	Gary Lewis & The Playboys
10	8	DO YOU BELIEVE IN MAGIC	The Lovin' Spoonful
11	--	GET OFF MY CLOUD	Rolling Stones
12	7	TREAT HER RIGHT	Roy Head
13	12	IN THE MIDNIGHT HOUR	Wilson Pickett
15	15	UNIVERSAL SOLDIER	Donovan
15	28	MAKE ME YOUR BABY	Barbara Lewis
16	9	WE GOTTA GET OUT OF THIS PLACE	The Animals
17	21	JUST A LITTLE BIT BETTER	Herman's Hermits
18	22	POSITIVELY 4TH STREET	Bob Dylan
19	16	THE WAY OF LOVE	Kathy Kirby
20	27	YOU'RE THE ONE	The Vogues
21	26	I KNEW YOU WHEN	Billy Joe Royal
22	23	I LIVE FOR THE SUN	The Sunrays
23	17	EVERYONE'S GONE TO THE MOON	Jonathan King
24	18	AGENT O-O SOUL	Edwin Starr
25	25	THERE BUT FOR FORTUNE	Joan Baez
26	29	RESPECT	Otis Redding
27	30	A LIFETIME OF LONELINESS	Jackie DeShannon
28	40	RESCUE ME	Fontella Bass
29	39	ROUND EVERY CORNER	Petula Clark
30	31	FOR YOUR LOVE	Sam & Bill
31	38	BUT YOU'RE MINE	Sonny & Cher
32	34	ALL NIGHT LONG	Palace Guard
33	--	I FOUND A GIRL	Jan & Dean
34	--	ARE YOU A BOY OR ARE YOU A GIRL?	The Barbarians
35	--	STEPPIN' OUT	Paul Revere and The Raiders
36	--	TASTE OF HONEY	Herb Alpert and The Tijuana Brass
37	--	MY GIRL HAS GONE	The Miracles
38	--	FOR YOUR LOVE	The Righteous Brothers
39	--	WHERE DO YOU GO	Cher
40	--	ROAD RUNNER	The Gants

KRLA ARCHIVES

KRLA Edition BEAT

Volume 1, Number 33   LOS ANGELES, CALIFORNIA   15 Cents   October 30, 1965

Bill and Bob – Giving Their Act A Face-Lifting
Another $1,110 Football Quiz Inside!

KRLA BEAT

Los Angeles, California — October 30, 1965

BILL AND BOB ... Changing Their Image

Righteous Bros. Expanding Act

The Righteous Brothers are expanding their act and changing their image a bit.

The image change is mainly in the clothes department. They are giving up the knee length jackets with high flat collars and "stingy" brim hats that used to be their uniform.

Their new image, which they haven't explicitly explained will be seen for the first time this fall on their nation-wide tour of colleges and on their scheduled appearances on the Danny Kaye and Andy Williams television shows. They'll also appear in a color musical special with the New Christy Minstrels titled "Something Special."

Their new image is expected to be something more along on the college line and less in the soulful category.

The Brothers—Bill Medley and Bobby Hatfield—already own a music publishing company, a record production firm, a Beverly Hills office and a costume merchandising organization.

They also appear as often as possible with their busy schedule on *Shindig* and have made two motion pictures, "A Swinging Summer" and "Beach Ball" as well.

Another Venture

Another new venture for the Righteous Brothers will take place next January. They'll do a one month stand at the Sands Hotel in Las Vegas starting Jan. 5. This is a big break for the boys because Frank Sinatra will be performing in the Copa Room of the Sands at the same time.

They may be expanding but their style never changes.

"Our approach is with one specific quality in mind—the heart of the song. We stick to our bag—no surf, hot rod or skate board," explained Bill.

Inside the BEAT
- Barry McGuire's New Songs 4
- The Shindigger 6
- On the Beat 7
- For Girls Only 8
- Casey Kasem Story 9
- Football Sweepstakes 10
- British Top 10 11
- Dear Susan 13
- Tips To Teens 14
- Fab Fashions 15

The KRLA BEAT is published weekly by BEAT Publications; editorial and advertising offices at 6290 Sunset Boulevard, Suite 504, Hollywood, California 90028. Single copy price, 15 cents. Subscription price, U.S. and possessions, $3 per year or $5 for two years. Canada and foreign rates, $9 per year or $14 for two years. Application to mail at second class postage rates is pending at Los Angeles, California, with additional entry privileges at San Francisco.
Exclusive distribution handled by Miller-Freeman Publications, 6325 Lewis Avenue, Long Beach, California. Inquiries should be directed to the attention of David Thomas.

New Music Poll

This Time It's Girl Vocalists Being Selected

Balloting continues in the second week of *The BEAT*'s first annual International Pop Music Awards Poll.

This week we're voting to select the ten most outstanding female vocalists of 1965, with a special "newcomer" category for those whose first big pop record came during the current year.

You'll find a complete ballot at the bottom of the page. Just put a check beside your choices and mail them in. When balloting has been completed in all categories and the results tabulated, the field will be narrowed to ten names on each list.

Ballot Below

Then a complete ballot will be printed in one issue of *The BEAT* and you can vote on your top choice among the finalists.

Afterward *The BEAT* will present the winner in each category with International Pop Music Awards in formal presentation ceremonies.

Last week's balloting was for male vocalists. Other categories will include Best Vocal Group, Best Duo, Best Instrumental Group, Best Vocal Record, Best Instrumental Record, Best Vocal Album and Best Instrumental Album.

Public Appreciation

The BEAT is founding the International Pop Music Awards to give you, the public, a chance to show your appreciation for outstanding accomplishment by those in the pop music field.

Be sure to mail in your ballot so that your favorites will be included in the top ten finalists. Only ballots submitted on the official *BEAT* entry blank will be counted by the judges.

... SAM THE SHAM

LORD SNOWDON NOW ROYAL MOD

While self-styled moralists splutter over the dress and long hair styles of Americans (male and female) of the younger generation, a virtual revolution in the ruling class has erupted in Merrie England.

Leader of the one-man uprising at Buckingham Palace (or at least within a stone's throw of it) is none other than Anthony Armstrong-Jones, Lord Snowdon. To the British press, Snowdon is now Lord or Royal Mod.

Corduroy Smock

The husband of Princess Margaret, made an earl after he married the princess, Snowdon has emerged as one of the leading Mods of London, according to leading fashion editors there. Recently Snowdon was shown in the London press clad in corduroy smock-top, large check shirt, knee pants and high leather boots.

Such duds are strictly for his
(Turn to page 13)

Today's Singers Urged To Dance Way To Fame

MGM Records believes that it takes a little dancing skill to be a hit popular singer today.

Mort Nasatir, president of MGM, has ordered dancing lessons for the Animals, Herman's Hermits and Sam the Sham and the Pharaohs.

Top Teachers

The lessons are being given by Chick Minor, former Fred Astaire dancer, and Connie Poll and George Demaria of the Killer Joe Dance Studio.

Sam the Sham and the Pharaohs take lessons whenever they are in New York, according to their manager Len Stogel, because they "look so well individually we thought they'd look better if their movements were co-ordinated. Anything that can make the group better, we do."

Killer Joe is also reportedly creating a new dance step to be called "Sam the Sham."

Sam used to jump down from the stage into the audience and go into a really wild dance.

Would Go Crazy

"He's a fantastic dancer," Stogel said. "The kids would go crazy. But now that's impossible on account of the size of the audience the group attracts since their hit record, 'Wooly Bully.'"

The group is now working on new routines for all their numbers. In fact Stogel is even considering taking a dance instructor with them on tour.

Another MGM recording artist who is working on improving his talents is Johnny Tillotson. Although established professionally already, he is broadening his field by taking voice and acting lessons.

BEAT Pop Music Awards Poll
CATEGORY II: OUTSTANDING FEMALE VOCALIST
(Please Check 10)

		NEW FEMALE VOCALIST
☐ BAEZ, JOAN	☐ LESTER, KETTY	(Check Maximum of 10)
☐ BASS, FONTELLA	☐ LEWIS, BARBARA	☐ BAEZ, JOAN
☐ BASSEY, SHIRLEY	☐ LYNNE, GLORIA	☐ BASS, FONTELLA
☐ BROWN, MAXINE	☐ MASON, BARBARA	☐ BASSEY, SHIRLEY
☐ CHER	☐ MILLER, JODY	☐ CHER
☐ CLARK, PETULA	☐ PAGE, PATTI	☐ CLARK, PETULA
☐ DAVIS, SKEETER	☐ PHILLIPS, ESTHER	☐ DUKE, PATTI
☐ DE SHANNON, JACKIE	☐ SANDS, EVIE	☐ ELLIS, SHIRLEY
☐ DUKE, PATTI	☐ SHARP, DEE DEE	☐ FAITHFULL, MARIANNE
☐ ELLIS, SHIRLEY	☐ SHAW, SANDIE	☐ GILBERTO, ASTRUD
☐ FABARES, SHELLEY	☐ SIMONE, NINA	☐ KIRBY, KATHY
☐ FAITHFULL, MARIANNE	☐ SMALL, MILLIE	☐ LEWIS, BARBARA
☐ FRANCIS, CONNIE	☐ SOMMERS, JOANNIE	☐ MASON, BARBARA
☐ GARNETT, GALE	☐ SPRINGFIELD, DUSTY	☐ MILLER, JODY
☐ GILBERTO, ASTRUD	☐ STEVENS, CONNIE	☐ SANDS, EVIE
☐ GORE, LESLEY	☐ THOMPSON, SUE	☐ SHAW, SANDIE
☐ GORME, EYDIE	☐ TURNER, TINA	☐ SIMONE, NINA
☐ HOLLOWAY, BRENDA	☐ WELLS, MARY	☐ WRITE-IN: _____
☐ KIRBY, KATHY	☐ WRITE-IN: _____	☐ WRITE-IN: _____
☐ LEE, BRENDA	☐ WRITE-IN: _____	

MAIL TO: Pop Music Poll, KRLA BEAT - 6290 Sunset, Suite 504, Hollywood 90028

Win $1,110 in KRLA Football Sweepstakes—p. 10

KRLA ARCHIVES

TWO BEAT EXCLUSIVES!

BEAT Photos: Chuck Boyd

Barry McGuire In Action . . .

...THE AGONY

On a recent night in Hollywood, our trusty BEAT photographer—along with many members of the Hollywood "In Set"—fell by a new night club on the Sunset Strip, known as The Trip. The object: to see and hear the dynamic new sensation in the field of folk and roll, Barry McGuire.

Well, our photographer went, saw, and shot just so that you too can have a glimpse of this exciting new entertainer.

So now, exclusively in The BEAT, the first action photos of opening night with Barry McGuire.

...THE STRUGGLE

...THE ECSTASY

...THE SORROW

...THE JOY!!

KRLA ARCHIVES

...And His Latest Hits

Upon A Painted Ocean
By P. F. Sloan

Come gather 'round those who feel it's time for savin'

The cardboard cowards who'd have you feel like they do—

Help wake up the sleepy and quiet the ravens,

But look at what they've turned the world into—

(CHORUS)

So come on, come on, let's sail upon a painted ocean

Captain set the wheels of love a spinnin'—

For those who are losers soon will be winnin'

A place in the sun upon a painted ocean.

Let your hair hang down—'til it rolls on the ground—

You won't be needin' your maps for where we are bound—

And for those who place tradition on pedestals

Will be chained to the docks and be ridiculed.

(CHORUS)

And I'll preach to you love until you can hear hate—

Whispering in the ghettos of our own mistakes—

And until enough people become aware

Then we'll stop standin' still and start going somewhere

(CHORUS)

Just as there are two sides to every coin, so are there many sides to every man. Barry McGuire is a many-sided man with a multitude of thoughts and opinions which he seeks to express through his music.

With his first smash hit, "Eve of Destruction", Barry managed to stir up a great deal of controversy and concern. The song was labeled a "protest" song, and "a message" song. He was accused of preaching hate.

Now, Barry has a new record, penned for him by the author of his first hit, P.F. Sloan. Entitled "Upon A Painted Ocean," and "Child Of Our Times." Barry's new record also has an important message, but it is in direct contrast to "Destruction." This time Barry is singing about a world full of love, a world full of promise, a world which is very far from the brink of any destruction whatsoever.

Read the lyrics, exclusively here in *The BEAT*, and decide for yourself: Is it really the "Eve of Destruction," or are we all to take a pleasant voyage—along with Barry McGuire—"Upon A Painted Ocean?"

Child Of Our Times
By P. F. Sloan

Take your first look around and see the world you're comin' into.

Oh, have a good cry, I sympathize with you.

Forever gone is your serenity.

For the fleeing fawn there's no sacred tree

They'll try to make hypocracy your heredity.

So choose your views most carefully

The future's hope is on what you turn out to be.

Child of our times—Child of our times

Product of our society—In your burnin' turnin' mind

You are your own worst enemy

SECOND VERSE:

What will you grow up to respect?

What will you grow up to protect?

Ah, don't wave banners, you don't believe parasites

You'll have to discover your own wrong and right.

Just color your perspectives black and white

They'll label you weird

But that's all right—they'll thank you in the end

After they see the light.

Every minute you're alive you're that much closer to death

So try to make the most of each precious breath.

Now the heroes of the past were all good guys

But the leaders of the next war no one will memorize.

Only the orphan child will sound a cry

Of a mistake that never could be rectified.

I'm tellin' you now 'cause you can stop it if you try

Child of our times.

...BARRY

Yeah, Well Keith...

By Tammy Hitchcock

This week's Yeah, Well Hot Seat is occupied by that Stoney guy—Keith Richard. Ready, Keith?

Keith seems to be suffering from an acute case of sweet tooth, or maybe it's just that he doesn't like the taste of American coffee. Anyway, whatever it is Mr. Richard plops *seven* cubes of sugar (I know because I counted them, and so did Keith and so did Mick—out loud yet!) into his coffee before he even tastes it.

Yeah, well listen, Keith, why not forget the coffee and just drink the sugar—that's all you can possibly taste anyway!

Keith is the Stone who got appointed the countdowner—that is, the one who starts the Stones all off together by counting "1-2, 1,2,3,4." Yeah, well listen, Keith, why don't you surprise your buddies one day by counting *backwards*? On second thought, maybe you'd better not, Mick might bop you over the head with one of his $7 maraccas!

Keith says he will never move permanently to the States because he "couldn't stand hamburgers everyday." Yeah, well with your money, Keith, I should think you could afford an occasional hot dog!

Of personal appearances, Keith says: "We will continue to tour no matter what happens in the future." Yeah, well then how come it's taking you so long to get out here? Man, I'm waiting.

Keith reveals how most of the Jagger-Richard compositions emerge: "We usually write our songs in hotel rooms after dates, sometimes staying up till six in the morning and with a bit of luck a couple of hits come out of our sleepy efforts."

Yeah, well if you can write those songs when you're tired, I'd sure like to hear what you could write when you're awake!

'Course, one of Keith's favorite subjects is girls. But surprisingly enough when asked about them he merely replied with a grin: "Mmmm." Yeah, well "Mmmm!"

All boys like to talk about cars and so does Keith. "I like them comfortable, well-upholstered but most important there's got to be a record player installed."

Yeah, well listen, Keith, I've got this really neat looking car which I tried unsuccessfully to sell to Brian. Anyway, it's comfortable (you only feel every *other* bunp!) it's well-upholstered (I got all my mom's old rags covering the holes!) and it has a record player (only it doesn't work). And for you Keith, I'd sell it real cheap!

Keith says: "People seem to think because we've got long hair it's all right to have a go at us." Yeah, well people who haven't got much hair get kinda jealous when they get an eyeful of all you guys have got to spare!

Many entertainers don't bother with their fan mail especially when they receive as much as the Stones do, but Keith says: "We do answer our fan letters." Yeah, well then how come you didn't answer my letter, Keith? And after I enclosed seven cubes of sugar, too!

BEAT Photo: Robert W. Young

...YEAH, WELL "Mmmm!" KEITH

KRLA ARCHIVES

OUR ROVING REPORTER
THE BRITISH SCENE: A COMPLETE REPORT

Editor's note: The BEAT has another one—a roving reporter, that is. Our newest rover is Sharon Richardson and she has just returned from a vacation in England. Sharon has written us an extremely interesting report on the English scene so naturally we're sharing it with you.

By Sharon Richardson

Anyone who has been around the country and listened to the different radio stations has probably been very happy to return home where, I believe, there are not only the best disc jockeys but also a very good selection of radio stations. Hence, if you don't like the record being played, you can change the station and come back to it when you feel the record is over.

Not so in England. If you don't like the record being played, tough teddybears. There is no other station to turn to.

Portions of Discs

Listening to Radio Luxembourg is very frustrating. They have a few commercials, but for some reason, they don't always play the entire record. They'll play two, maybe three, verses and take the record off, talk, and then play a portion of something else.

Radio Caroline (a pirate station) is much better. However, it only runs certain hours of the day. Occasionally, they will stop a record in the middle, play a commercial and then continue the record where it left off.

The music played is pretty much the same as here although there is a much larger selection of English groups, naturally. The disc jockeys generally do not talk to you about how they feel about this record or that group. On the whole, listening is rather dull when you compare it to American radio.

Sonny and Cher are getting far more play than the Beatles. It seems that Sonny & Cher can do no wrong. There are a large number of articles and pictures about them in the record trade papers.

McCoys and Walkers

"Hang On Sloopy" by the McCoys and "Make It Easy On Yourself" by the Walker Brothers get a lot of play, as does "Satisfaction" by the Rolling Stones. As you know, it has just been released over there after being such a big hit here in the States.

Speaking of the Rolling Stones, they took over for one whole show of "Ready, Steady, Go!" And what a show! Charlie Watts and Bill Wyman danced with each other while Mick Jagger and Brian Jones did a lip sync to "I Got You Babe."

The last three numbers they did on the show employed some very interesting camera work. Something similar to that used in "HELP" in the Alps, when the camera puts one singer in focus while everything else is out of focus.

They also did a lot of close-ups of each of the Stones, while girls in the audience charged at the boys and hung on until they were pulled off by studio personnel. It was really quite exciting!

Three TV Shows

In the course of 10 days, the Stones were on three different TV shows—"Thank Your Lucky Stars," "Top Of The Pops" and "Ready, Steady, Go!"

Herman's Hermits were on the first two of these shows with the Stones. Both groups have just released singles in Britain and thus are on these different shows to promote their records. Why can't we get video tape showings of these great TV shows since these performers cannot be in the States too much and some can't get in at all?

Once you drive in England, if you're brave enough, you'll see why they have such small cars. Even main roads are only two, at the most three, lanes wide. Other roads are just one lane and you often have to pull to the side to let an oncoming car pass. You really don't mind, though, because the scenery is so beautiful and green.

Since a large majority of their highways are built through farm land, the driver cannot just pull off anywhere to get gasoline. Thus, services have been built every so many miles. These are rest areas where you can refuel, eat, freshen up, and sometimes even sleep.

Over Highways

As you approach them, they appear to be bridges over the highway but once you get closer you see that it is actually a restaurant built over the highway with parking facilities off to the sides. Quite handy, interesting and convenient.

Liverpool is terrific. It has a large, pleasant shopping area, a number of good theaters and a lot of scenery connected with the Merseyside Beat.

The Cavern looks just as it does in pictures I have seen. However, it is not quite as close to the docks as I had expected it to be. The alley is quite narrow with warehouses on both sides. But the sign indicating the Cavern is so small I walked passed it before I realized it.

In London, I had expected it to be very easy to find the offices of many of the groups and record artists in which I was interested. Not so. The phone book does not list the addresses of the fan club offices, so if you don't know you generally don't find out!

Fan Club Mail

In a lot of cases, the fan club mail is handled through the agency office, thus it helps if you know what agency handles your particular favorites. You even have to know which newsstands sell the trade papers you want. It seems to be a very IN group!

The agency offices are in very unlikely spots, too. The street where the Beatle Fan Club Headquarters is located looks quite residential and a little run down.

While on the subject of British groups and music I would like to say something about "Passion Flower Hotel" the West End play in which Jeremy Clyde (of Chad & Jeremy) is appearing. The theater, the Prince of Wales, is right in the very center of Picadilly Circus with three stories of the theater ablaze in neon lights proclaiming the name of the play.

I had expected Jeremy to be undisputed star of the play with a good deal of billing. However, Chad & Jeremy do not enjoy as much popularity in England as they do here in the States. In fact, in the three weeks I was in England I never heard one of their records.

No More, No Less

Jeremy was given no more or no less billing than any other cast member. But as the play progressed, it became very obvious that he had the leading male role. He played a young, inexperienced lad of 16 living at an English boarding school having his first encounter with love.

There are a number of good songs from the play which could become hits. Jeremy sang a couple of these. It is a colorful, fast moving musical comedy. The show has only just opened but I believe it is doing very well. Audiences seem to be enjoying it and Jeremy is a good actor, accomplished singer, fine dancer and delivers a comedy line with polish.

During a party scene in the play the cast was dancing. Jeremy was doing the Jerk and the Swim while most of the other dancers, like the young people I saw, just sort of swayed. They do sort of a very loose twist rather than letting their bodies pronounce the beat as in the jerk.

The shops in London are fabulous with quite reasonable prices. The shops change their windows very frequently. The window dressers are usually girls and most of them wear black stretch pants with colorful print overblouses. These girls must have studied their trade very hard as the windows are always very attractively set up.

Carnaby Street

Carnaby Street is where a number of the British beat groups shop. Most stores carry only men's clothes although one or two have a small ladies department. Music courtesy of the Rolling Stones, Beatles and Beach Boys can be heard in the majority of these mod shops.

On the whole the men are very well dressed. The business men wear bowler hats and carry umbrellas and brief cases. Younger men have neat clothes and wear their hair a variety of lengths—none of it is exceedingly long.

The women for the most part are well dressed and always carry umbrellas as you can never tell when it will rain for a few minutes, hours or days! The one thing I noticed all over England was that the heels of most women's shoes were very badly worn down. Even some of the well-dressed women wore shoes badly in need of repair.

Some of you may have wondered what the Beatles were spelling in semaphore on the cover of their "HELP" album. The line-up on the American cover spells "NSUT." The British version lines up George, John, Paul and Ringo spelling "NUTS." I'd say rather typical, wouldn't you?

BEAT Photo: Robert W. Young

...**STONES** (l. to r.) Brian Jones, Mick Jagger, Keith Richard—and passing friend?

Success Is Word For Sonny & Cher

How do you measure sweet success?

One way is money. Another way is by taking a look at the fantastic career of Sonny and Cher whose record sales and personal appearances have put them on top of the pop world in the past year.

Put money and Sonny and Cher together and you get success spelled out like S-U-C-C-E-S-S. Last year, for example, they figure their annum earnings came to about $3,000; their fiscal report for this year will read a total earnings picture of over $2 million.

If that isn't success, we just don't know the meaning of the word.

KRLA ARCHIVES

EVERYONE STARES
Keith Allison Looks Like Paul But Sounds Himself

By Louise Criscione

The first time I saw Keith Allison was backstage at the Rolling Stones' show. I did what everyone does upon sighting Keith for the first time—blinked and looked again! For, you see, Keith has the most uncanny resemblance to Paul McCartney and you just *can't help staring!*

The next time I saw Keith he wasn't such a shock—but still he gives you a kind of weird feeling. I don't know exactly how to explain it—I just know it's there.

Besides his looks the thing which impressed me most about Keith was his modesty, or maybe it was just shyness. When I say modesty I don't mean the phony Hollywood kind of modesty, I just mean that he wasn't in love with himself—he didn't think he was God's gift to the girls.

Probably, it's just that he's a nice guy—I don't know, but whatever it is I like it!

Or Was It Paul?

Anyway, I'm not always quick to spot potential but after seeing the way the girls reacted when that curtain parted and there stood Keith Allison (or was it Paul McCartney? From the back of the auditorium you just couldn't tell!) I knew that sooner or later someone would discover Keith in a big way.

Putting all these facts together I decided *The BEAT* could do with a few shots of Keith by himself (at this time he was playing with the Crickets). So, I grabbed our reluctant photographer, who was extremely unhappy about coming with me because he was then shooting pictures of Cher whom he considered better looking than Keith!

But after much pleading and begging on my part, he finally plodded along behind me. I spotted Keith standing at the side of the stage totally absorbed in watching the band rehearse.

When I asked Keith if he'd mind posing for our *BEAT* photographer he looked surprised. Mind? No, he wouldn't *mind* at all!

Photog Cuts Out

After the pictures were taken our photographer again deserted us for Cher so I had a chance to talk to Keith alone.

He speaks very softly, the way most Texans do. He seems to be very straightforward and direct and there is nothing pretentious in his attitude.

I asked Keith if he had ever been mistaken for Paul and actually been mobbed. He grinned: "Well, a couple of times—but I got away!"

At this point a gentleman standing behind Keith turned and said: "Come on, Keith, tell the truth. He's been mistaken for Paul plenty of times. Why, I remember once . . ."

Keith Embarrassed

Keith was embarrassed. I could tell by the way he pivoted his eyes to the floor during the man's long speech. He didn't say anything but it was obvious that he wished that man had never opened his mouth.

. . . KEITH ALLISON

Well, all that happened some months ago and, although I'm not much of a fortune teller, my prediction about someone discovering Keith in a big way has come true.

Keith happened one day to wander into Hollywood's Whiskey A 'Go Go in search of a friend who was then appearing at the club.

The singer didn't find his friend but someone did find him. Her name's Rosalind Ross and she's production executive of Dick Clark's "Where The Action Is."

'Action' Filming

"Action" just happened to be filming that day at Whiskey and Miss Ross was desperately in need of people to fill the club's chairs and act as an audience for the show.

Keith didn't seem to be doing anything special so Miss Ross asked him to sit down. It would be nice to say that Miss Ross was knocked out the minute she laid eyes on Keith. It would be nice but it wouldn't be true. The truth was that she saw nothing extraordinary in Keith—he was just another long-haired guy. The kind of long-haired guy that Hollywood was full of. So?

The show aired several weeks later and, sure enough, when the camera panned the audience it picked up one Keith Allison. That's all—no fanfare or anything, just one extremely quick shot of Keith sitting at a table.

That's all there was—but that's all there needed to be, for the very next day Dick Clark's offices were buried under an avalanche of mail —all asking the same question: "Was that Paul? And if not—who is he?"

And to be quite frank, Clark didn't *know* who Keith was but he did know one thing—he was going to find out! So, he set Miss Ross on Keith's trail and it was not long before she found him playing the Thunderbird in Las Vegas with Jerry Naylor and the Crickets.

Miss Ross remembers: "I was prepared to meet with a good-looking lad with no special qualifications for show business. When I found that Keith could sing and play and dance, I practically fell on my face! How lucky can you get?"

Of course, the minute she found Keith she signed him for "Action" and soon Keith began appearing regularly on the show.

The phenomenal amount of fan mail continued to stream into Clark's office. Dick was amazed, he told me he had never seen such tremendous response as that which greeted Keith's appearance.

Got Talent Enough

"And he doesn't have to rely on his resemblance to Paul McCartney either because Keith's got talent enough of his own," Dick continued.

Miss Ross, too, was astounded at what had happened. "I couldn't believe that one brief, anonymous appearance on any TV show would meet with such a response from viewers," she recalled.

Keith is not stupid. He knows full well that his resemblance to Paul got him his big break, but he also knows that now he's got to make it on his own.

Once again typical of a Texan, Keith has set his professional ambitions sky-high. He wants simply to be successful in everything he attempts.

The Shindigger

Howdy hi Shindiggers. I was beginning to think that you'd never get here tonight. C'mon, let's go in now. OOPS!! What was that body I just tripped over? Oh, it's Carole Shelyne. Hey Carole, the break's over now, what's wrong with you? Why is everyone asleep on the floor?

"We had a slight extension in hours last night—we worked till 3:30 this morning . . . and had to be back on the set at 8:00!!! So everybody around here is just dead today."

Sit Down, Carole

Gee Carole, I'm sorry to hear that. Listen, if you're not due onstage right away, why don't you come and sit down with us and fill us in on all of last night's happenings?

"Okay. It was sort of like a nightmare that just wouldn't end. We were all dancing, and singing, and working, and screaming for food and water—which almost never came!

. . . CAROLE

"It was really unbelievable, 'cause the dancers had to dance and sing and everything, and then double for the audience as well!!

"At one point we all really just collapsed from sheer exhaustion and there were bodies cluttering every aisle; you couldn't even walk through them. And just at that moment, a tour of the studio came wandering in, and one lady kind of leaned over and whispered, 'Are you *sure* this is Shindig?'"

Horrible Death

"The kids were all joking about the time and wondering how late we were going to stay—this was early in the evening—and then the Wellingtons decided to have a pool to guess what time we would all leave. Some people said 10:00, some said 11:00, and some real joker came up with a guess of 2:00 and we all laughed. Then Dean Whitmore —our producer—said 3:00 and all of a sudden everybody died a slow and horrible death!!

"Finally, just before we did the last take of the finale, George Patterson of the Wellingtons went up to the microphone to announce the winner of the pool. First he presented the booby prize to the person whose guess was the farthest away, and then he made a big presentation of the first prize—the pool, which came to all of about ten dollars!—to the winner, who was Jean, of the Blossoms. Jean went up to the mike and it was just like a Presidential nomination or something. She made a great big acceptance speech, and we all applauded and yelled.

Lying On Floor

"You usually think of Shindig as being nothing but action, but can you imagine seeing all of us lying on the floor, completely without any energy at all, while they were playing 'Twist and Shout' over the loudspeaker? It was really weird."

Yes, I bet it was. Y'know—Shindig just doesn't look the same today with everyone half asleep. But here comes someone who looks very familiar—Hi, Bobby Sherman.

"Hi kids. Listen, I'm gonna have some really great news for you next week, so I hope you'll all hang in there till then."

. . . THE BLOSSOMS

But Bobby, what about *this* week?

"Just my love and kisses!"

Alright then, Bobby, we'll see you here next week.

New Guest Hosts

By the way Shindiggers, what do you think of the new guest hosts we've been having on Shindig? We're all pretty excited about them around here.

Just before we go, here's a little question for Kirby: What's a spoolie, Kirby?

Till next week then, Shindiggers—maintain your soul, and remember, no matter what *anybody* says:

ROCK ON!!!

KRLA ARCHIVES

On the BEAT
By Louise Criscione

The ultimate has now come. Maybe you thought it had come when Ed Sullivan actually booked Sonny & Cher on his famous Sunday night show.

Incidentally, both Sonny & Cher told me that they were a little nervous appearing on Ed's show. Cher even went so far as to reveal: "Before we did the show I wasn't sure if I liked Ed Sullivan but now I do—he's very nice and we hope to do his show again."

Well, now I've gotten entirely off the subject. What I meant to tell you was that the ultimate had not yet come with the Sullivan Show. The absolute ultimate is that *five* movie companies are out after Sonny and Cher.

It's about time producers woke up to potential, isn't it? Anyway, nothing is definite or even semi-definite—but I'm sure it will come eventually and can't you just see the wild movie Sonny & Cher could turn out?

Evie Doll

That doll, Evie Sands, is 18 years old and has only been singing professionally for the past fourteen months!

Evie just graduated from Brooklyn's Tilden High School this past June and if all goes as planned Evie will enter college in February to study music and history. But with the success of "Take Me For A Little While" it is unlikely that Evie will have much time to crack those books!

Paul Revere and the Raiders who, of course, sport an extremely patriotic name, are now really becoming patriotic by working for good old Uncle Sam.

Without pay, Paul and his Raiders will tour the Orient on weekends performing at military bases including Vietnam. The group will also play to support such government sponsored activities as the Job Corps, the Peace Corps, the USO and the "stay-in-school" movement.

When not performing for the government, Paul Revere and the Raiders will continue to be seen on "Where The Action Is" since their initial 65-show commitment has now been expanded to two years.

...REVERE

Donovan's mother says: "Donovan is mad on children—especially young children. He would cut his right hand off for kids and is very sympathetic. In the streets if kids were playing he would always stop to talk to them. He would always protect a child, whatever the cost might be."

QUICK ONES: The McCoys have signed a three year deal with Andrew Oldham's Immediate Records for British release of their recordings. Also, the group is planning to make a visit to England in mid-November... Brian Epstein is bringing the play, "The Amen Corner" to his West London theater, the Saville... The Everly Brothers-Cilla Black tour now playing England is expected to bring in a total audience of 100,000 which is pretty big for Britain... Also currently touring England are the Rolling Stones who are, of course, selling out every show and evoking the same riotous response which they always do... Freddy Cannon told me that he thinks Paul Revere and The Raiders will soon be the biggest thing going Stateside... Jackie DeShannon finally got that jeep she wanted so badly, but she had to settle for a yellow and black one.

Paul Doesn't Dig

Paul McCartney declares that he doesn't dig those protest songs because they "make me concentrate too much on the lyric—which I don't like. These labels late 'protest' become ridiculous."

Always there is someone waiting to cash in on a little bit of free publicity. Like when the Byrds went to England an English group there tried to sue them because they claimed the Byrds were taking away the English Birds' popularity, etc.; which was a complete bunch of rubbish because these English Birds had enjoyed total obscurity before our Byrds went over there. The entire thing was made up for publicity reasons and everyone knew it.

Well, now it's happened again. Only this time it concerns the Rolling Stones. A Bristol country and western group are claiming that *they* registered the name "Rolling Stones" first!

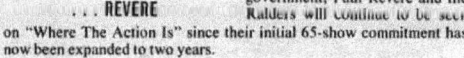
BEAT Photo: Chuck Boyd
...PAUL

PORTMAN'S PLATTERPOOP
By Julian Portman

HOLLYWOOD... The Blues Season Sets In, or... The First TV Ratings are Released. **Shindig**, Number One of the teen dance shows, has sagging arches. *Hullabaloo*, bolstered by big name adult emcees, is faring little better. Other teen dance shows, local or otherwise, nothing to write home about. I guess the fad has run its course.

Sonny & Cher made the gold record class for the second week in a row. Their "I Got You Babe" sold more than one million discs... **Roy Orbison** goes the celluloid route in a MGMer "Fastest Guitar in the West". Plans are for Roy to do some singing in this country/western musical... **The Leaves** next for Mira records is "Be With You". It's a sizzler!

Do Yourself a Favor Dept: Do buy yourself a copy of "Honey" by **Tony Harris** on Dee Gee records. It's getting huge airplay in San Francisco, Minneapolis and Chicago. It's getting big!

Barry McGuire, striking while he's still hot, signed for two Smiley Sullivan appearances on October 31 and December 5 and agreed to emcee the **Hullabaloo** shindig on November 15... **The New Christy Minstrels** creator, **Randy Sparks**, is seeking new undiscovered talent, singles and groups. Call **Barry Friedman** at 474-3565, not me! Whenever I place a "talent call", I usually wind-up with many of the telephone calls. Not that I don't enjoy speaking with y'all, but call Barry.

Ruth Conte, the beauteous boss-lady of Chattahoochee records, came into *The BEAT* office with a lovely teen-ager **Cathy Brasher**. After introduction, Cathy handed me her first single "SHHH...Listen" b/w "He Told Me He Loved Me". You can hardly say that, Cathy, we just met!

Nancy Sinatra made her recording debut on **The Dick Clark Show**. A wonderful gal, with a limited voice... **The H'wood Argyles** on Chattahoochee may re-release their old hit "Alley-Ooop"... Lovely **Deborah Walley**, a former Gidget that went Hawaiian and now the star of the various bikini pictures playing at your local theatres, came by *The BEAT* office with her first release for Dee Gee records "I Just Got To Love You." The record sleeve has a "fab" picture and autograph of Deborah for all you photo collectors... Another child star now maturing is **Patty Duke**, whose newest release for United Artists is "Funny Little Butterflies."

Handsome **Tommy Cooper** has Reprise records panting for his signed pact, but he's waiting to hear about his forthcoming appearances on the Tonight and Sullivan TV shows... "Blow Your Mind" by **The Gas Company** is rising high on the charts... **Dick Howard**, the Scarlet Pimpernel of the **Shindig** set, reports that **Eddie Hodges'** "Love Minus Zero" on Aurora records can make the top of the ladder... at the same time Agent 000½ Howard announced that the delightful French rocker **Jean Paul Vignon** is heading for one of the **Shindig** outings. Watch the gals hearts flutter!

"God, Country and My Baby", **Brad Berwick's** first offering for Deem Records, received an enthusiastic reception on **Dick Clark's** October 16th show. It's a great platter and worth the investment... **Jordan Christopher**, better known as Mr. Sybil Burton Christopher, has split from **The Wild Ones**. He's trying for a screen career, probably like Sybil's first hubby, a chap called Richard... **Petula Clark** had to cancel her October 7th appearance at "It's Boss" in Los Angeles, but did make her opening at the Copa in New York on October 14... hmmmm!

The rumor that the parents of **Herman's Hermits** may come over to visit the boys in the U.S. was probably due to the enthusiasm generated by their press agent when he discovered that **President Johnson** was signing the "Immigration Bill." Ohhh those Democrats... **Tony George**, the handsome hero of the former "Checkmate" TV series, pacted with Epic records... And December 22 is the date "When The Boys Meet The Girls" hits the L.A. movie houses. This is **Herman's Hermits** newest picture that also stars **Connie Francis**.

Bill Dana goes the Jose Jimenez route in "Make Nice", his first effort for A & M records. It's sort of a protest song, the Dana-way... **Elvis Presley's** soundtrack album of "Harum-Scarum" will be released to the public by Thanksgiving. It also happens to be the time that the motion picture makes the local screens... Cameo-Parkway's **Mike Clifford** goes thespian for the ABC-TV "Never Too Young."

ABC-TV continues to try and lure the teen market. Their next effort is a youth-oriented special, with a French background, "The Young Sounds of Paris." They're hoping to snare **George Hamilton** to emcee. Why George, nobody knows! But ABC continues to make small errors along the way as when packaging a teen dance show last year, they inquired and determined that the most popular disc jockey in Los Angeles was **Dave Hull**. So what happened, they went out and hired someone else. Ratings of that show, almost nil. What's new pussycat? Later baby!!

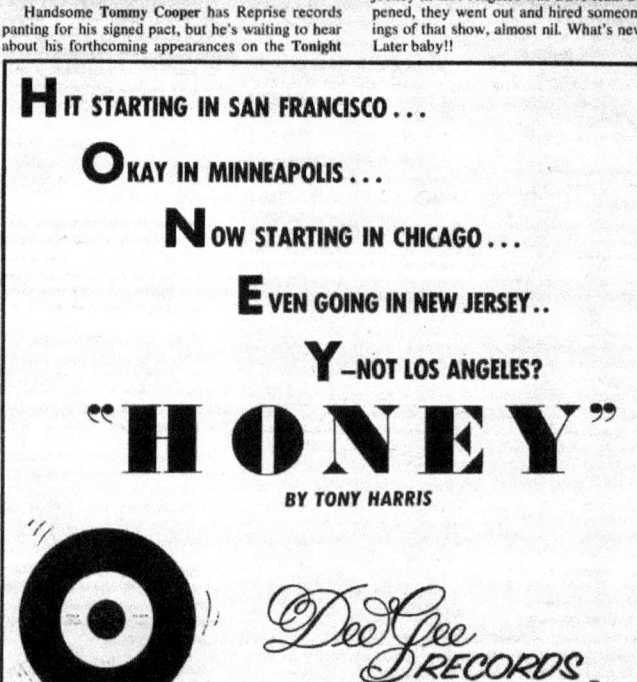

HIT STARTING IN SAN FRANCISCO...
OKAY IN MINNEAPOLIS...
NOW STARTING IN CHICAGO...
EVEN GOING IN NEW JERSEY..
Y—NOT LOS ANGELES?

"HONEY"
BY TONY HARRIS

Dee Gee RECORDS
ROLLING RECORDS
LOS ANGELES, CALIFORNIA 90025

KRLA ARCHIVES

For Girls Only

By Shirley Poston

Boys, go away. This entire column is going to be devoted to subjects you couldn't care less about (isn't it always?), but I'll try to come up with something fascinating for you next week. Like complete instructions on how to give yourselves a pedicure, for instance.

Well, now that we're rid of them, I can start blabbing.

I'm telling you, I've *never* been so amazed in my entire life! Remember when I wrote that thing about wondering if I were the only nut who stayed up nights making up meetings with George Harrison? (Or other stars, natch.) Well, at first the letters straggled in. Enough of them to prove that I at least wouldn't be all by myself in that padded cell. But now all of a sudden they're literally *pouring* in! Guess it took most of you a while to 'fess up, huh?

All I can say is I hope that padded cell is similar in size to the Sahara Desert because there are sure going to be a lot of us in it.

Your Wild Letters

I've been cracking up all week (cracking up even more, that is) over your wild letters and please don't stop now. I wish I could print every single one of them right here in this column, but if I did that, The BEAT would *also* have to be as big as the Sahara Desert.

But there is one I just can't resist printing word for word, and here goes.

"I just read your column about George Harrison and I had to write you about my 'dream'.

"The main guy is Rudolph Nureyev (you know, the ballet guy). In my dream I'm a reporter (15 years old) (sure thing). I'm on my way to the airport to catch Rudolph's plane to New York when who should I meet but Sonny and Cher!

"They just happened to be on the same plane. (Along with Chad and Jeremy, the Beatles, the Stones and Gene Pitney.) (Quite a coincidence, don't you think?)

Love Story

"Well, to make a long story short, we become good friends, fall in love and then have a fight. As I stormily get up from my seat, he puts his hand on my head (oh brother) but I pay no attention to it. (Incidentally, we were up in the air for six weeks).

"I go home. From then on his dancing is positively *lousy*! Needless to say, it's because we had a fight (cough, choke).

"When his company dances at the Bowl, I go to see him. I get front row box seats. For the first half of the program, he's his same lousy self. Then he sees me in the audience and he dances magnificently. Oh, well.

"P.S. You're not alone in your cell."

Isn't that the most gastric thing you've ever read? I about died. I've made so many people listen to that hysterical letter, it's hanging in shreds. (So are the people.) I'd print the girl's name, but she might kill me. Besides, there's no sense in horning in on her and Nureyev (isn't he *something else*!) at a time like this.

Message to the girl who composed this side-splitter: If you have any more where that came from, PLEASE write soon! Also, you have a fab flair for putting words together. Keep it up and I may be out of a job!

Dreams In Print

Hmmmm. Just thought of something. Since this is such a popular subject, why don't I print a 'dream' every now and then? That means you'll all have to keep me supplied with goodies, but that'll be a ball!

Just keep it down to as few words as possible so I won't create any more of a space problem for The BEAT than I already do every week with my ravings.

Besides telling me that many of you have this same habit, your letters also revealed something else. Some of you worry that all this might be slightly balmy, maybe even dangerous. And most of you are running out of new ideas for ways to meet you-know-who (George Harrison rules).

Well, stop worrying about it. These are private little dreams that won't turn into nightmares if you won't let them. This isn't something you'd want to do 24 hours a day. If you did, I wouldn't blame you for wondering if you'd dropped one (that's British for a loss of marbles). I mean real life can be just as much fun, but a little fantasy never hurt anyone unless you get too carried away and daydream your life away.

I see nothing wrong with creating a few spectaculars when you can't sleep at night, or when there's nothing else to do. After all, that's exactly what *I* do, and *I'm* perfectly sane. (There's a nasty rumor going around to the opposite effect, but don't you believe a word of it.)

And about that running out of meeting places, why don't we sort or compare notes? I can try a few of your wild ideas and you can return the favor.

For a starter, here's my very favorite (with the exception of the time I'm trapped in an elevator with George for three hours—WOW!).

I'm walking down a street in London and it's raining and foggy and all that. (Maybe it can't be rainy and foggy at the same time, but I just don't know any better.) I decide to cross the street and I'm about half way across when a car zooms out of nowhere and hits me!

Not awfully hard or anything. Just enough to knock the wind out of me.

Well, I'm lying there, whimpering softly, when George leaps out of the car. He's all alone (naturally, what do you think I am, crazy?) and although he tries to call for help, everyone seems to be away for the evening.

Of course he has to tenderly help me into the car and spend several hours with me to make sure I don't have a concussion or anything.

Well, you get the idea, right?

Runs Into John

My second favorite is when I just happen to run into John Lennon on the ski slopes and it starts blizzarding. (Forgive me, George, but after you and after Donovan who comes next, John, who is a little bit of all right, is following close behind.) (Cynthia, you'll forgive me too, won't you?) (Cynthia?)

Anyway, I have a million of them, so you tell me yours and I'll tell you mine, which sounds like a song and probably is.

Before I sign off, I want to answer a couple more questions asked in a lot of the letters.

I'm too embarrassed to tell you how I managed to meet George. I know someone who sort of knows him, and I threw a series of hints until he introduced me. And that's all I'm *about* to admit, *ever!*

Sigh, Blither(?), Gulp

About him holding my hand for thirty seconds, nope he didn't keep shaking it all that time. Someone else said something to him and he kept ahold (that is a word, isn't is?) of my hand while he looked away and answered their question. Oh sigh, blither and gulp. I'll never forget that moment. Or wash that hand!!

Oh, about that singing group I mentioned. Guess that's another popular subject. If we can find a way to get to the Sahara Desert to practice, let's really start one. We could call it the Oasisters—(oasis... sisters... right?) (Sorry about that.)

Adults Vote 'No' On Beatle Cuts

As we move deeper into the first school semester it is rapidly becoming clear that the "battle on bangs" (BEAT, Oct. 16) is barely joined.

Now the world renowned Gallup Poll has gotten into the act.

We don't for one moment blame the Gallup folks, whose business it is to taste the opinion of the U. S. public, but their findings on the subject of long-haired young (male) persons brings us up somewhat short. It so startles us not only for the overwhelming disapproval registered by U.S. adults in the national poll, but for the vehemency with which a great many registered their opinions.

Here is the breakdown of opinion as collected by Dr. George Gallup's American Institute of Public Opinion:

DO AWAY WITH BEATLE HAIRCUTS
Yes, should . . . . . 80 per cent
No, should not . . . 17 per cent
No opinion . . . . 3 per cent

The question was put this way: "As you know, many boys today wear their hair very long. Do you think the schools should require boys to keep their hair cut short?"

In no uncertain terms the adults questioned laid down why they feel the way they say they do.

"These young jerks," snorted one such adult, "think they're revolting against something. Actually, since so many are already doing it now, it's not revolt but pure conformity."

"If my son wore his hair like that," snapped another, "I'd make him wear a skirt until he got it cut."

And again: "There's a theory that people tend to live up to their appearance—to act the way they dress and look. I'm against long hair cuts because they make boys look like animals, and they act like animals, too."

Finally, on the negative side, we find this proposition: "These long haircuts are the best argument I can think of for universal military training. These sissies would keep their long hairdo's about 10 seconds after they landed in an army camp." (Well known singer, Joey Paige, who recently spent time serving in the U.S. Marine Corps Reserve, might have a thing or two to say about the last comment. See The BEAT, Oct. 16.)

Not all those polled were anti-long hair on boys. Noted one sympathizer: "I don't like either long hair or beards, but I don't think they should be required to cut them. After all, Abraham Lincoln had a beard and wore his hair pretty long."

Then there is the neutralist and Practical Man:

"If they were all as successful as the Beatles, I'd comb it myself," according to this worthy. "Most of them, however, have no talent and no brains under that mop."

Four out of five school authorities questioned are flatly opposed to boys wearing long hair in their schools. Yet many of these adults sneer at the idea of a young peoples' revolt. What, they ask mockingly, is there to revolt about?

The BEAT asks in return: When the spirit of independence and revolt against the world they never made is stamped out, talked out or quashed in any way in the young persons of the world, what kind of a world will we be left with?

Would *you* want to live in it?

HEY, JOEY PAIGE . . . the Russians are coming!

KRLA ARCHIVES

THE CASEY KASEM STORY
Casey Traded Bat For A Microphone
By Eden

This week Beaters, in the second article of our series on the disc jockeys of KRLA, we have the privilege of speaking with the man they call "Mr. Sincere" – Casey Kasem.

It is unusual to find a person so genuine and so genuinely interested in others as this handsome young man of Lebanese descent. Although his real first name is Kamel, the nickname "Casey" was given to him as a result of his burning desire to be a baseball player as a child.

Having gotten over his childhood ambition to tear up the world of baseball, Casey went on to school. "I graduated from Wayne State University with a degree in Speech Education and I didn't get a chance to teach because I went into radio immediately and was working in radio professionally as an actor on such shows as "The Lone Ranger," "Sergeant Preston," and "The Green Hornet." I did teach as a student teacher, and once as a substitute and I realized then that I made a better announcer or actor than a teacher. I think that to be a good teacher takes a lot of devotion and you really have to like what you're doing. So anytime you think of a teacher as being a good one, why that's a real compliment. That's like winning an academy award for an actor. Good teachers are hard to come by."

Fantastic Knowledge

Casey is well-known for his fantastic knowledge of almost every performer in the industry. But Casey indulges himself in one of his infectious laughs as he explains:

"Oddly enough I didn't know anything about music until I became a disc jockey in Korea. There I floundered around – not knowing *what* I was doing, didn't really know who Frank Sinatra was or some of the other people. I knew that they made records, but I was more interested in baseball when I was in high school. I was lucky enough to be able to be a disc jockey while I was going to college, so I put myself through school that way. And it became my ticket to Hollywood."

As much as he knows *about* the music industry, Casey claims that he can't do much of anything *in* it. "I can't play *any* instrument. I tried playing the drums and they threw me out of class when I was in grade school. I tried the clarinet and the same thing happened! I have absolutely no talent for playing an instrument. And I can't sing, either. I once had to sing in a play and they laughed me off the stage; they decided to let me hum!"

Definite Opinions

Although he may never make any earth-shaking endeavors in the field of music, Casey does have very definite opinions about it. In regard to the recent influx of music from across the Big Pond, Casey says, "The British acts and the British music did the same thing for popular music that years ago Elivs Presley did. That's why it's 'popular' – because whenever popular music needs a shot in the arm – some adrenalin to move it along – there's a Beatles, a twist with Chubby Checker, an Elvis Presley, and so on. And every few years it needs it. When the demand is there, why the supply just seems to be right around the corner. So, the British music was that adrenalin that popular music needed."

After the Beatles four left Los Angeles this summer and headed back to England, Casey found that he had acquired an even greater admiration for, and appreciation of them than he had had before.

"I was impressed with the Beatles at their press conference because so often they're asked and looked down upon by the press who think that it's awfully clever to make fun of their hair, to make fun of their music. And it's *so* unfortunate that these people are narrow-minded and can't seem to appreciate the music and their songs. I think we're all guilty of this; we can't blame the newsmen.

I was awfully proud of them in their interviews here in Los Angeles because they were straight-forward, and when someone asked them a question and wanted a serious answer they were ready and willing to give it. Such as Dave Hull's interview for *Shebang*. But too often newsmen want to be clever and they'll sacrifice a good interview just to be cute and clever, thinking that the people are on their side. Well, fortunately they *aren't*. Too many people are too smart for that; nobody wants to see someone else put down. I would say to people who don't like the Beatles as yet, or don't like our popular music of today that they give it the same chance that very many of us give to serious music; we give it no chance at all. We hate it. Something we don't understand we usually hate. But usually if a person would like to appreciate something, would like to have a feeling for it – if they will make the *motion*, the *emotion* follows. And that's usually a solution to some people's problems about music, or anything. That seems to be an answer to some people who would like to enjoy the Beatles but who don't; they won't give them a chance.

(End of Part I. To be continued next week.)

```
* * * * * * * * * * * * *
*   Great Western       *
*   Exhibit Center      *
* "Battle of the Bands" *
*     Nov. 17 - 20      *
*   For Info: RA 3-3678 *
* * * * * * * * * * * * *
```

WANTED: TEEN TALENT
Open auditions for teen-age music groups and vocalists.
Wed., Oct. 20 4-9 p.m.
CORONET THEATRE
366 N. La Cienega
No Phone Calls
Come Prepared to Perform

AFTER COMPLETING HIS KRLA SHOW (12-3 p.m.) Casey Kasem dashes to Channel 11 for his daily afternoon television show, Shebang. Here, minutes before broadcast time, he gets a helping hand from Dick Clark with some minor emergency repairs.

AT THE END OF THE DAY, after his daily radio and television grind, Casey finally relaxes in his stylish new apartment.

Pssst...
HAVE YOU HEARD ABOUT THE
HOLE IN THE WALL

here's a hint for you
- it's not a new movie
- it's not a new restaurant
- it's not a new dance joint

the IN crowd "says"
- here's where they get dresses
- here's where they get sportswear
- here's where they get **REALLY GREAT CLOTHES**
(in sizes 3 to 14)

HOLE IN THE WALL
2867 S. Robertson Blvd.   422-24 N. La Cienega Blvd.
839-1311   652-7562
La Cienega Store open Mon., Thurs. Eves 'til 9 P.M.

ON THE SHEBANG SET, surrounded by the "regulars" on his show, Casey chats with one of his featured guests, Neil Sedaka.

KRLA ARCHIVES

KRLA $11-10 Football Sweepstakes

The KRLA BEAT will award $1,110.00 to everyone accurately predicting the scores of 10 of the 11 games listed below (games to be played Friday, Oct. 29). This contest will be repeated each week for the remainder of the high school football season.

ENTRY BLANK

1. Wilson_____	Huntington Park_____
2. Jordan_____	Gardena_____
3. Franklin_____	Belmont_____
4. Los Angeles_____	Manual Arts_____
5. Palisades_____	Hamilton_____
6. Westchester_____	Hollywood_____
7. Monroe_____	No. Hollywood_____
8. San Fernando_____	Poly_____
9. Granada Hills_____	Van Nuys_____
10. Canoga Park_____	Birmingham_____
11. Chatsworth_____	Taft_____

Weekly Contest No. 2

Name_____ Telephone_____
Address_____
City_____ State_____ Zip_____

$11-10 CONTEST RULES

1. Scores for all 11 games must be filled in. Everyone correctly guessing the scores of any 10 of these varsity games will win the jackpot of $1,110.00.
2. Entries should be addressed to: KRLA BEAT 11-10 Contest, 1401 S. Oak Knoll, Pasadena, Calif.
3. Entries for this week's contest must be postmarked no later than 12 p.m. Wednesday, Oct. 27, 1965.
4. Enter as many times as you like. Each entry must be made on a BEAT official contest blank or on a hand-drawn facsimile.
5. Employees of KRLA and The BEAT, and members of the families of employees, are not eligible to compete.

Hear the scores of all varsity football games every week on the KRLA-Herald Examiner Sports Line. Listen for Danny Baxter's Weekly Predictions on KRLA—"The Station That Knows The Score!"

KRLA BEAT SUBSCRIPTION

you will SAVE 60% of the regular price!
AN INTRODUCTORY SPECIAL . . . if you subscribe now . . .

☐ 1 YEAR—52 Issues—$3.00 ☐ 2 YEARS—$5.00

Enclosed is $............
Send to:..Age:........
Address:..
City:................State:..........Zip:..........

MAIL YOUR ORDER TO: KRLA BEAT
1401 South Oak Knoll Avenue
Pasadena, California 91106
Outside U.S.: $9.00—52 Issues

KRLA'S EMPEROR BOB HUDSON, dressed in his famous flowing royal robes, discusses nuclear policy and alligator wrestling with recording star Roy Head. Roy was one of the first guests to appear on Bob's popular new television show, Hollywood Discotheque, Fridays, 9 p.m., Channel 13.

FAN CLUBS

BEATLES
c/o Debbie Frame
3218 Drew Street
Los Angeles 65, Calif.

ROLLING STONES
c/o Suzi Knoll
3028 Coolidge
Costa Mesa, California

MIKE SMITH
c/o Mariann Kuwahara
1762 Windsor Lane
Santa Ana, California

**KEITH RICHARD
(KEITH'S FEMIES)**
c/o Linda Fletcher
7506 McConnell Avenue
Los Angeles, California

BRUCE SCOTT
c/o Linda Lee Mino
3332 Kenilworth Drive
Los Alamitos, California

DAVID McCALLUM
c/o Marci Karzen
727 N. Fuller Avenue
Los Angeles, California

SONNY & CHER
c/o Robin Hatoff
1206 E. Haven
Anaheim, California

DAVE CLARK FIVE
c/o Kathy Moore
8538 Syloan Drive
Riverside, California

NO ADMISSION
NO AGE LIMIT
PANDORA'S BOX
8118 SUNSET STRIP

Personals

To Chris Jones:
John English's former group, the Heatherns, has a new lead singer, Don Roberts. They are located somewhere in Buena Park. John has gone solo now, and is living in West Hollywood. You'll hear about him soon. By the way, he doesn't have a London accent. It's a Manchester accent.
—Jody

To Bobby Tanner, Santa Monica:
Hi friend! I wanted to let the world know that I'm your pen pal and The BEAT is the best way I could think of to do it. Luv ya! From a Midwestern (Beloit, Wisconsin) BEAT luver.
—Julie

Dear Vaughn, Clarence, Captain Hobkins, Teenage Dictator, etc.:
Will the "real" Mr. Filkins please rise? Thank you. Eeegads!! Oh well, your nose is darling compared to Denise's or Gaby's!! It's too bad such places as Boyle Heights and Anaheim aren't fictitious. Ha.
I'm looking forward to your reappearance or "rea-hear-ance" on the Dave Hull show.
—Rosie and Kathy

To Any Seed Fan:
I want to know if they are still having the weekly get together with the Seeds and if so, I would like to know where. Please write. Connie Chubinski, 1831 Grovecenter, Covina, California.
—Connie

To Peter & Gordon:
We're sorry about the trouble we caused you. Hope your "Red Skelton" taping turned out all right.
—The Two Girls at CBS

To the Starfires of Downey:
You guys are out of sight! Do you have a fan club? If not, I'll start one. If so, send the address to The BEAT.
—Lesa Lynn

To Billy of the L.A. Fair:
Your ring-toss booth was great. Just like Disneyland! We've got 42 rings to remember you by, but we still want a teddy bear!
—Brian & Shari

BEAT BACK ISSUES

YOU DON'T HAVE TO MISS OUT . . .
on any great pictures, fab interviews or newsy items appearing in any of the following KRLA BEATS which you might have missed. For a limited time only, these BEATS are still available.

ISSUES AVAILABLE
3/31 —BEATLE TITLE CHOSEN
4/14 —INTERVIEW WITH JOHN LENNON
4/21 —INTERVIEW WITH PAUL McCARTNEY
5/5 —HERMANIA SPREADS
5/12 —HERE COME THE BEATLES
5/19 —VISIT WITH BEATLES
6/9 —BEATLES
6/16 —BATTLE OF THE BEAT
6/30 —PROBY FIRED
8/7 —DYLAN
8/14 —HERMAN
8/21 —STONES TESTIFY
8/28 —KRLA PRESENTS THE BEATLES
9/4 —BEATLES . . . IN PERSON NOW!
9/11 —THE THREE FACES OF BOB DYLAN
9/18 —PROTESTOR BARRY McGUIRE
9/25 —SONNY—HE & CHER HAVE 5 HITS
10/2 —WAS YARDBIRDS' ORDEAL IN VAIN?
10/9 —PAUL & RINGO—NOW SOLOING
10/16 —ELVIS—KING OF POP?
10/23 —BEVERLY BIVINS—WEE ONE OF WE FIVE

To order a back issue, send 25c (15c plus 10c postage and handling charge) to: KRLA BEAT, Suite 504, 6290 Sunset Blvd., Hollywood, Calif. 90028. IT IS NO LONGER NECESSARY TO SEND STAMPS OR SELF-ADDRESSED ENVELOPES

KRLA ARCHIVES

Dodd Still No. 1 — But Manfred Catching Up

Although Ken Dodd's "Tears" is still the chart-topper this week, the record that everyone is excited about is Manfred Mann's "If You Gotta Go, Go Now" which landed in the number two spot.

The Mann is once again proving that controversy sells records. Critics have labeled the record "suggestive and obscene."

Paul Jones, lead singer for the group, hit out at critics saying they were all wet.

And this week Manfred Mann took a swing at his knockers but Manfred's views on the record are completely different than Paul's.

Manfred admits: "The words of this song mean exactly what most people think they mean. But the only thing I can say is that the message is open, clear and healthy. There is no disguise."

That smoothy, Andy Williams, moved up again this week falling in at number four with his "Almost There." Looks like those British teens really dig Andy!

A fast climber and possibly a future number one record is Sandy Shaw's "Message Understood." The record debuted last week at number 17 and this week moved into the top ten at number seven. Sandy seems to be one of the most popular, if not *the* most popular, female singer in England.

Sonny & Cher continue to do fantastically well in England with back to back records on this week's charts. The re-issue, "Baby Don't Go," moved up to number 11 while "I Got You Babe" fell down to number 12.

British Top 10

1. TEARS — Ken Dodd
2. IF YOU GOTTA GO, GO NOW — Manfred Mann
3. MAKE IT EASY ON YOURSELF — Walker Brothers
4. ALMOST THERE — Andy Williams
5. EVE OF DESTRUCTION — Barry McGuire
6. LOOK THROUGH ANY WINDOW — The Hollies
7. HANG ON SLOOPY — The McCoys
8. SATISFACTION — Rolling Stones
9. MESSAGE UNDERSTOOD — Sandy Shaw
10. IL SILENZIO — Nini Rosso

Top TV Show To Be Dumped

One of the most talked about television shows in the world for the last few months has been Britain's "Ready Steady Go."

Produced by Elkan Allen for Rediffusion, the show has over 12 million viewers faithfully tuning in every Friday evening.

Although the show itself has always been live, it has only been since the beginning of this year that the artists have begun singing live, rather than miming to their own records.

Now it has been announced that the show will be dumped by Rediffusion at the end of the year in order to make way for a new show which will feature less emphasis on new records.

Cathy McGowan, the 20-year-old ex-secretary who was boosted to stardom as the hostess-interviewer of RSG, is also scheduled to be dropped, although she will assist with some ideas for the new show.

Regarding his decision to cancel RSG, Executive Producer Elkan Allen said: "I would rather take the program off in a blaze of glory than let it out-stay its welcome. We are planning a new show with a lavish production which will probably be pre-recorded. It will have a little audience participation, but that will be incidental compared with the part the audience plays in RSG."

Ready Steady Go is the only one of the British pop shows which has received widespread international coverage, and it has received many awards in its field.

THE BEAT'S READERS SPOKE— SO WE HAD TO RE-RUN OUR AD!

A TWIN HIT

 IN

SAN FRANCISCO • WASHINGTON, D.C. (Johnsonville, U.S.A.) • BOSTON • PHOENIX • LOS ANGELES

Mirr Records

9145 SUNSET BLVD. • • (213) CR 8-1125 • • LOS ANGELES, CALIF.

KRLA ARCHIVES

Opinion

To the Editor:

In your Sept. 11 issue a reader wrote, and I'll quote, "To me, a boy who wears his hair long or dresses differently is showing that he is not a nonconformist but an individual".

If everyone wears their hair long to be individuals, doesn't this make all the individuals "conforming, nonconformists"? They can't all be individuals, can they?

An individual is someone who makes up his *own* mind how he wants to be an individual, not by having someone else tell him how. If everyone does the same thing to be individual then no one *is* an individual. Right? Just a nonconformist conforming.

I am by no means condemning long hair. On most boys it is very appealing. And on some, more than others. It's most appealing on the boy who sincerely wants long hair for a cause. Long hair on a boy who has it long just so people will look at him would be better off with no hair at all. He might even start a new nonconformity.

"Donkinni'

Dear BEAT:

I was reading an article the other day about the way kids dressed for the Beatle concert. The writer said that he noticed when he was watching the crowd at the concert that the girls there all looked very Mod or very "Cher". He said they were trying so hard to be different they all looked the same. I think he was right.

Why can't we forget about being "different"? I don't mean we shouldn't be individuals but why try so hard. No two people are exactly the same in looks, actions, or the way they think. In fact, we're all very different. So why can't we all just be ourselves?

That, to me, seems to be the only real way to be different or to be an individual. And it's the only way to really have, or be, any fun.

Gale Saastad

To The BEAT:

A couple of nights ago, I was watching Shindig, which is what I call a good show. I enjoy it, but all I heard from my mother and father was, as always, criticism. They call it Jungle-Bunny music. Where they got that I don't know. I think if I enjoy it, and grown-ups don't, they should let me enjoy it, at least. I've sat through their kind of enjoyment and brother, well, I think it's funny. There is one thing that I'm glad about and that is that everyone does have some type of enjoyment. Grown-ups seem to think our type of pleasure in music isn't pleasure at all 'cause they don't like it.

Also, the grown-ups at my house think that the entertainers I like have no talent—only long hair. I think that groups are liked because of their talent and their records. Even though the Beatles did start the style (and I like it) I have also noticed that not *all* groups with long hair become popular.

So, let's live and let live and enjoy and, etc.

Pat W.

....The Walker Bros.

Liverpuddles
By Rob McGrae
Manager, The Cavern

LIVERPOOL, England—What a fantastic night we had here in Liverpool recently when that fabulous American trio, the Walker Brothers, came to town.

This was their first appearance here and judging from their reception they'll be back again soon. The show took place at the New Brighton Tower and over 4,000 teenagers crammed the ballroom to see the fantastic show.

The show was emceed by Billy "Spin-a-Disc" Butler, the Cavern D.J., and his first job was to introduce the Richmond Group. The group had the crowd roaring and when their lead vocalist Dave went wild in the middle of one number the girls tried to pull him off the stage.

Delight Audience

Butler next introduced the Hideaways who delighted the audience for 30 minutes. Then, as the Masterminds came on stage you could feel the atmosphere building up as the time drew near for the Walker Brothers.

The Masterminds put on a really professional show and received great reaction from the crowd especially for their latest recording, "She Belongs to Me".

Then Butler introduced the Escorts who had Pete Clarke back on drums with them. Pete left the group eight months ago and this was his first appearance after he had decided to rejoin the group. They drew a battery of screams which one thought would be impossible to better.

But Liverpool's top group, the Clayton Squares, came on stage to a deafening roar. Denny Alexander, their lead singer, just saved himself from being pulled off the stage. So great was the noise that it was impossible to hear them. Their act is so great that they no sooner got on stage than it seemed their act was over.

Zero Hour Approaches

Then Butler came back as zero hour was fast approaching. Butler did a tremendous job of keeping the crowd in order while he introduced the backing group, Johnny B. Great and the Quotations. They did two numbers—and the time had come.

Garry, the drummer of the Walker Brothers, came on stage and nearly brought the house down. Then John and Scott came on stage. This was too much for the fans and they suddenly broke through the cordon of men holding them and rushed toward the stage.

For the next ten minutes the scene was chaotic as officials tried desperately to stop the girls from climbing on stage. Girls were fainting all over the place and Bob Wooler, who organized the show, saw that there was a risk of people getting injured and decided to get the Walker Brothers off the stage. So the great night came to an earlier end than everyone had expected.

Now I want to take this opportunity to answer some of the questions about the Cavern Club which I have received.

The first one is from Laura Rider of Castro Valley, Calif., who asks how old the kids are who come to the Cavern.

Under Twenty

Well, this is an easy question to answer. Most of them are within the 16 to 20 age group.

Another question from Pam Oliphant of Costa Mesa, Calif., who asked if a Keith Norton owns part of the Cavern Club. A number of people have asked me this so I feel that I must tell you that the Cavern Club is owned solely by Raymond McFall. He has no partners at all. No one here at the Cavern has ever heard of this mysterious Keith Norton.

No "Help" For CBS

The Beatles can do anything. Now they have made the simple word "Help" a valuable piece of property.

CBS-TV is working on a half-hour situation comedy series for next season and wants to call the series "Help."

Producer Sherwood Schwartz has already signed Phil Silvers to star in it.

But United Artists, which released that fabulous Beatle film "Help" have advised CBS that the use of the word could involve them in some legal conflicts.

CBS has since notified producer Schwartz that it would be "inadvisable" to use the title.

The Beatles not only conquered the world, now they own a word.

Is Best Best? You Decide!

It is no longer just a rumor that Pete Best may tour America on the very heels of his former associates. It's a fact!

When ex-Beatle Best appeared on the New York scene last week to meet the press at a conference sponsored by Mr. Maestro Records, it was announced that a U.S. tour is definitely being arranged.

The powers behind Pete are going all out to promote this artist who recently filed an eight million dollar libel and slander suit against Ringo Starr and the other three Beatles. And a similar suit against Beatle manager Brian Epstein.

His First Disc

His first record on the Mr. Maestro label is titled, not unappropriately, "I Can't Get Along Without You Now". Although Best's backers are predicting Pete's American tour will be a smash success, the teenage population is less optimistic on the subject. Many feel that Pete has, through his recent actions, made it impossible for fans to like both him and the Beatles. The Beatles have ruled the American pop world for nearly two years. Many other groups have enjoyed great popularity during this time, but none of the additional royalty has ever made it necessary for fans to choose between their sound and the permanent roar of Beatlemania.

Co-Existence

It would seem there *is* room at the top for all, providing that those at the summit practice peaceful co-existence. And the possibility of any other arrangement seems unlikely.

Thusly, Pete Best, almost an "unknown" in this country until now, begins his climb surrounded by a whirl of controversy.

Will he make it? That is, as it should be, entirely up to those who will make or break the choice. You.

KRLA ARCHIVES

Dear Susan

By Susan Frisch

Dear BEAT Readers:
To all of you who have written to me concerning certain fan clubs for your favorite individuals of the groups, here they are, and thank you for writing. George Harrison, 3976 Ridne Pike, Collegville, Pa., Ringo Starr, 4244 Lakewood Blvd., Long Beach, Calif., Paul McCartney, 4949 Lordi, Long Beach, Calif., Mick Jagger, 3028 Coolidge, Costa Mesa, Calif.

Can you please tell me if "HELP" is doing better than "A Hard Day's Night?"
Jackie Genovese

Dear Jackie,
The people working with both of the movies have predicted that "Help" will bring more to the box office than "Hard Day's Night."

Can you please give me the addresses of some record stores in England?
Lynette P.

Dear Lynette,
I hope that these will be able to help you. Sherwins for Records, Market Square, Hanley, Eng., Gould's Music Stores, 97 Liverpool Rd., Stroke-On-Trent, Eng., Beeston's, 38 Bampton Street, Tiverton.

Can you please give me Sonny and Cher's home address?
Laura Flanders

Dear Laura,
Sorry; but I cannot.

Is it really true that George is not dating Patti anymore?
Judy Gondorcin

Dear Judy,
From the time I wrote in my column about George and Patti I have received many letters. Some thanked me over and over, some hated me for saying that. The source of this information will have to remain a secret. I can only say that what I told about them is the truth so far as I know. Of course; maybe it was not the truth. Only time will tell, and when George marries we'll find out who was telling the truth . . . George, or your reporter.

Will you please give me Herman's home address in England?
Karen Fontana

Dear Karen,
Here is the new Home address of Peter (Herman) Noone: 9 Chestnut Avenue, Roby, Liverpool, England.

I read in a recent magazine article that Barry Whitman's parents were Mr. and Mrs. Bean. Are they his foster parents or what? Also is he married?
Carol Tysky

Dear Carol,
Barry's nickname is "Bean." That is why you read this about his parents. All the other Hermits call him by that name. No, he is not married or going steady.

What kind of cigarettes does Mick Jagger smoke, and how tall is Chris Shrimpton?
Chris Hanson

Dear Chris,
When the Stones were out here a few weeks ago for a recording session I noticed Mick smoking Marlboros. Chris is 5-feet five-inches.

Will you please tell me what Ray Davies named his baby?
Susan Smith

Dear Susan,
Ray named his baby girl Louise.

Want English Pen Pals...

Tom Jacobson
85 San Juan Avenue
Daly City, California 94015

Pen-Pal
40 Maxwelton Road
Piedmont 18, California 94611

Pam Thompson
335 - 4th Avenue
Venice, California 90291

Anne Maloney
2310 - 7th Street
Atwater, California

Criss Salcido
11-A Taylor Street
San Rafael, California 94901

Kathy Hopkins
50 Pikes Peak Drive
San Rafael, California

Karen Tello
171 Andover Street
San Francisco, California

Please send in your AGE as well as your name and address to this column.

IS IT? IS IT THE BYRD'S NEW SINGLE? Is it growing before their very eyes? Byrd Jim McQuinn, producer Terry Melcher and engineer Ray Gerhardt of Columbia Records watch with fascination (?) as the Byrd's soon-to-be-released single is played back in the studio.

LORD SNOWDON NOW ROYAL MOD

(Continued from page 2)

off-duty moments, of course; we mean, what would they say at the palace if he showed up in *that* outfit?

They say that in Rome one must do as the Romans do. Well, on vacation with Margaret there recently, he outdid the natives as he disported in a light summer suit of Norfolk jacket, slim pants and a dark shirt and tie.

Shocked Scots

We never hear of doing as the Scots do in Scotland, but Tony caused Scottish eyes to pop on a skiing vacation as he dressed in a thigh-length furry coat, slender, courduroy trousers and a Scandinavian peaked cap.

With all this colorful, "mod" manner of dress, it is understandable that the more stuffy bowler-and-umbrella set of stolid Britishers may sniff in disapproval, even view with alarm this revolutionary in their palace set. But not Britain's teenagers. To the Young Mods of today's England, Tony is a real gear chap.

Miller Bedded By Bad Throat

Roger Miller, "King" of the Road" in both country and popular music, has joined the sick list.

He recently had to cancel two days of appearances at the New Mexico State Fair because of strep throat and a very high fever.

Both shows had been advance sell-outs of over 10,000 persons each.

Miller's physician confined him to bed in his Los Angeles home and ordered him not to sing or talk for at least a week. That's a rough order for a man who likes to sing so much.

World Record Quiz

Any where-it's-at Californian knows what's happening all over the nation, but do you know Who's Who this week in the rest of the world? Musically speaking, that is.

Below you'll find a list of five songs and five countries. Each of the five songs is the Number One Hit in one of the five countries (which has to be the most confusing sentence ever to reach print) (if it ever does).

If you have any idea what we're talking about, see if you can match the songs and the countries. (Huh?) Then drop us a line and tell us what we're talking about, will you?

1. "What's New Pussycat" (Tom Jones)   a. Mexico
2. "Satisfaction" (Rolling Stones)   b. Norway
3. "Help" (The Beatles)   c. Canada
4. "Wooly Bully" (Sam The Sham)   d. New Zealand
5. "Eve Of Destruction" (Barry McGuire)   e. Holland

RECORD QUIZ ANSWERS: (AND DON'T THINK WE DON'T KNOW YOU'RE PEEKING AGAIN) 1 - d, 2 - e, 3 - b, 4 - a, 5 - c. If you got three or four correct answers, you really do know what's happening. If you got all five correct, we have a suggestion. You come in and write The BEAT and we'll go to school. Drop by just as soon as you finish bragging.

A UTILITY DELIGHT, if you dig their gassy sounds, The Gas Company — Greg Dempsey (l.) and Kathy Sinclair, pictured here in pensive mood — and their new single, "Blow Your Mind" for Mira Records has caught the fancy of BEAT readers. No, reports the Gas Company, they are NOT listed on the Stock Exchange.

KRLA ARCHIVES

Tips to Teens

Q: Most shampoos I've tried leave my hair clean for the first two days, but I can't stand it after that. I shampoo every third day, but my hair is still very greasy by then. What can I use or do? Also, is there anything harmful about ironing your hair? My mother and I get into an argument every time I want to do this. (Which is after every shampoo.)
(Marilyn M.)

A: Why don't you try using one of the special shampoos for oily hair? If even this doesn't work, you'll probably just have to grin and bear it on the third day until it's time for your shampoo. Incidentally, many people have a "phobia" about clean hair and can't even think straight when it's any other way. So don't feel lonely. As for ironing your locks, we don't know of anything harmful about this practice if you use a warm-not-hot iron. Why don't you try an experiment to convince your mom? Put a wall thermometer inside the hood of a hair dryer and then put it very near to the iron. See how much difference there is in the two degrees of heat, if any.

Q: I have a **terrible** problem. I can't get rid of my dandruff no matter what I do. It's very embarrassing and none of the medicated shampoos I've tried seem to work. Please, please help me.
(Kay T.)

A: This won't be the first time we've recommended beauty supply houses and it won't be the last. Products used by professional hair stylists are available in such shops (look in the Yellow Pages) and they are usually much better than the treatments you'll find on the market. If you have to pay a little more for your purchase, it will be more than worth it. Just explain your problem and they'll be happy to help!

Q: I have a fairly nice complexion except for one thing. I have a red dot right on the end of my nose. It isn't a lump or anything and I can't imagine what causes this, but it's always there. What can I do besides cover it with makeup, which always fades away anyway, leaving me looking like Rudolph.
(Kathy C.)

A: The first thing to do is find out what's causing the spot. It could be just the pigment of your skin, but something else could be creating this problem. Silly as you might feel going to the doctor about a spot on your nose, go anyway. Once he's determined what the spot is, he can advise you how to remove or cover it safely.

Q: I have a problem that many teenagers share. I have freckles on my face, arms, legs and large ones on my back. Could you suggest some way of fading them? It's very embarrassing when I go swimming, etc.
(Ronnie M.)

A: You didn't say whether you are a boy or a girl, which confuses us slightly (we know a girl named Ronnie). If you are a gal, try covering the largest freckles with a waterproof makeup (try some of Max Factor's theatrical makeup if all else fails). If you're a guy, we honestly don't know of a way to help you. There are products available to help "fade" freckles, but we don't know of one that really works. If anyone reading this knows of a way to solve this problem, please drop a line to this column immediately. Ronnie's waiting!!

HINT OF THE WEEK

Attention all dieters! I've wanted to have my say on a certain subject for ages, so I hope my hint will get into *The BEAT*.

If you're dieting very strictly, forget it and start over. You can whittle yourself down to a size 9 in no time, but I've found out (the hard way) that weight that goes off fast goes back on even faster.

I have two more months to go on my first "sensible" diet, and it's not only coming off, its' staying off! Slow down and you'll get there faster.

If you have a question you'd like answered or a hint you'd like to share, please drop a line to Tips To Teens, c/o The BEAT.

Fugitive Seeks Another 'Arm'

David Janssen must have a thing about arms.

As everyone knows, he spends his days in front of the TV cameras as Dr. Richard Kimble, fugitive extraordinaire. A guilty-but-innocent fellow in hot pursuit of the one-armed man, while the long arm of the law follows in even hotter pursuit.

Sounds like enough action to keep anyone busy, doesn't it?

Seeking Another Arm

Well, not Janssen. He's now spending his evenings in search of another sort of arm. That being the long arm of the phonograph! And he'll be making his debut record on the Epic label soon.

Will the Janssen sound become as big a hit with the younger set as his "Fugitive"?

Good question. Which can only be answered with a rousing WHY NOT?

The Nebraska-born actor sure hasn't made a wrong move yet!

Had Actress Mom

His moves in the right direction began at an early age when David went on the road with his actress mom. He made his acting debut at the age of eight (in a Johnny Weissmuller movie), and by the time he'd graduated from Fairfax High School 10 years later, he knew exactly which way he was going to go from there.

A Giant Step

It took him awhile and a blur of unimportant roles to get there, but one day he took a giant step by becoming TV's "Richard Diamond" and he kept right on climbing!

Course, we can't expect the good doc to record "our" kind of songs. But seeing as how he's such a warm, great guy who thinks teenagers are the most, maybe we could be *needled* into listening to "his" kind!

Who knows? He might even make it all the way to the top 40 too! If that dang Lieutenant Gerard will mind his own business for a change, that is.

A "FAB" RECORDING—
FROM A "GEAR" M.P.C.*

Judy Thomas Singing

"HE'S MY HERO"

on Tower Records

From the "Home of Teen-hits"

LOWREY MUSIC CO.
ATLANTA, GEORGIA

*A HIP MUSIC PUBLISHING COMPANY

Her Silent Love: How She Learned

DEAR *BEAT*:

In a September issue of *The BEAT* there was a letter from a girl who told how she solved a problem which resulted from her love for a star. As I read the letter, I knew I could fully understand her feelings, because for me, the past two years have been the happiest and yet the saddest years of my life. For the very same reason as hers.

For these two years, I have loved a very famous person. He has become much more than a star to me. At times, I feel as if he is the only friend I have in the world, especially when I'm feeling depressed. But I know he is always there for me to confide in, and he will never turn away.

Began To Write

Like this girl, I too began to write to him. Letters of friendship, of appreciation, and most of all—love. However, instead of sending them to him, I keep all my letters together, according to date and under lock and key. I write him as often as possible, telling him about what happened during the day, how I feel about a lot of things, and all the mixed emotions inside of me. I keep the letters as sort of a diary which no one else has read.

In doing this, I find peace of mind and something to look forward to at the end of each day. This also gives me the opportunity to go back a few months and read some of my previous letters to see how my feelings for him have changed.

Last week I made a startling discovery. I feel just the same way now as I did almost two years ago, only the feelings have grown a little.

Learned A Lot

These letters have taught me a lot about myself. And I know more about love and friendship now.

I hope you'll print this letter in *The BEAT* because it is something I want to share with other girls. It has helped me immensely and I'm sure lots of teenagers would benefit from it.

Please withhold my name for very special reasons.
(Name Withheld By Request)

Fab Fashions for Fall

Ribbed Sweater

Long Grannie

What are you going to wear to school tomorrow to make that adorable boy in your history class notice you?

You say you've tried your mother's expensive perfume and all he did was ask who brought their chemistry experiment with him. And you tried accidentally bumping in to him in the hall, but since he's over six feet tall and the star of the football team he didn't even feel the bump even though you sprained every muscle in your shoulder.

Why don't you try wearing one of those new "poor-boy" sweaters that are so popular today? They look great with the hip-rider skirts and maybe some textured stockings. Perhaps you can even find some stockings to match your sweater.

Total Look

The big thing in fashions for school this fall is the Total Look. The Total Look is the sweater-and-stocking matched outfit, usually with a short, hip-rider skirt.

The Total Look can be found in clothing stores, but many clever girls buy separates, carefully searching for knee-high or over-the-knee socks to go with their ribbed or "poor-boy" sweaters.

Many schools now have regulations regarding skirt lengths since the hems have risen even higher than last year. Some schools state that skirts must touch the kneecap. Others allow shorter skirts if worn with hose. Be sure you know what your school's regulations are before you try anything too extreme.

Boots The Thing

Another big item on campuses which has caused some concern with school authorities is boots. Boots are really the thing now, particularly with the Courrege or "little girl" look. However, many school authorities don't think they are appropriate for school. The regulations on them range from absolute banning to all right if they're below mid-calf.

So far the boots have been seen mostly in black, with a few white ones, but colored boots are expected to come in soon to go with the colorful sweaters and stockings of the Total Look. Most schools are a little more lenient on rainy days and the Courrege rain boots are becoming quite popular.

An attractive addition to the Total Look is the new jockey hats popping up everywhere. They're usually not allowed in classes but are great for before and after school and strolling around campus boy-watching during lunch period.

"Stove Pipes"

Other popular clothes ideas this fall include the ribbed sweaters with either short skirts or hip-rider pants, and the new "stove-pipes." "Stove-pipes" are perfectly straight legged pants, available as hip-riders, both with and without cuffs.

Another really popular fad, though definitely not for school wear, is the grannies. Last summer mu-mus were the thing to wear during the lazy summer months, but now the mu-mus have slimmed down a little and dressed up a little and are being worn to the beach, casual parties, shopping and to Beatle concerts.

Grannies have originated in several different places at the same time and are now seen practically everywhere. The idea seems to have come from the Hawaiian mu-mu as well as the London Look, particularly the bell bottoms. Singers like Cher and Marianne Faithful have done a lot to make them popular also.

Grannies Are Here

No matter where they came from, the grannies are here. The most popular styles seem to be the small polka dot with puffed sleeves, the small floral prints with long sleeves and cuffs and the empire waist outfits that hang straight. Scooped necklines are being seen more than the high neckline now and lace trim on the sleeves is becoming quite popular.

Many girls have been making their own grannies, but for the less talented seamstresses, they are now available in many stores such as the Broadway Department Stores, which feature all of the latest in teen styles.

A new idea for the grannies is to use them as hostess dresses and dressier party dresses. This will probably give rise to grannies in all sorts of new materials. Until now they have been mostly cottons, but for hostessing wool and even velveteen looks great.

Slit Slightly

Although the grannies have been seen frequently on teen dance shows on television, many girls think they are too awkward and too hot to dance in. Some girls solve this problem by putting slight slits in the bottoms of their grannies to allow more movement.

So girls who complained last year that their legs weren't attractive enough for the real short skirts can now hide them while still calling attention to them by wearing the textured hose or can even hide them all together under a grannie.

Poor-Boy Sweater

The Total Look — matched stockings and sweaters.

Short Grannie

KRLA ARCHIVES

THE BEAT GOES TO THE MOVIES
BUNNY LAKE IS MISSING

By Jim Humblin

The family has just moved into London. Movers are loading and unloading furniture, and all the things you have to do to get settled are crowding the day. And it's your daughter's first day in school.

But when you arrive at the private school, there is such confusion that the cook says she will keep an eye on the little girl so you can get to your next appointment in a busy day.

Where's Bunny?
Nowhere To Be Found

Afternoon arrives. Time to pick up your daughter Bunny.

She's not there. No one has seen her. The cook who was watching her quit and went home in a dispute over gelatin salad.

Scotland Yard arrives. And from this moment, one of the year's most exciting movies gets into high gear. Superintendent Newhouse, of the Yard, is skillfully played by Sir Laurence Olivier. Olivier is so good you don't really need anybody else, but his performance is perfectly supported by others in the film.

Hair Hanging Down
Through Entire Movie

Beautiful blonde Carol Lynley moves through the entire picture with her hair hanging down and is put through exhausting scenes in this dramatic study of mystery and arch-suspense, released by Columbia Pictures.

Soon the audience begins to wonder the same thing that the police are asking themselves: Is there *really* a Bunny Lake or is she a *childhood imagination* brought to England by this American woman?

Final Answer In
Closing Moments

The answer is found in the final moments of the film—and depends on what you saw in the first five minutes. That's why they don't want you missing *any* of it.

Otto Preminger doesn't know how to make even a mediocre movie, and this is no exception.

Nothing is missing from this excellent photoplay.

Except Bunny Lake.

CAROL LYNLEY co-stars in the Otto Preminger suspense movie, which traces a story that leaves everyone wondering if Bunny was ever **real**.

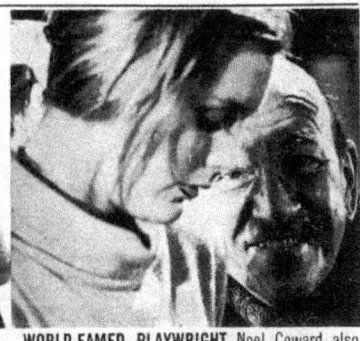

WORLD-FAMED PLAYWRIGHT Noel Coward also stars in BUNNY LAKE, and looks like **Attila The Hun**, and snorts around like an Outer Mongolian.

KEIR DULLEA objects to questioning by police inspector, played effectively by Sir Laurence Olivier.

KRLA ARCHIVES

KRLA Tunedex

EMPEROR HUDSON

CHARLIE O'DONNELL

CASEY KASEM

JOHNNY HAYES

BOB EUBANKS

DAVE HULL

DICK BIONDI

BILL SLATER

KRLA BEAT
6290 Sunset, No. 504
Hollywood, Cal. 90028

This Week	Last Week	Title	Artist
1	1	YESTERDAY/ACT NATURALLY	The Beatles
2	2	LOVER'S CONCERTO	The Toys
3	11	GET OFF MY CLOUD	Rolling Stones
4	7	KEEP ON DANCING	The Gentrys
5	4	HELP/I'M DOWN	The Beatles
6	3	THE "IN" CROWD	Ramsey Lewis Trio
7	6	LIAR, LIAR	The Castaways
8	5	HANG ON SLOOPY	The McCoys
9	15	MAKE ME YOUR BABY	Barbara Lewis
10	9	EVERYBODY LOVES A CLOWN	Gary Lewis & The Playboys
11	20	YOU'RE THE ONE	The Vogues
12	12	TREAT HER RIGHT	Roy Head
13	17	JUST A LITTLE BIT BETTER	Herman's Hermits
14	8	MOHAIR SAM	Charlie Rich
15	13	IN THE MIDNIGHT HOUR	Wilson Pickett
16	18	POSITIVELY 4th STREET	Bob Dylan
17	22	I LIVE FOR THE SUN	The Sunrays
18	14	UNIVERSAL SOLDIER	Donovan
19	16	WE GOTTA GET OUT OF THIS PLACE	The Animals
20	31	BUT YOU'RE MINE	Sonny & Cher
21	19	THE WAY OF LOVE	Kathy Kirby
22	10	DO YOU BELIEVE IN MAGIC	Lovin' Spoonful
23	21	I KNEW YOU WHEN	Billy Joe Royal
24	36	TASTE OF HONEY	Herb Alpert & The Tijuana Brass
25	26	RESPECT	Otis Redding
26	29	ROUND EVERY CORNER	Petula Clark
27	28	RESCUE ME	Fontella Bass
28	30	FOR YOUR LOVE	Sam & Bill
29	33	I FOUND A GIRL	Jan & Dean
30	—	ONE, TWO, THREE	Len Barry
31	39	WHERE DO YOU GO	Cher
32	35	STEPPIN' OUT	Paul Revere & The Raiders
33	38	FOR YOUR LOVE	Righteous Brothers
34	37	MY GIRL HAS GONE	The Miracles
35	—	MAKE IT EASY ON YOURSELF	Walker Brothers
36	—	MR. JONES	The Grassroots
37	—	TURN, TURN, TURN	The Byrds
38	—	LET'S HANG ON	The 4 Seasons
39	—	LOVE MINUS ZERO	Eddie Hodges
40	—	PIED PIPER	The Changing Times

KRLA ARCHIVES

KRLA Edition BEAT

Volume 1, Number 34   LOS ANGELES, CALIFORNIA   15 Cents   November 6, 1965

David McCallum—'UNCLE' Hero America's Teen Heartthrob

Vote Now for Your Favorite Group

KRLA BEAT

Los Angeles, California — November 6, 1965

...SONNY & CHER — BEAT Photo: Chuck Boyd

Shindig Out! Hullabaloo?

Vocal Groups Spotlighted In BEAT Poll

The 1965 *BEAT* International Pop Music Awards Poll moves to Category III this week—Outstanding Male and Mixed Vocal Groups—and this may produce the fiercest battle of all.

It matches all the big groups, including the Beatles and Rolling Stones from England and the Beach Boys and Byrds from the U.S. You'll find them all listed on the ballot at the bottom of the page, along with spaces for write-in votes for any group not listed.

Ten Groups

Everyone voting in this week's poll is asked to check the names of 10 groups. The 10 receiving the most votes will then be in the finals.

Balloting during the past two weeks has been for Outstanding Male and Female Vocalists. Other categories to be featured in future issues of *The BEAT* will be Best Female Group, Best Duo, Best Instrumental Group, Best Vocal Record, Best Instrumental Record, Best Vocal Album and Best Instrumental Album.

When first-round balloting has been completed in all categories, the field will be narrowed to the top ten names on each list. Then a complete ballot will be printed in one issue of *The BEAT* and you can vote on your first choice.

Pop Awards

Afterward *The BEAT* will present the winner in each category with 1965 International Pop Music Awards in formal presentation ceremonies.

The BEAT is founding the International Pop Music Awards to give you, the public, a chance to show your appreciation for outstanding accomplishment by those in the pop music field.

Be sure to mail in your ballot so that your favorites will be included in the top ten finalists. Only ballots submitted on the official *BEAT* entry blanks will be counted by the judges.

The nation's major television networks seem to be playing a game of Russian roulette with the top teenage pop music shows, *Hullabaloo* and *Shindig*.

Rumors have been flying fast and furious lately about the fate of both shows. One is rumored to be on it's way up; the other is out.

Word came out of New York that *Hullabaloo*, taking advantage of *Shindig's* drop in ratings, may expand back to the hour show that it used to be.

It was also rumored that the show would be moved to Friday night along with a proposed move to make Friday night a "teen night" on NBC.

Date Night

The *BEAT* wonders if the NBC executives who dreamed this up ever considered that Friday night is a traditional date night for teenagers, the very audience they are trying to attract. Friday, of all nights, seems the least likely to be a big night for teenage television watching.

However, NBC vice president Mort Werner has denied any plans to expand or move *Hullabaloo*.

Meanwhile, informed sources have reported that *Shindig* has had it. *Shindig* host Jimmy O'Neill will remind viewers to "rock on" for the last time on a show which will be filmed in November and aired sometime in December.

It seems even with the switch to special guest co-hosts *Shindig* couldn't make it.

Another Show

Still another of the many reports flying is that *Shindig* will be replaced by another rock and roll show called *TJ's*. The pilot of *TJ's* was filmed quite a while ago but put on the shelf by ABC.

The show features Sal Mineo as host. It's produced by Emmy award-winning Jimmie Baker and directed by Steve Binder from the Danny Kaye Show.

TJ's policy will be to feature one young star or group each week. Starring in the pilot show are the Dave Clark Five.

At least one person who saw the show before it was shelved reported that is is better than either *Shindig* or *Hullabaloo*. If it does replace *Shindig* it may turn out to be quite a hit.

Word Gets Around

On top of all this comes a report of still another new pop music show. Boy, the way the word gets around in this business!

This one reportedly will be called "Way Out" and will feature Joey Paige as host and the Bees as regulars. It's a Four Star Production syndication. It's hard to tell who will be the winner, or winners, in this game but it sure looks like there are going to be

(Turn to Page 12)

NOW IT'S THE MOVIES FOR SONNY AND CHER

The pop world's most popular married couple are climbing even higher up on the golden ladder of success.

Mr. and Mrs. Salvatore Bono, better known as Sonny and Cher, have finally decided to branch out from their fantastic singing career and do a motion picture.

Finally Caught

They have had no less than five movie companies after them trying to sign them to a movie and it looks like someone finally caught them.

That someone is movie producer Steve Broidy who just associated himself with Capitol Records. Capitol has just entered into the movie business by announcing that they are going to make a movie starring the Beach Boys, under contract to Capitol.

Sonny and Cher aren't under contract to Capitol but they have signed to do the movie which will begin filming Jan. 10. No script or co-stars have been announced yet. We'll just have to wait and see.

Meanwhile, Sonny and Cher have been adding to their collection of golden hits.

Over A Million

Their Atco album, "Look At Us," has just been certified as having racked up sales of over $1,000,000. The album was just released here in August and is now being released in Canada, England, Italy, France, Germany, Holland, the Scandinavian countries and the Far East. It's expected to sell over two million copies. That's a lot of looking.

Their single "I Got You Babe" was certified for sales of over a million almost a month ago.

Those Bonos really know how to keep the hits rolling.

Inside the BEAT

"In Crowd" Left Out	3
Liverpuddles	3
Yeah Well, Yardbirds	4
Chad Without Jeremy	5
P. F. Sloan Portrait	6
For Girls Only	8
Dick And DeeDee	8
Dear Susan	13
Bees Look For Honey	13
British Top 10	14

The KRLA BEAT is published weekly by BEAT Publications; editorial and advertising offices at 6290 Sunset Boulevard, Suite 504, Hollywood, California 90028. Single copy price, 15 cents. Subscription price, U.S. and possessions, $3 per year or $5 for two years. Canada and foreign rates, $9 per year or $14 for two years. Application to mail at second class postage rates is pending at Los Angeles, California, with additional entry privileges at San Francisco.

Exclusive distribution handled by Miller-Freeman Publications, 6328 Lewis Avenue, Long Beach, California. Inquiries should be directed to the attention of David Thomas.

BEAT Pop Music Awards Poll
CATEGORY III: OUTSTANDING GROUPS (MALE & MIXED)
(Please Check 10)

☐ ANIMALS	☐ HOLLIES	☐ SPINNERS
☐ BACHELORS	☐ HULLABALOOS	☐ SPOKESMEN
☐ BEACH BOYS	☐ IMPRESSIONS	☐ STRANGELOVES
☐ BEATLES	☐ JAY & THE AMERICANS	☐ SUNGLOWS
☐ BEAU BRUMMELS	☐ JIVE FIVE	☐ SUNRAYS
☐ BYRDS	☐ KINKS	☐ TEMPTATIONS
☐ CASTAWAYS	☐ LETTERMEN	☐ THEM
☐ CHANGING TIMES	☐ LEWIS, GARY & THE PLAYBOYS	☐ TIKIS
☐ DAVE CLARK FIVE	☐ LITTLE ANTHONY & THE IMPERIALS	☐ TURTLES
☐ DINO, DESI & BILLY	☐ LOVIN' SPOONFUL	☐ UNIT 4 PLUS 2
☐ FONTANA, WAYNE & THE MINDBENDERS	☐ MC COYS	☐ UNIQUES
	☐ MIRACLES	☐ VEJTABLES
☐ FORTUNES	☐ MOJO MEN	☐ VOGUES
☐ FOUR TOPS	☐ MOODY BLUES	☐ WALKER BROTHERS
☐ FOUR SEASONS	☐ NEWBEATS	☐ WALKER, JR. & THE ALL STARS
☐ FREDDIE & THE DREAMERS	☐ OLYMPICS	☐ WE FIVE
☐ FULLER FOUR, BOBBY	☐ PALACE GUARD	☐ WHISPERS
☐ GENTRYS	☐ REVERE, PAUL & THE RAIDERS	☐ WHO (THE)
☐ GERRY & THE PACEMAKERS	☐ REFLECTIONS	☐ YARDBIRDS
☐ GRASSROOTS	☐ ROLLING STONES	☐ ZOMBIES
☐ GUESS WHO	☐ SAM THE SHAM & THE PHARAOHS	
☐ GUILLOTEENS	☐ SEARCHERS	☐ WRITE IN _____
☐ HERMAN'S HERMITS	☐ SEEKERS	☐ WRITE IN _____
	☐ SILKIE	☐ WRITE IN _____
	☐ SIR DOUGLAS QUINTET	☐ WRITE IN _____

MAIL TO: Pop Music Poll, KRLA BEAT – 6290 Sunset, Suite 504, Hollywood 90028

Win $1,110 in KRLA Football Sweepstakes—p. 10

KRLA ARCHIVES

'In Crowd' Left Out

There was a slight disagreement between the Ramsey Lewis Trio and the producer of *Ninth Street West* and *Hollywood A-Go-Go* last week.

Ramsey Lewis and his trio just recently broke into the popular market with their recording of "The In Crowd," were on the West Coast for an appearance at the Lighthouse, a Hermosa Beach night club.

Agreed To Appear

Lewis talked with Milt Hoffman, executive producer of the two television programs, on the phone and agreed to appear on *Ninth Street West* while he was here, according to Hoffman.

A short time later he called back and said he wouldn't appear on the show.

He was reported to have said "I don't want to lose my feeling of being a jazz artist, I couldn't care less about the teenage kids."

A Different Story

Lewis, however, had a different stoy to tell. He says he was contacted by Hoffman weeks ago and had agreed to do the show but leter changed his mind.

Lewis said he told Hoffman, "At this point, I'd rather wait awhile because I'm more interested in a different caliber show."

So the show was cancelled. But Lewis said he was contacted later by Hoffman about trying again. He said he was told that the show would be built around him.

Lewis explained, "My main criticism is not of the teenagers — God forbid! — they bought a lot of 'In Crowd.' And I am not trying to create an image of a jazz musician, as Hoffman contends I said. Not until you can rid yourself of that connotation can you enjoy success in most instances. Sixty percent of those who bought 'Crowd' were not necessarily jazz fans as such.

Says Mis-Used Terms

"Hoffman mis-used these terms when he says I told him I wanted to solidify my image as a jazz musician. I told him we were not directing our music particuarly to teenagers. But I said I felt I owed it to he people from 22 to 35 to continue along those lines. The shows we have worked in the past few years definitely are not geared to teenagers."

So the Ramsey Lewis Trio never appeared on the show. Freddy Cannon came down at the last minute and filled in.

So far nothing more has been done to get the trio on the program, but Hoffman said that Lewis "will always be welcome to come on the show. He has an open invitation but he says he doesn't want to marr his image."

...RAMSEY LEWIS TRIO

On the BEAT
By Louise Criscione

The Yardbirds have, without a doubt, one of the weirdest sounding records around — "Still I'm Sad." And in case you think it sounds an awful lot like a church hymn — you're right. Sam says it's a 13th century Gregorian chant! There's one thing which Sam forgot to mention and that is, 13th century Gregorian chant or not, "Still I'm Sad" is one heck of a hit. And that only figures since the Yardbirds are one heck of a group and if you ever get the chance to see them perform "live" — do yourself a favor and don't miss it.

As if he didn't have enough to keep him busy, Bill Wyman has now turned co-manager. Right before joining the Stones, Bill played with a group called the Cleftones. Well, now the Cleftones have changed to the Preachers and Bill has become their co-manager. Interesting to see what a difference a couple of years makes, huh?

Another Beatle Success

Now that "Yesterday" has topped the charts and proved itself yet another Beatle success Paul admits the Beatles' doubts about the song. "We didn't know at first whether to release the number as a single or not. So I was very relieved indeed when I heard it had gone to Number One."

Guess by now you've figured out that I dig the Rolling Stones but I've got one small bone to pick with Keith Richard 'cause he said about pop papers: "They're all written by people who don't know what they are talking about." Not a nice trick, Keith.

...BILL WYMAN
BEAT Photo: Robert W. Young

Remember a couple of weeks ago I said if something doesn't give we'd have three dead Walker Brothers on our hands? Well, something's given all right — the Walkers have given up all ballroom appearances because "it's too dangerous."

Latest mishap belonged to John's leg and a spokesman for the group says: "He's been in agony ever since." And the cause of all this trouble — unruly fans who insisted on charging the stage and all but massacring the Walkers in the process.

One of Hottest

Since their smash "You Were On My Mind" the We Five have become one of the hottest groups on the scene. They recently tore 'em up on a Righteous Brothers' tour which hit colleges from Oklahoma to Louisiana.

QUICK ONES: Did you know the Dave Clark Five wanted to record "Hang On Sloopy" but the McCoys beat them to it ... Tom Jones used to play drums and guitar ... Funny scene — Tom trying to explain why some teens get the wrong impression when they meet their favorite groups ... Isn't one of the Grass Roots trying awfully hard to look like Brian Jones? And you know something else — he's succeeding! The group really is good, though, and they sure tear it up when they do "I Need You" ... Saw Bobby and Randy Fuller driving down the street the other day looking great as usual ... Tip to the Regents — dress a little sloppier and I think you'll make it.

The cat's out of the bag — John of the Walker Brothers is married to 19 year old Kathy Young and has been since June.

What a see-saw Wayne Fontana is riding on! First of all he announced to the world that he and the Mindbenders were splitting up and then the next week he turned around and denied that he had ever said such a thing. Now he's back to the breaking up bit again. This time his manager, Rick Dixon, was quoted by an English paper as saying: "The group will cease to exist on October 31." What's *really* going on is anybody's guess!

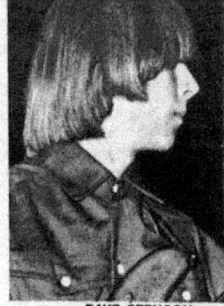

...DAVE STENSON

Memo To Big Wigs

Special memo to "Hullabaloo": George Maharis, Paul Anka, George Hamilton as hosts? You must be kidding! Wise up and snatch people like Herman, the Rolling Stones and Beatles (so dream big) — these people make for ratings while hosts such as Maharis, Anka and Hamilton make for laughs and switched channels.

Liverpuddles
By Rob McGrae
Manager, The Cavern

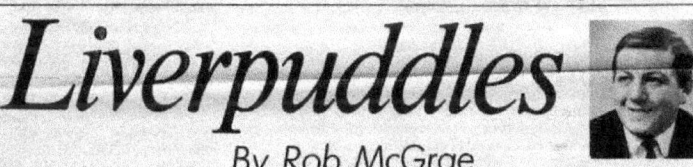

LIVERPOOL, England — "Come and Get It." That's what all the record stores in Liverpool are proclaiming in their window posters this week.

What's the reason for this? Quite simple, Liverpool's top group, the Clayton Squares, have their first record release this week, and the title is "Come and Get It." The record is certainly causing a lot of interest here in England, particularly since the Squares performed it on the television show "Seen at the 630."

So popular are the Squares that on the day the record was released nearly 100 of their most ardent fans formed a queue outside one of Liverpool's biggest record stores over an hour before the store was due to open. They were determined to obtain the record as soon as possible.

Overjoyed

The boys themselves are overjoyed with the reaction to the record and Mike Evans, their leader, told me all the boys are keeping their fingers crossed that it will be a big seller.

The day before the record was released the boys performed it for the first time at a dance. Many celebrities in the show business world came to wish the boys luck with the record but judging from the reception they received there is going to be no need for that. Over 1,000 teenagers who crammed themselves into the small ballroom showed their appreciation of the number.

My opinion of the number is that it is going to be very big indeed. It is a very catchy song which Danny Alexander performs with great zest. The big sound of the Squares is solidly behind Denny and makes the number a cut above the normal record.

The 'B' side was written by the Squares themselves. It's a really moving slow ballad with a flute introduction. The words are really poetic and beautifully handled by Denny. Both sides of this record are so good that I think it is possible that it could be a double-sided hit.

Big Prediction

By the way, the record is soon to be released in the States on the MGM label and I'll predict that as soon as you have heard it you will agree that it's going to be a big, big hit.

Many people have written asking me to write an article on the Escorts, another fab Liverpool group. This I will do very shortly for they are a great group and deserve all the support they have gotten. I was wondering if any of you Escort fans would be interested in a souvenir of one of their appearances at the Cavern.

The souvenir is a four by five foot poster that was put up in the club to welcome them home from Germany. I will send it to the person who sends me the most original request for it. So put on your thinking caps and send me a really clever request. The winner will receive not only the poster but also an autographed photo of the boys.

Question Time

Miss Marsha Fewny of Belmont, Calif., writes to ask whether the Stones and the Yardbirds have ever played at the Cavern. Yes, they have. Both groups have played a number of times here. The Stones caused such interest that over 1,000 people had to be turned away.

Rosemary Almada of San Francisco asks what dances do they do at the Cavern. Well, there are a great many dances being done here but the Shake is by far the most popular.

Lots of readers have asked whether they can become members of the Cavern and I want to say that this is quite possible. All you have to do is send $2.00 and your name and address to me at either 17, Heydean Road, Allerton, Liverpool 18 or at 8/12 Mathew Street, Liverpool 2. You will receive by air mail a Cavern membership card. You can also buy Cavern pens for $2.00 each or three for $5.00 from the same addresses.

KRLA ARCHIVES

The Shindigger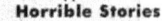

Howdy Hi, Shindiggers. You're just in time to say hello to a beautiful girl named Dinah Lee. Dinah is currently the number one female singing star in Australia and New Zealand.

Hi Dinah. Hope you're enjoying your visit to the Land of the Stars and Stripes. Have you noticed any differences between the teenagers of our country and the teens Down Under?

"They all sort of appreciate the pop music, and they all scream and go to town at concerts and shows. They're a little more subdued in Australia and New Zealand."

"Hi everybody."

Hi Jimmie O'Neill. Are you going to join us for a little while? By the way, I hear that you and your wife Sharon had quite an experience the other evening. Will you tell us all what happened?

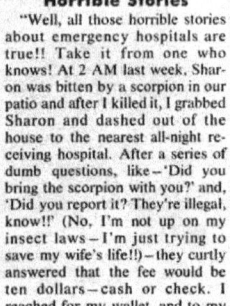

...JIMMY O'NEILL

Horrible Stories

"Well, all those horrible stories about emergency hospitals are true!! Take it from one who knows! At 2 AM last week, Sharon was bitten by a scorpion in our patio and after I killed it, I grabbed Sharon and dashed out of the house to the nearest all-night receiving hospital. After a series of dumb questions, like—'Did you bring the scorpion with you?' and, 'Did you report it? They're illegal, know!!' (No, I'm not up on my insect laws—I'm just trying to save my wife's life!!)—they curtly answered that the fee would be ten dollars—cash or check. I reached for my wallet, and to my stark terror, realized that in my panic I had dashed out of the house without a penny on me! Believe it or not, they refused to treat her without full payment in advance. Then they gave us the wrong directions to another hospital! So finally, in desperation, I stopped at a local store and cashed a counter check, then returned to the original hospital and threw the money in their faces!! They then called the Health Department to find out what to do for a scorpion bite. At last we learned that California scorpions are non-toxic and that Sharon would live! They then sent us to an all-night drug store ten miles away where we filled her prescription and bought the suggest ice pack to soak her ankle. She'll be sick for three days but thank God—she'll be all right."

That's quite a story, Jimmie, but we're all glad that Sharon is feeling better now.

Breathless Waiting

Which reminds me—last week Bobby Sherman promised that he would have some kind of big news for us this week. All right Bobby—we're waiting breathlessly!!

"Hi kids—be looking for a new show coming out on ABC called 'In,' on which yours truly will be the host! It will be on five days a week and at about 4:30 or 5:00 in the afternoon. It will consist of just about everything that the teens are doing, including their fads, fashions, groups, music, ideas, and problems, etc. Also it will take in all of the happenings of the teens in other countries around the world. It will be strictly for you so your participation will make the success of the show. See you there? Thanks."

"Hi everybody."

Hey everyone—it's Joey Paige. Hi, Joey, what's happening?

"Well, I just dropped by to go over the songs I'm going to sing on the show next week so I thought I'd come over and say hello. By the way, I'd like to say thanks to all of my fans for remembering me while I was away in the Marine Reserves. All that mail was great."

Well, it's good to have you back, Joey.

Shindogs' Message

Small aside to Jane Nelson: You've been very patient so far, and the Shindogs will be here to deliver that message to you in person next week. Thank you for waiting!

One more small aside to George Patterson of the Wellingtons: You'd better tell Eddie to start keeping his dates—but check it out with Kirby first!

...JOEY PAIGE

If you're at all interested in fun, Shindiggers, then you aren't going to miss next week's show, 'cause it's gonna be really great! Dropping by for the festivities will be Joey Paige, Len Barry, the Rolling Stones, Barbara Lewis, the Gentrys, Ian Whitcomb, David Jones, Donna Loren, the Righteous Brothers, the Turtles, Sandie Shaw, and Dusty Springfield.

Till then, maintain your soul, Shindiggers, and remember—no matter what *anybody* says: ROCK ON!!!

Yeah, Well Yardbirds...

By Tammy Hitchcock

When the Yardbirds threw a party they invited *The BEAT* staff to come and hear them play so I suppose you know we spent the whole darn afternoon getting ourselves ready.

Anyway, when the party was over we said our goodbyes to each of the Yardbirds and the funniest scene of the night had to be when Keith Relf told us: "Thank you for even bothering to come."

Yeah, well listen, Keith, we'd *bother* to come if you guys were playing in that big hole they're busily digging across the street. I admit I'd look rather funny climbing down a 100 foot hole but to hear you guys I'd climb... I'd climb!

Chris' Designs

Chris is not only a talented musician but also one heck of a shoe designer and a big shoe manufacturer is currently featuring one of Chris' designs. Yeah, well listen, Chris, how about designing a pair of shoes for me—*cheap*.

Jim pointed to his picture on the cover of the Yardbirds' British album, grinned from ear to ear and asked me: "Isn't this guy handsome?" Yeah, well I 'll say he is—but, of course, I'd *never* tell him that, instead I told him all the rest of the guys were sure good looking but he was U-G-L-Y! Typical of Jim—he just laughed!

Did you ever listen very closely to the last note of "Still I'm Sad?" Well, the last note is no note at all—it's somebody laughing! Yeah, well own up—which one of you is the funny man—Jim or Jeff?

During one particularly cold London day Keith and the rest of the Yardbirds were dreaming of moving to a deserted island. "We'd work our passage to somewhere miles away where it's always hot," Keith explained. Yeah, well I've got just the place for you, Keith—my office!

Stealing Fans

The Yardbirds really dig their fans only they can't quite figure out why some are so thoughtless. "One night we were signing autographs for fans in the dressing room and we turned around to find forty pounds worth of stuff missing, including our bongo drums," Sam revealed.

Yeah, well listen, Sam, I'm gonna have a talk with our telephone girl, Susie, 'cause she came trippin' in here the other morning with a pair of bongoes sticking suspiciously out of her purse!

When Jeff was up in our office he was feeling kind of sorry for himself so he jokingly asked one of our girls if she had a knife.

Yeah, well don't get excited, 'cause when our girl produced a sharp letter opener you should have seen Jeff run! I mean, he was out the door and into the elevator faster than you could say Yardbird!

Keith made the understatement of the year when he announced unceremoniously: "Nowadays, I suppose, we are very interested in the money we are making." Yeah, well I guess so! Fact is, I'm kinda interested in money too so if you have any leftovers...

Chris is so sweet, really everybody likes him. He looked so cute the other day when he shyly admitted: "We always wanted a hit." Yeah, well I know what you mean, Chris, I always wanted a hit too but the only one I ever got was on the top of my head when I was trying to get gracefully out of the boss' Stingray and I forgot the top was up!

Happening

By Eden

Hullabaloo has a family spirit these days, and dropping in for return visits will be the sensational Supremes on December 6, and Barry McGuire will take over the hosting honors on November 15. Certainly looks like the "Eve of Production" for this talented young man.

* * *

If you're wondering where everyone is going these days—take a fast look Down Under. Yep, Australia and New Zealand are pulling 'em all in and it seems to be quite a haul! Sonny and Cher have signed for 12 dates next April, the Stones are planning on Rolling by 'long about February, and Herman's Hermits will fall in with the rest come January. Sounds like all those kangaroos—or *somebody*—will be having lots of fun!

* * *

Chad Stuart, of Chad and Jeremy, stopped by with some news items for *BEAT* readers.

Concerning their new record, Chad says: "It's a break from our old ballady tradition; it's the first one that Jeremy and I have written for a long time, and it is the first single on which I play harmonica."

These are the words of one half of a talented British singing duo, whose new disc looks like a "smashing success!" Entitled "Should I?" b/w "I Have Dreamed," this new disc is another of a series of beautiful records from the pair.

Chad also had a few words for Beaters regarding the rumors currently flying about concerning his citizenship. It has been rumored hereabout that Mr. Stuart had filed for American citizenship. However, Chad explains that this was due only to the demands of the musicians union here—without whose cooperation Chad is unable to work in this country—and he currently has a lawyer in Washington attempting to straighten the entire situation out. In the meantime, Chad declares that he loves America—and "especially California"—but he has no plans for becoming an American citizen at this time.

* * *

Barry McGuire and P.F. Sloan are still on tour in England, but their smash tune—"Eve of Destruction"—continues to be banned by the BBC. The pirate stations have done so well in keeping this disc alive, that it now places high in the top ten on charts all over England.

* * *

Currently taking all top honors as one of the most sought-after couples in town are Mr. and Mrs. Salvatore Bono. Who are they, you ask? You might be somewhat more familiar with them as Sonny and Cher. And there are now five producers—Joe Pasternak, Steve Broidy, Peter Lawford, the Mirisch Bros., and Allied Artists—who would like to be familiar enough with the popular duo to have them star in a movie.

See there—who *said* Long Hairs were out of style??!!!

And that's Happening, this week.

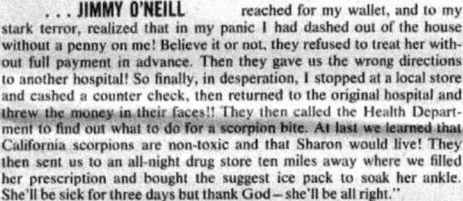

CHAD WITHOUT JEREMY

Chad And Jill In Love With U. S.

It's a beautiful, wind-blown afternoon in Southern California. Trees are gently waving to the people on the street. Everything is peaceful and quiet in the warm, mid-afternoon sun.

We have an appointment with an extraordinary young man in a few minutes. He is young (handsome in a boyish sort of way) British, and one half of a successful recording duo. His name is Chad Stuart.

As we arrive in the courtyard beneath his apartment, he appears above us on the balcony and invites us to come upstairs. "Welcome," he says with a smile as he throws open the door.

Inside the apartment, we see yellows, oranges and lots of fantastic multi-colored stuffed animals everywhere we look. They belong to Jill, who belongs to Chad. She is Mrs. Stuart.

Witty Cat

It is very easy to talk to Chad, because he is an extremely witty and intelligent person. So, it isn't very long before we find ourselves plunged headlong into a fascinating conversation with our talented friend.

He begins speaking of his childhood in England and of the partnership he eventually formed with Jeremy Clyde:

"I was born September 10, 1941, in the Lake district, a very beautiful part of England. It's very rainy and very beautiful, and it has lots and lots of tall trees. My father was in timber—in forestry—and he used to chop trees down, so I had an idyllic childhood! Later on, I went away to boarding school—the conventional fate for a moderately wealthy Englishman's son. I went to Durham school. I was also a chorister from the ages of 10 to 14 at Durham Cathedral where I picked up all my music, because I was reading and writing music very fluently at a tender age, due to the bullying of our choir master.

"We formed a duo at drama school, at the Central School of Speech and Drama. We nearly formed a trio because I met Jill there as well, and I married her. I went there with a guitar and Jeremy had one—he was there a year before me—and we just naturally teamed up. And we used to sit around in the coffee bar between the classes singing folk songs and generally being like the Byrds—very beat and hip!! This was four or five years ago. Gradually we formed a rock 'n' roll group. We decided that it was good for a laugh. It split up in the end. Out of the group, I was the only one who stayed with music. I used to play with a lot of groups in London. I used to work as an arranger and stuff like that. And we only teamed up professionally when Jeremy had been out in the professional theatre for a year and he wasn't getting much fame, so he came back and we started singing in a coffee house."

Temporary Separation

So many questions have been raised as to what has been termed the "temporary separation" of Chad and Jeremy, that Chad seems anxious to have an opportunity to clear up this matter once and for all.

"You've caught me in a very strange moment in my life; I think you may detect my voice is slightly depressed today. We're in the middle of a turmoil: this doesn't mean that Chad and Jeremy have gone bust or anything. I think we've been very honest with everybody about our problems, and that is this problem of being a musician and an actor, and the actor wanting to act and the musician wanting to 'musish!' It's very difficult to combine; it's going to work out—eventually—but right now it is a problem, because I'm having to run things my end and he keeps saying: 'What are you doing, and I hear awful stories about this and that,' and it's a big, big hassle right now. But I'd like to go on record as saying that we'll be seen in a TV series next year, and probably films, and this kind of thing, because this is our bag, this is what we can do. We don't just simply wiggle our hips and waddle. And we're not breaking up.

"But with Chad and Jill, I want to try and keep that separate from Chad and Jeremy, but I want everybody to know that it's not a 'rival' or anything like that. It's sprung up out of a gap which was created by Jeremy leaving."

Talented, Sensitive

As we listen to Chad speaking, it is quite apparent that he is an unusually talented and sensitive young man. A man with hopes and ideas for his future. Just what are these ideas, Chad?

"What I have ambitions to write is something altogether more serious. I think that Dylan paved the way to make people think, lyrically speaking, and I think there's no reason why the kids who are really eager not to learn so much as to listen to all sorts of weird things—won't listen to anything you care to create.

Different And Original

"I just want to try and keep different and keep original. I think that as a songwriter I dried out when I heard Dylan. I think I just stopped and I sat down on the floor and said 'What am I doing?' And I think there are an awful lot of songwriters around who should shut up and take note. I *don't* mean that everyone should start writing Dylan, that's not the point. It's just that he had something to say and he somehow made me feel inadequate. I've only written two good songs, I think, in my life, which were 'Yesterday's Gone,' and 'Summer Song.' Jeremy and I have written six on the album out now. We've written a lot of songs, possibly good songs, but they weren't hits or anything, and they didn't tear anybody's world up! What I've decided to do is shut up and live a bit and then when the urge comes on me to say something, then I'll say it musically. But as of now, I'm just content to arrange other people's things, gifted people.

Together, Chad and his wife Jill made the journey from their native England to our own fair American shores. Were there any first impressions for the Stuarts? Indeed there *were*, Chad explains:

"When we first came over it was a shock; we were overwhelmed by the size of everything in New York, and it didn't take us very long to get very fed up with New York because it's not really a way of life. It's really grim and it just scares me. You can't see the sky or anything like that, and we don't want to go near the place.

Beautiful Continent

"We've found that it's the most beautiful continent we've ever seen. It's unbelievable, it really is. Especially California, which has everything. Another thing which impressed us was the fact that Americans must have big things.

They park their enormous, enormous cars in their enormous garages, and then they go into these teeny little houses. I just don't believe it. They all exist in tiny little rows of little houses, and yet size is important. I don't get it; it doesn't fit with the national character!"

...CHAD AND HIS JILL

CHAD AND JEREMY... BACK TO BACK

KRLA ARCHIVES

A PORTRAIT
P.F. Sloan—A Many-Colored Personality Revealed Here

By Eden

At some time during your childhood, you may have had the experience of peering through a kaleidoscope with its multitude of shapes and designs. Part of this was probably beautiful, part of it weird, another part fascinating, and part of it, perhaps, somewhat confusing.

Life is often like that kaleidoscope, and so are people—some of them. P. F. Sloan is such a human being.

If you were able to take all the myriad elements which compose the character and being of P. F. Sloan and enclose them in this cylindrical toy, you would have a fascinating kaleidoscope which would incorporate every color in the spectrum—and then some—in it's many patterns.

Let's peer into that kaleidoscope then, and view some of those designs and patterns which are passing through the life of P.F. Sloan.

Soft colors of yellow and pale orange: his friends call him Flip...

"I was born in New York in Jamaica, Long Island. I was the most rebellious child—at two I hated everything. I was a terrible walker—that's how I got my name, Flip; Flip Flop! I used to trip over every rock. If there was a rock in the middle of the street, I'd find it and trip over it, no matter *where* I was, I'd trip. I was always on the floor."

Greys, and browns, and patterns of thought and irritation: he is surrounded by adults...

"The word "adult" is a dirty word, being an adult is not something to be desired. Because all adults are cowering in their own closed-in boxes and they're narrow-sighted and closed-minded. But *mature* is the word I'd rather see. I'd rather be a mature-thinking person. I think we should all be little kids, but mature enough to face the outside world. Kids don't mind who they play with; and kids don't start riots in Watts."

Deep pools of purple concentration, and thoughtful hues of blue, penetrated by a flash of fuschia; emotions are the life he lives.

"Can I hate? Not really. I *dislike* many things and people strongly. But I can never say, 'I hate,' because I'm dual-sided and I always picture myself in the other person's shoes. I always say there's something in him to like no matter *how* much I hate. It's really hard to hate *anything*. Everyone's going to build up an image of me as a person with total hate inside. But I don't; I have written a lot of songs I felt were total love. I have very, very deep love feelings—and I also have very, very deep hate feelings. I think we all should. But it's the 'hate' that I *hate!* I don't go to bed at night thinking it's the end of the world or anything like that; but I've thought about it. Like the song on the reverse side of my record 'Sins of a Family'—'This Mornin'—I was very, very excited to get up that morning, and I was just thanking God that I was living to see another morning. It's a deep sensitivity to people."

A jagged bolt of flaming crimson, burning across a blazing field

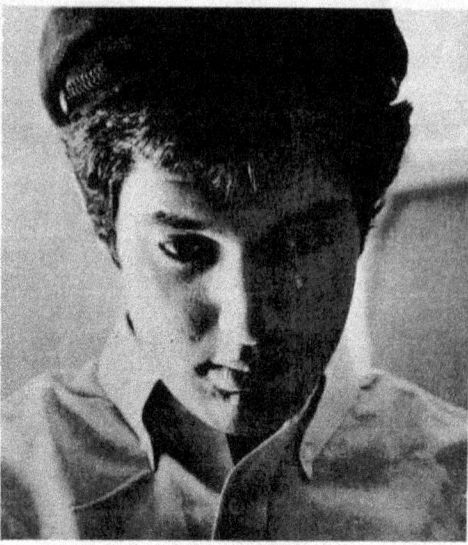

...DEEP, DEEP FEELINGS

of orange: Listen...

"Censorship? I don't think it's their right. If it's obscene—fine. I don't think kids should be subjected to obscenity over the air. But the very person who is *censoring* it (the "Eve of Destruction") is the person I'm writing this about. I'm saying 'Open your eyes and start looking around you!! And this guy doesn't want to even *listen* to the record and find out what I'm saying. We're going through pretty troubled times now, and if someone has to throw a couple of mud pies at you to open your eyes, then that's what's gonna have to be done. I feel that this record is a mud pie and it's gotta be thrown at the people who have their eyes closed."

Gentle patterns of understanding and a longing to communicate; friendly bands of green and yellow.

"I think the younger generation is fantastically hip. Philosophical folk songs could have *never* gone over before, you never would have had a chance to say anything. They have to be hip, because we're so much closer now. You don't have to send soldiers over there now—bombs can come over here. You have to think about it. I really want to do something about it—I'd just love to have a teenager's club, of a million kids, and send a letter to the President and say the kids are really against it—all the war. This is our country and I believe we have a right to shape it. We're not old enough to vote yet, but I think we should have the right to say something about it. I still think that America is the greatest country in the world, but there *are* places like Selma, Alabama."

Geysers of color foamin to a peak and overflowing in pools of rainbows; one figure emerges from a sea of many colors...

"Bob Dylan was my catalyst; he woke me up out of my ridiculous sleep. But Bob Dylan really deals in images, rather than in words. I deal in *words* rather than *images.* I come out and say exactly what I mean. I *feel* in images; my basic concepts are all images. But I put them into words. I usually picture dream sequences—that's images to me. Then I'll just let myself free-write—three or four pages—and then take out what makes sense to me."

"The most important thing in your life is when you stop *reflecting* and start *shining your own* views. You're just a sponge for other people's ideas. But it's the person who takes these things in and then wakes up one day and says, 'By God—I really disagree with that, and for these specific reasons.' Not just for the sake of being called a non-conformist. Everybody wants to be a non-conformist, but are they really? You walk down Hollywood Boulevard and everybody's a non-conformist; they're *conformists* being non-conformists!"

Many blacks and whites; an entire sphere of gray...

"All this controversy over 'Eve of Destruction'—I just can't believe it. I've been getting phone calls; everybody reads something into it—something they don't want to hear, something they don't want to believe. It's kind of hard to take—most people can't take it. I think our whole generation is straying away from all accepted norms: straying away from organized religion—not religion in itself, but *organized* religion—just as a means of expressing themselves. 'Eve of Destruction' doesn't mean that we're all gonna be destroyed tomorrow, but it's an eventuality that we have to prepare for and discuss and do something about. I believe *if* we *don't do* something, we're on the 'Eve of Destruction.'"

Turning, turning—you keep on turning, for there is so much more of him to see. But all of P.F. Sloan cannot be contained within a one-dimensional kaleidoscope.

MAIL BOX

Dear Editor:

I would like to express my gratitude for saying what we teenagers really have been trying to express for a long time in your article "Maybe It's Time to Protest". I would also like permission, as editor of my school paper, to publish this article in our paper. I feel this is what the majority of teenagers feel and I think it should be shared with everyone.

Thank you very much and I would appreciate your reply.

Donna Smith
Editor's Note: Permission granted!

To *The BEAT*:

As the saying goes, it takes more than one tree to build the temple. So, a little note of thanks to you at *The BEAT* for doing such a great job with my story of introduction to your readers. I only hope I will become the kind of artist, and most of all, the kind of person that *BEAT* staffers will have been proud to have introduced to the kids.

Frankie Albano

Dear *BEAT*:

We are writing to the most talked about, read about paper ever published—*The BEAT*—because we think we can accomplish our ideas and projects through you.

Our project is just this: Several of us have an idea and would like Beatle fans to help. We want to start a "Beatle Quilt". Seven of us will put the quilt together but would like scraps of material big enough to make a fairly good size quilt square. With the material we would also like their name and address.

We want as many fans as possible to participate in our and their project.

Write to Kathy and Janet Abbott, 1277 Shelley Ave., Upland, aliformia 91786.

Dear Editor:

I am somewhat tardy in congratulating you on the superb editorial in your newspaper—"Maybe It's Time to Protest."

I have been a teacher (history and English and Psychology) for 37 years in the California high schools. The ideas and ideals you mentioned in your editorial are those I tried always to inculcate in all the young people who sat in my classrooms over the years. Can you imagine my surprise and delight to find these so succinctly expressed in a teenage publication which seems to be devoted to the current music and other teenager's mores. I salute you!

I understand that we in the peace movements are going to be using this editorial to distribute at gatherings where many young people can be contacted.

Mrs. Frances Nelson

To Readers of *The BEAT*:

My English pen-pal has a friend who would love to have an American pen-pal. She would like to write to a girl with the same interests. She likes folk singing and one of her favorites is Joan Baez. She doesn't particularly like the Rolling Stones or the Kinks but has an average admiration for the great Beatles. Her name and address are: Alison Sandifer, "Goldenacre", Silver Street, Needingworth, Nr. St. Ives, Hunts, England.

Gayle Holland

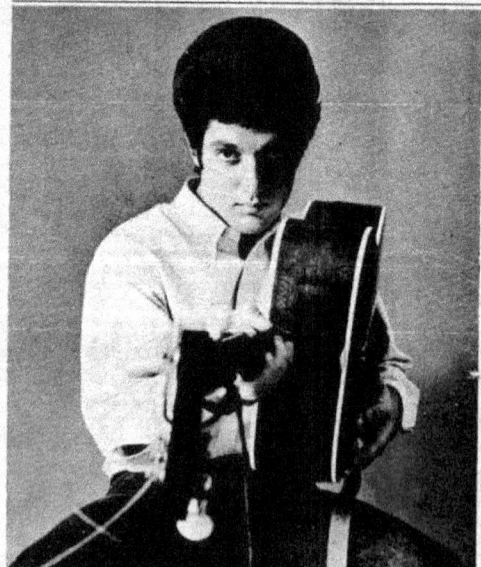

..."DESTRUCTION" IS A MUD PIE

The colors in this little toy must fade now, but the light of their source will never die.

You want to see more, know more, hear more of a fascinating and complex young man named P.F. Sloan—*listen*, then, to his records, to the things he has to say. Watch him as he goes from one pattern to the next.

For, like the kaleidoscope, he is beautiful, and fascinating, weird, and confusing...and great—*very* great.

But most of all — he is P.F. Sloan.

KRLA ARCHIVES

The Hermits At MGM

HERMITS (l. to r.) Barry Whitman, Keith Hopwood, Herman, Karl Green and Lek Lekenby.

BEAT Finds Herman Hungry and Hammy

By Susan Frisch

How many of you have wished that you could spend an afternoon with Herman and his Hermits on the set of their MGM movie, "There's No Place Like Space?" About a million I'd guess!

Well, let me tell you it was hard to gain admittance to Herman's very closed set but once again *The BEAT* scored and we were invited to visit Herman on the set.

Our visit began in the studio commissary where the boys were hungrily wolfing down huge quantites of food. While they were shoveling down mouthfuls I managed to uncover a few hidden facts about the Hermits.

The Heartbeats

First off, they were not originally called the Hermits, but were known around the Manchester area as the Heartbeats. Thinking that name wasn't catchy enough, they switched it to the Hermits.

Next the hunt was on to find a suitable name for Peter, something which would sound good with "Hermits." It wasn't an easy search but a name was hit upon which was a natural.

It seems that the Hermits considered Peter to be a perfect lookalike for Sherman of the Bullwinkle cartoon series and so had taken to calling him Sherman. You must admit that Sherman's Hermits was quite a mouthful. But by simply dropping the "S" they came up with Herman's Hermits and the boys had a new name!

After finding a new name things moved rather fast. They found a manager, a hit and suddenly they were known throughout England. Soon America fell to the boyish appeal of Herman—or Peter as he would rather be called—and his lovable Hermits.

There are probably only two things which Herman has done in the course of his career to make his fans bite their fingernails. The first was to lose his famed tooth and the second was to strike up a friendship with British singer, Twinkle.

Biggest Splash

Herman made his biggest splash by singing simple songs with a strong Cockney accent 'ala "Mrs. Brown" and "Henry the VIII."

Either intentionally or unintentionally, Herman has projected a "little boy" image here in America. Herman reveals that in England "they won't put up with it" and so in his homeland he drops his little boy act. But once he lands Stateside again the little boy in him gushes all over the place.

As always when interviewing boys the subject somehow gets around to girls. On this subject the Hermits expound!

All five boys agree (which they rarely do) that American girls are definitely friendlier than their English counterparts. But since they have to return to England and since English girls *do* read *The BEAT*, they admitted sheepishly that English girls are more sophisticated than American girls.

Mad About Red

Besides girls, Herman has several other things which he is currently mad about. The first of these is the color red—Herman loves it and buys everything red in sight!

The other thing which Herman seems to be particularly fond of is his huge number of fans and especially those who scream and yell at the Hermits' personal appearances. In fact, they would like *The BEAT* to convey a message to all their fans—Keep on screaming!

British and American television differ considerably and during the course of their career the Hermits have had plenty of opportunity to sample both. When I asked them for a favorite show they thought hard and then replied: "The commercials!" Figures, doesn't it?

Biggest Ham

About this time the Hermits had finally finished devouring their lunch so we stepped outside to take pictures which was the most fun thing of the afternoon—especially for Herman who has got to be the biggest ham in the world!

And all you Herman fans—don't you dare miss "There's No Place Like Space"—it has got to be one of the funniest movies ever.

Restless Reporter Asks... The Question of the Month

IF ACTOR ROBERT (NAPOLEON SOLO) VAUGHN WERE A CANDIDATE FOR THE OFFICE OF GOVERNOR OF CALIFORNIA, WHY WOULD YOU URGE ADULTS TO VOTE FOR HIM?

Answers:

"Because he could make the bad guys say 'UNCLE!'"
— Jay Dravenstadt, Millbrae, Calif.

* * *

"If they didn't vote for him, they might be taken for THRUSH agents."
— Nancy Davis, El Cajon, Calif.

* * *

"Governor? Why not head of the F.B.I.?"
— Janet Barnum, Hayward, Calif.

* * *

"Because David (Ilya Kuriakin) McCallum would, of course, be his press agent."
— Kathie Hancock, Littlerock, Calif.

* * *

"I wouldn't. I'd urge adults to vote for a Republican candidate like Ronald Reagan."
— Lisa Mason, Manhattan Beach, Calif.

* * *

"Anybody's better than Ronald Reagan, you gotta admit!"
— Jeff S. Hawley, Hayward, Calif.

* * *

Readers of *The BEAT* are invited to send in answers to the Restless Reporter's next QUESTION OF THE MONTH, which is:

If guys wear long hair and get away with it, why shouldn't gals adopt the crew-cut for themselves?

Please mail your answers to THE QUESTION OF THE MONTH, *The BEAT* — no later than Friday, November 5, 1965. Thanx, dear hearts.

KRLA ARCHIVES

... DICK AND DEEDEE

IN LOVE WITH LONDON
Dick and DeeDee Dig England Hard

By Louise Criscione

A California duo which has remained active on the American record scene for a number of years without enjoying all that many hit records (although it must be admitted that they've had their fair share of hits) have now fled to England where they haven't had all that many hits either! The duo in question? Dick and DeeDee, of course.

You needn't blow your cool because Dick and DeeDee are not abandoning the States at all, they've just gone over to England for a promotional visit. However, the trip will be a pleasure for the two as well as some hard work.

DeeDee admitted the couple's liking for England when she said: "We love it so much that it sounds corny if we say so. We dread being asked to give our views on London because we see looks of doubt and suspicion cross the interviewer's face when we start gushing over this beautiful city.

Just Everything

"But honestly, it's true. We adore the place—and the people and all the traffic muddle and the old buildings and the rain and the easy-going tolerance of the show business crowd. And just everything," DeeDee continued enthusiastically.

The duo really fell in love with the country when they visited it in December, 1964. In fact, DeeDee admits that of all the countries they have visited (and they've visited practically every country there is!) England and particularly London is their all time favorite spot.

"We paid for that trip ourselves because we wanted to experience the excitement of the land of the Beatles and the Rolling Stones and all the other big, new, exciting groups. We never regretted a penny of what it cost us—which was several thousand dollars," DeeDee explained.

The first time they arrived in England they found it terrifying but they soon renewed their friendships with some of the English groups whom they had met here in America and spent the rest of their stay visiting all the "in" clubs, meeting loads of interesting people and DeeDee must have ventured out to every dress shop in the country.

Loads of Clothes

"I bought loads of English clothes—I must have spent a thousand dollars on them—and we explored Oxford Street, Bond Street and Chelsea hunting for new European fashions which were, and are, so coveted in America," DeeDee said.

Perhaps you've noticed DeeDee's new English look. She's traded in her sweaters and skirts for "Courreges" and white boots. And you know something? She looks great in them!

While DeeDee was chasing around the country digging up new fashions, Dick was soaking in the friendly atmosphere of the English pubs.

"There's an openness and friendliness in the English pub which we would never find in an American bar," Dick commented.

Mixing Freely

"People of all ages and all types seem to mix together so freely. Old, grizzled men smoking pipes solemnly at their regular tables, seem so toleant of the bright young things," Dick added.

Dick and DeeDee could hardly wait to return to England to see all their friends and especially Cathy McGowan and Vicki Wickham of "Ready, Steady, Go", Brian Jones of the Stones, DJ Alan Freeman and all of the Searchers including their former lead singer, Tony Jackson.

It won't be long before Dick and DeeDee wing their way back. They'll probably be glad to get back 'cause no matter how much they rave about England they're only too happy to plant their feet firmly on Stateside ground.

For Girls Only

By Shirley Poston

Out, boys!!! Every single one of you! The way I feel today, I may never *speak* to another male again as long as I live.

I'll get over it, of course (see, this isn't your lucky day after all) but for the moment, o-u-t, OUT!

So what am I so steamed up about anyway? Well, I have rather long hair and sometimes I wear it in braids. Hanging ones, I mean. (Oh WHY can't I ever explain anything SENSIBLY??? Hanging ones . . . oh comma brother.)

Anyway, I went to the supermarket last night to buy an orange popsicle. (Honest, I did. I have this thing about orange popsickles.) And this *man* wouldn't let me buy one! He said I had to buy the whole box of popsickles or nothing.

One Last Plea

After muttering about what on earth I would do with *twenty* orange popsickles, and coming up with a few pretty good ideas at that, I made one last plea to the checker.

You know, I said something original and clever like "Aw, be a sport."

Well! Do you know what he *said?* He said, "Sorry, Becky Poo, I can't do it."

"Becky Poo???" I thundered. He laughed. "Those braids make you look just like Rebecca of Sunny Brook Farm."

Well, did I storm out of *that* store! I mean, what a thing to *say* to a girl. After all, I like to at least *think* of myself as the sultry, dangerous-woman type. I know better, but do people have to go 'round (still going through that English phase, I am) telling me I'm absolutely *harmless?*

Days Numbered?

But, you know, come to think of it, it was pretty funny. Do you also know that I have just spent numerous inches of type talking about *orange popsickles?* I have a feeling my days are numbered . . .

Speaking of things being funny, isn't it funny how everything is so funny sometimes? Which made about as much sense as most of my sentences. I'm trying (very) to say that sometimes very unfunny things are hilarious. Like *most* of the time, for instance.

You know how you can be driving down the street with a bunch of friends in a car (which somehow figures as it is somewhat difficult to drive down the street with a bunch of friends unless you *are* in a car) (huh?). Anyway, you'll look out the window and see a *tree* just standing there minding it's own business and everybody absolutely *cracks up!*

Isn't that weird? Maybe its just being young and full of fun and all that makes this sort of thing happen so much. You never see adults getting hysterical over just nothing. Do you "grow up?" I sure hope not. There are so many things I hope never change. Come to think of it, in 10 years I might not even like *orange popsickles.* (Good grief, there I go *again.*)

Middle Name

Well, I know one thing for sure. I still like George S. Harrison. (The S. stands for Slurp.) Say, that reminds me. I don't even know what his middle name *is!* Of course I don't know what *mine* is either, most of the time, but that's beside the point. So if anyone reading this *does* know what comes between the G. and the H. (besides Slurp), please let me know.

While I'm on the subject of George (well, it's better than orange popsickles, isn't it?) I have another question. I got a letter from another Harrison addict who said her main mission in life is to "keep George from making the terrible mistake of marrying Pattie Boyd."

I'm still wondering about that one. I don't know much about Pattie, by choice, because the more I know about her the more time I'd spend thinking about how well she knows MY (and yours too, of course) George. But now I'm curious. Is there something about Pattie that the rest of you Georgeites *especially* don't like? Other than the fact that she has him and we don't!

It must be something else. After all, Cynthia has John and we still like her in spite of this fault (ahem). Let me know if I'm missing something (besides a few marbles), okay?

Another Confession

Before I leave the subject of George (which I may never), I have another thing to confess, like that I lie-awake-nights-and-dream-up-meetings bit. Only this one is *really* weird, and I just may be the *only* one who gets this feeling. Anyway, sometimes I get this odd sensation that George is *watching* me! So help me, I do!! I know he's in England and I'm in California, but I *still* get the feeling. And when I do, I always act sort of "cute" and try not to do anything too un-cool like scratching or something like that.

Does that ever happen to you? I hope so, but I doubt it. I also hope you aren't wondering about me.

For reasons explained elsewhere (elsewhere?) What was in that *coke?*) In *The BEAT*, I have promised to not rave on indefinitely in my column from now on, and keep it down to a few million words. And I promise to keep that promise. (At least for a week.)

One More Thing

But before I say farewell, there's just one more thing. And I've been meaning to say this for about a hundred years.

Isn't it just incredible how much difference there is between *looking* pretty and *feeling* pretty? I just can't understand it, but sometimes I'll get all daped up (I used to call dresses dapes when I was a kid) (a very *sick* kid) and everyone will tell me I look great. But underneath it all I feel like an absolute snerd!

Then, other times, I'll wear something I especially like or have my hair a certain way and no matter how many people point and say "What's *that?*", I feel perfectly beautiful!

I even have "beautiful" clothes—you know, things I wear when I'm more concerned with feeling good than I am with looking good. I mean they're not exactly rags (almost), but they're not exactly anything to write home about. I always wear them when I have to do something I'm half-scared of and need an extra dose of self-confidence. And they really help.

Snerdsville

I also have a couple of outfits which are reasonably sharp, and I know good and well that no sooner than I put them on, I'll be in snerdsville.

Someday I hope I will be able to figure a lot of things out. With the help of a competent psychiatrist, that is.

Something tells me I just broke my promise about keeping down to a dull roar. Oh well, I do have my good points. And, if I wore a hat, no one even notices!

Bye for now, keep writing and I'll see you *next BEAT*.

McCallum Wins Dress Award

Well girls, it looks as though you aren't the only ones who dig David McCallum, co-star of "Man From U.N.C.L.E."

The people who dress the stars also think he's pretty great.

McCallum has been named winner of the annual Adam 'N Eve award for television for 1965 by the Motion Picture Costumers.

KRLA ARCHIVES

THE FASTEST TEAM IN THE WORLD — KRLA'S twin entries in the racing world draw admiring crowds wherever they're displayed. The Horsepower Engineering Dragster (left) is regarded as the fastest in the world. The KRL "A" is not only fast but also the classiest thing on the road. Incidentally, model car builders are all talking about the KRL "A" contest. Entry blanks are available at all model stores.

BEAT BACK ISSUES

YOU DON'T HAVE TO MISS OUT...
on any great pictures, fab interviews or newsy items appearing in any of the following KRLA BEATS which you might have missed. For a limited time only, these BEATS are still available.

ISSUES AVAILABLE

- 4/14 — INTERVIEW WITH JOHN LENNON
- 4/21 — INTERVIEW WITH PAUL McCARTNEY
- 5/5 — HERMANIA SPREADS
- 6/9 — BEATLES
- 6/30 — PROBY FIRED
- 8/7 — DYLAN
- 8/14 — HERMAN
- 8/21 — STONES TESTIFY
- 8/28 — KRLA PRESENTS THE BEATLES
- 9/4 — BEATLES ... IN PERSON NOW!
- 9/11 — THE THREE FACES OF BOB DYLAN
- 9/18 — PROTESTOR BARRY McGUIRE
- 9/25 — SONNY—HE & CHER HAVE 5 HITS
- 10/2 — WAS YARDBIRDS' ORDEAL IN VAIN?
- 10/9 — PAUL & RINGO — NOW SOLOING
- 10/16 — ELVIS — KING OF POP?
- 10/23 — BEVERLY BIVINS — WEE ONE OF WE FIVE
- 10/30 — RIGHTEOUS BROTHERS — NEW IMAGE

To order a back issue, send 25c (15c plus 10c postage and handling charge) to: KRLA BEAT, Suite 504, 6290 Sunset Blvd., Hollywood, Calif. 90028. IT IS NO LONGER NECESSARY TO SEND STAMPS OR SELF-ADDRESSED ENVELOPES.

Smash! Crash! For Hermits and Animals

Herman's Hermits and the Animals had a smashing night in the Hollywood Hills a while back.

The smashing part was a closed sliding glass door that one of the Animals managed to walk through.

Beatles' Place

The Hermits were renting the same Hollywood home the Beatles were in during their stay and Herman and the boys had the same problems with girls and guards.

Herman reports that one of the guards got a little tipsy one night and allowed a group of estatic young girls to get in the house.

With typical British hospitality the Hermits and the Animals turned the whole incident into a swinging party. But during the confusion one of the Animals walked through a sliding glass door he thought was open but wasn't.

Not Serious

But Herman said he luckily wasn't cut seriously in the accident. The girls had a fantastic time and will probably never forget their encounter with the Hermits and the Animals.

WANTED
PIANIST OR ORGANIST
TEEN-AGE MALE, WITH ELECTRIC INSTRUMENT, TO JOIN ROCK 'N ROLL GROUP — CONTACT
JO-ANNE ZITO — 279-2103

Help!

HELP!
Anyone having Beatle Books 1 - 20, or who knows someone who does (ask your English pen pals), please get in touch with Sylvia DeFresne, 5520 N. Parmerton Ave., Temple City, Calif. I'm willing to pay 50c each for them.

HELP!
Anyone having color or black & white pictures taken at the Beatle Concert at the Bowl please contact Pattie Gigenheimer, 23216 S. Adolph Ave., Torrance, Calif. Only one of mine came out and I would like to have some pictures to remember the Concert by.

HELP!
I am an 18 year old boy who would like to organize a band with at least four boys and a couple of girls. If interested contact — Ron Wynne, 8421 Leroy St., San Gabriel, Calif. Please state musical interest.

HELP!
Anyone interested in joining a fan club for the Turtles, please write to Dorene Hutchinson, 6441 W. 83rd Street, Los Angeles 45, Calif.

HELP!
My hobby is making gum wrapper chains out of gum wrappers (obviously). Please send me any gum wrappers you may have and I will help you with your hobby in return. Thank you, Aggie Acker, 1111 Bella Vista, Pasadena, Calif.

HELP!
I am making a scrapbook on Herman and I don't have enough pictures and articles on him. Anyone wanting to help out write to: Deanna Thomas, Rt. 1, Box 184, San Luis Obispo, California.

HELP!
I am collecting pictures of Joey Paige. If anyone has any I can have please send them to: Sally Frazier, 4551 Point Loma Ave., San Diego, Calif. 92107.

NEW!! NEW!! NEW!!
AT THE "HOLE IN THE WALL"
BIRD SUN GLASSES
COMES IN TWO COLORS: GOLD OR SILVER, WITH CASE
$7.95 PAIR

WE WILL MAIL TO YOU PREPAID
SEND MONEY ORDER OR CHECK

NAME: _____
ADDRESS: _____
CITY: _____ STATE: _____
CHECK COLOR WANTED: GOLD ☐ SILVER ☐

422 N. La Cienega
Los Angeles 48, Calif.
HOLE IN THE WALL

PUT A TIGER IN YOUR TANK
-LISTEN TO KRLA-

THIS WEEK'S CARTOON WINNER is Rex Morache of Long Beach, who wins a record album for sending us this excellent sketch.

KRLA ARCHIVES

KRLA $11-10 Football Sweepstakes

The KRLA BEAT will award $1,110.00 to everyone accurately predicting the scores of 10 of the 11 games listed below (games to be played Friday, Nov. 5). This contest will be repeated each week for the remainder of the high school football season.

ENTRY BLANK

1. SYLMAR____ SAN FERNANDO____
2. CLEVELAND____ POLY____
3. BANNING____ CARSON____
4. EAGLE ROCK____ MARSHALL____
5. DORSEY____ LOS ANGELES____
6. HOLLYWOOD____ FAIRFAX____
7. VAN NUYS____ MONROE____
8. NO. HOLLYWOOD____ GRANT____
9. TAFT____ BIRMINGHAM____
10. CANOGA PARK____ RESEDA____
11. WASHINGTON____ JEFFERSON____

Weekly Contest No. 3

Name_____ Telephone_____
Address_____
City_____ State____ Zip____

$11-10 CONTEST RULES

1. Scores for all 11 games must be filled in. Everyone correctly guessing the scores of any 10 of these varsity games will win the jackpot of $1,110.00.
2. Entries should be addressed to: KRLA BEAT 11-10 Contest, 1401 S. Oak Knoll, Pasadena, Calif.
3. Entries for this week's contest must be postmarked no later than 12 p.m. Wednesday, Nov. 3, 1965.
4. Enter as many times as you like. Each entry must be made on a BEAT official contest blank or on a hand-drawn facsimile.
5. Employees of KRLA and The BEAT, and members of the families of employees, are not eligible to compete.

Hear the scores of all varsity football games every week on the KRLA-Herald Examiner Sports Line. Listen for Danny Baxter's Weekly Predictions on KRLA — "The Station That Knows The Score!"

KRLA BEAT SUBSCRIPTION

you will SAVE 60% of the regular price!
AN INTRODUCTORY SPECIAL . . . if you subscribe now . . .

☐ 1 YEAR — 52 Issues — $3.00   ☐ 2 YEARS — $5.00

Enclosed is $..............
Send to:...Age:..........
Address:..
City:..........................State:..............Zip:..........

MAIL YOUR ORDER TO: KRLA BEAT
1401 South Oak Knoll Avenue
Outside U.S.: $9.00 — 52 Issues   Pasadena, California 91106

THE CASEY KASEM STORY, PT. 2
Years At Turntable, Yet Yearns To Act

A great deal of discussion lately has centered around Bob Dylan and around the so-called "message," or "protest" songs. When I asked Casey what he thought about all this, he thought for a moment before replying: "I don't know a lot about Bob Dylan, but what I know about him is what I've read and what I've heard in his songs. To say that he's just a deep thinker isn't enough; to say that here's a man who knows why he gets up every morning is even more important. How many of us know *why* we're here? He *knows*, I think. He's a man who is tolerant and who has shown that he has little respect for material things. I think a man who is tolerant of other people, and who places little importance on material things — must be headed in the right direction. Because after all, we live with people, and people are the most important things to us in life. If we can learn to love them — and apparently that's what he's saying — why then our lives can be fulfilled. It's not enough to say that he's an individual. You can slap

. . . BUSY OFF THE AIR

OOPS!

Gert the Gremlin went and did it again last week. In our first installment of the Casey Kasem Story our Gert got her tricky fingers on the type and messed up the caption on one of our photos. The result was that we said Casey's show, *Shebang*, aired on Channel 11. For shame, Gert! We almost caused Casey to show up at the wrong studio. *Shebang* is broadcast over Channel 5 — daily at 5 p.m.

a label on the man, but it's not fair. I think if you listen to his songs, you'll find that he seems to be headed in the right direction — philosophically. And I think that maybe there's a lesson in that for all of us — that we all have to find it out for ourselves. He certainly has — he *knows* why he gets up in the morning!"

When Casey is not at KRLA on the air, and when he has finished his nightly session at *Shebang*, he still occasionally listens to the hi fi in his apartment. "It just depends what I'm in the mood for; my tastes in music range from one end of the spectrum to the other. There's no limitation — I'm willing to listen to all kinds of music; it all supplies entertainment. I listen to popular music radio because I know what I'm going to hear; that's one of the reasons for the success of KRLA."

I think that we can all agree that Casey is a great disc jockey, but The Caser has other plans for himself as well.

Wants To Be Actor

"You asked me about ambition: I would love to be an actor, but I'm in no hurry. I think that I would like to continue working as though I'm going to live forever, and praying as though I'm gonna die tomorrow. I would like to learn to love people more than I do now, and it's a hard thing to do sometimes. I think more and more every day, I'm learning that there's no greater thing in the world than love. I think the more *my* life takes this direction, the happier I am. And I find out that some of the things that were major problems before no longer are major problems, and that I'm a lot happier for it."

Casey has one other ambition which has stuck with him for a good many years, and although it has an element of humor to it, it is also a good example of Casey's character. He says, "I've always wanted to be a waiter, and I think that I'd make a *good* waiter! I think anyone should be proud of anything he does well. To be a waiter takes no particular talent — it takes an attitude. The attitude is wanting to help other human beings. Maybe it's selfish, 'cause when you see they're happy and pleased, well then you can mirror that happiness, too. So, I think I would make a good waiter."

This has been just a brief introduction to some of the many sides of Casey Kasem. But there are many others, and they are all just as fascinating. Casey is a warm, sensitive, intelligent young man who is headed right for the top rung on the success ladder, and certainly there is no one more deserving of being called, "Mr. Sincere."

Public Invited To Band Battle

The "Great Western Battle of the Bands" will be held Nov. 17 through 20 at the Great Western Exhibit Center.

The competition is open to band groups, either amateur or semi-professional, teenage or older. Prizes include $100.00 for first place, $75.00 for second and $25.00 for third.

The public is invited to watch the final competition which will be held Nov. 21.

Groups interested in entering may contact H. F. McGruder, General Manager, Great Western Exhibit Center, P.O. Box 22108, Los Angeles 22; telephone RAymond 3-3678.

GREAT WESTERN
EXHIBIT CENTER
"Battle of the Bands"
NOV. 17-20
FOR INFO: RA 3-3678

NO ADMISSION
NO AGE LIMIT

PANDORA'S BOX
8118 SUNSET STRIP

KRLA ARCHIVES

HEAD BEACH BOY
Brian Wilson Turns Serious
By Jamie McCluskey III

A funny thing happened to me as I was sidewalk surfin' the other day. At the crucial moment, just when I was about to hang eight—Alas!—I slipped!! Well, actually, I sort of *slid*—right into a building which just happened to be conveniently standing nearby. Oh hevvins, what a coincidence *that* was, especially since Brian Wilson of the Beachboys also just *happened* to be there.

So, being ever ready with super fab ideas, I immediately trapped Brian with my trusty Secret Agent Kit and secured him to the edge of my giant, transistor-powered skateboard, whereupon we rapidly sped off to a nearby Cloud Nine in the skies, at which time I was fortunate enough to obtain the following exclusive interview for *The BEAT*. (Phewwww!!)

Somewhat puzzled by the many different "sounds" currently circulating the airwaves, I queried Brian as to the reasons behind the Beachboy sound, the British sound, and the type of music which he prefers to listen to.

His Voice Quality

"What is unique about our sound? Possibly the quality of my voice, the higher range of our total voices, the different variations in production techniques and arranging, and of course, in song writing.

"Personally I like a certain kind of orchestrated sound, like Nelson Riddle (Did we hear you right, Brian???), and contemporary popular music. Actually, I enjoy all kinds of music, but I enjoy creating in that popular vein of orchestration. I personally prefer to sing a group ballad kind of a number.

"I think the British influence in American production has been stimulating because a lot of the creative producers were eclipsed, and a lot of their artistic records lost their significance, and I think they tried that much harder to make a unique-sounding record that stuck out. For that reason alone I think the British influence—in the end—produced a good result. I think the Beatles' influence is so far-reaching that it's hard to say what their influence is to date. I think it'll show up even in the next five years.

Speaking of Dylan

Speaking of Bob Dylan, and of the current trends of folk and protest music, Brian confided to *The BEAT* microphones:

"Bob Dylan stands for such a large segment of the folk industry. He stands for the contemporary and liberated minds—I think—of today, and so many people are considered 'Dylan people,' but there are 'Byrd people,' and 'Stone people.' I think it's all really part of a movement of liberaion—of self-liberating feeling. And I think he's definitely the king—by his talents alone.

"The protest records are very direct—outside of Dylan—I think that Dylan is very implicit, and his lyrics have to be read into for quite a time. I think in that protest bag, most of the protest songs are very direct, and they can only mean one thing."

Brian is a talented writer—of both songs and prose—as well as being an accomplished producer and Number One Beachboy-type. He is a very thoughtful and introspective boy, and he furrowed his brow very introspectively as he thoughtfully began to speak of his composing endeavors:

"Sometimes I just sit down at the piano and write, and before I even start writing I know that I'm not writing for commercial reasons, so I'll just write to explore some of my musical capacities. I'm always doodling at poetry and thoughts—mostly prose. I'll probably write a book on something; that's the only way you can really pass on what you know. Musically I'm still searching for a new thing, a new bag, a new field. I don't know what's coming, but I know what's here. The Dylan cult is now a realization, and other than that—things like the Phil Spector approach to production, and the Burt Bacharach style of writing.

Soon it was time to clamber back aboard our Super Constellation Skate Board for the return flight home.

Brian admitted that he didn't *really* mind too terribly being kidnapped in this fashion, and he promised to stop in and visit *The BEAT* of his own free will again very soon.

And with that, he stood erect (hanging nine), threw back his noble head with a defiant toss, gave out with a mighty "Hiyo Surfer Joe," and disappeared into the Cloudy Surf.

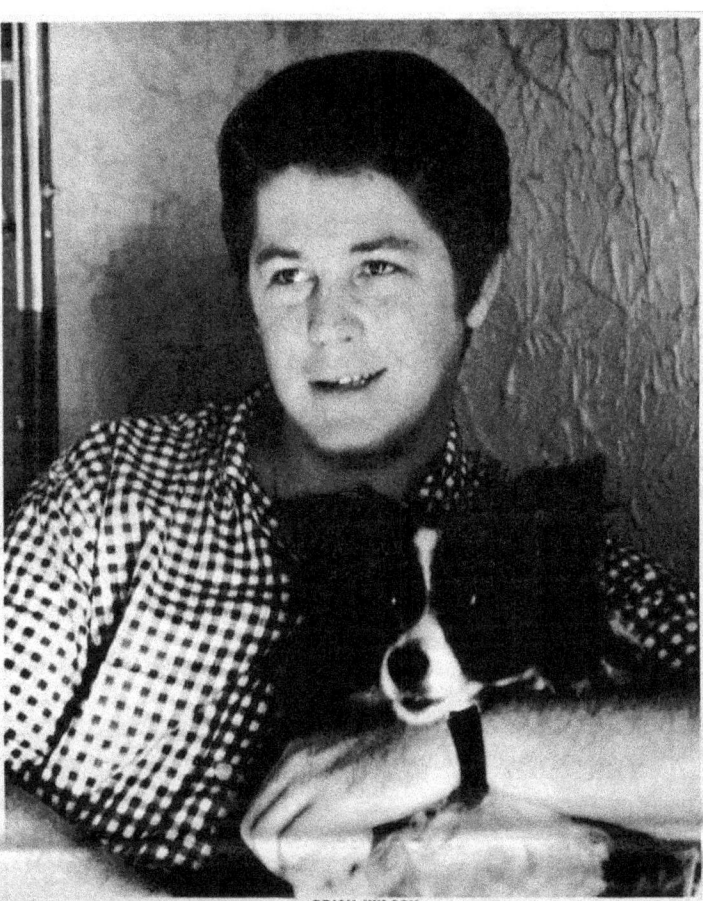

...BRIAN WILSON

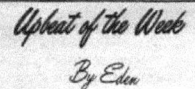

By Eden

Have you heard Barry McGuire's new single yet? It's filed under "Positively Out-of-Sight" at your local discery, and it comes complete with two great sides—"Upon A Painted Ocean," and flip-sider "Child of Our Times."

This one's a winner at *twice* the price! The Byrds are flying high and wide these days, and after hearing their new single—"Turn, Turn, Turn"—it's absolutely certain that these boys aren't about to have their wings clipped! And just for the record, the lyrics to this great new disc aren't just beautiful by accident. The words are taken from the *Book of Ecclesiastes*, and set to music and arranged by one Mr. Peter Seeger. This is one to watch, 'cause the Byrds are going to soar up the charts with this unusual record.

Passing quickly down the line of sounds 'n' singles this week, some of the best of the new include the Stone's new blockbuster—"Get Off Of My Cloud"—and a catchy new item by Paul Revere and the Raiders, entitled "Steppin' Out." This one shows signs of becoming really big.

Also on the Discs-To-Watch list is a two-sided beauty by Chad and Jeremy. The talented Britishers have joined their voices in harmonious song once again and offer "I Have Dreamed," and "Should I?" for your listening enjoyment.

PORTMAN'S PLATTERPOOP
By Julian Portman

HOLLYWOOD ... Sensational rumor hitting Sunset Blvd. **THE ROLLING STONES** have inked a Christmas and New Year date for "It's Boss" nitery. Pleeze make my reservation **Mr. Raffles** ... Legendary **Phil Spector**, the man whose music created the **RIGHTEOUS BROS.** and the **RONETTES**, is opening a chain of Karate parlors in Los Angeles ... **Elke Sommer**—does three songs on the Nov. 3 **Jack Benny** special. It's a first for the lovely doll.

Capitol records goes into the motion picture business. Their first epic will feature **THE BEACH BOYS** ... Speaking about **Louise's** favorite boy singers, **THE STONES**, they kicked off their tour of the North American continent October 20 in Montreal, the home of my mother's relatives. Lots of excitement for this largest French speaking city in this part of the world. The "Gendarmes", if you're inclined towards the French, the "Bobbies" if you're inclined towards the British, the "Mounties", if you're just plain Canadian, had their hands full. The boys broke all attendance records. They hit Los Angeles December 5. Are you ready Mr. Parker?

Frank Sinatra, Jr. first effort for Reprise records, "Young Love for Sale", is just an effort. He hasn't the "soul" yet, and it's a waste of wax ... The **Modern Folk Quintet** signed with Philles records, and maybe a few karate courses, too? ... **Sonny & Cher**, the world's newest millionaires, will tour till December 3 and then come back to the new big house they bought ... **Joannie Sommers** switched record labels from Warner Bros. to Columbia.

THE BYRDS did landslide business during their appearance at "The Trip" ... Warner Bros. **Freddy Cannon** sings the title song for the flicker "Village of the Giants" ... The huge album — selling **We Five** depart for a six-date tour ... The name of **Elvis Pres**ley's new movie "Harum Scarum", was changed to "Harem Holiday" for European release. It'll not effect the title of his newest RCA album ... The night before Christmas will find **Sonny & Cher, Joey Heatherton,** and **Frankie Randall** cavorting on the one-eyed TV monster ... Era records has a good one in "Wait Till Spring" by **Jimmy Lewis** ... **Frankie Randall**, the brightest young prospect on the Victor label, has been asked to do two more **Dean Martin** appearances. He'll introduce his latest record effort during one viewing.

Didja enjoy **Zsa Zsa Gabor's** singing of "High Heel Sneakers" on the Oct. 14 *Shindig*. It was hysterically funny!

Ian Whitcomb, the English lad that came to the American shores to make good before the British would accept him, was sensational in his Oct. 25th opener at "It's Boss." He was also snared for a Nov. 11 *Shindig* appearance ... **Lloyd Thaxton**, the American-lad that made good in America, takes-off for a two week tour of England. Of course, he'll film English artists ... The **Dave Clark 5** have signed to appear at the Carousel Theatre in West Covina on Nov. 22 ... Everyone ready!

Herman's Hermits go to the horses. At least they'. be doing a segment with the talking horse of TV, "Mr. Ed." ... "Mom Always Liked You Best," the **Smothers Bros.** Mercury album is headed for the million dollar sellers.

Have you read where several radio stations in the U.S. have hired British d.j.'s to try and boost sagging ratings? Baby, if you can't do it with glib Americans—and this is spelled with a big "A"—why bother! After all, they're not the **Beatles** or the **Stones** ... A youth oriented TV show is in the works at N.B.C. It'll be a la the **Dean Martin** format, with **Frankie Avalon** (at this writing) considered as the host. It appears someone at that network reads *The BEAT*.

KRLA ARCHIVES

FROM FOLK TO ROCK

MFQ Members Are Zany Philosphers

By Carol Deck

The MFQ visited *The BEAT* recently and revealed their plans for breaking into the rock 'n' roll field.

MFQ, for those of you who may not know, stands for the Modern Folk Quartet. That is, it used to. Now they have added a drummer and are officially the Modern Folk Quintet, but prefer to be known as the MFQ.

The group started seven years ago when three of them, Cyrus Faryar, Chip Douglas and Tad Diltz were splaying in a Honolulu coffee house owned by Cyrus. Then about three years ago they came to Los Angeles, met Jerry Yester and became the original MFQ.

They had great success as a folk group and traveled quite a bit. But the boys believe in change. The group goal, says Cyrus is "never to be the same."

Verges On Poetry

Cyrus is really the philosopher of the group. He sometimes verges on poetry when he talks.

I asked Cyrus to explain the change from folk to rock 'n' roll.

"We play rock 'n' roll as a logical outcome of how we think. We would have had to change our whole mental attitude to stay where we were," he said.

So when the four guys, the original three from Honolulu and Jerry, who is from Los Angeles, met Eddie Hoh, a drummer from Chicago, about two months ago they decided to try the rock 'n' roll field.

Now With Spector

They are getting off to a great start with Phil Spector, who produces a lot of the Righteous Brothers' records, producing their first single titled "This Could Be The Night."

These five guys are really a bunch of characters. The first thing Jerry did when he walked in the offices of *The BEAT* was to ask for some tape to tape together a one dollar bill he had accidentally torn in half. He's a thrifty one. He also told me that the man-in-the-moon doesn't smoke, a fact I hadn't known.

Tad, who bears a remarkable resemblance to John Sebastian of the Lovin' Spoonful, plays an electric banjo which he invented himself. He says it bites sometimes. He had an odd looking symbol on a chain around his neck. I asked him what it was and Jerry told me it was the key to his apartment. Tad explained that it wasn't really. It's an old Egyptian symbol that was given to him.

Cyrus, the deep one of the group, tried to explain more about the group's goals.

New Vocabulary

"We hope to become a part of the new vocabulary. We want to stay as new as we can so people will have trouble describing us, except in superlatives."

"We're lucky because we're free," he went on. "We can talk and dress the way we want. When you live in the world you have to play other people's games but now other people are playing our games and I have to admit it's nice."

Cyrus has a natural tendency to act as spokesman for the group and the others don't mind.

"It's always a pleasure to sit down and hear Cyrus say what I'm thinking," explained Jerry.

The boys believe in protest songs but feel that they are more sympathetic toward the whole movement than many of today's protest singers.

Such A Poet

"Dylan can say what he wants because he's such a poet," noted Cyrus. "But even Dylan's not too sympathetic. We feel a little more sympathetic toward the whole protest bag."

Besides Tad's electric banjo, the group has three guitars, a six string, 12 string and bass, drums and a "bozouke."

The "bozouke" is Cyrus' and he explained that it is a "cross between an oud and a sitar." He swears it's real. I asked him what it looks like and helpful Jerry threw in that it resembles a "pregnant mandolin." Cyrus added that it has butterflies on it.

Cyrus also revealed that he has a particular fondness for kangaroos. He wouldn't say why but he did say that he hoped the group gets to go to Australia sometime so he can see some that aren't behind bars.

The boys have got a busy schedule already set up for them. They just finished a stint at a West Coast club and have filmed a *Shindig* show which aired Oct. 14.

Concert Tour

They are leaving now for two weeks of concerts at college campuses across the country. The campus concert tour was booked for them before they decided to change from folk to rock.

"We're going to lay some new stuff on them," Tad said.

They are going to try to bring some of their folk fans over to the rock n' roll side with them.

"It's the folk fans that come to our concerts," Tad continued, "And we are going to introduce them to some new stuff."

After the college tour they will do night club appearances and film another *Shindig* and a *Hullabaloo*.

This group has a great sound. They've got good voices and know how to use them. While they were at *The BEAT* they serenaded us with an archaic Spanish liturgy, sung acapella, without instrumental accompaniment, which was beautiful. They also sang for us a Delco battery commercial they had done some time ago.

This group can sing anything — folk, classical, rock n' roll and even commercials. Watch out for them. They are on their way to the top.

PLAYBACK... (l. to r.) Cyrus, Jerry, Chip, Phil Spector, Tad, Eddie.
BEAT Photo: Robert W. Young

Shindig Out!

(Continued from page 2)

some major changes in the teen television scene.

England, a country credited with starting this whole phase of television programs aimed at teenagers and featuring top recording singers and groups, may also take credit for backing out first.

The top British teen show, *Ready, Steady Go*, has already been cancelled. Is this some kind of omen?

The American versions of these programs used to ride high in the ratings with no problems. But now they are changing the lengths of shows, the nights they are on, hosts and everything else. Is this a last ditch effort to save them?

Is this the beginning of the end of rock and roll stars on their own type of TV shows?

The BEAT hopes not. These shows are the best opportunity for rock and roll groups, both stars and new comers, to be seen by mass audiences.

Liverpool Five To Settle Here

The Liverpool Five, one of the newest and fastest rising singing groups from England, have decided to make California their new home. The "five" who are, Steve Laine, Dave Burgess, Ron Henley, Jimmy May, and Ken Cox, have leased an apartment here where they plan to go when they have a few days to relax and unwind from their hard and exhausting tours.

Their newest release is a Bob Dylan composition entitled, If You Gotta Go, Go Now. This boomed to the charts within the first week of release. Some numbers which are to be recorded on their album are, "Sister Love," a new kind of sounding ballad, "Everything's All Right," "Crazy World," "That's What I Want," their first record, and many, many more new sounds.

Q: This summer we went on a trip to Minnesota and before I left, I wrote a "friend" of mine and told him where I'd be. I got one letter from him while in Minnesota, but none since we've returned home. I've written a couple of times since, but he doesn't answer. Do you think he's trying to tell me something, or is he just too cheap to buy stamps?
(Judy E.)

A: Wish we could say he's probably just short on nickels, but it sounds as though he's even shorter on tact. And is "trying to tell you something" without coming right out and saying it. Don't think too badly of him, though. Ending any kind of relationship is a difficult process, and something most of us try to get out of doing "in person." Don't write him again. If you don't hear from him soon, look for a new pen pal.

Q: I have two questions I'd like to ask. I'd like to wear my hair "pouffed" on the top, but my set never turns out right. My hair always splits right down the middle. Teasing doesn't even help this problem. Do you have any suggestions? Second, I bite my fingernails, which makes my hands look awful. What can I do to stop?
(Teresa J.)

A: First, there are many wave lotions on the market which can solve this problem. Buy one which clearly states that it adds body to the hair. A lack of body is what's causing your hair to droop instead of pouff. Second, we suggest you buy a set of false fingernails. Not the dime store variety; the kind that become a part of the nail after they're glued on. The cosmetic section of most department stores carry this product.

Q: I read an article in The BEAT that recommended conditioner and an electric air comb as a method of straightening hair. Would it be possible to purchase such a comb from a beauty supply house, and how much would it cost?
(Jane K.)

A: Electric air combs can be purchased from most beauty supply houses and cost about five dollars. And they've been known to work wonders!

Q: I am fourteen years old and people are forever asking if I'm eleven. I'm only 4'8" tall and I hope you'll be able to give me some hints on how to look my age.
(Mary N.)

A: Experiment with hairstyles until you find one that looks more fourteen than eleven. The latest styles are so popular because of their youthful effect, but in your case, you may have to choose between being fourteen and being fashionable. Try something upswept and away from your face. This will add height, and so would shoes with an inch or so of heel.

HINT OF THE WEEK

I read the letter from the girl who had troubled skin and I have some good news to pass along to you. I had some very bad skin problems until I discovered a certain soap. After I started using it, I could see the difference in two days! I now sell the soap, but I'm not allowed to have the name in print. If you'd like to try this product, write to me or telephone after school (3:30) or on weekends. My name is Richard Hamilton and I live at 226 Isabel St. in Los Angeles. My phone number is 223-2631. The soap, by the way, sells for 60c a bar.

If you have a question you'd like answered or a hint you'd like to share, drop a line to Tips To Teens c/o The BEAT.

KRLA ARCHIVES

Bees Look For Honey In Strangest Places

By Jamie McCluskey, III

Warning to all the high-flying Byrd types: You're about to get some powerful competition from another winged group, so watch out!

Buzzing around the ladder of success, the Bees are keeping an eye on that top-most rung, so stand back everyone, and give them soaring room!

The Bees are five in number, and if you were to drop in at their hive, you would be greeted by George Caldwell—"King Bee," lead singer, and founder of the group; John York, resident comic-philosopher and "apprentice human being;" Peter Ferst, guitarist and reknowned falconer; Ron Reynods, serious member of the Bees and an almost-engineer; and Cary Slavin, skin-beater for the five and "an exchange student from Mars."

Meet At Party

The quintet was formed by George about two and a half months ago, at a party where he met Ron and Cary. Since that time, the group has played several live dates, and recorded it's first single—"Leave Me Be"—and are now hoping for a big chart success with this initial disc.

All five Bees are in possession of the standard Beatle Bob-type top knot, but when John was asked if he had recently cut his lengthy locks, he swore he hadn't and explained: "I just had my shoulders lowered!"

The type of music which the group sings and plays is very important, so they must choose good material. John was asked if he wrote for the group, and he deadpanned—"I type." Ron patiently shook his head at this, then explained that all of the boys write songs together. "We write folk songs—our style. It's folk-rock."

Good-Time Sound

At one of their concerts, a guard told John that the group had real "Blue-eyed soul," but George disagrees slightly with that as he brands their music "a happy-bird sound." Ron simply disregards them all as he thoughtfully defines their sound as being "a twelve-string, good-time sound."

All five of the Bees have great respect for Bob Dylan, and they commented briefly on him for The BEAT:

Peter began by saying, "Since he started swing towards rock 'n' roll, he's getting the message across to more of the kids;" to which John added, "I think he's a genius, but he's putting everybody on."

Pete brought up the subject of protest songs and declared that, "I think it's time for a new era—of construction!" And Ron joined him by saying that he felt these songs were dated. Would he like to sing protest, or message songs? "I don't think we'd like to tell anybody anything. We don't want to push anything on anyone."

Poverty On Influence

John had been silent for a few brief, but brooding moments, and now he suddenly sat upright in his chair and defiantly stated that, "Poverty has influenced our sound." But after thinking it over briefly, he revised that slightly and explained: "Elvis influenced me the most; it was my complete *dislike* for him that made me take up the other kind of music!"

All of the boys have, at one time or another, given some fleeting consideration to the days ahead: George wants to "make a lot of money," and Cary seconds the motion by agreeing that he, too, would like "to be successful." Ron claims that "I just want to play in front of people." All five Bees feel that the future holds "breakfast and many socks in the laundry" for them.

In all probability, it holds a great deal more than that, so if you should hear a loud buzzing sound around the pop scene, watch out! The Bees are coming!!

Dear Susan

By Susan Frisch

How do I find out when my favorites are in town, and is there any other place where I can write to Peter Asher, other than his home, where I can get a personal reply?
Pam Lord

Dear Pam,
As to your first question regarding your favorite groups, the best I can say is listen to the radio stations that usually broadcast the arrivals of the groups. About Peter, his home address is the best I can give you.

Can you please tell me who plays background on the Sonny and Cher records; the music is great.
Carla Mahakian

Dear Carla,
The people who play the background are session people. Professionals who just work on certain records.

When I was in San Francisco there was this English group called the Liverpool Five playing in a club. I've been reading The BEAT lately and always seem to notice their name. Can you please tell all you know about them, and their music?
Evelyn Lew

Dear Evelyn,
The boys in the group are Steve Laine, Dave Burgess, Ron Henley, Jimmy May, and Ken Cox. They have just finished their first album for RCA Victor. Their new single should be released in about two weeks. They are all from England and have been together for about two years. Steve is the lead singer; Dave, who is bass guitarist, sings, too. Ken is on rhythm guitar, Ron plays the electric piano, and last, but not least, Jimmy, on the skins. Besides playing in various nightclubs they will soon be starting a new tour of the U.S.

Can you tell me if Tom Jones has been in California lately, within the last month? And when he will be making personal appearances again here.
"Pussycat"

Dear "Pussycat,"
Tom has not been here that recently. As for his appearances, I do not know, this is known only to his agency.

Will David McCallum be in any shows, other than Man From U.N.C.L.E.?
Susan Love

Dear Susan,
Yes, David will be appearing in a new movie called, "Around the World Under the Sea." From what I've heard it should be a great new movie with a lot of action and suspense.

When is the next time the Beatles will be on television? Also, is their Christmas special going to be broadcast out here?
Jackie Hibler

Dear Jackie,
They are trying to bring the special to America, but as of yet I don't think anything definite is set for their television appearances.

Will Bobby Sherman be doing any T.V. shows this year other than Shindig? Are there plans for him to make an album?
Kim Leighton

Dear Kim,
Bobby will be hosting his own show some time this year. As for plans for an album, none have been made.

Can you please give me the ages of Paul Revere and the Raiders.
Ellen Oldell

Dear Ellen,
The ages are as follows: Paul, 24; Mark Lindsay, 22; Mike Smith 21, Drake Levin, 18; and Phillip Volk 19.

Can you please tell me the color eyes of Mark Lindsay and Mike Smith of Paul Revere and the Raiders? Also, where were they born and raised?
Christine Fisher

Dear Christine,
Mark has hazel eyes and was born and raised in Eugene, Oregon. Mike has brown eyes and was born and raised in Portland, Oregon.

Can you please tell me if Brian Epstein and the Beatles accepted Sid Bernstein's offer of $500,000 for two concerts at Shea Stadium in June?
Beverly Anisowicz

Dear Beverly,
I have heard nothing as of yet about Brian accepting the offer.

When will be the Beatles be back in California?
A Fan

Dear Fan,
The fabulous foursome will be back here next summer, probably the end of August.

An Explosive Combination
Eddie Hodges' Greatest Hit
Bob Dylan's Greatest Composition

"Love Minus Zero"

Aurora Records
Los Angeles, California

KRLA ARCHIVES

THE SUN RAYS are America's newest group sensation. Their "Follow The Sun" has become one of the big hits of 1965.

Dave Clark Considers TV Drama Series

Well, just guess who might have a TV series next season? None other than Dave Clark and his four! Their agent is currently wrapping up the deal and if all goes as expected an English filmed, *Dave Clark Five Show* will hit the airwaves in the not too distant future.

Of course, this won't be the first acting venture for the Five. They were the stars of their own movie, "Having a Wild Weekend." They say they all enjoyed acting so a TV series should be right up their alley. And, naturally, the Five's fans will love it!

Of all the English groups to hit it big in America the DC5 are the first to go dramatic via a regular television series. But if the show catches on you just might look for other groups to suddenly acquire shows as well, which isn't a half-bad idea at all.

Will "Tears" Ever Fall? Andy Williams Now No. 2

You guessed it, "Tears" is still Number One!

Well, the British are up to their tricks again. Right when you think you've got their charts all figured out and you've studied and studied all the records and you are absolutely positive "If You Gotta Go, Go Now" is gonna be the next number one — what happens? It falls!

The song has been climbing up rapidly every week that it has been on the charts and last week it almost dumped "Tears" from the top spot. But, alas, this week finds the Manfred Mann tumbling down to three being replaced at two by Andy Williams! And if next week finds Andy at number one it will be the upset of the century!

A new entry into the top ten belongs to that wailer, Dusty Springfield. "Some Of Your Loving" has been on the charts for four weeks, each week etching it's way higher and higher up the ladder. It's interesting to note that Dusty is a tremendous singer as well as an all around performer and in her native England she is extremely popular. But here in America Dusty has been having her share of troubles even getting on the charts.

Watch for the Yardbirds to really fly up the charts with a double-side hit. Strangely enough, the side which is really causing a stir Stateside is "Still I'm Sad" but apparently it is the other side of the British single, "Evil Hearted You," which is storming up the English charts, moving this week from 26 to 15.

The other side, "Still I'm Sad," is also on the British charts debuting this week at number 20!

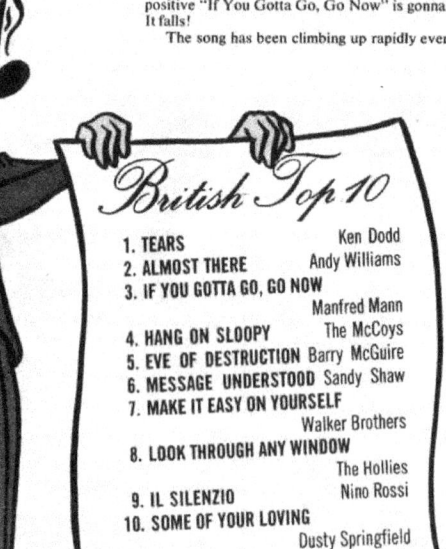

British Top 10

1. TEARS — Ken Dodd
2. ALMOST THERE — Andy Williams
3. IF YOU GOTTA GO, GO NOW — Manfred Mann
4. HANG ON SLOOPY — The McCoys
5. EVE OF DESTRUCTION — Barry McGuire
6. MESSAGE UNDERSTOOD — Sandy Shaw
7. MAKE IT EASY ON YOURSELF — Walker Brothers
8. LOOK THROUGH ANY WINDOW — The Hollies
9. IL SILENZIO — Nino Rossi
10. SOME OF YOUR LOVING — Dusty Springfield

KRLA ARCHIVES

CAST OF THOUSANDS (almost) in Paramount's "Beach Ball" includes, clockwise from the left, the Supremes, Edd Byrnes and Chris Noel, the Hondells, the Four Seasons, Aaron Kincaid and Chris Noel and the Righteous Brothers. Put them all together and they spell a fun-filled movie with six new songs and a lot of swinging dancing.

THE BEAT GOES TO THE MOVIES

BEACH BALL

By Carol Deck

Take a dozen or so beautiful girls in bikinis and a group of good-looking guys, add several of the nation's top singing groups and what do you have? A "Beach Ball" of course.

The girls, including Chris Noel, Gail Gilmore, Mikki Jamison and Brenda Benet, are trying to get the guys, Edd Byrnes, Robert Logan, Aron Kincaid and Don Edmonds, back into school. But the guys are more intent on winning a rock and roll music festival so they can use the prize money to keep their instruments from being repossessed.

Scenes and Songs

Tossed into the middle of all this are some great scenes and songs by the Supremes, the Four Seasons, the Righteous Brothers, the Hondells and the Walker Brothers, who are currently making it big in England.

Sportswise this movie has something for everyone. Of the four leading guys, one is a surfer, one a sky diver, one a skin diver and one a hot-rod racer. The surfing scenes at the beginning of the movie are breathtaking, and the sky diving scenes will either thrill you or make you dizzy.

Wild Chase Scene

There's a chase scene toward the end of the movie that is worthy of the Keystone Kops. It takes in a police car, a super car-of-the-future and some construction workers and ends up at the festival with the guys, who call themselves the Wigglers, performing in the wildest costumes you could imagine.

The Paramount picture is produced in Technicolor by Bart Patton and directed by Lennie Weinrib.

"Beach Ball" is really a ball and includes five new songs and the old favorite, "Dawn," by the Four Seasons.

Will the Wigglers be successes, or go back to school, or both? See "Beach Ball" and find out.

BRENDA BENET is featured as Samantha, a calm, sane coed who gets changed a bit herself while trying to help change the Wigglers from drop-outs back to students.

BEFORE Susan, played by Chris Noel, met the Wigglers she was a prim and proper coed member of the scholarship committee. And after she met them . . .? Well, it's all in good fun.

EDD BYRNES is the arranger, manager, general friend and jack-of-all-brains behind the Wigglers who would rather spend what money he has on instruments than education (or would he?)

KRLA ARCHIVES

KRLA ARCHIVES

KRLA Tunedex

EMPEROR HUDSON

CHARLIE O'DONNELL

CASEY KASEM

JOHNNY HAYES

BOB EUBANKS

DAVE HULL

DICK BIONDI

BILL SLATER

KRLA BEAT
6290 Sunset, No. 504
Hollywood, Cal. 90028

This Week	Last Week	Title	Artist
1	1	YESTERDAY/ACT NATURALLY	The Beatles
2	3	GET OFF MY CLOUD	Rolling Stones
3	2	LOVER'S CONCERTO	The Toys
4	4	KEEP ON DANCING	The Gentrys
5	11	YOU'RE THE ONE	The Vogues
6	5	HELP/I'M DOWN	The Beatles
7	9	MAKE ME YOUR BABY	Barbara Lewis
8	8	HANG ON SLOOPY	The McCoys
9	10	EVERYBODY LOVES A CLOWN	Gary Lewis & The Playboys
10	6	THE "IN" CROWD	Ramsey Lewis Trio
11	13	JUST A LITTLE BIT BETTER	Herman's Hermits
12	7	LIAR, LIAR	The Castaways
13	30	ONE, TWO, THREE	Len Barry
14	17	I LIVE FOR THE SUN	The Sunrays
15	20	BUT YOU'RE MINE	Sonny & Cher
16	12	TREAT HER RIGHT	Roy Head
17	25	RESPECT	Otis Redding
18	15	IN THE MIDNIGHT HOUR	Wilson Pickett
19	19	WE GOTTA GET OUT OF THIS PLACE	The Animals
20	18	UNIVERSAL SOLDIER	Donovan
21	16	POSITIVELY 4th STREET	Bob Dylan
22	37	TURN, TURN, TURN	The Byrds
23	24	TASTE OF HONEY	Herb Alpert & The Tijuana Brass
24	26	ROUND EVERY CORNER	Petula Clark
25	27	RESCUE ME	Fontella Bass
26	23	I KNEW YOU WHEN	Billy Joe Royal
27	36	MR. JONES	The Grass Roots
28	29	I FOUND A GIRL	Jan & Dean
29	31	WHERE DO YOU GO	Cher
30	35	MAKE IT EASY ON YOURSELF	Walker Brothers
31	34	MY GIRL HAS GONE	The Miracles
32	32	STEPPIN' OUT	Paul Revere & The Raiders
33	38	LET'S HANG ON	The Four Seasons
34	40	PIED PIPER	The Changing Times
35	—	MY HEART SINGS	Mel Carter
36	—	I LOVE HOW YOU LOVE ME	April & Nino
37	39	LOVE MINUS ZERO	Eddie Hodges
38	—	STILL I'M SAD	The Yardbirds
39	—	YOU'VE GOT TO HIDE YOUR LOVE AWAY	The Silkie
40	—	UPON A PAINTED OCEAN	Barry McGuire